A

Power

John W. Holmes

RLETON LIBRARY NUMBER 98 / $5.95

Canada:
A Middle-Aged Power

John W. Holmes

The Carleton Library No. 98
*Published by McClelland and Stewart Limited
in association with the Institute of
Canadian Studies, Carleton University*

THE CARLETON LIBRARY

A series of Canadian reprints, original
works, and new collections of source material
relating to Canada, issued under the editorial
supervision of the Institute of Canadian Studies
of Carleton University, Ottawa.

JX 1515
H 65

Contents

Introduction

"I am only a medium medium" was a haunting plaint Hermione
Gingold used to sing into her crystal ball in a drab London suburb. So
here we are, alas, in Canada, middle-powered, middle-class, and now
middle-aged. It's a sad fate for young Lochinvar who came out of the
North such a short time ago to put the world right. The mood is
menopausal. There are the fantasies about youth, a time of golden
accomplishment or a time when the profligate gave away his wealth.
There is the feeling of impotence measured by illusions of fantastic
potency. The disposition is bitchy. Agonizing is preferred to delibera-
tion. Everyone is wrong-headed, including ourselves. Woe is us.
    As is well known, of course, this is a phase from which people and
countries of sound constitution recuperate. There are many hopeful
signs, particularly the disposition of a younger generation, bored by the
posturing and the abstractions. A government which was determined to
tear our foreign policy up by the roots has replanted it, having
rediscovered that the earth is round and not easily remade to
accommodate the internal compulsions of a large empty country. It was
a healthy exercise for both critics and defenders of traditional policies.
There has, in the process, been a reinterpretation of those principles of
functionalism which have stimulated Canadian foreign policy since the
Second World War, but which got lost in the arguments of the 'sixties
over roles and stances. This, in no sense, means a reversion to policies
which fitted the world and our circumstances as they were in the
'forties, the 'fifties, or even the 'sixties. The challenges of the
'seventies are different, and it is even harder now for us to duck them.
Our contemporary foreign policy is more closely concerned with the
national interest, not because the collectivist policies of the early
postwar period failed to serve the national interest in their time but
because the big issues of the 'seventies—distribution of resources and
population in the world at large—cut closer to our bone. The decisions
we have to take about food for Bangladesh and the extent of the
continental shelf affect the basic preoccupations of the electorate in
ways which the Suez crisis never did. Enlightened internationalism is
going to cost more—in dollars and in votes.
    The inclination to abandon "the role of a middle power" as a
guideline of Canadian foreign policy was timely. It is true that a
government which had talked a little disdainfully of "helpful fixing"
found out soon enough that helpful fixing could hardly be avoided. It
may have learned that the "role of a middle power" was not one which

Canada had in the first place sought but for which Canada was invented by the United Nations to serve a common need. It was perhaps not middlepowerism against which the new government was reacting but roleism. Does a country need a role? There is something to be said for it, but a preoccupation with posture is a weakness of middle age. The concept of having a role as middle power was developed to a large extent after the fact. It had at least one good purpose and that was to give Canadians a sense of proportion, to convince them that they need not be mere ciphers in the international community, and to warn them also against assuming that they could model their tactics on those of the great powers.

That was the real point of middlepowerism. It was complicated by a *double entendre*. The middle-sized powers found themselves with a mediatory vocation which became part of the mystique. The idea of such a vocation reinforced Canadian self-confidence in diplomacy, and justifiable pride served a purpose—until it became over-stuffed. As medium mediation became something of a cliché, sourness set in. Some people saw a soft-spoken conciliator as one who failed to defend vigorously the national interest or who could not distinguish right from wrong. Others thought we were a little over-anxious to solicit mediatory business for Canada. Peacekeeping had come to be regarded as the quintessence of the middle role, but our boys had been thrown out of Egypt and scorned in Indochina. Surely this was a fall-guy's role in which nice Canadians were bound to be tricked by foreign powers great and small. To most people's surprise, however, when the calls came again for peacekeeping in the Middle East and Vietnam Canadians did not feel any better able to say no than they had when they were young and starry-eyed.

Perhaps after these ups and downs we shall come to see the mediatory function of foreign policy not so much as the special vocation of one country or another but rather the normal habit of the international community, standard practice for all members of the United Nations. The required objectivity is *ad hoc*. So long as our foreign policy is not informed by the jealous defensiveness of some of its critics, we shall go on being an honest broker in hundreds of small and large ways just by doing what comes naturally, seeing it as an aspect, not the whole, of a good foreign policy. We can act our age, less self-conscious about role and identity, accepting all the facts of life, including the inescapable fate of being a middle power.

Although the middle-power mediator "role" was not sought by Canadians after the war, it fitted our philosophy. According to our well-defined version of "functionalism," countries accepted special responsibilities and had special status in organizations and activities for which they were especially fitted or in which they had special interests.

The generalization of middle-power status which became common was a misinterpretation of a theory, according to which any country could be a major, middle, or minor power depending on the function. Canada was a minor power in international shipping, a middle power in military and security affairs, and a major power in relief and rehabilitation. When we started to think there was a standard role for a middle power, a concept which had been functional became dysfunctional. Now the idea of middlepowermanship is being rejected because it is not seen functionally. Our "declining" power, however, is not across the board. We may no longer be a military power of consequence, but we have to be reckoned with when the subject is coastal waters, fishing, nuclear reactors and other energy resources, or even money.

The idea that Canada had been temporarily a mini-major power in the immediate postwar situation, and then had lapsed into a less authoritative position as the United Nations expanded and other states became middle or major powers, was a healthy corrective to grandiose thinking but it, too, has become a deadhand legend. It is a handy excuse for inaction on the international scene, a nice theme for the melancholics who enjoy our tragic situation as a lost cause. It ignores the fact, however, that we are a country of increasing importance in most economic issues (well behind the great powers but rarely below the top ten in the charts). Nor is this a "role" the responsibilities of which we can escape by our favourite plea that we are owned by foreigners and have no control over our resources. Independence is a relative affair and it is doubtful if Canada's "dependence" is greater than that of Japan, which hasn't even oil that foreigners own.

Fortunately, there is evidence in our policies on the law of the sea or outer space that there is a new breed of functionalists in Ottawa who understand how to apply our functional power in our own interest and in that of the international community. Although our bureaucrats are constantly criticized for clinging to old shibboleths, in many of these important international issues they are again, as they were in the late 'forties, bolder than the politicians and the press. The conceptualizing of roles is remote from the onerous activities of the players at international conferences. Independence or alignment seem unreal as aims of foreign policy. Quiet and unquiet diplomacy are ways of life for all participants, not issues to be debated. Relations with the Americans are a matter of manoeuvre, supporting them for our purposes, lining up allies to oppose them, or, most of the time, trying to get them to alter a paragraph. It isn't at all like sleeping with an elephant.

We are in an age which is not only post-Cold War; it is also post-détente. Security issues cannot be ignored to concentrate on economic and social questions, but security is largely a problem of maintenance in which the Canadian part is functionally minor. Because

viii CANADA: A MIDDLE-AGED POWER

it is less important for us, however, it does not follow that it is unimportant in the scheme of things. It has to be seen in the new dimensions of a United Nations which is now at last universal. Our part will not be decisive; it never was. Any power in the system can provide leadership. We can do that, and we can also act as a catalyst—as we did in the swing towards relations with Peking. We are not likely to do so, however, unless we raise our sights and abandon the self-indulgent concern with our psyche. That is an appropriate preoccupation during puberty and the change of life. President Nixon invited us to have a mature relationship with his country, and it must have been one of the few bits of good advice he ever gave.

This is a collection of essays written since the last such volume was published in 1970 as *The Better Part of Valour*. The essays were written for various audiences, foreign and domestic. Some are included as period pieces for historical reference. The subjects are those which seemed of most interest to editors and to the courageous organizers of meetings abroad on so unsexy a subject as Canadian foreign policy. For sound reasons I am not often asked to write about economics. This volume does not pretend, therefore, to cover the full range of foreign policy issues for Canada.

I am indebted to Peyton Lyon of Carleton University, as is the whole foreign policy community in Canada, for wise counsel and encouragement in writing and collecting these pieces. My thanks are due to all my students at the University of Toronto and at Glendon College for the way in which they have honed my opinions and rescued me from error, and to Marion Magee, who has probably saved more authors from more errors than any Canadian editor. Gayle Fraser, without whose constant help not a word would have been written, let alone printed, served as research assistant, secretary, and editor-in-chief. I have been very fortunate to have all the resources of the Canadian Institute of International Affairs at my disposal, but that venerable institution has no responsibility for the opinion of its erstwhile Director General. This volume and a study in process of Canada's postwar foreign policy have been made possible by a grant from the Izaak Walton Killam Memorial Fund administered by the Canada Council to whom I am most grateful.

Part One:
Foreign Policy Reviewed

It might be said that Canadian foreign policy has been twice reviewed since the process was inaugurated with trumpets in 1968. The Trudeau government's review, which culminated in the "white paper," *Foreign Policy for Canadians,* set out to devise a policy for new circumstances, but it seems from the perspective of the mid-'seventies, to have been preoccupied with themes of the past: independence, alignment, counterweights, regionalism. In a few years after 1968, the world situation altered so drastically that a review of the review has been forced on the government and people of Canada. Whereas the first review served a purpose by re-examining foreign policy in the light of a new calculation of the national interest, the infinitely more difficult review into which we have been plunged reminds us of the danger of assuming that we can shape a world to suit the interests of Canada. We are the world's oyster although an oyster can, of course, express its own vitality and produce pearls.

The first essay, for purposes of perspective, deals with the second stage review. The particular assignment was to provide something like "over-the-horizon radar" for a discussion of resources policy by a distinguished group of Canadians assembled in Edmonton in 1974 for the CIIA annual conference. The other essays in Part 1, which have more to do with the first review, were efforts to provide some answers to questions raised by British and American editors about the directions of Canadian foreign policy in the Trudeau era.

1:
The Canadian Role as Usurper

I should like to take my text this morning from Jean Jacques Rousseau:

> How can a man or a people seize an immense territory and keep it
> from the rest of the world except by a punishable usurpation, since
> all others are being robbed, by such an act, of the places of
> habitation and the means of subsistence which nature gave them in
> common?[1]

Although this statement sounds like the platitudes we have heard from
preachers and politicians for a long time, it is a revolutionary principle
which threatens the basis of the Canadian state. Instead of remaining an
abstraction of moralists and philosophers, it is now being taken seriously as a political principle by the aroused population of a good deal of the
world. If you don't believe so, tune in on the recommendations from
the developing countries at the recent special session of the United
Nations General Assembly called to deal with "the problems of raw
materials and development."

You will find virtually nothing about it in the Canadian papers. They
couldn't spare space from the scandals of Washington, the significance
of which for Canada's international relations is infinitely less than what
the General Assembly was talking about. The obsession with the
United States and the total preoccupation with continental issues which
has gripped Canadians, whether they are pro- or anti-Americans, has
made us parochial. It has veiled from us the real challenges and
menaces for Canada—Canada which cannot help being a world power,
both fortunate and vulnerable.

To get any attention in Canada the President of Algeria had to put his
speech in the Canadian papers as paid advertising. He called "the
allocation of world resources" a central issue. "Any approach to a
concrete, definitive solution to the problem," he said, "implies as a
prerequisite that an appropriate stand be taken regarding the recognition of human priorities. This should in the end lead to a profound
reorganization of economic relations between rich and poor countries,
tending toward a distribution of the benefits of growth and progress . . . ." He added that "the problem of raw materials can no longer

2

be formulated in purely commercial terms.'' Mr. Boumediene is one of the moderates because he holds out the offer of co-operation.

The espousal of Rousseau's revolutionary principle could totally upset present Canadian calculations about resources and population. It would mean the application to the whole world of a principle of sharing to which we are still painfully trying to adjust within the Canadian confederation. It presents problems which make freight rates or fuel prices across this bountiful land seem insignificant dilemmas. For the Canadian nationalist, furthermore, it presents a challenge which makes the suggestions out of Washington for a continental resources policy sound utopian by contrast. It could make our finely calculated immigration policy totally impossible to administer and Canada a pariah nation with about as much sex appeal at the United Nations as South Africa.

I can be accused of the kind of shock tactics which I deplore when the ecologists use them because they tend to induce people to despair rather than inspiring them to remedial measures. My kind of argument carried too far might just persuade Canadians their best bet was a tightly defensive continental resources policy with the United States to preserve Fortress America's high level of beefsteak consumption from the barbarian hordes. My purpose is exactly the contrary. It is to make Canadians more aware of the implications for us of rapidly changing attitudes on other continents. As the events of the past year have made clear, the international climate in which we try to carry on as one of the world's leading trading nations is drastically altered.

I am not suggesting that the national and continental issues on which we in Canada now concentrate are unimportant. The argument for strengthening Canadian control over our own resources can be a petty nationalist argument. It can also be an internationalist argument for acquiring the capability to accept responsibilities thrust upon us by a global situation. In our agitated concern over oil or beef, we ought not to lose sight of the wider international context.

The world community is, of course, a long way as yet from accepting the ultimate implication of Rousseau's moral. There were dozens of proposals put forward by the developing countries in the General Assembly, but none of them at this point suggested the establishment of a world body to ration and distribute equitably the world's resources on a one-man, one-mouth basis. They simply pointed in that direction. The so-called Third World is far less monolithic than we tend to assume. We have witnessed of late, for example, the differentiation of what is called the "Fourth World," those developing countries who don't possess oil or other resources with which they can bargain. The developing countries, paradoxically perhaps, insist vehemently on utter sovereignty over their own resources while they seem to be suggesting that the policies of the developed countries must be subject to some higher law. The debate was confused because the subject is vastly confusing. What we have to note, however, is that the thrust is towards a principle of international sharing and it is directed against those countries which have the most resources and space per capita.

The heat may be turned off the superpowers and on the rich, middle-class, middle-power, middle-aged countries like Canada. (We are in fact so pre-eminently a target that it is hard to find another country which one could describe as "like Canada.") As far as I can see we are not at the moment or in the immediate future likely to be confronted with anything very concrete in the way of international "legislation" compelling us to ship off our oil and wheat as some UN body determines or pay UN taxes to feed the starving. What is being challenged, however, is our right to dispose of our resources and to use our land simply in accordance with traditional principles of a free international economy or in accordance with our own calculations of the particular interests of the few million people who happen to live here. We at least have to talk the language of sharing and that means that we do have to think in that dimension even while we are figuring out what is best for Canadians and how best to hold this country together. It is clear from Canadian statements at the Assembly and elsewhere that flat confrontation is recognized as unwise, that a disposition to be accommodating, to go as far as possible in helping to alleviate the worst situations, may help avoid demands and international controls in the future which would require much greater sacrifice. It is hard to say just how these weak countries, even if they could make common cause, could force us to comply. On the other hand their bitter hostility could make life for the rest of us on their planet very uncomfortable.

Clearly it is politically impossible for the Canadian government or the government of any other developed country, coping with inflation and shortages themselves, to undertake at present anything very drastic in the way of resource sharing. When you get down to the ways and means of it, the noble principle of sharing resources for the benefit of mankind is somewhat difficult to implement and is full of ambiguities. It is inequitable that I should pay so little for hydro-electric power compared with a Bengali, but I don't quite know how I share the Ontario Hydro-Electric Power Commission with him. I could, of course, give up driving my car so that he could have more fuel and fertilizer, but I for one don't know how that is worked out. I could invite ten Bengalis to come and share my small heated apartment. But if every household in Canada took ten Bengalis, the population of the Asian sub-continent would be little affected. The easiest thing for the government to do is to quadruple its foreign aid spending, but even quadruple amounts remain marginal to the problem.

The most serious issue is food. The threatened world crisis over food shortages seems more imminent and catastrophic than the longer term crisis over metallic resources. It seems now widely accepted gospel that the planet is going to be hard put to produce enough food to feed the expected population, even if birth control is successful beyond all expectations. Canadians are being urged at the moment to grow things like mad because there is tremendous demand. Demand, of course, makes prices go up. What do we do if we have the food and few people can pay for it—if Canadian dollars are beyond reach? When the United States met that situation in the obvious way in the postwar years by giving it away Canadians squawked like hell. I am far from being able to recommend a specific agricultural policy to meet this situation. I am merely suggesting that in our calculations of an agricultural policy we will have to recognize that there will be strong international pressure, as well as strong moral obligation, to cultivate every conceivably arable acre of this craggy land of ours to turn out more and more food, and our practices cannot be determined only by the traditional calculations of the market place. We may even have to help feed the Americans.

There is another aspect of what Rousseau had to say which applies directly to the Canadian plight. That has to do with population. Although I recognize that the concept of resource-sharing is hard to implement, one notes increasingly the view, not only in the Third World but even in Europe, that a small ration of population to resources in a country is not to be tolerated. If we can't figure out ways of sending off the resources, it would be expected that we allow more people to share them here. Everybody knows that the most generous possible Canadian immigration policy could provide relief for no country larger than Barbados. We are right to insist that the effort must be to increase drastically the resources in Asia, Africa, and Latin America. That is what the developing countries say they want too. Nevertheless, Canadian actions to keep people out of our treasure house will be regarded as inhumane if not criminal.

The trend in Canada, however, for reasons of employment, ecology, and increasing concern for the maintenance of our political cultures, is in the direction of restriction. This comes at a time when the pressure on the northern developed countries from restless people of the south is presenting problems of increasing seriousness in Europe as well as in North America. We treat our immigrant labourers far better than the *Gastarbeiter* in Europe—as we damn well should—but we want to inspect them first. Illegal immigration has become one of the major problems of government. The surge of desperate people is not going to relax, and the gates are being shut in Europe and the United States as well. We are going to do the ugly things we dislike, establishing firmer controls at the border, sending back planeloads of people, coping with a veritable slave trade, and deporting individuals whose sad plights will be reported all over the world.

It has been one of the internationalist achievements of which we can be proud that Canada has removed racial discrimination from its immigration regulations. What will be our attitude, however, if, as seems quite likely, people from the United States and Western Europe, facing more critical fuel shortages, want to come to Canada in increasing numbers? When we established racial equality we thought we were establishing equality among those we would admit. It is harder to apply it as a principle of exclusion. It seems to me that the pressures to let in Aunt Elsie from Birmingham or Boston, not to mention Gina Lollobrigida, are likely to be highly political. As an indication of what the rest of the world would think of such a policy, one might consider the angry reaction among Americans to moves of Canadian provincial governments to restrict the sale of land to foreigners. It isn't the sovereign right of Canada to do these things which will be attacked. It is the callous inhumanity of people with so much fresh air and water, fuel, and, yes, even houses.

One of our troubles in Canada is adjusting to power and wealth. We have regarded ourselves as poor relations for so long, and we have taken a rather Presbyterian view of admitting affluence. Our philanthropic tradition is far behind that of the United States. We are increasingly conscious of the disparities within our own population and we grow concerned with too large cities and too much garbage. (Have you ever talked to a man from Osaka about our pollution problems?) Evidence of a national indisposition to face reality can be seen in that it is usually the same people who crusade against big cities and high rises and want all of Toronto to live in Anne Hathaway cottages, who think we should be much more liberal in our immigration admissions policy. Well, the more immigrants, the more garbage, and the more likelihood that they and their rose bushes will spread out over all the arable land in Ontario. Even high-minded people have to have a consistent policy on population.

It is a time when in Canada the national interest is glorified. The internationalism which characterized Canadian foreign policy a few years ago is disparaged. That internationalism, one must recall, was based on a very hard-boiled calculation of the Canadian national interest rather than on woolly-minded idealism. It was a simple belief that Canadians could neither survive nor prosper in isolation in a fire-proof house because the rest of the world just wasn't going to let them be so lucky.

Notes

[1]David Corbett aptly drew this quotation to the attention of Canadians in his *Canada's Immigration Policy* (Toronto: University of Toronto Press, 1957), p. xi—and then went off and became an Australian.

2:
The New Perspectives of Canadian Foreign Policy

One result of Canada's decision to withdraw some of its forces from Europe was the passing interest in matters Canadian that it roused in Western Europe and even in Britain. During five months which I spent in Geneva in 1969 there must have been well over half-a-dozen stories about Canada in The Times *and the* Neue Zürcher Zeitung *while* Le Monde, *which gives the best Canadian coverage of any foreign paper, had twice that number. Even more extraordinary were invitations to talk about Canadian policy in London. This article is based on talks to the Foreign Affairs Club, a cordial but sceptical assembly of ex-diplomats and practising journalists; at Chatham House to an audience which was, needless to say, largely Canadian; and for the Foreign Affairs Committee of the Conservative party, which was deprived of my stirring message because the division bells rang each time I got under way—after having explained twice that Mr. Mackenzie King was no longer with us (at least, I didn't think he was). This is a somewhat more one-sided defence of Canadian policy than I might have produced for a Canadian audience, induced by increasing exasperation with the European perception of Canada's "failure" to accept its obligation to defend the Europeans. The article originally appeared in the October 1969 issue of* The World Today, *the monthly journal published by the Royal Institute of International Affairs, London.*

On 23 April 1969 the Canadian Prime Minister made a statement in the House of Commons in Ottawa on foreign and defence policy which changed Canada's international position very little but suggested an important shift in perspective.[1] Instead of being ignored abroad, as is customary with most Canadian declarations, this statement had the rare privilege of being denounced by the NATO foreign ministers in conclave. Editors and political figures in Europe and the United States complained or lamented. It was called isolationist, neutralist, and continentalist. In the words of the distinguished Defence Minister of what one is tempted of late to call Canada's "mother-in-law country," it was "passing the buck to us."

Mr. Trudeau's stated purpose was to repatriate the perspective on Canadian defence policy, which he thought had shifted its base from Ottawa to Brussels. He said that Canada was acting in a responsible way when it observed that the European members of NATO now had a combined gross national product of $500,000 million and a combined population of 300 million, and that, apart from the United States, Canada was at present the only member of NATO carrying out a NATO military role on two continents. He thought the remarkable recovery of the states of Western Europe since the Second World War had considerably increased their capability of defending "their own region." The word "region" is the key to the perspective. Whereas in the eyes of its allies the NATO region is obviously Europe, Canada is insisting that the Canadian region, much the largest of any national region, must be regarded as a vital part of the Atlantic community. Mr. Healey's clumsy statements certainly helped to rally the support of Canadians to the new policy.

Mr. Trudeau's speech was made on a motion to support the government policy of "continued Canadian participation in the North Atlantic Treaty Organization and the intention of the government, in consultation with Canada's allies, to take early steps to bring about a planned and phased reduction of the size of Canadian forces in Europe." The intention was to put the defence policy in the context of a coherent policy announced a month earlier before the NATO anniversary. Although Canadian governments had always insisted that the defence of Canadian territory was their first priority, the view of the new government was that previous governments had never shaken off the assumption of fifty years, that Canada's first line of defence was bound to be in Europe. Its commitment to a NATO military policy, it was believed, had come to dictate its foreign policy. Now the defence of Canada and co-operation with the United States in the defence of the continent of North America were to take a larger share of its resources and come first in its calculations. It would still be prepared to undertake UN peacekeeping operations, but an impression was given that this would have a somewhat lower priority. Whether this is largely a reaction by the Prime Minister to the somewhat exaggerated rhetoric about the significance of peacekeeping by Canadian spokesmen in recent years is hard to say. It undoubtedly reflects the Canadian disposition, since the end of UNEF, to be more tough-minded about the terms of commissions accepted. It is unlikely that Canada would, in a moment of crisis, reject a call to serve.

Since April, the Minister of National Defence, Mr. Cadieux, has discussed these intentions with his NATO colleagues, and he has had a rough time. Only the French could not disagree, but they have preferred to act for some time as if Mr. Trudeau did not exist. Just when the reductions will take place is still uncertain; these are in a state of negotiation. The government has made various protestations of a desire to accommodate the wishes of the allies but has reiterated that the decision to reduce is not negotiable. At present Canada has in Europe an armoured brigade of about 6,000 men and an air division of about 4,000 men. Both of these have nuclear capability, and, although the intention has not been made explicit, it seems likely that they will become (if they remain) an entirely conventional force—to some extent out of anti-proliferation principles but more so because of the impracticability of a smaller power being thus involved. Mr. Cadieux's statements emphasized the transformation of the brigade into a smaller, more lightly armed, air-mobile force, stationed in Europe for possible duty on NATO's flanks. The air division would probably be reduced to fit this pattern. One objective is a force for Europe whose training and equipment would be compatible with that of other Canadian forces so that they would be more readily exchangeable. This emphasis on mobility and availability for service in various parts of the world is not new; it has been the theme of statements on Canadian defence policy since the important white paper of 1964. It is an approach well designed to suit the internationalist direction of Canadian foreign policy; how practical it is militarily is a matter of dispute.

These positions on NATO and defence policy were taken after a review of all aspects of Canadian foreign policy which Mr. Trudeau promised when he assumed office and which is continuing. Although the review is directed to all foreign policy questions, public attention has been centred to a large extent on our NATO membership. There is in Canada some opposition to the very existence of NATO, the arguments being similar to the opposition in other countries to military alliances in the belief that détente and conciliation would be hastened by their dissolution. But the real issue in Canada is whether or not Canada should be in NATO and about its contribution to forces stationed in Europe.

The principal arguments used for our remaining in NATO are as follows. First of all is the view that we joined the collective security club in our own interests and it is our duty to continue "paying our dues" in kind. Many Canadians take considerable pride in their forces' role in Europe and in their high quality. Second, it is insisted, particularly by the professionals, that only in this way does Canada have any influence in European questions. Somewhat more important is the argument that membership makes it an "insider" with the great powers in military questions, in the development of technology, and in grand strategy. This argument is more effective when it is stated negatively, by pointing out the extent to which Canada would suffer as a party in world politics if it were excluded from this kind of confidential arrangement with the great powers, and with the United States in particular. Canadians are strongly resistant to pressures from the United States, but there is a basic instinct that tells them life will be easier for them in many ways if the Americans consider them good chaps, friends, and allies rather than unreliable. A somewhat more sophisticated argument is that Canada needs armed forces, as all countries need them, simply to protect and demonstrate its sovereignty, and if one has armed forces they must have something to do. They are happier themselves when they are sent abroad, and they can be housed and looked after in Germany just about as cheaply as at home. Finally, there are, Canadians have heretofore believed, political advantages in being a member of a multilateral alliance rather than being associated alone with a very great power in a bilateral alliance.

Against these views are those who do not recognize the collective security argument. This represents to some extent a difference in generations. Those who lived through the last World War comprehend the conscious decision made by Canada after the war to entrust its defence to a collective security organization and they are therefore less concerned if the Canadian military contribution is hard to justify as a national defence programme. A younger generation has not the same consciousness of an investment in security and tends to think rather of NATO as involving Canada in activities controlled by and for the benefit of others. There is also a good deal of scepticism about the real extent of the influence which Canada is able to gain in Europe or even the value of having that influence. As for being a military "insider," there are those who consider this simply a means of being dragged along by the American or NATO military machine. The argument expressed most vigorously against NATO is that it involves Canada in a large and useless expenditure and that it might far better save the money and turn its attention to economic development abroad and the living standards of Canadians. Some critics of present policy would like it to withdraw from all alliances in the belief that it could be more effectual if it were nonaligned. Others consider that Canada has no real place in Europe and it would be better to withdraw its forces in order to strengthen its contribution to North American defence. Canada's economic and cultural ties with Europe are increasing considerably, but Europe's political problems interest the new generation of Canadians far less than their parents. Others have no objection in principle to its being involved in a military alliance with Europeans but believe for various reasons that its military contribution no longer makes any sense and is in fact a wasted effort.

This view was stated effectively in a recent article[2] by Mr. Dalton Camp, former chairman of the Progressive Conservative party. Mr. Camp here touched upon an aspect of the Canadian reconsideration of its role which has not been noted very much abroad. Canada has been faced with major decisions on equipment in the near future which make impossible a policy of simply carrying on as before. To do so would soon involve decisions on the replacement of aircraft, tanks, and destroyers which, inflation in the arms business being what it is, would enormously increase its military budget for NATO. The new equipment would not be usable elsewhere, and it would find itself committed in Europe for another decade or two by its military investment. There has been a lively debate on this topic and conflicting opinions, particularly on the timetable for re-equipment and its nature. The general conviction, however, that such decisions were looming inevitably provoked anxiety to have a hard look at the purposes of being in Europe. At the same time comes the prospect of having to co-operate with the United States on the new Airborne Warning and Control System (AWACS), the ABM programme, and other expensive operations.

Escalating technology in arms is posing questions about the role of all lesser powers in an alliance and their relationship to the ''leader'' in ways for which the old formulae of partnership, joint policies, and shared decisions and obligations do not provide the answers. Europeans have the same problem vis-à-vis the United States, but they hope to find a way out in a European arms establishment—a logical but unlikely solution. Canadians are not going to escape this dilemma simply by withdrawing from the European aspect of the problem to take, as Mr. Trudeau advocates, their ''fair share'' of the defence of the North American continent. To take such a ''fair share'' would involve us in astronomical costs which one leading expert has estimated at an additional $1,000 million over the next five years. Defence spending has been frozen for three years, and it is doubtful if any government which proposed a substantial increase, however importunate its allies, would survive.

The principal significance of the new policy may be in the abandoning of a historic assumption—the theory of Europe as counterweight. Canada promoted and joined NATO in 1949 for the common cause but also for reasons of its own. It had been rent for years between continentalists and trans-Atlanticists. An alliance in which it was joined with its large neighbour and its two mother countries suited it excellently, and it gave Canada a long period of consensus in foreign policy. It also served the concept of the alliance by converting what would otherwise have been a United States aid-to-Europe scheme into a defence community of twelve or fifteen countries. Canadians were the most dedicated believers in the Atlantic community and wanted it to have economic and cultural implications as well. They were bringing in the Old World to redress the imbalance of the New.

In these hopes they have been disappointed. NATO has become a cause of conflict between Britain, France, and the United States. It has turned out to be an aid-to-Europe scheme after all. The Strategic Air Command, based in the United States, was never regarded as part of NATO. More important for Canada, NORAD (North American Air Defence), when it was established in 1957, was excluded from the NATO military framework, in spite of the strong wishes of many Canadians. This was the fault not of Europeans but of the United States military, and Canadians seem to be paying for it in the apparent inability of Europeans to grasp Mr. Trudeau's argument that the shifting of Canadian forces from the European region to the Canadian region is not a withdrawal from NATO. Being part of a multilateral defence organization did not shield it from the impact of direct defence relations with a superpower. The cultural and economic counterweight it does need is not seriously affected by its relations to NATO. If it is to guard its sovereignty, the road does not lie through Brussels. On the other hand, in the world of international politics, Canada still gains from working in a forum where it can form combinations against the great powers; this advantage would disappear if a European bloc were formed in NATO.

One reason for changing Canadian attitudes to NATO and Europe has, of course, been the rise of the doctrine of Europeanism. Some years ago there were vociferous but not very widely or deeply held objections in Canada to Britain's joining the EEC. These have been muted by the declining importance for Canada of the British market. It is still important and there is no enthusiasm for losing existing favourable arrangements with Britain without compensation, but this attitude is counteracted by a wide belief that the development of the EEC with Britain could increase the purchasing power of the whole market. There is interest in Canada in ideas for an international free trade area, or even the more limited idea of a North Atlantic free trade area, and this could be further stimulated if there were more indications of sponsorship in Britain and the United States. These changing attitudes to Britain and Europe on the whole reflect increasing Canadian self-confidence. There was a time in the past decade when it feared that the rest of the world would be organized into continental or regional common markets and it would be left outside. However, the fact that Canadian exports have continued to rise on a scale comparable to those of Japan has modified an earlier anxiety that countries not involved in broad common markets were lost.

The development of "Grand Design" thinking both in the United States and Europe led Canadians to wonder if they had any place in the conventional pattern of Atlantic thinking. The so-called dumb-bell or twin-pillar concept of a united Europe and a united America in partnership was neat and attractive although it ignored the fact that neither a united Europe nor a united North America existed. Europeans tended to posit a North America in the singular as a mirror image of their own fantasy about Europe. Many Europeans still do not seem to realize that there is no common market in North America—except in automobiles. There is no single voice on world affairs and no interest in either Washington or Ottawa in creating one. Canada-United States relations are based on a principle the reverse of what Europeans—or at least what one might call Europeanists—proclaim as their intentions. Ours is an effort to develop international co-operation or rather to exploit each other's resources in the most mutually profitable way, and in doing so to avoid integration, supranational institutions, and interference in the separate institutions, laws, and languages to which each of us is devoted.

Although the "Grand Design" is unattractive to Canadians, they realize that the pattern of North Atlantic relations cannot be designed to their taste. If Britain is successful in creating a European group within NATO, Canada will naturally be less interested in NATO as a political forum. That is not a decisive argument against a European group if it has other merits. It is ironical, however, that those Western European (including British) ministers who do so much huffing and puffing about something called "Europe," about "its" rights and "its" interests and "its" voice, feel no shame in reprimanding a non-European country of middle size for not being willing to go on defending Europe indefinitely.

I must not give the impression that Canadian defence policy, unlike that of others, is determined entirely by reason untouched by political passions. The revulsion against the military option and military expenditure is as strong in Canada as elsewhere. The demand that money be diverted to eradicating poverty at home and to development abroad is strong and cannot be ignored by any government. It is no secret that some members of the cabinet favoured getting out of NATO altogether and putting the money into saving their own country. This is a time when the very continuation of Canada as a nation may depend on the provision of more funds to the provinces, and on maintaining, among other things, an educational standard in two languages which enables Canadians to compete with Americans. Differences of opinion on defence policy cut across ethnic divisions, but there is a firmer consensus against defence commitments among French Canadians, and this fact cannot be ignored by a government which is striving hard to prove that it is the legitimate voice of French- as well as English-speaking Canadians. Canadians are much more concerned over a divided Canada than a divided Germany.

Another political factor is the vigorous nationalism, and a kind of restless "independentism," among Canadians, particularly among the more articulate if not necessarily the most representative. This is more resistant to the United States than anti-American, but opposition to military relations with the United States is at least strong enough to make political leaders sensitive. Opinion on Vietnam is divided, but even those more sympathetic to Washington's plight have been made aware of the advantages of Canadian independence. There has been some vociferous opposition to continuing the association in NORAD. The view which prevailed, however, was that nothing Canada could do would in fact remove it from involvement actively or passively in United States defence of the North American continent. This being the case, it is better to have some formal machinery which guarantees it a right to know and a right to be "consulted," even if all this can mean is that we have some pipeline through which we can indicate where Canadian interests might be affected. Policy will be made by those in control of the technology, a fact which has to be faced. The tentative United States decision to place Safeguard ABM missiles near the Canadian border is a case in point. The danger of fall-out, if nothing else, concerns Canada. In the Senate Foreign Relations Committee hearings, Senator Fulbright tried to find out whether Canada had been involved in the decision. It was made clear that it had been *informed* of the decision, and Mr. Laird said that there would never have been any question of Canada's having a veto. There was no dissent when Senator Fulbright concluded that if Canadians did not like it, "they could lump it." Some Canadians were indignant; none was surprised. They were less disposed than ever to be tied to a missile programme determined entirely in Washington—if they could avoid it without doing Canada more harm than good.

To turn now to some of the more specific criticisms of the new Canadian policy. First of all, is it neutralist? The first point of Mr. Trudeau's speech was a reaffirmation of Canada's belief in NATO. Seen in the context of the Canadian debate, this was a major decision. He had been obliged to resist the wishes of many of his closest supporters, and revealed that he himself had been through a process of convincement. He stressed the role NATO should play in the cause of détente with the Warsaw Pact and in promoting arms-control arrangements. In his view he was not supporting a unilateral reduction of NATO forces but proposing a regrouping in the course of which every effort had been made to avoid rocking the boat. His statement that the unilateral decision to reduce was not negotiable may sound unco-operative, but it must be asked which other NATO government can with an honest conscience proclaim that it never took a unilateral decision and treated it as non-negotiable.

The charge that the timing was bad deserves consideration. It was at least a better time than the autumn of 1968, when the new policy might otherwise have been announced. In the views of other members it would never be a good time, and some moment would have to be seized. The argument that Canada could have bargained its reduction with the Eastern Europeans is too ingenuous to be taken seriously. Reciprocal withdrawals are at any rate more likely to take place without negotiation. The best justification of the timing may be that the pressure in Canada for withdrawal could have built up to such a point that it would later have acted in a less responsible way. A considerable majority of Canadians now favour staying in NATO, but the budgetary implications have not yet been faced. To act after the Americans have done so is a kind of humiliation Canadians always seek to avoid. Canadians know about the German problem and the need to keep down the percentage of German troops, but they find it difficult to understand why they should pay to keep troops in that radiantly prosperous country. Unlike the United States or the United Kingdom, Canada has never required financial compensation from Germany. If it is symbolism that is required, that can be taken care of by the efficient little force Canada will probably leave behind.

The argument that this is a dangerous precedent was not disregarded; it was not considered decisive. As for the European countries, they cannot follow the precedent of withdrawing their forces across the Atlantic. They have, in fact, been bringing their own forces back to their continent at a rapid pace these past twenty years, and Europe has become, it might be argued, the most isolationist of all the continents. As for the precedent in Washington, Canada's reasons for withdrawal are its own. It is possible that its action will encourage United States politicians to press for reducing their own forces, but it is likely to be no more than a minor debating point for them. Their knowledge of Canadian foreign policy is normally so thin and conjectural that it does not matter very much what Canada actually does. The European way of seeing Canadian troops as a proxy for the United States is the kind of European thinking about Canada that is partly responsible for the alienation that has taken place. There is, furthermore, a basic difference between the Canadian and American military involvements in Europe. Europe is one of many areas in which American forces are deployed as part of a global strategy and the United States has always felt very possessive about NATO. Canada has had its fair share in the formulation of NATO policies, more than its public realizes, but military strategy is predominantly decided or predetermined by the United States. The attitude of Canadians and that of Americans are therefore bound to be different. Those Canadians who helped found NATO and feel it is their creation have largely retired.

To say that the policy is isolationist is to accept the highly Eurocentric connotation this term has acquired—as applied to the Americans when they are concerned about Asia, and to Britain when it devotes attention to Malaysia or New Zealand instead of isolating itself in Europe. There is little real isolationism in Canada. Those who want to get out of alliances want to put the money they think would be saved into a deeper involvement in Africa, Latin America, and Asia. The impulse is to become a more world-minded country after snapping what is left of the umbilical cord. The Trudeau government set out to establish relations with China and sent off large ministerial missions to Latin America and to Japan; French Canadians, who have been traditionally isolationist, are interested in francophonie; the Commonwealth as a field for economic aid and development has an appeal to many English Canadians. The Canadian aid programme has multiplied in recent years, and it is the declared intention of the government to reach the magic figure of one per cent of gross national product shortly. Whether it is strategically wise for Canada to lower the priority in security matters for Europe is debatable. It should not be called isolationism.

It is true that the new policy looks like continentalism, because Mr. Trudeau emphasized that Canada's defence policy must give priority to its own continent. Is there any NATO member which does not do the same? What Mr. Trudeau wanted to say was not that Canada had abandoned a world view of security but that it is taking a new look at the world map. Canada, he has pointed out, is not just an Atlantic country; it is a Pacific and an Arctic country. In many ways the last is the most important because that is the way the missiles come, and it is these missiles which are the main threat, not the Red Army. Canada's primary contribution to preventing an exchange of missiles is on this front, in North America, at the heart of the system of deterrence—the deterrence which protects Western Europe as well. Europe remains an important front, not "the front."

Mr. Trudeau also spoke of the necessity of preserving Canadian sovereignty. Paradoxically Canada defends this against the Americans by collaborating with them. The prospects of Arctic oil and nuclear submarines and ice-breakers have reminded Canadians that their occupation of the Arctic areas is less than overwhelming. By proposing to assume a larger responsibility for surveillance of this vast region,

Mr. Trudeau acted in accordance with the traditional Canadian belief that it must bear its share of continental defence lest the Americans insist on coming in to do it for Canada. This may be a kind of continentalism, but it could hardly be described as a turning away from the Europeans to embrace the Americans. It is the Canadian way of coping with *"le défi américain."*

North America is itself less peaceful than it was in 1949. Mr. Trudeau may have had in mind—though it is not something nice Canadians talk about—that we live beside a country in the throes of violent civil disturbance. Canada too has its own civil conflicts, much less violent as yet than in other countries. It is a first duty of military forces to assist the civil power. Planning to restrain the kind of violence which can accompany civil conflict ought not to be interpreted, however, as planning to put down rebellion or secession.

All these intangibles of the future Mr. Trudeau undoubtedly had in mind—including the challenge of the Third World, the promise and threat of technology, the questions raised about the survival of government itself—when he said that Canada should have a role in the world "which will acknowledge that humanity is increasingly subject to perils from sources in addition to an east-west conflict centred in Europe." He also said: "Those . . . who say that our defence policy represents a turn toward isolationism are proclaiming only that, in their fixation on old wars and on old problems, they are isolated—isolated from the world of now and the world of the future."[3]

There is justification for a reorientation of Canadian defence policy—and that of all NATO members—from a fixation on the cold wars to concern over the greater threats to humanity. So far the Canadian government has done no more than make a gesture to clear the way. The questions which arise are about how it is to be carried out in positive terms. Withdrawing forces from Europe can indicate an intention to *reculer pour mieux sauter*—but where and how to jump and at what cost? The significance of withdrawing a few thousand troops, one is inclined to think, has been exaggerated both by Canadians who call it a "new" policy and by their critics. Only ten per cent of the Canadian forces have been assigned to Europe, and it can be argued that the priority for North America is not at all new. It is easier to show how the previous "Establishment" was NATO-oriented than to prove that Canadian policy was in practice much distorted in that direction. What is significant is the challenge to orthodoxy, the blunt scepticism about the priority of European security in our worries about the 1970s. Perhaps it is the realization by West European governments that many of their own citizens share this scepticism which has caused them to react so sensitively.

The one European complaint that deserves a hearing is the charge that Canada is simply planning to cut its financial contribution to "western security," althought its percentage already ranks low among the allies. Part of the Canadian rebellion, of course, is against the assumption that a NATO member must keep its defence spending at a certain level to prove its virtue, regardless of the strategic value of the contribution—not a whole but at least a half truth about NATO policy. It remains a substantial charge that Canada, under cover of a plausible theory of altered priorities, is reducing its burden. The will to turn money for swords into money for African ploughshares has to be proved by the deed. It should be noted that Mr. Trudeau himself has not given much comfort to those who argue that foreign aid is a simple alternative to defence spending. If money is to be saved by defence cuts or spending stabilized, there may have to be an even more significant reconsideration of the contribution to continental defence. The laudable intention of doing a fairer share in North America could be frustrated by the rising cost of joining in military exercises with a superpower. The negotiations with the Americans, of which Mr. Trudeau spoke, have yet to take place. They are likely to go on for a long time. In the end, Canadians might have to consider the granting of United States bases on Canadian soil as the only feasible means of collaboration which would not tie Canada to the tail of American escalation.

What we have had as yet is the adumbration of a defence policy which should be judged in those terms. Government statements suggest that that is the way they look at it. The hardest decisions are yet to come. We may find the challenge and the cost of continental defence much greater than the simpler and perhaps even less expensive participation in Europe. This prospect, however, is an even stronger argument for the shift of priorities.

Notes

[1] Canada, House of Commons, *Debates*, pp. 7866-70
[2] "Canadian-American Interdependence: how much?", *Canadian Forum*, XLVIII (February, 1969), pp. 242-4.
[3] Canada, House of Commons, *Debates,* p.7870.

3:

Canada:

The Reluctant Power

The Americans seemed less concerned than the British over Canada's foreign policy revision, and the officials who did view with alarm were wise enough to realize that American criticism would be counterproductive. When in the spring of 1971 the editors of the distinguished American quarterly, Orbis,* *produced their fifteenth anniversary issue, they asked a number of foreigners to comment on their country's foreign policy in the light of the "Nixon Doctrine" proclaimed in February 1970. This article was designed to respond to the questions being asked by those Americans who were largely concerned with international security issues. Later, Americans concerned with economic issues became alarmed by reports from their sanitary inspectors that a malady called nationalism was reaching epidemic proportions north of Buffalo.*

Inquiry into the appropriate role of small, middle, and great powers in the maintenance of world order has been overtaken by uncertainties about the categories themselves. Which is now the model of a modern "middle power," Germany or Canada? It has been overtaken also by doubts about the art of rolemanship and even the concept of "world order." There is still a strong argument for a state less than super to acquire a perspective on what it should and should not seek to achieve and see its power in relative terms. Typecasting, however, has encouraged posturing. Efforts to categorize the uncategorizable have confused as much as they have clarified. And states are left, whether aligned or nonaligned, to find their own balance between national and international demands, alone and unique. At least that seems to be the

---

*Journal of world affairs published by the Foreign Policy Research Institute, Philadelphia.

current mood at a time when disintegration has affected the categories as well as the alliances, except for the superpowers locked in their strange embrace.

That Canada's role in the world is unique and therefore not interesting has been a persisting assumption of European and American students of international affairs. Like all countries, Canada is unique but its case is illustrative. Europeans, believing Canada no more than a frontier province of America, have disregarded a valuable laboratory for the study of foreign investment. Americans, for their part, have never realized that the problems that plague Canadians as allies, although complicated by the continental relationship, resemble those that bother their allies in Europe and the Pacific. For the foreign policy establishment, plagued with troubles, Canada remains vaguely in the mind as a temperamental but loyal and eminently forgettable tract. The anti-establishmentarians, the revisionist historians, curiously ignore Canada also—perhaps because the long history of the Canada-United States struggle for control of the territory of North America had such a happy ending for the lesser power that it raises doubts about the innate American appetite for imperialism.

The point of these introductory remarks is not pique. The advantages of being a lesser power and forgettable are more evident today to Canadians than they were in the days of their adolescence. It is simply to suggest that the throes in which Canada finds itself over foreign policy are both typical and illuminating. Which is not to say, as Canadians have been wont to say, that they are typical of the throes of a category we have been pleased to call "middle powers." What is typical and perhaps interesting is not the Canadian role but the Canadian dilemma about that "role."

Among internationalist Americans it is now customary to observe that Canada has a distinct mediatory role in world affairs and that is a good thing. It is a way of defining the uniqueness and making further consideration unnecessary. Canadians should not complain, because they have, for the past decade, been trying to convince their allies that they have indeed a special role as a middling and moderating force in world politics. Basic concepts of international relations, however, take a long time to be transmitted even to neighbours. After three-quarters of a century the Soviet Union seems to have come around to the views of Admiral Alfred T. Mahan when Americans are growing weary of them. Americans who, in the 1950s, regarded the independence of Canadian foreign policy as not playing the game, are being converted to the Canadian thesis about diversity in unity and the role of the middle power at a time when Canadians—especially those in high places—are turning away from the idea of a role of any kind. The recent government white paper on foreign policy rejects the Canadian image of the country as the "helpful fixer." The reference is less derogatory than it sounds. The paper was not designed to question the intermediary part Canada played in the UN (at the time of the Suez crisis, for example), over Commonwealth differences, and even occasionally in NATO, or its general peacekeeping function. Rather it expressed revulsion against excessive rhetoric about middlepowermanship, against a shift of emphasis from a Canadian diplomacy which had tried to be useful because world order mattered to Canadians to an unhealthy emphasis on the Canadian role as an end in itself in a kind of diplomatic Olympic games.

Revulsions have set in in Canada as they have in other countries. There is a weariness not so much with the actual structure which Dean Acheson, with a little assistance from others, created after World War II as with the twenty-year-old clichés about that structure and the Canadian part in it. The Canadian response to a call to serve is likely to be as co-operative and as reluctant as it was when Canada was called upon previously to do dirty jobs, as for example to man the International Control Commissions in Indochina. That the compulsion to mediation is still stronger than the revulsion against it was illustrated by the widespread expectation that Prime Minister Trudeau would take the lead in holding the Commonwealth together in Singapore. This sort of thing is less likely to be seen, however, as the central purpose of Canada in world affairs.

Canadian commentators on foreign policy are obsessed now with two ideas. Canadian influence in the world, they insist, has declined from an inflated position after the war because of the recovery of the defeated powers and the expansion of membership in the United Nations. A masochistic delight is taken in puncturing their own pride. The other fashionable argument is that Canadian foreign policy has paid too little regard to the national interest and has given its priority to pretentious international diplomacy. These are different from but similar to trends of thinking in the United States and Britain. In the growing disillusionment about the Canadian role there has been some flirtation with Gaullist philosophy, the argument being that Canada's quiet diplomacy failed to move the great powers, especially the United States, whereas de Gaulle by his bluntness made Washington shake. That de Gaulle got larger headlines in the American press than did Lester Pearson is beyond dispute. That American policy-makers responded any more favourably to loud than to quiet diplomacy is not proved. Canadian nationalists are crying out for a posture of defiance against Washington, but this kind of rhetoric is also dated. It is associated with the claustrophobic debate of the 1960s about independence and influence as ends in themselves and the advantages of alignment and nonalignment which appear increasingly irrelevant in the 1970s. In any case Canada has for a prime minister the most noted non-Gaullist in public life, as uninterested in that kind of nationalism as he is in national role-playing. It is significant that in the past two years official comments from Ottawa about the Vietnam war have virtually ceased, but one would be mistaken to assume a greater sympathy with any American policy except withdrawal. The silence is rather a reaction against a Canadian role as moral adviser and a practical calculation that public calls from Ottawa are not for the moment likely to help President Nixon get the boys home.

The charge that Canadian foreign policy and diplomacy have neglected the national interest reflects illusions about "priorities" which afflict Americans, British, and others. Problems of the cities, ethnic tensions, and economic paradoxes force themselves upon the attention of governments. Domestic problems are probably less serious in Canada than in almost any country in the world, although it would be hard to convince many Canadians of this. The idea that they can or should drop foreign policy to turn to domestic policy is a fallacy that persists in all countries. The issues of world peace, commerce, and development do not pause while political leaders deal with slums. The notion that governments and bureaucracies can turn their minds to only one or the other, the interests of the people at home or those abroad, is particularly strong among Canadians, who have rarely regarded foreign policy and defence expenditure as a life-and-death matter for themselves. There is in public statements these days a rather forced note of *Realpolitik,* a determination to put the interests of Canada first, that nicely catches the nationalist mood but need not be taken seriously by allies who never shared the widespread Canadian view that Canada has been the patsy of international politics.

Canada happens to be one country that can, or whose people think it can, leave world security to others without getting into serious trouble. Canadian governments for sixty years have notably refused to adopt that position, but it is always tempting them. It is particularly tempting at the present time because Canadians have grown sceptical of the role they chose for themselves. Serious questions are raised about all the pillars on which their international commitments were built. They find it hard to discern a role in the SALT age. If there is a drift away from traditional commitments to international security, it may be attributed to several causes. First there is a more aggressive demand for aid at home from those less benefited by the rich Canadian economy. More shrill but less important is the Canadian variation on the theme of disengagement from "American imperialism," although this cry cannot fairly be called isolationist because it demands Canadian involvement and expenditure on behalf of the unliberated in distant continents. Most important may be an involuntary cause, failure to find an answer to the question: what can a smaller ally do in the 1970s that makes sense? Most Canadians would probably still like to go on trying, but changing circumstances cast doubt on old answers, and new ones that seem practical and consistent with the preservation of identity are not forthcoming. So the temptation is strong to turn to the internal revolution and justify the downgrading of a role in world security by a significant but not too painful rise in the contribution to aid and development.

Americans may find it difficult to understand why Canadians would not happily accept their good fortune as part of a North American economy burgeoning from the technological revolution, and as a partner in defence against common enemies which is allowed to pay only a small share of the cost. Anglophone Canadians, incidentally, persist in asking almost the same question, and with the same blind spots, about Quebec. In the New World we are intolerant of all nationalisms except our own. In the United States nationalism was turned into a state religion. Canada, on the contrary, was designed, as all states should be, for comfort and convenience rather than for a moral purpose. Canadians, even at some cost, are reluctant to get involved in a continentalism which at present looks uncomfortable. This is not a kind of nationalism that looks worthy to the heirs of Jefferson, but it has some of the frontier optimism the United States has mislaid.

Another problem of timing is that although Canada may in recent years have been too big for its boots, it is now trying to get into a smaller pair that will not fit. In military terms Canada is not only a lesser power; it is without ambition to be anything else. The ambition of most Canadians is probably to be the smallest possible military power. Unfortunately for a country getting over its adolescence and recognizing the happiness to be found in modest means and seclusion, greatness is being thrust upon it. In those things that matter increasingly—territory, resources, industry, and trade—Canada is rapidly becoming a great power. This fact is obscured by the inevitable comparisons with its neighbour. The persistent problem of the Canadian image is chiaroscuro.

Before this decade is over, Canada, according to present trends, may have a larger gross national product than either of the two European countries with permanent seats in the Security Council. Canadians debate whether theirs is an adult economy, whether their ability to play a major role is inhibited by foreign control. A larger share of Canadian ownership of industry and resources might well strengthen the Canadian hand, but descriptions of the Canadian condition in drastic terms as powerless or satellite are wide of the mark. Control by Canada of resources desperately needed by the United States and Japan gives the country its own kind of power. The growing importance of Canada in international bodies concerned with monetary or commercial issues, or in conferences on questions like the law of the sea in which vast geography is a factor, suggest that, however diminished its military strength, it will be a country of increasing consequence in the kind of world affairs that are beginning to matter most.

One reason Canada has been conducting an extensive and, on the whole, healthy review of its foreign policy is that serious questions have been raised about the bases on which that policy rested: the United Nations, the Commonwealth, NATO and the continental partnership.

The universal worry over the United Nations has a special dimension in Canada because it has always been the ideal place for a creative lesser power to find a role compatible with national interests and national pride. In the function of peacekeeping Canadians found an outlet for their idealism and a satisfying use for their military forces. The rhetoric about peacekeeping, like the rhetoric about middlepowermanship in general, has been overdone in recent years and the disposition at present is to play down its significance. On the other hand a tragic stance about the United Nations is avoided. Canadian governments had tended to view the United Nations as a valuable diplomatic instrument to be developed rather than as a world government in which they could put their total trust. They are less disposed therefore to write it off now. Canadians are continuing to take UN causes seriously, especially those having to do with economics or disarmament. All that is needed to revive interest in peacekeeping is probably another invitation. If such an invitation comes, there will be a more sceptical examination by Ottawa of the provisions for the operation, but the government is not going to find it much easier to say no than did its predecessors—although there may be more countries now than there were ten years ago with an interest in this kind employment for their troops, and the ban on great powers may be lifted.

Recent unilateral Canadian gestures to extend authority over larger areas of ice and sea have been looked upon by Americans in particular and by members of the international law community as a Canadian retreat from the role of international good boy. The Canadian argument is that it is nothing of the kind; it is simply a gesture by a reasonably powerful country to defy the domination of international law by large powers with special maritime and naval interests, an insensitive domination which has encouraged international lawlessness among the developing countries. There is room for argument here, but the Canadian position is not that of the calculated outlaw. Like most countries, Canada will identify its national interest with the general interest, but it still recognizes that there is a general interest and that international law is important. One might sense a disposition to join forces with the developing countries, and Canada may play this part again when opportunities arise. Unless the Ottawa government becomes a great deal more revolutionary than it seems, such opportunities are not likely to arise often. Because Canada has an enormous coastline and few ships, its interests on maritime questions are contrary to those of the United States and other major powers, but usually it will be pulled by its own interests into their camp.

As for the Commonwealth, Canadians are proving tenacious because they consider themselves to some extent creators of the modern Commonwealth. It has been easier for Canada than Britain to accept the looser Commonwealth because Canada had not regarded it as a monolithic structure and its function as a consultative body has not ceased to be useful for Canada. A few years ago one might have thought interest in the Commonwealth was moribund in Canada, but few external issues have attracted as widespread attention as the Nigerian war and the controversy over arms to South Africa. With a strong emphasis on the Canadian role in francophonie as well, it could be charged that these are areas of a modest kind of Canadian imperialism. In both cases there has been some contest with the mother country. The Secretaries-General of both the Commonwealth and L'Agence de Coopération culturelle et technique are Canadians. Because it is in a sense the Canadian as much as the British Commonwealth which is at stake, Trudeau was forced by Canadian opinion and African expectations as well as conviction into opposing the British over the sale of arms to South Africa.

Few Canadians question the right of the British to say goodbye to their imperial past and to plunge into Europe, but a renunciation by the Heath government of one of the great creations of British political genius would deny the validity of a long experiment in international relations in which Canada played its own honourable part. At any rate, the Canadian response to this challenge to the Commonwealth shows that the mood is not really as isolationist as it may seem to be—although of course there is little cost involved. There is the cost of economic aid and development programmes both in the Commonwealth and in francophonie, still not adequate for an economic "great power" but rising faster than those of other developed countries. Any suggestions that Canada might take over leadership roles from Britain and France in these last phases of their empires get little encouragement in Ottawa. Canadians are anti-imperialists not so much by conviction as by laziness—and a surfeit of territory. They prefer to be a supplementary rather than a leading power.

For Canada the Commonwealth has been part of a philosophy of counterweight. NATO was another aspect. Canadians made no secret of the fact that although their primary purpose for going into NATO was its urgent necessity in 1949, it was also an answer to their own need for a multilateral rather than an unequal bilateral alliance. The service of NATO as a counterweight is now questioned. The United States insisted on divorcing NORAD from NATO, and there has been no practical way for the Europeans to correct the imbalance in continental defence. Counterweight is a neat political idea without much relevance here. There is scepticism also about the value of acquiring "influence" through alliances. NATO may, as its advocates argue, have given Canada some voice in European affairs, but the critics are asking what national interest that serves. Europe as an economic and cultural counterweight is more interesting, but these advantages are unrelated to the NATO tie.

The reduction of Canadian forces in Europe should be attributed not so much to Canadian isolationism as to the sheer irrationality in the 1970s of Canada, with its own vast land to control or defend, maintaining troops in Germany. It has made sense to those who lived through 1949; but it is difficult to convince present Canadian voters that an emergency situation of twenty years ago, attributable to the weakness of France, Germany, and Italy, is still an emergency. This is not because the Soviet threat has diminished but because the capacity of the Europeans has increased. The case of the United States is different because the United States is more than a Western Hemisphere power; it is a world superpower, and its influence in NATO councils is commensurate with its power. So is Canada's for that matter, and that is why it is hardly worth maintaining. The argument that Canada's presence in Europe is that of proxy for the American presence is insulting.

The assumption in Europe that Canada is withdrawing in order to enter into a more comfortable defence relationship with the United States is the reverse of the truth. The philosophy expressed in the Prime Minister's defence statements is that we should keep our forces at home so that we can look after our surveillance ourselves rather than rely on our neighbour to do so. In that way we preserve our independence from creeping continentalism and American wrath. Serious questions about the basis of continental defence have been raised which cannot be discussed adequately here. Suffice it to say that the logic of joint continental defence is still accepted but not taken for granted as readily as it was fifteen years ago. Partly this is because there is not the same certainty of consensus in designating the enemy. Partly it is because the escalation of technology and cost has made anything resembling military partnership or joint control of policy impossible. Some Canadians think that by rejecting a defence relationship they can exorcise the United States. The majority, while unhappy about the present situation and puzzled, are not clear about safe alternatives. At most, the established machinery of joint defence might move along unobtrusively. It is not a political climate that encourages new initiatives, new roles, or even the refurbishing of old ones—or participation in expensive new joint projects.

A preoccupation with the dilemmas of the continental relationship has prevented Canadians from contemplating the impact on them of a weakening of the pax Americana. A problem for the allies is that the United States in the age of the American empire behaved, insofar as the allies were concerned, not so much like a governor as a governess. It did not impose NATO on any of us. In a sense of common danger we got together and created an alliance. Because the United States paid the piper it came to call the tune—not entirely, but to a considerable extent. It tried to get as many contributions as possible from the poor relations, encouraged and praised them when they did well, and reminded them of the awful dangers when they strayed into heresy. An unhealthy reliance on the United States developed. It was inevitable that people would come to think, especially after the excessive Cold War ideology of the 1950s, that Washington had created the alliance for its own purposes and that the Soviet threat was the product of American imagination—an assumption encouraged in recent years by certain political and historical writings even in the United States. We became dependent upon the United States even for intelligence, a disabling situation for any ally. As the age of the superpowers developed, the allies, or at least their voters, became less and less preoccupied with the Soviet "threat." They thought it exaggerated or they thought it was something for the United States to cope with. Sheltered from the Soviet Union, governments became preoccupied with their relationship with Washington. It was not that the United States threatened them in the same dire way, but it raised more complicated problems.

This is particularly the case in Canada. The Soviet threat in the Mediterranean may have stimulated the Europeans into anxiety, but it has less impact on Canada. Increasingly, Canadians see themselves as Arctic neighbours of the Soviet Union rather than as separated from the Soviet land mass by Europe, but this awareness, this ultimate abandonment of Mercator's view of the world, leads their attention to a frontier where they cannot see clearly. The greatest physical threat to

Canada is not a Soviet invasion of Europe but a nuclear exchange between the Soviet Union and the United States. The former might trigger the latter, but the former is a problem for the Europeans. The exchange of missiles between the United States and the Soviet Union is almost entirely a problem for the United States. Canada had a role in defence against the manned bomber on which doubt is now cast. For twenty years Canada has accepted a supplementary role in defence of the United States nuclear capacity, but this has grown less important. Canadians once thought their partnership in continental defence would give them some share in defence policy, but their bargaining power has been reduced. In the age of the superpowers lesser allies can do little more than protect some of their own immediate interests. The United States alone makes the decision to go into an ABM programme, although it will listen to Canadian complaints about how this might affect Canadian territory.

Canadian influence in the SALT talks is not likely to be important, and Canadians look for a more active outlet in the disarmament negotiations in Geneva. As in the argument over the placing of arms in coastal waters, they sometimes find themselves in assocation with lesser powers against the United States and the Soviet Union, but the philosophy is that while the superpowers alone can maintain the deterrents, other countries can best use their brains exploring arms control agreements. Canadians do not see themselves as antagonists of the United States, but sometimes they are allies of certain forces within the United States against others—a situation that makes relations with the United States government tricky indeed.

Taking a fresh look at the fundamental problems of defence, Canadians ask: Who, if anybody, does threaten us? To judge by the decibels of the debate one would conclude that the answer is the United States. The dilemma is that while Canada considers the conventional problems of its security in a dangerous world, it must also consider the defence of its independence, sovereignty, and identity. The traditional associate in the former struggle is the country that poses the largest threat in the latter. The fact that the threat to Canadian independence is not a calculated policy of the United States government, but an amalgam of economic and cultural forces over which the United States government has little control, diminishes the ill will but not the problem. Regionalist answers to world security problems which seem sensible elsewhere would be suicidal for Canada. The United States impinges so much more than the Soviet Union that defence against its far less mortal threat preoccupies Canadian attention. Furthermore, it is a threat Canadians can and must cope with on their own.

The long-term challenges, however, are different from those perceived twenty years ago. Canada is vulnerable because it is a country with a small population, enormous territory, and vast resources. It is exceedingly dependent upon a world safe for commerce. Its relatively good image in the Third World is threatened by its international activities and its own "neo-imperialism." It is one of the few under-populated countries in the world and there is likely to be a great scramble on the part of the major industrial powers for Canadian resources. The challenge is not of flying missiles, invading armies, and submarines, but of a general threat to those who are unfairly rich in a desperately poor world. The guerrilla arm has already struck at us viciously. The threat of international anarchy to the specific Canadian need for "world order" was never more clear, but this is not at all like the kind of Cold War threat against which our security arrangements were established in the postwar years.

Few developing countries now see emigration as an answer to their problems, but they are nonetheless likely to resent the Canadian proportion of resources and investment to population. The only country that could conceivably provide a threat of mass immigration to Canada is the United States—an unlikely possibility but one which, in the light of civil unrest and pollution, is at least imaginable. (Canada has civil unrest and pollution but more space for it.) There is some fear that the United States will withdraw into its own continent where the pressures for resources of energy and space will become such that Americans might put intolerable pressures on their underpopulated neighbour. In addition, uneasiness about the turbulence across the long thin border has made Canadians fearful of, rather than frightened by, the United States. It is to some extent the malaise of the comfortable suburb. It is keeping the attention of Canadians off distant continents and worldly roles.

Because their capacity to contribute much to world security in the conventional sense has diminished, Canadians will find their role to be much more in the realm of economics, but as economic pressures grow more threatening, the issues of world security may be largely economic. One would like to think that the Canadian capacity for intermediation could be displayed in this area. There is an obvious will in Ottawa to be the enlightened world citizen in international economics, but here Canadian interest is much more basic and direct than in military questions, and the pressure of domestic forces is likely to make it more defensive. The Canadian standard of living is involved as it never seemed to be over Suez. For this purpose Canada is in a paradoxical position. Its favourable balance of trade and payments has been increasing spectacularly, and in international terms Canada is a rich and fortunate country. At the same time unemployment and regional disparity are increasing, and the difficulty will be for Canadian governments to behave abroad with the assurance and generosity other countries have a right to expect from a major and confident power.

The Nixon Doctrine for Canadians, as for other associates of the United States, has contradictory elements. The majority of Canadians probably feel that United States power was overextended, especially in Vietnam, and that a withdrawal from the role of world policeman is all to the good. There may, however, be shocks accompanying that withdrawal which will remind us all of the extent to which we had come to rely on the Americans' capacity to intervene—when we wanted them to as well as when we thought they should not. The notice from Washington that others are expected to assume a larger share in the maintenance of world order and the combating of world catastrophes may have an effect in Europe. There are signs it is doing so. However willing sensible Canadians might be to accept such a call, it is hard for them to know what they could do except perhaps maintain their capacity for peacekeeping should the occasions arise again. Token contingents are more trouble than use. The white paper advocates a Canadian orientation toward the "Pacific rim," but in spite of the willingness to become more involved, no one has advanced any serious suggestions about a role Canada could play in Pacific security. A brigade or two in Vietnam might once have been the suggestion from Washington, but the Nixon Doctrine indicates that is not likely in future to be the kind of help required. There is no prospect of a North Pacific treaty organization and no apparent disposition in Washington to share its Pacific supremacy with allies who could be troublesome. In looking for a role here there seems little else than to fall back on remedies which may sound old-fashioned but may still be valid: economic aid where it is needed, mutually beneficial bilateral trade, and efforts at political and cultural understanding for which lesser people have some advantages.

Canadians would argue that their establishment of relations with Peking is of this order. Some have apocalyptic illusions about what one medium power can do to bridge that great gap. In more influential circles, however, the move is seen as a valid if small contribution that could help eventually to get Americans and Chinese talking to each other. It is ironic that now, when the tendency in the country is to minimize the international influence it can exert, Canada has demonstrated again the powerful effect even a lesser power can have as a catalyst. The formula for recognition that Ottawa and Peking agreed to accept has been adopted by Italy and Chile and has led to a climactic situation in the United Nations. Whether this was a move in the right or the wrong direction is arguable, but that it has been influential is beyond dispute. When conventional wisdom is to minimize the impact of lesser powers on the superpowers, we tend to gloss over the impact of Cambodia or Israel, not to mention Albania and Canada. What indeed is a middle power?

4:

Canada and the Crisis
of Middle Powers

The editors of Worldview, *published in New York by the Council on Religion and International Affairs, wondered what had been happening to the concept of a "middle power" and asked for an article "with particular, but not exclusive, reference to Canada." As is their wont, they stimulate an author with provocative questions, as for example: "At what point is the role of conscience compromised or confused by the fact that middle powers also have their own games to play?" This piece was an effort to look at middlepowerism as an international phenomenon. It is reprinted, with permission, from the June 1972 issue of* Worldview.

If the superpowers are, as is commonly suggested, passing through a time of crisis, so inevitably are the "middle powers," for the states that for twenty-five years have been collectively but erratically referred to as middle powers are groping for their place in a system determined by the giants. At San Francisco in 1945 the middle powers seemed to have found a mission in frustrating the great-power determination to brook as little interference as possible in their ordering of world politics. When the great powers fell apart, the middle-power front was also broken. Its members found their niches in alliance with the great powers or in a status they called nonalignment. Alignment and nonalignment make sense, however, only in relation to the great powers' division.

We middle men chafed at our dependence, but, for the most part, flourished and survived nicely within the framework of mutual deterrence, of pax Americana or pax Sovietica-Americana. Now that framework is in transition. If the superpowers lose their grip or if, for that matter, they act together to tighten their grip on the system, do we resume our San Francisco stance? The prospects force us out of our habitual rhetoric to honest self-examination. How much do we really want to float free? Do we want to revive the discredited illusion of universal collective security? If not, what can we do for the cause of peace that makes sense? Assuming we are ready to play a real part in maintaining international security, what can we do when technology has largely restricted the arms race to the top two or maybe three? There was a time when the concepts of alliance and collective security gave us rational purpose, but they no longer seem so rational. If we resume our compulsive and automatic resistance to the superpowers, is that in their interest? or ours? or the world's? Finally, as the unfrozen issues of international relations become more economic than military, maybe we have to re-think what we mean by "superpower" and "middle power."

The concept of middle power came out of a peculiar history. It is a term of convenience with no standing in international agreements or organizations. It is subject to a confusing ambiguity, its significance is in a play on words. It may or may not have a future.

Although the concept was recognized in the structure of the League of Nations more clearly than in the United Nations, the term middle power became current at the end of the Second World War. It was an unofficial way of describing countries which did not have the veto rights of great powers in the United Nations but could still contribute more than small powers. Sweden, Brazil, and Canada were clearly middle powers, but the term was frequently extended to include a country like India which, although enormous in population, was neither economically nor militarily a great power.

Canadians embraced the term more enthusiastically than others, arguing in 1945 that there must be no permanent right of the great powers to privilege and veto in all aspects of international relations. The strong military powers should be accorded rights in line with their function in the Security Council only. Countries with special colonial responsibilities would have their place in the Trusteeship Council, and it was hoped that countries with economic power would have special status in the Economic and Social Council (ECOSOC) and the functional organizations. The rule would be, "To each according to his capacities." Geographical and regional pressures, however, soon succeeded in overwhelming the rule. Powers of middling military strength were not even recognized as having a greater right to election to the Security Council, as Canada had insisted. Nevertheless, the persisting value of the concept, at least for those who professed it, was that it defined for themselves a sensible attitude to responsibility. They did not presume to be great military powers, but they knew they had duties beyond those of the small and weak. They would demand a larger voice than the great were disposed to accord them, and they would earn it through services in the cause.

Enter the ambiguity. Many issues—Kashmir, Indonesia, Palestine, for examples—arising out of the break-up of empires required states or individuals with less vested interests to play the role of intermediaries. The middle-sized powers filled the bill because, while they did not have interests or power enough to be threatening, they did have sufficient diplomatic and military resources to mediate conflicts. The term ''middle'' originally denoted size, but now took on the connotation of intermediary. Countries which proved useful as intermediaries, however, soon included Norway, Ireland, and Tunisia, states which are hardly medium in resources or population. The term middle power is no doubt ambivalent; some think it ambivalent to the point of being meaningless.

The 1970s promise only to intensify the ambivalence. Now that the British and Germans—but never, of course, the French—are informally referring to themselves as middle powers, it is time to take a new look at the hierarchy. Instead of the great powers designated by the Security Council in the 1940s, we now seem to have this line up: two superpowers; China, which is *sui generis;* Britain and France, still recognized as great powers in the Security Council but far from super; Japan, an economic if not a military power; India, a great power in political influence; and Brazil moving up fast. In economics we have, for example on monetary questions, the Group of Ten, which includes among the financial great powers some of the classical middle powers of the postwar period.

If the term middle power means anything useful now, it is probably with reference to countries like Yugoslavia or Sweden which have by nature or situation intermediary capacities. Intermediation, however, has become much more ad hoc. As the concept of world-embracing alignments declines, nonalignment becomes more regional and specific. One hopes of course, that as many nations as possible will cherish their capacities and responsibilities. On the other hand, the idea that certain countries are suited by nature for this role in most if not all world conflicts may be of diminishing value. Even Canada, which has clung to this mission as its best definition of foreign policy, is turning away from the idea of mediation. A new generation is bored with the role and the reputation that goes with it. Also, since Canada is now a major economic power, it is less likely to play the part of disinterested mediator in the great commercial and monetary conflicts of this decade. It is not easy, however, to escape the habits of a generation or the expectations of the international system. Prime Minister Trudeau, shortly after expressing scepticism about the role of "helpful fixer," was drawn into mediating between Britain and the African states over arms to South Africa and the status of Rhodesia. Being viewed as a professional mediator has it drawbacks, but it is finally mediation that keeps the planet from blowing up.

Before we discard the concept of middle power we should consider its past contributions to world politics as well as its failures. It should be emphasized that, although the middle powers did struggle at San Francisco to establish their second-class voice in the hierarchy, the mediatory role was more thrust upon them than sought. The role was largely defined *ex post facto*. The issues that arose in the United Nations required an intermediary force. The great powers persuaded the middle men to act, and the victims of conflict welcomed their interventions. Greece, Indonesia, Lebanon, and Indochina are among the better known interventions, but the functions of the middle powers (in the late 'fifties *The Economist* called them the "Sanitavian Bloc") were demonstrated persistently if less visibly in the regular work of the UN and other international bodies: getting together sponsors for compromise resolutions, lobbying to avoid dangerous confrontation, collaborating with the efforts of the Secretary-General, and in a thousand ways seeking to reduce tension. It can be argued that, insofar as it can be worked, the middle powers made the UN work. They made possible the "peacekeeping" which emerged in the 'fifties as one way the UN could act to prevent the spread of conflict. To be sure, these were chapter VI functions of conciliation rather than chapter VII functions of enforcement, but they were the best that could be done.

Or were they? Perhaps peacekeeping, while it dampened immediate conflicts, prevented settlements. It could be argued that peacekeeping has prevented for over twenty years a settlement in Kashmir, whereas the sharp military surgery of the Indian government in 1971 made a settlement possible in East Bengal. But such logic is perilous. The wars that did not take place are never as vivid as the conflicts that continue; a strong case remains for the policy of damping brush fires during an inflammatory period in the world's history. In any case, the middle powers were doing what the great powers and a strong majority of UN members wanted them to do. The instinct of the United Nations to interpose a mediatory force in any conflict is deeply rooted. While less often practised in recent years, another conflict could revive the process instantaneously—particularly a conflict that powers which have in principle disliked peacekeeping want to have extinguished.

The middle-power function was not confined to the major councils of the UN. The same practices have been prevalent in NATO, the Organization of American States, and the Commonwealth. The middle-power function is also evident in the disarmament negotiations in Geneva. It is sometimes hard to preserve a distinction between middle powers and nonaligned powers, since middle powers, whether aligned or not, have some responsibility to restrain superpower assumptions which threaten the legitimate interests of the weak. Italy and Canada, for example, neither of which could be called nonaligned, have frequently joined with Third World forces to press the nuclear powers at Geneva. They ganged up to pressure and defeat their betters in securing the admission of new members to the UN in 1955, and perhaps they deserve some credit for getting Peking seated in 1971 when both superpowers had reason to be less than enthusiastic. (There have, of course, been other occasions when the so-called African-Asian bloc has enforced its will, but that is something different from middlepowerism.)

If in the age of SALT there is a resurgence of superpower authority, a coalescence of all lesser powers may become a more frequent phenomenon; the coalition might also include European powers with veto rights, nervous or jealous of the presumptions of Washington and Moscow. But such schematizations should not be pushed too far. Just how the antagonism to superpower domination felt by Britain, France, or Germany might be harmonized with the not very similar feelings of, say, Tanzania, Uruguay, or Rumania is hard to envision. Of course, Western Europe itself might become a superpower. The greater danger, however, is that the members of the European Economic Community, incapable of the discipline of a single voice, will use the "voice of Europe" theme for blackmail while refusing to accept the responsibilities of a unified superpower. One unhappy consequence of this pretense is that the authentic voices of some very useful European middle powers will be silenced. The international community would be the loser, for it needs conscientious middle powers more than it needs a new superpower—especially an unreliable superpower.

At least one of the superpowers is going through a devastating examination of conscience. The citizens of the middle powers should follow suit. A certain moral arrogance has crept into the concept of middle power. That might is not right all would agree—but neither is weakness. Middle powers are middle powers because they are weaker, not because they are more virtuous. Many of them (and I think especially of my own countrymen) boast that they have no imperial aims, they threaten no one, and therefore they are widely loved. But they forget that they threaten no one because they are incapable of doing so. Stated so bluntly, this is too harsh a judgment, for middle powers have indeed shown judgment, objectivity, and dedication. Nonetheless, the basic difference between us and the great powers is functional rather than moral.

Among the less pleasant psychological manifestations of middlepowerism, all too evident in Canada at present, is the "David versus Goliath complex." The facile assumption is that David is justified in using any means to beat Goliath simply because Goliath is a giant and David is self-evidently on the side of the angels. This attitude is generally encouraged by UN Assembly rhetoric, and it is at least more understandable when proclaimed by very small and weak powers, although it is of doubtful validity even then. It is thoroughly unwarranted and undignified in the case of middle powers which are, in relation to the world at large, rich and greedy. The Canadian reputation for good sense and proportion has been threatened by an obsessive chauvinism which has taken hold even among socialist and liberal circles where one customarily expects expansive internationalism. Resistance to Americanism masquerading as internationalism is entirely justified. However, an obsession with the need to protect our interests in competition with a very powerful neighbour seems, to an articulate minority of Canadians, to justify a policy of national self-interest in which we lose sight of our responsibilities in the wider world. We have more land and resources and coastline per capita than any other country in the world, but when it comes to the protection and extension of our coastal waters, our fish, our seabed, and our protective tariffs we tend to behave in an aggressive manner more appropriate to a developing nation in Africa. Fortunately, Canadians are not aggressive enough by disposition to sustain this posture, and the government has for the most part resisted these pressures. Whatever the future of middlepowerism, most Canadians still realize that a reputation for fair-mindedness remains their most valuable asset.

An additional temptation for middle powers is to cling to the Cold War which made us. It is a greater temptation for the nonaligned, because changing alignments undermine the very concept of nonalignment by which they defined themselves. Dependent countries may be even more attached to the Cold War because of their notable success in getting support by playing one side off against the other. It is easy to exaggerate this temptation, but it calls for vigilance. A good world citizen should, for example, watch the Peking-Washington rapprochement with relief and enthusiasm. Some countries might be excused a few unworthy *arrières-pensées*. Scandinavian and Eastern European countries which have been important as messengers and interpreters may find themselves unemployed. While Canada did not enter into diplomatic relations with Peking in 1970 in order to mediate between Peking and Washington, there is no doubt that Ottawa had some worthy hopes of helping to heal that breach. Mr. Nixon, however, got to Peking even before Mr. Trudeau.

Canada has long had something of a "linchpin" fixation. It once saw itself as the interpreter between Britain and the United States, but Messrs. Churchill and Roosevelt put that idea to rest many years ago. There is much to be said for renouncing bridge-building as a national profession. But something worse could replace it. The need of lesser states for a mission may be deplored but it can't be ignored.

The healthier aspect of the new Canadian nationalism is a determination to be ourselves, not to be judged as extensions of Britain, France, or the United States. The mood is caught in a popular Quebec song, *"Mon pays, ce n'est pas un pays; c'est l'hiver"*—sung not regretfully but exultantly. Such a mood hardly promotes international brokerage as a national mission, however. Burgeoning nationalism is a volatile force that can turn swiftly in various directions. With the Canadian GNP approaching $100 billion, we are tempted to a hard self-assertion that could spawn its own brand of middle-power imperialism. Foreigners, Americans in particular, can help turn Canadian nationalism sour by deploring it. Americans have a habit of disparaging any nationalism except their own as emotionalism, of assuming that nation-states, except their own, are anachronisms—an assumption that has in the past decade become one of the more anachronistic clichés of our time. What Canadians—and other middle powers—need from abroad is encouragement of their better instincts, of self-confidence, and a moderate, medium but inspiring sense of mission. Such a mission must be unique, appropriate, discrete. It can be complementary or even supplementary, but it must not be just a matter of pitching in and sharing the work that a great power has defined for itself. That is what the Australians did in Vietnam, and it is not a precedent they or others will want to follow.

Fortunately for Canada, as for most other middle powers, our first national interest is in a world order that secures the greatest combination of peace and prosperity for all. Our secondary interests are competitive. Our interests are in freedom of the seas and of commerce and in the stability that comes not from conserving the status quo but from controlled change and development. We need not see foreign policy as a zero-sum game. There is no basic incompatibility of interest between us and the large or small, developed or underdeveloped countries, although this assumption is much less clear to those for whom the present is much less satisfactory.

Narrower conceptions of national interest, however, are bound to assert themselves, and the very high percentage of land and resources per capita in Canada compared with other countries in a crowded world will put our large-mindedness to a severe test. Economics increasingly dominates world politics, and our responsibilities for constructive leadership are enormous and increasing. As for matters of security, our responsibilities are probably decreasing. The technology and exorbitant costs of fleets, planes, and missiles reduce the military options of middle powers to little beyond peacekeeping, relief, and patrolling our frontiers. In a missile age even our real estate is less essential for bases. Our military contribution through multilateral alliances once seemed sensible, but the utility of such alliances is unclear beyond the immediate future. NATO for example, may become primarily an instrument for maintaining equilibrium in Europe in order to counterbalance the Warsaw Pact. Our role in international security will be more and more economic or diplomatic, and thus our power depends less on armed might than on our GNP and our wisdom in international policies.

Meanwhile, we should try not to be inconsistent in our tensions with the great powers. It is true that most of us recognized early the disastrous American miscalculation in Vietnam, but few of us recognized the general responsibility for a situation into which the United States so wrongheadedly plunged. We foreign friends seem unable to make up our minds whether the United States is a bogeyman or a fairy godfather, whether we want Americans to pack up, go home, and stop bothering us, or whether we want them to intervene all over the world in favour of the good guys—or at the very least to accept our volatile conceptions of which guys are at the moment good and bad.

We need some rigorously honest thinking about pax Americana, or whatever one chooses to call an international system marked by a considerable, although limited, United States hegemony. The sensible response is obvious. Pax Americana may have provided some stability in the postwar years, but it is inequitable, untenable, and, at any rate, its *raison d'être* has been destroyed in Vietnam. It must be replaced by a world order in which power and authority are shared by the strong and the weak in fair proportion. Americans and non-Americans can all agree about that. But how do we get there?

We are where we are because the United States acted as trustee for world authority while other powers were gathering their resources. That is the creation at which Dean Acheson thought he was present. We have learned some hard lessons since 1945. We have learned, of course, that even the most benevolent superpower cannot for long distinguish between its own and the international interest. The rest of us have also learned how comfortable and inexpensive it can be to leave the basic structure of world order to the superpowers. This is not the customary statement of gratitude to the United States for generously defending us, for one cannot be sure whether it has been defending us against our own or its own enemies. We are protected not by one superpower but by the system of mutual deterrence. The point is that we lesser powers have discovered distinct advantages in a system wherein we had to maintain only a minimum police force and had to accept no responsibility except that of watchdog in the critical decisions about missiles and fleets and in the dilemmas of intervention. We have made two efforts to implement the principle of universal collective security. We have been disposed to blame the great powers for their failure, but we know in our hearts that the principle was unsound. In the new constellation we shall, for better or worse, be more on our own and without the easy concept of alliance that gave us a definition of our role and some share in policy-making.

So long as we have superpowers, most Canadians want the United States to be a superpower. Of course we might want to get rid of the superpowers, but not one at a time. A little isolationism in the United States would be a good thing. The United States ought to rationalize its commitments, to give up trying to do the impossible in Asia, to stop trying to manage Europe and Latin America and the world at large. But the United States has little need now of our advice to do just that. We should be very careful to avoid driving the United States into isolationism. We must appeal to the benevolent, internationalist spirit which is the persistent greatness of the United States. To play that large-spirited role, the United States must remain strong and respected, and we must respect its need to remain strong, even militarily. We may not like the pretensions of the United States Navy, but if there are going to be superpower patrols of the Seven Seas—and there are—we would much rather there be more than one world-girdling fleet and that one of them be American. The United States must keep its place in the arms equilibrium in order to play a forceful role in the constant effort to scale down arms all around.

To say that the middle powers should be the conscience of mankind is presumptuous only if we presume to be its exclusive custodians. Because our specific national interests are rarely engaged directly in international conflicts, we are less subject to internal pressures than are the great powers, and we ought to, even if we don't, maintain more balanced perspectives. It is always hard for Samaritans to avoid being Pharisees. We in Canada and Sweden and other middle powers are encouraged by anxious citizens of the United States to act as the conscience of mankind because we haven't their power and their temptations. We have our own. Pettiness is a sin like overweening pride. Still, virtue may be less costly for us. It is hard to take seriously the idea of urbanized twentieth-century Canada as the new Walden

Pond, but we do have a duty to give sanctuary, for example. That includes sanctuary to some refugees who may be imposters. Contrary to American opinion, which sees this as an unfriendly act, it is not as a judgment on United States policy in Vietnam that Canada admits deserters and draft-dodgers. It is in simple accordance with the historic and honourable principle of sanctuary which the United States and other liberal powers have always themselves respected in the case of other nations' straying recruits. It is one of many precious principles which have mitigated the severity of the international system; like the conventions of the Red Cross, or white flags, or hot lines, it must not be sacrificed for temporary expediency.

We have a right and a duty to offer opinions, privately and publicly, to the great powers and, if necessary, we can combine to put stronger pressure on them. Advice is not effective, however, if it is automatic, cantankerous, and hypocritical. Above all, it must be based on our own considered scheme for world security, a calculated consideration of the proper part for the great powers in that structure and a due appreciation of the actions they must take and the resources they must maintain to do what we expect of them. In short, we have to be credible.

In sum, we have reason to fear the superpowers in concert but less reason than we have to fear the hegemony of one or a world without leadership. The superpowers in concert may sacrifice the rights and positions of lesser powers. Some countries—Taiwan, Cuba, Yugoslavia, Israel, or Egypt—have grounds for concern. West Europeans and Canadians, lying as they do between the Soviet Union and the United States, should be vigilant, but the advantages for both of superpower accord so far outweigh the dangers that obstruction on our part would be unforgivable. Of course we should seek to have some voice in negotiations, both to protect our national interests and to discourage backsliding, and, if the United States does not want to rouse the grudging spirit in us all, it will make sure that our appropriate participation is respected. The United States has set itself a good precedent in its consultations with its NATO partners on the SALT talks; these consultations helped to diminish the antagonism building in Western Europe against superpower bilateralism.

Our relative weaknesses as middle powers also make us perilously dependent on the strengthening of the United Nations system. That system is deeper and broader than the UN as an organization; it is a maze of international laws, rules, and prescriptions, of international habits and expectations. It is everything implied by the Charter, however imperfectly observed. Its gaps and weaknesses are well known, but its tenacity may be best demonstrated by the fact that, after all these years, the régime of Mao wanted to take its place in that system. The UN is threatened by a revived spirit of national assertion, a contempt for world opinion and for international restraints which are "only" moral. By defying the system, the great powers can do more damage, but middle and lesser powers have also contributed to today's perilous cynicism about world order.

5:

The Role of Diplomacy

To the middle-power concept of Canada, diplomacy was intrinsic. The medium was a good part of the message. Much attention was paid by the advocates and antagonists to the process by which Canada would persuade, manipulate, or just command the Gabonese or the Americans or the whole United Nations to see things the Canadian way. The role of Canadian diplomats was a subject of contention during the foreign policy review. In the prejudiced opinion of an ex-diplomat, the argument was largely inconsequent. Ministers, professors, and editors sounded off, frequently with a dubious grasp of the functions of diplomacy, not to mention Canadian constitutional practice. The diplomats, silenced by that sound constitutional practice, could not retort—save for the splendid statement of one young officer to a gentleman of the press during the Biafra crisis: "And if you tell me I don't care whether African babies starve, I'll punch you in the god-damn face." Unhappily, stereotypes on both sides get in the way of the constructive exchange between academics and civil servants which the country badly needs in the dilemmas we face. It is a situation which has been improving rapidly, partly as a result of the effort put into it by the Department of External Affairs through its Academic Relations Division and partly by the good work of bodies like the Centre for Foreign Policy Studies of Dalhousie University, which arranged in 1973 a conference on "the changing role of the diplomatic function in the making of foreign policy." Some thirty academics and civil servants were closeted for a lengthy weekend on the rocky coast of Nova Scotia where point-scoring gave way to what the poli. sci. chaps call consensus-building. This essay was a sermon delivered to the conference by a schizophrenic with a foot and heart in both camps. It was printed and distributed as an occasional paper, along with the more scholarly presentations, by the Centre in June 1973.

This paper is a simple plea for the application of common sense and responsibility to the study of diplomacy and foreign policy, together with some suggestions for areas of exploration. It is an appeal to diplomats and professors to abandon the futile effort to score points against each other, to recognize that the function of diplomacy cannot be exorcized, that its satisfactory performance is a life-and-death matter for all of us, that the functions, habits, and priorities of diplomacy are mutable, that kinds and breeds of diplomats or interlocutors are likely to multiply and the role of the ambassador does need serious rather than captious re-examination. It is not a scholarly paper but a sermon, personal and prejudiced, reflecting the schizophrenia of one with a foot in each camp.

The basic assumption of this paper is that diplomacy is inevitable (if not necessarily diplomats as we have known them). Let us speak of interlocutors if the word diplomat is regarded as pejorative or expendable. The assumption that diplomacy has been abolished by the invention of Telex and participatory democracy and other modern improvements is widely and glibly held and provides considerable satisfaction to those who cling to romantic notions of the diplomat as a villain—and perversely prefer a machine. Diplomacy, it is here assumed, is a primitive instinct. The question for consideration is the always changing role of the people who act as interlocutors, whether they are professional diplomats, private citizens of good (or ill) will, or the members of prime ministers' and presidents' personal staffs and entourages, who, contrary to fashionable assumptions, have been a prominent feature of international relations since long before the reigns of Messrs. Trudeau and Nixon.

Another glib assumption is that diplomacy is moribund with the nation state. To begin with, it seems clear the state is far from dead, however much its sovereignty is inhibited by international agreements, economic or military dependence, or by powerful neighbours. Diplomacy, in any case, struck its roots in the city state and would presumably survive the so-called nation state. As far as Canada is concerned, it is not and never was a "nation state." The multiplication of transnational links is undoubtedly a challenge to the authority of the state and the efficacy of its diplomats. It is a challenge, however, which has re-emphasized the importance of the state as the defender of its people's interests. In the other direction, the diplomacy of the state, particularly a federal state like Canada, is challenged by the loosening of its internal structure. The result is not the death of diplomacy but rather its multiplication and its complication. The relations among the provinces and of provinces with foreign bodies increasingly look like diplomacy on other levels. The consequences of this diversity can be the spread of anarchy by the abandonment of rational means of communication or the adaptation of diplomatic rules and practices to serve the purposes of a universe in the process at the same time of integration and disintegration.

We must concern ourselves with all these changes in what is regarded as classical diplomacy, although it would be wise to bear in mind that adaptation has been proceeding pretty rapidly in the last quarter-century and what exists today is replete with un"classical" features. Defenders and critics both distort the discussion by dealing in stereotypes. The effect of technological changes in communications on the conduct of diplomacy for example, is important. The frequent assumption that the part played by the ambassador in policy formation has been downgraded if not eliminated is one example of the superficial treatment of a subject scholars have too often disdained to take seriously. Communications work in both directions, and the part the ambassador can now play in the devising of his own instructions has been greatly increased. The question to be considered is how technological change can be best exploited to improve the policy-making process or, if one prefers the chaster role for political science, to analyse the consequences to date on the policy-making process.

Likewise, there is needed a more pragmatic look at the changing function of the embassy or consulate in the light of the increasing complexity and specialization of negotiation. The easy assumption that as neither the ambassador nor his staff can comprehend the issues of nuclear power or salmon fishing they are expendable is another of the fashionable conclusions too ingenuous to be taken seriously if they were not repeated by scholars and politicians who ought to know better. The increase in the quantity and the intricacy of negotiations has already had a profound effect on the role of professional foreign service officers. It can be argued, however, that it only emphasizes the need for greater competence in their own professional stock-in-trade: diplomacy and international know-how. The complementary functions of the specialist assigned ad hoc and of the permanent establishment in a foreign capital ought not to be difficult to define. At any rate, what we should be looking at closely is change and adaptation. Investigation must not stop short with irresponsible conclusions about the death of diplomacy.

We must concern ourselves with good and bad diplomacy, competent and incompetent diplomats, as well as anachronistic diplomats and diplomacy. Critics of diplomacy are particularly given to extreme conclusions about the value of a diplomatic service based on their direct experience of one or two incompetent members of this profession. Like all professions, diplomacy has its duds—perhaps more than most because the profession as now practised is a peculiarly corrupting experience. Too often, however, criticism is based on a hazy idea of what duties and services our representatives abroad are expected to perform and the scope and limitations of their advisory function of the government. The assumption by many citizens that embassies abroad are intended to provide free travel, legal and medical services is one which diplomats have grown used to living with. More serious, from our point of view, are the misapprehensions of those who should know better: as, for example, that the primary function of missions abroad is to send back political reports in competition with the *New York Times*.

The primary function of any diplomatic mission abroad is negotiation, and that includes the constant preparation of the ground for possible negotiation. Reporting is valuable in that context. The kind of information Ottawa needs to have about personalities and policies in Bogota before embarking on a trade treaty with Colombia or a joint initiative in the United Nations is unlikely to be carried in any one of the public media. In any case, all competent diplomats read the *New York Times* and even better papers like *Le Monde* to supplement the specialized reports from their missions. That the members of the Canadian or any other foreign service might be occupying themselves more usefully than they now do, that their training and experience might be of a different kind, goes without saying now and forever more. That there are paradoxes, contradictions, and priorities to be considered ought also to be taken for granted. The question of whether a foreign service should be composed of generalists or area specialists is a case in point. A continuous re examination of the advantages and disadvantages of either practice is required. All bureaucracies need outside stimulation to consider changing traditional customs, but the retention of customs which are still valid is not to be written off as inertia. Not all good practices are new; some go back to the Garden of Eden.

The disrepute into which diplomacy has fallen is a matter for serious concern on the part of lovers of peace in all countries. Stupid diplomats and blundering diplomacy can properly but only partially be blamed for this ill reputation. Diplomats, like journalists, rally too often to defend their profession as indiscriminately as critics attack it. Attitudes of glowering suspicion and intolerance have built up. What seems undue conservatism on the part of diplomats is often an outraged defensiveness provoked by the irrelevance and misinformation of much of the criticism. There is also to be considered the helpless frustration of diplomats themselves with diplomacy as it is widely practised. Few experienced diplomats would want to abandon in principle the concept of protocol. Established rules of precedence have averted wars and ruptures of friendly relations among states. Few diplomats doubt, however, that the social customs of diplomats, which earn them envy and contumely, require sober re-appraisal.

Such a re-appraisal, if sober, would acknowledge the inestimable value of happy social relations among diplomats along with the needless escalation of eating, drinking, and the bending of calling-cards occasioned by the escalation of the number of diplomats. The United Nations has initiated useful progress in improving or establishing rules and customs of international intercourse, and it might some day tackle the anachronism of protocol. The abolition, for example, of the term "Excellency" for an ambassador would be a first step in the right direction, as it would remove one of those factors which tend after years of chancery life to corrupt even the nicest of guys from Medicine Hat and their wives. It should be acknowledged, however, that it is hard for a country to make progress unilaterally, and that the stoutest defenders of antique rituals and indefensible privileges are the newcomers on the international scene rather than the bored old relics of the Congress of Vienna. It is easy enough to encourage our own foreign service officers to break away from the herd and act humbly and austerely on their own, but such an injunction does not always accord with the equally admirable advice to adapt to local customs rather than offensively to impose abroad the preferred habits of Medicine Hat or Rockcliffe. It is unlikely to be consistent either with the popular injunction of the moment, which is to put first the Canadian commercial interest. It is the Canadian businessman who most frequently laments the cocktail partying of the "striped-pants boys" and most extravagantly practises this form of salesmanship in his own trade. Some sensible cost-benefit analysis of this kind of nonsense, which most diplomats would happily escape, should be possible if the aforementioned desire to score points could be abandoned.

It would be helpful if "diplomacy," like "appeasement," could lose its pejorative overtones—which is not to say that there are never occasions which require loud challenges rather than diplomacy and stubborn confrontation rather than appeasement. In popular fantasy, diplomats are charged with being by profession both warmongers and appeasers. The latter charge is a great deal more apt. Their duty has always been to prevent conflict, and this instinct is much stronger now than it ever was before because an increasing proportion of their time is involved in the creation of international structures and their way of life encourages broad perspectives. A continual problem with diplomats today is that they tend to put the international above the national interest, to be carried away by the spirit of Geneva or Brussels or Peking.

There are some particular problems of Canadian diplomacy which require disentangling. These may be partly attributable to the confusion in Canadian minds between diplomacy and foreign policy and the consecration of diplomacy as foreign policy. The so-called middle-power diplomacy of Canada in the postwar period was a response to international needs and can be defended as a service to the international community. For a country which can survive only in a world where there is constant brokerage among states, it remains a service to be performed on call in the national and international interest. It is not a role chosen; it is doing what comes naturally. The glorification of diplomacy into a basis of foreign policy was a response partly to the Canadian need for definition. Technique was exalted, ends and means were confused. Middle-power diplomacy can still be a facet of our foreign policy. Its relationship to a "foreign policy" is in fact a subject which would profit from the kind of co-operative analysis by political scientists and practitioners which this essay recommends. The present tendency to reject the intermediary function in principle rather than just the fantasies of middlepowerism threatens to undermine what is, after all, merely a disposition to help avoid conflict and confrontation.

Especially in the present wave of assertive nationalism in Canada, the government and its instrument, the Department of External Affairs, are being urged to renounce diplomacy in favour of the strident demand: instructions to other states to stop their wars, the unilateral assertion of rights over waters and fish and other resources. Diplomacy, it is too easily forgotten, is a game of skill in which countries without adequate weight to be decisive in world politics and economics play whatever hands they can muster. To do so they need more friends than enemies. Canadian short-sightedness on this point is attributable partly to the fact that we have never been threatened or pilloried to the extent that we desperately needed the help of friends. We are too little aware that even in our internationalist activities we have needed friends.

The Canadian initiative in the Suez crisis would not have been successful if Canada had not been able to put together majority support in the United Nations Assembly. That support did not come instantaneously. It was built up laboriously over the past years by fraternizing with and showing understanding of the interests of Indians and Arabs, Latin Americans and Yugoslavs, and even of the defendants in the case, the British, French, and Israelis. You don't get that kind of support if you run around international conferences with your fists up and your chips in place on the shoulder. He whom you denounce will welcome the chance to denounce you. Increasingly in a world dominated by the pressure of population on resources we are going to need friends, not just to stop someone else's wars but to help us establish international rules to protect our own vital interests. But even this argument for sweet relations in the national interest is not a simple one. Countries which sacrifice consistency and principle and never stand for their convictions lose credibility and respect. The Canadian initiatives which gained us a reputation for good international citizenship have lost us friends but so long as this reputation persists (and it endures longer abroad than at home) it does strengthen our position in international councils. Canadian commentators on diplomacy have been too reluctant to accept paradox.

The confusion over the functions of Canadian diplomacy has been nowhere more foolishly illustrated than in the controversy over "quiet diplomacy," a controversy, incidentally, which is not to be found in those terms in other countries. There has, of course, been a legitimate debate since at least the days of Woodrow Wilson about open covenants openly arrived at. The persistent problem for opponents of secret diplomacy is that every one, from Left to Right, who assumes power realizes that secret diplomacy is both dangerous and indispensable. A Hoare-Laval pact secretly arrived at to dismember Ethiopia is easily recognized as evil, but there are few people who would not concede the right to confidentiality of Henry Kissinger and Le Duc Tho if they can thereby bring peace to Vietnam. It was the Chinese who particularly requested secrecy about the talks with Canada in Stockholm. Few Canadian critics of "quiet diplomacy" complained, because most of them wanted Canada to be successful in establishing relations with Peking and recognized that regular reports on the state of play, as on the chess matches in Reykjavik, would not contribute to that end.

What has confused the issue badly is that the argument in Canada over "quiet diplomacy" is a genuine argument over foreign policy and the diplomatic instrument but it is not an argument about "quiet diplomacy." It is an argument about how to deal with the United States. The criticism is based on a belief that Canada did not stand up firmly enough to American pressures and was ineffective in persuading Washington to the Canadian point of view on world problems. This is one of the most important subjects for discussion and analysis in Canadian foreign policy, but useful analysis has not been promoted by this kind of over-simplification. Confidential diplomacy is practised by every government on earth, as well as by every private organization and institution, including the family. If Canada were to abandon such a practice, it would become a pariah nation, utterly impotent. The apparently absolutist argument against "quiet diplomacy" has undercut the essential discussion about the abuses of privacy and the frustration of public discussion. The childish assumption that because Canada was unable, in private discussion, to persuade the Americans to clear out of Vietnam, public denunciation would have done the trick has diverted us from a sensible calculation of the most appropriate instruments to use. Which methods have proved most effective: an ambassadorial plea before United States policy has congealed, a public request in a speech in Philadelphia, a threat to withhold resources, or an offer of collaboration under certain terms? There is a case for each tactic.

At the heart of the problem is the calculation as to the extent to which Canada can go it alone and the extent to which we need, without being unduly submissive, to retain the good will of Washington—and of Brussels—and how much, if anything, we should be prepared to sacrifice to maintain it. This fundamental issue is not being treated seriously enough in the current caricaturings of both "continentalists" and "anti-continentalists" (whatever those caricature terms mean) because they avoid the realities of diplomacy. Blaming the diplomats is also a handy means of avoiding hard decision. Diplomats involved in the tough international game, far from St. George Street, or Point Grey, or St. James Street, know that one rarely gets concessions without making at some times concessions. There is legitimate argument about whether Canada has made too many or the wrong concessions and about the stewardship of the Department of External Affairs. It would be a better argument if it were based on more impartial research. Paradoxically, it would also be better if the successes and failures of "quiet diplomacy" did not remain, by definition, quiet for some years at least. (How long is in itself a subject for argument.) An examination should also be made as to whether the argument for loud diplomacy is reciprocal. Canadians who anguish over our quiet diplomacy were the first to protest when the State Department in 1962 issued a press release questioning some conclusions of the Canadian government. President Kennedy was also rebuked for saying in Ottawa that Canada would be welcome in the Organization of American States.

This is not, however, essentially an argument about quiet or loud diplomacy. It is the much bigger, the endemic Canadian problem of how to use our wits to live as a nation on a continent in which we have always been vastly out-numbered. It should be noted, incidentally, that our diplomats on the whole take a much less defeatist attitude on our capacity for survival than do the doomsters in the academies. Diplomacy is to a large extent the science of living by one's wits.

The question of public opinion and foreign policy is, of course, much in need of investigation. The complexity and intricacy of international relations, and perhaps the increasing need by governments to integrate their resources and play strong hands in international negotiation, do not make the problem easier. Obviously the exigencies of the situation encourage élitism among the practitioners and bureaucratic contempt for the public's fumbling approaches. On the other hand, the assumption of other élite groups, in the academies, chambers of commerce, or other professional organizations, that they are the true voice of the people is not acceptable. Can we at the same time talk about opening up the policy process and demand that the government formulate integrated policies—on resources, for example—and play successful poker? We probably do have to do both, but we had better not pretend that the conflicts involved can simply be blamed upon the stupidities or arrogance of our governors or a bunch of professors. We are going to have to resist increasingly the managerial presumptions of the governing classes because of the increasing complexity of issues but it is dangerous to do so by reviving ingenuous notions about the people's wisdom.

Related to this question is the position in government and society of our foreign service. What should be their role in the policy-making process? If the bureaucrats themselves are confused about their role, so too are the critics, and the game of point-scoring gets in the way of clear thinking. The classic concept of the civil servant in the Canadian/ British tradition may not be good enough, but it had values which should not be mislaid in the process of revision. It should command more respect than it does from critics who fear the excessive influence on policy of the bureaucracy. It affirms the supremacy of the elected ministers and assigns to diplomats the role of advisers. The contradictions are apparent in discussion of the relationship of the Department of External Affairs to the public. Is it the function of these professional advisers to incorporate in their advice the vagaries of public opinion, or is it their duty to set out for the government the consequences of their action on the international community and on the long-range interests of Canada regardless of internal politics? A good civil servant surely has the responsibility of warning the government, however unpopular his warnings may be. It cannot be assumed, of course, that his views are unbiased, but the conflicting views of the professionals within a service which has been kept healthy and uncowed is some guarantee of hard advice. The fashionable caricatures of foreign services as monolithic preserves of reactionaries or nests of disloyal pinkos have not only been wrong in fact; they have obscured the issues for consideration about the function and composition of foreign offices. So remedies and definitions proposed tend to lack sense. Neither the idea of the foreign office as a politically virginal élite nor of the elimination of the professionals in some pure exercise of the people's will in foreign policy is acceptable. Diplomats far removed from the political realities of their country or contemptuous of their fellow-citizens are incapable of giving advice which a government can accept. Should the citizen, however, seek to affect policy by influencing the bureaucracy or his elected representatives?

Academic critics in Canada too often encourage the heretical idea that foreign policy is made by the Department of External Affairs by talking and acting as if this were so. The purist argument, however, that no effort should be made to persuade the bureaucrats begs too many questions. The Department of External Affairs cannot, unless it unhealthily isolates itself, avoid being something of an agency of transmission of ideas and opinions between the government and the people or at least the foreign affairs élite. It is not, strictly speaking, their function to act in this way and they ought not to be assigned it. The first principle in this matter is perhaps to avoid strictly speaking altogether.

How do these processes actually work, and how might they work better? These are the questions which the practitioners and political scientists, historians, and journalists should be working at together. We are, in Canada, far from having done adequate descriptive work. Behaviouralist techniques of analysis have lagged, not only because of the persistent scepticism of their value on the part of Canadian academics and bureaucrats, but also because the raw material for quantification is lacking. Whatever the methodology, what is needed most of all is objective research. The age of the clam seems to be passing in Ottawa. There is a much greater disposition in the relevant departments to make material available. Closer association, as we well know, between officials and scholars is producing a new attitude of confidence. Officials and politicans are more likely to offer information if they believe that it is not going to be misused in their disfavour. For the scholar, as for the journalist, of course, there is the constant fear that he will be used in this way. He cannot compromise his integrity by promising to conclude what the official wants him to conclude. Here lies and will continue to lie the heart of this problem. There is no solution for it. As in all issues of foreign policy there is only the need to recognize that there are and will remain inescapable conflicts of interest.

6:

After 25 Years

In 1970 the International Journal *of the Canadian Institute of International Affairs celebrated its twenty-fifth anniversary as the unique English-language quarterly on international affairs in Canada with a world-wide reputation acquired by its editors for the past fifteen years, Robert Spencer and James Eayrs. This introductory contribution to a volume devoted to Canadian foreign policy was an effort to see in historical perspective recent changes as well as the looming challenges which would require a more drastic review of our place in the world. It appears in volume XXVI, winter 1970-1.*

In contemplating the Canadian position in world affairs over the quarter-century since this Journal was established, it is hard to decide whether we have moved into a new age or just completed another of our familiar manic cycles. Both conclusions are no doubt valid. The dimensions have changed enormously, but the persistent themes are reappearing. We are back with the three hundred and fifty year old dilemmas over dividing a continent across the middle. We struggle again with the paradoxes of independence and collectivism—the unsolvable but acceptable paradoxes of trying to control our own destiny and share, as well as pay for, the advantages of the pax Britannica or the pax Americana or the United Nations system or the new era of SALT. The debates over Reciprocity or the Naval Bill or sanctions against Italy are relevant. In fact, what seems more strange from 1970 is the euphoric mood of the late 'forties.

Whether we have passed through golden decades or silver or base metal (the sell-out theory) is a matter of perspective, loyalty, or even mood. The middle power has become middle-aged, more sceptical of its capacities and its accomplishments. The mood is introspective. In international affairs, one is tempted to call it unadventurous, but it is also, and not only in Canada, utopian and apocalyptic and perhaps unadventurous only in the intergovernmental relationship. There is much confusion and perplexity over what the state can do in this bravura new world—especially what our particular kind of state can do. Canadians exalt and ignore their own foreign policy. A perverse compulsion to identification with American political and social processes is accompanied by an insistence on utter independence. The right and left seem to have misplaced the Canadian identity in their thrilling contemplation of other people's revolutions, but the chilling contemplation of our own recent *événements* may repatriate their concern. The pragmatic majority is properly puzzled about the best way to be good Canadians and good world citizens. We have been through this kind of debate before with Goldwin Smith and Sir George Parkin and Sir Robert Borden and Mackenzie King—but without television.

It is easy to be depressed, even humiliated, by much of the current debate over foreign policy, especially if one looks at it from abroad. Foreigners seem often to hold us in contempt both for the extravagance of our nationalism and for our lethargy in the face of threats to it. They find it hard to tune in on our shrill debate. Nevertheless, our re-examination of ourselves is not unhealthy. We were getting out of step with our own philosophies and needed a new look at our place in the world. We are, it is to be hoped, going through a stage. We would be wiser to acknowledge a menopause than to go on at age 103 claiming exemption for adolescence. Some corrective was required to the illusion of middle-sized superpower, and recognition that foreign policy is more than a diplomatic high-wire act—a view, incidentally, which is dearer to the heart of the public who found it cheap and comfortable, than to the diplomats, who found it exhausting. We shall pass through this awkward stage, no doubt, but not until we rediscover the world around us.

Our temper seems closer to the late 'thirties than the late 'forties. The latter is the period, however, when, it is now charged, we were selling ourselves to the Yankees. But it was an age of much greater self-confidence than the present or than the 'thirties. We were not disposed to doubt our ability to keep company with larger powers and stand up to them if required. In this respect St. Laurent and Pearson were more like Borden and Meighen than like Mackenzie King or the present articulate, if less highly placed, "nationalists" who give the ingenuous but high-minded Canuck no more chance to stand up to IBM or the CIA than the colonially-minded nationalists of a generation ago gave him with a British lord. Their innocence reminds one of the political mileage Mackenzie King got out of the "plot" of Lord Halifax in 1944 to ensnare us in a closed empire—and the obsession about imperial threats is just as peripheral to the hard world issues of now as then.

There is everything to be said for beginning a calculation of our national interest and our consequent foreign policy from bang in the middle of the northern half of North America, with our very own polar view of the importance of Europe and the Arctic and the Gulf of Aqaba. We have been too much disposed to get our strategic concepts second-hand from mother countries, large neighbours, and dominant allies. Looking at the world from Beaver Lodge, however, need not limit our vision to the continent around us. Nor ought it to fix us in permanent fascination with *le défi américain.*

So preoccupied have we become with standing up for our little rights to the Americans that we are in danger of ignoring the real scope of our international plight. The essential issue for Canadians in the next few decades is how to live with our riches in a world more and more preoccupied with the gap between population and resources. The question of Canadian ownership is relevant and important but incident-al. Our relationship to the United States market for energy and other resources is only one aspect, and by far the easiest to resolve, of the resources issues which will come to worry us. We must at last give up the illusions of being poor and undeveloped and recognize the responsibilities and the vulnerabilities of extreme affluence. It is we, not the Americans, who may be regarded as the arch-imperalist power of the 'eighties, even though there will still not be many of us. We are feeling first the pressures of the Americans and the Japanese, but they already have, in the eyes of the rest of the world, much too large a share of what the earth provides. The argument against a sharing of resources on a continental basis is much deeper and wider than our nationalists seem to realize.

One of the truths to which we cling is that our status at the end of the last war was inflated but that, since the restoration or rise of Germany, Japan, France, and other countries, we have had to give up illusions of middle power and behave like the dependent and dependable but ornery youth we have some natural disposition to want to be anyway. It has been wise of us to accept this demotion, but as an argument for caution rather than self-indulgence. The decline in our stature is relative, not absolute; and the trend is deceptive. While we have been adjusting ourselves to a lower standing in the world league, our GNP has been rising so rapidly that by the mid-'seventies it is approaching that of Britain. What kind of power do we call ourselves then? It isn't a question of vain boasting but of accepting responsibility. Most Canadians would probably prefer not to have to be a great power; we have for centuries known the comforts of being sheltered, the luxury of a supplementary foreign and defence policy. But the country which sits on vast sources of energy, land, and resources will have to get used to thinking and acting for itself.

Standing up for our rights against the big guy, assuring our claim to more fish and more undersea resources per square mile of coast and head of population than any other peoples, stretching our sovereignty to keep out intruders, is not an adequate end for Canadian foreign policy. It may be an essential means to a higher end. Fortifying Canadian nationalism and assuring Canadian sovereignty are reactionary if their purpose is to allow us to sit on our hoard and drive off poachers. They are necessary steps, however, to enable us to behave as enlightened world citizens. The dilemma for the Canadian internationalist is that his well-intentioned sermons against nationalism and sovereignty may save the world in the long run but may lead Canada into committing suicide in the short run, to no good internationalist purpose at all. Maintaining foreign policies at various levels is, however, the key to survival for powers of all shapes and sizes.

Part Two:
International Institutions

The idea of the middle-power "role" grew out of Canadian participation in international organizations, especially the family of the United Nations. The fashionable thesis of Canada's decline in the world is popularly associated with the belief that both Canada and the United Nations have grown decrepit. Both those assumptions are strongly contended in the first article. The other articles in this section consider the two major functions of the United Nations as Canada saw them in 1945, collective security and mediation. The extensive attention given to the mediatory function is justified on the grounds that it has been and is likely to remain our Canadian habit if not our role in middle age.

1:
The New Age of Functionalism

As one who carried a briefcase in the Canadian delegation to the First General Assembly of the United Nations in London in 1946, and was on hand for the crises over Berlin, Korea, Suez, Hungary, and Lebanon, I ought to have been disillusioned early about the United Nations. I was not, because I was trained by a remarkable group of men in a practical, functionalist concept of a United Nations responding to and building itself on challenges. So in the 'seventies I saw it not so much as an institution as a now ineradicable habit. My mentor, Hume Wrong, put it thus to the last session of the League of Nations in 1946: "The troubles of the world are not, and never have been, at bottom a question of the nature of the existing international machinery, of the processes whereby issues are brought forward for discussion and settlement, of the Covenant or the Charter of the rule of unanimity or the veto power . . . The League of itself could accomplish nothing. The United Nations of itself can accomplish nothing. Both are instruments for collective action of their states members. We must seek to avoid that mischievous fallacy which at times in the past led many people to make excuses for the inaction of their own governments on the ground that the question at issue was one for the League to settle. More cannot come out of any internationl organization than its members are ready to put into it." This article was provoked by the dangerous attacks on the United Nations in 1974 by well-intentioned people without historical perspectives, and also by the failure of the Canadian press and public to pay adequate attention to the extraordinary if undramatic contributions Ottawa bureaucrats are making to the most important contemporary activities of the United Nations family of institutions. This is an extended version of an article entitled "The World" which appeared in* Saturday Night, *July/August, 1975.*

*Canada, Department of External Affairs, Conference Series, 1946, No. 2, *Report of the Canadian Delegates to the Twenty-First Assembly of the League of Nations,* Geneva, April 8th-18th, 1946, pp. 24-5.

In its thirtieth year the United Nations is not expiring. It is, in fact, in one of its most creative phases. What is more, the Canadian contribution is as effective and constructive as it has ever been. That, admittedly, is not conventional wisdom. The UN is said to be in a precarious state and Canada's part in it that of an ineffectual observer relegated to third-class status. The "golden decade" after the war, when the UN really worked and Canada was heeded, is regarded either with nostalgia as a busted dream or as an overrated tour de force remote from the real interests of the country.

People who talk that way are usually looking in the wrong direction. They may be obsessed by particular issues, the fate of Israel or the price of oil. Or they are mired in traditional values of the age of the Cold War, preoccupied, as far as Canada is concerned, with archaic questions of alignment or independence. Paradoxically, those who cling most doggedly to the Cold War perspectives are those who think they have opposed them most vigorously. The Cold War provided the mindless Left as well as the mindless Right with their point of reference, their one sure indication of goodness and badness. A UN no longer dominated by the Cold War or even by détente—in which, for example, the deadliest rivalry is between Moscow and Peking—is hard for them to cope with. No wonder; it is hard for anyone to cope with, and the temptation is strong to throw up our hands. The posture of the cynic is always tempting. Its uncompromising stance so easily disguises its essential naïveté. It is easier to holler "Doom" than to think through the complex ways of avoiding it. Articulate Canadians are incurable denouncers.

The basic problem is, as always, that people never seem to get through their heads what the United Nations is. It is neither an avenging God nor a dispenser of divine justice. Nor is it the devil incarnate. It is more they than it. The UN is a loosely linked network of institutions and agencies within which member states can do or not do what they can find a consensus or a majority or enough great-power agreement to carry out. It is also, of course, a Charter, a common bond to good behaviour among sovereign states and in that sense something greater than the sum of its parts. But as the UN it cannot act, and the system is not responsible for the actions taken within its component parts. The UN did not recognize the Palestine Liberation Organization. A large majority of members invited Arafat to state his case and, abetted by the temporary President of the Twenty-Ninth General Assembly, gave him preferential treatment. The wisdom of doing so is debatable. It may be regarded as an unholy blessing on terrorism or a bid to offer the PLO an alternative to terrorist action. It was one of many wise or unwise decisions that have been made since 1945 by majorities of various kinds in the hundreds of assemblies and committees that make up the UN system. The General Assembly is one of the principal organs of the UN, but it is not "the UN," and it cannot on its own admit or expel members.

The recourse is not to abandon the institution but to seek ways of altering the majority or the majority view. To talk as if the UN were dispensable is to misunderstand what has been happening in this century. The habit of multilateral collaboration is so deeply in-grained—not just because it is desirable but because it is unavoidable—that in a vacuum new institutions would re-form like a spider's web or flesh over scar tissue. The problem for the West is that they might not again be universal and we would be on the outside. A Middle East settlement might be juggled for a time by the great powers on their own but not the control of epidemics, nuclear proliferation, civil aviation, or meteorology. These latter are the critical issues of international surviv-al, so successfully managed within the UN system that we take them for granted. They are not to be dismissed as its secondary purposes.

The worst enemies of the UN have always been both the utopians and the cynics. The former insist on seeing it as a world government asserting its will over sovereign states. The trouble with that perspective is not just that it bears no relationship to world politics in the foreseeable future. By positing an "all or nothing" approach it stunts the growth of the UN as an organism of enormous vitality constantly finding ways and means of dealing with diverse problems, building up the infrastructure by experimentation rather than seeking to impose a philospher's dream which would shatter at the first unsuccess-ful challenge. The cynics, on the other hand, like to pretend that the UN is a world government in order to score points against it by proving that it does not act like one. If the UN is to be blamed as an "it" for not stopping the wars in Vietnam or Bangladesh or, by a wave of its hand, closing the gap between rich and poor countries, it might be given credit for seeing to it that more of us failed to die of cholera than were ever killed in these wars. We rarely think either of the millions who did not die in the wars frustrated by preventive action in UN bodies.

Without any alteration of the Charter, the Security Council and other organs could be used for practically all the purposes their critics have in mind. We have to work for consensus because the UN is a voluntary system, and no change of the rules on paper can alter that fact of life. None of us can be forced by a majority, although we can be subjected to strong moral pressure. The UN was invented not to abolish international politics but to provide a setting in which they might be conducted more harmoniously. One may well ask whether the present cacophony does more harm than good. It is surely preferable, however, to the terrifying reverberations in the void which could follow the dismantling of a system which forces the powers to split their differences and be called to account. It is this enforced association which matters most and its best results are rarely expressed in formal resolutions. It is too often forgotten that the UN Charter does not insist that all peacemaking take place in its formal sessions. By article 33 parties to a dispute are enjoined "first of all" to seek a solution by "peaceful means of their own choice." There is nothing essentially contrary to the Charter in Henry Kissinger's efforts to find solutions in Jerusalem and Cairo or in the efforts to do the same in Geneva. It is the results that matter.

To pretend, of course, that present problems in the UN are routine would be as dangerous as giving up the struggle. We do need perspective, however. The UN is going through another and perhaps more critical period of agonizing adjustment, as members try to come to terms with a changed political configuration. Majorities form and re-form, and the UN has adjusted quite well. The danger has always been that those in control of a majority will exploit their temporary advantage to alter the universalist structure. In the late 'forties there were heedless politicians in the West who wanted to force the Soviet Union and its friends out of the system because they were frustrating the will of a majority which wanted to do things in its way. The Canadian government was among those which stoutly resisted this pressure, arguing that the UN must be preserved as the one forum where deadly antagonists would have to talk to each other so that, if the temporary rivalry could be contained, the UN could carry on its essential purposes. They regarded NATO not as an abandonment of the UN but as a means by which countries which felt themselves threatened could provide for their own collective defence, thereby frustrating those who would turn the UN into a non-communist military instrument in the name of collective security.

Without saying so, the Russians did the same in the Warsaw Pact, and in the UN members were thereby enabled to devote their attention to keeping the world as peaceful and prosperous as possible. Feeling more secure and confident, they wisely abandoned the effort to turn the UN into an agency of enforced collective security. There were successes, failures, and stalemates, but undoubtedly much less fighting than there would otherwise have been. That the long-range gamble on universality is paying off might be proved by the fact that the United States and the USSR are not only still sitting together in UN bodies; they are actually collaborating in efforts to control nuclear proliferation as well as brush-fire wars. Their progress cannot be regarded as entirely satisfactory, but their accepting such a programme is something we would hardly have dared hope for twenty years ago. It is a curious kind of partner-/antagonist relationship and it certainly doesn't solve all the issues in the UN, but the essence of international collaboration in the UN is the recognition that we are all natural antagonists and competitors who have to restrain our competition so that we don't tear each other apart. It is a higher level of civilization than is envisaged in concepts based on the fantasy that men and tribes are by nature loving and complementary, frustrated in their longing for peace by self-seeking leaders.

The universalism of the UN is, of course, part of its present problem. The balance has again swung too far. The grossly under-represented "Third World" has acquired an unhealthily swollen majority in the Assembly. Power and responsibility—especially the responsibility for paying the bills—are out of joint. A majority has been using its power somewhat recklessly and threatened the principle of universality, the basic conviction that we are all sinners at times, that membership in the UN is a discipline, not just a privilege. Countries like Israel and South Africa cannot hope for fair-mindedness, while states of the majority could practise genocide without censure. The United States can expect only its sins to be noted by Assembly orators. It is time for the Americans and friends to resist, to set limits to what is tolerable, and remind the exasperated of the essential role they have played. In doing so it is wise, however, to realize that the current abuse of the majority must be compared with the exclusion of the real government of China for two long decades. Present misbehaviour ought not to be justified by bad precedents, but recollection of the latter should keep us humble.

Over thirty years the UN has developed a remarkable set of checks and balances. The Third World is using its Assembly majority to correct what they regard as imbalances in the international structure, and specifically to compensate for the barrage of vetoes by which the First and Second Worlds control the Security Council. Yet the veto itself is one of the useful checks in the system, a means of breaking the circuit when the system is over-heated.[1] When the United States, Britain, and France vetoed in the Security Council the effort in 1974 of the Assembly majority to expel South Africa, they were not supporting apartheid. They were reminding a temporary majority that this way madness lay. Unless temporary majorities resist the temptation to fling into outlawry states they dislike, the UN could be eroded. Learning to live with the UN system is the justification of the system.

Fortunately the reality of UN politics is never the caricature it is made out to be. Current assumptions to the contrary notwithstanding, the UN was never at any time the plaything of the United States. Nor is it now the tool of a united and vengeful Third World. The latter, which must already be distinguished as Third and Fourth Worlds, unite only on certain issues. Many of its leaders are as aware as any Western statesman of the need for restraint to preserve the UN. They resist Western domination, but they know perfectly well that the Russians and the Chinese can offer them little more than verbal support, that their wish to use the UN for their economic development will not be abetted if the industrialized countries are driven into sullen resentment. So majorities form and dissolve, but the structure survives if the majorities have shown it sufficient respect.

It is, of course, the lash of the Third World and the energy dilemmas of the First that have propelled the UN into what I have called its most creative phase. It is always most creative when it is most dangerously challenged. The planetary issues—food, population, pollution, the seas, and outer-space—cannot now be avoided. Governments are just beginning to grope with them in the established UN organs and agencies and by special conferences on resources, population, food, and "the law of the sea." If the UN did not exist something like it would have been invented under pressure in 1974. That our governments have barely come to grips with the life and death issues is obvious from the rudimentary—though mostly positive—steps taken last year in Geneva, Bucharest, Rome, and Caracas. But the UN is ready and available, with its infinitely flexible machinery and its chastening but encouraging experience, to support just as much change and progress as national governments, or more particularily their frightened electorates, are prepared to sanction. It has been said of peace that it is no longer a "whether" question; it is a "how" question. The same is true of the equalization of economic advantage. We have to get out of our pulpits and into committees of the whole. One value of the UN forum is that in the end it induces pragmatism and reveals the irrelevance of the closeted doctrinaires, capitalist or Marxist. Nobody foresaw the world we are in. Flogging our guilt complexes, avoiding thought and sacrifice by blaming OPEC or the CIA or Kurt Waldheim may be fun, but they are distractions we cannot afford. In Canada we shall not think straight until we can lift our sights beyond our stultifying obsession with the United States and contemplate a world in far worse shape than a continent—in which we are an independent and responsible major power.

In such bewildering circumstances one favourite scapegoat is the bureaucracy, paralyzed, it is said, by inertia and its effortless preference for the status quo. Such a generalization would be a gross misjudgment in Canada at the present time. The agenda of the UN, more than ever before, occupies the attention not just of the Department of External Affairs but of a dozen ministries. It would be easy to cite examples of lethargy and unimaginative responses no doubt, although it should be borne in mind that the need to defend the interests of Canadian farmers and fishermen quite properly complicates bold international initiatives. The best kept secret in Canada, however, is the extraordinary degree of successful initiative Canadians have taken in recent years in the most fruitful area of UN activity: extending the infrastructure of international law and regulation.

The subjects may seem more mundane than those dealt with by the great powers in the Security Council, or the Suez crisis over which Canada gained respect in 1956. But are they less important to people? There was, for example, the Canadian-Swedish initiative to get UN consideration of the effects of direct satellite broadcasting, or the Canadian initiatives to get international action on the sensing of earth resources by satellites as well as fixing responsibility for damage from fallen space objects. Such things are essential for an international community in a new age and for the defence of Canadian culture, economy, and sovereignty. Canada, concerned over the role of multinational corporations but realizing that this was world-wide and not just a Canada-United States issue, was responsible for getting a discussion of the legal aspects under way in the United Nations Committee on International Trade Law. It has co-sponsored proposals to cope with hijacking in various UN organs. Its proposals on the control of pollution were the basis of international action at Stockholm. These are only a very few of the activities in which Canadians have been actively engaged. None may seem decisive on its own. Compounded, they are a calculated and well-reasoned campaign. It is closely related to the national interests of Canadians, but it reaffirms the traditional Canadian conviction that the interests of Canada, an inescapably international country, are best protected by the development of world order and the extension of international rules.

The main Canadian thrust in the UN has shifted from the highly visible issues of the Political Committee of the General Assembly or the Security Council of which we have not been a member for some years. It is master-minded by a remarkably able team of international lawyers, abetted by the collaboration and criticism of their academic colleagues across Canada. The most notable of these has been J. Alan Beesley, former Legal Adviser and at present Ambassador in Vienna where he is more readily available for the kinds of meetings at which he is required. More and more it is Geneva and Vienna rather than New York where the fabric of the United Nations is being woven. When Geoffrey Stevens of the *Globe and Mail* ventured to the Law of the Sea Conference in Caracas last summer, the central focus of Canada's new UN diplomacy, he said of Beesley, "Brilliant would not be too extravagant a word to describe his performance," and "By any yardstick, he was among the half-dozen most effective delegation leaders in Caracas."[2] He had been made chairman of the conference drafting committee in recognition of the fact that he and his able colleagues had for over four years been probably the most creative thinkers in the Seabed Committee. There they laboured patiently to bring off a conference the significance of which is hard to exaggerate. It was a first effort to establish an international régime by the consent of the whole world, which would replace the "international law" of the sea established by the custom of major powers. The project is so bold it may well be an incomplete success at the present series of conferences. The Canadian planners would be disappointed but not dismayed. They have been working nearly twenty years on the sea law. Their approach is to build on whatever agreement they can get, to widen areas of regulation, bilaterally, multilaterally, or regionally as proves possible, working towards universality but not sacrificing all progress to perfectionism.

Although this philosophy is concerned largely with an aspect of the UN to which Canadians in the earlier stages paid less attention, it is in the traditions of "functionalism" with which Canadians approached the world structure at the end of the war. As Beesley states it, international society will not develop into an international community by settling first the problems of the use of force. "The process, in my view, will, on the contrary, be that of regulating so many fields of conduct so effectively that there will be less and less reason to resort to force, and thus less resistance to the gradual acceptance of real constraints upon its use." This is no ingenuous utopian speaking. "States abide by the law because it is in their national self-interest to do so." He insists defiantly: "It is a fact of international life that states do not take their treaty obligations lightly."[3] That can be proved even by the conduct of the superpowers.

Such optimism is also in the Canadian tradition. Without ignoring the problems ahead or the failures, try to build on what has been accomplished. That was the essence of the Pearsonian approach, and also that of Dag Hammarskjöld. Some spokesmen of the new approach like, in the fashionable preoccupation with the national interest *über alles,* to see in the new campaign a departure from the "timidity" of earlier Canadian policy. Others, like Beesley, prefer to cite Lester Pearson's statement in his memoirs: "Everything I learned during the war confirmed and strengthened my view as a Canadian that our foreign policy must not be timid or fearful of commitments but activist in accepting international responsibilities. To me, nationalism and internationalism were two sides of the same coin. International cooperation for peace is the most important aspect of national policy."[4]

For the nationalist, suspicious of the Department of External Affairs' susceptibility to foreign (i.e. American) and internationalist (i.e. the big bad great powers) blandishments, the history of Canada's seminal contribution to the Law of the Sea conferences should be illuminating. The working paper with draft articles on basic issues which Canada presented at Caracas was co-sponsored by Norway, New Zealand, Mexico, Mauritius, Indonesia, India, Iceland, and Chile. So much for Canada's inhibiting "alignments." The whole conference, much of the impetus for which has come from Canada, was an assault on the law of

68 CANADA: A MIDDLE-AGED POWER

the sea as established and vehemently defended by the great seafaring powers, including the United States, Britain, and even the Soviet Union. So much for Canada's "satellitism."

The agenda involves so many aspects of the sea that generalization is too hazardous. At the heart of the matter was the insistence of the great powers on a narrow territorial sea and unlimited "freedom of the seas," positions which the major coastal states, like Canada, and the developing countries firmly opposed. Technology has raised new issues vital to coastal states—the prevention of oil pollution and the protection of fisheries far beyond a three- or even twelve-mile limit, as well as the exploration of oil and mineral resources on the sea-floor. The concept almost certain to prevail if agreement is reached is that of the "economic" or "patrimonial zone," some two-hundred miles beyond the 12 mile territorial sea in which the coastal state would acquire not sovereignty but the right and duty to police or regulate pollution, fishing, and mining, with some special claims on the products of the area. Central to this formula is the concept of "custodianship," as distinct from sovereignty, which Canadians developed out of the controversy over the Arctic voyage of the *Manhattan* and the Arctic Waters Pollution Prevention Act of 1970.

When the *Manhattan*, owned by Jersey Standard, set out on an experimental voyage with Canadian approval and supervision it was widely regarded in the Canadian press and parliament as was the pocket battleship, *Graf Spee*. There were chauvinistic outbursts in the House and External Affairs Committee from Right and Left. The government was commanded to declare sovereignty unequivocally and plant maple leaves up to the Pole. The lily-livered bureaucrats were accused of capitulating, as usual, to the Yankees. The bureaucrats were, in fact, avoiding the grand showdown, the polar Grey Cup the fans wanted, because they weren't sure we would win it. The frontal challenge might serve only to provoke opposition far wider than that of the United States. The bureaucrats were painstakingly preparing an approach with which, in the end, Canada would achieve much more than a score against the Americans. It would convert them. Persuading Americans—or any other people—to see things our way is rarely if ever achieved by putting them on the public spot.

The new approach was the hundred-mile zone towards which we took a "functionalist" approach. Sovereignty we did not need out that far. What we needed to do for ourselves and for the international community was to accept a responsibility to prevent disastrous oil spills. It was an approach we applied also to the protection of coastal fish from extinction. It is the concept of custodianship which became a major component of the various proposals for an "economic zone" at

Caracas. The United States did not like our Arctic Waters Act at all. They compared it with the 200-mile territorial seas the benighted Peruvians had established.

Until a few months before Caracas it looked as if Canada and the United States were locked in confrontation. Ottawa did not blink. Canada had many allies—including some in the United States. Eventually the Americans realized that the "economic zone" was the only feasible alternative to an anarchical extension of the territorial sea by one state after another. The great powers had to recognize their vital interest in international rule. It was the second time Canada had persuaded the Americans to give ground for that reason. At the Geneva Law of the Sea Conference of 1960 there was a Canada-United States proposal for a six-mile territorial sea plus a six-mile fishing zone. This is the kind of event which casual scholars list as one more example of Canada supporting the United States. What they fail to note is that in this, as in many cases, Canada votes with the United States only because alone, or more often in company, it has persuaded the United States to move to more acceptable ground. To get the Americans to abandon their fanatical insistence on a three-mile territorial sea was no mean feat.

Although there remain considerable differences between Canada and the United States over the law of the sea, and, of course, the whole proposal could still break up in disorder, the history so far is instructive about Canadian diplomacy. To confront a great power in the UN we need allies, we need to use our wits and imagination, and above all we have to build up a sound case. The United States cannot be ordered or threatened to change its policy, but it can be persuaded to see its interests in a different light—particularly, of course, if some interests in the United States are arguing our case. Some compromise on our part will be necessary, but instead of starting with the assumption that it is a zero-sum contest, it is better to look for an alternative proposal which could satisfy the legitimate interests of both parties. Steady nerves are required, for the Americans can be intimidating even when they are bluffing. The Canadian hankering for a brawl is best confined to hockey. Our shrill demands often make it harder for a United States administration to give ground.

In these various Canadian efforts to build a world order from the foundations up, the creation of a revolutionary régime for about three quarters of the earth's surface, the seas, is only the most significant. Taken altogether, it is as important as any Canadian contribution to international organization in the 'forties or 'fifties. It is a new application of the peculiarly Canadian interpretation of functionalism. In matters of sea and space Canada is not a minor but a major power; we have so much of both. Power in international diplomacy must be regarded functionally. That is what we always argued. Instead of prattling on about how Canada lost its status as a semi-great power, we should relate power to functional capacity. When it comes to Strategic Arms Limitation Talks (SALT), ours but to keep a vigilant eye. In questions of trade, resources, food, or even money, we are a much more significant power than we have been since the brief emergency period of 1945-6. Military capacity has very little to do with the major issues of UN concern at the moment. The boldest idea for a new law of the sea, that of the oceans as the "common heritage of mankind," was put forth by Malta.

For Canadians it is the cumulative importance of many campaigns which needs to be understood. Unless the particular subject matter grabs the interest, it is all rather boring, but it might be said that the UN is at its most effective when it is most boring. As Alan Beesley has described Canadian policy: "There is an emphasis on concrete problem-solving and a lesser concern with doctrinal attitudes, particularly those stemming from traditional concepts. On a number of continuing problem areas, there is evidence of consistency and perseverance over a lengthy period . . . There is a deliberate attempt on virtually every issue to develop the basis for accommodation between conflicting interests, in particular between the interests of Canada and those of the other members of the international community. A common characteristic throughout is a conscious tendency towards pragmatism, functionalism, and flexibility, most notably in responding to the need for change."[5]

In many ways this is harder slugging than it was in the 'fifties, when UN policy was to a considerable—and probably too great—extent designed by the Secretary of State for External Affairs and his staff. The big issues now vitally concern ministers and officials dealing with fish, communications, wheat, or defence ad hoc. What is more, the provinces have to be involved in policy formulation in a way regarded as inconceivable even a decade ago. So also do non-governmental organizations like trade unions, farmers, and fishermen. Before the big conferences in 1974 such as that on population at Bucharest, exercises in cross-country consultation were carried out. At the World Food Conference in Rome, there was a large attendance of representatives of private Canadian organizations. The delegation at Caracas included various ministers and deputy ministers, provincial representatives and politicians on rotation, representatives of trades unions and business.

It goes without saying that the efforts at consultation were roundly criticised and the government accused of disregarding good advice. Canada, like all countries, has domestic interests which are irreconcilable. It may be that these elaborate and expensive efforts to secure consensus will prove too confusing, and time-consuming, but they are still in the stage of experimentation. It is certainly good for the bureaucrats to rub shoulders with the special interests. It is also good for the latter to learn by experience at an international conference the reasons why our diplomats cannot always have it our way.

Because Canadian diplomats have played so constructive a part in thinking out international devices, they have to act in these conferences on two levels—just as Lester Pearson or Paul Martin did when they sponsored and managed plans for a Korean armistice, the universality of UN membership, or a UN Emergency Force. Geoffrey Stevens noted of Alan Beesley at Caracas that, "He found himself playing two, not entirely reconcilable, roles. He was expected to promote Canada's views vigorously. At the same time, he became a sort of honest broker trying to reconcile divergent views among the 137, particularly between the developed countries and the developing nations."[6]

This is presumably the way most equable Canadians would like our men to act. Their hand is inhibited, however, by that parochial form of nationalism which feeds on the self-indulgent myth of victimization (by Americans and multinational capitalists or by Ottawa do-gooders and Afro-Asian swindlers) and unable to see Canada as others see us, a very rich and major power. The apologists for Canada's "current approach" argue, however, that there is no fundamental distinction between the pursuit of national goals and international objectives, or between self-development and world order. According to Allan Gotlieb and Charles Dalfen, both of whom have been involved in these efforts to extend "international law," self-interest requires the betterment of Canada and it implies a world order which is favourable to or compatible with such betterment. The promotion of national self-interest fuses the planes on which government objectives are pursued. It not only fuses the goals; it fuses the activities that are undertaken in pursuit of these goals.[7]

Needless to say, Canadian policies in these fields are open to criticism. What is needed, however, is critical consideration of what our diplomats are actually up to. A good approach can be carried *ad absurdum*—as happened perhaps to middlepowerism. We have had some failures and frustrations, not all of them unworthy. Once at a conference in Brussels where we advocated stringent measures of international responsibility for oil pollution we found ourselves in a minority of one. Unless we are prepared to take a more generous position about the produce of our own enormous continental shelf and the needs of countries hungrier for fish than we are, not to mention the Third World's interest in the seabed as "the common heritage of mankind," we may jeopardize the whole effort to get a law of the sea.

Generosity with domestic interests is a matter for the politicians and the citizenry, not the diplomats, to decide. That is why it is essential to have a wider understanding of what is at stake. It is no less than the survival of the attempt to maintain and extend international regulation over the increasingly perilous activities of mankind through the flexible instrumentalities provided by the United Nations system. The alternative is to lapse into anarchy. The struggle to discipline ourselves with international law has been going on, not just since the UN was founded, but over at least three centuries. International law is changeable but not expendable. Because it is based on voluntary acceptance rather than imposition by force, as is the case in domestic law, it is always vulnerable. A people so utterly dependent as Canadians on the international exchange in tranquillity of goods and services dare not lose sight of our vital interest in a structured international community. As a country with a future we should recognize also that what we are dealing with is not just the prevention of calamity but the exploitation of boundless opportunity—the two faces of nuclear power, the revolutionary technology of space and the oceans.

Notes

[1] See Inis Claude, *Swords into Plowshares: the Problems and Progress of International Organization*, 4th ed. (New York: Random House, 1971), p. 136.

[2] *Globe and Mail,* 31 August 1974.

[3] J. Alan Beesley, "War, Peace and Law in Today's Divided World," Leonard Beaton Memorial Lecture, University of Toronto, 26 February 1973.

[4] *Mike,* the Memoirs of the Right Honourable Lester B. Pearson, Vol. I (Toronto: University of Toronto Press, 1972), p. 283.

[5] "The Sixties to the Seventies: the Perspective of the Legal Adviser," in R. St. J. Macdonald, Gerald L. Morris, and Douglas M. Johnston, eds., *Canadian Perspectives on International Law and Organization* (Toronto: University of Toronto Press, 1974) pp. 935-6.

[6] *Globe and Mail,* 31 August 1974.

[7] "National Jurisdiction and International Responsibility: New Canadian Approaches to Internationl Law," unpublished paper, portions of which were presented by A. E. Gotlieb at the First Annual Conference of the Canadian Council on International Law, 13 October 1972, p.6.

2:

Canada and "Collective Security"

As it will be clear to anyone reading the subsequent essay that, in my view, the idea of collective security is one which, as a specific theory, the United Nations wisely abandoned, a question arises as to why it is worth a whole lecture. The topic was assigned by the National Defence College in Kingston, and as a former member of its Directing Staff, I do what I am told. The purpose of the essay is to examine why the theory wouldn't and didn't work and to grapple with the collectivist approach to defence and security which Canada adopted during and after the Second World War—and which is what most Canadians mean when they talk loosely about "collective security." The lecture was delivered on 19 April 1973.

First of all we must decide what we are talking about. Collective security is one of the most misused terms in the political science vocabulary. It has a precise meaning, but in popular as well as academic and political parlance it has been used to mean many things. I suspect you want me to talk not only about Canada's relationship to the classic concept of universal collective security but also about the idea as most Canadians seem to think about it—that is, the idea of not going it alone, of joining forces with others to assure our protection, perhaps of paying dues to a protective agency (or getting a free ride?). I expect you also want me to say something about our alliance relationship, of NATO, and of continental defence but these, as I shall explain later, are *not* collective security institutions; they are something else.

I shall begin with a definition by one of the best writers on the subject, Inis Claude. "The concept of collective security may be stated in deceptively simple terms: it is the principle that, in the relations of states, everyone is his brother's keeper; it is an international translation of the slogan, 'one for all and all for one'; it is the proposition that aggressive and unlawful use of force by any nation against any nation will be met by the combined force of all other nations."[1]

It is a noble, logical, and beautiful concept which we have discovered after several tries is too rigid and even dangerous for a world which is so far from being a community. Few people take it seriously as a concept applicable to our present situation, but many people persist in the belief that it is what we are working towards. Although it is discredited, a belief that it isn't applicable but ought to be confuses the thinking of too many people and the most serious result is the use of this argument to discredit the United Nations. Even people who do not believe in collective security belabour the United Nations because it does not act as if it was an agency of universal collective security. Canadians are probably more confused than most on this subject. As the same political scientist put it: "Collective security has gone the way of most other ideal concepts; respectable people insist upon believing in it, but they also insist upon retaining beliefs which are incompatible with it and rejecting beliefs which are fundamental to it. In these circumstances, the problem of evaluating the principle of collective security as an approach to peace requires especial care."[2]

Canada suffers from schizophrenia of various kinds. One variety has to do with collective security. We gyrate wildly between isolationism and internationalism, to some extent cyclically, depending upon events and the national mood, but also even in the course of a single political speech. On the whole we have tended to favour collective security for others.

For a century or so we survived on the delicate balance of power between the British and Americans. Then the British and Americans decided, with our encouragement, that they weren't going to fight each other any more and we subsided into the security provided by the Anglo-American pax or empire. Secure as we felt then, it is hard to understand why we rushed to fight in 1914 and 1939. In spite of our isolationism we enjoyed then our own form of internationalism, the Empire. In 1914 we did believe that the framework which protected us was undermined by the German challenge. It was the same thing in 1939. By 1945, however, we were beginning to see collective security in broader terms—the United Nations, with Anglo-America as its core.

The first effort at collective security in which we were involved was the League of Nations. It gave us a recognized position in the world, but we had grave doubts about an organization which in our view was designed to protect a European status quo of dubious justice. Both Conservative and Liberal Canadian governments showed the gut Canadian view when they struggled persistently against article 10 which put teeth, or presumed to, in the provision for collective security. The League was too Europe-centred and not sufficiently universal to be effective. We were reluctant even to get involved in sanctions against Italy or Japan. Mackenzie King is blamed for Canada's "failing the League," but it is pretty clear that he reflected uncannily the political wisdom of a people whom he never consulted on foreign policy. He passionately supported Chamberlain's appeasement policy and went to see Hitler out of his conviction that face-to-face talks would settle all disputes. In doing so he struck a note which persists in Canada's international policies to this day. Canadians are not pacifists, but they do believe in the settlement of conflict by almost any means or on almost any terms. Like the theory of collective security this is an approach which has a great deal to be said for it—especially now that we live in a nuclear world. However, like collective security it must be applied with discrimination.[3]

The Second Word War, of course, had a lasting effect on Canadian thinking. The conclusions drawn were these: if we were always going to be drawn into wars we ought to have a part in trying to prevent them by offering forces in advance and having a hand in policy; and secondly if the aggressors had known in advance that there would be a coalition of free peoples against them there would have been no war. By the end of the war we were thinking of the great allied effort as a collective security operation, and the United Nations, it should be recalled, was set up during the war to perpetuate this wartime united nations alliance on behalf of peace. In 1945 the talk was about a universal collective security system "with teeth." Fortunately, although there was much rhetoric about universal collective security, those responsible for designing the United Nations were wise enough not to establish such a body. The United Nations was conceived as the continuing alliance of the great powers who together could resist threats to world security like those we had suffered from the Nazis and the Japanese. Canadians did resist the spread of the veto to non-military subjects, but they clearly accepted this principle of great-power supremacy in the Security Council. What we approved was not a universal collective security system. There was no provision for a great United Nations army but only for military contributions negotiated with the United Nations and voluntarily made available when required.

The United Nations, it is important to remember, had a mixed programme for security. It was a system to prevent conflict in the first instance. That was to be its main purpose. In the background there was to be the threat of economic or, as a last resort, military force against the misbehavers. It was a concept of deterrence. Canadians indicated their willingness to play their small part in the latter function but they saw their role as mainly in the first. That is the role which remains to the United Nations.

The Canadian schizophrenia on collective security was particularly apparent in the first decade after the Second World War. The strongest possible rhetorical support of collective security was combined with the strongest possible effort to reduce military forces to a bare minimum. It was not deliberate hypocrisy. It seemed as if leaders believed that pledges alone would deter aggression. The question of "credibility" had not yet been expressed on such terms. In the late 'forties Canadians developed their reputation as the strongest supporter of the United Nations, but in June 1950 when the call came for the UN force in Korea, the cupboard was bare. The same illusion was notable with regard to NATO, the belief that entry into a collective defence agreement would reduce the Canadian military establishment and budget—if that was possible. You could scare hell out of an aggressor just by threatening to mobilize several of those terrifying Canadian divisions if he misbehaved. One has the impression sometimes that the politicians and the officials, as well as the military, were leading quite separate lives.

Very shortly after the United Nations Security Council was set up, it was realized that collective security was not going to work as intended—if not necessarily as expected. I need not go over the reasons it failed. The Security Council, for one thing, was designed before all but a few international statesmen knew about nuclear weapons, and the configuration of power in the world was particularly unsuitable for a universal scheme. The lack of a world community was reflected in an inability to get a consensus on aggression. The idea of universal collective security, it has been argued, turns out to be an arrangement by which all conflicts are universalized. The United Nations job was in fact to localize them.

Canadian officials were among the first to realize that things were not going to work out as they had hoped and to argue for a self-defence agreement of those countries willing to do something about it. Far from wanting to abandon the United Nations, however, they wanted to save it. They wanted to out-manoeuvre those who would turn the United Nations into a "free world" organization. If the United Nations couldn't act in accordance with chapter VII, which deals with enforcement of peace, they would retreat to the second position, chapter VI, which deals with peaceful settlement. In its first term in the Security Council under a distinguished soldier, General McNaughton, Canada established an enviable record for progress in conflict resolution. It was very important in our eyes to keep the United Nations alive for these purposes and for the promise of some future day when great powers had had their heads knocked together. Canadians were among the strongest, therefore, to insist that NATO must be designated as a self-defence organization in accordance with article 51 of the Charter rather than as a rival to the United Nations.

That really marked the end of Canadian dedication to the principle of universal collective security—except confusingly in speeches. We reverted to our faith in alliance, essentially to a concept of the Atlantic world which was an expansion of our old Anglo-American shield.

NATO is not a collective security organization because it is not primarily designed to keep peace in its own area. It is an alliance against an outsider in a collective defence scheme. It was a way round the Soviet veto, an effort to make it possible for those United Nations members who would defend what seemed to them important to be able to do so.

The United Nations effort in Korea is sometimes seen as its one effort to enforce collective security, but in fact it was more an effort on the part of one of the great powers, strongly supported by two other of the great powers, to organize broad support within the United Nations for a crusade operated by the Atlantic alliance. At any rate, even those who hoped that it would launch the United Nations on a career of collective security recognized, after the military stalemate and with a perceived threat of Soviet aggression in other parts of the world, that however desirable collective security might be it was, as a United Nations operation, a strategic impossibility. What should be said, however, is that Canadians responded to the call in Korea in a belief that they must do so in order to fulfil the collective security promises of the United Nations. There was still in 1950 a strong conviction that if any aggressor were allowed to get away with it in any part of the world the hopes of peace would collapse. That concept belongs to the theory of universal collective security. As a conviction it survives, having outlived any confidence in the means of enforcement. It was the conviction which took the Americans unilaterally into Vietnam. Our dilemma is that the conviction may still be justified even though it seems un-enforceable.

One point might be cleared up here about Canada's attitude to NATO at this time. It is frequently said that Canada insisted on article 2 because it was ashamed of belonging to a purely military alliance.[4] This was a part of the truth for internal political reasons but in fact the point of article 2 was that countries which were to have a military and political alliance must accept a decent regard for each other's economic interests as an essential part of that bargain if they were to stick together. The idea was never more relevant than in 1973.

The real, if unacknowledged, removal from the United Nations of responsibilities for what we called "collective security" after 1950 perhaps helped the United Nations because it had a lively and useful decade in conflict resolution and in developing the concept of peacekeeping. The United Nations was helpful in reaching a peace settlement in Korea. A great many conflicts were not only solved but prevented by United Nations diplomacy in the chamber and in the corridors and in all this Canada developed its considerable reputation as a mediatory power. The inability of the United Nations to do anything effective about Hungary in 1956 did not mark the failure of collective security. It simply revealed starkly what could and what could not be done under this banner in any organization. Denunciation of the United Nations as such for failure to stop aggression in Hungary was just silly—or deliberately mischievous. The United Nations could not order force to be used because the countries with armies were not prepared to fight a hopeless battle. The sending of a United Nations peacekeeping force to the Middle East at the same time was not a collective security effort but a part of conflict resolution.

Associated with this surge of United Nations activity was the development of what the books call "preventive diplomacy." By preventive diplomacy I mean what we usually lump together as "peacekeeping," ranging from observer missions in Lebanon, Indochina, or Kashmir to emergency forces as we have known them in the Middle East and Cyprus. Theirs is a function of peaceful settlement rather than collective security and it is particularly important for Canadians to understand this fact and also to persuade other peoples to understand it. Misunderstandings about what such a force is expected to do have been all too obvious in Vietnam, for example. I need not discourse here on the Canadian aptitude for, Canadian affection for, and perhaps now the Canadian distaste for peacekeeping. Those with responsibility for Canadian policy in peacekeeping always understood, I think, that what was being developed was not a collective security role of the United Nations. It was something the United Nations might usefully do when it was quite obvious that it could not take on a collective security role.

In Ottawa there was always, of course, enthusiasm for developing the strength of the United Nations and at times perhaps the idea that this nucleus of an international force, if it could become permanently established and accepted by all the great powers, might lead to the revival of ideas about collective security embodied in article 43 of the Charter. The Canadian military who were engaged in peacekeeping wanted for obvious reasons a permanent establishment in New York which would save them from the perils and problems of improvisation. External Affairs officials sympathized with this wish and would probably have favoured some kind of standing United Nations force for this kind of service if they had thought it was politically possible. The objections of the communist powers and many of the nonaligned to such a move made it seem unwise even to try. The Canadian view tended to be that in times of emergency the United Nations would accept steps which it would not accept in theory and success would lead to further success. Or of course failure could lead to further failure. Canadians tended to favour also a clear distinction between peacekeeping and mediation although they insisted that the mediatory process should be undertaken firmly at the same time so that peacekeeping would not go on forever.

I think it can be said that Canadians, both officials and the public, warmed to the peacekeeping role because it seemed to fill a particular need. Canadians by and large did not want a free ride and they wanted to make some kind of contribution to what they thought of as "collective security." Insofar as possible also, they were feeling a need for doing something helpful which was their own thing. They had been finding that, without particularly seeking it, a role for them as a mediatory middle power was being created by the United Nations diplomacy of the time. They had no desire to be "neutral," but objectivity in the particular issue was what was required here rather than neutrality. The idea that they might play their allotted part in a United Nations collective security force had vanished. They were engaged in a contribution to NATO, with troops now in Europe, but already by the mid-'fifties there was talk of withdrawing forces which had been sent for a transitional period until the Europeans could get on their feet. The idea of joint continental defence with the United States was pretty well accepted on the eve of NORAD (in 1957) but this seemed primarily a function of radar chains, of the air force and the navy. Up to 1954 Canadian contributions to United Nations peacekeeping forces in Kashmir and the Middle East had been pretty easy. A few officers, some out of retirement, were sent off to New York where they worked under United Nations direction. When the first major call on the Canadian forces came for Indochina in 1954 the army was busy trying to get a force together for Europe. There was little enthusiasm for this new role, which seemed unconventional. To the great credit of the army a first class effort was made—and of course they suffered the reward of a first class effort—further demands. By the time the United Nations Emergency Force (UNEF) was established in 1956 the Canadian forces were beginning to see this as a regular function, an interesting one, an overseas assignment, a means of promotion, and a form of activity they were beginning to take pride in. Altogether this was a laudatory response to particular requests in particular places. When at a later stage—and there was less peacekeeping to do—it became glorified into a kind of national mission, scepticism developed.

A word might be said about the idea of a special force which evolved in Canadian thinking about 1950. Whether it was a good military idea is not for me to say. It has been a good foreign policy idea. When it became clear in the summer of 1950 that Canada had no forces to send to Korea, it had to raise them fast. Mr. Pearson was anxious to demonstrate Canadian fidelity to the United Nations and also to strengthen the idea of the United Nations as a body which could call on forces for its own purposes. It was thought Canadians, French- and English-speaking, would rally with fewer complexes to a United Nations call. Because we also needed to raise forces at that time for the new NATO demands this special force was raised for service at the call of international organizations—the United Nations or NATO—although of course there never was any intention that the sacred Canadian principle of having parliament decide on our commitments would be abandoned. This idea has gone through various changes, becoming eventually the idea of holding certain troops inoculated and ready for service and specially trained in the ways of keeping the peace. Whether it makes good military sense or not, it is a persistent idea because it is a response to the Canadian feeling of a vague responsibility to do things in various parts of the world to help the forces of law and order, good guys in trouble, without knowing where the next call might come from. However difficult mobility may be to achieve in practice, those who design Canadian foreign policy, as long as it remains internationalist, will be attracted by the idea.

I have emphasized that in the minds of those who established the United Nations—and the League as well—there were various ways of keeping the peace and collective enforcement was only one. With peaceful settlement I have dealt. In the days of the League of Nations the idea of economic sanctions had been ever present as the most painless means of collective security. The general consensus of scholars has been, I think, that except in time of war when there is an economic blockade, sanctions simply do not work. The idea of sanctions persists, however. There is an instinctive reaction to strike out against and to punish wrongdoers. But there is rarely a consensus about wrongdoing. Ottawa has always been pretty sceptical about the efficacy of sanctions rather than about their desirability or their morality. Critics argue that it is the Canadian anxiety to make fast bucks that keeps them from joining these worthy campaigns—whether it is against Cuba on the Left or South Africa on the Right. In the various sanctions issues which have arisen over the past fifty years or so, however, it is hard to find a case where Canadian trade was sufficient to matter very much. South Africa may be an exception, but the pragmatists in Ottawa are quick to point out that Canadian trade with South Africa is so heavily in Canadian favour that the result of a boycott would be to punish Canada rather than South Africa. Rhodesia, being a small land-locked country, seemed the one case where a universal boycott might work—especially as nobody loved Rhodesia. Given the Canadian position in the Commonwealth and in the United Nations it would have been impossible for Canada, even if it had wanted to do so, to stand out alone against these sanctions. The effort has generally not been considered a great success although the judgment of history in long range may be different. At any rate the results to date are not such as to encourage a belief that sanctions against South Africa would achieve their end. The Canadian decision to give special help to Zambia as the victim of Rhodesian sanctions seemed a more practical approach.

Now what is the present Canadian position on whatever might roughly be called "collective security?" After the Second World War I think there can be no doubt that the Canadian government, supported by a consensus of the Canadian electorate, made a solemn decision for collective security defence in principle rather than going it alone. Ideas about collective security, as I have tried to point out, were confused (not only in Canada but generally in the Western world) but the belief was clear that the only sensible way for Canada to defend itself was in collaboration with others, making its own contribution to general schemes whether in the United Nations or NATO. One attraction for Ottawa was that this was also believed to be by far the cheapest way. The other strong attraction was the belief that by participation we would earn a voice in policy. It is necessary to emphasize this point because it is missed too often by younger critics not only in Canada but in the United States and elsewhere. The idea that the whole "collective security" network, and particularly NATO, was a single-minded creation of the United States into which Canada was forced or sucked, is altogether too prevalent. At the time NATO was conceived Canada thought very much in broad Atlantic terms and not at all about docilely following American leads. At that time the principal aim was to make sure the Americans remained committed to "collective security." Canada is still free to decide whether or not it wants to continue this commitment after calculating the profits and losses. It was healthy that a new look was taken at the NATO commitment in 1969 so that when it was made again it was clear that it was done so for Canadian reasons and for reasons that still seem valid. It is unfortunate that the decisions on NORAD have always been hasty and unaccompanied by appropriate debate. Such a discussion would make clear that this was an entirely voluntary commitment on Canada's part and we can continue to determine whether or not we regard it in our interest. The lack of debate over the renewal of NORAD probably reflects not a government disposition to secrecy but rather a lack of interest and controversy at the present time over continental defence when all brains are absorbed in continental economics.

In connection with the debate over the withdrawal of forces from Europe there is one historic point I should like to make here. Whether it makes military sense to emphasize defence and surveillance of our great land mass as a first priority I leave to the military. It should be noted, however, that this priority is by no means as original as both the champions and the critics seem to assume. To anyone going through the record it is perfectly clear that Canada made the point very strongly that

NATO was a reciprocal pledge of Europeans and of North Americans and that North America was an area to be defended. It is perfectly clear also that in the beginning it was not expected that Canadian troops would serve in Europe and that when they were sent after the Korean war it was taken for granted that their stay would be temporary. If one looks furthermore at statements on Canadian defence going back to 1945 one will find that the home base has always been given priority.

What was also quite clear was that NATO applied to the Atlantic region only. Security in the rest of the world was left to the pax Americana with some informal help from a dwindling pax Britannica. Whether or not this was an arrogant assertion of American imperialist tendencies rather than a benevolent security effort is a matter of widespread debate (in the United States as elsewhere). I think it is fair to say, however, that although in Canada there have been increasing misgivings about American policies and many efforts to influence American activities, there was a basic feeling that any pax was better than no pax in the kind of world we were living in. It was beyond our control and there was little we could do to help, but we should be careful about knocking it. The Vietnam war has, of course, stimulated doubts about this concept, most particularly in the United States.

The relationship of the NATO allies to United States worldwide commitments has always been a matter of ambiguity. Although there has been continuous consultation and exchange of views among the major NATO partners on worldwide issues, it certainly cannot be said that American policy in the Far East in particular was multilateral. Divisions of policy among the major allies were a matter of particular concern to Canada which, especially during the 'fifties, strongly emphasized the desirability of consultation and co-ordination. This just wasn't possible. The paradox was that for constitutional reasons alone the United States had to act unilaterally. Canada and other countries were inevitably affected by what the United States did but they could not admit the principle of being committed without any share in the decision. This seems to be a paradox to be accepted rather than a grievance to be aggravated.

In the case of Vietnam, NATO allies had to decide their moral responsibilities to their powerful friend. They were under absolutely no formal commitment to join the Americans, even though Americans did regard this as a crusade to teach aggressors a lesson in accordance with the classic principle of collective security. It was the Americans themselves who made their unilateral position clear at the beginning. They specifically and categorically refused to be made in any way responsible to NATO for consultation or decision on their policies outside the NATO area. Here is the endless circle about "collective defence" which has always been a problem for Canadians. If you haven't a voice in policy you can't be expected to contribute, but if you don't contribute, you haven't a right to a say in policy. After years of staring at that paradox I think it best to leave it unresolved in theory.

Canada has had security agreements which apply to three of its four frontiers. The Arctic, Atlantic, and American are covered in one way or another through NATO and arrangements for continental defence. It is perhaps worth noting here that the basic texts on continental defence date back to 1938. In spite of a continuing debate on the implications of NORAD and our defence arrangements with the United States, I think that the reciprocal pledges given by President Roosevelt and Mr. King before the last war remain unchallenged. President Roosevelt's pledge was that if Canada was threatened from abroad the United States would not stand idly by. Mr. King's pledge was that although Canada obviously wasn't going to attack the United States it would consider that it had a responsibility to see that Canada was not used as a base from which any other power could attack the United States. Our agreements on continental defence are within the NATO framework and are not collective security agreements either. They are practical arrangements to meet a common enemy. They do not, as alleged, tie Canada to the tail of American policy. It is for us to decide the extent to which we think United States interests coincide with our own.

A dilemma of joint defence is that if it is to be convincing there has to be some reasonable agreement on the direction from which the threat comes. It was quite clear in the first couple of decades after the war that we were jointly defending ourselves against a perceived threat from the Soviet Union. When it comes to China or North Vietnam or Cuba, however, agreement is not quite so clear—and at any rate there was a Canadian fear that the United States was picking its own enemies who weren't necessarily ours. The official view that there is a Soviet military threat against which we need to be defended has certainly not been abandoned. On the other hand, at a time when the United States and the Soviet Union are discussing defence policies between themselves in the Strategic Arms Limitation Talks (SALT), the earlier assumptions get fuzzier. These developments, along with the technology which has made collaboration more difficult and a general sense of détente—whether well based or not—certainly diminish the sense of solidarity. The economic conflicts which Canada had hoped to control under article 2 of NATO don't help.

On the Pacific front Canada has had no agreement which could be called even incorrectly a collective security pact—other than the United Nations. During and after the war Canadians were quite happy to let the Americans regard the North Pacific as their lake. They recognized the United States-Japan treaty as fundamental but there was no point in our horning in on it. Canada has in a sense been nonaligned in its trans-

Pacific activities and this has been useful in that it has done some helpful mediating and peacekeeping. There has never been much doubt where our interests were believed to lie, but the fact is that we had no commitments in SEATO or any other security organization applying in that area. The Commonwealth was a moral commitment which led to some support of the Malaysians during the period of confrontation with Indonesia. In the different political circumstances there could not have been a North Pacific treaty organization which, like NATO, contained the major powers. Without such an organization, however, it is difficult for a small or middle power to find any meaningful role in "collective defence." If the new kinds of relationships developing between the United States and China, the Soviet Union and Japan, continue there is very little likelihood that anyone will talk about new multilateral security agreements. (The vulnerability of our best friend in North Asia, Japan, is basically economic. As that is where our strength lies, there is a good argument that the best Canadian contribution to stability and security in that part of the world lies in the realm of economics—if we can figure out how to interpret that truism in practical policies.)

For a lesser power a basic principle is that even though we recognize that we live in a world in which trouble anywhere can affect us and in which the security of Europe or of Asia or of Latin America might affect our own security, nevertheless, it does not follow that we should assume obligations everywhere. There may be a moral argument for doing so, but the strategic arguments are all against it. In fact, this may be the lesson which even a superpower, the United States, is learning.

In conclusion I should like to go back to Inis Claude and collective security. The pure theory has to be discredited, but there is something in the idea which one is reluctant to disparage: "Yet, the point remains that the theory of collective security has inspired the growing recognition that war anywhere is a threat to order everywhere . . . As a doctrinaire formula for a global panacea, collective security is a snare as well as a delusion; as a formulation of the reality of global involvements and the ideal of global responsibilities, it may be a vital contribution to the evolutionary development of the conditions of peace through international organization."[5]

Now let me suggest that our current issues of "collective security" are more issues of tactics than principle, and the former ought not to be taken as the latter. Whether our NATO forces are in North America rather than Europe, for example, is a question as to where they are most effective—for political as well as purely strategic reasons—and ought not to be regarded simply as a test of our loyalty to the collective principle. The problems are how to make an effective and appropriate contribution to the defence organizations we belong to at a time when there have been technological shifts and political developments (like the enlarged EEC) and when the old rationale is open to question. Things were simplest when we just kept up our defence spending to the respectable level expected at the NATO Annual Review and used the soldiers where they obviously seemed to be needed.

Questions about the conventional roles we had in NATO, NORAD, or peacekeeping do not necessarily reflect détentiste illusions or a careless desire to get a free ride. Expectations of détente, whether realistic or unrealistic, do account, I suppose, for the lesser urgency of the defence discussion at the present time. On the other hand, the moves to SALT, Mutual and Balanced Force Reduction (MBFR), and the Conference on Security and Co-operation in Europe (CSCE) have produced a wider understanding of the requirement to maintain defence forces as an element of deterrence and in a negotiating situation.

What does a medium power like Canada, an economic major power and a military minor power, do to pay its way in promoting world security? I have no answer. I suggest that people who argue that we might just as well give up being a military power altogether and throw our weight behind economic measures which are of increasing importance in deterring revolution and aggression are not necessarily being irresponsible. What they fail to recognize probably is not so much the essentiality of our military strength in "collective security" as our need as a nation—or twin nation—for armed forces which are permanent, self-confident, and multicompetent.

My purely subjective impression is that the country at large is reasonably content with the present disposition of forces and the defence budget. They feel rather than think the need for collective action with friendly countries. They are confused by the technical arguments about equipment and disposition and they would be happy to continue as we are, provided costs don't escalate. If they have to face issues of defence policy again soon it will be because there have to be tactical decisions about equipment in Europe and North America. These decisions involve questions as to the amount Canadians are willing to pay for collective defence rather than their belief in the principle. That is as it always has been.

It would be better if we all recognized that problems of Canadian defence policy are complex. It doesn't help to dramatize them as issues between warmongers and peacemongers. It certainly doesn't get us very far to say again that we must stand shoulder to shoulder against a threat which is constant, pay for our ride, and gird our loins. It is even less helpful to say that the Cold War is over and we can make love rather than war—for which we presumably ungird our loins.

If we are going to attend appropriately to our loins we have to cover them with a maple rather than a fig leaf—and there's a problem. The most logical courses might be to tell the Americans we would just pay a certain percentage of their defence budget and let them get on with it—or to do away with our forces altogether and go in for economic aid, as suggested. Neither course is viable for a state with a national consciousness and, what is more important, a national responsibility. The reason we have to make our own kind of contribution, do our thing in a collective effort, is not just to satisfy emotional nationalism. It is because we have to maintain reasonable control over its size, shape, and cost. We cannot allow it to be escalated by the technological and purchasing decisions or the grand strategy of a government elected by another set of taxpayers. How to reconcile that set of facts with the other set of facts, our need for the security of collective action and our relative inability to determine grand strategy, is the inescapable dilemma—and it is not solved by pretending that it doesn't exist.

Notes

[1]Inis L. Claude, Jr., *Swords into Plowshares: The Problems and Progress of International Organization*, 3rd ed. (New York: Random House, 1964), p. 224.

[2]*Ibid.*, p. 227.

[3]See "Mediation or Enforcement?", p. 88 for Mackenzie King's view of the League of Nations as a body the purpose of which was conciliation, an attitude reviled during and after the war but which sounds remarkably like a conventional speech now about the United Nations.

[4]Article 2 required members to "seek to eliminate conflict in their international economic policies" and "encourage economic collaboration between any or all of them." The popular assumption has been that it was the Canadian intention to give NATO economic functions, but the essence of it was that allies who might have to fight together ought not to be weakening the alliance by conducting trade and monetary wars with each other.

[5]Claude, *Swords into Plowshares,* p.259.

3:

The United Nations and the Frustration of Conflict

During the summer of 1969 I had the good fortune to be a Visiting Research Fellow at the European Office of the Carnegie Endowment for International Peace in Geneva. While there I served as rapporteur at the Conference on Mediation, Talloires, France. It was sponsored by the Endowment and the participants were men with wide experience in mediation. The following two articles on the role of mediation in international organization were the result of a summer's contemplation for which I am deeply grateful to the Carnegie Endowment. The first article originally appeared in International Journal, *volume XXV, spring 1970. It is intended for the general reader. The purpose of including the second "report" is that it makes available for anyone interested in the art, science, or craft of mediation, international, industrial, or familial, the views of some very distinguished practitioners. It is not possible to identify them, however, (and the report must be abstract) because it was recognized that a good mediator, if he is to be trusted by the parties, must swear not only to be discreet at the time but also never to reveal the offers and responses made to him in confidence.*

i) Mediation or Enforcement?

"There is undoubtedly much that is attractive and persuasive in the conception of a world united to prevent by force a breach of the peace by an aggressor." This much was acknowledged by Mackenzie King in 1936, but he added, of course, that it was only a hypothetical argument and bore no relation to the actualities of the day. "It may be that eventually some such rule of law will be established in the international as has been established in the national field, or at least in those countries where law and the free expression of the people's will still prevail. But clearly that time has not yet come, and to pretend that it has is only to make for disillusionment and misdirected effort.''

For such sentiments Mr. King and his generation of thinkers have been reviled ever since it was apparently made clear in 1939 that without a system of tight collective security war would come at least once a generation. But over thirty years later these views are coming back into fashion. Mr. King's long speech in the House of Commons on 18 June 1936 bears re-reading. It is much more intellectually respectable than has been assumed—the product probably of his two brilliant advisers, O.D. Skelton and Loring Christie. He did not dismiss the effort at international organization but defended it in words strikingly like those used by defenders of the United Nations in 1970: ''If it [the League] cannot become the international war office, neither need it become a mere debating society. It can emphasize the constructive side of its task. It is of great value to have at Geneva a world-wide organization where the machinery for conference and conciliation is always available, not having to be improvised in the midst of a crisis; where representatives of fifty countries meet periodically and come to have some appreciation of the difficulties and the mentality of other lands, and slowly develop the habit of working together on small tasks leading to greater; where, in spite of all the criticisms we often hear as to vaguely worded resolutions and hotel bedroom conversations, the statesmen of great countries are forced to come into the open and defend in public, before a world forum, the policies of their governments. It can press on to its task of disarmament, or at least to the halting of armaments. It can develop and apply the instruments of conciliation and of arbitration in settling specific disputes before they lead to open challenges and entrenched positions. It can provide a forum for the discussion of economic grievances.''

We seem to have come full cycle. We dare not forget that these were the views of a man who, along with the like-minded, has been accused of having ''killed the League.'' There may be a horrible parallel between the triumph of such convictions in the last days of the League and the scepticism which is affecting the United Nations in 1970. Are we repeating the same mistake or are we finding the same truth a second time? Must we grapple again with the stark reality that the only way for an international organization to serve our needs is by conciliation rather than by force? The answer is by no means clear-cut, but there is much to be said for asking questions about our assumptions and seeing where the case for a United Nations devoted to conciliation leads us.

Is it possible that our various efforts of the past half-century to create a better world order have failed because they were too preoccupied with war? Have we been too much concerned with disease? Has our attention been directed unhealthily to solving disputes and to settling conflicts, dedicated to the triumph of right over wrong, to defence against aggression? Has this preoccupation led us to see world government in terms of institutions rather than of process, bent on the creation of supranational enforcement rather than providing for people and tribes to govern themselves by infinite negotiations, accepting a continuous state of brokerage as the basis of international relations?

There is not a whole truth here certainly, but perhaps a way of looking at things. These are questions provoked by meditation about mediation and its place in the experiments in international institutions in which we have been engaged during this century. There has been a slow process of disillusionment with the formulae: collective security, the pacific settlement of disputes, all those devices enumerated in article 33 of the Charter—"negotiation, enquiry, mediation, concilia-tion, arbitration, judicial settlement, resort to regional agencies." Disillusionment produces the kind of cynicism about international institutions which threatens us now with anarchy. But the shedding of illusions leads us to the beginning of wisdom, and one likes to hope that what seemed like disillusion has been rather an unravelling. We may be reaching the heart of the matter, the identification of mediation not as a device but as a way of life, a habit of mind, not as an institution in itself but institutionalized in the process of world government, world gov-ernment which is not a constitutional entity but a kind of self-discipline.

Generations exposed to the horrors of the two world wars have naturally thought of the promotion of good relations among peoples in terms of the prevention of war, but war may no longer be the major issue because it may be destroying itself. That is not to say that it has done so or is certain to disappear from the earth. If it is banished, however, it will be as a result of its own technological exaggeration not because we have outlawed it by international institutions. If war becomes an irrelevant concept in the endeavour to make life on earth endurable and even enjoyable, then is peace an irrelevant aim? Do we take peace for granted, thereby exorcising it, and get on with the serious problems of humanity? Do we cease to think in terms of settling disputes and concentrate on regulating and harmonizing interests? "The lesson of the twentieth century," according to Inis Claude, "is not so much that the world needs better arrangements and devices for pacific settlement, but that pacific settlement—however well in-stitutionalized—is not a sufficient remedy for what ails the modern world."[1]

All this is, as suggested above, only a way of looking at things, not the definition of a new orthodoxy. As a corrective to cynicism, it may serve a purpose. Is it because we have linked the idea of mediation with the prevention of war or the settlement of disputes that we have found it wanting? That may be a partial explanation. Wars and disputes continue. But most of the mediation which goes on in the world today has nothing to do with the prevention of war or the righting of wrongs; it is part of an infinitely complex process of adjustment. The struggle for peace has been negative. It was a struggle against war, not for a better society. As the prospect of war recedes, the instruments for peaceful settlement weaken. But antagonisms remain malevolent and interests are at cross purposes even if they are unlikely to lead to large wars. The need for mediation is greater than ever, but the need is not basically the prevention of war. That is still one requirement, of course. The prospect of war may be receding, but it has not disappeared. Even in a transitional stage we have bloody fighting in South Asia, the Middle East, and west Africa. These wars have been subjects of intensive mediation and without successful mediation they are unlikely to end. To end wars and to forestall them we still need mediation. There remain many concrete disputes over territory or resources which require arbitration, mediation, or conciliation. Perhaps we are shedding, however, that concept of a world in which peace and brotherhood would dawn as soon as we knew how to settle disputes and right wrongs.

The fixation on war created first the illusion of collective security as the goal of international organization. True believers in the League struggled to enshrine the dogma against the sceptics, the opponents of the Geneva Protocol, those who have been considered the enemies of international organization. But objections to an automatic commitment against an "aggressor" look wiser since we have come through the learning experiences of Korea, the debate over article 19, and the failure of a long effort to define aggression. Whatever might have been said for collective security in the days of Munich, the development of nuclear warfare has made a conceivable theory inconceivable. Conventional wisdom on that subject is now that of Hans Morgenthau: "By the very logic of its assumptions, the diplomacy of collective security must aim at transforming all local conflicts into world conflicts . . . Thus a device intent upon making war impossible ends by making war universal. Instead of preserving peace between two nations, collective security, as it must actually operate in the contemporary world, is bound to destroy peace among all nations."[2]

As dogma, collective security was as wrongheaded as are all dogmas about international relations. As an ideal, however, it must be rec-. ognized as having had its impact on the consciousness of the world in a wider assumption of responsibility for the protection of others. If we are beginning to think of guidelines for a postwars era, an era that could be as sanguinary and unjust as the era of wars, we must recognize the contribution to international solidarity of the struggle to outlaw wars. We shall need that sense of responsibility in what might be a long era of transition with fewer wars and more murders. Collective security principles may still be applied by moral or economic sanctions, although doubts about the efficacy of such sanctions have been reinforced recently. The idea of collective security is likely to be tried for some time on a regional basis. Such application of the principle can be helpful although it may not always be for the best, as illustrated by the 1968 invasion of Czechoslovakia, which, from the point of view of the regional alliance, was a collective security operation.

The dogma of "collective security" was based on an assumption that moral issues were black and white and aggression identifiable. It was, however, a principle of last resort. Out in front was the provision for "pacific settlement of disputes." It was an age when international relations were dominated by lawyers rather than social scientists. The rigidity of the League was tempered by the concept of "peaceful change," a more radical idea than that of the "pacific settlement of disputes." The League was dominated by those who wanted to preserve the status quo and who believed, therefore, in the settlement of disputes according to the laws and treaties they had made. The principle of "peaceful change," unlike "collective security," recognized the ambiguous nature of dispute and conflict. The League made little progress in its endeavours to change, if not to legislate, intolerable situations into situations better adapted to new conditions—although the conditions in Danzig, Memel, and the Saar might have been considerably worse without League management. A good deal of progress was made, particularly in the first decade, in designing and using instruments for the peaceful settlement of disputes. The Council explored methods of mediation and developed programmes for intervening in disputes and interposing third-party assistance, even sending peacekeeping forces, long before these methods were rediscovered by the United Nations.

Understandably the statesmen of the League counted heavily on an international court to settle the disputes which caused wars. Much was done to develop and improve concepts of international law. The belief in judicial settlement as a means of preventing wars persisted into the San Francisco Conference and the new International Court of Justice, more broadly based than its predecessor. Whether its decisions have prevented wars is open to question, but they have played their part in easing tensions. International legal procedures must be an important feature of an international order which seeks government through mediation and conciliation, but they are unlikely to be central. It is not surprising that the Court has almost ground to a halt at a time when there is strong pressure everywhere for changing the structures which confine us—whether this be pressure against what is perceived as a structure imposed by the strong against the weak or simply the pressure of countries like those of Western Europe to create a new structure for themselves. International law is essentially conservative and has its place—but only if the institutions it helps conserve are at the same time subject to peaceful change.

The United Nations Charter was in one sense reactionary. Conceived in the shadow of a war which by 1945 looked very much like a collective security operation against aggression black and identifiable, the framers were dominated, as were their publics, by the determination "to put teeth" into the organization and establish a police force against aggression. They seemed to have turned their backs on the progress made in the mediatory processes under the League, although they did try to provide in the Charter for everything in the League which seemed to have worked. The public was in a vengeful and tough mood about warmongers and there was heavy concentration in United Nations rhetoric on the collective security function. The founders of the United Nations were in fact more sensible than the rhetoricians have implied. They did not try to set up a world government with a police force. Those who insist on positing the United Nations as an institution designed to impose universal collective security have been to a considerable degree responsible for the disrepute into which it has fallen. It should not be accused of failing to do what we never intended it to do. As an agency for peaceful change its record is better—far from perfect but good enough to justify its existence. The United Nations did not legislate the transformation of empires after 1945 which has been the most phenomenal example of peaceful change in history, but it did help keep it peaceful. The United Nations, abetted by the establishment of the Commonwealth idea, provided a framework of assumptions based on the Charter and an infinite variety of forums and conciliatory procedures to ease the transition for the imperial powers as well as the dependencies. Of course it was and still is a bloody business, but nothing compared with what it might have been. We know about Vietnam, but we don't know how bad the situation might have been in Indonesia without United Nations assistance.

In the perspective of a hundred years, the United Nations record in this transition may well look better than it does now when we are all too conscious of what we cannot do through it. It is hard to see a body so resonant with unconciliatory voices as a force for conciliation, but that is what it has been in rude embryo. The debate is probably more violent precisely because the danger of war is less. The violence of the argument may also be attributable to the preoccupation of the founders with war. It is to some extent true to say that there can be no peaceful change unless the victim of injustice screams and threatens the peace to get a hearing not only under chapter VII, which deals with breaches of the peace, but even under chapter VI, which deals with the pacific settlement of disputes. Has this emphasis discouraged preventive mediation?

Collective security as a universal principle has been abandoned, although it is still used to signify a sense of international responsibility for peace and order. Efforts at the pacific settlement of disputes continue and much is accomplished in the ambiance of the United Nations by quiet bilateral and multilateral diplomacy, but this is divorced from the function of keeping the peace. The United Nations is much more disposed to "peaceful change" although the term is considered old-fashioned. The United Nations is not, as was the League, dominated by those who have their major vested interests in the status quo. The trouble, of course, is that peaceful change can be just as unlikely when there is a majority in favour of change at almost any price. In either case mediation, conciliation, even-handed justice are sacrificed to political pressure.

And so, in the twenty-fifth year of the United Nations, the struggle for world order seems in a discouraging phase. Hopes founded on universal collective security, world federation, the compulsory jurisdiction of an international court, the pacific settlement of disputes as the key to peace have been found wanting. Efforts to "legislate" peaceful change produced a dubious and uncertain arrangement for the former Italian colonies but have failed to provide even that for southwest Africa or to control the evolution of a minor country like Rhodesia. The catastrophic world war has been averted, but there have been savage if limited wars, riots, and carnage. Even the progress made in the very limited contribution to security known as "peacekeeping" seems to be in abeyance. We have reached either the end of the age of idealism or the end of the age of illusion. Unless we resign ourselves to chaos, we have to decide that it is the latter.

We are, after all, entering the SALT age, and anyone who foresaw that possibility a decade ago might have been considered a foolish optimist. The Strategic Arms Limitation Talks between the Americans and the Russians are likely at best to make slow progress but they could change the international climate because they are based on an acknowledgment of the validity of a basic tenet of the Charter, the fundamental common interest of great powers in international security. There is serious talk of getting back to article 43 and what was really the basis of security in the Charter, not universal and automatic collective security but a grand effort at the mediation and conciliation of international tensions led by the great powers. The four-power talks on the Middle East have revived the classic concept of the United Nations function as seen at San Francisco, and it is a concept of pressure used not against the aggressor but against both parties to a dispute. It is an effort to find not a "settlement" of a dispute but a possible means for countries to live with each other.

Perhaps the shift in the centre of United Nations gravity from New York to Geneva and to Vienna is part of the pattern for the optimist to discern. There is conflict enough in Geneva, but it is not the dramatic and posturing clash which accomplishes nothing; it is the conflict of real interest in hundreds of subcommittees where the rough texture of a new world order is being fabricated. The horrid facts of life have shown us not only that collective security and world federation are impossible. They have taught us that life on the planet is made possible not just by the banishment of war but by the bargaining, arranging, calculating, negotiating, mediating, conciliating, arbitrating of interests which by the nature of things conflict and go on conflicting. Pacific settlement of disputes must be a continuing process, and there is rarely settlement. Even in New York things are changing. The Security Council operates less and less by vote and veto and more and more by consensus achieved quietly by the president. It is to be hoped that the Council is preparing itself for the situation when neither the threat of war nor the promise of instant peace is a credible inducement to peaceful change.

Optimism must, of course, be based not on illusion but on the end of illusion. Nuclear war has not been banished, and violent rather than peaceful change may be expected in Africa, Latin America, and Asia, not to mention in the body politic of the great powers. Another superpower may well challenge the equilibrium in a world from which it has been excluded. The new world revolutionaries oppose the very idea of world order as it has evolved. Powerful economic consortia are challenging the authority of governments. International political and security institutions seem unable to cope, and it is quite possible that a failure of the great-power effort to drive the Middle Eastern countries into a lasting truce will discredit finally the United Nations system.

Out of this appalling complexity of an overpopulated world comes, nevertheless, a realization that there are no simple answers—no answers at all. The threat of war may no longer be the major problem and peace may no longer seem an end in itself. Coexistence is what we are after, not the pacific settlement of disputes but the pacific living with them. We are forced by a society red in tooth and claw to seek not punishment but mediation and reconciliation. This does not seem like an age which encourages sweet reasonableness, but the disposition to mediation may be more soundly based on despair than on wishful thinking, on a recognition of our common greed and above all the need for common action to curb our instinct to corrupt the life process and destroy the planet.

So where do we go from here? How best can the mediatory function be strengthened to reduce and forestall conflict and to make for a more productive and co-operative international society? Ways and means must be found because, as we have realized again, mediation, broadly conceived, is the United Nations' basic method of dealing with conflict and forestalling conflict.

First of all there is the question of what can be done by scholars, practitioners, and politicians to understand the practice and purposes of mediation. We are still groping out of simpler concepts into a maze. Clearly the approach must be more interdisciplinary, involving lawyers, sociologists, political scientists, psychologists, and the help of all sorts of people from family court judges to experts in linguistics. Most difficult of all, the academics and the practising international politicians and diplomats must learn to talk to each other. The scholars should be attached to formal mediatory exercises and immersed in the mediatory politics of the United Nations Delegates' Lounge. Diplomats should go to the academies to inject more realism into the scientists' quantifications. United Nations diplomats should be encouraged to talk to each other and, when they can, to the general public about their experiences, about their failures as well as their successes. They should spend as much time as possible with mediators in other fields, particularly labour. They should be willing to look at the results of scholarly research in the spirit of the injunction: Know thyself. Mediation is a hard subject to talk about because it is a chameleon. It changes colour and disappears. Sometimes one finds oneself grappling with sophisticated ideas and more often merely stating the obvious. Mediation suffers from too precise definition because it is essentially a human approach, not an institution.

It is easy to reach the conclusion that mediation and conciliation must increasingly become the basis of our institutions if life is to survive on the planet. But what kind of institutions are required to make this possible? The most obvious solution, the creation of a supreme body which supersedes national sovereignties, is the worst of all because of its rigidity and its totalitarian inclinations. Any system, however, which provides for mediation only among sovereign states seems inadequate when conflicts of interest increasingly cut across national boundaries. Those conflicts which seem most likely to disturb the peace, furthermore, are often internal issues with international complications: Biafra, Tyrol, Quebec, Vietnam. To regard national sovereignty, however, as the villain and assume that life would be beautiful if it could be abolished has for too long distracted men of good will. As the Biafra issue has demonstrated, it is not impossible for outside powers to reach in to an internal dispute and even to urge mediation upon the parties. We are not likely, however, to get far by pressing for institutions of mediation which violate the basic principle of national sovereignty. Many Canadians, for example, imagine they are in favour of such institutions when they think about Biafra, but not when they think about Quebec. The whole Biafra affair showed how frustrating it is for good people to accept the inability of the international community to force countries to act as the community wishes because we can rarely count on a consensus of the community, although it may have demonstrated that the moral pressures of the community are not without influence. The illusion of collective security dies hard, even when it is applied to pacific settlement and peaceful change rather than to the punishment of aggression. It is hard to reconcile ourselves to persuasion, knowing that persuasion may not be enough.

Fighting against sovereignty may be the same kind of distraction, essentially negative in approach, as fighting against war. Sovereignty may seem to divide mankind, but its more immediate function in international society is to protect the weak against the strong. The liberal internationalist fails to realize that his crusade against sovereignty can serve the ends of imperialism. About the only way most of us can in fact divest ourselves of our sovereignty without perishing in limbo is to become frontier provinces of the American or Soviet empires, subject to the centrifugal forces of Washington and Moscow. However defective a system of international mediation based on the assumption that only sovereign states can be parties, it works better if there are one hundred and twenty-five parties rather than four or five. The world could presumably be re-planned so that centres of population were more rationally tied to resources, but so long as communities are based on historical circumstances, not only past circumstances but unpredictable present and future circumstances, there are going to be pockets of people of various tribes whose defiant intention to go on living can be protected only by sovereign governments. The power of these governments to stand up to the pressure of stronger governments, as well as stronger non-governmental forces like international corporations, is of course limited, but their right to participate in the mediation of their own interests is a defence with which they dare not dispense. The present state of international relations is not entirely unfavourable to them because of the mutual deterrence of nuclear force and the play of international politics. A world of sovereign states is not an ultimate condition of man, but it grew up in response to real needs and should not be abolished until there is something better to take its place. There is nothing essentially reactionary, therefore, about concentrating for the time being on the promotion of mediatory institutions among sovereign states.

This means essentially bolstering and if necessary adapting the United Nations system. The need is not for new institutions but for the will and the disposition to use what are provided. One thing that is needed is for members to settle down in recognition of the fact that they can no more achieve their ends by the imposing of majority decisions in the Assembly than by the organization of collective security in the Security Council. They can only press for conciliation and mediation in the search for peaceful change. Since the establishment of the League there has been a continuous weakening of the decision-making role of the third party, from the imposition of peace to the laborious unravelling of interests. If conflicts are to be prevented rather than solved perhaps we should direct renewed attention to articles 10 and 11 which permit discussion by the General Assembly of any matter within the scope of the present Charter. The heavy emphasis in the early days of the United Nations on resisting aggression and keeping the peace, and consequently on chapters VI and VII of the Charter, tended to rule out consideration of issues which were not a threat to the peace. There is still everything to be said for the insistence that parties try to solve their disputes by less dramatic means before they bring them to the Security Council, but the test of an important issue should no longer be whether or not it threatens world peace. To encourage the inscribing on the Assembly's agenda of every cause of conflict in a very conflictful world would be to open a Pandora's box and wreck the Assembly in a flood of passionate language. There must be priorities, but these could be accorded to issues which are subject to conciliation rather than those about to trigger fighting.

The shift of attention to the forestalling of conflict by removing the causes before birth is notable in the attention to outer space, the seabed, and the non-proliferation of nuclear weapons. In provisions for these purposes processes of mediation will be of great importance. To make clear that mediation is the intended basis of the operation there is an argument for enshrining it in prescribed institutions but here the case of UNCTAD is illustrative. It was solemnly launched by the Assembly with elaborate provisions for mediation which have never been used. Nevertheless mediation, informal and continuous, has been the basis of its operation.

There seems little to be gained by establishing new institutions of mediation for the United Nations. The United Nations Panel of Conciliation still stands although mediators have only on rare occasions been chosen from it. In 1950 the Assembly provided also for a Peace Observation Commission which could be sent with the consent of the territory to "observe and report on the situation in any area where there exists international tension the continuation of which is likely to endanger the maintenance of international peace and security." International politics have not favoured its use, but it could presumably be employed in situations which need straightening out even if they do not directly threaten the peace. It isn't the lack of consensus to back them. Such a consensus may be more likely in the SALT age, even though it is a kind of consensus which would have to be regarded with constant vigilance by all but the superpowers.

If the United Nations is to make the great leap forward to conflict prevention then its agenda will have to be enormously multiplied. Unless it is to be strangled by even more talk, it will have to develop ways and means to cope: subcommittees, supervisory bodies, ad hoc investigations, and endless missions of mediation. In a sense this is what is happening by the enormous proliferation of activity in Geneva. Much of it seems and is futile—just as futile as most of the debates in national parliaments or in the interminable sessions of academic committees. Good government is essentially boring. The less dramatic and the more normal it is, the better.

Having said that, one realizes with dismay how alien the present intellectual climate is to the proliferation of mediation. The opposition to war has never been stronger, but so also is the hostility to peaceful change. Radicals and reformers seem to oppose war and glorify conflict, partly it must be noted, in despair over the possibility of peaceful change by mediation when conservative forces seem too deeply entrenched. The concept of neutrality and objectivity at the basis of mediation is rejected. Force and violence are coming back into favour, with new illusions about collective strength deployed in the cause of justice—this time by the alignment of pressure groups not governments. It is hard to see what arguments could divert this great moral fervour behind the cause of mediation—except perhaps experience of the ambivalence of force and a greater disposition on the part of those with power to demonstrate concretely that the weak have more to gain by mediation than by violence.

Cynicism about mediation is too often justified. When advocating the importance of a mediatory approach to the problems of international society it is essential to recognize the dangers of the mediatory mentality. It can lead to the assumption that Solomon's judgment is always the most satisfactory. But the way of mediation is the hard and complex way, not the easy and simple solution. Truth and justice are not to be found down the middle. Even if one accepts the principle of seeking always to upgrade the common interest, one has to recognize that the sacrifices to be made are not just fifty-fifty. A major problem of a mediator is to deal with a situation in which one party has staked out preposterous claims in expectation of a solution based on splitting the difference. He may also find himself tempted to apportion blame equally to establish his position in the middle. When one reads, for example, that on 16 May General Odd Bull attributed the initiative for firing on the Suez Canal to the forces of the UAR and on 17 May to the

Israeli forces, one recognizes that this may well be in accordance with the facts but it might just be a United Nations "mediator" coping with very difficult facts in the manner most conducive to an eventual settlement. It is difficult to posit principles of justice to be followed when the issues are relative and subjective, but it is wrong to drift into the assumption that mediation is a simple matter of cutting the cake in two. If we have an hegemony of great powers in the next phase of our planetary experience, we may find that their anxiety to avoid trouble pushes them in this direction.

The concept of mediation as the promotion of a bargain, the division of a cake, or, in the professional patois, "a zero-sum game" is under attack and rightly so. The approach to mediation as an effort to upgrade the common interest, to promote or arrange a situation which, partly because conflict could be replaced by co-operation, would be a gain for both parties is being advocated as a revolutionary perspective on mediation.[3] It is sound and timely, particularly as mediation moves away from formal structures and as it is more influenced by sociologists and psychologists and less by lawyers. The only question is whether it is really as revolutionary as suggested. Bernadotte and Bunche and the long line of mediators in the Middle East have believed that they were working towards a situation in which both Israelis and Arabs could find greater prosperity. For Palestinians there has been, on the other hand, the stubborn question of territory which is theirs or someone else's. Territorial disputes among countries seem to be declining in frequency and importance as the aspirations of nations move in other directions. Nevertheless the value of resource-bearing land has become even greater and there are many economic resources which do have to be divided in some way among disputants even though formulae can be sought which would provide for joint profit. The principle of always seeking to upgrade the common interest can be promoted without necessarily claiming that it is universally applicable. It can be insisted that misperceptions are often at the bottom of disputes without insisting that therapy directed towards the altering of perceptions will clear away all conflict.

The advocates of the therapeutic approach may damage their case by overstating it, but it cannot be disregarded, especially as we are in an age when the authority of governments is more and more questioned. The problem of conflict-solving through therapy is whom to apply it to and how to get at the right parties: governments or peoples and which peoples? It is too easy to slide into the convenient assumption that conflict is the invention of self-seeking politicians and cynical diplomats rather than the suffering people. It can be, but more often it is the people rather than the diplomats who have to have their perceptions changed, and it is not easy for third parties to intervene in public opinion. Diplomats are by the nature of their profession more likely to see the common interest in a solution and they have a vested interest in pacific international relations. They are, of course, the servants of their political masters, not creatures in a political vacuum. Some are untrue to their calling and see their jobs as that of promoting the narrowly conceived interests of their own countries and parties, but these are more often the amateurs than the professionals or those whose lives have been spent in antique rituals in antique chanceries rather than in the newer diplomacy of international organizations.

Good diplomacy is absolutely basic to the cause of mediation. The increasing tendency to discredit the profession of diplomacy and its practitioners has become a serious menace to pacific international relations. Insisting that diplomats live up to the highest standards of their calling is something quite different. There can be no progress towards an international society based on the conciliation of conflict, preventive and therapeutic, without a large body of interlocutors whose loyalty to their own government is tempered by internationalist perspectives and a better grasp than most citizens of the inescapable compulsion to reconciliation in a nuclear world. "The function of pacific settlement agencies is not so much to let the people get at the diplomats as to protect the diplomats from the people."[4] One of the few hopeful signs for world society is that international organizations have in fact produced a new breed of diplomat and international civil servant whose way of life is the practice of mediation. There may well be, as has been said, a decline in the United Nations secretariat from the standards of internationalism maintained with conviction by the pioneers of the postwar period. It must be recognized, however, that the earlier secretariat was to a considerable extent unicultural and the institution itself dominated by the West. As it becomes multicultural it is less easily manageable. The concept of a civil service of internationalists has given way to that of a civil service which is internationalist because it is composed of representatives of various countries. The change was inevitable and there is the hope that a revived sense of common purpose in the United Nations will lead to a revival of the internationalist calling.

As stated at the beginning, the purpose of this essay has been to suggest questions and to speculate. To make clear that nothing is certain, it ends with a question which contradicts much of the trend of the argument. Is it possible that our traditional insistence that mediation is, by definition, voluntary might have to be revised or at least qualified? At the present stage there is little evidence in the international organizations that sovereign parties can be forced into mediation. It is recognized that one of the advantages of institutional mediation as in GATT or EEC is that a skilful and perceptive director can manoeuvre a situation which gets what is virtually a process of mediation started without the consent of the parties. Within regional organizations such as the Warsaw Pact or the OAS very strong pressure can be put on members by the most powerful member or by a majority of all members to patch up their differences. A Rumanian-Hungarian dispute over territory is unlikely to be allowed to threaten the peace, and when differences between Honduras and Nicaragua burst into violence a settlement is promptly forced on them. NATO pressure on Turkey and Greece to accept mediation was probably decisive. It happens in the United Nations only on those occasions when the superpowers want a settlement or at least control of conflict, as they did in 1956 and apparently want again in 1969. Whether the parties to the Middle East conflict will accept this pressure, or will be forced to, is the outstanding question. We may have to look again at a prediction which when made in 1961 by Jean Meynaud looked unrealistic: "But the development of the international organizations will gradually deprive the 'classical mediatory' procedures of part of their discretionary elements: the peaceful settlement of differences, resort to mediation and conciliation, are among the obligations imposed on signatories of treaties and conventions and, notably, on members of the League of Nations and the United Nations, expressions such as 'imperative mediation' and 'obligatory conciliation' cease being simple self-contradicting terms."[5]

Notes

[1] Inis L. Claude, Jr., *Swords into Plowshares*, 3rd ed. (New York: Random House, 1964), p. 221.

[2] Hans J. Morgenthau, *Politics among Nations* (4th ed.) (New York: Knopf, 1967), p. 402.

[3] Eg., John Burton, *Conflict and Communication* (London: Macmillan, 1969).

[4] Claude, *Swords into Plowshares*, p. 220.

[5] Jean Meynaud et Brigitte Schroeder, *La Médiation: tendances de la recherche et bibliographie (1945-1959)* (Amsterdam: North Holland Publishing, 1961), pp. 31-2.

ii) Mediation: Art or Science—
Notes on the Talloires Conference, 1969

The basic recognition of the essentiality of the mediatory process brought together in June 1969 at Talloires on Lake Annecy a group of mediators, experienced in both international and domestic mediation, to consider what had been learned over the years about this very basic vocation and what role it could or should serve in future. Along with the practising mediators were a few scholars interested in the subject. At a private session at which all participants were either mediators or mediationologists, there was no need to prove to anyone the virtue of the profession. After a searching and sceptical examination over five days of past and present practices and institutions, there emerged a sober consensus on the inescapability of the principle and the need to improve the practice if we were to escape damnation. The increasing complexity of international relations, it was recognized, made the study of mediation, the exploration of better methods, and the probing of an increased role for mediation in international society more difficult but also more essential. The United Nations had turned from the principle of enforcement to that of conciliation and from elaborate and formal structures of mediation to highly informal methods, often difficult to distinguish from ritual negotiation and other forms of international politics. It was pointed out that it was not so much the classical mediations like that of the Thai-Cambodian border or the Indo-Pakistan meeting at Tashkent which should concern us now but rather the amorphous conflicts like Biafra. It was not just the formal interventions in high policy but the everyday and highly informal ajudications and adjustments on which all international institutions justified their existence. In the course of reaching what were on the whole soberly hopeful conclusions about mediation, a good deal of evidence and opinion on many aspects of mediation were forthcoming, and it is on the evidence of this unique assembly that this essay will to a large extent rely in its discussion of mediation.

Scepticism about mediation extends even to the value of talking about it. Is it just human nature, instinct, the application to international differences of approaches learned from childhood? At Talloires there were about fifteen practitioners, those with experience of individual mediation and those associated with institutional mediation, from the United Nations and other functional and regional organizations and agencies, and they for the most part thought mediation was an art. The scholars, outnumbered four to one, were inclined to think, or cautiously to hope, that the analysis and classification of techniques could lead to the tentative definition of principles or guidelines. There were experienced labour mediators who, although generally on the side of art rather than science, did point out that labour mediation had in many countries become in the past quarter-century a profession with established institutions. It is not long since the same scepticism was applied to the idea that there could be a scientific approach to business, but business management is now universally accepted.

The problem here is, as usual, the overstatement of the two positions. Mediation is no more likely to become a computerized science than, say, business. Genius, sensibility, perception, timing, are intuitive and essential. If good mediators are not born, they are at least formed in childhood. They cannot be made. On the other hand they have a good deal to learn from each other's experience. The systemic approach of the political scientist offends the practitioner by the academicism of its categorizations and he cries out for flexibility. The wise political scientist insists that he is only groping after systems and rules and that the practitioner would understand his art better if he joined in the groping, for it is the groping rather than the body of dubious doctrine produced which is revelatory. It is perhaps significant that the practitioner who proclaims that mediation is indefinable genius is quick to generalize himself and to explain the principles he has deduced from his own experience. Mediation is by definition a lonely job, and the mediator, fortified by some study of what other lonely souls have tried in situations which, if never similar, are usually in some respects analogous, is more likely to retain the confidence he needs. Whether it is merely a question of swapping experiences or classifying situations and practices, there is considerable value, as the Talloires experience proved, in talking about mediation.

If the scholasticism of the social scientist is to be avoided, so too is the scholasticism of the legalist which has dominated this subject too long. Differentiation between arbitration, conciliation, or mediation can become an end in itself of little profit. One good man seeking to promote agreement is likely to mix a bit of all these ingredients into his recipe, and it is the results not the definition which matter. For the purposes of discussion, therefore, it is better to use the word "mediation" in its encompassing rather than its more limited and technical meaning. In the former sense it has been well defined by Jean Meynaud as "a considered and manifest effort taken by a third party with a view to resolving a conflict.'' Meynaud has provided two other useful definitions: ''The introduction of a third party distinguishes mediation from direct negotiations between parties and more diffuse methods of reconciliation such as the elimination of prejudice by education, etc. A second essential criterion is the voluntary character of the process, distinct, at least in principle, from judicial methods. According to general opinion, the methods of mediation and conciliation are characterised by an absence of precise, formal procedure, and by an opportunism in the elaboration of recommendations.''[1]

These form a loose and flexible definition for the purposes of this essay. It may be questionable also whether one wants to leave out of consideration those ''more diffuse methods of reconciliation such as the elimination of prejudice by education'' as the weight of emphasis on the subject swings away from the lawyer to the sociologist. The interesting efforts at mediation by the Centre for the Analysis of Conflict at the University of London, for example, are more like therapy than negotiation. The intention here is to concentrate on what is generally thought of as mediation as distinct from arbitration or negotiation, but, as semantic distinctions are not important, one has to look at a conciliatory concept that looks interesting. The subject matter is all the activities advocated in article 33 of the United Nations Charter: ''negotiation, enquiry, mediation, conciliation, arbitration, judicial settlement, resort to regional agencies.'' In the discussion one wants at times to distinguish for specific purposes between certain classical procedures and for this reason Meynaud's definitions are useful. In the case of ''good offices'' the third party does not intervene on the basic grounds of the dispute. In mediation, propositions designed to furnish the basis of a solution of the conflict are submitted, and the mediator enters directly into the negotiation. The object of inquiry is the establishment of the facts by a disinterested party without the formulation of the recommendations. Conciliation unites the task of the investigator and the privileges of the mediator.[2]

There are obviously some types of conflict which are more amenable to mediation, to the intervention of a third party, than others. The international balance of forces may be such or the character of the disputants and their independence such that the proferring of third-party assistance would be a waste of breath: the Soviet-China border dispute, for example. The time may come, however, even on the Ussuri. For years there was deadlock in the attempts at mediation over Trieste, but eventually the political situations in Yugoslavia and Italy changed and a settlement became possible. Dag Hammarskjöld was encouraged by his success in promoting a mediated solution of the border dispute of 1958-9 between Thailand and Cambodia to try to move into the dispute between Laos and North Vietnam, but the latter was no simple territorial dispute. It was a great-power contest in microcosm and there was nothing doing until there was a new president in Washington prepared for a different basis of agreement. Some few cases in which there is a legal dispute and the parties are disposed to honour international law are best left to arbitration: the disputes between Britain and Iceland or Britain and Norway, for example. Sometimes the mediator is less a mediator than a kind of balancer who tips the balance in the direction of compromise. That may have been the case with Ellsworth Bunker over West Irian when he obviously carried the authority of a superpower in the compromise he "recommended." It has been said that the World Bank "bought" a settlement of the Indus Waters dispute between India and Pakistan because the economic support and good will of the Bank made an acceptance of a compromise attractive.

There are some cases in which United Nations mediation is unwise because it takes the pressure off the parties to seek a compromise. When Sir Owen Dixon presented his report on Kashmir he recommended handing responsibility for the settlement back to the parties. As is the case with peacekeeping, mediation sometimes is an avoidance of responsibility. On the other hand, some disputes have to be lived with until they have lost their sting or become irrelevant. New generations grow up which care less about old quarrels and an arrangement can be made quietly. If a chronically unsuccessful mediatory mission, as in Kashmir, can help the parties through a non-violent transition it has probably been worth while. A peacekeeping mission can serve the same purpose, but it is so expensive it is unlikely to last a generation as required. Some disputes are smothered by friends and neighbours who will not let any really non-partisan mediators at them. Alan James suggests that there was no attempt at mediation over the Rwanda massacre because the other African states did not want to attract attention to an African massacre and the Secretary-General did not want to get involved in another Congo.[3] The United States, acting alone or through the OAS, frustrates outside mediation in Latin America, and border issues in Eastern Europe are unlikely to be mediatable.

In answer to the question whether some types of conflict were more amenable to mediation than others, there was a disposition at the Talloires meeting to consider rather the levels of conflict at which mediation might be effective and the different types of mediation required at different levels. There is a case for a mediatory approach to every conflict not subject to arbitration or judicial decision—or force beyond the present capacity of the international community to resist. Cases were cited, nevertheless, where the intervention of a mediator could be tactically unwise or on the wrong level of magnitude or authority. A problem is that sometimes the parties prefer to nourish their grievances for internal reasons and do not really want a settlement. One experienced mediator said that mediation should be attempted only where there was a reasonable chance of success; there was a case in some disputes for doing nothing, although even doing nothing should be a calculated tactic. Mediation could be successful in both negative and positive ways. It was not necessarily to be regarded a failure if it produced no solution but prevented things from getting worse, saved the faces of the parties, and allowed them to live with their conflict until it eventually might be resolved. Even when there seemed little chance of success, it was admitted, the pressures were often such that it had to be tried.

Mediation was easier and more routine, it was suggested, where values and interests were shared, as with the European Community. The more passionate issues of politics and security raised in the United Nations—the "to be or not to be" issues on which a nation's life depended—were less amenable than the economic issues in GATT, for example, where interests were easier to define and bargains to negotiate. The argument that economic issues roused lesser passions than political issues was not, however, left unchallenged. The involvement of the great powers and the polarization of the positions of the parties, as in the Middle East, certainly made mediation much more difficult. An "institutional" mediator said that the only types of conflict amenable to mediation were those where there was perceptible a common interest concealed by political passion; that was what mediation was about. He illustrated how a common interest could be found even where passions were strongest. The task of mediation, it was said, was to de-ideologize conflict; but another participant pointed out that political activists today, including students, are opposed to mediation for this reason.

There is an increasing trend towards viewing mediation in international relations as a continuing function, part of the way of life of a multitude of international organizations, designed more for preventing than solving conflicts, rather than as a procedure of last resort established ad hoc by some recognized international authority to prevent a war or to stop one. Nevertheless, there is still need of the latter and more traditional procedure, and at any rate there is value in studying the course of such mediations for what they teach us of method. What is being promoted now is in a sense just the multiplication to infinity of the process of mediation, and a code of practice based on more limited experience should be worth exploring. That is the argument for spending a good deal of time in this essay, as did the participants at Talloires, on kinds of classical mediation which we agree are less and less relevant.

A primary question which arises is by whom should the initiative in starting a process of mediation be taken. By one party, both parties, a third party, an international organization, a regional or other organization, or by the mediator himself? The answer at Talloires seemed to be that it could be taken by anyone with the authority to get the process under way. There is always a danger, of course, of the strong forcing the weak into a mediation which is really only an imposed solution—a description which some people might think fitted the West Irian "mediation"—and that is the best argument for the authority resting in the hands of an international organization and preferably the United Nations. That the United Nations is capable of imposing a solution of dubious justice at the insistence of the great powers in unison who prefer peace to justice or because of the partiality of the Assembly majority on colonial matters is obvious, but the general international organizations contain more checks and balances than the more limited, and particularly the regional, organizations. The right and obligation of the Secretary-General of the United Nations and of the directors of other international bodies to undertake mediation is clear. The Secretary-General's authority to do so is clearly stated in article 99 of the Charter although it is not often used. However, the impossibility or the disadvantage of placing certain critical subjects on the agenda of the Security Council or the General Assembly—the Biafra dispute, for example—makes private initiative essential. It is perhaps the principal value of the United Nations that it provides an ambiance for the mediation of disputes in its back rooms where parties meet on common ground to seek compromises on issues which are not on the agenda of any United Nations body.[4]

Only by private initiative is there likely to be hope of mediation which would treat the causes of conflict before a crisis erupts. A suggestion was made at Talloires that what was needed was an official like the man who used to sit in the tower of a Chinese town to detect the "tone" of the community. This, it was thought, was to some extent the function of the Secretary-General of the United Nations and there was evidence that increasingly the directors of the functional agencies were developing their sensitivity to conflicts which might arise. It was recognized, of course, that conflict could be functional as well as dysfunctional and that the role of institutional mediators was not only to forestall dysfunctional conflict but to control or even at time force functional conflict to a head to promote progress.

The question of the authority of the mediator, the source from which he derives his mandate, is of central importance. Those who have been mediators are virtually unanimous in their insistence on the backing they must receive from the institution which commissioned them. Ralph Bunche has said that he could not have done what he did in the

Middle East in 1948 without the moral authority of the United Nations. Other mediators have pointed out that their missions might have been successful had they received the continuing backing of the United Nations or, in particular, of the great powers who had pressed them into taking up the mission. On the other hand, there is the argument that the United Nations is more important than any mediator and it is better that the latter suffer as a scapegoat than that the world organization diminish its authority. It is an honourable position but of dubious value, as the gesture of a mediator in accepting blame is unlikely to prevent the public from seeing where the cause of failure lay.

There seems to have been a decline in the authority of the United Nations and its willingness to use its authority to promote mediation. The League Council approached mediation with the full panoply of its authority and had its special procedure for the purpose, with a "rapporteur" to find a solution which he could report back to the Council. In the early days of the United Nations mediators like Count Bernadotte and Ralph Bunche were the symbols of United Nations authority. But as the politics of the United Nations have become more contradictory there has been more reliance on mediation established by the authority of the Secretary-General, even if not undertaken by the Secretary-General himself. Gunnar Jarring, on the other hand, has been very much on his own.

At Talloires there was general agreement on the necessity of the mediator's commanding authority of some kind, but the very concept of authority remained ambiguous and contradictory. It was considered as based, in Weber's terms, on charisma, tradition, or the law, with the addition of power as another element. Law is an insufficient element; mediation is involved only where there is no law or the law is inapplicable, although treaties and general international law can play a role in the mediation. Attention was fixed on two ideas of authority. First is the authority derived from charisma, the quality, particularly the impartiality, of the mediator and his acceptance by the parties. Second is the authority derived from the means of suasion at his disposition, a combination of tradition and power. The view was also expressed that although the competence of the mediator mattered, what mattered most was not the authority behind him but the willingness of the parties to agree. Another opinion was that the classical definition of authority was alien to mediation; what the mediator needed was simply personal credentials, a "passport" of acceptability to the parties.

Whatever his auspices there is no doubt of the need for quality in a mediator. There was such a strong preference at Talloires for the single mediator that the discussion of mediatory commissions was confined largely to the re-examination of historical cases. If there were to be commissions, however, they should be composed of individuals, not governments, the latter experiment both in the League and in the United Nations having been discouraging. The individual mediator, furthermore, must be independent of his own government and invulnerable to political pressures. Whether charisma is what the mediator requires most remains a question. What counts is integrity, sensitivity to cultural variations, and a capacity to develop his authority by the respect he gains as he proceeds. Authority, it was said, is the weight a mediator is able to bring to bear on his work; it is something he has to build himself. He and his sponsors ought not, if possible, to be prejudiced in favour of a particular kind of world order, even the preservation of the present state system. It was objected, for example, that all those who had attempted mediation in Nigeria, whether from the OAU or the Commonwealth, had brought with them a bias against the division of existing states. There is doubt whether the kind of charisma that attracts publicity helps a mediatory process, although when the dispute has reached crisis stage it is probably necessary to bring in a distinguished figure as a dramatic gesture to divert attention or cool the crisis. Sometimes the parties will accept mediation only by a distinguished personality.

In most cases it seems desirable that the good mediator should strengthen his authority from outside as well. "Traditional" authority he derives largely from the institutions which sponsor him. The experience of labour mediation suggests a mixture of authority driving from the institution and from the mediator's successful career in the job. In the international field there are no professionally trained mediators as yet although a few men, chiefly members of the secretariat of international organizations, have acquired the authority of reputation and experience. Still, men outside the organization with a record of success can bring with them the reputation which builds up their authority.

Concern was expressed at Talloires over the declining authority of the United Nations, attributed, among other things, to a changing view of the Secretariat as no longer international but a collection of national persons. It was suggested also that the United Nations had been too available and ought not to be over-burdened with mediatory responsibilities, and that the Secretary-General was and should remain at the head of the United Nations mediators rather than become involved himself. Whether he could pass on his "charisma" to those delegated by him was disputed. Those who had had experience of mediation within the United Nations system felt strongly the need for the mediator to be assured of the support of the organization and of the major powers interested in the success of the operation. Such authority must not be just nominal, it must be involved, even though the mediator should be left as free a hand as possible. It was noted also that the very term, mediator, was becoming unattractive in the United Nations context. Those, for example, who were performing ostensibly mediatory roles in Cyprus and the Middle East were not formally "mediators." Countries did not like the idea of having their interests "mediated," and this was a sound reason for taking the drama out of the exercise and institutionalizing it into normality.

When it comes to special agencies of the United Nations family, the situation is more encouraging. Authority in such bodies as GATT, UNCTAD, or the Office of the High Commissioner for Refugees derives from the institution and ultimately from the common interest of the members to make it work. The mediatory function, informal and a mixture of negotiation, mediation, good offices, and the knocking together of heads, is increasingly the role of the directors and other members of the secretariat. Strong personality is obviously a major factor in this kind of mediation. The case of the EC Commission is special but interesting as it illustrates how a common interest in promoting integration reinforces the insitutional authority. The Commonwealth Secretariat's effort to resolve conflicts has been strengthened by the will of the members to hold the institution together. The situation of the International Committee of the Red Cross is different again. Its authority is in its weakness, in the fact that there is no coercive power attached to the Geneva Conventions but nations want in their own interest to keep this bridge open. The Geneva Conventions, it may be argued, do, however, provide an element of "law" in Red Cross authority which can be an asset but can, in certain cases, constitute an impediment to the mediatory function. The North Vietnamese, for example, will not deal with the International Committee of the Red Cross because they do not want to accept the Geneva Conventions, although they will deal with national Red Cross societies.

Authority by coercion is incompatible with mediation. The consent of the parties is essential, although it need not be explicit or verbal. Mediation has been described as "an instrument of constructive pressure." The force of world opinion and an appeal to humanitarian instincts is part of the authority of the United Nations and other international bodies, and, although it has to remain implicit, a prospect of sanctions. In labour disputes mediation is often invoked to forestall the application of penalties. There is the carrot also in the implied willingness of an organization like the World Bank to make it worth while for the parties to get together. On the Middle East the four great powers are meeting, with the threat of pressure or even sanctions on the parties, an exercise kept entirely distinct from the quasi-mediatory function of Mr. Jarring.

The legitimacy of the mediator is established by his personal ability to acquire it in the eyes of the parties, and by the prestige of the institution or other force backing him. The office would be strengthened by reinforcing both elements, and. there are various ways of doing this. The mediator's competence might be improved by some training in the art and/or science of mediation. He could be helped in the process of mediation by actions and declarations of the Security Council, the General Assembly, or other bodies. He might be assisted by the establishment of a peacekeeping mission to assure tranquillity. He himself, however, should have no other obligation. He should be divorced from any peacekeeping responsibility, because the need for firm action would compromise his reputation for impartiality. What might in some circumstances reinforce his authority could in other circumstances be a hindrance to mediation. Public discussions, in or out of a United Nations organization, could put pressure on the parties towards agreement, a kind of public mediatory operation accompanying the private effort. Often, however, it is best to take the glare off the mediator and what he is doing. Peacekeeping, although often essential to prevent bloodshed and escalation, may remove the pressure on the parties to move from rigid positions. So even could the establishment of a formal process of mediation. The mediatory process, however, is usually long, and sometimes the function of a mediation operation is to sit it out until time and events change the conflict situation.

From any external pressures, however, the mediator should be divorced, ostensibly at least. Furthermore, he should be given as loose a rein as possible, a blank cheque to negotiate and make proposals as he sees fit and as the attitudes of the parties permit, without having to report back to his principals for instructions. Examples were cited at Talloires of a situation in which a mediator was given a mandate by his principals but denied their moral support, and one in which the mediator had got from his principals a pledge to back whatever proposal he came up with. The former did not succeed and the latter did. The evidence that the latter was a more promising situation was strong, but it had to be acknowledged that the former was an inherently less tractable dispute.

Clearly a prescription for a solution laid down by the Security Council or another international institution would be an inhibiting factor. The advantage of the system of the rapporteur under the League was that he was a member of the Council from a disinterested state who went off and worked out with the parties a compromise which was then presented to the Council with the expectation that it would be accepted. The authority of the international institution to support the mediator's proposals must be distinguished from the insistence of the institution on prescribing in advance the lines of a settlement or keeping the mediator on a very short rein. On the other hand, it may be that the insistence of the Security Council that a settlement between Israel and the Arab states should be based on Security Council resolution 242 of 22 November 1967, which recommends the restoration of the 1967 frontiers and the end of the state of war, provides the element of compulsion necessary to induce realism on the part of intransigent disputants.

The question of the mediator's authority raises also the complex issue as to whether he should be guided by his conscience if he is faced with proposals which are unjust or not in the interest of the international community. This is a question which arises in labour disputes as well. There were practitioners at Talloires who insisted that it was not the role of the mediator to stop an agreement if the parties were going to accept it. His not to reason why, his merely to act as a transmitter. Perhaps this is a principle useful to lay down as an antidote to officious and presumptuous mediation, but it would be impossible to carry out as an absolute principle. Particularly where the mediation has been set up by an international body, a solution which set a bad precedent or was at the expense of third parties or just out of tune with contemporary ideas of international morality would seem to be unacceptable. At least one would like to think so, but, as the case of West Irian might illustrate, there are some disputes which the international community would like to get rid of at any cost.

It is a danger which may become greater if, as seems possible, we return in the SALT age to an international régime, briefly adumbrated in 1945, which is dominated by the will of the great powers for peace above all. It is a turn of international politics not likely to be left unchallenged by lesser powers who, as the behaviour of the General Assembly now suggests, may again combine forces as at San Francisco to try to frustrate great-power hegemony. On the other hand many of them too want peace at any price not their own. It is the prospect of these new alignments which makes the proposed "mediation" of the four great powers in the Middle East of such decisive importance. If they agree and are able to impose their will on the parties by using sticks and carrots, the United Nations may turn away from its trend towards voluntary mediation, and collective security without arms may be revived as an ideal. And we shall have to look to our semantics, for what the great powers are trying to do looks like mediation but cannot be called that if it is imposed. On the other hand, Gunnar Jarring, who is carefully not called a mediator but is just a representative of the Secretary-General acting in accordance with a Security Council resolution, is trying to do what is more classically known as mediation. That the two exercises can be complementary is obvious, but is it mediation—or does it matter what we call it if it works?

There was perhaps some paradox in the views at Talloires that the mediator should be protected by his sponsors (from the noise of international politics, from the press, and from the requirements of security) and the general opinion that he should consider himself expendable. The principle of mediation and its institutions were more important than the mediator, it was insisted. He should suffer calumny or offer a personal resignation if necessary rather than interrupt a process of mediation or lower the reputation of international institutions as mediatory bodies. Sometimes he should see his function as that of a scapegoat. He should not give up easily, however. The importance of tenacity, of trying again, was stressed, in particular by those with labour experience.

Different kinds of authority are required at different levels of the dispute. The earlier the mediation process could begin, the better, and there was much stress at Talloires, with examples from labour, on the great value of conflict prevention. This is happening increasingly among the functional agencies where conflicts can be spotted in advance and forestalled by the mediatory efforts of officials. It is a principal preoccupation of the EC. It is much harder in the political and security field of the United Nations, because most serious conflicts are internal-international and few member states are willing to accept any kind of intervention in internal affairs. Hope was expressed that the exploration of conflicts at an early stage might be attempted increasingly by private organizations but that the healing function of the United Nations should be developed nevertheless whenever possible. In spite of efforts in this direction, however, there are bound to be conflicts that erupt into crises which have to be dealt with by the classical procedures, the appointment of a mediator with personal and institutional authority. The improvement of these "classical" procedures as well as the development of more rational and progressive methods of dissolving conflict will have to remain a subject of study.

Closely related to the question of initiating mediation and the authority of the mediator is the matter of the timing of third-party intervention. Obviously the aim should be conflict prevention and this is the argument for institutionalization. Even here, however, it is recognized that conflict must often be forced to a boil so that progress can be made to a more satisfactory set of relationships. For disputes of the more classical type there seem to be two periods when intervention is likely to be most successful. One comes before passions have been roused to such a pitch that it is very difficult for governments to make concessions. The other comes later after publics have become bored with the issue. If a mediation has to be initiated during the passionate period because of the disturbance of international tranquillity it should probably be regarded as a holding operation only. That is not to say, of course, that the mediator can avow this aim. He must start hearing both sides and going through the rituals of mediation but, unless he is convinced that a sudden solution is absolutely essential to prevent bloodshed—and he should not be easily intimidated by hot language—he should bide his time before producing his proposals. A practical problem is, of course, that parties to disputes, especially the parties for whom the status quo is preferable, cannot be persuaded to accept mediation unless they are frightened of war or retaliation or the displeasure of the great powers or their closest associates. Consequently the mediation is usually set up during the passionate period when success is least likely.

There is an apparent conflict between the increasing emphasis on the institutionalization of mediation and the trend away from formalization of the procedure, but these two trends are in fact complementary. A good example is the case of the United Nations Conference on Trade and Development (UNCTAD). When the structure of UNCTAD was established in 1964 great trouble had been taken by the United Nations General Assembly itself to provide for conciliation procedures. These procedures, however, have never been used. Nevertheless, mediation and conciliation have been practised constantly within UNCTAD; it is the way the institution works. Mediation was constant but informal. The formal procedures were never invoked because members knew in advance they would not work in the particular case. In the international agencies mediation should be considered as an instrument of constructive international pressure, but it must not be construed as law, the imposing of legislation. Institutionalization is the provision of a framework where individual cases can be dealt with by a permanent staff of mediators in a continuing manner—on their merits and without undue attention to precedents. Formalization is the laying down of a *procedure* of mediation inside an institution. This procedure would provide rules which include those of interpretation, ie, the following of precedents. Thus one can have institutionalization without formalization, as is in fact the case in UNCTAD where procedure has been spelled out but never used.

On the subject of procedure and tactics for mediation a book could and perhaps should be written, but if it is to be at all scientific it will have to await a good deal of research. Perhaps a manual of case histories would be most useful at present or even a listing of alternative procedures found useful and not useful in the past. There is no getting away from the argument of "It all depends," although its constant use infuriates the political scientist. A serious problem is that the kinds of mediations usually compared and about which there are records are too few in number and disparate in character to produce results with much validity. What is perhaps necessary is to turn away from the classical cases and look at a fair sample of the thousands of mediations and submediations which are carried on every day within the United

Nations family and all other international organizations. It is significant that in the field of labour mediation we are closer to patterns and guidelines because there are hundreds of comparable cases which can be analysed. Almost any diplomat with United Nations experience could produce a dozen cases in which he has been involved, ranging from efforts to produce a compromise resolution to efforts to settle out of formal sessions a passionate dispute with a formula which can be submitted for ratification by a contrived group of sponsors. Procedures are less formal in this kind of routine mediation but the tactics of the third parties, their assessment of the facts, the attitudes of the disputants, and the timing of proposals involve psychological and other considerations relevant to the major issues and even more relevant to the institutional mediation which may be the wave of the future.

The practitioners at Talloires were reluctant to commit themselves to anything that looked like rules, but they were interested in the accumulation of experience. About the only "rules" they agreed on were that mediation should be private and flexible. It was just as significant, however, that they didn't flatly disagree about much, if anything, although there were differences of stress. Their experiences had varied greatly and they wanted to insist that procedures and tactics should be chosen to suit the particular conditions, but nevertheless their experiences seemed to have taught them similar lessons.

The need for privacy is basic, of course, although it runs counter to certain attitudes of contemporary thinking and is rarely accepted in practice by the press.[5] In spite of the insistence of the press, in the name of the public's right to know, to reveal anything they can get their hands on, it is hard to find anyone positively arguing that there can be hope of successful mediation if the mediator cannot talk to the parties in confidence. The parties themselves usually cannot be persuaded to keep quiet, although a mediator is off to a good start if he can get their agreement to let him be the sole spokesman to the public. One mediator suggested that in normal circumstances the parties were so busy giving their own versions to the press that it was better for the mediator not to compete. It has to be recognized that comments and leaks to the press are aspects of the vying for position and the organization of support by the parties which has to be expected as part of the mediatory exercise. They can also serve the purpose of preparing the public for concessions. (Mediation is rarely concluded because light has dawned on one or both parties. It comes when the balance of pressure is such that the parties are ready to give in or strike a deal.) The mediator may even find that although he must keep all details of the negotiation private he needs some public discussion to keep the heat on the parties. Bodies like the General Assembly and the Security Council are not designed as forums for mediation, but there are times when public discussion of the issues lets off steam or creates pressure for settlement. It can, of course, have exactly the opposite effect by making the parties more intransigent. One must reluctantly say that it all depends. However, one can also review the situations in which publicity helped and those in which it didn't to see if there are a few useful pointers.

The practitioners are likewise agreed on the need for flexibility and reject not only predetermined procedures but also any fixed rules about how to move from the first stage, that of information gathering, to the final stage, the release of an agreement, the preparation of a report, or the resignation of the mission. Nevertheless they have acquired some advice to give on all these subjects. The mediator must have a plan of attack in mind before he starts, even though he will have to adjust it as he proceeds. He should not, however, offer to the parties a fixed programme for he might then be stuck with it. He must keep in the driver's seat. One practitioner suggested the need to keep the disputants off balance, for mediation is something of a cat and mouse game. First of all, it is agreed, the mediator must set out to discover the facts, not only the facts as they are but as they seem to be to the parties. Whether he should be chosen for his familiarity with the area is a matter of difference, with a slight preference for the virgin mind not only unbiased but seeming to be so. He must interrogate the representatives of the disputants and supplement this direct method with his own investigations. In the latter endeavour he must be very careful to get at popular or minority opinions, even the views of the extremists who apply the pressure, not just the fixed positions of official representatives, but it is a delicate and often impossible task to make contact with non-official, and particularly opposition, sources. At Talloires scholars proposed various devious methods for acquiring essential information which the practitioners rejected as unbecoming or risky. The fact to be recognized, of course, is that there are many ways of acquiring impressions about the background to a dispute which cannot and should not be acknowledged before or after a mediation by those involved and the scholars might leave well enough alone. In interrogating the representatives of the parties, the mediator probably has to act with each privately although there are advantages in trying to get an agreed set of facts around a table whenever the parties are sufficiently civil to each other to make this possible. He may try to move as a first step to a version of the facts on which both sides will agree, but this can be a useless effort which serves only to aggravate the conflict. Parties can agree on a compromise without surrendering any of their convictions about the righteousness of their cause. Clarity about the terms of the agreement will forestall misunderstanding, but ambiguity about the nature of the conflict is probably desirable in any statements issued. It has been suggested that the result of a successful mediation is a misunderstanding acceptable to both sides.

At Talloires the vital importance of information to the mediator was stressed. A mediator has to know the dispute, and even more so the parties themselves. Pre-mediation briefing is important, but much information has to be obtained during the mediation. How to obtain this information was the subject of varying opinions. It was generally considered unwise to attempt a formal statement of the "facts," as this would initiate controversy and lead both parties to question the mediator's impartiality. Moreover, parties often create myths which become for them realities that no "inputs" of messages or information can shake. Some thought the mediator ought not to question the representatives of the parties on the facts; others considered this unavoidable and a good way to get the feel of the dispute. Other classes of information considered important included the basic goals of the parties, the extent to which their ideological protestations were rhetorical, the decision-making processes in the relevant governments, and the personalities of the negotiators. Before putting forward proposals, soundings should be taken to make sure they would be acceptable. It is important to show the parties that their grievances are not unique. There was considerable discussion as to whether the mediator should put forward proposals at all or whether he should be a mere transmitter of messages. It was agreed that it was best for the parties to be induced to ask for proposals. Sometimes they entered into mediation to get proposals they could use to obtain domestic acceptance of a settlement. The "practitioners" were disposed to think that in international, as in labour, disputes the mediator could rarely avoid making proposals in some way, and even that he should use the tacit threat to make public his proposals. As for transmitting messages, he ought not to be a "shuttlecock" and there is grave risk of each side assuming that he favours the messages he brings, but on the other hand if he is no longer trusted sufficiently to act as a go-between in this way, it is time to give up.

With whom should the mediator seek to deal? Obviously he should refuse to treat with anyone lacking in authority, but he cannot usually dictate whom the disputants will nominate to represent them. To insist on seeing the top man is not necessarily wise, as the latter is usually required by political factors to be more intransigent than anyone else. The popular but erroneous theory that ambassadors are merely useless mouthpieces does not hold. A good ambassador, much of whose skill is in the negotiation of compromises and who usually has a more international perspective than his homebound principals, is often the best man to draft a formula and persuade his government to accept it. Sometimes the more junior diplomats are freer to engage in speculative explorations than are their seniors. There are times, of course, when a mediator, particularly if he is a man of the status of the Secretary-General or his personal representative, must insist on talking to the head of government if for no other reason than to involve him morally in the exercise. A mediator usually has a staff provided by the institution which authorized him and he will want to pursue his explorations at various levels. Always he must bear in mind that he will succeed only if he comes up with a formula that the governments concerned can accept without losing their own authority. It profits little to get an agreement which is promptly upset by a *coup d'état*.

Mediation is normally a lengthy procedure involving hundreds of conversations with the parties on various levels. Obviously some record should be kept of these discussions and in particular of any agreements reached or promises made. The practitioners recommend against any effort to keep an official and agreed record. It is like the effort to get an agreed set of facts, the source of infinite delay and exacerbation. The mediator should keep his own private record. One very successful mediator kept a detailed diary which he found adequate for his purposes.

In the end the mediator may well have to issue a report. He will almost certainly have to do so if he has failed or if he is suggesting an intermission. What goes into the report will, of course, depend on whether the mediator hopes for a resumption of negotiations later or whether he feels that the parties or their sponsors need shock treatment. With due humility, the mediators themselves insist that the last thing to be considered is their own personal reputations, although it should be noted that the stock of men with the kind of international reputation and charisma to move into dangerous disputes it too limited for them to be considered lightly expendable. They are likely to be judged, in any case, not by what they say of themselves and their endeavours but by what the press has been reporting of their activities. Neither version is necessarily accurate. The strongest case is usually to be made for a report which is not inflammable, but although there is a case to be made in theory for a report which places the blame squarely on one of the parties or both or on their backers there are few examples of this having been done, possibly because it would be an act contrary to the instinct the mediator has been training himself to observe. Of course, the breaking off of a mediation is in itself something of a shock treatment. The threat of resignation is one of the mediator's most valuable tactics. but it cannot be used very often and must never seem the expression of mere petulance. Much more useful is the adjournment of active negotiations for cooling-off periods or to let the parties live a little longer with their troubles or cope with intransigent opinions at home.

The necessary pressure might be provided by the mediator's having his own deadline to meet, the expiration, for example, of his leave of absence from his regular occupation.

Recesses and cooling-off periods are obviously useful tactics, but there are times for heating-up periods as well. The practitioners are doubtful about imposing forced marathon sessions but if they happen they can certainly be exploited to induce a mood of compromise by exhaustion. The imposition of deadlines is considered risky also. Deadlines are, of course, often imposed by outside factors or even by the requirement of a report by a stipulated date on the part of the authorizing institution. Deadlines, however, can lose their force quickly if they are too often imposed and too seldom observed. It is often wise, however, when mediation has been stalemated on one point to move on to another and seek a more favourable situation to return to the former.

Some tactical options which attracted the scholars seemed to the practitioners too difficult or risky in practice to be considered. This is especially true with regard to such activities as mobilizing pressure by outside powers or affecting a disputant's decision-making processes by contacts with dissident members of the government or opposition elements. In certain circumstances, when the mediator is on the ground, it is hard to avoid some involvement in local politics. One participant at Talloires spoke of the necessity of dealing with extremist opinion, not just the moderates. The charge was made that mediators did much more of this than they admitted, but in response a difference was maintained between a recognized and acknowledged process of fact-finding in the community and clandestine contacts. There seemed a consensus, however, that it was better if pressures could be exerted by other powers or institutions, not involving the mediator. One mediator said that mediators should be careful not to become intriguers, but some of the scholars had a fancy for intrigue, without which, they thought, mediation would get nowhere. It was recognized, however, that the exertion of political pressure was difficult when the mediator was an ad hoc third party without continuing contacts with the countries and persons involved. It was more practical for the mediator when his organization was of importance to the parties because of the tangible benefits it provided and when its activities involved mediation on a day-to-day basis over the years. Officials of such an organization deliberately created contacts in various countries which could be brought to bear when needed. They even made discreet speeches intended to influence opinion, a tactic which was almost inconceivable for an ad hoc mediator. A difficult tactic under any circumstances is an effort to affect or use the press, by press conferences or leaks or the planting of editorials—although there are examples of effective use of all these. The risk of misinterpretation and the abuse of confidence makes this too risky. An association with journalists is better exploited to keep things out of the press than to get them in.

These are a few of the general principles of procedure and tactics on which something might at this stage be said. There are many other questions which might be treated in handbooks or investigated by scholars able to quantify the answers. How should a mediator start out, for example? Should he go straight to the central issue or try to get agreement first on something easier? Are there advantages in initial success which creates confidence and induces tolerance? If so, should this be sought on a procedural issue as seems to be the regular procedure of the superpowers when they sit down in conference? Would it be better, on the other hand, to postpone what looks like an easy question for a time when the exercise is threatening to break up? If the mediator is going to make a proposal himself should he work to develop a package? Should he for tactical reasons ever make a proposal the parties are unlikely to accept? Should he limit himself to ruling out unacceptable solutions and putting forward general principles of a compromise? Should he put forward proposals one at a time or are there advantages in issuing a stream of proposals as Ralph Bunche is said to have done in 1948, in order to draw out the parties? Should the mediator start off with his own conception of what a general settlement could be or let himself be led to a plan on hearing the arguments? How can a mediator help clear away any advance commitments by the parties which stand in the way of mediation? There are at present no available answers to these questions beyond the injunction to use common sense, but one detects on the part of practitioners a bias in favour of the mediator as one who draws out of the parties the framework of a settlement rather than one who is forward in putting up solutions for consideration. One of the principal reasons for this disinclination to suggest a solution is the fear that highly prejudiced parties will regard any proposal which is short of their demands as favouring the other side. This would be particularly true if the proposals, as is very likely, got into the press. The need for the mediator to preserve the confidence of both sides in his own impartiality is absolutely essential—provided, of course, that the parties are negotiating in good faith and not simply engaging in a ritual of mediation to prove to their own or the general public that there is no compromise possible with an opponent. If the mediator loses the confidence of one side, there is a general assumption that he might as well give up, but if this loss of confidence can be kept private he should do everything possible to regain that confidence before excusing himself from the assignment. He should have some leverage in that a party which is involved in mediation in good faith will be reluctant to accept responsibility for breaking it off.

Mediation may of course often serve purposes other than that of mutual agreement on some compromise. The value of stalling until passions have cooled or the cause has lost its significance has been mentioned. If the purpose is merely to prove that the other side is unreasonable the mediator should probably break it off when he becomes aware of this motive. He might come to the same conclusion if he began to realize that one or both parties would rather live with an exploitable grievance than receive satisfaction. Or he may conclude that for both parties it is easier to live with the conflict than to make the sacrifice or to face the loss of prestige involved in any settlement. Such a situation is unlikely to be critical enough to cause a war and might safely be abandoned to the parties. If it is the ostensible cause of a war, then it is only an excuse the solution of which would not prevent fighting. Sometimes the principal purpose of a mediation is simply to clarify the real facts about a military situation or internal developments in opposing countries to quiet fears. This was the function of Pier Pasquale Spinelli when he was sent by the Secretary-General to Amman after the Lebanese crisis of 1958 and he managed successfully to dissolve suspicions among the Arab states that had created a dangerous situation. When Dag Hammarskjöld brought the foreign ministers of Egypt, France, and Britain together in the autumn of 1956 he insisted that he was merely trying to help the parties see their somewhat obscured agreement. He got agreement in three meetings and might well have succeeded had other forces not been intent on bringing about another kind of settlement by force. Sometimes also the parties, or at least their representatives, are in agreement or close to it and simply want a third party to ''force'' them to accept a solution so that they might get moral approbation to cover a retreat or acquire a scapegoat for the benefit of their voters.

The present and the prospective institutionalization of mediation was a recurring theme of the Talloires conference. It was pointed out that the state mediatory institutions in the United States, available for mediation but not prescribed, in which the conference showed a good deal of interest, were only about twenty-five years old. The precedent of the International Court, set up when the United Nations was devoted to the belief that disputes were subject to judicial treatment, was cited; now that mediation was recognized as the wise approach, why could not a procedure for it be institutionalized?

The principal advantage of institutionalized mediation, even when practised without formality, was seen to be its constant availability. It avoids the often emotionally charged issue of selecting an acceptable mediator in time of crisis. (The need for the special man for the special case was, however, insisted upon.) More important, the institution has a much better chance of preventive mediation; it can even initiate a mediation without the consent of the parties. A multilateral institution can be more impartial. In institutions like the Commission of the EC, where common interest is strong, this was perhaps its major function. One "institutional" mediator said the charter of his organization was drafted with the intention of mediation in mind and he described the play of *forces* within the body to prevent conflict, stressed the need for "esprit de corps" in the Secretariat for this purpose, and estimated that of about one thousand substantive decisions taken in ten years only one had had to be put to a vote. Another "institutional" mediator claimed he had never been a mediator although he had spent twenty years mediating. He asked whether mediation was a process that was continuous, built into a system permanently, or a "one shot" operation turned to in an eleventh-hour crisis when other processes had already failed. The opinion of the conference seemed to be that it had to be both.

A danger from the multiplication of institutions is that they may become involved in conflicting ways in the same dispute. The case of Biafra was examined where there had been multiple involvement and perhaps some advantage from different approaches. In this case one organization refrained while the other was trying and they kept in touch. Passing on information by one mediating institution to another was difficult, however, as it had been given in confidence. There is a strong argument for co-ordination but not for limiting mediation in principle to certain institutions. There was no disposition, for example, to try to keep functional and regional agencies out of political disputes. Interest was shown particularly in what the ILO was doing in political conflicts and the hope was expressed that in some intractable political disputes a way in to mediation might be found by the economic and social agencies concerned with non-political aspects.

A new look was taken at institutions tried in the past when the acceptance of mediation was less clear—particularly procedures of the League whose progress in this field had been too often ignored. The advantage of the League, it was said, was that mediation had been made a normal *ex officio* part of the process of dealing with conflicts. The one League institution given extensive consideration was that of the Rapporteur, the member of the League Council designated to prepare a report on the dispute before it. There was some support for reconstituting such an appointment in the Security Council, at least on an ad hoc or trial basis, as a means of reducing tension within the Council. It was suggested, however, that the rapporteur had been a consequence of the rule of unanimity in the League Council and that perhaps the increasing practice of the President of the United Nations Security Council of expressing a consensus obtained by discussion with members out of session served a similar purpose. Another view was that the rapporteur had been invented at the League to shield the Secretariat from political involvement, but the United Nations Secretariat had developed a more active function and a rapporteur was less necessary for this purpose.

The most promising prospect seemed to be in the special institutions with built-in mediation, in the possibility, for example, that a High Commissioner for Human Rights might be fully "institutionalized" to take early initiatives in mediation. Consideration was given also to the possibility of informal third party interventions by private institutions, which could bring together officials or un-official people to seek agreement under circumstances in which they were not "playing for keeps." They could also, by patient probing of special conflict situations, seek to "upgrade the common interest." In spite of many worries expressed about trends in United Nations mediation there was a recognition that ways and means would have to be found because mediation, broadly conceived, was the United Nations principal method of dealing with conflict.

Notes

[1]Jean Meynaud et Brigitte Schroeder, *La Médiation: tendances de la recherche et bibliographie (1945-1959)* (Amsterdam: North Holland Publishing, 1961), p. 30.

[2]*Ibid,,* pp. 31-2.

[3]Alan James, *The Politics of Peace-Keeping* (London: Chatto and Windus for the Institute for Strategic Studies, 1969), p. 71.

[4]A homely but typical example of this function of the United Nations of which the author had experience concerned the disposition of the state treasures from Krakow stored in Canada during the war and held there for many years at the insistence of trustees who remained faithful to the "old" Polish régime. Discussions in Warsaw and Ottawa between officials made little headway because of the need for governments to stick to established positions, but at the United Nations they could hypothesize. Formal discussion in the General Assembly would only have hardened positions. The Canadian government, from being a party to the dispute, became the initiator of a mediatory process between the "old" and "new" Poles, the impetus provided by its anxiety to rid itself of embarrassment. Another mediator was the pianist, Witold Malcuczynski, whose charisma as a patriot with contacts in both camps enabled him to help in the devising of and pressing for a formula for solution.

[5]The reasons the examples cited in this article are less concrete than might have been wished is that the mediators at the conference insisted, with admirable integrity, that a mediator ought not only to respect confidentiality during the process of mediation but forever after. A politician willing to risk his career in the treacherous waters of concession must feel confident that his tentative position will not be laid bare shortly in the mediator's memoirs.

Part Three:
Counterweights

Canada grew up in traction. It was the product of a balancing act, and it is no wonder that the idea of counterweights pops up so frequently in calculations of our foreign policy. Although we cling to the legend of victimization by our great-power associates, Britain and the United States, in fact we skilfully used our leverage with one against the other. We developed the concept of mutual deterrence before a name was found for it, prospering on the uncertainty each of the powers felt about what the other party would do if we were raped. That fear of violation, when younger, encouraged us to embrace NATO in accordance with the theory espoused publicly at the time, that there was less danger of rape if one went to bed with eleven partners. It is a proposition which ought to have been subjected to quantitative analysis by some doctoral student—a challenging interdisciplinary project for the Carleton School of International Affairs in association with Masters and Johnson. At any rate, the validity of the counterweight as a defensive mechanism was severely tested in our youth. In middle age, however, divested of our chastity in one way or another,* we are offered the counterweight again in *Foreign Policy for Canadians,* this time with the Mysterious East as an added dimension. It is a recurrent note in the effort to establish an independent relationship with the European Community.

---

*In a lecture several years ago to the National Defence College I planned to explain how we had lost our early virginal aura when we got into the thick of UN politics, inevitably stepping on the toes of other countries who therefore contested our shiny image. My hastily scrawled and cryptic note for the lecture was transcribed with the following entry: "Loss of chastity by stepping on toes." The typist had added an oversize question mark.

1:

Odd Man out in the
Atlantic Community

The following are excerpts from a paper commissioned by the Brookings Institution for a study of the future of the Atlantic relationship, which had been inaugurated by the Committee of Nine of the North Atlantic Assembly. A report of the study was published in 1974, but the papers have not appeared in print. My co-author of this paper, who did the solid work but should not be held responsible for the more churlish opinions, was Robert Willmot, now on the staff of the Parliamentary Centre for Foreign Affairs and Foreign Trade and editor of International Canada.

It is necessary to look briefly at the Atlantic world as Canadians saw it during the period of "the Creation" from 1945 to 1950. Canadians were exploring the concept of a North Atlantic community even before the strategic imperatives as perceived in 1947-8 made an alliance necessary. For some years they had talked about the "North Atlantic triangle," and this was an expansion of the so-called "Anglo-American idea" that had been central to Canadian ideas of international security. Canada's continuing existence had become dependent in the late nineteenth century on harmony between Britain and the United States. Canadians, particularly after the First World War, were inclined to see the British Empire and the United States in tandem as the essential basis for peace, the core area of the kind of world which would be good for Canada.

The wartime experience of collaboration among the allies and growing concern over the domination of the triangle by the two major powers encouraged Canadians into the more international concept of a Western European-North American basis both for prosperity and for the deterrence of aggression. This somewhat regional concept was not seen as contrary to the interests of the United Nations, for while

Canadians had reluctantly accepted the necessity of NATO as a collective defence arrangement, they were at great pains to reconcile it with the terms of the Charter. Indeed, one of the reasons they espoused the North Atlantic movement and took an active part in preaching the doctrine was that they considered this far better than the transformation of the United Nations into a Western organization by the expulsion of the communists—a proposal being advanced in some influential quarters to cope with Soviet abuse of the veto.

Although Canadians recognized the military necessities of 1948, they assumed that their own military contribution would be limited. They had no reason then to think they would be expected to send troops back to Europe. Given their disposition towards the Atlantic community, however, they naturally were strong advocates of the idea that countries which were pledged if necessary to fight and die together must do everything possible to harmonize their foreign policies. Most members of NATO agreed on this in principle but Canadians had particular concerns which led them to press especially for inclusion of article 2 in the Treaty.[1]

That article and Canada's efforts on its behalf have subsequently been misinterpreted as unnecessary attempts to make NATO an agency for economic organization. It is true that some Canadians, including some high officials, did entertain hopes that NATO would develop into a close-knit, relatively co-ordinated international community. Whatever their merits, however, such hopes were not the operative concerns behind Canada's efforts. Canada's real worries arose from the simple calculation that adequate co-operation on security matters would be impossible if the allies were constantly confronting each other over economic issues. It was based also on the belief that NATO must offer something besides simple military deterrence to counteract the impact of communist expansion on the morale of Western European publics. That Canadians were not alone in these worries is suggested by articles 1, 2 and 3 of the Brussels Treaty.[2] Since the closing days of World War II, senior officials in Ottawa had been haunted by the fear that once the bond of wartime alliance was dissolved, the devastated European countries and the North American countries, whose economies had been stimulated by the war, would find their interests so different that they would inevitably engage in economic policies which would degenerate into somethign like economic warfare. As Canadians saw it, article 2 was designed to infuse into the spirit of NATO an acceptance of the view that the economic policies of the member nations should be guided by the same principles of mutual interest and respect as were considered essential in other aspects of their foreign policies.

Canadians also saw NATO as a counterweight. Along with the Commonwealth and the United Nations, it would give Canada a multilateral forum in which, by combining with other lesser powers, it could make its weight felt and so be relieved, at least psychically, of the inhibitions of life on a continent with one gigantic neighbour. Being grouped with Britain, France, and the United States in a common organization, it was hoped, would bridge the prevailing rift in Canadian opinion among imperialists, internationalists, and continentalists. To a very considerable extent it did achieve that.

A quarter of a century later, the one Canadian purpose in sponsoring and joining the North Atlantic Treaty which would not be widely questioned in Canada is that which inspired article 2. There is no question of a Canadian wish to turn NATO into a Western economic institution, for although NATO is itself now dealing with such matters as pollution, the functional divisions between NATO, OECD, and other bodies are entirely accepted. However, the reasons for concern over the possible isolation of the Atlantic countries into warring economic blocs are greater now than at any time since 1949. Canada has most to lose in such a situation because its identity as well as its trade is threatened.

Other reasons for being in NATO have either evaporated or considerably lost their force. In the greatly changed circumstances of the European members, military arguments for the stationing of Canadian forces in Europe are hard to support. They were sent there as a temporary gesture when Europe was weak. They are trapped there now not because they are needed but because of the symbolism which would be attached to their withdrawal. The argument that they give Canada a seat at the table and a voice in European affairs, emphasized by one school of thought, grows less convincing to Canadians who ask whether a peripheral influence on a continent more than ever determined to go its own way is relevant to the Canadian national interest. The military role is taken more seriously by Canadian diplomats, but in their case they probably see it largely as one way to keep a foot in the door of European ministries if they are not to be shut right out of the West European economy. They have good reason also to value the exchange of intelligence and the discussion of policy with major powers in NATO, about which the public is largely unaware and sceptical.

In the military field the counterweight did not work out as hoped. Canadians on the whole would have liked North American defence and, in particular, the North American Air Defence agreement (NORAD), to be part of the NATO framework, but the American military insisted on its separation lest they have interference from Paris or any semblance of multilateral control over the Strategic Air Command (SAC). At the same time Europeans, who rarely seem able to comprehend that North America is an integral part of the area of the North Atlantic Treaty, preferred to concentrate on their own continent. Therefore, NATO did not act as a counterweight to the imbalance of the

Canada-United States military relationship in continental defence. At a time when Canadians are obsessively concerned with the North American imbalance, this might be a more serious problem were it not that the growth of technology, and particularly the development of intercontinental missiles, has greatly reduced the importance of Canada in American military calculations for the defence of the United States.

Having no longer a very serious role to play in European or North American defence, Canada finds itself increasingly in a position of what might be called functional neutralism. Belief in détente has, of course, affected Canadian thinking as it has the thinking of the peoples of all North Atlantic countries. It is the lack of a clear military role rather than excessive optimism, however, which inclines many Canadians towards a position best described perhaps as non-involvement. This is not, of course, government policy. Fundamental strategic realities, as well as a variety of economic and political considerations, ensure Canada's continuing membership in the NATO and NORAD alliances. But as long as the widespread confidence in détente lasts, and as long as Canadians feel that they have little to contribute besides their bare presence—which is likely to be for the life of the alliances—this feeling of non-involvement and a certain longing to be free of essentially encumbering obligations may well grow. Its expression in policy will not be in the form of withdrawal but rather in the discovery of even greater elasticity in the obligations of alignment. The basic security considerations with which Canadians are concerned are, at any rate, much more economic than military, and it is economic issues that are likely to determine the degree of elasticity discovered.

With a heightened awareness of the ubiquitous American presence, and less faith in the efficacy of international role-playing, the old instinct for counterweights has reappeared. The recognition of Peking, the Prime Minister's visit to the Soviet Union, and Mr. Kosygin's return visit encouraged some Canadian neutralists and foreign critics into false assumptions about Canada's "realignment." There is a great deal of interest in Japan and the Far East, and an interest perhaps more rhetorical than actual in Latin America and Africa. Some counterweight may be found in a revived United Nations, more particularly in the economic and monetary institutions with broad international memberships. Yet it would be more realistic to think of Canada's actions in such agencies not in terms of counterweights, but more simply as the fulfilment of international responsibilities in areas of special interest and competence. At any rate, this would seem to be the government's view. For example, the strong Canadian initiatives at the Stockholm conference, though clearly directed to the extension and strengthening of international law in the field of environmental protection, were nevertheless visibly linked to Canada's vital national interest in challenging the whole concept of an unchecked freedom of the high seas.

The question arises, then, as to where Canada is to find the desired counterweights. Besides the obvious strategic value of pursuing as normal and healthy relations as possible with the Soviet Union, there are a number of areas for possible collaboration, particularly on common problems of northern development. But the potential for increased trade, though significant, is limited. China, it is hoped, will remain an important market for Canadian wheat, and Canada is seeking a foot in the Chinese market, in tobacco and airline communication, for example, before Washington and Peking become too cordial. Although Canada and China are exchanging enormous trade fairs this year it is doubtful if much can be expected as long as the Chinese show no signs of dropping their preference for economic self-dependence.

More might be expected from trade with the non-communist, industrialized countries of the Pacific but, aside from Japan, developments so far are not on a scale to promise important diversion from the United States market. The normal difficulties of finding counterweights are compounded in Canada by the lack of energy being expended for the purpose. One might almost say that the problem has not really been identified, for the focus of political debate is on the admittedly alarming extent of American investment in Canada, instead of on the extreme dependence on the United States market that constitutes our real vulnerability. The Canadian business community below the level of the large corporation is mainly unaware of the potential markets in the Pacific, including Japan, and seems unwilling to make the special efforts required for their exploitation. Canada and Japan now rank as each other's third largest trading partner, but on our side this is too much a result of the actions of international corporations and of Japan's need for the natural resources and semi-processed goods which we have in seeming abundance.[3]

In any talk of counterweights, Canadian thoughts ought logically to turn to the other side of the Atlantic, but the view towards Europe is still ambivalent: in political and security questions there is increasing detachment, as already noted, while in the fields of trade, culture, and especially tourism, the interest among Canadians is growing. Except during the period of Britain's first unsuccessful bid for entry, Canadian governments have taken a passive and deliberately correct view towards the EEC. Few Canadians have shared the messianic views of influential Americans about European union. They have been less inclined to see it as a giant step towards world order and more as a manifestation of economic and political regionalism or blocism. That *le défi Européen* has to be accepted is clear, but Canada has been paralysed by uncertainty. Trade with the United Kingdom last year was still larger than trade with the six Common Market countries combined. Part of the problem has been a general apathy in the business community, similar to that noted above regarding trade with Japan. Such an attitude was relatively easy to sustain during the 'sixties, the period of most rapid economic development in the EEC, because Canada's trade with the United States and Japan was expanding explosively. The present signs of change are to a considerable extent due to the imminent loss of traditional advantages offered under the Commonwealth preference system coupled with the fears that attended the measures announced by Pressident Nixon in August 1971.

Better intentions towards Europe may be welcomed, but they will not solve all problems. The growth and enlargement of the European Economic Community is variously regarded as a good or a bad thing in general, and whether in the end it will be helpful or harmful to Canadian trade and investment is much debated. But there is general recognition that it tends further to isolate Canada within the Atlantic community, and this may be more important in the long run than the loss of advantages in the United Kingdom or the structural difficulties of formal Canada-EEC relations. Canada's historic role in NATO was, as pointed out at the time, to convert what would otherwise have been an American aid-to-Europe scheme into a community of fifteen nations. If the Western Europeans now seek to speak with one voice, Canada is shut out from common causes with its most natural associates, the smaller European members. If the EEC is to be one of the "twin pillars" of the Atlantic world, then the United States must be the other. It cannot be "North America." There is no Brussels on this side of the Atlantic. Not only is there no common North American front—there is no basis for one, because the differences in power and economic interests are such that a common position on political, economic, or security matters can rarely be guaranteed. The United States and Canada will often be in agreement, but the agreement is coincidental and Canadians could not permit it to be regularized. The fact of being both North American is responsible for as much conflict as common interest. Even the on-again-off-again acceptance of the principle of a common policy by the many nations of the EEC is no model for a continent consisting of one superpower and one middle power.[4] Canada thus becomes the odd man out, the unsymmetrical element in the pattern. This creates a problem for Canadians of being disregarded. It presents a real problem for Americans and Europeans also of seeing how (or even remembering) to fit this stubborn piece into the framework.

In matters of security the notion of a triangular Atlantic community is nearing the end of a long death, and while Canadians have found it a painful process they are now adjusting. The same concept of triangularity may seem equally distorted when applied to non-security matters. Relations with the United States are, of course, of far greater importance to the European countries than their relations with Canada. As a trading partner, Canada is at present more important to the United States than is the EEC, but in broad international affairs the Europeans still carry more weight, and Canada tends too often to be left to fit into patterns worked out between the United States and the EEC as happened in the Kennedy Round of negotiations.

The situation which Canadians have come to accept in NATO is intolerable in the economic and monetary discussions within the Atlantic community. Because Canada is now an economic power comparable with the major powers of Europe this exclusion, however understandable, inspires a frustration which is partly responsible for the current wave of nationalism and emphasis on the national interest in Canada. In the issues which preoccupy Canadians now—exploitation of resources, fishing, coastal waters, monetary stability, trade restrictions—the antagonists tend to be the United States, Britain, and even our close political friends of postwar years, Norway and Denmark, not to mention the whole of the EEC. Older assumptions of a basic community with the other Atlantic countries are thus no longer accepted so automatically. Yet this itself raises problems for Canadians. The inescapable fact is that we need our friends, both politically and because it is essential that we establish good relations with the EEC.

The question arises nevertheless, whether the Atlantic community is now too narrow to be recreated as such. From a Canadian point of view the inclusion of Japan and Australia in the OECD and other organizations is very much welcomed, particularly if we are to be faced in these bodies with a common European front. (The supplementary question whether the EEC can continue to claim twelve or fourteen votes in international bodies if it is going to speak as a unit is one which Canadians will increasingly ask. Although their interests are by no means coincidental with those of the United States in monetary matters, they are not anxious to replace American dominance with European.) Because of their continuing conviction that a basic solidarity between Western Europe and North America is necessary, Canadians do not want a split either in the Atlantic alliance or in the Atlantic community. The decision to remain in NATO was an earnest of this conviction. The sublimation of the Atlantic community into something broader is a different matter, however, and it raises another set of questions. The inclusion of Japan and Australia and in due course, no doubt, other countries, suggests the evolution of a bloc not of Atlantic but of industrialized countries. Certainly this widening is in the particular interest of Canada, caught as it is between the twin pillars of the strictly Atlantic community. We must wonder, however, whether it is in the general world interest to have a bloc of industrial countries emerge. Such a group could bring disaster if its members placed the emphasis on the preservation of their privileges, but it could forestall dangerous conflicts and promote the evolution of a more equitable world, if they continued to recognize that, as rich and powerful countries, they have an obligation to assist developing nations.

A question very much for consideration is whether this larger grouping should continue the old Atlantic idea of forming a common front against the communist powers or other hostile blocs. The answer is probably that it would be futile to attempt to do so across the board, but the members might feel obliged to coalesce for resistance in ad hoc situations. There are no longer monolithic first and second worlds, and the effort of the Third World to form a common front in UNCTAD is having trouble. It is not a good time to encourage the first, or Atlantic, world into a coherence most people would consider anachronistic, and yet it has to be remembered that the original argument for that coherence was not a defence of privilege but a recognition of certain obdurate facts of international life, including the regrettable but undeniable existence of malevolent power.

A major problem is the tendency to think in terms of shapes and symmetrical designs, for one of the threats to the evolution of a more orderly world comes, paradoxically, from the compulsive constitution mongers and other tidy-minded people in universities and chanceries. The concept of a triangular Atlantic community, to take an example dear to Canadian hearts, is not so much distorted as out of date. The economic community which really matters has at least four major poles, and any attempt to encompass *that* system within a single grand design would have to resort to pre-Copernican epicycles to "save the appearances." It follows that the concept of the twin pillars should also go the way of all good metaphors, and the sooner the better. It has been cherished by the Americans because it offers them the illusion of escape from lonely power. The problem with such easy images is that they distort the perception of reality and tend to fulfil themselves until they founder on their own inherent contradictions. If they do not prevent, they at least inhibit, frequently rather severely, the development of what would otherwise be more normal and desirable processes and relationships.

A healthier attitude now would probably be to welcome a proliferation of agencies and of coalitions on a functionalist basis. In some agencies, as in the case of the Group of Ten, membership might be limited in fact, though not in principle, to the Atlantic or the highly industrialized states. Other bodies would include members from whatever part of the world or state of development was appropriate. To a considerable extent, this is a description of what is in fact happening.

What is necessary is to recognize it as on the whole a desirable rather than an anarchical principle. What Canadians had particularly in mind by promoting the functionalist principle when the United Nations was being established in 1945 was that although the major military powers would have a special status for security purposes in the Security Council, they would not presume to be an executive body administering the world. It was recognized, as it still should be, that major powers will participate in most of these functional international agencies. But this flexible system, or non-system, would be a better guarantee of responsibility than the impractical and unacceptable establishment of a hierarchy with special authority in all fields given to two or five superpowers.

Such a philosophy leaves open the possibility of collaboration among what have been known as the Atlantic powers when this is desirable, without maintaining their existence as the kind of bloc which will increasingly exasperate less favoured areas of the globe. It leaves room for countries like Canada and Japan to play roles and exercise influence in accordance with their real power, in a way that they cannot do in a two-pillared community. One of its key advantages—the one that may lead to its eventual adoption—is that it should make life easier for the Western Europeans. In the not-too-unlikely event that unity of policy becomes even more difficult to achieve in an enlarged EEC, with three major powers instead of two, the debilitating effects of compulsive concern with matching or forestalling American economic might will multiply. In any case, like everyone else, the EEC will have to diversify its markets and find new areas for investment. Sometime soon it will be forced to confront soberly the West's rapidly disappearing supplies of raw materials and energy resources. These and other problems, notably the accommodating of Japan, will be more easily managed when the EEC has freed its thinking and its policies from the obsessions which are both cause and effect of the twin-pillar mentality.

These are factors to be considered also when we remember that the continuation of détente, though it should be prayed for, cannot merely be assumed. The strength of NATO, and the deterrence implied by the continuing willingness of its subscribers to coalesce if necessary, remains a factor in détente. So too, the concept of NATO and the Warsaw Pact as complementary bases of European security, while it may or may not produce the desired results, is certainly not one to be dropped at this point. Whereas it is clearly not desirable to strain the bonds of the Atlantic community too far by expecting even the unity of policy achieved twenty years ago, it is essential to maintain enough community spirit to sustain the credibility of the pledges of 1949. If the military threat to the alliance seems less real, one has to bear in mind that in a world where security issues will increasingly be economic issues, there may be times when the Atlantic countries should seek to stand together against what seem to be calculated and co-ordinated threats to their legitimate interests based on a policy of playing one Western country off against another. We should of course be exceedingly reluctant to use this tactic against legitimate claims of the developing countries, but we cannot rule out the possibility that it will be necessary in confronting some of the malign forces now battling for power over the more indigenous revolutionaries in Latin America, Africa, and Asia.

If there is to remain enough community spirit among the Atlantic countries for these various purposes, the community will have to become less Eurocentric. There was some justification in the beginning for thinking of this as an aid-to-Europe scheme because there was reason to think that the major threat to Atlantic security was in Europe, and the North American members were in much better shape to contribute than were the European countries. Even though both these situations have changed greatly, there persists the assumption that NATO is designed for the protection of Europe. This was seen clearly when European members protested the removal of Canadian forces from Europe to Canada, which they insisted on calling "withdrawal from NATO." The Canadian government insisted, in a way in which it had unfortunately not done before, that this was a transfer from one area of NATO concern to another. As suggested above, Canada has rejected Mercator and in a missile age refuses to regard Europe as "the front."

The assumption that Canada would and should participate in the Conference on Security and Co-operation in Europe (CSCE), however, was not questioned. The Canadian government, by insisting on a seat, indicated that it has not shaken loose from old concepts—in spite of the attempt to put Europe in perspective in the foreign policy white paper. The United States as a superpower is intercontinental in its responsibilities and the arguments for its attending a European security conference are obvious. Canada, on the other hand, seems to have got itself included for the wrong reason—that is, to prove to the Russians that North American countries couldn't be excluded. So long as Canada is a member and has some troops in NATO, there is certainly an argument for attendance. But as the CSCE is presumably designed to establish some continuing security arrangements for the continent of Europe and its immediate environment, the question must first be explored whether Canada is to accept the idea of a permanent commitment to that continent, any more than to Asia, simply because of habits of mind developed in 1941 and 1939.

The United States, of course, by its unilateralism, its denial of NATO authority in North America, and its own espousal of the twin-pillar and similar concepts, has strengthened the Eurocentricity of the community. The attempt at cohesion of the expanded EEC, and the bloc tactics that will, to a greater or less extent, be its consequences, will make it more difficult to maintain, let alone develop, a pan-Atlantic perspective. For Canada the pan-Atlantic position has always been the most attractive. It will continue to resist the forces of continentalism, with or without the aid and comfort of its Atlantic partners. The defection of Canada would certainly not be fatal to NATO, but its continuing alienation might be regretted as a symptom of the decline of the Atlantic spirit which, although it is too narrow in itself to save the world, nevertheless remains one of the essential components of a peaceful and more or less prosperous international society. Canadians, for their part, have to shift back from negative to positive thinking, exploring new forms and practices for the complex relationship with their pervasive neighbour, adjusting imaginatively to the altered pattern of relations with Europe and reconciling that with the wider community of the OECD membership. Finding for themselves the definable place, comparable to no one else's, will be difficult. They would profit from a little more serious—and preferably critical—attention from fellow members, preoccupied though they are also with identifying themselves.

Notes

[1]The North Atlantic Treaty, 4 April 1949. *Article 2:* The Parties will contribute toward the further development of peaceful and friendly international relations by strengthening their free institutions, by bringing about a better understanding of the principles upon which these institutions are founded, and by promoting conditions of stability and well-being. They will seek to eliminate conflict in their international economic policies and will encourage economic collaboration between any or all of them.

[2]The Brussels Treaty, 17 March 1949. *Article 1:* Convinced of the close community of their interests and of the necessity of uniting in order to promote the economic recovery of Europe, the High Contracting Parties will so organize and co-ordinate their economic activities as to produce the best possible results, by the elimination of conflict in their economic policies, the co-ordination of production and the development of commercial exchanges . . .

Article 2: The High Contracting Parties will make every effort in common, both by direct consultation and in specialized agencies, to promote the attainment of a higher standard of living by their peoples and to develop on corresponding lines the social and other related services of their countries . . .

Article 3: The High Contracting parties will make every effort in common to lead their peoples towards a better understanding of the principles which form the basis of their common civilization and to promote cultural exchanges by conventions between themselves or by other means . . .

[3]For a fuller discussion of the problems of Canadian-Japanese trade see Lorne

Kavic, "Canada-Japan relations," *International Journal,* XXVI (summer 1971), pp. 567-81.

⁴Mexico is a major middle power in what is geographically called North America, but its affiliations are with Latin America rather than "North America" as conceived in the North Atlantic context.

2:

International Security: A Wallflower View

As the United States sought détente with both Peking and Moscow and a diminution of its own responsibilities in the world at large, there was talk out of Washington of a world balancing on five points, the United States, the USSR, China, Japan, and Western Europe. The pentarchical structure had its attractions after bipolarism, but it raised some questions, in general and for a Canadian in particular, which I sought to examine in a talk prepared for the Council on Foreign Relations in New York in June 1972, at the conclusion of the 1972 Annual Conference of the Committees on Foreign Relations. The theme of the conference was "The Changing Balance of International Relations."

I see my assignment as that of asking irresponsible questions from the northern flank. More important than the direction is the fact that the questions come from a country which is to an increasing extent outside the framework—a wallflower state, so to speak. Those countries which have been called middle powers are becoming the forgotten peoples of the international security system. We are outcasts. I suspect, however, that far from being the wretched of the earth we are the truly blessed.

It is necessary to begin with some *Weltanschauung* even if I do not plan to be original. May I assume a certain consensus of contemporary opinion about where we are at the moment. There is to begin with an assumption that the Achesonian "Creation" of the postwar years—the UN, NATO experiment in collectivism—is breaking up or at least being shaken to the roots. What is taking its place? A two- or a five-pole system? The escalation of military technology and the SALT talks seem to some people to confirm a shift from multilateralism to a *bipolar* hegemony of the *two* unquestioned superpowers. However, the capacity of these powers to impose order by the use or threat of *military* force was never more in doubt than now. The economic factor of power is looming larger, and that raises all sorts of questions about the configuration. So there is much talk about a shift from a bipolar to a three-

or five-power world—a "Pentarchy" as Coral Bell has called it: the United States, the USSR, China, Western Europe, and Japan.

Incidentally, what has been called the Third World seems to have disappeared from this five-power structure. It may be that the term Third World now means little because the first and second worlds are recognizing common interests and the old concept of non-alignment, which held the Third World together, is dissolving. If the Pentarchy, as defined, means that the Third World is no longer regarded as a pawn in the power game, that is all to the good. If it means we want to forget about the Third World just because we don't want its bases any more, or its votes in the UN, that is not so good. For one thing the first and second worlds are technologically fragile and the particular power of the Third World elements to attack us at our weakest point—with bombs and guerrillas and faith-healing ideologies—suggests that it is imprudent to disregard them as a factor in international security. Our estimates of power and conflict are still pretty conventional. They are slow, I think, to adjust to the looming struggle for food and air which are the new imperatives of a security system.

As for the postwar Creation which is said to be breaking up, I think it is fair to say that its broad United Nations aspects were intended to be permanent, though evolutionary. The NATO element, however, was hopefully regarded as temporary or transitional. The break-up of the broad international structure would be disastrous, but the replacement of NATO in due course by something broader and deeper might be welcomed. This is something, however, which all the NATO allies must think hard about and not just let things drift. I say "all the allies" deliberately because I am aware of a popular view of the moment—propagated especially by young Americans—that this whole postwar international system, and especially NATO, was imposed by American dogmatists pursuing the narrow interests of American imperialism. People of my generation know full well that Dean Acheson had many willing and foreign collaborators, much as he disliked the lot of us. The Creation did become far more of a pax Americana than we had intended, more than the American co-founders intended, but there has persisted a joint sense of responsibility for the pattern, however unequal our contributions to the structure. The inequality of contribution was basically due to the inequality of power. Allied governments still carry with them, as part of their framework, assumptions about an Atlantic security community as an entity, however fissiparous. The attitude of allies of the United States to the trend towards bipolarity has been ambiguous. Increasingly we have thought of the poles as the two superpowers, but on the one side it has always been more or less "the United States and friends." In the new Pentarchy, however, our pole is split in two, Western Europe and the United States. (Iceland and

Canada are out. In an age when everyone is madly seeking his identity, do you wonder why Canadians are enjoying a kind of mass nervous breakdown?) It is one thing to have the Atlantic alliance sublimated into something broader. It is less attractive to hazard in a split all the work done over the years to bridge the Atlantic.

The other current assumption I would like to note is that universal collective security is dead—with a domino serving as a tombstone. This view is shared both by those who consider the United States was wrong in Indochina and by those who think it was let down by its friends and by the UN. The favourite idea of 1946, that of policing the world, is discredited almost everywhere. The only people who believe in the domino theory now, it would seem, are the Russians in their attitude towards the countries of Eastern Europe. Now how much any foreign policy planners in the Western world really believed in universal collective security after the Korean War is hard to say. Unfortunately politicians kept it as a stock in trade of their rhetoric for such a long time that the public has been misled into thinking it is something that has been lost, betrayed by a cowardly United Nations or by the self-ishness of the great powers, or by the petty nationalism of the lesser.

It is fashionable now to look again at the concept of regional organization for defence as a more practical alternative to universal collective security. The more one looks at that assumption, however, the less practical it seems. The Lord did not oblige by laying out the world in regions, and military power is not distributed according to any rational plan. (A Canadian, of course, might be expected to have a somewhat jaundiced view of the concept of North America as a cosy region, its security determined democratically by a majority in a club of two.) There are some viable regions, but that does not add up to a universal pattern.

The United Nations was not, of course, based on the doctrine of universal collective security. It was based on a more sensible concept of great-power hegemony in security matters. Unfortunately, during the period when we needed that great-power hegemony it failed us. Now when, after painful experience, the greatest powers are beginning to grope towards consensus, their incapacity to impose their will on other states is becoming all too clear although they may do by economic pressure what they could not do by military deterrence. So we seem to be shifting back to the idea of equilibrium maintained by a concert of five centres of power—except that the cast of performers has shifted—and some of them have only economic muscle.

What of this new pentarchy, this new trend towards the maintenance of some kind of world order by the linking in a strange dance of five disparate partners? What are the views of those of us who are left out of the dance? We ought to disapprove, to demand a return to the democratic principles of the United Nations with a greater voice for the forgotten. To a certain extent I would complain on those grounds. This effort to maintain equilibrium by antique diplomacy is a poor way to run a world. It is precarious because it depends upon an intelligence which cannot be depended upon. It leaves a large part of the world voiceless and vulnerable. However, if one regards it as a holding operation it makes sense. At any rate one has to ask: What better? For the rest of us it looks better than a bipolar world because our interests are more likely to be balanced among five than among two. (At least I think that is true, but it may be just a congenial abstraction.)

It is fashionable and it is politically obligatory for spokesmen of the wallflower states to complain that their interests will be sacrificed in superpower negotiations. No country has a greater reason to be nervous than Canada because it is the one country which lies between the United States and the Soviet Union. The greatest military threat to Canada is not an attack on us by either of the superpowers; it is a war fought by the superpowers over our heads. (Or in the new world of desperate competition for natural resources, perhaps the greatest threat could be a Soviet-American economic deal which undercuts the Canadian interest.[1]) No country has a stronger vested interest in the success of the SALT negotiations than Canada. The Europeans do more complaining about superpower negotiations, but most of them recognize the same basic interest. In principle, yes, we must be vigilant against the sacrifice of ourselves in the achievement of superpower compromise, but I am prepared to be pragmatic and look an issue of this kind in the eye when it comes.

Nostalgia for universal collective security as an alternative can muddle our middle-power thinking. Even if it were possible, it had a built-in rigidity which made it not only impractical but undesirable. It might have looked like the only way of preventing wars, by the threat of unity in advance, but it was also a formula for guaranteeing that even a minor incident would become a world war. (Canadians conceived a particular dislike of this theory during the days of the League of Nations when it was in our eyes designed as a means of dragging the rest of us in to preserve a questionable status quo in Europe.) The pentarchical scheme could act as a deterrent to aggression without running the risks of collective security.

And yet there is always the paradox. In spite of the impracticality of a system of universal collective security, it has never been possible to duck the logic of the argument that aggressors should be dissuaded in advance. We are still hung up, of course, on our utter inability to agree on the nature of aggression.[2] Imagine the Security Council trying to agree on who the aggressors are in Cambodia. Frankly, I would have great difficulty myself. Surely we have learned the painful lesson that it takes two sides to make a war and wars are set off by actions and reactions. There is, I believe, a force loose in the world which may prove more persuasive of good behaviour than an unreal provision for an international army. It is the sense of prudence which links the pentarchs in a nuclear world and still gives meaning to the UN Charter. The bomb is a terribly blunt instrument and it certainly hasn't stopped wars. It hasn't prevented aggression and injustice but it has prevented unlimited wars. It has provided one common interest on which we might begin painfully to build. I admit that there is nothing new in that idea, but it has to be confirmed from time to time against cynics and utopians alike. Ideas don't have to be new to be sound.

My chief concern about the concept of the pentarchy is that it may be accepted too neatly. It is too evanescent to survive schematization. The United States and the Soviet Union may be like a whale and an elephant, but they are comparable. China is a country of enormous people-power and considerable ideological clout which may or may not develop comparable military and economic strength. Japan is becoming an economic giant, but its will and its capacity to become a powerful military force is viewed sceptically by the specialists. What is called Europe is largely a mythological beast. The Western European countries in collaboration can become something of a united—though not necessarily benign—force in world economics. To think of Europe, however, as if it were an entity in international security matters is a miscalculation of which we should beware. Some instrument may be created for formulating a combined European grievance, for stating what Europeans are against. A people having aspirations to superpower status of a diplomatic and military kind must have the capacity to accept and fulfil responsibilities. My worry is that a schizophrenic attitude to European and national interests and an inability to agree except on the lowest common denominator will serve only to reduce the strong and useful voices in international discourse of Britain, France, and Germany, not to mention the wise lesser powers of Western Europe.

The idea of Europe as one of the pillars of a five-power world, as I suggested earlier, particularly confuses those of us who have regarded the North Atlantic alliance as something of a pillar. Continentalist nationalism as threatened in the enlarged EEC is not going to strengthen the Atlantic partnership. The position of a country like Canada is particularly painful because we are clearly excluded from an Atlantic structure which is now normally defined as the relationship between something called Europe and something called America. Sometimes in the presence of a troublesome Canadian the term America is enlarged to "North America." There is, however, no political entity which is North America and that too is a miscalculation. There is in North America one superpower—super in all fields—and one country which is a minor military but major economic power. The two states recognize common interests in world security but they are forced by the disparity of their power and by some diverse interests to find their own ways in a pentarchical world.

I must show a due sense of proportion, however. The special embarrassment to Canada is not a priority reason for worrying about trends towards continentalism in Europe and in North America. What matters most is the maintenance of a spirit of partnership between the countries of Western Europe and the United States. Canada's membership has always been useful because it made the whole thing less like a United States aid-to-Europe scheme and more like a multilateral community of nations on both sides of the Atlantic. As things change, however, Canada might be more useful in a free float.

The question arises whether the lesser powers ought to serve the general scheme by attaching themselves in firm alignment to one or other of the pentarchs. Is the alternative that old and disgraceful condition called neutralism? What in fact does neutralism mean any more? If the Western Europeans seek to set up an independent basis of power from the United States, are they being neutralists? Is the United States itself not going neutralist? Who, incidentally, were the neutralists back in 1954 when the United States broke with its NATO allies over Indochina and set off on its own course? The problem about neutralism is that it has to be neutral of alignments, and if alignments are not very clear, neither is neutralism. The term might better be abolished from our international vocabulary.

I do not think Canada can detach itself from its basic interest in the security and prosperity of the United States, although a lot of articulate Canadians seem disposed to try. On the other hand Canada has important common interests with the Europeans and the Japanese. In a pragmatic way it is also forging over the pole a kind of community of frozen people with the Soviet Union. As the world of military power becomes, for technological among other reasons, more and more a region for superpowers only, a country like Canada finds itself by no choice of its own in a kind of functional neutralism. Its troops are needed in Europe only as a vestigal token. It hasn't much of a role in continental defence and although it has a vital interest in Pacific security there is really nothing military that it can do about this. What still remain valid are the basic Canadian and American pledges made to each other in the 1930s: that the United States would not stand idly by if Canada were threatened from overseas, and on Canada's part that it would never allow itself to be a base from which the United States could be threatened by another power. If we remain aware of and loyal to this fundamental commitment, then we must each seek our national interests and make our individual contributions to a better world order on a broad international scene. It stands to reason that the kinds of things a smaller power can do will be qualitatively as well as quantitatively different from those things which a superpower does. United Nations peacekeeping was the kind of useful, if minor, thing that suited us well, and it remains about the only useful contribution of a military kind we can make to international security. The problem is that we aren't gettting much to do.

But international security is less and less a purely military matter. Now I would like to offer a schizophrenic perspective from the vantage of a country which is a negligible military power but a major economic power. This is important because it is the lot of many of the wallflower states and at least one of the pentarchs, Japan. I suggest also that this schizophrenia about military and economic aspects of security afflicts Americans and other superpower people as well. In some contexts, we look at a world dominated by military considerations and at other times we look at a world dominated by economic considerations. They seem to be quite different worlds. The concept of the pentarchy reflects the confusion. It seems basically a calculation of military factors, including military power potential based on a large population or industrial strength. It is the world, shall I say, of Mr. Laird. It certainly does not seem to be the world of the former Secretary of the Treasury, Mr. Connally.

My admittedly jaundiced view of Mr. Connally's view is that in it neither the Soviet Union nor China is of great consequence; the enemies are Europe and Japan and there are no allies. At least it is not quite clear whether Canada is an ally or an enemy. Canada, it seems to be assumed, has cast itself in the role of an enemy, as would a wayward child unaware of where its advantage lies. Whatever is said publicly, the message that comes through to Canadians is that if they were not consumed by some childish fantasy called petty nationalism they would realize that North Americans are all in this together and must join in defending the continental fortress against the unscrupulous Japanese and Europeans. (In this vocabulary note that nationalism is always "petty nationalism"; great-power nationalism, which nobly disregards the anachronistic idea of the nation-state in pursuing its terrestrial interests, turns up as "internationalism." Well, you can't accuse it of being "petty internationalism.") Besides, it is suggested sometimes more heavy handedly: Where else do you think you can go?

It is not only Americans who look out at two worlds which seem irreconcilable. Europeans, Japanese, Canadians, are equally confused. For many of us there is *no* significant part to play in the world of security. Our national survival depends on the way we play our hand in the world of economics. This is a fact that may be as true of Japan as it is of Canada—and of the European Economic Community as a community. In the case of Canada there is a distinction to be made between the survival of our persons and the survival of our country. Canada could cease to be a political fact and Canadians could carry on hewing wood and drawing water at a bare living wage for the rich folk in Chicago and Houston. It is by playing the economic game that we maintain the existence of our country with a reasonable standard of living. Our first priority, of course, is that Canadians as people should not be blown off the face of the earth, but their protection depends on the international security game which we are not powerful enough to play. The economic world rather than the security world is the tangible world for us, but it does not necessarily follow that we have lost sight of the fact that global war is ever possible and we could be extinguished at any time. There is a temptation to believe in détente because that allows us to concentrate on economics. It is a different thing, however, to recognize that overriding military threats exist but find no meaningful role in coping with them.

We can make our minor contributions as in UN peacekeeping and constructive contributions to international organization. Our one alliance, NATO, is now an instrument for the promotion of détente. We have a little part in it, but it is mainly a matter for the Europeans. There are no alliances in the Pacific or elsewhere for us to fit in to. If we are to play our constructive parts in maintaining a world safe for peaceful change then we have to do so largely in a non-military way. What we have to remember, of course, is that the military considerations are real, that the strength of the American military bargaining hand is important to us. There are still areas for collaboration in guarding this continent. We are wisely recognizing that the old concept of an alliance in which policies as well as contributions were shared was an illusion because a superpower is bound to act unilaterally. But the alternative to the sense of alliance we had in the past must not be alienation. If we are cast in the role of observers, we can be sympathetic and constructive. Not being a superpower is a luxury which can corrupt or induce illusions of superior virtue.

Notes

[1] According to a *New York Times* despatch from Moscow reprinted in *The Globe and Mail* on 30 May 1972 "a high Soviet economic planner," Mikhail Misnik, suggested it was about time the United States and the USSR moved beyond the stone age of bartering a sheep for a camel "into large-scale arrangements in which the United States would provide plant and equipment and we would pay with raw materials and the end-products of such plants."

[2] The UN General Assembly did finally in 1974 after years of effort reach agreement on a definition of aggression, but there remain doubts about agreement when it comes to identifying the guilty.

3:
Shadow and Substance:
Diplomatic Relations
between Britain and Canada

In September 1971 the Institute of Commonwealth Studies in London and the Canadian Institute of International Affairs, with essential help from the Nuffield Foundation, held a conference at Cumberland Lodge of Windsor Great Park at which a group of British and Canadian parliamentarians, professors, journalists, civil servants, and one ex-Prime Minister, Lester Pearson, sought to explore the vastly altered relationship between two Atlantic countries of middle class. The British were preoccupied with their forthcoming marriage to Europe. The Canadians turned up in larger force, more in the mood for counterweights. This paper, which was prepared for the occasion, is due to be published in Britain and Canada: A Survey of a Changing Relationship. *It is reproduced here by permission of the publisher, Frank Cass and Company, London. (All rights reserved.)*

When the historic relationship between countries shifts, the substance is often obscured by shadows and foreshadows. This is the present case of Britain and Canada. Several reasons might be suggested for this obscurity.

Britain and Canada are out of phase historically. Although they are clearly bound together in the preservation or evolution of a common civilization, they seem to be moving in opposite directions. They are divided by a paradox in the present phase of world politics. A powerful movement towards transnational integration has been widely considered, in the past two decades, to be the wave of the future and the hope of mankind. Now, however, there is a reassertion of nationalism and particularism which is not merely reactionary but part of the revulsion against the inhumanity of technology, of central authority and great-power domination. It is impossible to regard one movement as good and the other evil. We must accommodate ourselves to this planetary ambivalence. Britain and Canada are being driven by both compulsions, but whereas the British have elected to move in the direction of continental integration, Canadians are resisting it.

Here we may be dealing more with national attitudes than with the basic facts of integration on the two continents. Perceptions, however, matter when one is concerned with a relationship between two countries which have really very few substantial grounds for estrangement. While Britons are in a state of enchantment and Canadians in a state of disenchantment with continental regionalism as the economic and political answer, their perspectives of each other lack sympathetic understanding. The British, having abandoned expectations of Canada based on Commonwealth loyalties, seem impatient and bored with the problems of Canadian nationalism. Canadians are largely indifferent rather than hostile to the development of the European Economic Community. Being anxious, however, to preserve as much independent action as possible in a world of superstates and blocs, they are uncomfortable about the emergence of a West European superstate which might swallow up not only an old friend and trading partner like Britain but also lesser powers on the continent which have been of late even closer diplomatic associates than Britain. Britain can, of course, hope to maintain much more of its sovereignty and identity in a European community of states than Canada could hope for in a very unequal integration with a superpower. The challenges which face the two peoples are analogous but dissimilar. For the moment, however, there are differences in perspective which put their short and long range thinking out of phase.

An historian might note that the old imperial relationship between Britain and Canada had always kept them out of phase, moving in different directions, one towards imperial solidarity and one towards independence. However, that struggle, if one could call it that, was more a civil debate in both countries than a confrontation of states and there was a complementarity in the process which held them locked in step. Paradoxically, the fact that these contemporary debates over intregration are being waged in different spheres prevents the friction of contact. It might, if the two peoples could change spectacles and see it that way, give them something to think about in common.

Another factor which works against sympathy is that the two countries seem to be moving in opposite directions in the hierarchy of power. The British have accepted with reasonable equanimity their relegation to a lower bracket. Canadians are confused about their own movement. They are inclined now to see in their recent past an exaggerated position of international influence in the wake of World War II, followed by a decline. What they cannot escape, however, is the consequence of being a country rising rapidly in economic power in a world more and more preoccupied with economics. Regardless of the terms of the Balfour Declaration, it is difficult for Britons and Canadians to regard each other as anything like equal powers on the world scene. Their international influence is still disproportionate even though their GNP's are drawing level. In the world of diplomacy Britain, for reasons of tradition and experience, has a much more effective voice than Canada. Britain is engaged in a ploy to regain world status through the European Community. Canada knows it cannot have much influence unless it acts in collaboration with others. It seeks, as the recent Canadian white paper on foreign policy indicates, to strengthen its ties with other continents. Canada is likely to be more energetic and more unilateral than Britain in cultivating its relations with the developing countries and with China, the Soviet Union, and Eastern Europe. The present intention is not to see this as a move away from Western Europe, but if Canada feels shut out from the EEC, it will take on that character.

The consequences of power are predictable, and Britons may gloat a little when Canadians suffer them. The richer Canada becomes in trade and resources, the more difficult it will be to maintain its reputation as an international "good guy." The protection of national economic interests is for the Canadian electorate a more serious business than diplomatic mediation, and Canadian diplomacy may be less high-minded—thereby perhaps removing one of the British complaints against Canada. Being neo-imperialist powers together could be a new bond.

A third factor which obscures the substance of the relationship is the tendency to concentrate on relative statistics. The fact that Canada and Britain are relatively less important to each other than they once were is incontestable. No one is allowed to forget that whereas in 1939 Britain took 34 per cent of Canada's exports it now takes nine per cent. What is rarely noted is that Canadian exports to the United Kingdom in 1939 amounted to $328 million whereas in 1970 they amount to one and a half billion dollars. Canada's population has doubled in that period, but its exports to Britain have increased five times. Canadian imports from Britain declined from fifteen per cent of the Canadian total in 1939 to five per cent in 1970, but the value multiplied over six times from $114 to nearly $800 million. The percentage shifts are obviously worth noting but not to the point that they hide the substance of the present trading relationship. The United States is obviously much more important to Canada economically and in all other ways than is Britain, and Europe is similarly more important to Britain than is Canada. No country survives, however, by limiting its associations to the one power with which it does the most business. Britons and Canadians seem hypnotized by the percentage figures into a belief that the relationship is dwindling and there is no future in it.

The British-Canadian diplomatic relationship over the past generation is hard to disentangle from the multilateral associations to which both belong. There is no time here to examine the whole scene, but a few selected observations might be in order because today's disaffection seems more rooted in the past than in any clash of present interests.

Up to 1939 there was, in spite of the Canadian insistence on a foreign policy made in Canada, a sufficient acceptance of diplomatic unity so that Canadians recognized a common interest in going to war together. This unity, incidentally, has been obscured by the nationalist mythology to the effect that Canada had to go to war although it had had nothing to do with the European diplomacy that led to it. This comfortable assumption should have been shattered by the publication in recent years of communications from Mackenzie King to Neville Chamberlain giving fervent support to British diplomacy in the immediate prewar years. Mr. King's prejudice against a united Commonwealth foreign policy was not so strong as his belief in appeasement, and it was he who bullied the Imperial Conference of 1937 towards a united front on this subject. The war revived the spirit of comradeship, but it never led to the recreation of Commonwealth institutions such as the Imperial War Cabinet of 1917. Efforts by the Australians and some at least of the British Conservatives to revive the concept of a single voice were frustrated by Canadian and South African opposition. This left a lingering resentment in Britain because there was hope that a united Commonwealth would bolster the United Kingdom's status as a great power. The Canadian view was that such a unified Commonwealth would be dangerously brittle, that Britain would have been the power to suffer most from the restraint. Further justification of the Canadian view seemed to come later when India and Pakistan brought new importance to the association.

The historic issue of a voice for the dominions, in any case, lost its meaning with the emergence of the United States and the Soviet Union on the world scene and the imposition of great-power hegemony on the postwar arrangements and on the United Nations. Canada had much less voice in the peace provisions of 1945-6 than it had had in 1919. It did, however, develop a new appetite for influence in world councils and found this in the United Nations, in the enlarged Commonwealth, and later in NATO. The old themes recurred in Canadian foreign policy—unity and independence, the relation between consultation and contribution—but in the new context of the Western alliance, the great powers in general, and more specifically the United States, were now the offenders. Britain had learned a lot from the Commonwealth experience and was more conscious of the rights of lesser powers—or of their capacity to be tiresome, a favoured word in the Foreign Office. The old imperial relation, it would seem, had ceased to be a source of friction between Britain and Canada. It is an association which has held the two countries in closer diplomatic association than would otherwise have been the case. Association, however, can breed friction as well as collaboration.

The Commonwealth has ceased to be a decisive factor in the diplomacy of Britain as well as Canada, and the fact that it is of secondary importance has obscured the fact that it is nevertheless valuable. Again the shadow of relativity obscures the substance. Because they are out of phase, Britons and Canadians tend to see the merits and the demerits of the Commonwealth differently. The transformation of the empire into the Commonwealth was a great achievement which gave Britain prestige and influence during a period when its military power was declining. This respect for Britain, however, was largely tacit on the part of the Third World, and it is not surprising that for the British people the critical reactions of the new member states were more apparent. The Commonwealth offered a formula which enabled Britain to disengage from its imperial commitments less painfully than other imperial powers. Bloodshed which has been prevented, however, is never as vivid as present trouble. It was a difficult and trying period and British embitterment with the Commonwealth is understandable if regrettable.

For Canada, on the other hand, there were advantages in the association and few disadvantages. Its economic assistance to new members was voluntary, whereas Britain was saddled with what was regarded as a post-imperial obligation. Successive Canadian governments did try to be helpful in intra-Commonwealth disputes. The Canadian reputation as a mediator enhanced Canada's position among the new nations of the Commonwealth, but the Canadian stance of impartiality sometimes looked to the British like betrayal or the calculated currying of favour for Canadian nationalist reasons. Canadians at the United Nations and in Commonwealth meetings felt that they were doing their best to mitigate attacks on the former imperial power and to create a Commonwealth which would be a helpful institution not only for the new members but for Britain as well. Canadians themselves had experienced the disadvantages as well as the advantages of colonialism. Their attitude was pragmatic and their "anti-colonialism" muted. They saw themselves as historically aligned not against Britain but with the liberal forces in Britain who had always been their allies against the Empire chaps. The view that Canada has been less than helpful to Britain in its relations with the Empire is stronger on the

Right than on the Left of the British political spectrum. The fact that
Canada has had no great sacrifices to offer and has been on the sidelines
of intra-Commonwealth disputes is the result of geographical and
historical facts of life. This incapacity for sacrifice made the Canadian
position seem pious to many Britons but it was not a respectable
argument for Canada to sit back and watch the fighting. The strength of
the Canadian position on Rhodesia, for example, was undermined by
the fact that whereas Britain suffered real damage from sanctions, the
Canadian stake was minor and the Canadian tobacco industry profited.
Membership in the Commonwealth and the United Nations, however,
obliged Canada to take a position. Where Canada could make "sacrifices" was in economic aid and assistance. Because of the Commonwealth, it gave much more aid to the Colombo Plan, to Commonwealth Africa and the Caribbean than it otherwise would have
done. It was less than might have been expected from a rich country and
admittedly not on a scale with what Britain lost in Rhodesia. Incom-
patibilities of this kind require an effort at mutual understanding and
good will which needs fostering.

During the 'fifties Britain and Canada worked closely together in
world diplomacy. The episode of Suez distorted this picture, but Suez
was an aberration. On the Asian questions which were of major importance in the decade or so after the war Canadian and British views
and policies were in harmony. Canada's policies in Indochina, in which
it was involved by membership in the control commissions, were much
closer to those of Britain than the United States. Both countries took a
more relaxed view of Asian communism than did the Americans. In the
Middle East, however, British attitudes seemed as possessive as the
Americans about China. Whereas to Canadians American attitudes to
Asia seemed excessively rigid, British positions in the Middle East
seemed unrealistic. In the eyes of those Canadians who were charged
with government responsibility at that time, and in the eyes of many
articulate British editors and political leaders, Canada contributed to
saving Britain from a disaster. The episode is best forgotten, but as it
has been regarded as the high point of Canadian diplomacy, this is not
easily accomplished. Suez may have marked the turning-point in an
easy and close association in international diplomacy which had roots
in a common foreign policy and a common foreign service. What is
required after fifteen years is a fresh recognition of common interest
based on factors more relevant than maternity.

For both countries during this period NATO was more important than
the Commonwealth although the causes of discord in the 'sixties were
more often of Commonwealth origin. Canada's part in NATO was
relatively less and differences with Britain, when they occurred, were
rarely bilateral. In the early days of NATO there were few serious

divisions between British and Canadian policies, although Canada found a natural alliance with the other smaller members. One thing the two countries had in common was that they were the closest allies of the United States. This was a relationship which at the end of the war looked as if it might develop triangularly. The Canadian experience of the triangle in atomic policy at the end of the war was so troublesome that it is just as well for all three parties that the triangle was absorbed into NATO. Canada has consorted ad hoc with one or the other on occasions to put joint pressure on the third in the normal game of diplomacy. The idea of Canada as a linchpin survives only as rhetoric. The Canadian instinct to keep the Atlantic narrow will no doubt be revived if the United States and the EEC drift dangerously apart, but it will be the European-American, rather than the Anglo-American, alliance which will be at stake.

Differences which developed in the 'sixties between London and Ottawa in the NATO context ought not to be exaggerated. There were some deviations in approach. Sometimes these were seasonal, ad hoc differences on tactics, dependent to some extent on the compatibility of the respective governments. The most noticeable dispute came when Britain, in the fury of its anti-Gaullism, took a hard line against France in NATO at the time of France's dissociation from the military aspect. Canada, in the year before de Gaulle came to Montreal, tried desperately to heal a breach which, it was feared, could have unhappy domestic consequences—and got no thanks in Paris or London. A sharp argument emerged in 1969 when Canada decided to reduce its forces in Europe. The Canadian action was so insensitively criticized by the British Minister of Defence that he strengthened the consensus in Canada for withdrawal. When the Conservatives returned to power at Westminster there seemed to be some variation in interpretations by Westminster and Ottawa of the strategic threat. Canadians have usually been less hawkish than their major allies. Britons and other Europeans tend to attribute this "irresponsibility" to remoteness from the threat. Canadians increasingly question this persistent Eurocentrism and argue that in present strategic terms Canada is as close and as vulnerable a neighbour of the Soviet Union as is the United Kingdom. Assumptions in London or Brussels—or Washington—that Canadians are naïve about communism are particularly exasperating. The persistence of the two-pillar concept of NATO, which posits a European entity and a North American entity, has been distasteful to Canadians. The disposition of Britain to favour a "European voice" to defend the European interest in NATO, whatever that might be, serves to isolate Canada. Europeans cannot be dissuaded from creating a European caucus because it makes the Canadians unhappy; it would help if they just showed better understanding of the consequences for Canada—and the Canadian distaste of being subsumed in a political unit called North America. To a considerable extent the existence of NATO has dissolved the bilateral relationship between Britain and Canada insofar as it was not already dissolved in the multilateral Commonwealth association. There is no argument for a special British-Canadian association in NATO except for the argument that all multilateral relationships have to be reinforced by bilateral understanding. This is an obvious truth which both Britons and Canadians seem perversely disposed to apply to countries with which they have not had an intimate historic association, not because a historic association is deemed to be sufficient but because it is *ipso facto* something to be cast off.

The most likely effects of British entry into the EEC on the diplomatic relationship are difficult to predict. During the period when the British have been forcing themselves to look East rather than West Canada has not interested them much. Now that a decision has been taken, the British may take a more secure look at the rest of the world. A Canadian fear is that West Europeans will be so preoccupied with the nuts and bolts of an exceedingly difficult and delicate operation that none of them will have much time to look abroad. Neither Canadians nor Americans could object to such a development because the preoccupation of Americans with serious internal questions and of Canadians with internal and continental issues has turned their minds inwards also.[1] A common assumption in Britain that Canada is withdrawing from Europe into its North American destiny is misleading. The Canadian half-withdrawal from Europe is intended to strengthen its continental posture vis-à-vis its powerful neighbour. The idea of Canada and the United States as partners in defending their continent still holds, but it is more widely challenged than at any time since the last war.

The official Canadian attitude on British entry into the Common Market has, in recent years at least, been determinedly correct. Some influential Canadians share the view that this triumph over old fashioned nationalism in Europe is a good thing in itself, but among those with an eye to Canada's own interests, there is no great enthusiasm. There is little reason why there should be. Canadian calculations are that there might be economic gains and economic losses, but their chief worry is the creation of another large power centre. This failure to share the messianic view of European unity as a great contribution to internationalism may pain Britons, particularly those determined that the new Europe will be "outward" rather than "inward" looking. The problem, as those who have been involved in federations know, is that whether the participants intend it or not, unifications oblige those being unified to look inward a good deal of the time. What is more, unification in the nature of things has to be against non-members. Unions look different to those included and those excluded. Canada doesn't feel excluded in the sense that it wants to be a member, but many of its best friends are banding together and erecting barriers. Emphasis on the sharing of a common European civilization and the need to protect the unique interests of Europe sound high-minded and internationalist to Europeans. They don't sound quite the same to the barbarians. A movement which in the eyes of its European exponents and American prophets is a triumph over bad old nationalism looks at times to outsiders more like the assertion of an even more fearful continental nationalism. When this assertion of the uniqueness of Europe is combined with a continuing assumption of the Canadian and American obligation to defend Europe, there is ground for aliena-tion. Fear and suspicion and lack of imagination on both sides are the problems, not an inevitable conflict of major interests.

What are the issues most likely to cause conflict between Britain and Canada—apart from the economic questions which are not the specific subject of this essay? These seem likely to be Commonwealth issues. A British "settlement" with Rhodesia which is rejected by the non-white members of the Commonwealth places Canada in a difficult position. The British government, it can be assumed, although not necessarily the whole British population, would bitterly resent Canada's lining up with the Africans or even withholding full support for the British proposal. Canadians might well withhold support in the hope that this was the only way to save the Commonwealth or mitigate international tensions, although no serious illusions are harboured in Ottawa about the capacity of the Commonwealth to survive British defection or rejection. The question of arms to South Africa could produce a similar crisis again. Many British regard Canada as a high-minded meddler in these matters with no interest at stake. Canada does have a stake of its own, though it may be less substantial, and Britons might try to understand it. Canadians believe they have as big a stake as anyone in the maintenance of communications and peace among the races and continents. Just because there is no specifically Canadian security interest in the Indian Ocean or a crucial economic interest in southern Africa, it does not follow that this aspect of Canadian diplomacy should have a low priority. Canada, as much as older countries, has a national interest in maintaining as strong an international position as it can acquire. Its reputation as a fair-minded white country is worth preserv-ing not only because Canada is no loner in world politics and needs friends but also because it has, in fact, been able to play some part in relieving international tensions. It is true that some Canadians have displayed such a mediatory megalomania in recent years that the nation's credibility has been affected, but these Canadian pretensions are tempered by a scepticism at home about the role of "helpful fixer," expressed even in the recent official white paper on foreign policy. The image of Canada as middleman remains so strong abroad that the Canadian Prime Minister could not avoid trying to play this part before and during the recent Singapore conference. It would be a real sacrifice for Canadians to give up this image, and it is important for London to realize that it is dealing here with something more substantial than a Canadian whim.

On the other hand it should be said that Canadian views on such questions, along with the views of other Western countries, have become more pragmatic. Sympathy for Africans remains strong, but the way seems more complex. In Canada, as in the United States and Europe, there is a turning away from other people's problems, partly selfish but partly a feeling that there is a limit to the extent to which outsiders can help countries to develop themselves. In such a climate the views of London and Ottawa might differ less than in the past. One is tempted to conclude that if the Commonwealth were to go out of existence an important obstacle to good relations between Britain and Canada would be removed. If the Commonwealth did not exist at the moment, it would clearly not be invented. There is, however, a difference between the gradual merging of the Commonwealth into a broader international system, thereby phasing out an honourable chapter of history and the break-up in wrath that is more likely over the African issues. The latter would leave some bitterness everywhere and an intensification of the shadow which clouds British-Canadian relations. It may be doubted whether the British and Canadian peoples think much about the question when they think of each other. Governments do, however, and so do the media.

European issues could, but need not, be a cause of dispute. Much depends on whether Britain will, as promised, be a moderating influence or be transformed into an over-zealous convert to European nationalism. Much depends also on the extent to which Canada will interest itself in Europe, whether its preoccupation with its national and continental dilemmas turns Canadian attention inward or revives the interest in Europe as a counterforce. The question of Canadian troops in Europe has been settled for the time being. There is no present disposition in Canada to withdraw from NATO. The transfer of the rest of the Canadian troops in a few years to what Ottawa insists is the Canadian theatre of NATO should suprise no one. Canada agreed, somewhat heedlessly, to take part in the proposed European security conference but if this should lead to continuing arrangements for European security Canada is likely to avoid further commitments. The Canadian view has always been that NATO itself, and particularly the stationing of Canadian troops in Europe, is an interim measure. If Canadian forces were withdrawn from the European theatre regardless of possible negotiations on mutual and balanced force reductions, there would undoubtedly be a renewal of irritation in Britain but no more so than in other NATO countries. The gradual phasing out of the Canadian military presence in Europe, however, seems unlikely to disturb very seriously the relations between the two countries. It is noticed only in chanceries.

As far as Canadian relations with Britain and with Europe in general are concerned, commerce and culture are of greater interest. The Canadian government is berated at home for neglecting to cultivate the EEC or for taking a fatalistic view of its consequences. Given the strong Canadian desire to strengthen its extracontinental economic and cultural associations to relieve the pressures of North America, Britain within the European context may become the object of Canadian diplomatic and economic offensives. The United States economic offensive of August 1971 revealed dramatically to Canadians how dependent they had become on one country. It quickened a new zeal to strengthen trans-Atlantic ties, moderated by a sober realization that Europe and Japan could not replace the giant neighbour.

Relations with France are not likely in present circumstances to be a serious cause of trouble between London and Ottawa. They matter less now to Canadians than they did a few years ago. That is not because Quebec separatism is declining but because the present breed of separatists is strongly québécois and takes a cynical view of France. Most important of all, however, has been the shift of French government policy towards better relations with Ottawa. The fact that Britain and France are now joined in their own political-economic association may not have much effect on the relations among anglophone and francophone Canadians, but it is at least a better situation than one in which Britain and France were in a state of hostility.

It is worth noting in this connection the agreement recently signed between Britain and Canada for British forces training in Canada. What is interesting about the agreement is that it attracted so little notice. A new agreement for American troops to train in Canada would be a matter for excited debate. At one time Canadian nationalists would have taken a dim view of such provisions for the British. Only a few survivors of prewar Canadian nationalism still fear the red coats. The fact that the lively Canadian nationalism of the day is directed to resistance against the United States has affected the view of Britain. There has been considerable discussion recently—more discussion than action—about the surfeit of American academics in Canadian universities. There was a time when this criticism was directed against British professors who had come out to elevate the colonials. Now British professors are regarded as a welcome leaven. (In this more favourable Canadian image of the British immigrant the decline of southern English has certainly helped.) There is not much satisfaction in noting that one neurosis may have killed another, but the more rational view of Britain might as well be exploited for its own sake.

If the British and Canadians have so much in common and if their differences are not of great substance, is there a need for new mechanisms of consultation? The issue of consultation, which pre-occupied Canadian thinking about foreign policy for such a long time, has suffered a change. The old dilemma as to whether Canada should be committed to British wars or other foreign policies without adequate consultation has of late been applied to the North American "partnership." Now that only a paranoiac Canadian could imagine that Britain would "commit" Canada, an old shadow has vanished from the question of Anglo-Canadian consultation. Certain illusions about con-sultation in general have in the meantime been removed by Suez, the Cuban missile crisis, and the many decisions taken unilaterally in Washington about defence and foreign policy which inevitably affect Canada. In a nuclear world, the leaders of major powers may not even consult their own foreign offices. Thus it is unwise to expect them to consult their friends or allies. This is a fact lesser powers must live with. The need is all the greater, however, for regular sharing of intelligence and opinion among partners who are likely to want to act together in a crisis. Among the professionals this has always been a habit. The Canadian Department of External Affairs grew up in close association with the Commonwealth Relations Office and the Foreign Office. Patterns of sharing involved constant communion not merely in Ottawa and London but also in other capitals where the two were represented. In the past decade the intimacy of the earlier days has been diluted, but the cause is to be found in personalities and attitudes rather than in the absence of opportunities for consultation. The merging of the two services in Britain means there will now be within the foreign service more senior officers conscious of and interested in Canada. (Whether they like the country or not is less important. Americans may desire to be loved. Canadians don't particularly care whether they are loved or not; they want to be noted. It is the tendency of British as well as American officials to forget about Canada that is the major cause of irritation.) It would be fatuous to suggest the setting up of special committees or practices to increase consultation. What is needed is just for the two countries to take each other more seriously. The reasons for taking Britain seriously as a major power of second class are fairly obvious. Britons may and do ask why, in present circumstances, they should take Canada seriously. The answer could be blunt: at least as seriously as you take any other country with a GNP of 95 billion dollars. Blood and tears are better not mentioned.

On the political level, however, the need for candid consultation is greater. Diplomatic issues are, of course, less important than economic, but questions like Rhodesia do require frank and bilateral discussion. It is interesting to note that Canada has joint ministerial committees with the United States, Japan, and Mexico which continue to meet and are regarded as useful. A joint ministerial committee with the United Kingdom was set up in 1967, met once, and has not been revived. Whether this failure represents a lack of interest on both sides or the inappropriateness of the body is a question to examine. It may be that there is so much traffic of ministers and officials between the two countries, so many functional meetings, professional and other kinds of personal exchanges, that such a body is unnecessary. On the other hand, the same could be said of the relations between Canada and the United States. A reason the joint ministerial committee is needed with the United States may be the difference between the Canadian and American structures of government and the extreme difficulty for any foreigner of penetrating the United States policy process. Because the British and Canadian systems are similar, and perhaps because there has been a long tradition of not regarding each other as foreign, penetration is easier. The traffic in ministers and officials is one-sided.[2] Whereas Canadians still tend to think of London as the first base for a European operation, British ministers, prime and secondary, maintain the irritating habit of touching down in Ottawa en route to and from Washington. They might, like Mr. Kosygin, sometimes consider Canada an end in itself—or combine the trip, as he did, with a visit to Cuba.

It is British and Canadian perspectives on international diplomacy which seem to have drifted apart in the past decade. Because their relationship has for most of this century been encased in multilateral relationships like the Commonwealth and NATO, as well as the League and the United Nations, it is difficult for the two countries to see themselves as partners. The shadow of the past makes it difficult for them to accept each other as comparable players on the world scene. British resentment of an upstart is no more serious a factor than a persistent Canadian preference for the postures and the maladies of adolescence: an infatuation with innocence and a preference for leaving serious decisions to others. Some voices to the contrary notwithstanding, Canada is really a very reluctant power. Neither side seems disposed to bother much about a relationship between two adjacent North Atlantic powers which might have seemed more obviously complementary if it had never been familial. Canadians find the British disinterested. A complaint from Britain is that Canada has not looked at the wider perspective of its relations with Britain or considered what importance should be attached to the relationship as a whole when the integration of Europe may lock Canada more tightly into a North

American system and its need for friends inside the European system will become more urgent. Canadians, it is complained, have concentrated on specific issues without any guiding principle about Britain's role in their international system. Some philosophy on both sides would help.

The range of common interests is perhaps too obvious to be apparent. It includes everything basic like the preservation of our kind of civilization, the maintenance of an international society free for commerce and ideas, and the struggle against international anarchy. Things seemed simpler when one spoke also of a common interest in the ''struggle against communism,'' but it is no less important now that one speaks of ''negotiation with the communist states.'' Neither Britain nor Canada could conceivably threaten the other, and each has a strong interest in the other's freedom. There are, of course, clashes of economic interest but not the endemic contradictions which Canada faces with the United States or Japan. Between an enlarged EEC and Canada there will be economic friction and competition, but Canada may find Britain a means of commerce and communication into the new organization. As for diplomatic and security cleavages, these would prove to be more shadow than substance if there were less generalized talk about the interests of Europe and the interests of North America. Britons and Canadians might, as a pilot project in consultation, sit down to determine what is a European interest and what is a North American interest and how, if at all, they diverge as continents.

It is not to argue against the continuation of the British-Canadian community within the Commonwealth and NATO to suggest that the two governments examine more often how they might work together. To start with they need to throw out the sepia prints and take new photographs of each other.

Notes

[1]Whether the rest of the world will allow any of us the luxury of withdrawal is a question.

[2]During the twelve months preceding this colloquium there were twelve visits to London by Canadian federal cabinet ministers, sixteen by provincial premiers and cabinet ministers, fifty-six by MPs and senators, and nearly two hundred by senior federal officials for bilateral purposes.

4:

Canada and the Pacific

We have a habit of conducting endless foreign policy debates about geographical abstractions which confuse the issue. This is particularly notable in our talk about that other "counterweight," Latin America. That Canada should have a policy applicable to Brazil, Cuba, and Mexico across the board seems a denial of our wholesome principle of functionalism. That Canada has some special link with Bolivia because of the way old geographers laid out the hemispheres is a notion that has provoked much sterile arguing over our position vis-à-vis the Organization of American States. A similarly confusing term of more recent vintage is the "Pacific Rim." Canada, it is said, must have a strong policy for the countries of this rim, for reasons of commerce and counterweight. That our agonizingly conceived policy towards China might have been applied to that other Pacific power, Chile, is perhaps a reductio ad absurdum. *What is really meant by all this talk about a Pacific counterweight is, of course, not the ocean but the continent of Asia. Australia and New Zealand are sometimes brought in to show that we do not acknowledge racial differentiation, but they are certainly* sui generis. *When the editor of* Pacific Affairs *asked for an article with this title, I knew what he meant. However, about the same time the editor of a Japanese quarterly asked for an article on "Canada and Pacific Security." What, he asked, was Canada prepared to do for Pacific security, as it had done for Atlantic security? We were, he reminded me, a Pacific as well as an Atlantic power. The question was logical in that precise Japanese way. Trying to explain why there is practically nothing we could do about "Pacific security" was a valuable exercise, nevertheless. The following article is the more general survey which appeared in* Pacific Affairs, *volume XLIV, spring 1971. The other appeared in* Pacific Community, *Tokyo, volume III, July 1972.*

Canada was discovered by mistake. French and British explorers who ventured up the St. Lawrence or across the top of Canada were looking for Asia; the symbol of their disappointment is the Montreal suburb still called, after three hundred years, Lachine. Although the venturers from Europe to Canada had to settle for the considerable resources available on this vast land obstacle on the way to Cathay, the romantic vision westward to the East persisted. Canada, like the United States, thrusts to the Pacific and when dominion was achieved from sea to sea by completion of the Canadian Pacific Railway in the 1880s, there was a revival in commercial and political quarters of the "gateway to Asia" mystique. When the second transcontinental railway was completed several decades later, the terminus was in the outpost town of Prince Rupert because this was 400 miles closer than Vancouver to Japan. In the early years of this century the Canadian government was seized with "the myth of the Japanese market" based on a conviction that once the Japanese experienced the high quality of Canadian wheat, they would forsake rice. Sir Wilfrid Laurier, the Prime Minister, declared to a cheering throng in Toronto: "Up to the present moment we have markets, chiefly in Europe, but the time has come when we must seek markets in the Orient, in Japan and China . . . We are in a position to profit more from this market than any other portion of the civilized globe."[1]

The Japanese did not give up rice, but the vision of Asia as a vast market for Canadian wheat and other produce was never quite lost. It was never realized in very exciting terms either, but in recent years both Japan and China have been buying Canadian grain in amounts sufficient to revive the vision. There are close parallels between Sir Wilfrid's prospectus and that inspired by Mr. Trudeau in the recently issued white paper on foreign policy.[2] The emphasis now being placed in Ottawa on cultivation of Pacific relations was dramatized by the Prime Minister's gesture in making his first extended official voyage not on a European tour but in an arc from New Zealand through Malaysia to Japan, signalling thereby both government intentions and his own predilections.

To see in these guildelines, coming at the same time as the establishment of Canada's diplomatic relations with Peking, a radical shift in Canadian foreign policy or a new approach to Asia would be at least premature. It is, as suggested above, not the first time Canadians have turned in that direction. However, Canada is now a much stronger economic power, and the facts of Asia have changed so greatly in fifty years that the consequences this time may be considerably more concrete, even if the rhetoric is familiar. The Pacific thrust is partly a gesture and partly a calculation of interest. As a gesture it is an assertion of national interest but also a recognition of internal politics, a response to the western provinces' claim that their Pacific frontier is ignored in favour of the rutted Atlantic preoccupation. What makes it somewhat unreal is an apparent assumption that the "Pacific rim" is a region, a political or geographical entity of any kind towards which Canada could have a uniform policy. There is nevertheless much to be said for it as a way of broadening the public's vision. Looking west and north instead of steadily gazing south and east is healthy for Canadians if they want to get themselves ready for the next century. The new Pacific direction, as described in the white paper, may seem limited. It has been criticized as largely commercial in content and inspiration, but the professed determination to expand cultural exchanges and increase understanding ought not to be regarded cynically.

What the white paper is not apparently concerned with is security. The question is raised whether the government simply does not see any place for itself in a Pacific security scheme or whether it does not see any Pacific security issue as such. It is not a question, of course, which can be very realistically discussed in an official paper because it requires blunt speech about other countries. The apparent assumption, therefore, that all members of the Pacific rim, including the Soviet Union, China, or Australia, may be looked upon alike as friends to be cultivated does not mean that the Canadian government is lacking a private concern about the forces loose in Asia. It is probably the realization that Canada is unlikely to be a decisive factor in these questions that has encouraged the Canadian authorities to ignore wider problems of security on their Pacific coast. Or they may have recognized, without specifically saying so, that "Pacific security" or even "Asian security" can no longer be contemplated in the tradition of Admiral Mahan. The white paper does display an awareness, in appropriately general terms, of the "inevitable tension between the forces of change and the forces of tradition" and that the "shifting power balance is thus only one aspect of the pattern of unresolved tensions in the Pacific"[3] and discreetly asks questions rather than offering prescription.

What does provide a solid basis for the new direction is the transformation of the commercial dream from romantic fantasy to a sound basis for trade. The principal factor here is, of course, the emergence of Japan as a great economic power. It has already assumed third place to the United States and Britain in Canadian trade and may well rise to second place soon. In the past ten years exports to Japan have risen from 150 to 615 million and imports from 100 to 460 million dollars. The economic relationship is becoming more sophisticated and more firmly based because of increasing Japanese investments in Canada. As the Americans have done in the past the Japanese are now seeking to assure themselves of supplies of Canadian coal, oil, and other materials by moving into the development and ownership phase. These moves are exceedingly welcome to the governments of the western provinces, hungry for capital to develop their resources. In the rest of the country wise old owls may be worrying over the kind of dependence this could eventually involve but this fear is counteracted by satisfaction that foreign investments in Canada are being diversified. The worry about mortgaging Canadian resources is lively, but it is directed almost entirely to the increasing pressures from the United States, now desperately short of water and sources of energy. If Japan, however, should become in another generation the giant industrial state predicted the competition for Canadian raw materials could turn ugly.

Another factor in the new look is, of course, the large sales of Canadian wheat to China in the past decade. The canny Canadian instinct is to look upon these as strokes of luck and to acknowledge the uncertainties of the Chinese market. Nevertheless there is still the vision of Cathay. The massive populations of Asia will have to be fed and Canada is among the countries which can massively overproduce food. To allow the western economy to become dependent, however, on so politically uncertain an area could be foolhardly. Canada is more dependent upon its export trade than all but a very few countries and it must beware of relying too heavily on any single market. Canada ranks about seventh in trade with China. In 1969 sales were $122 million, mostly wheat, but imports from China amounted to only $27 million, mostly textiles and peanuts. Federal trade officials are encouraging a more hopeful but essentially restrained vision of the China market in the new era of diplomatic relations, seeing prospects beyond wheat for raw and semi-finished materials, industrial machinery and transport equipment, but not consumer products.[4] At best China could be only one of a number of countries that could help Canada ease its excessive need for the American market.

Trade and investments are also growing with other countries of the Pacific rim—a term which curiously omits Chile, Peru, and even the United States. Although Canadians are not disposed to think of the Soviet Union in the Pacific context, nevertheless it is fifteen years since the two countries recognized with their first wheat agreement that it made better economic sense to import Canadian wheat from Vancouver to the Soviet far eastern region than to transport it there from the Ukraine. In fishing and whaling Canada recognizes the Pacific extension of Russia, but in commercial as well as political questions it is hard to break the habit of looking at the Soviet Union across Europe. Trade relations with South Korea, Hong Kong, Malaysia, Australia, and New Zealand have been increasing notably and raising many of the same questions first posed by Japanese exports. Textiles from Asian countries are forcing Canadians to face even more acutely the internal cost of free trade principles. The dream of Far Eastern trade included the importation of gorgeous silks but not Korean shirts at half the price of those made in Quebec. There are profits to be acquired undoubtedly, but also a great deal of trouble. As for Australia and New Zealand, the trade issues are quite different. The turning away by Britain from its erstwhile partners may bring the old "dominions" closer together. Certainly Canadians are taking Australia much more seriously now as a place not only for exports but for investments.

The inclusion of Australia and New Zealand, however, in the concept of the Pacific rim and in the Pacific section of the Canadian foreign policy white paper is sheer gesture. The concept of regions defined by hemispheres and oceans persists in spite of the doubt cast on their validity by modern communications and military technology. A common "Pacific policy" towards New Zealand and Korea would make no more sense than a common policy linking New Zealand and Poland. Canada's economic, and indeed its political, relations with Asian countries are all *sui generis*. There are some common elements, with reference to the textile industry for example, but these apply also to Latin American, African, or even East European countries and bear no relation to the waters of the Pacific. They might apply in Canadian relations with Mexico but certainly not because Mexico is a Pacific country. If the East Asian countries were themselves united in something equivalent to the European Economic Community or the European Free Trade Area, there would then be some basis for a Pacific economic policy for Canada, but such a development seems highly unlikely—unless of course some day Asian countries would feel a common interest in combined pressure on the North American countries. That the interests of Australia and New Zealand in such a situation would be with the Asians rather than with the North Americans can hardly be taken for granted.

Similarly there is nothing in the Pacific area comparable to NATO, of which Canada was a founder member. Without some Pacific treaty organization it would be hard to find a role for Canada in Pacific security. Canada has never been much interested in the skeletal security organizations which have been formed on the other side of the Pacific Ocean. Some of them seemed to Ottawa more provocative than useful. As for SEATO, Canada was not wanted because it was not a southeast Asian power in any sense of the word, and at the time of its formation in 1954 Canada had just assumed responsibilities in the International Control Commissions in Indochina which required it to avoid such commitments. If the United States, South Korea, and Japan, for example, were at any time to propose a North Pacific treaty organization, then Canada would undoubtedly have to think whether its interests required it to join and contribute. In the past Canada would have used almost any excuse to keep out of such an entangling alliance. In spite of the interest in shifting attention from Europe to Asia, it is highly unlikely that a Canadian government would be disposed or would have sufficient popular support to involve it in a new Pacific commitment. Insofar as Europe is concerned, Canadians have on the whole been eager *détentistes* and they emphasize NATO's function in mutual agreements on European security with the Warsaw Pact. As far as China is concerned the Canadian disposition seems to be towards understanding rather than provocation. It is not beyond the bounds of calculation that within a decade we might see the Soviet Union proposing a North Pacific treaty organization, but what any country would think of such a proposal depends upon so many other developments in China, in Japan, and in the United States that speculation from a Canadian perspective is unprofitable. If a middle power surrounded, as Canada is in the Pacific more so than in the Atlantic, by giants, leaves security initiatives to those giants and concentrates on economic issues in which it is a much more considerable factor, it is not necessarily blind to the possibilities of conflict and collision in that area; it may just be avoiding pretensions.

Perhaps the perspective of a lesser Pacific power serves to reveal the unreality of the concept of "Pacific security." Security is for people, not for water. There are ad hoc arguments for—and against—bilateral or even multilateral United States security agreements with Japan or South Korea or the Philippines. These are matters, however, of Asian security, not Pacific security. It is the Americans' belief, of course, that the security of the United States and of North America is involved as well and no doubt they are right. In an age of intercontinental ballistic missiles, however, one questions whether this danger has much to do with the Pacific Ocean. The heavy American involvement in Vietnam is attributable to convictions about the maintenance of world-wide, not Pacific, security. To get to their assignments in the Control Commissions in Indochina Canadians have found that it doesn't matter much whether they set out across the Atlantic or the Pacific. The old American—and to some extent Canadian—fear of invasion from the Asian hordes dies hard, but surely security concerns about Asia have to do with the world balance of forces, not the control of the Pacific.

Unless of course we are thinking about the protection of trade routes, and a major Canadian concern about "international security" is the maintenance of free commerce. With the increasing volume of trade across the Pacific, the freedom of those seas becomes more important. The queston arises, however, whether one could have a situation at sea in which escorts and convoys were required to protect shipping without full-scale war. It seems unlikely, but of course so many variations of limited war have been discovered that one could rule out nothing. Canadians, at any rate, do not now, or are not likely in the future, to carry much of their trade in their own ships, and would be disposed to think that the Russians and the Japanese whose ships they do use could be expected to protect their own bottoms. Even here, where Canada's interests are more obviously touched, it is hard for Canadians to see what they could do except whistle—and try modestly in their traditional way to ease tension and avert conflict.

For a country like Canada it is particularly hard to think in terms of "Pacific security." For the United States a vast ocean is and has been for three-quarters of a century within its calculation. There is in Canada no traditional military involvement in the Pacific, and its entire willingness to leave it to the Americans was demonstrated when Canada in the 'twenties played an effective part in opposing the renewal of the Anglo-Japanese Treaty lest the United States be offended. When the Pacific war began in 1942, Canadian forces were already deployed in Europe, and it made better logistic sense for them to stay there and leave the Pacific to the United States. The decimation in Hong Kong (in 1941) of the only Canadian force in Asia discouraged any interest in further token participation in Pacific security. As Canada did not have the chance to get involved on any scale in the fight against Japan between V-E Day and V-J Day, it was quite content again to leave that ocean to the Americans, who, in any case, showed no interest in sharing their responsibility. Canada contributed tardily but on a relatively large scale to the Korean operation, but this was regarded as an obligatory fulfilment of responsibility to the United Nations rather than as a joint Pacific operation with the United States. Canadians were disposed to recognize the Japan-United States relationship as a bulwark of their own security, but there never seemed any good reason why they should try to have a say in it. The Americans would do what they wanted to do in the Pacific anyway, and by being formally involved Canada would only lose its freedom from commitments. The principle of joint continental defence, accepted by Canadians as well as Americans long before it was formalized in NORAD in 1958, included, of course, collaboration in defending the Pacific coast. The fact that the continent can be threatened because of United States policy in Asia over which Canada has no control is a paradox which Canadians have preferred not to look at too carefully. That its smaller partner might have its own views as to who its enemy are is not an idea which has come naturally to Americans. An enemy of theirs—at least until recently—was assumed to be an enemy of the "free world." Most, but by no means all, Canadians would have agreed with them—before Vietnam at least—and they accepted therefore the illogic as well as the logic of continental defence.

North Pacific security is hardly distinguishable from Arctic security, and that is a subject on which Canadians feel more directly involved. Canadians' attention is increasingly being diverted to their Arctic frontiers, partly because of certain real issues of sovereignty, urgent and fashionable issues about oil transport and pollution, and partly because of a greater feeling of possessiveness in a period of nationalist assertion. In the Arctic Canadians are increasingly conscious of a kind of community of northern peoples with the Russians and with the Alaskans and Greenlanders. Here they are much more independent and assertive than in the Pacific area, more conscious that it is their own territory and their own resources which are to be protected for their own Canadian reasons and less inclined to think of themselves as a continental hostage bound to a world power with a habit of getting into trouble all over the world. But it is hard to draw a line where Arctic security ends and Pacific security could be considered to begin. Alaska fortunately saves Canadians a lot of problems. Although Seward, the Manifest Destiny braggart, has been a villain of Canadian history, he ought to be a hero. The pressures which would have been exerted on Canada if Alaska were Russian or Canadian, since Roosevelt in the late 'thirties began to grasp the significance of Canadian territory for the Pacific defence of the United States, would have been intolerable.

If Canada becomes more and more involved in exchanges across the Pacific, whether of trade or of people, the mutual stakes rise and it is bound to be more concerned with matters called "security." It will have an increasingly important stake in the survival of Japan as an economic partner and may increasingly develop special interests in its relations with Pacific countries which are not necessarily shared with the United States. Japan, for its part, may have a dependence on the availability of Canadian resources which will give it an interest in Canadian security—and Canadian independence. In spite of the present disposition to leave Europe to the Europeans, Canadians have not rejected the conventional wisdom that a stable and affluent Europe is essential to their own security and prosperity. For the next generation, however, Asia, or at least parts of it, are certain to become as important to Canada as Europe. The "gesture" towards the Pacific could turn into an essential commitment. Having been a sheltered and a supplementary power. Canadians have had a voluntarist[5] approach to their participation in world affairs. As they become an economic major power in a shrinking world, they begin to feel more exposed.

The Canadian tie with Europe has been a blood tie which is part of its strength. This too is changing, although not decisively. Nothing is more significant of the changed relations with Asia than the drastic alterations of Canadian immigration regulations in the past decade. Although Canadians were clever enough never to talk of a "White Canada" policy, for most of their history they have discriminated against non-Caucasians. After the last war the prohibition against Japanese was absolute, and ten years ago it was almost impossible for a

Japanese student or businessman to enter Canada even for a trip. Now Canada maintains an immigration office in Tokyo to encourage and assist Japanese immigrants. Because the Japanese have good reasons to stay at home, there is no large movement of population to Canada, but immigration from Hong Kong, India, Pakistan, and the Philippines has increased significantly and is already having a visible impact on Canadian cities.[6] During the past decade discrimination on grounds of race has been eliminated from Canadian immigration policy, but selection is on the basis of education and skill so that the flood gates towards Asia are unlikely to be opened. The Asians who have come to Canada are those best able to adapt themselves productively in Canadian society—a situation quite different from that in Britain. While the Canadian economy is expanding and there is still a need for skilled personnel, there is little evidence that the rise in the Asian population is provoking the kind of racial prejudices which disgraced the country before the Second World War. There is a predominating disposition to regard Asian-Canadians as a further enrichment of the Canadian mosaic—and with very good reason. The flow of well-educated Hong Kong residents, for example, could be a great help in the development in Canada of a better understanding of Chinese language and civilization. Canada has a better chance than most countries to develop a multiracial and multi-ethnic society, but racial relations are volatile and it is hard to isolate the Canadian experiment, with its more favourable conditions, from infection. Canadians are by no means free of racial prejudices; they just have fewer excuses for them.

Because it has had a long and special history, some comment is required on the Canadian-Chinese agreement on diplomatic relations. It would be a mistake to assume that this necessarily marked a reassessment by Canada of the Chinese role in the world or the way to deal with the Chinese fact and with real and pseudo-Maoism. What is significant is not the Canadian decision but the Chinese decision to let the exchange take place without demanding Canadian surrender on a matter of principle. The Canadian action should be regarded as the correction of an acknowledged error of twenty years ago. In spite of some lapses from time to time Canadian governments had always intended to recognize the régime in Peking, but they were prevented from doing so by many factors, including the outbreak of the Korean war just as they had decided to act, a lack of interest in Peking in making it easy for them to do so then and thereafter, and a Hamletian indecision[7] which settled upon Ottawa over the China question. Direct pressure from Washington was not so much a factor as Canadian uneasiness about provoking the wrath of the United States Congress. The new element in 1970 was a new prime minister come to power with a previous commitment to do something about Peking and a disposition to get on with it. The timing proved right, as far as Peking was concerned. Some lengthy negotiation was presumably necessary for both sides. The Canadians were prepared to make all the compromises they could. Canadians have never by and large had a feeling of commitment to the Nationalist government in Taiwan as the government of China. Their commitment was to the principle of self-determination. Faced with Peking's demand for a declaration about Taiwan they were not prepared to abandon that principle. They realized also that there was something preposterous about Canada solemnly disposing of the fate of that distant island.

The Canadian government had had its own political reasons for starting negotiations with Peking. There was little opposition in Canada to the move, and the Prime Minister would have been ridiculed if he failed to go ahead with his promise. It was not necessary for him to make a deliberate gesture of defiance of the United States, but he would have had to make clear that he was not, in office, submitting to American pressure. Negotiations having been started, however, and stalled by what in the eyes of Canadians generally were unreasonable demands from Peking, the government seemed quite prepared to sit it out. The experience of other countries, including Germany and France as well as Canada, had not indicated any close connection between diplomatic relations and expanding trade, and the particular Canadian national interest in establishing relations with Peking was not sufficiently demonstrable to goad the government to further compromise. The decision therefore to conclude the negotiations successfully was presumably Peking's. What is important, therefore, is how this reflects a revived Chinese interest in establishing better relations with Western countries and taking the Chinese seat in the United Nations.[8]

For Canadians who are endlessly debating as to whether and how they can influence the world at large and the United States in particular, it is an interesting example of the role of middle power as catalyst, for the Canadian action may well have started a movement which could lead to the transformation for good or ill of the United Nations. Not that it had to be Canada. Italy would have done the trick. During the Geneva Conference of 1954 Lester Pearson and Paul-Henri Spaak reached a tacit understanding that the most constructive step Canada and Belgium could take would be to recognize Peking at a time when such an action would be best calculated to ease the United States through an embarrassment which could affect Western security. It has taken a longer time than foreseen and it might better have happened sooner, but it may be that the vision of these two distinguished statesmen will be fulfilled. It has come at a time when the reaction from Americans has been much less hostile than was calculated in 1954.

The criticism has been made that the government acted heedlessly and without any clear disposition to spend its resources on exploiting the new opportunity of diplomatic, commercial, and cultural relations with China, or convictions about coping with the Chinese political phenomenon. There are undoubtedly illusions in the popular Canadian arguments for establishing contact with "one-quarter of the population of the world" when the latter are effectively forbidden contact. There is too little recognition of the disruption threatened by Peking's entry on the UN scene. The challenge to internal security which people claiming allegiance to the doctrines of the Chinese Chairman can pose even for Canada was vividly illustrated by events in Quebec at the exact time when the negotiations for recognition were completed. Canadians, both official and unofficial, however, have grown sceptical of the primitive idea of a monolithic communist enemy. They have long subscribed to the traditional view that one has diplomatic relations with régimes of which one does not approve—the case of China having been the exception to the rule. The case of Cuba has probably confirmed Canadians in this belief. In spite of a strong suspicion that terrorists in Canada were trained or sheltered in Cuba, it was an advantage to the Canadian government during the FLQ crisis to have regular relations with the Cuban government which, having reason not to disrupt these relations, proved very co-operative in arrangements for releasing the kidnapped men. The connection, if any, between Peking and its idolaters abroad, is a mystery, but the argument from Canadian terrorism against admitting Chinese communist diplomats seems to have been used largely by people who had already been opposing the step. Spokesmen in China seem to have ignored the FLQ entirely, perhaps in order not to disturb relations with Canada at this time.

There is no evidence that Canadian officials expect any great transformation after the establishment of relations. This act is merely a clearing of the ground for whatever might prove possible in the future. Canadians are painfully aware that they lack resources in Sinology and are ill-equipped to take a lead. The exchange of relations should give a considerable impetus to China studies in Canada and is welcomed for this purpose. An embarrassment Canadians face is pressure from American scholars to take advantage of a Canadian base to establish their own personal cultural relations with China. Canadians will presumably have to be careful to avoid the impression in Peking that they are acting for larger clients, but bridge-building is not a function to be shirked. As for a policy of reconciliation in broader political and strategic terms, the disposition is to do whatever seems possible, but the current Ottawa mood is to underestimate the previously over-estimated role of a middle power. Although its present action may prove catalytic, Canada is bound to be a minor player in the drama of

China. Whether China moves towards a more international role or retreats further into isolation is a riddle to those who do and do not recognize the Peking régime, but the Canadian assumption is that whatever China's intentions may be, it is better to be in communication. This is the foreign policy of a middle power, not a superpower. The considerations which affect United States policy are on an entirely different scale because action by the United States would be decisive rather than supplementary and because the United States, unlike Canada, has specific commitments to the Chinese Nationalists.

Canada's involvement in Asia has of course extended beyond the Pacific rim. Through the Commonwealth association its relations with India, Pakistan, Ceylon, and Malaysia have been closer than with the Pacific countries other than Japan. Its one security involvement in Asia has been the arduous and frustrating responsibility for the past sixteen years in the International Control Commissions in Vietnam, Laos, and Cambodia. However futile the work on the Commissions may seem to have been, it has had an important effect on members of the Canadian armed forces and foreign service officers, a considerable number of whom have served there over the years and acquired insights and perspectives as well as interest in Asia which have influenced them and toughened Canadian foreign policy. The Canadian government is not seeking an extended role of this kind in Indochina but, as the white paper makes clear, it would be prepared to do its duty by responding to a call, provided the provisions for the Commission were somewhat more responsibly laid down in the next "Geneva agreement."

Largely because the first Canadian aid programmes were within the context of the Colombo Plan, the bulk of Canadian overseas aid has gone to the Asian members of the Commonwealth. The fact that the largest proportion of Canadian aid goes to the Commonwealth, not only in Asia but in Africa and the Caribbean as well, is attributable both to an interest in maintaining this unique association and to the fact that the population of the Commonwealth forms a considerable majority of the total population of the non-communist developing world. Although Canadian enthusiasm for the Commonwealth seemed to be flagging in the new administration, the challenge presented to its future by British policy on arms to South Africa seems to have stimulated Canadians in general to a defensive posture and the Prime Minister to take the Commonwealth seriously. Whereas the Commonwealth at one time was the cause of some division among anglophone and francophone Canadians, the new policy of supporting francophonie and the Commonwealth as complementary expressions of Canadian biculturalism has given it a new validity in Canadian external policy. Although the attention to francophonie is directed largely to Africa, there is anxiety in Ottawa to pay special attention to Vietnam, Laos, and Cambodia when circumstances permit. If the Commonwealth survives the British Conservatives, and Indochina does not emerge as three Americanophone nations, Canadian interest in south and southeast Asia should carry on. Even though Canadians see these countries as part of the Asian scene, the political and economic ties that bind them have been conditioned by a special historic relationship. One of the reasons Canadian and United States policies in the Far East differed over the past twenty years is that when Canadians talked of the ''free countries of Asia'' they meant India, Pakistan, Ceylon, and Malaysia with their particular approach to China, whereas Americans when they used this term normally meant the Philippines, Taiwan, South Korea, South Vietnam, and Thailand. For Americans south Asia was perhaps part of the Pacific scene, but the Canadian approach was from the opposite direction.

Canada through the three hundred years of its existence has been involved in a permanent struggle against continentalism. Because it is so unequal in power to the neighbour with which it shares North America, the Canadian instinct has been to call in the Old World to redress the imbalance of the New. The tie with Britain, membership in the Commonwealth, and NATO were part of this intuitive response—as has been its rejection of the Organization of American States. In recent years Canadians have believed themselves threatened by a new exclusiveness on the part of the Europeans and the increasing economic and cultural thrust of the United States. The fear of being shut out of all trading blocs and markets has been acute for a decade, in spite of the fact that Canada's exports have been growing at such a remarkable pace that they have dislocated its monetary position. Regardless of the facts, whatever they are, Canadians have been looking hopefully at the wide world for counter-balance. The gesture towards the Pacific should be seen in this context. The countries on the far side of the Pacific are a fascinating area and their vast population and rapid development give promise of counter-balance of proportions adequate to relax Canadian dependence on its one great market and source of investment, the United States. Mr. Trudeau has been reminding Canadians that they have Pacific and Arctic frontiers as well as Atlantic. He is only drawing their attention to the obvious because Korea, Indochina, Japan, and China have in fact preoccupied and involved Canadians in the past two decades at least as much as Europe.

What is involved is not a Pacific policy but a Pacific direction. The so-called Pacific countries have little in common with each other and Canada's relations with them are largely ad hoc. No one expects Canadian attitudes to the Allende régime in Chile, for example, to be determined in a Pacific context. The section of the white paper dealing with the Pacific omits the Soviet Union entirely. ''The Pacific'' is no more than a chapter heading under which can be listed a number of disparate countries with which Canada would like to cultivate the best possible relations. The fact that Canada has a Pacific coast is not particularly relevant except in the stimulus it provides to the imagination. It would be difficult to argue that the Pacific Ocean is, as the North Atlantic has been described, a bond which holds together a community. What the Canadian white paper is trying to say may, however, be more to the point: that the Pacific Ocean need not be a barrier. We should seek to revive the philosophy of the former Institute of Pacific Relations, the purpose of which was not to establish a Pacific region for commerce or security or for any other reason, but to maintain and promote communications and understanding across this vast expanse of water.

Notes

[1] For this and further quotations and a vivid account of this episode see Robert Joseph Gowen, "Canada and the Myth of the Japan Market, 1896-1911," *Pacific Historical Review,* xxxix (February 1970).

[2] *Foreign Policy for Canadians* (six pamphlets of which one is entitled "Pacific"), Ottawa: Information Canada, 1970.

[3] *Ibid.,* p.8.

[4] *Foreign Trade,* fortnightly journal of the Department of Industry, Trade and Commerce, Ottawa, 10 November 1970.

[5] This term is well explained in the study by Professor Thomas Hockin of York University, Toronto, in Hockin, Lewis Hertzman and John Warnock, *Alliances and Illusions* (Edmonton: M.G. Hurtig, 1969), part 3.

[6] Immigration from Asia has increased from about 2,000 to 20,000 a year between 1963 and 1969, of which the largest groups are ethnically Chinese, Indian-Pakistan, and Filipino, with less than a thousand from Japan.

[7] A very apt phrase for which I am indebted to Michael Tucker of Mount Allison University.

[8] The "Canadian Formula" was to "take note" of the Chinese statement about Taiwan, explained by the Canadian government as a position of neither "endorsing nor challenging." It was subsequently adopted by Italy and Chile.

5:

The Illusion of Europe

One of the major problems of the counterweight policy on its main salient is that the European Community is neither fish, flesh, nor fowl and therefore very hard to waltz with. Its amorphousness presents serious problems for Canada. The note of exasperation in this article (reprinted, with permission, from the October 1973 issue of Worldview*) is explained partly by the long lectures suffered over the past decade from British, Dutch, or American friends on the moral superiority of European internationalism at a time when Canadians (those once nice people) were turning nationalistic and resisting the purifying rite of integration. My prejudices on the subject had perhaps been too much conditioned by the writings of David Mitrany, the theoretician of functionalism whose classic work was very influential in the Department of External Affairs during the period when the United Nations was being formulated. He wrote in 1943, "There is little promise of peace in the mere change from the rivalry of Powers and alliances to the rivalry of whole continents, tightly organized and capable of achieving a high degree of, if not actual, self-sufficiency. Continental union would have a more real chance than individual states to practice the autarky that makes for division."* Perhaps the mistake was to assume that such a union could ever be strong.*

During the excitement of expansion, members of the European Economic Community may be forgiven if their comments on Community policy are often more rhetorical than rational. In sober moments European leaders display an awareness of the dilemmas they face in achieving that ambiguous state of grace known as unity. What is less fully recognized is the dilemma the Community presents to outsiders, particularly those who are and wish to remain its friends.

**A Working Peace System: An Argument for the Functional Development of International Organization* (London: RIIA, 1943), p. 12.

How are we to deal with, how are we to accommodate, how are we to make provisions for this creation which, because it is in the process of shaping itself, does not know what it is going to be? Do we accept it for what it seems to be at this moment, a loose association of sovereign powers which already can exercise some authority in internal matters but is not acting in external matters like the unit it seems to want to be? Or do we make our calculations on the basis of the rhetoric?

EEC spokesmen at times stress the freedom of its sovereign parts. But they usually go on to talk about Europe speaking with one voice to defend *its* rights and *its* interests. They like to regard Europe as one of five great or superpowers, and they add up populations, resources, and trade, not to mention armed forces, to show that they count in a superclass. What distinguishes a superpower, however, is not its amalgamated resources. If one adds up the combined populations, resources, and armed forces of the continent of Asia, he gets something pretty stupendous.

What makes a super power super is the capacity to accept responsibility. Internal discipline enables government to behave effectively, whether it does so in its own or in the international interest. Internal differences indeed limit the effectiveness of both Washington and Moscow, and probably Peking. But none of them can evade the responsibility of power for the very reasons which, for the foreseeable future, will excuse the leaders of the European Community from fulfilling any but the blandest international commitments.

Once the celebrations are over, it is time for more candid talk about all this. West Europeans have been spoiled in the honeymoon period by their conviction (encouraged by Americans) that, since they were engaged in creating utopia in the obvious interests of humanity at large, they were entitled to indulgence. Who could be against unity?

Whether the EEC is a step forward in the long path to the brotherhood of man or just another effort to build an exclusive economic and political bloc is a matter on which opinion will continue to differ. There are many outside the bloc who may wish the Treaty of Rome had never been concocted. This is not to say, however, that the wiser among them would now wish the European Community to collapse. For good or ill, it has been launched. Having in mind the paralyzing schizophrenia which gripped Britain for the past decade, one is warned against the paranoia which could afflict the West European peoples if they were denied the chance to make something of their experiment. What they make of it, however, affects the rest of us in vital ways.

Ralf Dahrendorf has expressed surprise that relations between the United States and the European Community are shaped, not by the White House, or by the State Department, or by leading foreign policy specialists in Congress, but by the California and Arizona Citrus

Association.[1] What does he expect? The EEC is designed to protect and further the economic interests of certain countries in west-central Europe, and that is legitimate. Other countries will legitimately bargain with, make deals with, or form alliances against, the EEC in line with their understanding of their own interests. They can be expected to make concessions for the unity of "Europe" to the same extent that Western Europeans would sacrifice their farmers for the benefit of such political ideas as the Republican party, the survival of the Commonwealth, or the independence of Canada. It is the EEC, after all, which is incapable of political decisions and asks others to deal with a bureaucracy.

Unless relations with "Europe" are to be regarded as a zero-sum game, there must be a mutual disposition to act in the broader international, rather than the purely national, interest. Europeans, however, must be warned against the assumption that because the EEC claims to be international, it is acting more nobly when it furthers the special interests of its demicontinent than Austrailia, Japan, or the United States when they act in the name of national interest. Continentalism is not inherently more moral than nationalism and may indeed be more dangerous. It is not the willingness of the EEC to act generously and farsightedly that is worrying, it is their inability to do so.

The puzzle for outsiders—friends or otherwise—is to know which way they would like the Community to move. There are many good reasons for worrying about the emergence of a united European superpower. We have quite enough overkill loose in the world at the moment. We certainly don't want to be drawn any more into European civil wars. But the argument that the creation of a European Community would put an end to the danger of war in Europe has lost credibility. The rebirth of Germany and the creation of NATO settled that question long before the Treaty of Rome.

We might rather fear that differences will be exacerbated by efforts at amalgamation. Continentalist economics provoke economic conflicts, internally and externally. It would be unfair to blame the EEC alone for the more ruthless nationalism evident in American economic policy over the past couple of years, but there is an interaction between American nationalism and the threatening continental nationalism of the EEC—together with, it must be admitted, the nervous economic nationalism of lesser powers. When continentalist economics are accompanied by continentalist cultural assertion and the mythification of European history, the overseas barbarians have reason to shudder.[2]

One might wish the Europeans would just sensibly go on about co-ordinating their transport and rationalizing their neighbourly relations and forget about their mission as Europe. On the other hand, if they are going to take common actions without being able to accept common responsibilities, wouldn't it be better if they did indeed become something more like a sovereign power? As Herr Dahrendorf himself acknowledges: "The six European States have created a political reality which need not be defined as something different from them, but which, in accordance with the will of its architects, cannot be controlled by any one of them alone. This reality has an effect on the outside world, whether decisions are taken or not. The Six are therefore jointly responsible for seeing that what they have created does not adversely affect them individually or jointly, and above all for ensuring that it does not do damage in the world which they would find it difficult to repair."[3]

Belief in some general West European interest or in the defence of an EEC institution or practice will presumably, on occasion at least, prompt EEC members to close ranks and demand or force international organizations to accept certain policies or commitments. But the record of established governments in living up to their commitments is hardly impeccable. And the Community can be a special problem because, when conducting negotiations, it can always plead that it has no sovereign control over its members and to enforce discipline would be politically difficult.

Philippe Simmonot, writing in the London *Times* (20 June 1973), sees the main negotiating advantage of the United States to be "the indiscipline of the countries of the European Community" because "the people in Brussels are obliged to stop short at the point at which agreement between the Nine would bring down the European edifice in ruins." He fails to see the disadvantage to others who want to make mutually satisfactory agreements with European countries in the context of a complex relationship involving wider political considerations. How often have we all complained when the Americans used the excuse of attitudes in Congress to avoid commitments.

The response of Western Europeans to Henry Kissinger's recent (23 April 1973), statesman-like call for a re-examination of the Atlantic relationship has not been reassuring. What was clearly set out as an invitation to revise Atlantic relations on a more equitable basis was too widely regarded as not more than a crude effort to force economic concessions in payment for defence protection. Even the London *Times* (25 April 1973), which welcomed the initiative to lift discussion from "a largely technical level where conflicts of interest are unavoidable" to "the broad political level where the long-term common interests of the partners are more clearly visible," nevertheless pointed out that "Europeans have rightly resented attempts to link the military commitment with trade policies."

But who is doing the linking? Canadians have been led to believe that they must leave forces in Europe if they are to have any hope of a fair deal on trade from the EEC. And there can surely be little doubt that a withdrawal of American forces would promptly be used in Brussels as an argument to abandon generous consideration of American economic difficulties. Defence and economics are irrevocably linked in the Atlantic alliance, article 2 of which was intended to make clear that the spirit of co-operation and mutual respect which was essential to security was essential also in economic relations if the alliance was to hold together. Kissenger was simply reminding Europeans of a fact they too readily forget.

In an alliance based on give and take, North Americans tend to feel they have done all the giving. Both the United States and Canada sent troops to a European war, poured relief funds into the reconstruction of the continent, then sent more troops to hold the line until the Europeans could recover. When the Europeans did recover, they insisted the troops stay on, and their recovery took the form of an economic bloc which looks more hostile than friendly.

Even an internationally minded European like Theo Sommer of *Die Zeit* writes in *Foreign Affairs* that the preparedness of the Nine in principle "to conduct a good neighbor policy toward everyone will be subject to only one qualification . . . when in doubt act in the interests of the Community." Such a principle may be unavoidable, but it is doubtful if it is going to be reconcilable for many years with his further statement: "In the security field, there is no substitute for America's contribution to European defense."[4]

Comments in Europe on the Kissinger speech were not all parochial. The shrewdest may have come from the *Frankfurter Allgemeine Zeitung,* which asked *which* Europe would give the answer: "Pompidou's fading neo-Gaullism? Brandt, suspended between Atlantic loyalty and necessity and the temptation of the opening to the East? Italy, shaken by internal crises?" Raymond Aron reminded Europeans that they are vulnerable not only in defence but also in economics if they disavow the Atlantic tie, and he pointed to the need for the whole Western community to act together in face of the dire threat to their security posed by oil shortages. "It follows," he wrote in *Le Figaro* (2 June 1973), "that broad policy ought to be defined not only by defense against the commercial 'aggression' of the United States but by the search for common objectives. In the hypothetical situations of an economic war or of a Soviet-American condominium, who has the most to fear and to lose if not the Europeans, divided among themselves, who owe their wealth to the transformation of primary materials coming from the whole world?"

Unfortunately, this is not the language of the new breed of European chauvinist. Andrew Shonfield has noted the tendency in the EEC to live in a charmed circle, to think they can carry on their private world without affecting anyone else.

Friends of Europe must ask themselves, of course, whether it is premature to push questions about the long-range intentions of a single European voice. It may be that Europeans have in mind a long-term process by which the habit of working together would eventuate in a continental/national consciousness able to secure a consensus strong enough to permit a new Europe to act some day as a responsible unit in international politics. Even from this perspective, however, we must ask Europeans to clarify what they hope to achieve. Unity is not a sufficient end in itself.

When Jean Monnet set out on his crusade, few people doubted that the integration of larger units was the wave of the future. Now this is a more dubious proposition. Nationalism and sovereignty, which seemed bad things, have reappeared as the last defence of peoples against multinational economic forces and the aggrandizement of government. We may charitably regard the EEC as a supereffort to create a superstructure that can defend the interests of a "continent" against superpowers, specifically against the Soviet threat and the American challenge. And that may well be the only way Europeans think they can protect their standards and ways of life, the presumption being that they have common interests which are sufficiently distinctive to separate them from other countries struggling for similar protection. At the same time, however, they are creating another threat of superproportions. As far as lesser powers are concerned, the EEC, because of its amorphousness, may be harder to do business with than are the United States or Japan, China or the Soviet Union.

One of the spectres confronting us is the possibility that nationalism, having become continentalism, will become hemispherism. The fear of the consequences of the EEC's special agreements in Africa may be exaggerated, but even a careful and sympathetic observer of the EEC like Miriam Camps is pessimistic. She doubts "whether the growing European-African and European-Mediterranean special relationships could be broken except as a part of a large restructuring of relationships which included the withdrawal of the United States from the OAS system." Although she herself favours "a drastic shift to a truly multilateral system," she finds it hard to see it happening: "The more likely development is a continuation of special arrangements between the European Community and the less developed countries to its south, continuing American protests against this development, constant friction, and a general drift towards a world in which the main developed countries have in fact, fairly well defined spheres of influence—or spheres of responsibility if one wishes to be euphemistic—in the less developed countries.''[5]

The word imperialism has been flung about so casually of late that one is hesitant to use it in this case. Nevertheless, the proprietary attitude toward Africa adopted by some European leaders, and not only in France raises doubts as to whether, in the process of European continent-building, they may be carried away from their more laudable policies of relatively generous responsibility for assisting the Third World.

The political factor to be faced is the spirit of rivalry and even hostility inherent in the process of setting up any new community. The view is that there is nothing incompatible between a united Europe and a co-operative Atlantic world; in fact, a co-operative world is proclaimed, no doubt sincerely, by European leaders. But how else can one build a community except by emphasizing its exclusiveness?

The argument as to whether the Community would be inward looking or outward looking has been called ''*un faux problème.*'' True, but the reason it is false is that unless the Community is inward looking, it is nothing. The leaders can be inspired by a more or less liberal attitude on world trade and development, but the whole enterprise is meaningless except as an attempt to put a wall of some height around a community.

Members of the Community, having been for centuries world traders, travellers, and emigrants, have varied associations overseas. They can't, and say they don't want to, cut themselves off from old associates, but they are bound now to emphasize whatever interests they can find in common with their European neighbours. The idea that the British would bring international perspectives into the Community may be an illusion . It is the Germans of the Brandt régime who seem most aware of the extent to which the European countries are embedded in a wider community—perhaps because they have no extra-European ties to renounce. The French, from the beginning, have insisted on the primacy of the European loyalty. The British, until recently at least, have been busily denigrating their relationships with the United States, Canada, and Australia to prove their virtue as Europeans.

Community builders do need a few good menaces. The Soviet threat is less ominous at present. In any case, the Soviet threat is an argument for the strengthening, not of the European Community, but of the Atlantic alliance. To accept the Soviet menace as a reason for the Community's cohesion would be to accept responsibility for constructing a truly European defence system. It is both easier and cheaper to maintain the Atlantic system.

And so the Community's apologists reach for the threat to Europe posed by the collusion of the superpowers, but they are not very clear about how they will be collectively harmed by the Strategic Arms Limitation Talks or by Soviet-American trade negotiations. If there is no obvious enemy, one must be created. European zealots in Britain even managed to transform the Commonwealth into a threat, thereby doing permanent damage to a worthy and harmless institution and unnecessarily embittering relations between the British and those who had in the past perceived common interests when the threats to Britain were far from imaginary.

These questions of imagination and emotion may not seem important, but Europeans do not seem to grasp that their "economic community" is a matter not only of opening doors but of slamming doors as well. The consequences will be less dangerous if the members of the EEC recognize that they are engaged in an operation that is not necessarily complementary to Atlantic or wider international community building.

The need to emphasize barriers is what disturbs those who recognize the EEC as a fact but hope it will not accentuate the drift in the world at large toward national or regional self-interest. The creators of the European unity movement have certainly seen the movement as part of an overarching international system. Much of that spirit still inspires European leaders. The question is whether it can survive the transition period when the *European* interests of the members of the Community have to be emphasized or invented.

Europeans can in return call for understanding from others of what they are trying to do. In fact, they have had little cause to complain on this score. The United States, propelled by the illusion that it was creating a partner in the maintenance of world order, was more than generous in the formative stages. With the Community now established, the United States need not apologize for recognizing the EEC as a competitor, to be dealt with competitively. The Commonwealth, not being an entity, took no stand against British entry. British opponents of the Market holding antiquated views of the Empire used the Commonwealth as a weapon with which to beat the EEC. But the behaviour of the major Commonwealth countries affected was correct. They did not, by and large, share the illusions of Americans about the blessings of European unity, but they recognized Britain's right to self-government. Their approach on the whole has been pragmatic.

The institutions on which Europeans are now concentrating constitute only a part of the continent of Europe. They are cutting off the eastern, northern, and southwestern peoples of the same continent. Eastern Europe has, of course, isolated itself, but there is a question as to whether its present straining for pan-European institutions is getting the right response in the closing off of the EEC.

A more immediately relevant question is whether it is desirable to strengthen EEC institutions or those of the Organization for Economic Co-operation and Development. There is an advantage in the OECD concept which is perceived more clearly perhaps by those who are neither Europeans nor Americans. An unhappy consequence for Canadians, Australians, Norwegians, or Swedes of the Europeans' emphasis on continentalism is that they fasten this pattern on others. Canada and the United States do not claim to speak with one voice, for example, although their economies are closely intermeshed. Nevertheless, Canadians are continually finding themselves, to their own disadvantage, included in an entity called North America, which has no existence as a political or economic institution. For countries like Canada, Australia, Sweden, Switzerland, and many others the fashionable new two-power concept of Europe and the United States (or the three-power concept of Europe, the United States, and Japan) is unattractive and inaccurate. This concept seems particularly attractive to those Europeans who, especially in Britain, see the EEC as a way to maintain great-power status.

The OECD, on the other hand, not only gives major and lesser powers appropriate voices but also reflects more accurately the realities of the world economy, where resources count for more than guns. It may also be a less polarized and more flexible international system. Although it is itself too restricted in membership, it has always expressed the broad international responsibilities of its members.

The EEC answer to all this is, of course, that the EEC has no intention of renouncing these broader associations—from NATO and the OECD to the United Nations—but seeks only to co-ordinate the European voice within these institutions.

That is all very well in theory, but what does the co-ordination of the European voice mean? This is something much more than just a Central American caucus or an Arab lobby. Would the hardening of a European bloc within NATO do anything to strengthen the organization? Some Europeans have wisely recognized that an arbitrary insistence on all European members speaking with a common voice in NATO could lead to assumptions about European defence which they wish to avoid. Yet much is made of defence interests which European countries are supposed to have in common—even though NATO was based on the firm assumption that the defence interests of North America and Western Europe were common.

In other international bodies, whether the OECD, GATT, or the International Civil Aviation Organization, the formation of a disciplined European bloc cannot be accepted without unpleasant consequences.

Questions will eventually be asked about whether a group which acts in this way can go on calling itself a group or whether, if it wishes to speak with one voice, it should not, in accordance with prevailing rules of the game, have only one vote. In the United Nations, London and Paris might continue to claim special seats on the model of Minsk and Kiev. Voting blocs beget voting blocs. They don't necessarily strengthen the hands of those who participate. The position of the Atlantic countries was strengthened rather than weakened by their refusal to vote as a team in the United Nations. Immovable states, like those of Eastern Europe, have had little influence. The contrast with independent Yugoslavia has made that clear.

This brings us to the question of a common foreign policy for the EEC, one of the frequently proclaimed aims of founders and members. And in some ways the easiest to achieve because it requires no more than an agreement among governments that they will either define a common policy on major world issues and stick to it or caucus on each issue and, in the absence of consensus, accept a majority vote. Yet one has only to define what is necessary to realize how unlikely this is.

Foreign policy, as its practitioners know, is not just a matter of great principles but of deciding how to vote, speak, or act on thousands of daily issues. It isn't differences on principle that matter most; it is the variations of attitudes on tactics. No one has specified, and probably no one can specify, those natural interests which should keep Europeans aligned. So many world issues are ideological, and the present government of the Federal Republic of Germany might conceivably find harmonization of policies easier at one moment with the Australians than with the British.

Commonwealth citizens recognize this question of a common foreign policy as an old and sad story. The idea of "one voice" Commonwealth foreign policy was a favourite of British Conservatives and Australian Labourites at the end of the Second World War. British Tories thought it meant the dominions would, like sensible chaps, accept policies defined by the wiser and more experienced people in Whitehall. Australians thought it meant they would have a great deal more say in the determination of British foreign policy. The European member states might be warned that many British Tories are now talking the same way about the EEC—having been let down by the Empire.

In fact, the Commonwealth survived for many useful years because this concept of a single voice was rejected as not only impossible of achievement but also exceedingly divisive. Of course, no two situations are analogous. The EEC is creating a much more integrated structure than the Commonwealth was or wanted to become in 1945.

Nevertheless, many of the same difficulties in co-ordinating a common voice obtain. NATO in the 'fifties was a fairly tightly knit structure with vows of co-ordination, but it survived because a flexible attitude was taken toward foreign policy.

Judging by the so-called "Davignon principles" formulated by the six foreign ministers in 1970, one might assume that a fairly sensible attitude is being taken on this subject. Mention was made of "exchanges of information and regular consultations" and the harmonizing of points of view "when it appears possible and advisable, by trying to adopt common policies." Nevertheless, in Brussels the beavers are busy with committees, secretariats, and draft agreements on major items of policy. Again we recognize the illusion that afflicted the Commonwealth in 1945, the illusion that the problem is one of structure. It persisted too in NATO—the idea that if there could be ministerial instead of ambassadorial representatives on the permanent NATO Council we would have a common foreign policy.

Committees and secretariats, however, can do no more than draft compromise formulae. The real problem is a meeting of minds and a consensus on aims and tactics which is not forced. On most world issues it has been easier to get agreement between Copenhagen and Ottawa than between Copenhagen and Paris, and a Canadian may be forgiven for wondering about the advantages of a situation in which not only the Danes but the British and the Belgians would be obliged to support French policy toward Canada, whatever it might be. Perhaps countries like Canada, which have normally found among the smaller European powers their habitual collaborators in international policy, are most inclined to regard the creation of a rigid European caucus as purposeless.

Just what the basic principles of an EEC foreign policy would be is a problem. It is not difficult to define common interests of a security and political nature. It is more difficult to define interests which are unique to them and not shared by other members of the Western community and, indeed, by countries in other parts of the world.

The possibility of the Community having unique economic interests to protect and negotiate is clearer. These are not so much inherent European interests as created EEC interests. Although for the time being important monetary issues are debated in organizations broader than Europe, the question of whether the EEC will act as a unit in monetary questions is yet to be decided.

But the need to stand together on money does not necessarily imply standing together on Portuguese colonies or on the continental shelf. The creation of any kind of community, whether it be NATO or the Commonwealth or the Organization of African Unity, sets up expectations of loyalty. Not to vote with one's associates seems a particular form of unpleasantness which merits retribution. Most of the so-called disunity in NATO is attributable to expectations of unity which ought never to have been proclaimed in the first place. That members of the EEC should pay due respect to the wishes and interests of their partners in the Community is something which the rest of us can live with and understand. That they should be required to shut their ears to other friends and vote like sheep, however, is a demand that is likely to invite retaliation.

When one attempts in this way to probe the elements of a "common foreign policy," Europeans have a habit of reacting impatiently against what they consider caricature. This, we are told, is obviously not what they have in mind. Well, if not, then what do they mean by having a common foreign policy and speaking with one voice to defend the interests of Europe? These are the illusions which breed disillusion.

It is advisable to match limited expectations with limited rhetoric. The rest of us may not have a sure interest in the transformation of the EEC into a fifth power in the world, but we do not want a weak Western Europe. The effort to push too far the idea of a common foreign policy can result in a foreign policy of the blandest variety based on the lowest common denominator.

If we do not see the EEC as in itself a third or fifth power, we do nevertheless look to the great countries of Western Europe, and the smaller but wiser ones as well, as counterweights, as alternatives, and as constructive forces in the creation of international community. In the world we are facing it is not necessary to have military power to have wisdom and influence, although some superpowers will continue to be superstrong. When the British pull themselves together, we trust they will realize they do not need to have a fleet east of Suez to be the great constructive force they have been in international affairs. The voice of Germany, strengthened by its successes in European détente, should bring new hope to the United Nations. France shows some signs of emerging from its isolation into a new internationalism. What we do not want is to have these Europeans so intent upon the problems of their internal bureaucracy and so much preoccupied with producing an indigestible mash called a common European foreign policy that they vacate the field entirely to the real great powers.

I am tempted to end with a simple plea to Europeans to cool their enthusiasm for power and a role, to get on with the business of harmonizing their interests, and, out of their regional confidence, to behave in the world like the magnanimous and constructive countries their wealth and experience qualify them to be. If they can, ad hoc, act together in good causes, so much the better. It is the imposed obligation to unity and uniqueness which is mischievous. If they really have interests—economic, political, or military—which they do not share with others, obviously they must protect them in common. But if they do not resist the temptation to seek out or invent such interests, they will only isolate themselves and fall behind in the search for international community.

And yet I am worried by Dahrendorf's warning. If the EEC does not set about doing the impossible, forging a unitary instrument of government, will it not remain a mindless creature, capable of doing grave mischief but lacking the internal discipline to deal with the consequences? Can it move further in a common foreign policy than agreement on its basic grievances and resentments? In meeting the complex international issues we all face, how much could we expect from a peevish Europe?

The hope expressed by many Europeans is that the EEC will be an economic and social power, that in the new world equilibrium military power is unnecessary. It is the Japanese approach, as well as that of Canada and other lesser powers who are economically potent but whose military potential, even in alliance, is increasingly seen as negligible.

The argument against this is what the Americans call burden-sharing. This can no longer be understood in crude military terms, meaning that Japan and the EEC should take over United States security responsibilities in their respective regions. It is doubtful if, given the present state of the world, Japanese or West European public opinion would permit the increase in defence spending necessary for such a purpose—even if the United States disarms substantially. And the paradox of the American demand for security burden-sharing is, of course, that the United States does not want the EEC or Japan to control their own nuclear weapons. Nevertheless, these great economic powers will be decisively affecting international relations in an age when resources and commerce are the vital issues of national survival. On these subjects divergence between the United States, Japan, and a hungry, but headless Europe can be swift and drastic.

If the military burden cannot be shared, the burden of maintaining the essential structures of a mutually beneficial world economy must be shared. It is not good enough, as is common in both Europe and the United States of late, to disguise a reluctance to share burdens and international responsibilities as a renunciation of imperialism.

That the members of the Community will serve their own and the general interest best by acting as a bloc is an assumption that should be reconsidered. One thing is certain. If they use their power, in what can only be described as an old European tradition, to bully and blackmail weak governments in Africa or elsewhere, they will propel the world further into anarchy. United States policy toward Latin America could be cited as a precedent. But it is a bad precedent and one which now seems as moribund as the OAS.

We need to bury the mischievous two-pillar theory which John Kennedy and his Boston gamesmen and their European friends did so much to propagate. The American idea, which goes back to Dean Acheson and John Foster Dulles, was that a united Europe would share with the United States a benevolent hegemony in the world. Insofar as it meant accepting responsibility and sacrifice to promote a peaceful and prosperous world community, it was a noble idea. But it had two great flaws: it gave the Europeans the wrong idea of how they could act in the American model; and as has been revealed in the Vietnam disaster it demonstrated the gross error into which even a noble concept of hegemony can lead a great and united power.

The danger, of course, is the swing to the other extreme: renunciation by the United States and other Western countries of concepts larger than their own national or continental interests. The reasons why the United States might turn isolationist at this stage of its history are obvious. It is a time when non-interference in other parts of the world can look like a sound moral principle. That Western Europe is also in an isolationist mood is less frankly acknowledged, because Europeanism is portrayed as internationalism.

The rest of us are not in a position to preach sermons, but we nonetheless view with anxiety West Europe setting itself apart. Canada, in the throes of a reaction against its active internationalism, is no example to any country. We need European energies on a wider stage. Frankly, our historical memories do not permit total confidence in the political wisdom of Europe united and rampant; we would rather see the Europeans concentrating on something more useful and relevant than trying to transform themselves into a semi-superpower. The promise of a Europe wise, united, and responsible by the twenty-first century isn't much to count on for the issues crowding in upon us in the rest of the twentieth: multinational corporations, computer transnationalization, global television, global pollution, preprogrammed nuclear warfare, and the survival of government by the people.

Notes

[1] Ralf Dahrendorf, "Possibilities and Limits of a European Communities Foreign Policy," *The World Today*, XXVII (April 1971).

[2] See, for example, Max Beloff, "The European Course of British History,

The Round Table (October 1971) or Alain Clement, "Le temps des recriminations," *Le Monde* (25, 26, 27 April 1973).

³Dahrendorf, *op. cit.,* p.152

⁴"The Community is Working," *Foreign Affairs,* LI (July 1973), p.759.

⁵"Sources of Strain in Transatlantic Relations," *International Affairs,* XLVIII (October 1972), pp. 570-1.

Part Four:
North America

The question may be raised why this section is called "North America" when I argue in the essays against the excessive use of the term. The argument, however, is against using it as if it were a political or economic entity. It is an undeniable geographical phenomenon, and the relationship between the United States and Canada must be regarded as distinct in most, but not in all, ways from our relationship with other countries—but then all bilateral relationships are unique and therefore "special." Culturally and socially the problem is to identify and strengthen the peculiar features of the Canadian scene—or scenes— while sensibly recognizing that we are a native and not a conquered part of a branch of civilization one could identify as North American. The problem is partly terminological, the failure of the United States to get a proper name for itself. A Belgian can be a Belgian and see himself as European also. If the United States had called itself Washingtonia we could share the word American more comfortably—provided, of course, the southern part of the Western Hemisphere had not called itself also after that same troublesome Italian, Amerigo Vespucci. Nomenclature has plagued the Canadian nationalist. There was once the problem of being both Canadian and British, complicated by the fact that the citizens of the United Kingdom could never find a handy name for their island and a quarter.

1:

In Praise of National Boundaries:
The case against creeping continentalism

This is a revised version, which appeared in Saturday Night *in July 1974, of a lecture delivered on 8 April 1974 at St. Lawrence University, Canton, New York, which for the past forty years or more has earned the gratitude of Canadians for the opportunities it has consistently provided to discuss "the relationship." It is an audience to treat with respect, not to be bullied the way Canadian speakers usually manhandle American audiences on whose almost total ignorance of Canada they can rely. Residents of Canton are captives of Canadian television, with no CRTC of their own to protect them from foreign cultural penetration.*

What do we want to make of North America? It is not a question to which resisters of "continentalism" in Canada have directed enough attention. It requires positive as well as negative thinking, because we cannot exorcize or reject the United States. On many levels of policy and practice we have to think in continental terms. We have to identify where continentalism is appropriate and where it is not. The danger isn't well defined as "continentalism"; it is "continentalization"— and many who fight the former are backing into the latter. We are less likely to be continentalized by American investment than by assumptions on both sides of the border that North America is an entity rather than a community of two. The best way to avoid continentalization is to find ways of making the community work. It is more important to be non-American than to be anti-American, and mindless anti-Americanism could destroy a structure erected out of long experience. The threat to our identity comes not from the United States as much as from the idea of North America.

One problem of course is that the idea of continental unification has been widely regarded as the wave of the future. There is the false analogy with Western Europe. Europeans and Americans have rarely grasped the fundamental difference between the European Economic Community and what the political scientists call the Canada-United States dyad. The West Europeans deliberately seek political union through forced economic integration. In North America we are trying to preserve our political identities against the strong forces of economic integration which need no governmental encouragement. We have been intimidated by the almost universal belief in unity as an end in itself, by the insistence that internationalism requires the extinction of nationalism. The most over-estimated political value of our times is unity. Motherhood having become a questionable virtue in the light of the population explosion, there remains unity as the universal blessing. Who could hold unity in disfavour?

Well, I can, for one. We have, for example, the spectacle of the West Europeans aggravating their natural differences into dangerous frictions in the name of unification, losing sight of their own genius in the vain hope of asserting power and authority in a wistful dream of the Holy Roman Empire. Canadians are thrashing themselves into unnecessary frustrations in pursuit of what our leaders insistently call "national unity"—whereas the great advantage of being a Canadian is that we have never been unified.

Why does Canada exist anyway—and is it a defiance of the continental imperative, not to mention love and brotherhood, destined to be amalgamated or sublimated into a larger hunk of the planet as man moves to a higher level of civilization? Surely it is time for us to reject those world federalist concepts which have dominated too much idealist thinking—not because world government is unattainable but because it is highly undesirable. It is hard to imagine a more monstrous tyranny. God bless the nation state and, even more so, the two-nation state, and God bless nationalism, the emotional ingredient necessary to keep a sense of civic responsibility healthy. That has been an unfashionable view, but one could argue that the prejudice against nationalism, the idea that it is the cause of war, was propagated by great powers who resented lesser powers standing in their way. That is a very cynical view, and like all cynical views on international politics, it is half wrong—but half right also. Of course nationalism can be vicious. So can religion and wine and a lot of other good things.

If I am sceptical about unity as a universal good I am not arguing that disunity is a virtue. What I am arguing against is a universal prescription. We have a United Nations of very disparate sizes, some apparently viable, some apparently not. The patterns will change, but an orderly system cannot be imposed upon it. The dismantling of existing structures may or may not be advisable. The creation of some new unities may be a good thing. On the other hand, if the peoples of East

Pakistan or east Canada come to regard their existing structure as intolerable, it is doubtful whether a pre-existing unity can be maintained or imposed. There is a good deal to be said for the attitudes of new African states: that although they are the artificial concoctions of imperial powers, their stability and chances of development depend on starting from the status quo.

The world is not, and presumably never will be, laid out logically. All states—and not just Canada—are artificial products of the politics and economics of past generations. Economic and ethnic pressures may be expected to shift the present pattern of states from time to time. We are led astray, however, by an unthinking devotion to the idea that the more countries which can be wrapped up in bundles the better. The British tried that in the West Indies, Central Africa, and Malaysia when they were trying to launch successful nations out of colonial dependencies, but it didn't work very well. It had been successful one hundred years earlier in uniting the British North American colonies into Canada, but that was possible only because the United States scared the hell out of those colonies.

Internationalism too often has been a negative belief that barriers should be torn down, that national boundaries are unnatural and offensive to human dignity. It is particularly hard for people on this continent to realize that the customs and immigration controls which irritate us when they interfere with our swift passage across our famous unguarded frontier are in fact essential guarantees of our respective ways of life, including our jobs. It is a level of understanding we had better acquire quickly because the pressure of growing populations seeking diminishing supplies of goods has begun already to challenge our national legislation and regulation, and these frontier barriers are going to be harder rather than easier to penetrate.

To this prospect the unreasoning instinct of nice friendly people is to tear the nasty barriers down. That is the path to unity. It is also the path to the homogenization of mankind, the domination of great powers, and the crushing of smaller ones. It is the way also to the metropolitanization of society, the abandoning of resistance to the magnetic attraction not only of the big countries but of the big cities. Smaller countries do not exist only out of perversity. They exist so that government, even in a cybernetic age, can remain closer to the people. Their existence furthermore saves the great powers from intolerable responsibilities. Can you imagine the American president having to lunch regularly with the premiers of Alberta and Newfoundland and deal with Quebec over breakfast in French?

The threat of continentalization comes not from governments but from forces beyond the control of governments. The men in Washington insist that Canadian nationalists are flogging a straw man, that the United States has no intention of annexing Canada or interfering with the Canadians' perverse will to maintain a national existence, not to mention their questionable national identity and their habit of plastering maple leaves on their jeans. Many of them are fed up with the whining of Canadians about being pushed around by Big Brother and are inclined to tell them to run off and behave in unmentionable ways.

Much of that whining should be offensive also to Canadians who respect their country. I not only agree that there is no evidence whatsoever of a United States intention to annex Canada, I disagree strongly with the simple-minded assertion that the United States is planning to take over Canada economically. The United States, thank God, has no plans for Canada at all. It never had and I trust never will have a Canadian policy. There are real problems for Canada in the power and allure of the American economy and culture, but it is more a problem of sellout than takeover. Insofar as there is an American disposition to take over, it is more benign than malign. It is certainly not a conspiracy centralized in Washington. It is more likely to rest on a misplaced belief that Canadians as well as Americans would benefit from continental sharing—and that they don't like being regarded as foreigners. It isn't annexation by the United States we have to resist now; it is creeping continentalism, the incorporation of Canada by suction into an entity called North America.

If Canada ceases to exist it is more likely to be death by hypnosis than by foreign investment. The vitality of the American media, from NBC to *Penthouse,* is such that Canadians are losing consciousness of themselves. They tend, for example, to be so absorbed in Watergate that they neglect those urgent issues of confederation which are less like a daytime serial but our own. Paradoxically, the branch-plant mentality in Canada is most notable among many who regard themselves as anti-American. They have aped and envied the big-time radicalism of the American New Left, ignoring the poor of Newfoundland or east Montreal to picket and chant on behalf of such un-Canadian phenomena as black ghettoes, the draft, or California grape-pickers. We are in danger of becoming a zombie nation, our physical structure intact but our souls and minds gone abroad. Having gloriously resisted with our loyal muskets the Yankee invader on the slopes of Quebec and Queenston, Canada may well be conquered by American television. That's a hell of a way to die.

We are obliged to protect our media and our economy with formal restrictions on outsiders. The preservation of national distinctions, the maintenance of frontiers, is no more hostile than the sensible erection of fences to clarify jurisdiction between neighbours. This has all been said so often that I hesitate to say it again, but we do have to remind ourselves in 1974 of this central principle of North American co-existence because we are entering a new era when our relations may be fundamentally changed from those to which we are historically accustomed. Present trends indicate that the balance of advantage may now be shifting to the smaller country even though that country is bound to remain the weaker in aggregate power. Canadians ought not be over-confident of this trend, for the world is in an unpredictable state. So long as the weaker was the poor relation, we maintained a civilized relationship which was the admiration of the world. Americans are a benevolent people and kind to the poor. But if the Canadian way of living—as distinct from the standard of living measured in dollars per capita—seems to be higher than that of the United States in energy resources, space, fresh water, and urban tranquillity, what happens to the rules and assumptions we have lived by?

As a product of my generation I have an unreasoning faith in the civilization of this continent to meet the challenge, but I do think we should look hard at our basic philosophies and recognize new trends. Already there has been a dramatic shift in the flow of immigrants, altering a century-old pattern of a preponderant flow of Canadians to the United States. The numbers in both ways are not great and that is for the significant reason that it is harder now to move residence. Along with this are the measures now being taken by the Canadian provinces to restrict the sale of land to foreigners who have been buying it up—particularly lake and sea fronts—to an alarming extent. We must consider the possibility that a shift of economic advantage would invite a shift of population which could bring with it some baffling and disturbing dilemmas.

In the past the United States on the whole played the game with Canada (a few foul balls to the contrary notwithstanding). It does the Americans all the more credit because it was the historic view of American statesmen that Canada's existence was an affront to God's clear design for His own continent. Contrary to current assumptions in the United States and abroad, I do not believe that the United States is by nature an imperialist power—although a lot of Americans certainly have wildly imperialist notions. There is a dangerous American impulse to impose on other peoples what is regarded as good for them. Americans don't frighten me when they play *Yankee Doodle Dandy* or even *Dixie,* but the time to throw up the barriers is when they sing *The Battle Hymn of the Republic.* Canada survived because in spite of Manifest Destiny and the Fenians and "54-40 or Fight" there were enough Americans who believed that the founders of the Republic had intended their country to follow more enlightened principles of international relations.

These quiet Americans seemed to prevail in the end over the rabid senators and editors and generals who hollered at the Canadians to get in step or else. In any case, there was the ripe apple theory in which to take comfort. There was no need, it was said by a distinguished American, to push, because when the Canadians were ready Canada would fall like a ripe apple into the arms of the Republic. The natural assumption was that when Canadians were free of the shackles of empire they would choose liberty on its home ground, America. They didn't realize that the British weren't using Canada; the Canadians were using Britain as a deterrent and counterweight to protect Canadian independence. The British for most of the time would have been quite content to see Canada go as quickly and quietly and inexpensively as possible into the North American federation where they were sure it would eventually land. The British miscalculated, like the Americans, because they regarded Canada as an aberration, an assertion of bad politics against good economics which had no future. It is still Canada's problem to convince foreigners—and to some extent its own people—that it is for real.

There may have been something to be said for continental union at one time, although it would always have been an annexation rather than a merger. In any case, it is too late now—unless the world moves into really desperate times. Canada has created over several centuries its own *raison d'être* and, what is more, Canadians now know we have a good thing going for us. We are suspicious of continental projects. The oil of Texas or the coal of Pennsylvania were not regarded as continental resources when Canada was in short supply. So we are chary of United States proposals for a continental resources policy which we fear as an effort to apply to northern gas and water the principle of sharing Canadian surpluses and American shortages. Our fear may well have made us too dogmatic, however, for there is an argument, which is at least worth looking at, to draw up bilateral principles for disposing of resources in the two countries based on the idea of orderly adjustments rather than the sharing of resources and shortages on the present basis of population and industry. We have to rid ourselves of the notion that we always come out the loser if we negotiate with the Americans or the British. It is historically unsound, and it is demeaning.

The recognition of separate rather than common interests is in the historic tradition. North America (north of the Rio Grande, that is) never was a political entity. Neither was Europe, for that matter. Culturally and socially and, of course, geographically, North America is a valid concept. Constitutionally and politically, however, there is no such entity as North America. Our history is that of two separate strains of colonization pressing from the Atlantic to the Pacific in competition with each other for land and commerce. It was not, as romantic Canadians like to think, an heroic struggle of Canadian yeomen against ruthless American expansionists. It was more like a contest of rival territorial imperialisms in which the Canadian imperialists outfoxed the more populous American imperialists and gained more than half the continent.

This is the great epic story of Canadian history, the national dream. But although it was a struggle which helped shape the United States also, it has almost no part in American history books. Look at the index of any book on the history of American foreign policy. Under Mexico the entries are lengthy. Under Canada, one finds: "see England, war of 1812," or "p.715 under NATO." Even in those new pseudo-histories which seek to prove that "imperialism is as American as apple pie," Canada is ignored—and for a very good reason. How can you account for an honest-to-God imperialist power losing half a continent to a handful of scattered settlers who didn't even have a road or a language to hold them together?

It is in the Canadian national interest to seek accommodation rather than confrontation with the United States. The legitimate argument is over the gains and losses, short and long term. We must recognize the difference between interests which are coincidental and interests which are common, because the argument for "North America" is based on a dubious assumption of mutuality based on geography. There is no doubt of our fundamental common interest, but it does not follow that we have a common North American interest over fisheries or relations with China. Competition, the struggle for advantage, must be recognized as part of our living tradition. It is not the result of perverse and selfish interests interfering with a continental Garden of Eden.

Canadians and Americans have had in common a high regard for the virtues of competition. Reasonably restrained, it is healthy for nations as well as peoples and industries. Advantages shift, and I think that Canadians are learning that this is not a zero-sum game. One country's health depends on that of the other. Bargaining and negotiation are our permanent way of life. There is nothing either unneighbourly or contrary to the spirit of alliance in opposing each other or pressing our own interests. Canadians have a neurotic habit of screaming foul whenever Washington puts it own interests ahead of ours—as if Goliath is always in the wrong. Americans have sometimes thought Canadians should be docile in gratitude for protection. Neither attitude is self-respecting.

A question now is how Americans, suffering shortages, would regard Canadians enjoying not endless supplies but a more comfortable level of austerity. Will the idea that shortages should be shared gain strength? And to what extent are we both obliged to share the shortages of our European allies? Since the Second World War the United States in an era of alliance has in many ways recognized that a healthy and prosperous Canada is in its interests and has behaved accordingly. There is too little recognition in Canada of this fact. It is not so much a question of what the United States has done to help us as what it has refrained from doing in order not to crush us. I do not share the view that Canadians should be grateful to Americans for pouring all that nice money into developing our resources and modernizing our industry. At the same time, I can't feel any sense of grievance against Americans who did just that. The profit was seen as mutual.

Many Canadians fear that we went too far in losing control of our economy in the name of growth, but surely fair-minded Canadians would blame Canadians rather than the United States government for letting this happen. On the other hand, I believe that there was more foresight in Ottawa after the war than is recognized. The Canadian economy was precarious, having lost its markets in Europe and its hope of finance from that source. The risk of too great dependence on United States capital and markets was fully realized, but the gamble was that in this way—and there seemed no other way—the Canadian economy could grow strong enough to hold its own eventually. The alternative was an East German pattern.

There is no doubt the degree of control surrendered has been cause for concern. On the other hand, the fact is that now when western countries are facing grim economic prospects Canada is recognized as being in perhaps the most favourable situation of any. What is more, during the crisis over oil the Canadian government has shown that although it may not, any more than other countries, control the international traffic in oil, it can exert control on the export and import of its own energy resources, regardless of the nationality of the shareholders who seem to own them. Our lack of independence is a fact to recognize, but those who overstate it sap our will.

The fact that the position of Canada vis-à-vis the United States has been fundamentally altered in the past decade may be better realized in Washington than it is among Canadians—who tend to be reluctant and embarrassed millionaires. We shy away from the responsibilities of wealth and prefer the right of the poor to complain. President Nixon laid it on the line when he came to Ottawa in 1972. He said that Canadians and Americans must regard each other as mature and in-dependent nations. He and his advisers were well aware that Canadians had been growling about their threatened independence while at the same time using the old argument about a special continental dependence when they wanted concessions in United States legislation.

He borrowed Canadian language about maturity and independence. Canadians tended to regard this statement of the President's as an acknowledgement of our right to be ourselves, but I presume that he was issuing an American declaration of independence as well— independence of the obligations of a special relationship. It seems to me that Canadians have matured further since that was said.

It should be noted, nevertheless, that in spite of his acceptance of the continental divide, Mr. Nixon could still talk about the desirability of a continental resources policy. There is a dangerous clash of Canadian and American perceptions over those words. Canadians are in no mood to be denied the opportunity to exploit our new-found advantage in order to raise our industrial base, social infrastructure, income, and population. That includes the right to surpass the American level of consumption. Everything must be done within reason, of course. Luxuriating in too much oil and heat if the United States were short might or might not be a Christian thing to do; it would be untactful and provocative.

Although during the oil crisis Canadians insisted on their right to be self-sufficient before exporting, nevertheless they did not brutally turn off the tap when Americans were in difficulties last winter. Under stress they saw what they had always recognized in the past, that it is not in the interest of the weaker country any more than it was in the interest of the stronger to disregard the other's distress. To have cut off all exports would have upset the equilibrium of civilized behaviour on which the future of the continent—and particularly the lesser power—inevitably depends. Which is not the same as accepting the principle that Canadians must settle for the same level of per capita oil supplies as Americans.

The great epic of North America is not the sharing of a continent; we share only a border. It is that after having divided the continent by traditional rough and tumble methods we settled down to live with it like civilized people—inventing procedures like the International Joint Commission and thousands of ad hoc agencies to seek out equitable solutions for the issues we shall never cease to have between us. We have been wise enough to avoid supranational bodies which would impose their decisions. The IJC proposes, but Washington and Ottawa dispose. Supranational institutions may be conceivable for six or more states of Europe which can balance each other. They would never be acceptable between two countries, one of which is ten times as populous as the other. It is not American arrogance but the system's bias which Canadians would have to fear.

A world superpower like the United States could not possibly allow Canada an equal say—that is, a veto—in formulating its political and economic policies. And Canada in its own way has world-wide interests which by no means always coincide with those of the United States. We share a basic interest in the maintenance of economic stability and a world which lives by rule and regulation, but we have different views of what those rules should be. Canadians must and do recognize a responsibility to defer at times to the United States because a majority of Canadians regard the health and strength of our neighbour and the leading Western power as a Canadian national interest. But, in spite of our propinquity and our economic links, our economies are far from identical. The wide differences in our populations, in the nature of produce, the proportion of resources to people, the burden of communications, means that our needs in the world are very much our own. Perhaps the greatest difference between American and Canadian policies is that the United States, unlike Canada, does not have an American problem. The existence of a bordering superpower is an overwhelming factor for policymakers in Canada and introduces a defensive element which is not at all a consideration in Washington. Having a tiresome nag as a neighbour presents it own problems for the United States but they are different ones.

An example of the way in which our interests lead us not only to differ but to oppose each other in international conclaves is presented by the negotiations over the law of the sea. At the forthcoming conference at Caracas as at other meetings, Canada, along with Australia, will be opposing the United States and the other great shipping powers. We may all be North Americans, but one country has the interests of a great naval and maritime power and the other has the interests of a country with little shipping but an enormous length of vulnerable coast line.

So that is why Canadians must struggle against this habit of conjuring up an entity in world politics called "North America." There is no North America as there is an EEC, no Brussels on this continent, and Canadians must firmly resist the forces which press us into this formula. Canadians and Americans do have some positions to argue in common in world conclaves—including, for example, a mutual interest in opposing the protectionism of Europe and Japan. These interests should be regarded, however, as coincidental, not as permanent interests in common, just as we have coincidental interests with Australia over the law of the sea. We cannot allow others to assume that the United States is speaking for us.

We Canadians are, on the eve of revolutionary changes in the balancing of power and wealth, in a highly unfamiliar position, and alone. What other countries might have the same interests as we, with surplus resources to be defended or shared? Australia or Nigeria perhaps? In some cases the Soviet Union more than the United States.

We have one thing in common with the OPEC countries—oil to export. The relatively good relations we have had with the Third World, as a power too weak to threaten them, are at stake. Perhaps we may take over from the United States the role of imperialist enemy number one. We cannot avoid being closer than ever to the centre of international controversy. The historic triangle on which we balanced has changed its shape. The search for counterweights is still instinctive for Canadians, but the priority has declined—partly because the counterweights have not lived up to our expectations and partly because we feel firmer on our own feet. We are much more closely entwined in the American economy than we were when we conceived our place in a triangulated world after the last war. To say that we are more dependent on the United States, however, begs many questions. It is on the relationship that we are more dependent, not the United States. Within it our relative strength has greatly increased and the dependence of the United States on the relationship has also increased. We are a very long way from being equal. Still, the new balance could be a healthier one and, as Mr. Nixon perceived, more mature. The adjustment to a new status can be difficult, however. It may be difficult for Americans to accept the new Canada in place of the hunting and fishing preserve for which they had a condescending affection. What worries me more, however, is the capacity of Canadians to grow into a new status as an economic power with increased responsibilities in the world at large, shedding the shin-kicking postures of the adolescent past and the illusion of poverty.

Our obsession with the giant beside us has obscured our changing position in the world at large. We are being isolated by our unique good fortune. Our small population, traditionally regarded as an inadequate market and a source of weakness, has become, in an age of shortages and pollution, an advantage. It is an enviable position, but a country rich in resources and space and short on people is increasingly vulnerable. Can we live fatly while the Third and Fourth Worlds collapse of hunger and cold, while Western Europe and Japan, which are not only our friends but our markets, face industrial and social breakdown from inflation and lack of fuel? Preoccupation with the American problem has made us parochial. The negotiations between Edmonton and Ottawa and between Ottawa and Washington on resource issues are important, but they have to be seen in the context of the infinitely graver and more threatening situation in the wider world. Our fuel and food are needed for more crucial purposes than the health and strength of the Canadian state.

When it comes to resources we may be better off than the Americans but together we form the uniquely fortunate continent. A peculiarly seductive form of continentalism we may have to resist is the temptation to withdraw into Fortress American to protect our hoard from the barbarians. That mentality, bred of fear, would lead us inexorably to the philosophy of the efficient continent—a philosophy which has always posed the greatest threat to the Canadian dream.

2:

Political and Security Issues

In 1969 I was invited to appear before the House of Commons Standing Committee on External Affairs and National Defence to discuss "the non-economic aspects" of our relations with the United States which the Committee was setting out to study. My assignment was to pose questions rather than to answer them and suggest where the issues lie. In my introductory comments I said I would try to define the dilemmas and state the paradoxes rather than offer solutions. This may well have been a rationalization, but I defended it by asking whether we should be thinking in terms of solutions at all. Problems between the United States and Canada should be regarded as permanent. They would not go away when we had "solved" them or found a formula. It was a question of "process" rather than "solution." What we needed were the right perspectives on the process so that we could live with the problems. Whether the distinguished legislators bought this I don't know. They gave me some good lessons in the political and security issues as they had to see them. Feeling wiser after the event, and contemplating the things I wished I had said or had said differently, I produced a refurbished version of my testimony which was published in Behind the Headlines, *volume XXIX, March 1970.*

The present debate over Canada's relations with the United States is distorted by two schools of thought: anti-Americanism and anti-anti-Americanism. The simple desire to score points against the United States stands in the way of reason. So does the blind assumption that any relationship other than total commitment is unmentionable. Although I share neither of these attitudes I shall try in my analysis to take the existence of both into consideration. Some confession of faith, however, is necessary in advance.

I reject the view that the United States is a malevolent force, an attitude found not only in Canada but in the rest of the world and in the United States itself. It seems to me as intellectually wrong-headed as McCarthyism, which attributed all the evils of the world to the conspiracies of Moscow. Belief that the United States is wrong in some or many of its policies, for example Vietnam, is different, of course, from the fixed attitude that United States policies and American influence should be opposed and rejected on principle. If one holds the view that the United States must be purged of its sins, then certain conclusions on policy follow which have their own logic. It is not a view held by many Canadians, although a somewhat larger number, with less logic, borrow arguments from those who do. I have left it out of consideration because I don't believe it is likely to be a dominant opinion in Canada and because I cannot see any practical line of policy we could follow from this conviction. Ours is a long border on which to erect a Berlin Wall.

I do not believe that the United States as a state or as a society is a counter-revolutionary force. It is still the most revolutionary society of our century. Within it there takes place the conflict between revolutionary and counter-revolutionary forces. It certainly has its sicknesses, but these are not unique. Most of them are shared by other Western countries including Canada, but United States sicknesses are, like everything else American, extravagant. Even its sicknesses, however, are avant-garde, because the United States is engaged in a further expansion of democracy to include groups which did not previously share its advantages. The adjustment is exceedingly painful, but it is a process in which other democracies are or will be engaged.

Our sicknesses in Canada, social and constitutional, resemble but are not the same as those of the United States. We should profit by the exploratory errors of the United States and also be careful not to import their problems, racial problems in particular, from a compulsion to identify ourselves with them—a characteristic of the Right and the Left in Canada. To handle our problems in our own way we need to preserve our institutions and to change and reform them in our way. To do this, the preservation of national sovereignty is essential. We must beware of the bigoted defenders of sovereignty, but we must beware also of the woollymindedness of liberal internationalists who denounce sovereignty and nationalism in the abstract as evil.

Like most other things in life, sovereignty and nationalism can be good or evil depending on whether they are exploited to promote civic virtue at home and a sense of national responsibility abroad or uniformity at home and aggression abroad. There is no good argument in Canada for an archaic attachment to sovereignty of a kind which would inhibit international collaboration, but we do not promote the cause of internationalism by allowing the sovereignty of a lesser power to be drained into the national sovereignty of one larger power.

One fact of life that must be recognized is that Canada, if it continues to exist, will do so by sufferance of the United States. We shall continue as always to depend upon United States forbearance. If the Americans turned ruthless, they could extinguish us. They are unlikely to do so by old-fashioned military methods or positive economic sanctions, but by ceasing to take our economic interests into consideration they could make life for us as Canadians on our part of the continent unacceptable. In considering our policy towards the United States, we cannot forget the need to maintain the basic good will of the Americans and their government. From this principle one deduces a policy of good sense rather than of submission. History has shown us that we do not need to accept an attitude of hopeless dependence. We have, as always, certain cards to play. The manifest destiny of the United States has for nearly two centuries been curbed by internal politics and regional stresses within that country. The respect of Americans for themselves and their own good reputation inhibits the United States government, if not necessarily all its citizens. Increasing United States vested interest in the Canadian economy involves many Americans in the continuing existence of Canada as an entity. One reason we need to maintain our sovereignty and the strength of our government is that through that government we can negotiate with the United States government to protect us against Americans who, for economic or other reasons, do not care about Canadian sovereignty.

The good will which we need from the United States need not be entire. We can live with a United States that is irritated, unfriendly, or even hostile on specific issues. The question we have to bear in mind, however, is whether we could exist if Americans regarded Canada as they regarded Cuba in the early 1960s, a country which poses a serious threat not only to their way of life but to their security.[1]

Here concludes my credo. From now on I shall be endeavouring to analyse the political and military issues and speculate—with a few opinions but no convictions. We cannot divorce the political and strategic from the economic aspects of our realtionship with the United States, but, in the spirit of contradiction, this is what I propose to do. I shall speak of economic factors only as they affect defence and foreign policy. Of course they affect it enormously, probably decisively. The answers to the questions whether we can or whether we want to pursue foreign policies separate from or in close association with the United States are to be found largely in our economic interests and our economic conditions. The deductions from the economic factors are not, however, automatic or obvious. In this sense we have freedom of choice in our foreign and defence policies and it is not true to say that our "dependence" on the United States, whatever that means, makes us a "satellite," whatever that means. There are factors other than the economic which play a part in the determination of our foreign policy, in questions of security and in the protection of our national institutions. It is with the paradoxes involved in the political and security association with the United States that I shall be principally concerned, with the alliance and its significance, and with the contradictions between the need we have felt to join with the Americans in defence of shared interests and the need we have to protect the interests and the identity which we do not share with them and which are jeopardized by the partnership.

Identification of the Relationship

To begin with we have a problem of definition. What are we vis-à-vis the United States in the international context? Are we a partner? an ally? A tributary province? A colony? Or a natural enemy? A threat to satisfactory relations is that the relationship is changing in fact but our definitions are not catching up. Between the idea and the reality falls the shadow of misunderstanding. The change is largely in circumstances and should not be defined as if it were a simple change of attitudes and dispositions.

The definitions to which we cling, at least in rhetorical statements, are "allies" and "partners," but these terms were conceived in the circumstances of twenty years ago. During that period there have been the following changes, among others:

1 An explosion of technology has increasingly differentiated the superpowers from all others in military function and capability.

2 To a considerable extent as a result of these technological developments, the requirements for "continental defence" have been changing. The trend has been to lessen the importance of Canada in American plans to defend the United States, the continent, and the deterrent. This trend, however, cannot be assumed to be constant because technology can alter the situation. A requirement for Canadian participation in the Airborne Warning and Control System (AWACS), for example, illustrates the importance the United States government is likely to attach to Canada so long as there remains a threat of bombers from the USSR.

3 The changing relationship between the United States and the USSR inevitably affects the position of their allies. However one regards the reality of détente, there is the present fact of the Strategic Arms Limitation Talks (SALT), begun by the United States and the USSR in Helsinki in 1969 and due to be carried on in Vienna. It may be years before these talks produce results, but the fact that the two superpowers are consulting together about their armaments emphasizes the differentiation in function between the super- and the lesser powers. Whether or not SALT will eventually end the confrontation of the two

blocs, they may restore in the meantime the tendency, notable at the end of World War II, for lesser powers to draw together, as was already notable in the 1969 session of the United Nations General Assembly.

4 The Vietnam war has shaken the basic Canadian conviction of twenty years ago that when the United States is at war, Canada, whether it likes it or not, will also be at war. Although Canadians have been divided in their attitudes towards the United States role in Vietnam, the experience has accentuated a disinclination to be too closely allied with United States foreign and defence policies—either because these policies are regarded as wrong or because Vietnam is the kind of mess we would like to keep clear of.

5 The growth of a continental consciousness among Western Europeans, although it has not been institutionalized to the extent its devotees would like, tends to isolate Canada from its European allies and force it into a "North American" role whether it likes this or not.

The Implications of Alliance

The question is therefore: are we still an ally of the United States in the classical sense of the term? And, the supplementary question: should we still be an ally and does the United States want or need us as an ally?

To answer these questions we should look first at the historical basis of the alliance. The military alliance between the United States and Canada is a relatively new phenomenon and one that was quite unthinkable in the first century and a half of our two centuries of coexistence. The principles of the new relationship can be traced to Mr. Roosevelt's statement in 1938 that the United States "would not stand idly by" if Canada were threatened and Mr. King's reciprocal pledge that Canada would see that the United States was not attacked through or across Canadian soil. These are still the basic features of the North American compact. If they are now being questioned, it is largely because their relevance in an age of intercontinental missiles is less obvious than it was in 1940 and 1941 when the Ogdensburg and Hyde Park agreements committed us to the concept of partnership in defence and in defence production. In retrospect it might be argued that partnership leads inevitably to integration, but integration was not what was being talked about in the early 1940s, except of course in terms of the desperate need to win the war. Circumstances change in a generation, and it is important for Canadians to recall that at the time of these two agreements it was Canada, not the United States, which was pressing for the defence tie because in 1941 we wanted to involve the United States in our war. After the war, we were as keen as the Americans that the defence partnership should not lapse, partly because we wanted to have the cheapest possible military establishment ourselves. The defence partnership was never forced on an unwilling Canada, and in the field of defence production it was we who always took the initiative because it has always been to our economic advantage to do so. That is not a decisive argument that the defence partnership as it stood is still in our interest. It is intended merely to provide some perspective on Canadian interests when our vision has been clouded by the Vietnam War.

In looking at Canada's role as a military ally, it is essential to recognize that this is based on a compact. In the late 1940s, the Canadian government, backed by an unusual consensus of the Canadian people, consciously and voluntarily rejected the option of an independent defence policy in favour of a limited collective security agreement in the North Atlantic Treaty. Within this broader framework we set our military alliance with the United States, including the separate instrument for NORAD. The basis of the compact was the simple belief that defence would be more effective and also less costly if resources were pooled and that an aggressor would be more effectively deterred if he had to take into consideration an alliance with a disposition on the part of its members to go to the defence of each other. Canada's position was neither selfish nor altruistic. It was based on a cool estimate of Canadian national interests. It is proper that this compact should be re-examined because of the considerable change of circumstances, but it is important in regarding Canadian policy towards the alliance with the United States in particular and with NATO in general to recognize that a commitment was made and that our partners look upon us as fellow investors rather than as benefactors. Our policies in the past twenty years towards our allies must be regarded as having been based on this concept of mutual interest against a common threat. There is notable a considerable generation gap on this subject. Those of us who were conscious during the war and postwar periods accept the fact of the compact even if some may question its wisdom. The younger generation is less conscious of it and some of the confusion of the present debate rises from this misunderstanding.

We have to decide whether or not we consider it in the Canadian interest, broadly conceived, to continue the compact. If we acknowledge benefits we should pay dues—although the question is asked whether one incurs obligations through benefits inadvertently conferred. The nature of the benefits requires re-examination. So also does the nature of the threat against which the alliance is directed. There is no reason, furthermore, why the nature of the dues cannot change. They have changed in the past twenty years: we had, for example, no expectation of sending troops to Europe when we joined NATO in 1948. What we do have to bear in mind, however, is that so long as we subscribe to the idea of a compact and a pooling of resources, our defence policy is justified as a contribution to a broader scheme rather than as a strategy meaningful in purely national terms. The presence of troops in Germany or Canadian assistance in defence of the United States Strategic Air Command are not isolated operations but parts of a combined strategy, the sum total of which is assumed to be in the long-range interest of Canadians. It can be argued, of course, that Canadian interests have not been adequately catered for in the alliance programme or even that it was a mistake in the first place for Canada to take the pledge. What is essential, however, is to recognize that this was a way of defending Canada calculated as such quite freely by Canadians.

It is also necessary to ask whether Canada has already renounced the compact. Certainly its desirability is no longer unquestioned. Statements even by some government spokesmen seem to ignore it, but the recent renewal of commitments to both NATO and NORAD, although limited, suggests that the compact has not been renounced. Like all other members of the alliance Canada has continually altered its views on what its contribution should be, though we obviously must make some contribution unless we inform our allies that we have for good reasons renounced the commitment to collective defence.

A fair question for us to ask is whether our allies, and particularly the United States, have renounced the compact or acted in such a way that our renunciation would be justified or desirable. The compact, it must be remembered, involved participating in policy-making as well as in the offering of guarantees and the sharing of burdens. We have a right to ask whether we have had or continue to have our share in alliance policy-making. Here we wallow in the uncertainties of what would be the fair share for a country which carries only a small part of the burden—either of NATO in general or of NORAD in particular. (There is a controversial issue also of whether and to what extent we should participate in the foreign policy-making not of the alliance but of our allies.) As far as NATO in general is concerned, Canada has had as good a share as could be expected in the military decisions and political recommendations. As for North America we probably have a grievance in principle. The United States has not consulted with Canada as prescribed in the terms of the NORAD exchange. Basic to this agreement was the concept that if Americans and Canadians were going to fight together they should consult together about questions which were likely to cause the fight to break out: "The two governments consider that the establishment of integrated air defence arrangements of the nature described increases the importance of the fullest possible consultation between the two governments on all matters affecting the joint defence of North America, and that defence co-operation between them can be worked out on a mutually satisfactory basis only if such consultation is regularly and consistently undertaken."[2]

It would be hard to maintain that this pledge was observed by the United States at the time of the Cuban missiles crisis. Evidence is hard to come by which would prove that Canada has really been consulted on the major United States decisions concerning continental defence, in spite of the close and useful daily association of Canadian and American military personnel in Washington and in Colorado. Recently Mr. Laird made it clear that when he spoke of Canada's being "consulted" over the decision on ABMs he meant "informed." The basic question which this poses for Canadians, however, is not whether we have been wronged but whether the NORAD provision is realistic. Given the changing circumstances mentioned above, and especially the curious isolation and combination of the superpowers, can Canada expect any real sharing in the military policy of a superpower, however well intentioned the latter might be? And if there can be no real policy sharing, is it in our interest to make our contribution to the continental defence scheme—a question by no means simply rhetorical?

The "common threat" against which an alliance is directed requires consideration. Can we speak of a common threat when there is no single instrument but rather separate governments to perceive and define that threat? United States strategists, when talking about NORAD, seem to assume that this threat is a permanent fact of life. The question is inherent in the alliance structure, but it was of less importance when there was a general consensus in "the West" that the Soviet Union and its allies were in one form or another "the threat." Ottawa never perceived that threat in exactly the terms that Washington did and frequently differed strongly with Washington over the tactics to be used. The matter is even more controversial now when there are considerable differences of opinion about the Soviet "threat." As the superpower, the United States, draws away from its allies in its responsibility, how free do we remain to determine the threat as we see it? Are we obliged to play our parts in an alliance the posture of which is inevitably determined by Washington? Are not Washington's views of the Soviet Union and China, little affected by our interpretations, the determining factor in the international confrontation? As we increasingly accept the philosophy of deterrence and the logic which has led to SALT, are we not moving away from the simple conception of a threat initiated by the Soviet Union and responded to by the rest of us to a concept of Soviet-United States provocation and Soviet-United States response? Even if we are basically on the side of the United States, we must recognize that its actions, over which we have little or no control, could provoke the threat. But such logic leads to the sobering question: if we insist, as we have a right to do, that our own government will make its own assessment of the threat, where does that line of argument lead us? To splendid isolation, moral superiority, oblivion, or a better stance from which to use our bargaining power? Each conclusion can be argued.

The question whether NATO is the best framework within which to conduct our alliance relationship with the United States requires examination. Canadians made no secret of the fact that one of the advantages for them of NATO in 1948 was that it seemed safer to join a multilateral alliance than a highly unequal bilateral alliance. The question arises whether this was a valid calculation or just an instinctive response to the old adage that we must call on the Old World to redress the imbalance of the New. We have not been able to bring NORAD into the NATO structure. We are left unaccompanied to deal with a superpower in the difficult problems of continental defence. This naked confrontation is likely to become more acute as we switch our emphasis from Europe to our own land mass. So it seems, but there may be an argument which could be put forward by our military advisers to show that the ability to combine with other powers in NATO institutions strengthens our hand in dealing with the United States. Multilateralism is important in the diplomacy of NATO, where the combination with lesser powers has been more effective in affecting United States policy than has Canadian influence alone. In general our ties with Europe fortify our culture and our economy to resist United States domination. It must be asked, however, whether membership in NATO is at all relevant to matters of culture and trade.

A cause of confusion is that Canada's relationship is not only to a continental neighbour but to a superpower, a permanent member of the United Nations Security Council, an imperial system. It is hard to disentangle continental, NATO, and United Nations or other involvements of the United States and therefore to calculate our obligations as an ally to the whole of United States foreign policy. What are the implications of the NATO/NORAD compact outside the North Atlantic? There is no doubt that the area in which NATO applies is a limited one and members have, for example, never considered themselves obliged to support militarily their allies in their imperial problems in Africa or Asia. Although Canada allowed the Americans to keep NORAD outside the NATO structure, recent Canadian policy seems to have established the valid argument that the transfer of troops from Europe to North America is not by itself to be considered withdrawing them from NATO. The imperial powers within NATO, that is those involved in other continents, including the United States, may never have expected military support from their allies, but they have expected moral support or at least the absence of active opposition. But no NATO ally has given military support to the United States in Vietnam, and one of the causes of United States disenchantment with NATO has been the lack of even moral support from many of its allies. It has never been suggested that there was a legal obligation on a NATO member, not even Canada as a NORAD member as well, to put troops into Vietnam. The problem posed for the allies of the United States, however, is not whether they have a legal obligation to the United States in southeast Asia, Latin America, or elsewhere; it is whether their own national interests would lead them to save the United States from defeat or humiliation on the grounds that the weakening of the United States in Asia would weaken it also in the North Atlantic where we recognize its role in our security. The dilemma has not been acute because a superpower like the United States is not dependent upon the military support of others to avoid defeat. A few divisions of European or Canadian troops in Vietnam would probably have only complicated the command structure, although they would have been important in the diplomatic struggle. For Canada and other allies there remains however the consideration whether they should use whatever political and diplomatic influence they have to prevent the weakening of a power which, in other spheres including the United Nations Security Council, is regarded as an essential force. Whether United States strength can best be preserved by simple support of United States policy or by opposing it totally or partially when it is wrong is a legitimate question for those who consider the preservation of United States strength in the Canadian national interest.

A question which bothers Canadians is that of paying their fair share. Canadian social tradition frowns on those who get a "free ride." Getting a ride at half-price is perhaps more our way of doing things. Having accepted the compact, however, we tried to make a respectable contribution. As the question of nuclear deterrence seems to get farther and farther from the things the alliance deals with, the problem of a free ride begins to look different. The general assumption is that Canada is protected by the United States nuclear umbrella, and it is only right therefore that it should pay for protection or do whatever is required of it to keep the umbrella aloft. In the SALT age, however, it may seem increasingly as if we were protected not by the United States deterrent but by the system of deterrence itself, a system which enables not only Canada but all lesser powers to pursue their contribution to world politics relatively free of the threat of oblivion. Seen this way, there is an argument for saying that our payment for peace is to make our own best contribution to develop the kind of world which is in the interest not only of Canada but of the United States. This might be done much more effectively if we did not get involved in further military expenditure. There is always, on the other hand, the argument to be considered that the system of nuclear deterrence depends upon the effective performance of the United States and Soviet systems and that Canada is an essential part of the United States system. This may always be a matter of opinion, but it again emphasizes the necessity of finding out what the United States wants most from us.

Alternative Policies

Having in mind the questions raised concerning the compact or alliance relationship with the United States, let us look at various policies which might be considered.

1   We could try to continue, as before, a policy of close military co-operation, sharing contributions and expenses at about the present proportion. The advantage of such a policy is that we would not rock the boat and there would be less danger of the kind of ill will in Congress and elsewhere in the United States which would induce unfavourable treatment of Canadian interests. We would also be able to maintain the present special association with the American military and civil bureaucracy and the special consideration given to an ally in policy-making. Even if this special consideration is regarded as a wasting asset or less than just, it might be better than nothing. Even if its positive worth does not seem great, we should consider the negative results of being cut off the secret and confidential list altogether.

The principal question mark about such a policy is whether it is in fact possible to carry on as before a policy of sharing. We have never paid what could honestly be called our "fair share," even of NORAD expenses. If, as is possible, the United States takes off in a new escalation of military expenditures over which we have little or no control, can we carry on at about the same proportion without being caught up in a similar escalation? When these mounting expenses are the result of major technological decisions by the superpowers, would Canadians be prepared to multiply their defence expeditures? It seems clearly up to us whether we want to take part in an ABM system or an AWACS system.[3] If we do, our defence expenditures are bound to multiply unless, of course, we let the Americans pay even for the Canadian participation. If we do not, is there not inevitably some change in the nature of our defence relationship? An assumption is made here that although we may well be given a chance to state objections or put forward national interests which might be affected, decisions on these major strategic policies are bound to be made in Washington (or Helsinki or Vienna)—not because the Americans are inconsiderate but because these are American, not alliance, policies and cannot be shared.[4] In spite of this assumption, however, some calculation of advantages and disadvantages in going along is required.

It is advisable, furthermore, not to describe the policy-making process in too absolute terms. The opportunity for "consultation" on Mr. Laird's terms would never give us a veto but it may not be entirely useless.

2 We might continue as an ally, declaring ourselves to be still on the United States side but with a more clearly differentiated military and diplomatic function. We would accept an even more unequal partnership than we have at present—both in burden-sharing and in policy-making. First of all we should find out what the United States does need of us now for defence—defence of the continent, defence of the deterrent. We should not simply accept their prescription, but we are obliged as neighbours to take it into consideration. To have a differentiated military function is an attractive political idea, attractive in the way the unique role in international peacekeeping and mediation has satisfied our political needs. We work better and more effectively if we can do our own thing. There is a great deal to be said for this political prescription, but we have to find out whether the military facts allow us to fill it. Can we find a formula according to which we co-operate in continental defence on a shared basis without getting involved in the stratospherically expensive operations of the United States in the game of deterrence? Can we retreat to Mr. King's formula that we will look after our own defences and see that the United States is not threatened from our soil? We might quickly find ourselves faced with the question whether a people with the largest number of square miles per person to defend could in fact do so without going broke. Can we afford even to patrol our own country? If the Arctic is opened up and becomes as exposed a frontier as the Atlantic and Pacific,[5] can we afford to defend or even just to maintain all this land? Are we then driven back to an acceptance of the view that although we remain vulnerable no one is likely to violate us and the danger of their doing so is too small to warrant ruining ourselves in military expenditure? Or do we come back to the simple theory that we are protected by the game of mutual deterrence? If so, what interest in or responsibilities for the deterrents should we accept?

There is a question whether Canadian defence collaboration is a nuisance to the Pentagon. After the Cuban missiles affair, when Canadian collaboration was not quickly forthcoming, there was some disposition among the American military to prefer reliance on a unilateral defence even if this meant leaving Canada out of their calculations. That was in the period when the importance of Canadian real estate seemed to be declining. It would be desirable to find out whether this attitude exists and whether it is justified and whether it has been altered by the appearance of such new devices as AWACS. One alternative which Canadians would certainly find hard but might eventually come to see as the lesser of evils would be the granting of bases to the United States on Canadian soil. If we do not want to be whisked off in the escalation of American technology but are fearful of the consequences of the Americans resenting us as unco-operative or neutral, we could presumably let them establish bases where they need them—preferably in our wilderness—and let them use them as expensively as they please. They would become prime targets for an enemy of the United States but presumably no more so than if they were jointly run. Such a concession might tie Canada less closely to United States policy than it is tied by NORAD. It could hardly be said that the presence of Guantanamo inhibits the foreign policy of Cuba—a parallel which has some relevance but should not be pressed too far. It could be argued that the Canadian prejudice against having United States troops on Canadian soil is a nineteenth-century prejudice related to nineteenth-century fears. A greater twentieth-century threat is the loss of identity which comes from military integration in a collaborative effort. There is the precedent of American troops stationed in a number of European countries for twenty years, although countries separated by an ocean from the troops' source do not have the same acute concern for their sovereignty as we have because their identities are more secure. Such a proposal, it must be recognized, goes so strongly against Canadian inclinations, both of those who want to maintain and of those who want to break the American alliance, that it may not be worth considering. The pursuance of this logic, however, does help us understand something of our condition even if we end by rejecting it.

Finally, one of the advantages of this second course is an argument which admittedly goes counter to one of those advanced for the first course. There might be less danger of incurring American ill will if we clearly differentiated our function than if we pretended we were sharing and fell further and further behind in paying our dues.

3   There is the course of neutrality or non-belligerency. Non-belligerency is the position we have adopted vis-à-vis Vietnam and which we could adopt in other wars, declared or undeclared, when the United States was engaged in areas which do not directly threaten North America.[6] Neutrality is a name usually given to a policy of withdrawing from NATO and following the Swedish model. It is a term which becomes less and less meaningful as the world becomes less polarized. In Canada the argument for this position has to a large extent been based on the diplomatic advantages which would be achieved. This is no place to go into the contradictory arguments as to whether non-membership in NATO would or would not give us more ballast in dealing with the Third World. It may well be true that our military association with the United States makes us less attractive to Africans, and it can be argued that it makes Africans take us more seriously. The key con-

sideration in this context, however, is whether Canadians are likely to decide the fundamental question of our military relations with the United States on the basis of an uncertain calculation of our influence in the Third World, however much we are told that the future of the planet depends on correcting the balance between rich and poor nations.

It is not only our relations with the Third World which matter in this connection, of course. Similar inconclusive arguments are raised as to whether our independence from or close association with the United States enhances our influence in the international community at large. Our Western European allies seem to like us best in the role of loyal ally, although this position also causes them to ignore our special position in the alliance and lump us against our will in "North America" on the assumption that that is a single, constitutional entity. It may have been because General de Gaulle (as a result of our selling uranium to the United States without the restrictions required of France) regarded us as irrevocably committed to the Americans, that he switched from a benevolent to a malevolent attitude to Canada. It might be assumed that the Eastern Europeans would respect us more if we were neutral, but there is also evidence that they would rather have us as a member of the NATO team, involved thereby in a European security conference and NATO-Warsaw Pact bargaining, because of our reputation for flexibility. As for Latin America, there is a strong argument that our relations would be compromised by too close an association with the United States in security questions. Before committing ourselves to the Organization of American States and full participation in inter-American security and economic agreements it would be advisable to examine whether our NORAD and NATO obligations would in any way prejudice our freedom of action in considering inter-American security questions. What would be the American expectations of our behaviour as a special kind of ally in this system? As in so many of our dilemmas, the answers to all these questions are to be found not in blanket assertions but by carefully totting up the balance of advantages and disadvantages, all of which are still hypothetical.

The question of neutrality must be looked at in terms of direct Canadian national interest. It is for this reason we have rejected it for the past thirty years. It should be looked at again in the light of changing technology and international politics even if it is only to discover again in a new situation that military disengagement from the United States would not serve our interests in the 1970s any more than we thought it would in the 1940s. It has usually been dismissed with the argument that Canadians could not escape the holocaust if there were a war between the Soviet Union and the United States. It can be argued, however, that it is better to be a side-effect than a direct hit. If Canadian participation in continental defence is no longer crucial (and that is by no means a certainty), have we a right to look again at the possible advantages for us of contracting out from an expensive game? The game in any case is coming to be more and more a question of shadow-boxing between two players. One wonders whether, if SALT continues, we may not find ourselves in a position resembling neutrality not by deliberate choice but by a train of events which shunts us onto the sidelines. There may be nothing very useful for us to do and it may be more efficient for the United States and the USSR to play this game alone. United States strategic policy would then be determined in negotiation with the USSR rather than in consultation with its allies.

The threat to Canada, it can be argued, is not a nuclear attack upon us from the Soviet Union or from China, as we are unlikely to provoke an attack. The danger to us is nuclear war itself, particularly if this is a war between one or other Eurasian power and the United States over our country. Our principal defence interest, therefore, is not in protecting ourselves from the Soviet Union or China but in preventing a war breaking out. Should we consider the possibility that in due course, if SALT continues, we might serve our own interests as well as those of the United States and the world better by being not a military ally of the United States but the neutral area between the superpowers on which might be installed the devices of inspection or detection pointed in both directions[7] on which a strategic arms limitation agreement would be based. This again is one of those ideas which has political attraction for Canadians and which is worth exploring. However, there is no certainty that it would be militarily feasible or even helpful. That would depend on the technology of the superpowers and the trend of their discussions, and of course on their political perceptions. Some investigation of the military aspects of it could, however, be undertaken at this stage.

On the other hand, one cannot take for granted that the SALT trend is necessarily an argument for neutrality. Even if the United States and the Soviet Union are the single negotiators, they do in a sense represent their respective alliances. Negotiation progresses more surely when the negotiators play from strength. One cannot disregard the argument that agreement might be reached sooner if we stood behind the United States as an alliance just as the Soviet alliance is bound to stand behind its champion.

There is some question whether we might, like other and more neutral powers, exploit the cold war by playing off the Soviet Union against the United States. There are presumably some questions on which we might get Soviet support against the United States. If we should enter into a contest with the United States over Arctic sovereignty the Soviet Union would be likely to support our thesis. Calling in Soviet forces to prevent an American invasion is not a policy which is likely to become real under foreseeable circumstances. In a sense, however, we do profit from the cold-war contest. American good behaviour towards its neighbour is basically a product of their own best traditions; it is also stimulated by a cold-war desire not to behave like Russians. A suspicious Canadian might on the other hand see some sinister prospects in the way in which the United States deplored but accepted Soviet intervention in Czechoslovakia on the grounds that each superpower has rights in its own sphere.

The difference between American policy and the Brezhnev doctrine may be simply that the Americans are more sophisticated and allow their neighbours a great deal more latitude in political forms. Intervention in a neighbouring state where a form of government considered inimical has been established is not beyond the reach of the American mind. On the other hand there is an air of unreality about this speculation because the community of social and political attitudes in the United States and Canada, in recent years at least, is such that the likelihood of Canadians, anglophone or francophone, wanting to install a government totally alien in philosophy from that of the United States is remote. Social, political, and economic philosophies on this continent may, however, be in for drastic change and the competition for resources may be renewed more ruthlessly. Canada, with no concern over the growth of its population, and the United States, turning like Japan to controlling its numbers, could conceivably diverge in their social practices, and Canada could become much more defensive. It is still hard to see us turning for protection to the Soviet Union, but the instinct to turn somewhere for moral support would return if the endemic contest between Canada and the United States for the resources of the continent became too raw.

Paradoxes of Partnership

There is a paradox at the basis of partnership and alliance between unequal countries. Withdrawal from the partnership could leave us out in the cold. We can have little influence on United States policy if we do not know what that policy is or if we do not know what is going on in discussions among the great powers. It is worth, therefore, paying a price for influence, especially if that influence includes not only a voice in world politics but the protection of our own interests. However, if the influence we gain is minimal, is it worth paying the price? Do we lose our freedom of movement for an illusion? There are even certain advantages in not being consulted by the United States. Being involved in a process of consultation may mean being morally involved in supporting the conclusion. If we had shared in the decision to move to

ABMs, would we not feel moral responsibility to participate in carrying out this agreed policy—even if there had never been any real chance of our changing the American mind. We should be exceedingly wary of schemes, usually well-intentioned, which emanate from American political leaders offering to give us a voice in some body supposedly determining joint foreign or defence policy—or even a right to be heard in the Senate. Those who propose such things are rarely unscrupulous enough to realize that they are proposing a trap, but it is not one we should fall into. Nevertheless, in considering this question of policy-sharing and burden-sharing, it is advisable not to pursue the subject to logical conclusions. Good sense and long experience suggest caution and resistance to the principle of integration, along with a disposition to pragmatism.

In deciding whether an alliance is the most satisfactory mutual relationship between our countries, one could also compare and contrast our relations with the United States in the North Atlantic and in North America where we are bound by an alliance and in Latin America and the Far East where we are not. It might be argued that there has been less conflict and irritation over Latin America and the Far East because the Americans did not expect us to behave as military allies. From the time of the Korean war there have been very considerable differences between Canadian and United States attitudes on Asian questions and in Indochina we have had separate responsibilities. These differences would have been rubbed raw if we had been members of SEATO.[8] Furthermore, it would not have been possible for Canada to play the useful mediatory roles it essayed in trying to get and to establish armistices in Korea and Indochina if it had been an ally of the United States in those areas. These are similar to a reason used for our not joining the Organization of American States; the danger in friction caused by different perspectives if it is enclosed within an institution. There have been more direct clashes in NATO and on continental questions. However, one must recognize that there have also been a great many more causes for conflict because the interests are much greater and closer. The suggested contrasts in the various systems are worth looking at, but it is necessary to bear in mind that the North Atlantic and North America are or have been areas of primary concern to Canada, and Latin America and the Far East secondary. Whereas Canada is to a considerable degree a finite, a discrete state, the United States is an imperial system. This is to some extent a reverse of the prewar situation when Canada was involved in a world-wide empire and the United States, seeking isolation, did not want to be dragged into a world war by Canada. Whether we like it or not, the United States has assumed obligations abroad to maintain "world order." To some extent it has created a pax Americana. This is not an ideal way of maintaining world order, but it is a pax of some kind and it may be argued that it is better to move from a tentative pax to a more soundly and justly based pax than to relapse into international anarchy. One does not have to agree fully with United States foreign policy to recognize that its reserve of force might be needed. Even United Nations peacekeeping has been dependent upon United States military transport and logistic assistance. United States intervention in Vietnam and in the Dominican Republic may have been mistaken, but there could be other situations in which the Americans alone or through an international organization were asked to intervene by a wider consensus. United States pretensions to intervention arise to some extent out of its responsibilities as a great power in the United Nations Security Council. Canadians must ask themselves therefore whether they have some interest of their own in maintaining this pax Americana even as a transitional form. If so, then they must act in this recognition and consider how Canada might assist the transition to a more widely based security system rather than simply denigrate the present instrument.

There is an ambiguity at the heart of Canadian defence. This has been well stated recently by a young American, Roger Swanson, in the following terms: "National security must, if it is to have any contemporary relevance, include . . . survival of national identity and values . . . Indeed, in a strategic sense, Canada is caught in a dilemma of Kafkaesque proportions. Among possible threats to its national security are the United States and the USSR. The one force (United States) that guarantees Canada's security and thereby eliminates a second possible security threat (USSR) itself then constitutes a national security threat of a different nature and magnitude, but of no less relevance to Canada's existence and identity."[9]

Canada conducts a defence on two fronts. We are of course reluctant to equate the two threats and in fact we don't. The threat from an extra-continental aggressor may be greater to our personal lives, but the threat from the United States is greater to our national existence. The former may be more fatal, but the latter preoccupies us more. The acceptance of this paradox is surely the beginning of wisdom.

The Relevance of Independence

The question which obsesses Canadians is how independent we can be in our foreign policy. The first question of course is whether independence should be considered an end in itself. Most people would deny that it should be, but they often seem to act as if this were in fact the case. Others seem to think independence a frivolous aim. In itself it is empty, but a considerable element of independence and the image of independence are important instruments if Canada is to carry out a foreign policy which protects its own interests and contributes to the general good.

An answer to this question is that we can be as independent as we dare to be. The United States is not likely to specify the bounds beyond which we can move. Our freedom of movement is circumscribed not by orders from Washington but by our own caution. We could lose a good deal by being reckless. We always have to calculate carefully our various interests in determining the extent to which we want to differ from the United States. In making this calculation we have to ask ourselves two major questions.

1   Are we likely to provoke ill will in Washington and elsewhere which will jeopardize our interests?

2   Is it in our interest to weaken the United States or the credibility of the coalition to which we belong?

This is not to deny that there are other considerations which should guide the Canadian government to do what it thinks is right. A decision is particularly painful if Ottawa considers that Washington is morally wrong and such a decision requires particularly strong public support. Given the similar nature of Canadian and American societies and the transnational cultural influences, we are not likely often to face a situation in which our governments differ starkly over a major matter of foreign policy. In such a situation, we would probably be free to contract out of any association with United States policy. In the cases of Vietnam and the Dominican Republic, both in areas to which the alliance commitment does not extend, Canadian governments have remained aloof but have refrained from condemnation. In neither case was Canadian help seriously needed and in Vietnam Canada had the valid excuse of its obligation to the International Control Commission. The consequences for Canada have not been notable. Official denunciation by Canada or interference with defence production sharing would undoubtedly have provoked a dangerous reaction. It should be noted that a similar policy on Vietnam has been followed by most other Western countries, a fact which raises certain questions about the uniqueness of the Canadian position vis-à-vis the United States. In all cases, the reasons were probably the same: uneasiness about the American reaction to criticism, concern for the prestige of the "leader," a belief that United States policy was mistaken rather than wicked and could be influenced more effectively by persuasion than by condemnation, and divided opinion in the country about the Vietnam war. Whether this cautious attitude by Canada and other countries was wise or not, one cannot rule out the possibility that there will be occasions when Canada will feel obligated to dissociate itself flatly from United

States policy. Even in such a situation, however, the consequences should be calculated so that they can be coped with as well as possible.

My own conviction is that Canadian policy, as practised by governments and their diplomats, is a good deal more independent of that of the United States than is widely assumed. Those, for example, who talk about Canadian support of or "complicity" in United States policy in Vietnam concentrate their attention on the secondary (though not necessarily unimportant) factor of defence production and ignore the major factors, which are that Canada has not joined and has never considered joining the United States as an ally in this war—and has been free to do so—and that Canada acted contrary to American policy when it agreed to serve the Geneva agreements of 1954 from which the United States abstained. An examination of the positions adopted by allies of the United States on various international issues might be worth pursuing. I have no doubt that it would show Canada as having acted a good deal more independently than most of the others, Britain and Australia in particular. Those who want Canada to break free of the United States and follow what they consider an independent policy usually have of course something more drastic in mind than opposing United States tactics in particular situations. They differentiate between independence of manoeuvre within an accepted alliance relationship and a policy of "neutrality" in which the common interest and affinity with the United States would not be recognized. A basic question here is not only whether this would be in Canada's interest but whether it would accurately reflect the attitudes of the Canadian public which would have to support it—probably with a prospect of some personal sacrifice.

An assumption frequently made is that Canada cannot have an independent foreign policy because of United States "control" of Canadian industry. I will not touch here on the consequences of this "control" on our economic policy, which are obviously considerable, but rather on its effects on our general foreign and defence policy. Here we need a good deal more investigation. It is often stated as an obvious fact that United States control of Canadian industry must inhibit our general foreign policy, but this charge has been neither proved nor entirely disproved. It is necessary to be specific. What does United States control of our industry mean? There is no centralized control of American industry from Washington, and the control over Canadian industry comes from Houston or Pittsburgh or Denver on the part of people who are by no means in collusion with each other. These people in Houston and Pittsburgh may well have ideological objections to Canada's recognizing the Peking government or trading with Cuba, but the question is how effectively they can and do translate this personal bias into a real impact on Ottawa. Much has been made of the extension of United States trading restrictions to their Canadian subsidiaries. The United States government, as distinct from private United States industry, has been more co-operative and understanding in this matter than Canadians usually acknowledge, but it remains a genuine source of irritation. A source of irritation must be distinguished from a serious threat to the freedom of Canadian foreign policy. The export of a few Dodge engines to China is less important than the right to sell wheat to China or to recognize Peking, neither of which we have been prevented from doing. There are undoubtedly, as suggested above, inhibitions on our foreign policy arising out of our economic interests in the United States. Is it United States control of Canadian industries, however, which is the important factor or the power of Congress to ignore our interests? Certain American attitudes on world affairs are probably carried to the Canadian business community by its professional associations, but this is true of a variety of professions, including professional students.

The extent to which we are tied to the United States by defence production sharing agreements is a special matter. These agreements which, as suggested above, were sought by Canada and have been to our economic advantage, raised few questions until the Vietnam war, when the indirect supply of American matériel seemed contrary to the obligations of a member of the International Control Commission in Vietnam. Unless the whole broad series of agreements is renounced, it would be difficult for Canada to avoid the same kind of ''complicity'' in any other American war. There seems no practical way in which they can be suspended to cover only the particular situation in Vietnam. They would have to be removed entirely, and it would have to be seen whether this was possible, given the integration of Canadian and United States industry. For those who believe that this ''complicity'' is immoral, the economic consequences will not be the decisive factor. That these might be on such a scale as to weaken the national fabric and provoke United States ill will to a dangerous degree cannot be ignored. We may be saved this dilemma by a phasing out of the American war effort, but the question remains whether the likelihood of a similar situation arising in the future makes it desirable for us to become less dependent on defence production sharing. It may be, of course, that further differentiation of our military function, suggested above as a possibility, might diminish our claim for orders in any case.

Influencing United States Policy

The question of how to influence United States foreign policy has become a major preoccupation of students of Canadian foreign policy.

One has the impression sometimes that this is, in many minds, the sole aim of Canadian foreign policy—to find out what the Americans are doing and tell them not to. Because of the power of the United States, it is obviously important for Canada to consider its leverage in Washington as a significant element in its policy. Very often this is best exerted multilaterally rather than bilaterally. An examination of the Canadian record in the United Nations, from the ending of the Korean war to the present Canadian opposition in the Geneva disarmament commission to the United States-Soviet proposals on demilitarization of the seabed, suggests that combination with other countries is the effective way of resisting American policies. Occasionally, as in the question of sovereignty in the Arctic passages, the government is not confident of support from a majority of countries, and it must play its hand warily. There are many situations, both economic and military, in which Canada claims a special position vis-à-vis the United States and does not want to be lumped with the world at large. In most questions of world politics and strategy, in questions of economic development or international trade, working on the United States through international organizations seems the obvious path. On the other hand, on issues of continental defence or many financial and other economic issues there is not much help to be had from outside, and the best way seems to be to request special status in Washington. The danger is, of course, that this special status can be turned against Canada in the form of special obligations and expectations. ("We expected better of the Canadians whom we don't consider as foreigners.")

There are various methods of trying to have an impact on United States policy, one of which is through normal diplomatic channels, a method which has been misunderstood by critics of "quiet diplomacy" in principle. Diplomacy is by definition quiet. Every country in the world, like every individual and every private organization, rightly insists on the wisdom of discussion and of negotiation in confidence.[10] Canada would become a pariah in international society if its foreign service officers were not allowed to engage in confidential discussions with other diplomats. Governments can of course be too secretive; that is another issue. The possibility however that all diplomacy should from now on be through loudspeakers is a terrifying thought for peace-loving peoples. The United States normally seeks to influence Canada by "quiet diplomacy," but when it once used blunter methods, the issuance of the famous State Department "clarification" concerning Canadian policy on nuclear arms on 30 January 1963, it was denounced by Canadians of all parties for not observing the accepted rules of international behaviour. Sometimes quiet diplomacy is the wrong course because it has been tried and proved ineffectual, because public criticism of one country by another is more likely to have an effect in this particular circumstance, or because there is a moral issue at stake which requires a public pronouncement. Even when quiet diplomacy is being pursued and statements by government leaders are muted, this is not a policy which can or should in a democratic country be extended to the citizenry. But the role of Canadian citizens, either singly or in groups, in influencing the United States government and its citizens is of growing importance as the means of doing so multiply. A more effective use of extra-diplomatic channels to affect the United States Congress and administration, such as the Canadian-American parliamentary meetings, might well be explored. A problem for the citizen about "quiet diplomacy" is that if it is to be effective it has to remain quiet and he may not be aware of what has been done until the archives are released thirty years later. This is frustrating and unsatisfactory in a democracy. On the other hand instant disclosure might well weaken our position. This is another paradox of any diplomatic relationship with which we have to live.

A particular reason for quiet diplomacy in dealing with the United States on world issues is that the time when we are most likely to impinge on American policy formation is before the policy has been announced publicly. The formation of policy in Washington is almost like an international operation because of the many powerful agencies involved. An advantage of close association with the United States, based either on an alliance or on the continental status argument, is that we can often, though not always, fully or partially learn what the United States government is thinking before it has reached its conclusions. This is often the best time to strike. We would receive no secrets if we could not be relied upon to keep them to ourselves. Striking at this time is no guarantee of success, but influencing United States policy on a world issue is not easy by any means. Once policy has been formulated by agreement among the agencies in Washington and publicly announced, it is almost impossible to get it undone or revised. No country, certainly not Canada, likes to change its policy under public pressure from another. On the other hand, in certain circumstances public pressure from a number of countries, particularly friendly countries, can have an effect on Congress. Sometimes there is an argument for Ottawa to put on the record in the final stage its disapproval even if it no longer has much hope of changing the United States position. It could be useful in future—or it could just cause unnecessary irritation.

Diplomacy cannot be successful if it ignores the obvious rules of psychology. It involves not faceless forces but human beings. One pitfall of which we must be wary is too close identification with the United States opposition; another is the danger of being a nag. No country likes to think that the government of another country is in league with it opponents. The response of the Canadian government to General de Gaulle makes the Canadian attitude clear. The United States, like any other country, is run by political creatures. If Canadian spokesmen take public positions which give the impression that they are allying themselves with a party or individuals looked upon as antagonistic by the United States administration, then our public protests may be counterproductive.[11] It is not a question of whether American leaders ought to feel this way; it is a question of whether they as human beings do. On issues like relations with China or the war in Vietnam, Canadians are constantly being beseeched by American opponents of their own government's policies to speak up. This is not a request which can always be turned down, and sometimes it is wise to be associated with a certain world movement of opinion. On the other hand, from the viewpoint of tactical effectiveness, it may be the best way to gain the point.

The other factor to remember is that the president of the United States and the secretary of state are exceedingly busy men and there are approximately one hundred and twenty-five ambassadors in Washington anxious to see them. Canada has a special claim on some issues but not many. If we claim the special right of the Canadian ambassador to be at the head of the queue, then of course we are accepting a special relationship with the United States which can be turned against us when we want to be independent. Anyone who is submitted constantly to demands and complaints from another individual is likely to resent the other individual and be less disposed to agree with him or make concessions. Because of the breadth of the agenda of Canada-United States relations we are likely at any one time to have a large number of issues to take up. It will often be necessary, however, to establish priorities. If we want the Canadian ambassador or the secretary of state for external affairs or even the prime minister to make a personal appeal to the president, we have to save these appeals for the most important issues lest they lose their force.

The Structure of the Relationship

This analysis has been largely concerned with the questions of alliance which have preoccupied us in the past two decades. They will not go away just because we declare them old-fashioned, but one must wonder whether they are the major issues of the 1970s. Priorities will almost certainly shift to the dilemmas of the continental relationship. These are to a large extent questions of economics, but they pose intractable dilemmas about the structures within which the two countries exist and seek to flourish. The relevance of governments themselves is in question when the private connections are multiplying at such a rate as to threaten the authority of federal governments. The necessity of Canadian sovereignty becomes more apparent when it seems less significant.

Our problem as Canadians is that we cannot pursue logical conclusions too far. Logic often seems to point in the direction of integration, but integration is what we want to avoid. Our position is the reverse of that of the European countries under the Treaty of Rome. In their case they look to economic integration as a phenomenon which will encourage political integration.

Americans and Canadians on the other hand are seeking ways of rationalizing the continental economy without making political integration necessary. There seems little, if any, interest in the United States in political incorporation of Canada, and in Canada the advantages of a more tranquil state and a higher standard of living (as distinct from a higher level of income) have strengthened the will to political independence. At the same time, we are driven by the logic of proposals for North American solutions. The concept of a continental economy, for example, bears watching for political reasons. The continent developed unevenly in the past two centuries and when Americans have in mind a continental resources policy they no doubt think in terms of preserving the present balance. Canadians, on the other hand, have a strong interest in adjusting the balance in their favour. For this reason, therefore, American proposals based on the idea that water is a continental resource are quickly rejected in Canada. The Canadian aim has to be to develop its own industry not simply to feed the further expansion of American industry. The language of the continentalist is beguiling. Canada and the United States obviously have a common interest in developing peacefully and wisely the resources of the continent, but the fact should not be disguised that we are in competition as we always have been for a share of continental resources. This is not to say, of course, that in economics as in defence, there are not things which have to be tackled on a continental basis, but we must be cautious as well as sensible. We have to be careful also that other countries and international organizations do not, out of convenience, make us part of a unit called North America, because North America is not a political or administrative unit and if it is expected to speak in world affairs with one voice, the voice will not be ours.

The problem of integration as a principle for our structural relationship, either economically or politically, is that Canada becomes a minor shareholder in the policy-making instrument which is bound to be controlled largely by the major shareholder. Because of the implications of integration, however, the minor shareholder is bound by the decision. More appropriate to our needs has been the formula of the

International Joint Commission in which there is full recognition of joint interests through investigation by a common board of solutions which would be in the general interest. The decisions, however, are left to the two independent legislatures. The same principle and the same advantage was to be found in the Permanent Joint Board on Defence in its more active days. A question to be investigated is whether devices of this kind can cope with the enormously increasing volume of business. Should we look to a multiplication of such bodies? Should we try to co-ordinate the Canadian-American bodies and rationalize them into a single instrument of which they would be subcommittees, or is that the inevitable road to an experiment in supranational government which is bound for Canadians to prove an illusion?

These questions are beyond the scope of the present examination, but the answers we find will deeply affect our foreign and defence policies. If we decide that on balancing the advantages and disadvantages, the integrated continental economy is best for us or that we have gone too far to resist, then many of the arguments outlined in this paper become irrelevant. It might then be best to seek a special status in the making of foreign and defence policy as, it has been said, "a kind of extra-territorial Texas." The probability, of course, is that we shall do nothing so clear cut but will pursue our national genius for improvising conditions workable but undefinable. For the time being at any rate, the option of a reasonably independent foreign policy reasonably pursued, within reason, may retain our Canadian identity in international affairs.

Notes

[1] The important points to note in this analogy may be that in spite of its hostility the United States never used the military force at its command to conquer Cuba or drive out its government. It resorted to sanctions, which could be resisted by a country which had a totalitarian government and was an island. Its will to overthrow Castro was obvious, but for reasons which are worthy of study it never deployed its full military power to accomplish that end.

[2] From the exchange of notes of 12 May 1958 establishing the North American Air Defence Command.

[3] On 2 February 1970 Prime Minister Trudeau, in reply to an enquiry in the House of Commons concerning President Nixon's statement that his administration proposed to proceed with the second stage of the Safeguard ABM system, said that there was as yet no evidence that the earlier announcement by the United States had in fact created an escalation of the arms race, as the Canadian government had feared. Nevertheless, he stated that the government was not happy "that a friend and ally of such importance should be seeing its way to peace in this direction." The dissociation from the United States ABM programme was futher emphasized when Mr. Sharp, in reply to a subsequent

question, gave the assurance that this decision by the United States ''was made quite independently of any consultation with us.''

⁴The nuclear committee recently set up in NATO is cited as an example of improved means of sharing policy-making. This is undoubtedly true, but there is a question whether it can have much effect on American decisions to commit themselves to this or that form of technological development in continental defence. There is always, of course, the opportunity for Canadians to participate in the intellectual process by which doctrines are developed if they have adequate information.

⁵It can of course be argued that it has been ever since the last war but we have been slow to recognize it.

⁶It is presumably easier for us to be non-belligerent in a war which the United States wages without declaring war; a formal state of war by the United States would involve a change in the status of all their defence activities out of which it would be harder for their continental partner to opt. This is an uncertain area which requires investigation.

⁷The rationale might be similar to that of General de Gaulle's famous policy of *tous azimuts*.

⁸There has been in Canada official and even more vigorous public ill will over United States policies in various parts of the Far East and in Latin America, but the point is that the absence of an alliance has reduced the amount of intergovernmental friction.

⁹''The United States as a National Security Threat to Canada,'' *Behind the Headlines*, XXIX (July 1970) 9, 10.

¹⁰It is the Peking government rather than the Canadians who have insisted on the confidential nature of the discussions over recognition in Stockholm.

¹¹There is reason to believe that President Johnson's coolness towards Canada was attributable to the fact that he thought Canadians were playing Senator Fulbright's game.

3:

Canada, Latin America, and United States Foreign Policy

The need for Americans to put Canada into some category is admittedly a problem. Nous ne sommes pas comme les autres. The tendency to group us with other nations of the sacred hemisphere was understandable if wrong-headed. There is a considerable functional distinction between the issues that arise with Canada and those with the Latin countries, although there are always interesting parallels. That Canada is a burden they have to regard as unique is increasingly understood in Washington, as revealed in the special institutions they are now setting up to cope with it. It is disconcerting for Canadians to find themselves in sessions with all the other species of Americans. Canada, they are aware, has been invited as an afterthought and the patterns under discussion don't fit very well. However, under the inspiration of an ex-Ottawan, Barry Farrell, there is at Northwestern University a course on United States relations with Latin America and Canada in which Canada is very much a centre of attention. A visiting lecturer must cope with several hundred students in a class who are unexpectedly and uncannily aware not only of Canadian policies but also of Canadian ploys. So when in 1972 there was a conference at Northwestern on "Canada, Latin America, and United States Foreign Policy" it was not based on false assumptions. The purpose was to listen to Latin Americans and Canadians provide their perspectives on United States foreign policy. So, of course, the Americans listened while their guests argued among themselves—the Latins with the Latins and the Canadians with the Canadians. It provided an exceedingly useful perspective for a Canadian to look at the subject beyond the conventional attitudes of the debate within Canada, and the paper presented to the conference was considerably revised afterwards. It has been published only in Spanish in R. Barry Farrell, ed., Latin America, Canada and United States Foreign Policy *(Mexico: Fondo de Cultura Economica, 1974).*

231

Shortly after the last war the *Manchester Guardian,* commenting on British foreign policy, suggested that it seemed simply a matter of finding out what the Russians were doing and telling them not to. Americans must sometimes wonder whether their assumed friends work on a similar principle applied to the United States. This assumption that whatever the United States does is bound to be wrong seems, however, to be shared by many articulate Americans. A stubborn persistence in the past decade in courses which have proved wrong has offered some justification. Unless one accepts, however, a determinist interpretation by which all action of an imperial power is malevolent, such simplistic assumptions about the foreign policy of any country are unprofitable. Never having accepted the view prevalent in Washington twenty years ago that all the ill in the world could be traced to a switchboard in the Kremlin, I find the fashionable contemporary view that the CIA is the source of all evil even less convincing.

I do not think a significant number of people in Canada, or in Latin America accept this perverse theory about the United States. They too often talk as if they did, and therefore their criticism, lacking consistency, is counter-productive in Washington. I am not suggesting that logic and consistency necessarily prevail on the banks of the Potomac; or that United States policy is itself consistent. It seems at the moment particularly contradictory because some of it is so good. What I emphasize is the obligation on non-Americans to resolve our inconsistencies. The mistakes Washington makes are more consequential than ours. Nevertheless, we are under the same obligation to conduct our policies with due regard to the world community. We must co-operate with larger powers rather than contract out to enjoy the luxury of criticism.

We suggest often enough what we do not want the United States to be and do. We give too little thought to the difficult question: what role do we want the United States to play? We give the impression that we would like the United States just to go away, end the Cold War by abandoning one side of it, shut down its arms factories, demobilize its armed forces, and get all its troops off other people's soil. One principle that seems agreed upon is non-intervention. However, no sooner have we banished the Americans to impotence than we insist they intervene promptly in Bengal, Rhodesia, or Czechoslovakia. We cannot make up our minds whether to cast the United States as bogyman or fairy godmother. It must on no account intervene in other countries, but somehow it must support peoples' movements. These contradictions are not, of course, always mouthed by the same critics; I am thinking of the impression given by a chorus. If, as is likely, we assign to the United States a large and active role in maintaining world security and promoting prosperity, we should accept the fact that the United States must maintain armed forces and cultivate its own economic capacity and that it is likely to favour countries it regards as partners and expect some sacrifices to be shared. In a world as complex as ours it is bound, furthermore, to determine its policies without taking into full consideration the conflicting wishes of one hundred or more clamorous countries. It should listen to others more than it does but the exigencies of superpowerdom are facts we have to live with.

First of all we must ask ourselves how we regard the possibility of a United States retreat from its over-extended responsibilities. The balance of argument in favour of military withdrawal from the Asian continent has grown stronger the more we have realized the disastrous results of continuing involvement. The argument for withdrawal from Europe is less obvious because it remains the will of democratically elected West European governments to have American forces remain. American bases are being dismantled in Africa, and as far as Latin America and Canada are concerned there are few American forces or bases to withdraw. It is the possible intervention of American troops rather than their presence which has been a grievance in the Americas. The case for withdrawal of the American navy to home waters has been less strong. We may not like its landing marines here and there or threatening Bangladesh, but so long as other superpowers are active at sea the policing should be international. At the very least we should be grateful for United States strength abroad in the air and at sea when there is a natural or a human disaster. If the United States is to pull in its horns, it is essential to build within the United Nations an infrastructure for international action to cope with floods and earthquakes. If there is to be further UN peacekeeping, some substitute will have to be found for the transport largely provided in the past by the United States. A world so interconnected as our global village requires patrolling. It is easier and cheaper to leave these things to one, or preferably more than one, great power because if we want a truly international pax rather than a pax Americana or pax Americana-Sovietica we have to pay for it—and we know from experience how difficult it would be to make it work.

There is a case, nevertheless, for a little American isolationism. The West Europeans, if they accept the NATO strategy, must do more themselves. The United States, as the organizer of the Western alliance and the idea of a coalition of the righteous to maintain world order, was too bossy. In the early days other countries were weak and the United States had to bear the brunt. By cajoling other countries to make contributions, the United States provoked the idea that contributions to NATO were not to a common effort but to the United States. Even in southeast Asia the United States was begged to intervene by local authorities. But this historic truth can become irrelevant when a country so powerful and so mechanistic has taken charge of its intervention. We cannot return to attitudes which prevailed about the benevolence of

234 CANADA: A MIDDLE-AGED POWER

American protection before the Vietnam war, but there is good reason for withdrawal at least until it becomes clear that in places and in circumstances of another kind American help will be wanted and justified. This retreat towards fortress America would seem to please Rightists at home and Leftists everywhere. The latter have been crying, ''Yankee go home,'' for years, and a lot of old Yankees are welcoming the message.

The trouble is that when we come up against the harsh, rough voice of American isolationism we are frightened by its implications. Isolationism has not only military but also economic aspects. Consider the shocked response to the Nixon economic policies of August 1971. It was not so much the measures themselves which frightened us as the voices crying for protection and a reversion to the ruthless attitudes on American interests characteristic of United States governments before their view of their role was transformed in the Marshall Plan and Point IV. How much we need and want American investment may be a matter of debate. American trade, however, is something none of us can get along without. However much we prefer a variety of markets, the unique absorptive capacity of the United States is in the foreseeable future irreplaceable.

If one believes that the confrontation with the communist powers was the result of United States provocation and that the wars in Asia, Africa, and elsewhere are the deliberate gestures of neo-imperialism, then there is a logical case for welcoming total United States disarmament and withdrawal of all its forces and investments from abroad. That premise is too simple for me to accept, but for those who do, nothing I say will be relevant. It takes, of course, strong conviction to face the consequences. Whether or not Soviet arms were only a response to provocation, they are now of terrifying proportions, and the Soviet military machine is showing the same disposition as the American to strengthen itself. There are other awesome military machines in existence. These are not Cold War fantasies; they are Cold War facts. The problem of how to paralyse this weaponry is far from academic. No government in the world, not even the revolutionaries in Peking, seems disposed to pack up its arms and take a chance. Smaller countries may do so because modern technology renders dubious their chance to defend themselves anyway. The balance of power is not a policy one advocates; it is a situation one deals with. Those who say we can abolish war only by changing people are right, but there has to be some world-wide balance of the power of changed people. The Cold War now is a matter of reverberations which will set off explosions if they are not tranquillized. Finding out who was to blame for starting the vibrations is a useful exercise, but it doesn't eliminate the consequences.

We are dependent for day-to-day survival on an equilibrium arrived at by accident and by design. The paradox which brings the constant danger of war is that the confrontation may in itself become a framework to guarantee peace.[1] The SALT talks point in this direction. In the discussion about a European security conference, mutual and balanced force reductions, not unilateral disarmament, are the aim. How long the SALT game can continue in the face of China's emergence is uncertain. In principle, at least, one can see better prospects of equilibrium if it becomes multipolar. An advantage of this present tug-of-war situation over earlier concepts of universal collective security is that it is less conservative. It allows for shifts in the status quo without imposing universal war. Whatever we as individuals think of it as a way to run the world, we have to face up to the certainty that those now firmly in charge of governments, communist, non-communist, or neutralist, are going to play the game of balance for the foreseeable future — however beautiful and sincere their protestations that they are doing nothing of the kind.

We have to ask ourselves, therefore, whether the military impotence of the United States is in anybody's interest. It is not necessary to believe in the virtue of Western capitalism or the wickedness of communism to consider that it is healthier to have among the three or four pillars of the system one which is representative of what is called Western civilization. A deplorable aspect of the Vietnam aberration is that it has discredited American power and we cannot see it in proper perspective. It is hard to argue for the maintenance of American military strength when it is being used for abhorrent purposes. In predicting American foreign policy, however, we might better regard Vietnam not as a precedent but as a traumatic experience. The war has eventually proved that in the United States there is a system of checks and balances. We have been acutely conscious of how slowly it has worked, but it works in ways hard to discern in the more obscure superpowers. We ought to oppose by all means at our disposal the criminal lunacy of over-kill by both superpowers and the continuation of dangerous testing by four powers, but should we expect the United States to abandon its position in weapons technology?

One kind of limited isolationism sometimes suggested for the United States is a retreat into regionalism. A superpower cannot easily extract itself from the world-wide system of deterrence or renounce its economic as well as its security investment in other continents. The most one could expect would be a shift of emphasis, the according of a priority, in rhetoric at least, to the affairs of the Western Hemisphere. As Canadians and Latin Americans complain that the United States does not accord them the attention they deserve, we should be gratified. Or should we? To what extent do we really want the United States to concentrate its attention upon us? Some Latin American countries would still like an increased share of the diminishing United States public and private budgets for economic development, although others seem prepared to live by their conviction that United States economic aid does more harm than good. Canada has never received governmental aid from the United States. Whether it wants more private American investment is a question on which Canadians have not made up their own minds. What we all want are better terms of trade with the United States, but whether we should seek a special arrangement for the Western Hemisphere is doubtful. If the EEC, with Africa linked to it, eventually becomes a closed economic bloc and something similar develops under Japanese aegis in East Asia, then we might have to consider whether we want to defend our interests in a pan-American economic community. For the time being, however, the fight against economic blocism seems worth carrying on in universal forums.

If continentalism seems to be winning out elsewhere, we are more likely to be driven into continental than hemispheric solutions in the Americas. Latin American economic collaboration is a more concrete objective than an unnatural economic union of the two continents. Those in Washington who take a backs-to-the-wall attitude now about the enlarged EEC, the threat of Japan and other protectionist powers, seem more interested in a North American continental fortress. They emphasize to Canadians the common interest we are believed to have in protecting our joint economy against Europeans and Asians. Canadians think of a North American common market or similar schemes as a last resort, something to be avoided because of their political implications. For political reasons they might be more attracted by a pan-American economic agglomeration, as they have preferred multilateral to bilateral associations with the United States. Whatever the political attractions, however, the economic argument is unconvincing. Although Canadians are ambivalent about "continentalism" they would rather have their own relationship with the United States than be assimilated in a regional framework with countries whose anxieties and requirements are not parallel with their own.

In international politics and security our attitude towards regionalism is also paradoxical. Many people in Latin America and in Canada still look to the United States as our defender against both conventional and unconventional aggression from communist powers. However, fear of a military threat from overseas has diminished. If it came in a missile attack the question is whether the rest of us would be targets only if we are associated with the defence of the United States. Latin Americans who regard the United States as their protector presumably think of it more as a pillar of the "free world" in a terrestrial context than as a country which will rush to their defence against an attack from the

Soviet Union or some unforeseeable overseas threat. The concept of the United States as protector has diminished in Canada, but a majority still believe they have a stake in the United States deterrent and should contribute to its defence. The problem for Canadians is what meaningful contribution they can make in an alliance where the strategic decisions are inevitably taken by the larger partner.

In such circumstances it is hard to see a case for a hemispheric security organization. Even the case for a united front against guerrillas has weakened as the Left disunites. There is no urgent need to dismantle existing bilateral and multilateral security arrangements which associate us with the United States in the various ways in which we want to be associated. To what extent the Organization of American States should be strengthened or maintained seems largely a matter for Latin Americans to decide. The meeting at Viña del Mar in which Latin Americans caucused to present a unified position to the United States may give the organization a new *raison d'être*. It is not one, however, which encourages Canadian entry. Canadians would not want to be part of a North American bloc in the OAS. The suggested role for Canada of mediator between the United States and the Latin Americans should be regarded as an occasional rather than a professional occupation. If Washington wants to strengthen the hemispheric association it would be well advised in the present climate to listen but avoid leadership. The present untidy network of associations works reasonably well and is adaptable to such desirable moves as closer unity of Latin Americans. We should discourage compulsive organizers attracted to grand designs for a new Western Hemisphere. The trouble with a new Western Hemisphere regionalism is the same trouble there has always been. All parts of it have their own deep involvements in other continents. As a pole-to-pole area it is strategically and economically incomprehensible. In the age of intercontinental missiles, intercontinental guerrillas, and intercontinental corporations, it is hard to find a function even for the Monroe Doctrine.

For Canadians an American interest in continentalism is a more urgent concern. Fear has been expressed that the United States, rebuffed militarily in Asia and faced with powerful economic blocs abroad, will pursue a new manifest destiny, some signs of which are detectable. What worries Canadians is that the United States, short of power to maintain its fantastic industry and standard of living, will take a more ruthless attitude towards resources existing on this continent. The President has himself suggested that he would like talks with Canada about a continental resources policy, and Canadians have shuddered for reasons which are perhaps hard for Americans to understand. They have feared that the Nixon economic measures of August 1971 indicated an intention to force them into acquiescence. If we are to avoid serious clashes, Americans outside as well as inside Washington should understand this Canadian fear of "continentalism." Americans may well be confused because a debate rages in Canada on the subject. There are Canadians happy to exploit the American need for oil, gas, or water power to make a quick buck. They assure their American friends that economic nationalism in Canada is just the yacking of a bunch of feckless professors—but they are only partly right. The federal government is increasingly responsive to those who argue that Canada, if it is not to remain a subsidiary producer of raw material for a wealthy, populous American industrial state, must conserve these resources to develop further its own industry and population.

Americans may find it difficult to understand why Canadians would not be interested in continental planning based on fair shares. The Canadian argument is that if the Americans have used up prodigally their share of resources they ought not to consider Canadian resources, and in particular Canadian water power, as continental. If fair shares implies an acceptance of the status quo, that does not appeal to Canadians as they believe they have the wherewithal to increase their ratio of industry and population. Canadians have learned, furthermore, that it is unwise to have American industry and settlement become dependent on Canadian sources of energy. They know, for example, that if a large industry and new cities grow up in the American northwest on power and irrigation from Canada, to cut off the flow when it is needed at home would be a *casus belli.* It may take a good deal of understanding on the part of Americans if heating and lighting and air conditioning, as well as industry, in the United States should run down while Canadians enjoy the advantages of a larger ratio of resources to population. The United States has been a good neighbour of Canada when Americans had no obvious reason to envy the Canadian standard of living. How would they adjust if the Canadian quality of life is apparently higher?

There will be opportunities for Americans to play rough. There is a difference of view between Canadian provincial governments, including that of Quebec, and the federal government on selling resources to the United States and importing United States investment. The opportunities for American private as well as public interests to exploit this difference are obvious. A Canadian can only plead that Americans bear in mind their long-range interest in a healthy and reasonably united Canada on their border. Americans might bear in mind also that Canada was created and confederated by threats from the south.

A Canadian considering what he would like the United States to do or not do is confronted with the amorphousness and intangibility of "the

United States" or "the Americans." How can one persuade or force or even bargain with this "it" or "them?"

On questions of foreign and defence policy the government in Washington takes decisions, but the way to the decision-making process is difficult. The State Department, through which Canadian diplomats deal, is not decisive, and to secure attention a foreign government has to campaign on many fronts. It has to get involved in the political side of government but avoid the kind of involvement with opposition elements which would turn sour the powers-that-be. We cannot ask the United States to alter its form of government. We can plead for deeper understanding of Canada or we can make American legislators conscious of the strength of our bargaining hand. Well-meaning Americans from time to time suggest that Canada might have observer status in the Senate or some formal right to a part in the United States decision-making process. This is for Canadians the wrong kind of solution. It would simply commit Canada in advance—morally if not constitutionally—to share responsibility for policies in the making of which it had a more assured position but on which its influence could rarely be decisive. More interesting might be a special right to point out, before important American foreign and defence policy decisions are made, in what respects they could harm Canada. In the case of ABMs, for example, a Canadian opportunity to explain the consequences on Canadian territory was reasonable to expect. It would be a right of complaint only, not intended to imply that policy made in Washington should be considered joint policy. However, we would have to reckon with political assumptions rather than legal obligations. Favoured treatment based on a continental association would diminish Canadian independence because it would encourage an assumption of partnership which makes a Canadian government's decision to go its own way look like disloyalty.

Canadians talk too often as if it was their sovereignty which is at issue rather than their freedom of movement. Canada's sovereignty, its legal right to do what it likes, is limited only by international agreements to which it has freely subscribed. What we are concerned about is what a country can get away with in a world in which its sprawling interests drive it in contrary directions. Rivers across borders flow in both directions. Sometimes it is in our interest to maintain downstream benefits and sometimes it is in the interests of the United States to do so. That is what foreign relations across a long continental dividing line are largely about. There is nothing the United States need do to assure us of our sovereignty in general, although there are some specific questions of encroachment on our sovereignty in the north and by the extraterritorial application of United States economic legislation. These are, however, aspects of the manoeuvering for advantage which is endemic in a divided continent. The United States government has the absolute power to get away with what it wants. Canadians can appeal to its better instincts, take it to court, or retaliate. The threat of retaliation varies in effectiveness depending on the issue but, as the recent controversy over the surcharge revealed, there is a healthy realization on both sides that it involves an escalation which is in no one's best interest.

Dealing with the United States government is relatively simple. Our major problems result from the exuberant operations of American private enterprises of all kinds, industrial and cultural, over which Washington has limited control. The United States government can be an ally in seeking to restrain operations by American enterprises which do harm abroad. Not only in the State Department but also in other policy-making establishments in Washington there are people concerned with the global relationship with Canada and disturbed at Americans who upset this. Appeals by Canada have alleviated the impact of American legislation governing, in accordance with American not Canadian foreign policy, the American subsidiaries in Canada—notably in connection with sales to China. Some Canadians complain that their diplomats who deal with Americans turn soft. They forget the importance for Canada of the softening up process of their opposite numbers. Diplomats and other bureaucrats recognize more clearly than most citizens that we must not play a zero-sum game in North America.

Most Canadians are aware that the American economic threat is a hydra-headed creature. Nevertheless, too much political rhetoric implies that we are faced with a monolith, rather like Mr. Dulles's vision of the Kremlin, in a vast conspiracy against our independence and prosperity. The trouble with that assumption is not so much that it is unfair as that it is a wrong diagnosis. Even efforts to apply it systemically get awfully far-fetched because Canada is very awkwardly type-cast as the victim of imperialism. *Le défi américain* is the product of the enormous vitality of the American economy and the American culture. It is based not in Washington but in New York and Houston and Hollywood and Cambridge, Mass., and is anything but monolithic. The United States government could not bottle it even if it wanted to. This "threat" is regarded by most Canadians as a mixed blessing. Before we know what, if anything, we want the United States government to do about it, we have to decide what restrictions 22 million Canadians can agree on. And in most cases it is up to the Canadian rather than the United States government to do something.

Canadians too often think their problems are unique, but *le défi américain* is universal. We resent the way progress and modernization are regarded as synonyms for Americanization, but we make the same mistake in reverse by identifying the evils of industrialization and pollution with one country. American corruption is an advance case of a universal disease. We want to profit from American mistakes but we do not escape the disease by quarantining the United States. Consider, for example, the problems posed by the prevalence in Canada of foreign, especially American, corporations. The question of multinational corporations is a complex issue for the world at large. There is a growing opinion that these corporations must be brought under some control and that it is in the interests of the United States as well as other governments that this be done. However, the imposition of controls raises almost as many problems as it solves. Because of the ramifications, we are not likely to get at the main issues by a bilateral approach. There are plenty of Americans concerned with the problem in and out of Washington, and we are more likely to make progress if we regard this as a co-operative international enterprise rather than an anti-American campaign.

In the meantime there are advantages in that the American ''threat'' is undisciplined. None of the great corporations is guided solely by the national interests of the United States. The pressures and interests that determine their policies have become multinational even if special. Far be it from me to argue, like some romantic apologists, that multinational corporations ought to be left unchecked because in the process of the market they reflect the interests of the peoples of the world, but they are caught up in the paradoxes. There are advantages for host countries in these corporations competing against each other. Furthermore, their competitive stake in a country such as Canada obliges them to lobby in Washington for the Canadian claims in which they have an interest. There would be more cause to fear industrial manifest destiny if Washington had totalitarian control. A Marxist argues that the socialist ethic would take the sting out of the American threat. Perhaps it would if a state could be produced able or prepared in a naughty world to abide by classical principles of socialism. Examples we have had have not been encouraging. Americans have had messianic visions of their service to the world through free enterprise. Messianism can have capitalist or socialist labels to justify national advantage. So, aside from the fact that a socialist United States seems quite a way off, it is doubtful whether this slogan offers a precise solution. What we need is more pragmatism on the Right and on the Left.

For a healthy national life Canadians have to impose some restrictions on the entry of American industry, capital, and culture. It is better to act positively by developing our own resources, but such is the power of American industry and the American media that tender plants are strangled or brought out before they acquire roots. Our government has the power to do what seems necessary, subject to international agreements like GATT, provisions of international law, and its concern to avoid retaliation. As far as the United States government and people are concerned, all we can do is ask them to be understanding and not be cowed by excessive demands from their own special pleaders. We must ask Americans to recognize that we are not two equal states but one overdeveloped and one underdeveloped country, and it is not fair to expect in all things reciprocity. The anxiety to control our resources is not to be dismissed as "emotionalism" or "anti-Americanism." It is an assertion of the same civic ethic of self-reliance as that in which Americans are indoctrinated. History might have made us a single continental community, but it did not. This is not an error to be corrected but a blessing to be counted, for North America in the twentieth century is too vast to be governed from a single centre. Americans have an infuriating tendency to call Canadian resistance "nationalism," the assumption being that the cause of the American bank or publication which wants entry into Canada is "internationalism." Genuine anti-Americans are a small but shrill minority in Canada. They have the same views on American policy as radical Americans, but the latter come out as anti-nationalists and the former are called nationalist anti-Americans. If Americans do not want to swell their ranks they must distinguish between the predominant forms of nationalism in Canada and malevolent anti-Americanism.

If there are to be Canadian airlines and railways and a Canadian broadcasting and television service, we have to use the resources of the state because our private interests cannot compete against American giants. We can admire the good work done by CBS or NBC, but we could not expect that Canadian television in their hands would pay the attention to our own problems and policies essential for the nourishment of a healthy state. There is no question of banning American television. The majority of Canadians live close enough to the border to receive it directly. We have to prevent take-over of our newspapers. Alarm has been sounded about the publishing industry, control of which is being bought by wealthy American and French companies. It was a conservative, not a radical, government in Ontario which recently prevented the sale to Americans of an established Canadian publishing firm. It is wrong-headed to identify these defensive mechanisms with book burning. Canada is probably the most liberal country in the world in accepting foreigners, foreign culture, and investment. We have welcomed them so liberally into our universities that we are now concerned about the Canadian content in our education. If we do not want our young citizens to apply the standards of the American political system to our own, it is not because those standards are bad but because they are inapplicable. You cannot run a machine with parts from a different motor.

In all fairness I should add that Americans ought not to let Canadians get away with the "poor young country" stance, which is often disreputable blackmail. We are as old as the United States, and although we look poor in the continental shadow we are one of the world's great economic powers. The modesty we display is at times a front for our reluctance to accept the responsibility of a major power in world economics. The special consideration we request as an unequal partner at the bargaining table with the United States need not be extended by the world at large.

Many Canadians, if asked what they would like the United States to do, would put it negatively. The United States should stop pushing us about; it should allow us more freedom in our international relations. Asked to be more specific about the constraints placed on Canadian independence, the Canadian would be hard pressed to document his complaint. There is little available evidence of United States dictation. The extent of United States "control" of Canadian industry is often produced as evidence, but that foreign controlled enterprises determine our foreign policy is unproven. The implications of this foreign "control" for the freedom of Canada to manage its own economy is another matter. The United States consistently presses its views about policies it would like Canada to follow, but this is normal diplomatic intercourse among allies. It might be easier to list awards meted out to Canada by an American administration grateful for Canadian co-operation in international enterprises.[2] One would search hard for concrete examples of retaliations or sanctions handed out as punishment to Canada for misbehaving.[3] It might be argued, of course, that Canada has never sufficiently "misbehaved" to bring down upon itself such a reaction. The Canadian recognition of Peking was delayed until the American attitude had grown soft. The continuation of Canadian economic and diplomatic relations with Cuba was passive. Even so, it soured the attitude of some Congressmen on issues which would have benefited Canada.

But this kind of argument is unreal. The restraints upon Canadian diplomacy by the United States operate like the system of deterrence. It is doubtful if the United States has ever calculated a conscious Canadian policy of any kind. The strength of deterrence, however, is in the mind of the beholder. It is the restraints Canadians place upon themselves out of consideration for American attitudes or possible American attitudes which are the determining factor. These restraints, it should be understood, are not inspired only by fear or by the hope of favour. For the most part they are a consequence of the alliance diplomacy in which Canada has freely participated and an abiding conviction that maintenance of the strength and prestige of the United States is in the interest of the Western alliance in general and of Canada in particular. This conviction is not as universally accepted as it was twenty years ago but the assumption of basic common interest still guides official and majority opinion. What I am concerned with here, however, are the restraints imposed by worry over the consequences to the vulnerable Canadian economy of action displeasing to Americans. We have to judge on a basis of speculation, because the United States has never shown what it would do, and undoubtedly Americans do not know themselves what they would do if Canada provoked them seriously. Now if Canada were to join the Warsaw Pact or offer the People's Republic of China bases on Vancouver Island, drastic military action by the United States might be contemplated. But the most any substantial body of Canadians advocates is disengagement from a specific military association with the United States like NORAD. The chances of Canada actually wanting to join a coalition hostile to the United States are simply not worth thinking about unless one wants to be mischievous. In the present international atmosphere, and with the diminished importance of Canadian real estate to the defence of the United States, the worst Canadians could expect from such a move would be an erosion of the consideration accorded to an ally. More serious would be a conviction in Washington that a ruthless defence of American interests was now justified in all relations with its northern neighbour. Some Canadians would argue that that is the way Americans act anyway, but they should think hard over what the United States could do if its actions were restrained by no good will at all.

So Canadian policy towards the United States has been cautious. Its "independence" has never been put to the test because of a basic community of thinking. To see this as evidence of systemic bondage is a reasonable enough analysis, but the policy implications are beyond the grasp or the will of contented bondsmen. If Canada wants to disregard entirely the interests of the United States, it must reduce its present dependence on the United States economy. In fact Canada is already stronger than Canadians have assumed and its foreign policies have often been too timid. We cure this, however, by acting less timidly, not by telling Americans to stop doing what they are not in fact doing. Some Canadians now argue that we ought to make greater use of the cards we hold—in particular the growing dependence of the United States on Canadian resources and the stake of Americans in Canadian industry. Canadians, however, must ponder whether it is in the interests of the weaker party to start playing poker. Washington might be tempted to pull all its cards together and come up with a Canadian policy.

My point is that this kind of constraint is not something which can be ended by unilateral American action. It is a product of the sheer existence of enormous power, which is by nature intimidating. A dilemma for Canadians is to determine whether Americans will be less intimidating if one deals toughly with them or if one makes certain sacrifices to maintain their good will. There are sound reasons for combining firm defence of national rights with reassurance that no threat to the security and prosperity of the United States can come through Canada. The strongest argument for remaining in some form of military alliance with the United States is that a rupture would provide an excuse for Americans to refuse consideration of Canadian interests. It is foolish to talk about "solving" the problems of the Canada-United States relationship. A border of this extent goes on generating problems. If Canadians want to gain as many points as possible they have to keep their wits about them. They should avoid provoking the United States into having a Canadian policy. Canadian survival has depended on recognizing that Canadian-American relations comprise an enormous number of strands, that we negotiate sometimes from strength and sometimes from weakness, but our total weakness would be considerable if the United States was a phenomenon in the singular.

North America is not only two sovereign states; it is a systemic agglomeration, and its relations are a cobweb over which no government can have full control. One way Americans can help is to join Canadians in trying to understand the nature of this system and help improve it. If American political economists could take their eyes off the Western European system or the politics of even remoter continents to look more intensely at their own, Canadians would not have to consider Canadian-American relations in such a suffocatingly unilateral way. I have emphasized the importance of American understanding of Canadian problems, not only so that United States policies will be just and aware, but also so that Americans in and out of office will exercise forbearance when Canadians have to do things that look hostile. I realize that the United States involvement is world wide and Americans have to concentrate their attention on those countries which cause them the most trouble. However, when I read the news in American papers or look at the curricula of American universities I wonder if Americans ever look at a map. What on earth do they make of that great pink blob which is all over them and larger? When I find books on American foreign policy, even a recent book on American "imperialism," in which Canada does not appear in the index except in some historic references marked "See Great Britain," I wonder how Americans can begin to understand the history of their own country. It is curious and perverse that these histories talk much about Mexico where the American record is infamous and ignore Canada, the very existence of which inspires grave doubts about the proposition that imperialism is as American as apple pie.

What we need is a more adult relationship on both sides. We have to recognize that we are friends and foreigners and that foreigner is not a pejorative word. Our relations cannot be solved by good will alone. Our common interest in a peaceful and prosperous world must be assumed, but we are also natural competitors. Americans who believe in the competitive system must—and for the most part do—accept competition as a normal aspect of relations between friendly powers. The relations are complex and we have to work at them. They can go smoothly or roughly, but they will never go away. Perhaps North Americans are misled by the same romantic notions about alliance that we are said to have about marriage.

Notes

[1] For an effective argument to this effect see Gérard Bergeron, *La guerre froide inachevée* (Montréal: Les presses de l'université de Montréal, 1971).

[2] President Johnson's support for the auto pact Canada wanted in 1964 was partly attributable to the good will inspired by Canada's initiative in getting a UN force into Cyprus, although there was no bargain struck in advance.

[3] I am not suggesting that our close link with and dependence on the United States economy is of no consequence in our foreign policy, but it ought not to be thought of in these concrete terms. The spillover in attitudes from the American and Canadian business community may be more important. Intellectual subservience in Canada is to be found most often among the Old Right and the New Left.

4:

Impact of Domestic Political Factors

An encouraging development in recent years has been the attention now being devoted by American scholars to the nature of the relationship with Canada. That Canada is a boring phenomenon may remain a widespread conviction. The discovery is that the relationship is a fascinating international and transnational phenomenon—and the computers are beginning to click. It will be of great advantage to Canadian political scientists to have, at last, a dialogue on the subject, although the new American research will make it harder for Canadians to get away with those instant best-sellers on the subject for which facts are selected to suit the native appetite for victimization. A notable contribution has been made by the editors of the admirable quarterly, International Organization, *in its autumn 1974 issue (© 1974 by the Regents of the University of Wisconsin System). This issue, which was produced by the indefatigable Alfred O. Hero of the World Peace Foundation with the assistance of Annette Baker Fox of Columbia and Joseph S. Nye, Jr. of Harvard, scholars whose distinction has done a good deal for the cause, appeared after the editors and contributors had experienced conferences at Harvard and at Carleton where their drafts were refined in crossfire. The following is the approximately fifth draft of an essay in which my assignment was to provide an impression of the political factors on the Canadian side as an introduction to the scholarly examinations to follow. The hope of political science is, of course, that if the data on the relationship can be subjected to much more objective and ''transnational'' scrutiny and quantification, there will be less, if any, need for this kind of subjective writing.*

The major difference between Canadians and Americans on the subject of their relationship is in the intensity of their perceptions. There is bound to be conflict between a people who regard the relationship as critical and those who have scarcely noticed the other country. Firmly fixed in the Canadian view is the idea that a special relationship has come to an end. When the British contemplated the end of their special relationship with the United States, they were interested in an alternative—association with the European Economic Community (EEC). The problem for Canadians is that no alternative association seems clear, attractive, or promising. In light of their relative comfort in the energy crisis of 1973, however, the need for any special relationship has seemed less urgent.

The Special Relationship

There has been a notable Canadian ambivalence about the special relationship, and it is not surprising that some outspoken Americans are telling Canadians that they can no longer have their cake and eat it too. That means specifically that they cannot ask for special treatment on the basis of a continental relationship and then reject that relationship when the United States wants to talk about, for example, a continental resources policy.[1] When President Nixon spoke in Ottawa in April 1972, he picked up the fashionable Canadian formula with disturbing alacrity. He said it was time for both peoples "to move beyond the sentimental rhetoric of the past" and recognize "that we have very separate identities; that we have significant differences," that American policy toward Canada "reflects the new approach we are taking in all our foreign relations" and "that doctrine rests on the premise that mature partners must have autonomous independent policies."[2] Shrewder observers in Ottawa realized that he was not so much recognizing the Canadian right to independence as proclaiming an American independence of special obligations.

What Canadians forget too readily in the present debate is the terms of their own existence. Canada is an adventure of various communities that did not want to join the United States, a collective experiment in American living under different auspices and with different rules. From the beginning this was recognized as a risky experiment based on "unnatural" economics. It was and remains a defiance of the United States. Americans have come to take a reasonably civilized view of this perverse determination of Canadians to live unto themselves, but Canadians too often give the impression that there is some historic American obligation to support the project. Political annexation seems a dead enough issue, but, given the American belief in the removal of barriers to free enterprise, especially governmental, the boundary must seem to most of them a regrettable anachronism.[3] Canadians can expect Americans to play the international game more or less according to the United Nations Charter which they so strongly recommend for others. Within those rules, however, the United States will pursue its own interests and Canada may pursue its interests as it sees them. Competition and conflict are natural and perpetual. The basic facts have been concealed, especially in the years of alliance, by the stress on common interest. The sense of alliance partnership, the belief that the competition must be moderated by fair dealing and good neighbourliness, is a product of the last half century. Before the Boundary Waters Treaty of 1909 and the establishment of the International Joint Commission, the game was exceedingly rough. The Nixon administration may well lack magnanimity toward Canada, but Canadians might well compare Mr. Nixon's pledge to Mr. Trudeau in 1971—that the United States did not insist on a surplus trade balance—with the remarks about Canada's lack of a future made not only by Mr. Seward in the 1860s but by Mr. Taft in 1911. Canadians who make a villain of John Connally and Senator Hartke have forgotten those nasties of the 'thirties, Smoot and Hawley. On the other side, statements of Canadian politicians about Yankee greed and immorality were in the not too distant past a good deal more devastating than the somewhat restrained regret expressed by the Canadian parliamentarians over the bombing of North Vietnam in 1973. Plus ça change, plus il n'est pas exactement la même chose.

Even if one regards the present situation as a cyclical phenomenon, it is necessary to look for new factors. Because the two countries are less isolated from each other and the world at large, the proportions of the problems are enormously greater, and quantitative factors may have become qualitative. Among the differences the following might be noted.

End of the Atlantic Triangle

Canada is now a more independent country than it was during previous periods of confrontation. A feeling of aloneness, of being the outer one, has been an important aspect of the Canadian political perception in recent years. For a century or more Canadians have had an ambiguous attitude toward the United States—seeing it as protector and as threat. They regarded themselves as an integral part of an Anglo-American world, which guaranteed them security and some prosperity. Within that world their powerful protectors checked each other. British power was a counterweight that deterred the United States, even if the British on occasion sacrificed pieces of Canadian territory in the broader interest of preserving this special relationship between Republic and Empire. The movement of Britain into the EEC may or may not have important economic implications for Canada. It has had psychic effects. The British percentage of Canadian trade declined to such an extent in the last decade or so that the actual move into the Community was less worrying than had earlier been expected, but it was the fact of that decline that increased the Canadian feeling of alienation. The idea of the Atlantic community was for Canadians an extension of the concept of shelter in the Anglo-American world. And Western Europe was seen also as the counterweight that Britain and the Empire once provided. Ottawa officialdom still clings to the idea of Europe as a counterweight in economics and in international diplomacy. Most Canadians would welcome such a factor if they could believe in its strength. Japan and other Pacific countries are looked at wistfully. Trade with all these areas does increase, but not in percentages compared with North American continental trade. The sense of being left dependent on a giant, especially a giant which may be altering its familiar personality, tends to polarize Canadian opinion. In a minority it induces a determination for drastic steps toward autarky, and in another minority it induces a disposition to give up resistance. Most Canadians are still looking for broader internationalist arrangements, aware, however, that the old triangular pattern is inadequate and they are more than ever obliged to fight for themselves in a chaotic world.

Increasing Strength and Vulnerability

Another change of importance is the sheer economic strength of Canada at a time when this is a more salient factor than military power. This strength is seldom grasped by Canadians or others because it is always juxtaposed against that of a superpower rather than estimated with its peer group. Its GNP, projected at over $130 billion in 1974, and a total international trade one-third that of the United States make it one of the major commercial powers in the world, with a considerable voice in international monetary questions as well. Being a responsible member of the small community of states that can influence decision making, realizing more and more that Canadian interests in the world are unique, coincidental often with those of the United States but not sufficiently so to justify absorption into a bloc, has encouraged, at least in official circles, a new and tougher internationalism.[4] The shift of international priority from security to economics increases Canada's influence and its solitude. On many issues of the 'seventies, the seabed, maritime pollution, foreign investment, and the control of multinational corporations, Canada's major antagonists are more likely to be its military allies than its assumed military antagonists with which its economic relations are relatively uncomplicated. The need to find allies all over the world on an ad hoc basis to strengthen the Canadian hand in such matters has encouraged a new boldness in Canadian diplomacy vis-à-vis the United States.[5] As this is undertaken in defence of identifiable national interests about which Canadian politicians are concerned, this boldness is likely to have a stronger political base than past challenges to United States policies on broad international issues such as China or nuclear weapons.

The paradox for Canada is that its strength increases its vulnerability. Maintaining its greater industrial power makes Canada all the more dependent on factors beyond its control.

This vulnerability, however, is more vividly perceived in economic than in military calculations, where a sense of dependence is probably decreasing. The Canadian contribution to collective defence has been maintained in principle, but in practice it consists of token contributions abroad and increasing emphasis on defence of the vast home base as a part of the whole alliance area. The feeling of dependence on the United States for protection, however, has been counteracted by a declining awareness of a military threat. The view that Canada is indebted to the United States for its defence is less persuasive than it was, partly because of an increasing alienation from United States military operations and partly because of the shift of a new generation to the view that nuclear deterrence is a game, played by superpowers with each other, which allows powers that cannot defend themselves anyway to stop spending money uselessly trying to do so. The almost unchallenged assumption of twenty years ago—that if the United States were at war, Canada would be at war—has lost credibility, largely as a result of United States unilateral activities in Indochina. Because of the decline in the value of Canadian soil for the defence of the United States in a missile age, defence pressures from the Pentagon are less than they once were. It is a situation, however, that is not necessarily permanent. Technological changes may well alter the Pentagon's concept of the part Canada could and should play in North American defence. A challenge over the new Airborne Warning and Control System could come shortly in fact. Current assumptions about détente could also be shattered by shifts or accidents in the configuration of powers, and in a time of fear there seems little doubt that Canadians would return to the instinct to find shelter with friends. In times of crisis, they would as usual want to play honourably their own part, and as usual they would probably have to start again from close to scratch, their military capacity having again been reduced to the barest minimum. It is even harder politically for a country like the United States with the capacity for decisive military power. However, although the assault on alliance mindedness has been loud and righteous in recent years, it does not seem to have shaken the convictions or instincts of political leaders or a majority of their electors. Co-operation with conventional weapons continues. Neither withdrawal from NATO or of more troops from Europe nor disbandment of the North American Air Defence Command (NORAD) are under serious consideration in Ottawa.

The Canadian vulnerability is, like the Japanese, largely economic. The more prosperous it becomes, the more it depends on foreign trade and therefore the more vulnerable is the high standard of living. The increasing dependence on the United States market, and in particular on the auto pact, is a constant concern that conditions a great deal of Canadian foreign policy. It is probably a more important inhibition than the foreign investment on which the nationalists concentrate. It would be wrong to suggest that Canadian policy on, for example, service in the International Commission of Control and Supervision in Vietnam was decided by this concern over the vulnerability of the Canadian economy to American action. However, it was a factor much discussed at the time, and it is a factor for consideration in weighing the advantages and disadvantages of many issues. There are always voices in Parliament saying out loud or more often *sotto voce* that Canada should put its own direct interests in Washington ahead of international obligations. Herein lies a dilemma for any Canadian government. It must bear in mind the danger that can be done to Canadian interests by a hostile Congress or administration in Washington, but it must maintain the posture of a government pursuing a strong and independent Canadian policy. Its critics can be counted on to denounce it for one sin or the other. It is not only vis-à-vis the United States that the government of a major commercial power has to exercise discretion. Arab oil producers and Chinese wheat buyers require more consideration than in the days when Canada could be the free middle spirit in the UN.

Continentalist Pressures

On economic questions Ottawa's position is still aggressively internationalist. The spirit of article 2 of NATO is strong—the conviction that the Western alliance will founder if its members do not restrain their competition—and Henry Kissinger is regarded as an important convert to the traditional Canadian position. In practice, however, this almost doctrinaire approach is undermined by suspicion that the Europeans and the United States Congress will not play that way. The idea of Canada as martyr to its high principles is a vision seen more clearly in Ottawa than in Washington, Brussels, or Canberra. As a fallback from internationalism there is some sense of defensive continentalism in the country at large. The Canadian business community is susceptible to prevailing winds of opinion in the American business community. The hostility that this United States community and its political spokesmen feel toward the Japanese, the Europeans, and other people who, by means of cheap labour and other un-American activities, are threatening the good folk on the North American continent has its appeal. Japanese trade with Canada is now second only to that with the United States, but it is open to even stronger criticism in that Japan rejects Canadian manufactures and soaks up Canadian resources. The idea of a common front in Fortress America has its attractions in Canada. The Ottawa establishment resists it in favour of wider internationalism, and there seems little doubt that the continentalist implications run contrary to what articulate Canadians would like. However, if the going gets rougher, more Canadians may decide, although reluctantly, that this is the option to back. And so, as the sense of standing together against a military threat from the communist powers has diminished, a new concept of continental defence in the realm of economics, a realm, incidentally, where Canada could have a more influential role than it could ever have in defence, may take its place. In such an atmosphere the pressures for continental management, particularly in the resources sphere, could become less resistible.

The extent to which transnational integration has gone in practice without any government direction makes Canadians nervous. A fear that the situation is out of control tends to discourage governments' efforts to try, but the feeling that the Canadian community is being burrowed away forces them to see what could be done. The idea that Canadian citizens are being locked into a computer web, which puts their personal lives on file for instantaneous transmission to Pittsburgh or Chicago or San Clemente did prompt efforts in Ottawa to preserve some national privacy in the computer industry. The Ontario government is investigating the transmission of information from private security companies to their United States head offices, and it has shown some interest in seeing that school children are reared on Canadian textbooks. After much agonizing consideration the Trudeau government came up with a proposal for an agency to review foreign take-overs of Canadian companies. However, as the Minister of Finance assured a New York audience, "It's not a dam, it's a filter." As the time for action has come, both federal and provincial governments are facing the bewildering complexities of unravelling the cobweb.

One form of continentalist pressure that has traditionally conditioned Canadian calculations is diminishing somewhat. This is the fear that the Canadian standard of living can never be allowed to fall far below that of the United States lest Canadians pack up and move south. New factors are affecting the balance. Even in periods of depression and considerable inequality, Canadians were sustained in their long experiment by loyalty to their own political tradition and the desire to maintain what seemed to them, if not to others, a reality—their own way and quality of life. The flow of immigration has in fact altered. In recent years more Americans have moved to Canada than Canadians to the United States.[6] The brain drain flows in both directions. Whether this reversal is attributable to factors associated with the Vietnam war remains to be seen.[7] The United States, even in turmoil, retains its fascination for many Canadians who find even its sin and conflict big-time compared with their own pale imitations. Nevertheless, the advantages of living in a less turbulent country at slightly less pay are now more obvious. There is also a rejection of American values which, ironically, is largely inspired by Americans criticizing their own country. The fact that Canadians, although to a lesser extent than Europeans, tend to lump together as American the features of modern society that they do not like is grossly unfair but politically significant. The more bucolic image of Canada, both among Americans and Canadians, is partly myth, but it has its effect. Racial strife and other factors in the United States have increased the differentiation between Canadian and American cities in fact as well as in fancy. Living in Toronto and living in Cleveland are not as much alike as they once were. Windsor is less a suburb of Detroit because Windsorites are afraid to cross the river.

The New Canadian Nationalism

Contributing to this differentiation is a wave of Canadian nationalism different from anything previous. For one thing, it is for anglophone Canadians unilateral Canadianism untempered by multilateral imperial loyalties. For Quebeckers it is often not tempered even by Canadian loyalties. It is fiercest among the young. It ranges from a heightened awareness among the moderates of the values of the Canadian tradition and a desire to strengthen it against unattractive pressures not only from abroad but also from within to an irrational Americanophobia which is less in the Canadian tradition. In fact, the more neurotic Canadian nationalism has a distinctly American accent. Much of its dogma is, in the most colonial tradition, mindlessly transplanted from the American Left. Denunciations of the United States in the glottal tones and arid verbiage of lesser American graduate schools become, simply by hopping the border, nationalist rather than antinationalist. Even less neurotic Canadian nationalists have always been affected by the cultural impact of American-style nationalism, transferring the same credos, pledges, and convictions about government to a Canadian flag and an unwritten Canadian constitution for which they are peculiarly unsuited. The new manifestations are more intense and intolerant and directed toward rousing ill will rather than good.

Out of this confused nationalist debate, however, are emerging some genuine Canadian values. Some of these are excessively historical-romantical and some needlessly reject an American cultural heritage that has been shared rather than imposed. Nevertheless, there is a better understanding of the Canadian way of life, based perhaps on a recognition that the political identity of Canada is clear even if the cultural identity is perhaps subsystemic. The Canadian confederation was not an imitation of the American but a response to the American Civil War. It has developed more directly from its British roots and has its own strengths and weaknesses which make even good American examples inapplicable. The loose nature of the Canadian federation is its weakness, but it is also being perceived as its strength in an age when government is becoming colossal. It is the urban challenge and the challenge of regional governments, not only Quebec but the western provinces as well, to the federal structure that have forced Canadians into an argument about their own way of government, thus producing a curiously unifying effect. The debate does emphasize the frontiers between the provinces and between the provinces and the federal government, but because it is a demicontinental rather than a continental preoccupation, it draws an even heavier line along the 49th parallel. The greatest danger to the Canadian identity is a preoccupation with American issues to such an extent that Canadians lose sight of their individuality. The problems of Canadian federation force Canadians to concentrate on issues for which the United States experience is largely irrelevant.[8]

The Federal-Provincial Factor

Division of responsibility between federal and provincial governments, particularly in such important areas as resources and investment, and the relative decline of federal power are widely believed to have weakened Canada considerably in its effort to manage a national policy that could guarantee independence. There is justification for this view. The federal government is constantly being told that it must have a resources policy, an industrial policy, and a population policy if it is to play its cards intelligently vis-à-vis the United States and in the world at large. The government is apparently weakened by two factors. In the first place there are the divisive interests of the provinces. In the second place the regionalization of Canadian issues in politics has resulted in an almost chronic situation of minority government. The incapacity of a minority government to take bold risks in the long-range interest is obvious. In the present nationalist mood of the electorate, at least as diagnosed by the rhetoricians of all parties, a posture of resistance to the United States must be maintained.[9] A problem, however, is that the

need to maintain such a posture makes difficult the constructive compromise, conceding minimum disadvantage for a greater advantage,
regarding continental relations not as a zero-sum game but as a process
of bargaining and manipulating for mutual profit.[10] Yet Canadians are
adjusting, as many Western Europeans have, to minority government,
which has been for some years and is likely to be for many more the
normal way of holding together a sprawling people. The crisis over oil
exports in the autumn of 1973 revealed inevitable conflicts of interest
between the oil-producing and oil-consuming provinces and differences of attitude toward sales to the United States. However, the
need for the government to put together an acceptable national policy
was all the more clear because it had to be conciliatory to stay in office.

It has become conventional to say that Canadian nationalism is
largely confined to Ontario, that it is the expression of a confident and
sophisticated industrial area which feels capable of standing on its own
feet, and that it is resisted by less favoured provinces that want foreign
investment, growth, jobs, industrial development, and all those things
they think can come from welcoming United States capital. There is
truth in this assumption, but there is a danger now of its being repeated
as an absolute truth. Among intellectuals, nationalism is as strong in
Edmonton as Toronto. Apart from Ontario there are various regional or
provincial assertions of nationalism, directed partly against Ontario but
not basically continentalist in thrust. Alberta and British Columbia
have been regarded as the provinces with the strongest American
orientation. But they are under new management. So, in fact, are all the
provinces. The old set of demagogic provincial premiers (''provochi-
al,'' they have been called) has in the last few years been replaced by a
set of pragmatic, managerial types, more disposed to pay due regard to
the national interest than were their predecessors. Three of the four
western premiers, where continentalism is believed to be most
rampant, are from the New Democratic party, which is the most
anticontinentalist of all the parties. Premier Barrett (NDP) of British
Columbia, it is true, went direct to Washington to talk with the authorities there, but with the intention of defying them on the Alaska
pipeline rather than snuggling closer. He has taken a tough line about
the export of British Columbian water to Washington state. Premier
Lougheed of Alberta, a Conservative, challenged not only Ontario but
to a greater extent the United States with his insistence on more returns
for Alberta's energy resources. He has struck a nationalist note with an
Alberta accent and showed a willingness to accept a national priority.
The Social Crediters, who have been thrown out of power in Alberta
and BC, were far more American and continentalist in their philosophy.

The north-south industrial ties seem to be growing stronger, but there
is a countervailing force. It was once the St. Lawrence system,

extended to the Pacific by the railways, that created a Canadian economy. The east-west ties of trade and people are deeply rooted. The phenomenon that now holds together Canadians (to some extent against their will) may be less the St. Lawrence route than the extraordinary phenomenon of Toronto, one of the fastest growing metropolitan areas in the world, whose economic vitality retains its magnetic effect on businessmen and industry, on the professional and nonprofessional labour force from Vancouver to Halifax. To a lesser extent this is true in the arts as well—for Anglo-Canadians. Whether Toronto is the capital of an independent system or a subsystem attached to New York and Chicago, it is of some consequence that it is still to a considerable extent a transcontinental system of its own.[11] The relative decline of Montreal, however, exacerbates internal tension. The greatest threat to Canadian independence is that its divisions should increasingly associate themselves with regions in the United States so that for all practical purposes the continent is divided not into two countries but into subdivisions of an essentially continental society and economy.[12]

Fear of American Nationalism

The provinces, and particularly the poorer provinces, have as much as Ottawa to fear from the rough attitude taken by members of Congress and by Washington officials toward Canadian federal and provincial policies to widen the geographical base of industrial development within Canada. When special tax concessions were given to the Michelin Tire Company to build a plant in Nova Scotia rather than in central Canada, the United States Treasury Department imposed countervailing duties on its export of tires to the United States. The rules of the game seemed unclear, or unfairly applied, since the United States Congress had already passed legislation in 1971 authorizing Domestic International Sales Corporations (DISC). Under this law comparable tax incentives were made available to American companies to increase exports if they met certain conditions. American officials have made it very plain to Canadians that they are not prepared to take a benevolent view of what they call Canada's "industrial strategy" if it is contrary to their perception of the American national interest. As the "industrial strategy" that the Canadian electorate increasingly demands includes regional development as well as corporate taxation and foreign take-over legislation, there could well be a basic confrontation and a trial of strength.

Canadians have been able with some success, particularly in the postwar years, to argue with American officials that they should restrain their power so that a more prosperous good neighbour could establish itself as a trading partner. That plea is less likely to be heeded when those officials regard Canadians as prosperous enough to look after their own interests. When Americans talk about a more mature relationship, the message reaches Ottawa loud and clear. One aspect of this mature relationship seems to be a greater disposition on both sides to shift the argument into multilateral forums where no special relationship applies and where allies from other continents can be enlisted by both sides.[13] This is notably the case over the sea and seabed controversies.

The shift toward nationalist positions on almost all fronts in Canada in the early 1970s has been to a large extent a response to what Canadians widely regarded as an assertion of nationalism[14] in the United States. Members of the Canadian business community who, in Toronto and elsewhere, have on the whole deplored economic nationalism as a left-wing aberration have been shedding some of their hopes and expectations about partnership. It is less easy to argue now that the best way for Canada is the way of economic integration, because the United States looks less prosperous and much less disposed to share anything but its shortages with a partner. There is hardly a consensus in Canada on this much debated subject, but consensus may be a little closer. The fortunes of the extreme nationalists of the "Waffle" Left have declined considerably, but the bourgeoisie are being radicalized, in a moderate Canadian way of course. They are not disposed to find socialism and nationalization the key to Canadian independence. They are impressed, however, and alarmed by the roughness of the Nixon administration. The special relationship they have favoured seems to have been ruled out by the current leadership in Washington. Many business leaders are pressing the government toward toughening its bargaining position, even though this is seen within the framework of a civil continental association rather than the noisy confrontation encouraged by the more leftish nationalists.

The Concept of North America

The Canadian problem is partly semantic. For instance, a Dutchman can call himself a Dutchman and a European without confusion. A Canadian is unable to use the term American to describe the cultural community of which he is a historic part rather than a subjugated victim. Too much identification with North America, on the other hand, submerges the Canadian individuality. Continentalism is a pejorative term in Canada whereas elsewhere there is a wide, if not very well based, belief that it is the blessed wave of the future. Even those in Canada who would like some joint management of resources, perhaps a

North American free trade or common market area, are wary about being called continentalists. Statements by Mr. Nixon and others that they would like to discuss with Canada a continental resources policy are regarded as sinister. Americans think of such proposals as equitable because they have in mind a fair division of resources. They do not realize the system's bias inherent in any scheme of sharing when one element is ten times larger than the other. Canadians realize this with their historic instincts. Americans have been vague about what they mean by a continental resources policy, and Canadians are so frightened by the concept that they do not want to be seen considering what may be under any other rubric sensible proposals.

The strong Canadian preference remains for bodies like the International Joint Commission, which has equal representation and is relatively apolitical. Its function is to find formulae for mutual advantage and recommend these to the two sovereign governments rather than to impose them. The complexity of border issues, pollution in the Great Lakes for example, is raising the frequent question of whether the time has come for international authorities that can impose their will. Many of these subjects come under provincial or state jurisdiction and would seem to provide opportunities for ad hoc, bilateral, transborder agreements that do not challenge the Canadian resistance on the federal level to continental institutions. There are usually ramifications, however, that affect federal control over national resources. Canadian resistance to extending the institutional framework is reinforced by the worry that federal power is itself disintegrating. This fear may have made Canadians rigid when there is a requirement for imaginative improvisation and experimentation with national and even continental institutions. Canadian unity has been one of the false gods of Canadian politics of late. The flexibility achieved in Canada by the growing responsibility and competence of the provincial governments should be seen as an assertion of the Canadian way of life. It provides grass roots interest in Canadian independence and a stronger disposition to preserve the sacred Canadian constitutional principle of looseness against the centripetal forces in the continent. It is in the Canadian tradition for citizens to want to preserve the Canadian framework in order to live more securely as Quebeckers or Nova Scotians or British Columbians.

A problem for Canadians on the world scene, however, is presented by an increasing tendency in Europe and elsewhere to regard North America as an entity. The EEC presumptuously considers itself an entity called Europe. Being primarily interested in the United States but vaguely conscious of Canada, the EEC posits an entity called North America that it assumes, for convenience and in the interest of symmetry, speaks with a single voice because it has a common interest.

Canada has many interests coincidental with those of the United States—free entry to the Japanese and EEC markets being among them. But on a large number of important issues, from maritime regulations to foreign aid or relations with India or Vietnam, its position varies from contradictory to divergent. In many trade and other questions its relationship with the United States is competitive. In official or unofficial discussions involving, as is so often the case at present, Europe, North America, and Japan, Canada must resist being lumped as North America not from a petty desire to show the flag but because it would be a sacrifice of Canadian interests to allow the Washington government or any group of private Americans to speak for North America. There is not and cannot be a Brussels in North America. As far as culture and society are concerned, there are sound reasons for talking about Europe. There is an unfortunate tendency, however, to ignore the differences between common issues and values and coincidental issues and values. What matters most in this context is not the similarities of accent and dress but the difference in national interests of two countries and the fact of two separate governments with no common institution. It cannot be taken for granted, for example, that Canadian interests would be served by a North American position on Middle Eastern oil, although on this or other subjects there is always the possibility of working out a common front on an ad hoc basis with the United States as with Japan or Australia.

So while international pressures and the mood of the times drive Canadians toward a continental identity, they also stimulate resistance. The rise of nationalism in the 'sixties has been partly a felt need to reject the conventional wisdom of the rest of the Western world and of Manifest Destiny in the guise of Frankenstein. A problem of the 'seventies is that an odd man out risks being regarded as a tiresome bore. He is alienated from his friends because his problems are so often very different from theirs.

Quebec

Most of what has been said here about popular attitudes describes English-speaking Canada in particular. It would probably apply to most of the million or so francophone Quebeckers. This is not a time when there are wide divisions on foreign policy among those Canadians, liberal or conservative, eastern or western, anglophone or francophone, who think in terms of a federal Canada. The wide division is between those who think of Quebec and Canada as destined to have separate existence in the community of states and those who do not. Even among separatists, however, there are those who think of hostile separation and those, probably a majority, who assume some kind of special relationship with Canada—and presumably also some sharing in special relationships with the United States. In the meantime Quebec has its own form of nationalism that is not identified with Canadian nationalism, although an indeterminate proportion of voting Quebeckers would not consider their own nationalism and that of Canada incompatible and would prefer, with varying degrees of scepticism, to share also in a Canadian nationalism that was reasonably bilingual and bicultural. The attitude of the Quebec nationalist to English Canadians on the grounds of their "economic domination," "arrogance," and "neglect of French Canada" is remarkably similar to the attitude of English-Canadian nationalists toward the United States. The Quebec nationalist tends to be contemptuous of the English Canadian's nationalism and minimizes his identity, and the English-Canadian nationalist is frustrated because the Quebec nationalist will not make common cause.

Paradoxically, however, one may argue that there is in 1974 less confrontation and more separation, and perhaps that is cause and effect. Economic rather than constitutional issues are now dominant; and there is, for the time being at least, less sense of crisis, although the relationship between economic and constitutional issues is by no means disregarded. Issues such as the energy crisis tend to emphasize the importance to Quebeckers of a healthy national economy, a fact reflected in the support given the Bourassa government in the provincial election of 1973. Emphasis is now on the cultural identity of Quebec, the flowering of which raises few questions affecting Canadian-American relations. The intelligentsia of Quebec live just about as separate and independent an existence as they would in their own state. Other Canadians are adjusting to this fact of life and, inspired to some extent by the Quebec example, have been making rapid strides in the creation of a more indigenous culture of their own. An unprecedented surge of drama, cinema, and literature, based on the experience of Newfoundland or Toronto or the Yukon rather than a mythical Canada or a revamped Surrey or Illinois, has in the past year or so given the Anglo-Canadians more self-confidence; the works are less preoccupied with the theme of survival from the Yankees and therefore less boring. Quebec nationalism is becoming less French, more native, and therefore more self-confident, less petty, and more serene. It has rediscovered its rich sense of humour and has ceased to reject its own language, American French or *joual*. This is healthy except that *joual* is so little comprehensible even to Anglo-Canadians, let alone Frenchmen or Americans, that it does in some ways isolate Quebec from all its neighbours. It is a private joke, like Switzerdietsch. The neighbours, however, have some reason to hope that Canadian culture, of both communities, will grow more rewarding and less obnoxious.

Attitudes in Quebec toward the United States vary considerably. Quebeckers accept their North American destiny. Although dedication to the preservation of a French-language culture is basic, France is of declining importance. Resentment of Parisian snobbery is an emotional element in Quebec nationalism. The English Canadians and the French rather than the Americans and the British are the butts of the Montreal chansonniers. The standard of living and much of the way of life of the Quebeckers are North American, and they are more willing than English Canadians to acknowledge this fact because they have less fear of their identity. Members of the large middle class of Quebec who drive their big cars off to Miami as do other North Americans have a pretty relaxed view of the United States. On the left wing of the separatist movement, the antipathy to the United States is expressed in the conventional language of Guevarists, but it is directed with even more bitterness against Anglo-Canadian capitalists. On the conservative wing are less revolutionary leaders, some of whom see in the United States a counterweight to English Canada. Proposals for an economic union or free trade agreement with the United States have been put forward.[15] For some it may be a flirtation intended to prod and irritate an arrogant and neglectful spouse. The provincial Liberal government has frequently stated its opposition to the Canadian nationalists who would deny American investment, although in its anxiety to protect the Quebec economy it is nervous about American as well as Ontario domination. This Quebec view is identifiable with the view of other less favoured provinces, but suspicion of Ontario does not make them all avid continentalists. They are less confident than the Ontario industrialists of their ability to compete internationally. There is probably less anti-Americanism in Quebec than elsewhere in Canada, but there is less identification with the United States.

Except from a radical minority, Quebec nationalists have not felt much warmth or encouragement from Americans. The tendency in the United States to identify Quebec nationalism with the Front de Libération du Québec (FLQ) and Cuban mischief is a gross over-simplification that discourages the moderate Quebec independentists from a dialogue with the southern neighbours with whom they have to live whether federated or not. From the point of view of other Canadians, it is less mischievous than would be the rousing of American sentimentalism about an oppressed minority. Although anti-American Canadian nationalists dearly love to see CIA plots in Quebec, there has been no convincing evidence of any official or unofficial American dispositions to play with separatists. Franco-Americans of New England seem even less disposed than Franco-Ontarians or Acadians to favour the Parti Québécois. Fear in Washington of a Quebec Cuba would presumably, if a crisis arose, lead any American administration to support a Canadian federal position. The Quebec situation, however, is so volatile that one does not know in what form confrontation might present itself. It may well not present itself at all. Canada may just go on in its well-known preference for evolution rather than revolution but evolve itself into something that does not look much like the Canada of today. The relationship of Canada and Quebec to the United States is bound to be a factor in the calculations or negotiations about Quebec's position vis-à-vis the rest of Canada, a unifying or a divisive issue among Canadians and Canadiens. The evolution is not likely to be placid, and given the very large American interests in Quebec and in Canada as a whole, the United States government and Americans in general may find it harder to maintain a totally neutral position. If their relations with Ottawa become nasty, as they may, temptations could be less resistible. Even not very well founded suspicions among English Canadians that American official or private interests were playing the separatist game could increase tension. (There is more suspicion at present of their playing with Alberta.)

A factor of importance to the continental relationship is that the strong Quebec stand on its social, economic, and cultural powers is being matched or supported by other provinces. There is a historic Ontario-Quebec axis vis-à-vis Ottawa or the western provinces. These forces cut across the idea of an Anglo-French confrontation, and they provide the possibility of accommodating Quebec quasi independence in a quasi-federal structure. As suggested above, the conventional view that the federal-provincial division of powers weakens Canadian resistance to the forces of continentalism depends on how one looks at it. The finding of a formula for a relatively independent and reasonably contented Quebec in a loose federation would strengthen the Canadian position. Canadian resistance to continental suction has been weakened by a lack of confidence in the future of the country as an entity. Part of this has been the association Canadian nationalists have tended to make between a strong Canada, national unity, and the affirmation of the federal power. This position is no longer tenable. Among other things, the Quebec nationalist has forced the Canadian nationalist to an agonizing reappraisal of the nature of Canada's political virtue. Some of the latter's more dogmatic assumptions about the management of the Canadian-United States relationship may be shaken up in the process.

The New Factor: Resources and Population

We seem to be on the verge of conceptual changes, both in the facts governing the relationship and in attitudes, requiring rapid adjustments of policy. They are related to altered attitudes in the world at large to growth and to the new Malthusianism. Typical of the impact is the shift within one year, 1973, of the nationalist Canadian complaint that the United States imposes unfair restrictions on imports of energy resources and agricultural produce from Canada to the demand that Americans be prevented from draining Canada of the materials that its citizens need to maintain the standard of living to which they have an independent right. At the same time, the American grievances have shifted from Canadian advantage in the balance of trade to Canadian reluctance to sell energy resources. Policymakers find it difficult to see the long-term interest clearly as their attitudes to buying and selling fluctuate. Only dimly foreseen at present are the implications for traditional attitudes to population as well as resources.[16] The extremely unequal distribution of population on the continent has always been a worry to Canada, but it has not been a serious source of friction between the two countries while there was relatively free movement across the border. United States doubts about an increase of its own population have been apparent for some time and for understandable reasons. The new factor is that Canada, of all countries, is having second thoughts about an increasing population because of compulsive urbanization, endemic unemployment, and the ecology factor. To citizens of a crowded world, including Americans, such an attitude must seem inexcusable. The Canadian attitude is getting to be something like that of the Swiss, a nervous desire to protect a way of life and standard of living against too many people who want to share in it. Canadians had nourished for so long the myth of victimization that they were slow to realize that a mere 22 million people have a very good thing going for them.

What could provide, therefore, an important domestic political factor is the emergence of the United States in the past few years as the largest source of immigration to Canada.[17] The irritation about draft dodgers is, it is to be hoped, over. Ill feeling has been roused among some Canadians by the fact that it is easier for an American to immigrate to Canada than for a Canadian to get into the United States and take employment. Canadian nationalists, however, are not unhappy with the latter provision. One may foresee a surge of Americans from their crowded and polluted cities toward the Canadian "wilderness." The idea that Canada is a land of wide open spaces for settlement is contradicted by the fact that Canadians themselves are leaving the land to crowd the cities, and that is where the immigrants go as well. This romantic motivation for moving north may be less important than a practical reason for moving to a country where fuel is more plentiful. The irritation over the Canadian permissiveness in admitting American "delinquents" may be replaced by anger over the solid Americans Canada will begin to keep out.

Americans have many advantages as immigrants, along with one disadvantage. They are the immigrants least disposed to realize that Canada is a country unlike the one they have left. They are often benevolent missionaries who want to bring Canada up to date in their image. Already their well-intentioned desire to "modernize" Canadian universities has inspired resentment of some political consequence. Some of them want to turn Canada into their own idea of anti-America. Either way old Canada would be engulfed. English Canada was, of course, a creation of American refugees, but 300 years of separate history has created a state dedicated to something more positive than simple opposition to American institutions. Waves of immigrants, including American immigrants, have been absorbed over two centuries. The Americans continue to supply a special kind of zeal that the more relaxed native Canadians appreciate and tolerate—up to a point. The present 22 million, by no means all of whom are native born, could be swamped. Persistent unemployment and new attitudes to population growth indicate a trend in Canada to more restricted immigration. Pressures of illegal immigration and the painful readjustment it is forcing in attitudes to population are creating one of the major political issues of the day.

Immigration to Canada from the United States has to be considered alongside the powerful thrust all over the world of peoples moving from regions of lesser to higher development, from the Mediterranean to northern Europe, from Latin America to the United States, from Asia and the Caribbean into Canada. Because of its relative security and ratio of people to resources, Canada is probably the world's most vulnerable country. Until very recently it has been one of the easiest to enter. Over the past decade racial distinctions have been eliminated from Canadian immigration laws. There are grounds for selection based on skill, education, or family ties, but no country or region is given preference over another. When Canadians removed all racial discrimination from immigration regulations, they thought in terms of adding new categories to the flow. They thought of equitable admission rather than equitable exclusion. If, as seems likely, they move increasingly to control the total flow, Britons, Frenchmen, or Americans have to be kept out or deported on the same basis as more exotic peoples. The only white country from which immigration is increasing is the United States. (Black Americans have shown less disposition than white Americans to cross the border.)

Neither Americans nor Canadians are used to harsh frontier controls. A spokesman from the United States Department of State recently suggested that Canadians be exempted from the Western Hemisphere restrictions. Barbara Watson, administrator of the Bureau of Security and Consular Affairs, said adverse reaction had been "particularly marked in Canada which, because of our traditionally open border, has long felt itself to have a special relationship with the United States."[18] Reciprocal preferences would presumably be expected. That sounds reasonable enough, but Canadians would have to examine the implications. Would they be moving toward the most continentalist of all conceptions—a free flow of people, a continental labour market? Not necessarily, but trends of that kind are incremental.

When it comes to keeping our Americans, Canadian popular attitudes are likely to be ambivalent. Hardship cases will make the headlines, and members of Parliament and congressmen will cry out. At this point one can only note the storm warnings. The tendency of American corporations to run their Canadian branches as regional plants is complicated by the barriers to the transfer of personnel. Opposition in Canada to the importation of American professors and plant managers suggests that many Canadians would not be unhappy in theory to frustrate in this way the continentalization of their economy. On both sides, however, there have been assumptions about personal mobility that would be challenged by the imposition of stiffer border controls of all kinds and the erection of the kinds of barriers that all North Americans associate with the more restrictive society of the Europe they rejected—and at a time when, in Western Europe, border restrictions are being eased. Neither federal nor provincial governments in Canada have been persuaded as yet to enact special legislation on the employment of Americans, but a climate of opinion has been created that has modified the personnel policies of universities and corporations. The tide, for the moment at least, is against continentalism in people.

It is also against continentalism in land. Strong pressures are building up on provincial governments to prevent or restrict the purchase of Canadian land by foreigners, with a special eye on Americans buying up farms in Saskatchewan, resort country in British Columbia and Nova Scotia, as well as the already well-populated lake country in Ontario. This emerged as a major subject of concern when the provincial premiers met in Charlottetown in August 1973. As in the provincial talks about the control of resources and outside investment, there is also in the land question an ambivalence about whether foreigners are people in another country or another province.

The forces of continentalism are like powerful forces of nature. The pressure of American capital and American hunger for resources are phenomena of which Canadian politicians are well aware. In the earlier years Canadian lands were filled up with American settlers pushing west and north with little regard for ill-defined frontiers, and Canada had a hard time establishing its sovereignty in some areas. For the past half century Americans have been enjoying their own prosperity, and Canada has been making itself viable with more assimilable, or docile, immigrants from overseas. American immigrants are likely to compete directly with Canadians for jobs, whereas the West Indians and Portuguese and the Pakistanis and Greeks will do the support jobs native Canadians are spurning. The population of the continent, however, is still very unequally distributed, and Americans have a historic tendency to press toward frontiers. Canadians have traditionally thought they would like to have a larger share of the continent's population, but they have to cope with an increase in the work force from their own citizenry, which is larger in absolute terms than that of Britain or Germany.[19]

Alliance and Partnership

Shifting attitudes toward the United States role in the world have, in recent years, inevitably altered Canadian attitudes toward the relationship. Partnership is a word less used now. The Canadian disposition seems to be toward more independence in foreign policy, and the shift of emphasis from strategic to economic issues fixes attention on areas where there is more conflict. The concept of partnership flourished during the war and postwar decades when the need to stand shoulder to shoulder against a clearly perceived threat from abroad was regarded as the basic national interest. That threat has grown more ambiguous.

Some of this change, however, is more apparent than real. It is of significance that Canadians and Americans both seem to think that the foreign policies of the Trudeau government are more nationalist and independentist than those of its predecessors, although a strong case can be made that the United States was in fact defied more stubbornly by the St. Laurent-Pearson policies of the 'fifties. On the continental front, for example, the United States was pressed into collaboration on the St. Lawrence Seaway because the Canadian government decided to go it alone. In world affairs the St. Laurent government took advantage of its considerable leverage to oblige Washington to accept article 2 of the North Atlantic Treaty and to oppose the United States over Korea with more courage than was required to recognize Peking in 1970 when the United States no longer cared. A difference may be that there is now less confidence in Ottawa, and probably in Washington also, that the benevolence of an ally or a priority accorded to the common interest will prevail over a perceived national interest. Even those Canadians who concede that quiet diplomacy paid off among people who respected each other in the heyday of the NATO spirit speculate now as to whether the goodwill of allies is a commodity to be counted on. Has that gone with the Cold War?

That priority once accorded to the alliance spirit was less in a continental than an Atlantic context. The broader trans-Atlantic spirit has soured even more certainly than the North American partnership. As a result, a bilateral partnership of sorts, wanted or unwanted, may be thrust upon North Americans by the exclusiveness of the West Europeans. It would be wrong, furthermore, to take for granted that Canadians as a whole and in the middle of the night have abandoned their reliance on North America as their bastion in a volatile world. Attitudes of the 'fifties have been abandoned. Canadians have learned that American military power can be employed in disastrous ways and is beyond their control, that there are almost insuperable strategic and logistic obstacles to the simple military collaboration they thought they once agreed to, but nevertheless most of them would rather have the United States stay as strong as the devils they do not know. NORAD was renewed in 1973, although for only a few years, without very much discussion. Unless and until overseas challenges look more menacing, or the cost escalates dramatically, NORAD is likely to look more like one of many sensible structures for handling transborder problems than the political commitment to common causes here and abroad that it appeared to be a decade or more ago. It may be all the more soundly based for being regarded as a practical mechanism and enduring convenience rather than as a gesture of solidarity dependent on shifting calculations of a threat.

It should be noted also that the new Canadian nationalism is a bourgeois as much as a left-wing phenomenon. The greater emphasis on the national interest paradoxically provides as strong an argument for being nice to the Americans as for standing up to them. That Canada's essential interests are economic and depend on United States policies is a proposition widely taken for granted. Many tough Canadian nationalists, therefore, advocate Canadian foreign policies designed not necessarily to please Washington but to avoid irritating it and thereby risking something they regard as important, like the auto pact. They put the Canadian interest ahead not only of internationalism but also of mere anti-Americanism. Their nationalism is based on a vested interest in the Canadian economy and polity rather than concern for the image of Canada in world councils or support of the United States as bastion of the "free world."

The divergences of the past few years have sharpened conflict, but they have also been a learning, and a sobering, experience. The crunch revealed how much each country had become dependent on the other. Canadians learned by standing firm against Mr. Connally that the

American government would not or could not be as ruthless as they had feared. Having a better appreciation of their own strength and the areas of American dependence, they are more likely to seek agreements on the basis of mutual and balancing interest than by the enervating plea of special vulnerability. The energy crisis has been stark enough to cut through a lot of bluster and illusion. Among the things Canadians have learned is that they are not powerless to control their own resources even if these are owned by Americans. While Canada may at the same time be involved in an international network of corporations, governments, and institutions that restricts its range of choice it is less so than most other middle powers.

Just as Mr. Connally and his associates retreated as it became clear that drastic measures for Canadians were double-edged, so too those Canadians who wanted to hold the Americans ransom for Canada's resources realized when the chips were being counted that there were two sides in that game. Using Ontario's plentiful hydro-electric power as a counter, for example, was rejected by the authorities of the Ontario Hydro-Electric Power Commission who pointed to their dependence on supplies of cheap coal from Pennsylvania. Diverting western oil entirely to eastern Canada was risky as the pipeline goes through the northern United States. Most important of all perhaps was a realization, when a showdown could be contemplated, that although Canadian energy resources were not the solution to America's problem, cutting them off with no regard for a neighbour's distress was not an act to be undertaken glibly. Aside from the danger of retaliation, there was a rediscovery under stress of the truth that the weaker power in the dyad is better off in the long run when the doctrine of mutual consideration is maintained.

At the same time, however, the Canadian government was driven in the course of a few months to take drastic measures in the direction of self-sufficiency that were heretofore politically impossible. Preserving and strengthening the Canadian advantage in resources is likely to be the endeavour of any Canadian government. A straw in the wind is Ontario Premier Davis's prediction at the end of 1973 that the greater availability of energy in Ontario will give a great advantage to the heartland of Canadian industry in the continental context. The continental spirit of give-and-take may be preserved in an era of hard bargaining, but the trend is against continental solutions. It may well be toward a more expedient approach to policymaking. In an interview of 1 January 1974, Donald Macdonald, minister of energy, mines and resources, said, when asked whether the Mackenzie pipeline was not "the spearhead toward continentalism," that: "This is very much argued between two poles, the continental energy policy on the one hand and no truck nor trade with the Yankees on the other. Of course the reality does not exist at either pole. The best Canadian position exists in the middle, that is to be able to assess at any one time what is in our best interest in terms of sales and energy to the United States."[20]

The United States, considering its enormous strength, has been a remarkably good neighbour over two centuries. A question Canadians seriously ask themselves is whether this will continue to be the the case if for the first time the Canadian standard of living becomes a reason for envy. That may depend on whether or not Canadians can keep their heads in such circumstances.

Notes

[1]Canadians generally regard the proposed Burke-Hartke bill as a menace, but when the Canadian section of the United Steel Workers of America discussed the subject, what they demanded were exemptions for Canada, ie, protection on a continental basis. *Globe and Mail,* 1 June 1973.

[2]Canada, House of Commons, *Debates,* 28th Parliament, 4th sess., vol. 2, 1972, p. 1328.

[3]US Assistant Secretary of State for Economic Affairs Thorp and Under Secretary of State Lovett, 8 March 1948, on a proposal under secret discussion to eliminate trade barriers between the United States and Canada: "The present may offer a unique opportunity of promoting the most efficient utilization of the resources of the North American Continent and knitting the two countries together—an objective of United States foreign policy since the founding of the Republic" (US Department of State, *Foreign Relations of the United States 1948,* vol. IX *The Western Hemisphere* [Washington, D.C.: United States Government Printing Office, 1972], p. 406).

[4]See, for example, Allan Gotlieb and Charles Dalfen, "National Jurisdiction and International Responsibility: New Canadian Approaches to International Law," *American Journal of International Law,* LXVII (July 1973), 229-58. In the currently fashionable anxiety to emphasize, as in the United States, that Canadian foreign policy is being dictated now by tough-minded national interests rather than by soft-minded internationalism as in the past, the extent to which the national interest was in fact subordinated to do-goodism by previous governments has been considerably exaggerated. The same argument may well apply in the United States, but the two mythologies are political forces nevertheless.

[5]For a contradictory aspect of this situation, however, see p. 252.

[6]For statistics, see footnote 17.

[7]Certainly the popular assumption that most recent American immigrants to Canada were draft dodgers has been widely exaggerated.

[8]For example, the move to integrated schools has been a great goal of liberals in the United States. In Quebec, Ontario, or New Brunswick, any threat to the right of the English and French to their own schools would be regarded as reactionary. Paradoxically also, it is the factor of the United States as an outside challenge that makes the problems of the Canadian confederation so different from those of the United States, which has no such challenge. The argument for governmental control of communications, for example, has no counterpart in the United States.

[9]Not to be confused with genuine anti-Americanism. Resistance to the United States is a *sine qua non* of the existence of Canada. It does not require a belief that the United States is sinful or intentionally hostile. It emphasizes differentiation rather than superiority. Anti-Americanism is more ideological, a conviction of the far Left or far Right or far liberal that the United States is based on false premises or has grown degenerate.

[10]There is evidence, for example, that the government could improve the Canadian-U.S. relationship on trade questions by conceding certain safeguards of the auto pact that have ceased to be meaningful but it does not dare risk accusation from the opposition parties of giving in to U.S. pressure.

[11]When the United States went on year-long daylight saving time in January 1974, the other provinces waited for Ontario's decision, and when Ontario decided not to follow the U.S. example, British Columbia reversed its decision to do so.

[12]A straw in the wind could be the agreement between premiers and governors of the Atlantic provinces and the New England states, meeting in August 1973, to press their respective governments to allow a free flow of power, generated in Canada, between the two regions. *Globe and Mail*, 17 August 1973.

[13]See particularly a report on United States tactics in the *Globe and Mail*, 17 June 1973.

[14]It is a word Americans tend to use only about other countries, but Canadians do not see much difference between the increasing emphasis on U.S. interests and what Americans pejoratively call nationalism in Canada.

[15]See Rodrigue Tremblay, *Indépendance et marché commun, Québec-Etats-Unis* (Montréal: Editions du jour, 1970).

[16]The Canadian percentage of the total population of North America (north of the Rio Grande) is rising rapidly. At the beginning of the century it was 6.6 per cent. In the decade of the 'sixties it rose from 9.2 per cent to 9.6 per cent.

[17]Immigrants in 1972 from four largest sources: United States—22,618; United Kingdom—18,161; Portugal—8,737; Hong Kong—6,297. According to the 1973 annual report of the visa office of the U.S. Department of State, Canadian immigration to the United States has declined steadily from 40,013 in 1965 to 7,278 in 1973.

[18]*Globe and Mail*, 29 March 1973.

[19]See UN *Statistical Yearbook, 1972* (New York: Statistical Office of the UN, 1973), pp.95-6.

[20]*Globe and Mail*, 1 January 1974.

5:

The Vietnam War and Canada

When the Canadian Association for American Studies met in Montreal in November 1970, I was asked to discuss the broad question of the Vietnam war in Canada. The lecture, in which I tried to summarize our own supervisory role and the consequences of the war on our foreign and defence policies, was published in War and Society in North America, *edited by J. L. Granatstein and R. D. Cuff (Toronto: Nelson, 1971). What appears below is the final section of that essay in which I tried to calculate what the war seemed to have done to our relationship in other ways. The mood in Montreal was sober. Our gratification at avoiding our neighbour's ghastly experience had been checked by the violent events of that autumn.*

Much of the impact on Canada of the Vietnam war is a spill-over or a mirror image of its impact on the United States. One must be careful in one's deductions because the Vietnam war is only one, although perhaps the major, element in the transformation of American society and attitudes in the past decade, and it is part of a world-wide movement, not just a North American phenomenon. The effect on Canadian-American relations has been curiously ambivalent; Vietnam has stimulated in Canada both alienation and identification. It would be hard to say how much of the increasing anti-Americanism—or at least strong criticism of the United States—in Canada is attributable to the Vietnam war and how much to the racial issue, United States policy in Latin America, or its heavy investment in Canada. Critics usually draw these aspects together in a gross charge of "imperialism." It is the exercise of great military force in another continent, however, which especially seems to confirm the diagnosis of "imperialism." It is the aspect which seems inexcusable to those who would concede to the United States, as to any country, its domestic failings and its assertion of regional predominance. In spite of the articulateness and the passion of the critics, however, probably just as many Canadians regard the United States endeavour to "resist aggression" in other parts of the world as justified and worthy of moral support—even though they may increasingly consider it a losing cause.[1]

The Vietnam war has raised the level of anti-American feeling in Canada and it has also tended to polarize attitudes towards the United States. For the majority, however, it has probably just stimulated Canadianism, of both the affirmative and perverse varieties. It could once be assumed that all Canadians, with the exception of a few last-ditch Loyalists, regarded the United States as a frequently arrogant, not particularly lovable, but basically harmless and essentially benevolent power and, provided they were not expected to say so too loudly, a good friend to have on our side. Few doubted that the United States was a good deed in a naughty world. For a large number of less articulate Canadians there was also a strong urge to share the higher standard of living in the United States or to make it in the big time.[2] Now that the higher standard of living includes the possibility of compulsory military service in the Indochinese jungles and a much higher liability to municipal violence, calculations have shifted. Fewer Canadians are moving to the United States and more Americans are moving to Canada.[3] It is hard to say whether this trend will outlast the Vietnam War, because the motivation is ecological and romantic as well as political. It is hard also to say whether calculations will be altered by the threat of civil commotion in Canada.

In Canada anti-Americanism was traditionally a phenomenon of the Right. Now the Right, disillusioned in its dream of Empire and tied closely to the industrial and financial community of the United States, has reconciled itself to continentalism and is sympathetic to the American cause in Vietnam. On the whole it is suspicious of the economic aspects of nationalism. The swing of the Left to attitudes varying from virulent anti-Americanism to a more-in-sorrow-than-in-anger disapproval of United States foreign policy is part of the world-wide phenomenon of the Left. The United States and, to an increasing extent, its fellow superpower, the Soviet Union, are the villains of left-wing thought in the world at large and Vietnam has played the most important part in creating this image. It has given anti-Americanism a wider respectability than it previously had in Canada.

Canadian liberal intellectuals are affected by the mood of American liberals, an apparent state of despair about American civilization. The Canadians do not know whether to respond by rejecting the United States and finding their own way or by wallowing in sin with Americans. This dilemma is attributable to one virtue, fairmindedness—the realization that we share the horrid bourgeois civilization and the Cold War and it is not decent to attribute the wickedness to the United States and the virtue to Canada. It is attributable also to the hair-shirt hangup which makes it impossible for some Canadians to accept their more fortunate circumstances. Renata Adler, film critic for the *New York Times,* has pointed to the determination of people to claim guilt for violent political events. "Claiming responsibility for the acts most remote from one seems a way of trying to assert control over things, of denying that events can be random, pointless and chaotically horrible."[4] Out of a laudable effort to avoid hypocrisy, Canadian critics of United States policy in Vietnam have been anxious to blame their own government for complicity. In doing so they have got things out of proportion. They ignore the remarkable degree of detachment from the war in Indochina which the Canadian government has maintained and the part it has tried to play in keeping peace in that area and centre their attention on the less important fact that Canada has not denounced the United States or broken off its defence production sharing agreements. The latter are perfectly valid (if debatable) criticisms, but they divert attention from the more significant event, that Canada, contrary to earlier assumptions, did not have to participate in fighting an American war.

Identification with the United States and its conflicts is to be found most notably on the extreme Left and the extreme Right, although it is probably the Lumpen Middle, brain-washed by television, that is least aware of the fact that Canada is not itself at war in Vietnam. Or faced with problems of conscription and racial violence. If Canadian radicals join anti-Vietnam parades in the streets of Washington, other Canadians will assume an identity of interest with the United States government by calling for the exclusion of draft dodgers and deserters. To describe these inconsistencies is not to suggest there could be perfect consistency. It is simply to suggest that we are here in the thick of paradoxes of which we have to be aware. The extreme Right and the extreme Left do not worry about consistency. They both regard the United States and Canadian governments as linked inseparably in defence of the capitalist system and they must be destroyed together or preserved together in accordance with values more important than the preservation of national sovereignty. The dilemma is for the more pragmatic Canadian nationalist. The Vietnam war, which has given a strong stimulus to Canadian nationalism, could in the end contribute to the erosion of Canadian sovereignty or at least the idea of Canada, not by American intervention but by the refusal of Canadians to accept their condition as non-Americans.

Finally, what impact has the Vietnam war had on Canada's view of itself, of its place in the world, and on the view other people, including the Americans, have of Canada? So many elements have gone into the changes since 1954 that one has to be wary of ascribing them all to Vietnam. How much, for instance, of the increase in nationalism and self-confidence in Canada in the past sixteen years is attributable to the expansion of our economic growth to near great-power figures, and how much to our neighbour's misfortunes? Canadians have suffered in the past from not so much an inferiority complex vis-à-vis the United States as a consciousness of smallness or perhaps of small-townness. Like small-towners they felt poorer and less sophisticated but had no doubt of their moral superiority. The Vietnam war may have encouraged smugness, but I am not sure that it has, in fact, aggravated our sense of moral superiority. As I have suggested, those Canadians most convinced of the immorality of American policy are those most determined to associate Canada with the crime. Other Canadians think we are letting the Americans fight our crusade and they, therefore, feel morally inferior. One can find parallels in the argument fifty years ago between those who believed it was the obligation of Britain to maintain the pax Britannica for our benefit but without our help and those who believed we should contribute to the great imperial cause.

What has shifted is the Canadian view as to who has the luck. Many Canadians grow sceptical of the North American assumption that bigness, whether of population or of industry, is an unquestionably good thing. The comforts of a quieter life and in particular the freedom from the terrible obligations to keep the peace in all parts of the world become daily more obvious. Others, paradoxically, see our luck in the bigness of our resources. We have certainly not shaken off the impetus to economic growth, but we covet less the status of great power because we have become more aware of its dreadful responsibilities and its vulnerability. We seem to be in a period of retreat from the ambitions for world influence which characterized us at the time of the Geneva conference of 1954. Whether this is a renunciation of world responsibility or a seeking after a different or a more appropriate responsibility for a country economically rather than militarily strong remains an unanswered question. Strengthening of the desire for independence or neutrality, for a non-military role, has certainly been encouraged by the Vietnam war, partly by the desire to keep out of something so messy and partly because of the apparent demonstration of the futility of military force.

The Vietnam war still rages and the final results are uncertain. If it ended in a new Geneva agreement with a responsible part for Canada, an adjustment to reasonably independent régimes in Indochina, and an American withdrawal without too great loss of face, we might all resume our active and constructive role in the building of a strong United Nations by experience. On the other hand an American withdrawal in disarray accompanied, or perhaps preceded, by upheavals in the United States would drive us into a frantic effort to isolate ourselves from contagion or, impelled by the death wish which plagues many Canadians, to jump into the flames in order not to be unlike the

Americans. Whatever the shape of events, we are likely to feel a cold chill from a collapse of the pax Americana. Whether we have liked it or not, and it is far from the ideal way to keep the peace, we have regarded it as a bulwark. Canadians who considered that American power was unwisely or wickedly used in Vietnam have, at least subconsciously, thought of diverting it to better causes. *Sub specie aeternitatis* we may regard the disintegration of the American empire as a good thing, but at the moment it would leave Canada more exposed and vulnerable than it has ever been part of our philosophy to regard ourselves. The shock waves alone could be devastating. This is not an argument to join the Americans in the way they are going; it is simply to underline our vital interest in their fate. Canadian calculations about our own situation in the world, whether they are neutralist or alliance-minded, for the most part assume a strong and internationally active United States—as well as a strong Soviet Union in counterpoise. A shift in the capacity, stability, or disposition of either superpower would bring us hard up against the brute facts of survival as an over-resourced and under-populated entity. Our present obsession with independence as the principal theme of foreign and defence policy may then seem to ourselves as heedless as it now does to most foreigners.

Preoccupation with Canada has never been an American obsession, but there is evidence of a changing attitude to us in the age of Vietnam. Persistent in American mythology, although never very high in profile, has been the vision of Canada as the tranquil frontier. It is a view which may be destroyed by recent events in Quebec, but Canada is a vast country and this element is now unpredictable. It is disconcerting to find Americans viewing Canada as an over-sized Walden Pond or a womb-like area where they might find the bliss of childhood. It is a bucolic vision of Canada which Canadians have been anxious to cast off, but it is not unattractive these days to be a haven where brilliant and attractive Americans come to find rest and help fight our expressways. The idea of Canada as America with a second chance has been suggested by no less a person than former United States Secretary of the Interior, Stewart Udall. He told the Montreal Canadian Club Canada ought not to try to win the race of bigness with the United States but should provide a lead in avoiding the galloping, unplanned growth in that country. "Canada has a built-in head start if you should elect to give priority to the creation of an over-all environment of balance and order and beauty."[5] Most sober Canadians realize that we face many of the issues of American society and would like to avoid American mistakes. Many of the American immigrants, especially the intellectuals, see their mission in helping us do exactly this. But we are not just the United States in the days of its innocence and we need different cures for different illnesses. Desegregation is no panacea for our ethnic differences, and, as for Vietnam, our national sin is under- rather than over-involvement in the affairs of other states. We must some time shake that paralyzing conviction that Canada's national purpose is catching up with the United States. Vietnam may have helped.

One is tempted to conclude, trying to avoid smugness, that the Vietnam war and all it has done to the United States, its soul and its image, has given Canadians more confidence in the quality of their own country or at least made them value more their habitat. But has it? Our liberation will not come through any form of obsession with the United States, even if it is hostile. Our artists and writers remain infatuated by the excitement and drama of Vietnam and the race riots—all of which they most vividly deplore. The most successful Canadian play of the year is about the Chicago trials, a phenomenon which one critic described as "the ultimate U.S. cultural invasion of our country." The expatriate actor, Donald Sutherland, whose views, if he were in Canada, would be called anti-American, says, "America is the most exciting country in the world because it is so volatile." Europeans may have been attracted to the United States by its republican virtues. Canadians have been more attracted by its excitement. The United States has always been better theatre. The Vietnam war and the American tragedies it has provoked have fascinated Canadians and drawn their attention away from the incipient tragedy in their own country. And so the Canadian reformers—the Anglophones at least— have only foreign remedies for domestic maladies which are unique. That seems to me a sell-out by English-Canadian intellectuals with consequences as threatening to the Canadian survival as the sell-out of our physical resources with which less purely intellectual Canadians are charged.

Notes

[1]As late as 1966, according to polls of the Canadian Institute of Public Opinion (Gallup), only 31% of Canadians thought the United States should withdraw its troops from Vietnam whereas 18% favoured carrying on at the present level and 27% were for increasing the attacks. By 1967 these figures had shifted to 41%, 16%, and 23%. In 1968, 35% of Canadians said they were grateful to the Americans for their efforts in Vietnam and 37% disassociated themselves from what the Americans were doing there. In May 1970, 36% said their opinion of the United States would go up if they withdrew all their troops from Vietnam and the same per cent said it would have no effect on their view of the great neighbour. In spite of the assurance of an articulate majority on both sides of the issue, it is hard to detect firm convictions on Vietnam by the Canadian public. Shifts of opinion in the last few years probably reflected shifts in opinion in the United States. There has certainly not been mass disapproval of

278 CANADA: A MIDDLE-AGED POWER

United States policy but a desire to remain uninvolved can probably be deduced from the fact that assistance to the United States war effort has been championed by no political party and rarely even by those who speak up in strong defence of American action.

[2]It is interesting to note a similar compulsion among virulently anti-American radicals in Canada who are contemptuous of the pettiness of Canadian grievances and are infatuated with American causes and campuses.

[3]Since 1964 the annual immigration of Americans to Canada has doubled from 11,000 to 22,000, whereas the number of Canadians believed to have moved to the United States has declined from 50,000 to 30,000.

[4]*New York Times,* D 15, 23 June 1968.

[5]*Globe and Mail,* p.b1, 24 October 1967.

6:

Quebec Nationalism and Canadian-American Relations

It is temptingly easy to forget about Quebec when discussing Canadian-American relations. The reason is not just an arrogant rejection of the Quebec fact. It is hard to know how to deal with it. So long as Quebec is part of Canada, then the cultural variations within Canada are not a crucial factor, at least in defence, economics, and foreign policy. If Quebec becomes a state, then, as Canadians like to say in their quaint American way, we are confronted with a whole new ball game. When the Centre québécois de relations internationales and the World Peace Foundation of Boston met at Saint-Marc-sur-Richelieu in June 1974 to continue their exploration of "Québec-Etats-Unis," I was asked to stare at this very difficult subject, "The Significance of Quebec Nationalism for Canadian-American Relations," and say something. These are the remarks prepared for that occasion.

It is impossible to talk of Quebec or of Canadian nationalism without recognizing that the mere existence of the United States—either as a challenge or a threat—is of central importance. The most significant aspect of Quebec nationalism on Canadian-American relations may be the impact it has had on the nationalism of English Canadians. It is shaking up our certainties, sending us back to discover the nature and purpose of the Canadian state. We are, I hope, passing through the stage where fear and the instinct of resistance drove us simply to reaffirm the certainties of the past generation. I hope we are coming to recognize that the sacred principle of evolution we have regarded as our special virtue means that we continue to be an experimental phenomenon, that our genius lies in adaptation to new circumstances and that the circumstances are new. Not only Canada but the whole of North America has been an evolving experiment in government, and

279

we have to see our own evolution, now as always, in the context of a continent.

In the present situation, under the impact not only of internal pressures on the Canadian concept of government but also of rapidly changing facts of international life, we should be open to almost any suggestion. The only sure thing is that the status quo is no place on which to stand. Too many shibboleths stand in the way of fresh thought—national unity is a good thing; nationalism is a bad thing— and our dialogue is inhibited by too many unmentionables: separatism, special status, or continentalism. We need to unplug our ears to each other—Québécois, Americans, or those conglomerate Canadians who grew up speaking not really English but what one might call "harse," roughly translated as "joual."

It is my intention, therefore, to be extremely tentative, to express no certainties, to ask questions and raise possibilities about which I have no fixed convictions. Because my subject is nationalism, which is generally recognized to have an uncertain relationship with economics, I am disposed to accentuate the political and ask whether economic realities can conform to the political will—as it is generally believed they have done in the past in the Canadian-American relationship.

I think it is fair to say that the reaction to Quebec nationalism of what for want of a better term I shall have to call English Canadians—or of most of them—has been to fall back on the assumption that if Canada is going to survive and prosper on a continent where it is unequally paired with a superpower, it can do so only by strengthening the power of the federal government to control and manipulate the economy. There is justification for the assumption because such a philosophy in Ottawa did lay the basis of Canada's evolution as an independent country and its postwar emergence as a major economic power in the world. Even those who argue that we built up not an independent but a satellite economy blame the central government for not being stronger. National unity is accepted in rhetoric as the unquestioned goal. Hypnotized by the United States, English Canadians have been losing sight of the other assumptions of the Canadian system. They are victims of the Americanization of Canadian nationalism, which imposes American philosophy on what was a very different experiment in government. They have accepted even the blackmail of the tranquil revolutionists, that Canada without Quebec would have no identity. They have got themselves out on a long limb—and lost contact with their roots.

For what is Canada? It never was an effort to create the new man or even a readily indentifiable Canadian. The purpose of the founders was to put a protective roof over their heads so that they could live their North American-style lives under different rules from those of the Great Republic which for varying reasons they disliked. Eventually they came together to erect a joint and presumably stronger framework for the same purpose. The purpose of this structure was peace, order, and good government, based on common sense, compromise, and collusion rather than the miasma of national unity. Unhappily American imperialism provoked Canadian imperialism in the late nineteenth century, and the healthy pragmatism of the founders was lost sight of. I suppose we needed that all-Canadian fanaticism to build the Canadian Pacific Railway, and I don't regret our making it from sea to sea, but I do regret some of the consequences. We have lost sight of the fact that the purpose of the Canadian state was less to create Canadians than to provide a framework within which Nova Scotians, Quebeckers, or Vancouver Islanders could flourish as securely and prosperously as international circumstances would allow. If New-foundlanders joined later to get Ottawa's family allowances, that was not cynical; it was a recognition of the purposes of the Canadian state—a progressive and civilized concept of the purposes of a state: to serve its people.

It is a purpose which requires a high degree of flexibility, a sensitive distribution of power in accordance with changing functions and circumstances. It is destroyed by dogmatism, in particular the dogmatic belief in central authority. Obviously decentralization carried to extremes means the end of the experiment, but this does not require fanatical resistance to decentralization in principle. Timidity ought not to close the mind to a restructuring of the experiment. Canadians have never adequately recognized their own genius for constitutional adaptation. In addition to our considerable contribution to the theory and practice of federal and of multicultural states, we virtually invented the Commonwealth which, whatever its future, played a notable historic function as a framework for constructive disintegration. Here at home we have not seen the end of the experiment which began with New France, was at one time the Dominion of Canada, and is reshaping itself into who knows what.

It is hard for English Canadians to accept this matter of fact interpretation of the meaning of their existence when they are hot after a Canadian cultural identity. I think they are somewhat confused between the need to construct a Canadian culture and the need to protect and nourish culture in Canada. We cannot allow the metropolitaniza-tion of culture, which is a world-wide phenomenon, to suck away our talent, and we must keep our artists focused on our own life so that we do not see ourselves falsely through foreign prisms. If our artists discover certain common features of Canadian life, the product of a shared political experience, so much the better, provided they realize that such uniformity is not essential. It is knowing ourselves in all our particularities that makes us healthy. Here English Canadians, as in so many things, have learned from Quebec. Awareness of, envy of, the burgeoning Quebec literature and cinema based on the native experience has been the major stimulus for a similar revolution in Toronto, Winnipeg, Vancouver, and even London, Ontario. The self-conscious Canadianism of the recent past, which had meaning only as defiance of Hollywood, Chicago, or London, is giving way to a critical and even amused examination of real people in Newfoundland, a small town in Saskatchewan, or of Nova Scotians in Toronto. It is not so much nationalism as nativism. What we have in common is the searching for ourselves. The most popular contemporary playwright in Toronto is Michel Tremblay.

So English Canadians have moved, I think, to the point where it would not be difficult for them to accept the comfortable concept of cultural autonomy for Quebec within a federation or union of some sort based on economics. It has been made very clear to them that the artists and intellectuals of Quebec, by and large, want to live unto themselves. The cultural autonomy of these Quebeckers is such an obvious fact, the question may be asked whether constitutional autonomy is required. English Canadians begin to wonder also if bilingualism is worth while, and they relax. Life might be easier all round if Quebeckers could do what they like and the rest of us did not have to feel guilty about doing what we like. If someone could come up with a formula which would organize that way of life, it might be very successful politically.

Cultural autonomy with economic union are obviously attractive also to many Quebeckers, but one cannot ignore those who say they are not compatible, that culture and economics cannot be separated, especially by a people who have been economically disadvantaged. I certainly do not reject that argument, but I wish we could do a little more exploring of the contradictions involved. The trouble is that neither federalists nor independentists can, for good enough political reasons, admit that any compromise is possible. This is particularly the case for the independentist who must encourage his followers to take a bold risk. They must not be beguiled with the possibility of an easier way out. The anglais must remain maudits.

For the independentist the dialogue can be permitted only after independence is an accomplished fact. With the logic of that position I sympathize. The trouble is that the economic and political factors on this continent are so much entwined that no new state could be immaculately conceived. There has to be preliminary negotiating or preliminary fighting among all three parties. The latter certainly ought to be regarded as a last resort. By that I do not mean that Ottawa or even Washington should regard armed force as the ultimate weapon to prevent the independence of Quebec. What I mean is that we ought to look before it is too late at imaginative and pacific arrangements for relationships which would give us all optimal satisfaction.

What sort of relationships might they be? Must they for example, be based on the present bilateral division of the continent? The principal argument in the 1970s for an arrangement which preserves a basic division along the 49th parallel is the shifting balance of advantage to the north in the looming world crisis over resources and population. That crisis has already affected drastically the working habits of the Canadian constitution. The balance of power and advantage on which the federation rests has been strengthened by the dissidence of Alberta and by the Quebec interest in a national energy policy. The conferences of first ministers have become a major element of the constitution. One can regard these meetings as evidence of disunity across the country or of a persistent will to compromise when a national policy is clearly required. Whatever it is, it is the denial of the old thesis that a national policy can be achieved only by the assertion of the authority of Ottawa. The reserve power of the federal government is certainly a factor but it is used to obtain an inter-provincial consensus. In the economic sphere Alberta is asserting rights to discriminate against other Canadians which go beyond anything Quebec has demanded. Quebec assertions in the fields of education or even international relations must henceforth be seen in that light. In other words, the changing climate of federal-provincial relations suggests that there are better chances than there were in a more doctrinaire period for the accommodation of Quebec and Canadian nationalisms in a structure, federal or quasi-federal, which maintains the common resistance to continentalism.

What of the school of thought which regards a period of constitutional separation as essential while both parts of Canada come to terms with themselves and understand better their own interests in each other—to be followed by negotiation for reunion or partnership on a more equitable basis? It is an idea that is attractive because it is based on good psychology. A danger, however, is that the haggling over the disposition of effects associated with the divorce and remarriage could poison the relationship indefinitely. What is perhaps more relevant to our subject today is the fact that the centripetal forces of continentalism are such that Quebec and Canada could hardly hope to maintain during a prolonged interim sufficient control over their own polities to come together again. So without any desire to be unhelpful, the Americans, by their mere existence, limit the freedom of choice we have to experiment.

What about options in a broader continental context? A state of Quebec which had cut the economic and political ties with Canada would be relatively stronger than most independent states, but the maintenance of its high standard of living and the fact that it has been embedded in a North American economy would create special problems. Assuming that a close association with the EEC is unobtainable or undesirable, a special economic relationship with the United States could be attractive—Quebeckers because of their greater cultural assurance being less nervous than other Canadians about becoming economically integrated. Although Washington seems not at all disposed to encourage Quebec nationalism, it is not inclined to be very sentimental about Canada because Canada is fat and rich. Faced with a fait accompli, Washington would have to live with a state of Quebec and pursue its own special interests. The common assumption that a truncated Canada would have no alternative than to be swallowed up in one or two parts in the great Republic cannot be dismissed but should not be taken for granted. Canadians would suffer from a wounded image, but they would retain many of the natural advantages of remaining on their own, e.g. more oil and less homicide. There could be a feeling of relief. The idealists would feel deeply the failure of the bicultural endeavour but others might see a new world of opportunity opening up—rather like the Dutch and the Belgians when they looked back on lost colonies as a burden rather than an advantage. This new national enthusiasm, however, would, by reason of the exigencies of a curious geography, be tempered with pragmatism.

Anything like an EEC model has been deemed inappropriate for North America because of the unsymmetrical nature of the political division. The imbalance of economic power would perhaps be aggravated rather than narrowed by a division of Canada, but the idea of three rather than two countries forming an economic community is more attractive in principle. Suggestions that Mexico might be drawn into a tripartite partnership with the United States and Canada have never been more than figments of the post-prandial imagination because the Mexicans have needed, even more than Canada, to protect their economic life. However, there is no need to close our minds indefinitely to speculation in that direction. We are presumably talking about an evolution of governmental structures, but in times when change can be rapid and drastic.

A loosening of the federal structure in Canada could, as federalists have always maintained, lead to a gradual regionalization of the continent, not by government action but by business and societal forces. Our affiliations would be determined not by our elected governments but by the disposition of American corporations, of Kiwanis International or the World Football League to lay us out in sales regions which defy the border. Quebec is better protected here by its linguistic identity. It has even given something approaching a special identity to an American baseball team. For the rest of Canada, this kind of regionalization is highly subversive, but the answer could be in the affirmation of our own provincial orders as well as resistance on a national level.

I need not add that my speculations beg more questions than they answer, and I do not propose here and now to defend them on constitutional or economic grounds. They are just part of an argument that in considering where the forces of Quebec, Canadian, and American nationalism are leading us we should look forward constructively rather than backwards defensively. Government for the people is a North American principle we all have in common. It is a principle which requires constant adaptation because the people's will keeps changing. What is required most of all is constructive dialogue. Quebeckers and Americans have never talked enough to each other, have tended to let English Canadians handle relations with the United States. Americans, terrorized by Canadian nationalists into keeping their hands off Canada, are afraid even to be helpful. English Canadians and French Canadians maintain their contacts in the political zone, but the dialogue among academics and intellectuals has almost ceased. Too many subjects are taboo.

There is also a central paradox for many English Canadians. They find themselves often sympathetic with the political concepts of the Quebec independentists, recognize that they resemble their own views vis-à-vis the United States, and have a sneaking suspicion that they would be in that camp if they were Quebeckers. Nevertheless, they are at cross purposes because they don't want the independentists to be successful in amputating a part of the flesh and blood of the Canada to which they are deeply attached. That English Canadians have an economic interest in the maintenance of the federation is undeniable. That their attachment to Quebec is also one of emotion and affection is too little recognized. But the emotions, like the economics, are inequitable. Quebec is a part of the Canadian legend whereas the English provinces are dispensable for Quebeckers seeking their roots. In such circumstances it is not easy to discuss the terms of divorce, new rules for cohabitation, or a ménage à trois.

Part Five:
In Conclusion

Tributes to youth are so ritual and perfunctory it is hard to sound honest. Nevertheless, I wish to say that whatever there is of wisdom in the contents of this book derives in large measure from the opportunities I have had to engage in seminars during the past eight years with a quite remarkable crop of students. They consistently oblige me to dismantle and rebuild my structures. They are respectful and sceptical and more inclined than their elder brothers to treat me as an equal. Constant association with them sharpens the mind and is good for the soul. I suspect it would induce even the editors of the *Globe and Mail* to cheer up. I find them reassuring because they have the capacity to come to grips with the future far better than I have. The following remarks were delivered to a 1973 Convocation of Lakehead University in Thunder Bay on 26 May—with some variations taken from an address the following month on a similar occasion at the University of Western Ontario

Convocation Address

I am greatly honoured to be present at this particular occasion in this particular place. Here at the Lakehead one knows he is in the heart of this country, North and South, East and West. The permanent Canadian condition is here vividly reflected—with the solemn land to the north and the unsolemn land to the south. Each is in its own way intimidating, and our national problem is how to live with both.

Convocation is a solemn occasion. I wish you all the success I know you deserve and if I say simply that I have great confidence in what you will do for yourselves and this country I hope you will accept that as something more than the solemn pronouncement which an occasion such as this requires.

My confidence is based on more than faith. Perhaps I should admit that I am by nature an optimist. Like C.S.Lewis, "I am an optimist because I believe in the fall of man." People like Mr. Lewis and me don't believe the world was beautiful just before we were born, and we are more inclined to notice progress than regression. Furthermore, my work of late has led me to closer study of the history of Canada's relations with the world outside and it is hard to avoid the one obvious conclusion. Any people who have not merely survived but have triumphed over challenges to their personal and national existence much more forbidding than those they now face ought not to be cringing defensively but should be leading the march towards a better international community. The other reason for optimism is that at an age when I should be taking up basket-weaving I have taken up teaching—if one can use that word for the experience of one who conducts seminars in a modern university. Six years direct exposure to college youth gives one an entirely different impression from the portrait on which the glossier periodicals thrive. It is of some slight comfort to me to realize that those of my generation could spell better and we knew how to put a verb in a sentence. Intellectually, however, we were much less sophisticated—appallingly so. I should hate to have one of my students see one of my college essays on how to save the world for peace—even though he could learn a little grammar from it. Incidentally, I trust that in the great concern you are all going to show for ecology you will awaken to the serious consequences of verbal pollution. If not, we are going to have a generation of Canadians which isn't even unilingual.

Now I don't want to fall into the fashionable habit of so-called "concerned adults" who take the temperature of youth at intervals and devise forecasts of hope or despondency for the world on the basis of what students are doing or being or consuming this season. I rather suspect that what students are doing most of the time is pulling our leg. However, as you probably know, it is being said at the moment that in the 'seventies you are growing apathetic, conservative, exhausted with causes except the promotion of your own welfare. Among professors I detect even a nostalgia for the obstreperous days when your elder brothers and sisters were locking them up for days in their own filing cabinets. All I can say is that unawareness and acquiescence are not the qualities I note among the students to whom I am at present exposed— and I doubt if the intellectual climate on the old Ontario strand differs much from that on Lake Superior. I have never known such a combination of healthy scepticism, honest enquiry, and intellectual integrity. My optimism in the country is based on solid evidence that in spite of reduced subsidies, the permissive society, foreign professors, and mixed bathing, the universities of this province are turning out people with the qualities we badly need to run this fractious country. I sometimes wonder frankly whether the graduate's good sense isn't a product of his survival—survival from professors, professors of a previous generation whose absolute convictions about absolute causes have fortunately contradicted each other. It is perhaps by growing up absurd that you see the light, the light being the realization that truth is not so easily established as those professors thought.

The trouble with all those crusaders, confident of the truth divinely revealed to them, is that they would blow up the country or the world for a principle. Now I should like to make a small plea for pragmatism, not as the one absolute philosophy but just as a corrective. If this country and this world of ours are going to survive they need a lot of management—management by intelligent, educated human beings with blood in their veins and a sense of proportion, masters of the computer but not its slaves. The beginning of wisdom is the recognition of complexity, the need to live with paradox. That seems to me the Canadian way and the only way for a country as happily diversified and elongated as ours.

There are admittedly less attractive strains in our national tradition which we can identify—a certain niggardliness of spirit for example. We are being told now that ours is a tradition of beautiful losers. But our myths and traditions are what we make them and there is a lot to be said for identifying and perhaps even for exaggerating certain national virtues in order to propagate them. Our national disposition to compromise may have been overstated, but it is worth cultivating. We shall expire if we work away self-destructively at negative myths, finding our virtues only in being not as other men are—especially our nasty neighbours.

290 CANADA: A MIDDLE-AGED POWER

As on old-fashioned nationalist with deep roots in the clay and rock and, more particularly, the marvellously unhomogenous peoples of this province and this country I am disturbed over some aspects of contemporary Canadian nationalism. I am disturbed not because, like many of my generation, I think nationalism is evil. I think it is essential to good citizenship. By profession I am an internationalist and I have seen what morbid nationalism can do to the peace of nations. The answer, however, is not to ban national emotion but to keep our nationalism from being morbid. World peace is not to be found in the homogenization of peoples but in the protection of peoples in all their healthy diversification. This protection can in the foreseeable future come only from the maintenance of sovereign states, another institution, like nationalism, which has got a bad reputation of late from dogmatic internationalists. The purpose of a good state is the peace, order, and good government of the people it shelters. As such it is an essential and constructive element in an international community of states.

The nationalism we need to pump blood into our Canadian state need threaten no one—unless it turns sick. If it is to accommodate the kind of free and easy country which it is our good fortune to be, it should be relaxed, self-confident, generous, and tolerant, equipped above all with a sense of proportion which means a sense of humour. Its aim should not be, as we too often say, national unity. It should be national harmony, equilibrium. Those who are preoccupied with the Canadian identity should realize that this kind of nationalism is about as Canadian and as un-American as you would want. The United States, by its Declaration of Independence, is dedicated to a world mission and to unity. That's fine for them. No Canadian should disparage the enormous contribution to the world made by the ideals proclaimed in that Declaration, however imperfectly they have at times been applied. But we have our own thing to do. Ours is a very different political experiment—to set our kind of example. We have to prove that a state can have good government without national unity, that flexibility and looseness are political virtues in the complex world we face.

Too much Canadian nationalism is just hand-me-down American nationalism, even when it sounds anti-American. Some of our more simple-minded nationalists want to create a Canadian identity which is just a mirror image of American nationalism adorned with a maple leaf. A fig leaf would be more appropriate. What are we anyway if our bosoms swell with pride only when an ill-advised group of drum majorettes from Saskatchewan, dressed like West Point cadets, wins a prize in Pasadena or a bunch of American baseball players do their stunts in a Montreal park instead of in Milwaukee? Whether sewing maple leaf flags on the backside of one's jeans swells the bosom is a problem I leave to the physiologists.

More worrying, however, than this kind of adolescent nationalism is the effort of some of our more fanatical nationalists to divorce us entirely from the North American society of which Canadians are just as native as the Americans, to imagine that we are or could ever be a nation undefiled by the contagion of contemporary society. We must profit from the mistakes of the Americans and not meekly assume that our national goal is just to catch up to them. But identifying all our troubles as American in origin is not only bad diagnosis; it leads us to the wrong kind of cures. We cannot shut out infection by closing the 49th parallel. Infection would in any case reach us by air or sea from Europe or Japan, which, like Canada, are struggling with problems of industrialization, modernization, pollution, capitalism, or whatever you want to call it. The United States has always been a pioneer society—even in sin.

It seems to me that too many of our contemporary nationalists start with the wrong premise. Our problem is not how to divorce the United States but how to live with it. The continental relationship was not fastened on us by gutless politicians and bureaucrats who sold us out for a fast buck—according to current myth. It was established by the glaciers. And it was our own Canadian forefathers who decided to co-habit this continent and to carve out a separate constitutional existence. We cannot hold the British or Americans responsible for our success or failure; we are no more their victims than we are their foster children. Our forefathers knew perfectly well that if we were going to be Canadians we had to find ways of living with that giant force to the south. They knew that we had no right to expect the Americans to be our patrons or our benefactors. We chose the terms on which we would try to live. We shall exist and prosper now and forever more by a combination of manipulation, confrontation, and, more often, mutual accommodation. There is no solution to, no fixed formula for, the Canadian-American relationship.

There is a fashionable current assumption that this is a zero-sum game, that any American advantage is bound to be our disadvantage, that the way to deal with the Americans is to tell them to run away, to cease and desist—to join Mexico. But this is the fantasy of those who have not faced up to the reality of relations among states. The weaker country has to survive by its wits, its brain power—and that is where you come in with your well-furbished brains. Our problem, as ever, is to devise the kinds of treaties, agreements, bargains, joint commissions, or even trade unions which will provide the greatest possible satisfaction to both countries. The assumption that any agreement reached with the Americans about resources or defence is bound to be to our disadvantage is not only craven; it is unhistorical. But if the Americans see no satisfaction of their own interests, they won't accept it. In these days even the East and West Germans are seeking ways of living with each other for mutual benefit. The peoples of this continent will not tolerate a wall. We are too restless and inquisitive.

A good, sound border, however, is not an impenetrable wall. We need a border to keep us politically separate and live in our own way. There is no need to feel apologetic about insisting on our separate institutions. This sprawling continent is far better governed in two parts and we Canadians have many reasons of comfort, convenience, and emotion to want to preserve our kind of government. Our distinctive contribution to the United Nations is a good enough justification in itself. Don't be beguiled by the sentimental anti-nationalism of those who think the world would be more peaceful if we abandoned our nation states and amalgamated. It is a statistical fact that more people are murdered by members of the family than by strangers. And don't be beguiled either by Americans or by subsidiary Canadians who think it would be so much more efficient if Canada were run as a branch plant and the continent put on a cost benefit basis. Those who deplore economic nationalism as if it were a virus are not always, as they claim, internationalists. Many of them honestly confuse industrial progress with human progress and are impatient of all obstacles put in their way by human beings. Sometimes they mistake United States or continental nationalism for internationalism. (A generation of Canadians horrified at the kind of nationalism which caused the World Wars has been understandably somewhat susceptible to this anti-nationalist plea.)

These critics of nationalism would not make headway, however, if so much of what passes for Canadian nationalism at the moment did not have ugly spots on it. It is too often a sick chauvinism without the magnanimity befitting a country that, whatever its problems with a larger neighbour, must regard itself as a responsible and constructive force in the international community. We need allies if we are going to stand up to the great powers. The good reputation and the friendships we have acquired in the world are essential to the promotion of our national interests. They are dissipated all too quickly when we strike the posture of the neurotic poor relation for whose miseries someone else is always responsible.

It is indeed fortunate that you are in a position to comprehend the dilemmas of international life more intelligently than my generation was because in forty years Canadians have moved out of shelter into the mainstream of international complication. We are more alone than we once were, with the lives and the fate of our country dependent upon the way in which we chart our own course. We are not a military power of consequence, but we are one of the major economic powers of the world—a fact too often obscured for us by the shadow of a unique superpower. That is a fact to induce not vain boasting but a sense of responsibility. The looming issues of the future have economic roots. The central dilemma of Canada's existence in the last quarter of this century will be how to live as the people who in all the world have more land and resources per capita than any other. And this in an age when the pressure of population on resources is more likely than the simple lust for empire to determine whether the universe will continue in something resembling tranquillity. In Canada our myopic obsession with the control of our economy in a purely North American context has shaded our eyes from the universal problem. The question we now debate, for example, about the share of our energy fuels the Americans can have is not irrelevant but it is only one aspect of a global issue in which other continents may play the decisive role.

Our obsession with the United States gives us a permanent squint. The anti-Americans are just as obsessed as the so-called continentalists. We shall never be liberated until we cast off this obsession and look out at the broad world. In that world our problem isn't that we are weak and dependent but that we are filthy rich. Our proper concern for the distribution of income within our country does not affect the status of fat cat which Canada occupies in the community of nations. Because we have had to struggle vigilantly to maintain our national existence in the rough embrace of a pachyderm, we have developed an inferiority complex which looks self-indulgent from the perspective of Rangoon or Port-of-Spain. Our nationalism of late has turned too easily into jingoism when we stridently warn off from our sacred shores and somewhat less sacred continental shelf hungry peoples who just might need our fish and oil a lot more than we do. In their eyes we are in no sense a victimized people.

Isolationism is no longer either a personal or a national alternative for Canadians. We are in the thick of things, not because larger powers have dragged us in to them but because our greatest national interest is a world in which we can peacefully trade. What we need are Canadian nationalists who recognize that if we pursue the national interest too narrowly we lose the way, for the world is wide—who recognize that the way is hard to find and there are no simple maps. Above all they must realize that it is only by accommodating our interests to those of others that any of us can survive. And it is largely because that is the prevailing attitude among students as I know them in 1973 that my confidence in you and the country is an empirical conclusion rather than just what seemed the right thing to say on this very happy occasion.

In John Holmes, experience, wisdom and wit have combir
produce the most admired commentator writing today on
ada's external relations. His first volume of essays, *The*
Part of Valour (1970) confirmed that here was a former
Canadian diplomat who was able to discuss Canada's f
relations not from a polemical standpoint but as one who
stood the changing international system and its consequenc
Canada's role. In this second volume of essays, written
1970, Holmes examines the new challenges confronting C
as a middling power in a much more complex and inter
dent world than the one which emerged from the Second
War. The essays in this collection concern themselves wi
Trudeau foreign policy review, the recent frustrations i
United Nations, the Vietnam war, Quebec nationalism and
dian views of the United States.

After almost twenty years in the Department of Ex
Affairs, John Holmes is now Director of Research for the
dian Institute of International Affairs. He also lectures
University of Toronto and Glendon College of York Univ

FIRST REPRINT

0-7710-9798-0

McCLELLAND & STEWART LIMITED

BETWEEN MAN AND MAN

Other books by Martin Buber

I AND THOU

GOOD AND EVIL

TWO TYPES OF FAITH

PATHS IN UTOPIA

THE WAY OF MAN

THE KNOWLEDGE OF MAN

BETWEEN
MAN AND MAN

MARTIN BUBER

With an Afterword by the author
on "The History of the Dialogical Principle"

Introduction by Maurice Friedman

THE MACMILLAN COMPANY
New York

Translated by Ronald Gregor Smith

Afterword translated by Maurice Friedman

Second Printing, 1966

PRINTED IN THE UNITED STATES OF AMERICA

The translator has pleasure in acknowledging the generous help of Mr. Kurt Emmerich, who gave unstintingly of his time and knowledge in the earlier stages of the translation, and of the author himself, who read not only the entire MS. but also the proofs, and made countless valuable suggestions.

CONTENTS

CONTENTS

FOREWORD

THE five works which I have brought together for English readers in this volume have arisen in connexion with my little book *I and Thou* (1923),[1] as filling out and applying what was said there, with particular regard to the needs of our time.

The first of these works, *Dialogue* (1929) proceeded from the desire to clarify the "dialogical" principle presented in *I and Thou*, to illustrate it and to make precise its relation to essential spheres of life.

The Question to the Single One, which contains some political inferences, is the elaboration of an address which I gave to the students of the three German-Swiss Universities at the close of 1933. The book appeared in Germany in 1936—astonishingly, since it attacks the life-basis of totalitarianism. The fact that it could be published with impunity is certainly to be explained from its not having been understood by the `appropriate authorities.

There follow two addresses on major problems of education, the first given at the Third International Educational Conference at Heidelberg in 1925, the second at the National Conference of Jewish Teachers of Palestine at Tel-Aviv in 1939. Both addresses treat of the significance of the dialogical principle in the sphere of education, the first for its groundwork, the second for its most important task.

The volume concludes with my inaugural course of lectures as Professor of Social Philosophy at the Hebrew University of Jerusalem (1938). This course shows, in the unfolding of the question about the essence of man, that it is by beginning neither with the individual nor with the collectivity, but only with the reality of the mutual relation between man and man, that this essence can be grasped.

MARTIN BUBER

Jerusalem

[1] English edition (R. & R. Clark, Edinburgh), 1937, 3rd impression, 1945.

INTRODUCTION

by Maurice Friedman*

When Dag Hammarskjöld's plane crashed in Northern Rhodesia, the Secretary General of the United Nations had with him the manuscript of a translation that he was making of Martin Buber's classic work *I and Thou*. It is because of this book and the philosophy of dialogue that it presents that Dag Hammarskjöld repeatedly nominated Martin Buber for a Nobel Prize in literature. *I and Thou* is recognized today as among the handful of writings that the twentieth century will bequeath to the centuries to come, but for many readers this compact and poetic little book needs an introduction to be properly understood and applications to concrete fields of human experience to be properly appreciated. More than any other work of Buber's, *Between Man and Man* provides this introduction and these applications. The opening essay on "Dialogue," in particular, with its contrast between "dialogue" and "monologue" and its personal anecdotes, represents the best introduction to Buber's philosophy of dialogue, while the other essays in this volume show its applications for such concerns as religious ethics, politics, social philosophy, marriage, education, psychology, art, the development of character, and philosophical anthropology, or the study of the problem of man.

In his Foreword to *Between Man and Man*, Martin Buber states that the five works brought together in this volume fill out and apply what was said in *I and Thou*. "Dialogue" clarifies the "dialogical" principle presented in *I and Thou*, illustrates it, and makes "precise its relation to essential spheres of life." The terminology and scope of *I and Thou* are different from those of "Dialogue," however. In *I and Thou*, Buber contrasts man's two primary attitudes—the two ways in which he ap-

* Author of the comprehensive study *Martin Buber: The Life of Dialogue* (New York: Harper Torchbooks, 1960).

proaches existence. One of these is the "I-Thou" relationship, the other the "I-It." The difference between these two relationships is not the nature of the object to which one relates, as is often thought. Not every relation between persons is an I-Thou one, nor is every relation with an animal or thing an I-It. The difference, rather, is in the relationship itself. I-Thou is a relationship of openness, directness, mutuality, and presence. It may be between man and man, but it may also take place with a tree, a cat, a fragment of mica, a work of art—and through all of these with God, the "eternal Thou" in whom the parallel lines of relations meet. I-It, in contrast, is the typical subject-object relationship in which one knows and uses other persons or things without allowing them to exist for oneself in their uniqueness: The tree that I meet is not a Thou before I meet it. It harbors no hidden personality that winks at me as I pass by. Yet if I meet it in its uniqueness, letting it have its impact on me without comparing it with other trees or analyzing the type of leaf or wood or calculating the amount of firewood I may get out of it, then I may speak of an I-Thou relationship with it. The person that I meet is, by courtesy of our language and our attitudes, a "person" before I meet him. But he is not yet a Thou for me until I step into elemental relationship with him, and if I do not step into this relationship, even the politest forms of address do not prevent his remaining for me an It. I cannot, of course, produce an I-Thou relationship by my own action and will, for it is really mutual only when the other comes to meet me as I him. But I can prevent such a relationship from coming into being if I am not ready to respond or if I attempt to respond with anything less than my whole being insofar as my resources in this particular situation allow.

I-Thou and I-It stand in fruitful and necessary alternation with each other. Man cannot will to persevere in the I-Thou relationship. He can only desire again and again to bring the indirectness of the world of It into the directness of the meeting with the Thou and thereby give the world of It meaning. So long as this alternation continues, man's existence is authentic. When the It swells up and blocks the return to the Thou, then man's existence becomes unhealthy, his personal and social life inauthentic. This applies equally to the contrast between "dialogue" and "monologue" that Buber makes in "Dialogue." However, here the concern is basically the relationship between man and man and, only insofar as the term is extended to art, the relationship between the human and the nonhuman.

In defining "dialogue," Buber introduces a concept that exists only implicitly in *I and Thou*, that of "experiencing the other side" of the relationship. This act of "inclusion," as Buber calls it in "Education," is that which makes it possible to meet and know the other in his concrete uniqueness and not just as a content of one's experience. In "technical dialogue," of course, no such experiencing of the other side takes place, since here the concern is only with what is communicated and not with the partners in the dialogue themselves. Still less is there "inclusion" in "monologue disguised as dialogue," that absolutization of oneself and relativization of the other that makes so much conversation between men into what Buber, in a later essay, calls "speechifying." The mark of contemporary man is that he does not really listen, says Buber. Only when one really listens—when one becomes personally aware of the "signs of address" that address one not only in the words of but in the very meeting with the other—does one attain to that sphere of the "between" that Buber holds to be the "really real."

"All real living is meeting," says Buber in *I and Thou*, and *Between Man and Man* again and again points to this seemingly evanescent sphere of the "between" as ontological reality. To say that "all real living is meeting" is not to say that one leaves one's ground in order to meet the other or that one lets oneself get swallowed up in the crowd and trades in one's individuality for a social role. "In the graciousness of its comings and the solemn sadness of its goings"—gracious because one cannot will both sides of the dialogue and sad because every I-Thou relationship must inevitably turn into an It, while the It need not become a Thou—the I-Thou relationship "teaches us to meet others and to hold our ground when we meet them." This means that experiencing the other side, or, as Buber later calls it, "imagining the real," goes hand in hand with remaining on one's own side of the relationship. Therefore, even the imaginative experiencing of the blow that I give to the other or of the pleasure that the other's skin feels beneath my caress must not be confused with "empathy," in which I give up my own ground for a purely aesthetic identification. Also, as Buber points out in "Education" and further develops in his "Postscript" to the second edition of *I and Thou,* in the helping relationships—those of teacher and pupil, parent and child, doctor and patient, minister and parishioner—this experiencing of the other side cannot be expected to be mutual without destroying the relationship or converting it into friendship.

It is this emphasis upon the ontological reality of the "between" and upon the possibility of experiencing the other side of the relationship that distinguishes Buber from such existentialists as Kierkegaard, Heidegger, Sartre, and even Tillich. "The Question to the Single One" makes clear a fundamental critique of the existentialism of Kierkegaard, who posits an exclusive I-Thou relationship between the "Single One" and God and leaves the relationship between man and man secondary and inessential. But in "What Is Man?" Buber shows that even Martin Heidegger, for all his emphasis upon solicitude and upon *Dasein ist Mitsein* (being-there-in-the-world as being-with-others), does not reach the ground of genuine dialogue. In fact, as I make clear in the "Intersubjectivity" section of *The Worlds of Existentialism,* the concern of thinkers like Sartre and Heidegger with "intersubjectivity" does not imply the I-Thou relationship, for many interpersonal, intersubjective relations remain fundamentally I-It. One need only contrast Sartre's attitude toward love in *Being and Nothingness* with Buber's attitude toward love in "Dialogue," "The Question to the Single One," and "Education" to recognize how Sartre limits human relationships *a priori* to my knowing the other as subject only when he knows me as object or, at best, to my recognizing his freedom only as a freedom that I wish to possess and dominate by my own freedom through seducing him to incarnate his freedom in his body. Buber, in contrast, sees love as precisely the recognition of the other's freedom, the fullness of a dialogue in which I turn to my beloved in his otherness, independence, and self-reality with all the power of intention of my own heart. It is this recognition that makes Buber the leading representative of those existentialists, such as Gabriel Marcel, Albert Camus, Karl Jaspers, and Franz Rosenzweig, who see dialogue, communication, and the I-Thou relationship not as a *dimension* of the self but as the existential and ontological reality in which the self comes into being and through which it fulfills and authenticates itself.*

But what is the reader to make of the fact that Buber extends the I-Thou relationship from the meeting with man, nature, and art to that with God? Can creation's "signs of address" really be compared with the conscious address made to me by my fellowman? Yes, if the concept of dialogue is properly understood. Dialogue is not merely the interchange of words—genuine dialogue can take place in silence, whereas much conversation is really monologue. It is, rather, the response of one's whole being to the otherness of the other, that otherness that is comprehended only when I open myself to him in the present and in the concrete situation and respond to his need even when he himself is not aware that he is addressing me. The God that speaks here is the God one meets only when one has put aside everything one thinks one knows of God and is plunged into the darkness, when the "moment Gods" fuse into the "Lord of the Voice." This "Lord of the Voice" does not speak to us apart from creation but right through it. Woman may be the "temptation to finitude," as Kierkegaard thought when he sacri-

* Cf. *The Worlds of Existentialism: A Critical Reader,* edited and with Introductions and a Conclusion by Maurice Friedman (New York: Random House, 1964), Part IV: Intersubjectivity and pp. 535–44 of Part VII: Issues and Conclusions.

ficed his fiancée Regina Olsen to God, but the road to God is through "fulfilled finitude." "The Regina Olsens of this world are not the hurdles on the road to God. They are the road." Marriage is the "exemplary bond" through which we touch on the real otherness of the other and learn to understand his truth and untruth, his justice and injustice. Each man's shortest road to God is the longest available to him—the creation in which he is set and with which he has to do.

God is not met by turning away from the world or by making God into an object of contemplation, a "being" whose existence can be proved and whose attributes can be demonstrated. God is met only as Thou. As I know the person of the other only in dialogue with him, I know God only in dialogue. But this is the dialogue that goes on moment by moment in each new situation, the dialogue that makes my ethical "ought" a matter of real response with no preparation other than my readiness to respond with my whole being to the unforeseen and the unique. I can know neither God nor moral values as transcendent realities knowable in themselves apart from the dialogue in which I meet God and discover values. For this reason, Buber is best understood not as a theologian—he has no theological assumptions or dogmas on which to build—or even as a philosopher of religion, but as a philosophical anthropologist, an investigator of the problem of man.*

It is as a philosophical anthropologist that Buber approaches *I and Thou*. He is concerned there not with deducing man's place from some over-all concept of being or the cosmos but with that twofold attitude that makes man man. Man becomes man with the other self. He would not be man at all without the I-Thou relationship. And man becomes more fully human through moving

* Buber himself makes this point in all explicitness in his "Replies to My Critics," translated by Maurice Friedman, in *The Philosophy of Martin Buber* volume of The Library of Living Philosophers series, edited by Paul Arthur Schilpp and Maurice Friedman (La Salle, Ill.: The Open Court Publishing Co., 1965).

from the separateness of the man who is no longer a child to the mature I-Thou relationship. Similarly, in the works in *Between Man and Man*, the genuineness of man's existence is seen as dependent upon his bringing all his separate spheres of activity into "the life of dialogue," a life in which one does not necessarily have *much* to do with others but *really* has to do with those with whom one has to do. In "The Question to the Single One," man is recognized as the one creature who has potentiality, the potentiality of each man to realize that unique direction and task that only he can. "When I get to heaven," said the Hasidic rabbi Susya shortly before his death, "they will not ask me, 'Why were you not Moses?' but 'Why were you not Susya?'" Why did you not become what only you could become? This is the existential guilt that comes when one realizes one's vocation and fails to respond to it.

The true teacher is not the one who pours information into the student's head as through a funnel—the old-fashioned "disciplined" approach—or the one who regards all potentialities as already existing within the student and needing only to be pumped up—the newer "progressive" approach. It is the one who fosters genuine mutual contact and mutual trust, who experiences the other side of the relationship, and who helps his pupils realize, through the selection of the effective world, what it can mean to be a man. In the end education, too, centers on the problem of man. All education worthy of the name is education of character, writes Buber, and education of character takes place through the encounter with the image of man that the teacher brings before the pupil in the material he presents and in the way he stands behind this material.

"What Is Man?" is the culmination of the philosophical anthropology of *I and Thou* and the earlier works in *Between Man and Man*. Here the problem of man is dealt with historically and analytically. The ages when man is at home in the cosmos are set in contrast to those when he is not at home, those when he becomes a problem to himself. Our age is seen as the most homeless of all because of the loss of both an image of the world—modern physics can offer us only alternative equations—and a sense of community. The split between instinct and spirit that Freud and Max Scheler take to be the nature of man is actually the product of the decline of trust in communal existence, of the divorce between man and man. The real problem is not the conflict between the individual and the society but is the individualism or collectivism that in equal and opposite ways destroys the true life of dialogue. Man is neither a gorilla nor a termite. He is a creature of the "between," of the happening between man and man that cannot be reduced to a sum of two individuals or to a merely psychological reality within the minds of each.

"What Is Man?" also lays the groundwork for the last important stage of Buber's philosophy, his systematic development of his philosophical anthropology in *The Knowledge of Man*.* The essays in this volume—"Distance and Relation," "Elements of the Interhuman," "What Is Common to All," "Guilt and Guilt Feelings," "The Word That Is Spoken," "Man and His Image-Work," and "The Dialogue Between Martin Buber and Carl Rogers"—represent a new development in Buber's thought, and their significance can hardly be overestimated. They bring Buber within the ranks of "technical philosophers," in the strictest sense of that term, and they show in all fullness and concreteness the implications of Buber's anthropology for theories of knowledge, social philosophy, language and speech, art, education, and psychotherapy. Yet they would be unthinkable without the method of the philosophical anthropologist that Buber has developed in "What Is Man?": the participation of the knower in that which is known, the recollection of the whole event as opposed to the psychologist's attempt to observe his own experience as it is happening,

* Martin Buber, *The Knowledge of Man,* edited with an Introductory Essay by Maurice Friedman, translated by Maurice Friedman and Ronald Gregor Smith (London: George Allen & Unwin; New York: Harper & Row, 1965).

the toleration of the strictness of solitude and aloneness as well as of the belonging to groups in which one still retains a boundary line of personal responsibility.

Between Man and Man is itself a classic, one whose reissuing has long been demanded. Walter Kaufmann makes central use of Buber's essay "The Question to the Single One" in his study of Nietzsche, and William Barrett acknowledges in *The Irrational Man* that Buber has put his finger on the weakness of Barrett's own master, Martin Heidegger, in the criticism of the latter in "What Is Man?" Aristotle, Feuerbach, Nietzsche, Kierkegaard, Scheler, Freud, Augustine, Pascal, and a host of other thinkers of the present and the past are encountered and brought within the focus of Buber's developing dialogical thought in the five works in *Between Man and Man*. This new edition of *Between Man and Man* contains an Afterword on "The History of the Dialogical Principle." In it Buber presents the first account in English of the development of the I-Thou philosophy from the eighteenth-century philosopher Jacobi and the nineteenth-century writers Feuerbach and Kierkegaard to such eminent thinkers of the twentieth century as Gabriel Marcel, Karl Löwith, Hermann Cohen, Franz Rosenzweig, Ferdinand Ebner, Karl Jaspers, and Karl Barth. This Afterword adds richly to the understanding of Buber's own thought and of the central place he holds in the ever-broadening movement of thought in our age that is concerned with the life of dialogue.

BETWEEN MAN AND MAN

I

DIALOGUE

Section One: Description

Original Remembrance

THROUGH all sorts of changes the same dream, sometimes after an interval of several years, recurs to me. I name it the dream of the double cry. Its context is always much the same, a "primitive" world meagrely equipped. I find myself in a vast cave, like the Latomias of Syracuse, or in a mud building that reminds me when I awake of the villages of the *fellahin*, or on the fringe of a gigantic forest whose like I cannot remember having seen.

The dream begins in very different ways, but always with something extraordinary happening to me, for instance, with a small animal resembling a lion-cub (whose name I know in the dream but not when I awake) tearing the flesh from my arm and being forced only with an effort to loose its hold. The strange thing is that this first part of the dream story, which in the duration as well as the outer meaning of the incidents is easily the most important, always unrolls at a furious pace as though it did not matter. Then suddenly the pace abates: I stand there and cry out. In the view of the events which my waking consciousness has I should have to suppose that the cry I utter varies in accordance with what preceded it, and is sometimes joyous, sometimes fearful, sometimes even filled both with pain and with triumph. But in my morning recollection it is neither so expressive nor so various. Each time it is the same cry, inarticulate but in strict rhythm, rising and falling, swelling to a fulness which my throat could not endure were I awake, long and slow, quiet, quite slow and very long, a cry that is a song. When it ends my heart stops beating. But then, somewhere, far away, another cry moves towards me, another

1

which is the same, the same cry uttered or sung by another voice. Yet it is not the same cry, certainly no "echo" of my cry but rather its true rejoinder, tone for tone not repeating mine, not even in a weakened form, but corresponding to mine, answering its tones—so much so, that mine, which at first had to my own ear no sound of questioning at all, now appear as questions, as a long series of questions, which now all receive a response. The response is no more capable of interpretation than the question. And yet the cries that meet the one cry that is the same do not seem to be the same as one another. Each time the voice is new. But now, as the reply ends, in the first moment after its dying fall, a certitude, true dream certitude comes to me that *now it has happened*. Nothing more. Just this, and in this way—*now it has happened*. If I should try to explain it, it means that that happening which gave rise to my cry has only now, with the rejoinder, really and undoubtedly happened.

After this manner the dream has recurred each time—till once, the last time, now two years ago. At first it was as usual (it was the dream with the animal), my cry died away, again my heart stood still. But then there was quiet. There came no answering call. I listened, I heard no sound. For I *awaited* the response for the first time; hitherto it had always surprised me, as though I had never heard it before. Awaited, it failed to come. But now something happened with me. As though I had till now had no other access from the world to sensation save that of the ear and now discovered myself as a being simply equipped with senses, both those clothed in the bodily organs and the naked senses, so I exposed myself to the distance, open to all sensation and perception. And then, not from a distance but from the air round about me, noiselessly, came the answer. Really it did not come; it was there. It had been there—so I may explain it—even before my cry: there it was, and now, when I laid myself open to it, it let itself be received by me. I received it as completely into my perception as ever I received the rejoinder in one of the earlier dreams. If I were to report with what I heard it I should have to say "with every pore of my body". As ever the rejoinder came in one of the earlier dreams this corresponded to and answered my cry. It exceeded the earlier rejoinder in an unknown perfection which is hard to define, for it resides in the fact that it was already there.

When I had reached an end of receiving it, I felt again that certainty, pealing out more than ever, that *now it has happened*.

Silence which is Communication

Just as the most eager speaking at one another does not make a conversation (this is most clearly shown in that curious sport, aptly termed discussion, that is, "breaking apart", which is indulged in by men who are to some extent gifted with the ability to think), so for a conversation no sound is necessary, not even a gesture. Speech can renounce all the media of sense, and it is still speech.

Of course I am not thinking of lovers' tender silence, resting in one another, the expression and discernment of which can be satisfied by a glance, indeed by the mere sharing of a gaze which is rich in inward relations. Nor am I thinking of the mystical shared silence, such as is reported of the Franciscan Aegidius and Louis of France (or, almost identically, of two rabbis of the Hasidim) who, meeting once, did not utter a word, but "taking their stand in the reflection of the divine Face" experienced one another. For here too there is still the expression of a gesture, of the physical attitude of the one to the other.

What I am thinking of I will make clear by an example.

Imagine two men sitting beside one another in any kind of solitude of the world. They do not speak with one another, they do not look at one another, not once have they turned to one another. They are not in one another's confidence, the one knows nothing of the other's career, early that morning they got to know one another in the course of their travels. In this moment neither is thinking of the other; we do not need to know what their thoughts are. The one is sitting on the common seat obviously after his usual manner, calm, hospitably disposed to everything that may come. His being seems to say it is too little to be ready, one must also be really *there*. The other, whose attitude does not betray him, is a man who holds himself in reserve, withholds himself. But if we know about him we know that a childhood's spell is laid on him, that his withholding of himself is something other than an attitude, behind all attitude is entrenched the impenetrable inability to communicate himself. And now—let us imagine that this is one of the hours which succeed in bursting asunder the seven iron bands about our heart—imperceptibly the spell is lifted. But even now the man does not speak a word, does not stir a finger. Yet he does something. The lifting of the spell has happened to him—no matter from where—without his doing. But this is what he does now: he releases in himself a reserve over which only he himself has power. Unreservedly communication streams from him, and the silence bears it to his neighbour. Indeed it was intended for him, and he receives it unreservedly as he receives all genuine destiny that meets him. He will be able to tell no one, not even himself, what he has experienced. What does he now "know" of the other? No more knowing is needed. For where unreserve has ruled, even wordlessly, between men, the word of dialogue has happened sacramentally.

Opinions and the Factual

Human dialogue, therefore, although it has its distinctive life in the sign, that is in sound and gesture (the letters of language have their place in this only in special instances, as when, between friends in a meeting, notes describing the atmosphere skim back and forth across the table), can exist without the sign, but admittedly not in an objectively comprehensible form. On the other hand an element of communication, however inward, seems to belong to its essence. But in its highest moments dialogue reaches out even beyond these boundaries. It is completed outside contents, even the most personal, which are or can be communicated. Moreover it is completed not in some "mystical" event, but in one that is in the precise sense factual, thoroughly dovetailed into the common human world and the concrete time-sequence.

One might indeed be inclined to concede this as valid for the special realm of the erotic. But I do not intend to bring even this in here as an explanation. For Eros is in reality much more strangely composed than in Plato's genealogical myth, and the erotic is in no way, as might be supposed, purely a compressing and unfolding of dialogue. Rather do I know no other realm where, as in this one (to be spoken of later), dialogue and monologue are so mingled and opposed. Many celebrated ecstasies of love are nothing but the lover's delight in the possibilities of his own person which are actualized in unexpected fulness.

I would rather think of something unpretentious yet significant—of the glances which strangers exchange in a busy street as they pass one another with unchanging pace. Some of these glances, though not charged with destiny, nevertheless reveal to one another two dialogical natures.

But I can really show what I have in mind only by events which open into a genuine change from communication to communion, that is, in an embodiment of the word of dialogue.

What I am here concerned with cannot be conveyed in ideas to a reader. But we may represent it by examples—provided that, where the matter is important, we do not eschew taking examples from the inmost recesses of the personal life. For where else should the like be found?

My friendship with one now dead arose in an incident that may be described, if you will, as a broken-off conversation. The date is Easter 1914. Some men from different European peoples had met in an undefined presentiment of the catastrophe, in order to make preparations for an attempt to establish a supra-national authority. The conversations were marked by that unreserve, whose substance and fruitfulness I have scarcely ever experienced so strongly. It had such an effect on all who took part that the fictitious fell away and every word was an actuality. Then as we discussed the composition of the larger circle from which public initiative should proceed (it was decided that it should meet in August of the same year) one of us, a man of passionate concentration and judicial power of love, raised the consideration that too many Jews had been nominated, so that several countries would be represented in unseemly proportion by their Jews. Though similar reflections were not foreign to my own mind, since I hold that Jewry can gain an effective and more than merely stimulating share in the building of a steadfast world of peace only in its own community and not in scattered members, they seemed to me, expressed in this way, to be tainted in their justice. Obstinate Jew that I am, I protested against the protest. I no longer know how from that I came to speak of Jesus and to say that we Jews knew him from within, in the impulses and stirrings of his Jewish being, in a way that remains inaccessible to the peoples submissive to him. "In a way that remains inaccessible to you"—so I directly addressed the former clergyman. He stood up, I too stood, we looked into the heart of one another's eyes. "It is gone", he said, and before everyone we gave one another the kiss of brotherhood.

The discussion of the situation between Jews and Christians had been transformed into a bond between the Christian and the Jew. In this transformation dialogue was fulfilled. Opinions were gone, in a bodily way the factual took place.

Disputations in Religion

Here I expect two objections, one weighty and one powerful.

One argument against me takes this form. When it is a question of essential views, of views concerning *Weltanschauung*, the conversation *must* not be broken off in such a way. Each must expose himself wholly, in a real way, in his humanly unavoidable partiality, and thereby experience himself in a real way as limited by the other, so that the two suffer together the destiny of our conditioned nature and meet one another in it.

To this I answer that the experience of being limited is included in what I refer to; but so too is the experience of overcoming it together. This cannot be completed on the level of *Weltanschauung*, but on that of reality. Neither needs to give up his point of view; only, in that unexpectedly they do something and unexpectedly something happens to them which is called a covenant, they enter a realm where the law of the point of view no longer holds. They too suffer the destiny of our conditioned nature, but they honour it most highly when, as is permitted to us, they let themselves run free of it for an immortal moment. They had already met one another when each in his soul so turned to the other that from then on, making him present, he spoke really to and towards him.

The other objection, which comes from a quite different, in fact from the opposite, side is to the effect that this may be true so far as the province of the point of view reaches, but it ceases to be true for a confession of faith. Two believers in conflict about their doctrines are concerned with the execution of the divine will, not with a fleeting personal agreement. For the man who is so related to his faith that he is able to die or to slay for it there can be no realm where the law of the faith ceases to hold. It is laid on him to help truth to victory, he does not let himself be misled by sentiments. The man holding a different, that is a false, belief must be converted, or at least instructed; direct contact with him can be achieved only outside the advocacy of the faith, it cannot proceed from it. The thesis of religious disputation cannot be allowed to "go".

This objection derives its power from its indifference to the non-binding character of the relativized spirit—a character which is accepted as a matter of course. I can answer it adequately only by a confession.

I have not the possibility of judging Luther, who refused fellowship with Zwingli in Marburg, or Calvin who furthered the death of Servetus. For Luther and Calvin believe that the Word of God has so descended among men that it can be clearly known and must therefore be exclusively advocated. I do not believe that; the Word of God crosses my vision like a falling star to whose fire the meteorite will bear witness without making it light up for me, and I myself can only bear witness to the light but not produce the stone and say "This is it". But this difference of faith is by no means to be understood merely as a subjective one. It is not based on the fact that we who live to-day are weak in faith, and it will remain even if our faith is ever so much strengthened. The situation of the world itself, in the most serious sense, more precisely the relation between God and man, has changed. And this change is certainly not comprehended in its essence by our thinking only of the darkening, so familiar to us, of the supreme light, only of the night of our being, empty of revelation. It is the night of an expectation—not of a vague hope, but of an expectation. We expect a theophany of which we know nothing but the place, and the place is called community. In the public catacombs of this expectation there is no single God's Word which can be clearly known and advocated, but the words delivered are clarified for us in our human situation of being turned to one another. There is no obedience to the coming one without loyalty to his creature. To have experienced this is our way.

A time of genuine religious conversations is beginning—not those so-called but fictitious conversations where none regarded and addressed his partner in reality, but genuine dialogues, speech from certainty to certainty, but also from one open-hearted person to another open-hearted person. Only then will genuine common life appear, not that of an identical content of faith which is alleged to be found in all religions, but that of the situation, of anguish and of expectation.

Setting of the Question

The life of dialogue is not limited to men's traffic with one another; it is, it has shown itself to be, a relation of men to one another that is only represented in their traffic.

Accordingly, even if speech and communication may be dispensed with, the life of dialogue seems, from what we may perceive, to have inextricably joined to it as its minimum constitution one thing, the mutuality of the inner action. Two men bound together in dialogue must obviously be turned to one another, they must therefore—no matter with what measure of activity or indeed of consciousness of activity— have turned to one another.

It is good to put this forward so crudely and formally. For behind the formulating question about the limits of a category under discussion is hidden a question which bursts all formulas asunder.

Observing, Looking On, Becoming Aware

We may distinguish three ways in which we are able to perceive a man who is living before our eyes. (I am not thinking of an object of scientific knowledge, of which I do not speak here.) The object of our perception does not need to know of us, of our being there. It does not matter at this point whether he stands in a relation or has a standpoint towards the perceiver.

The *observer* is wholly intent on fixing the observed man in his mind, on "noting" him. He probes him and writes him up. That is, he is diligent to write up as many "traits" as possible. He lies in wait for them, that none may escape him. The object consists of traits, and it is known what lies behind each of them. Knowledge of the human system of expression constantly incorporates in the instant the newly appearing individual variations, and remains applicable. A face is nothing but physiognomy, movements nothing but gestures of expression.

The *onlooker* is not at all intent. He takes up the position which lets him see the object freely, and undisturbed awaits what will be presented to him. Only at the beginning may he be ruled by purpose, everything beyond that is involuntary. He does not go around taking notes indiscriminately, he lets himself go, he is not in the least afraid of forgetting something ("Forgetting is good," he says). He gives his memory no tasks, he trusts its organic work which preserves what is worth preserving. He does not lead in the grass as green fodder, as the observer does; he turns it and lets the sun shine on it. He pays no attention to traits ("Traits lead astray," he says). What stands out for him from the object is what is not "character" and not "expression" ("The interesting is not important," he says). All great artists have been onlookers.

But there is a perception of a decisively different kind.

The onlooker and the observer are similarly orientated, in that they have a position, namely, the very desire to perceive the man who is living before our eyes. Moreover, this man is for them an object separated from themselves and their personal life, who can in fact for this sole reason be "properly" perceived. Consequently what they experience in this way, whether it is, as with the observer, a sum of traits, or, as with the onlooker, an existence, neither demands action from them nor inflicts destiny on them. But rather the whole is given over to the aloof fields of æsthesis.

It is a different matter when in a receptive hour of my personal life a man meets me about whom there is something, which I cannot grasp in any objective way at all, that "says something" to me. That does not mean, says to me what manner of man this is, what is going on in him, and the like. But it means, says something *to me*, addresses something to me, speaks something that enters my own life. It can be something about this man, for instance that he needs me. But it can also be something about myself. The man himself in his relation to me has nothing to do with what is said. He has no relation to me, he has indeed not noticed me at all. It is not he who says it to me, as that solitary man silently confessed his secret to his neighbour on the seat; but *it* says it.

To understand "say" as a metaphor is not to understand. The phrase "that doesn't say a thing to me" is an outworn metaphor; but the saying I am referring to is real speech. In the house of speech are many mansions, and this is one of the inner.

The effect of having this said to me is completely different from that of looking on and observing. I cannot depict or denote or describe the man in whom, through whom, something has been said to me. Were I to attempt it, that would be the end of saying. This man is not my object; I have got to do with him. Perhaps I have to accomplish something about him; but perhaps I have only to learn something, and it is only a matter of my "accepting". It may be that I have to answer at once, to this very man before me; it may be that the saying has a long and manifold transmission before it, and that I am to answer some other person at some other time and place, in who knows what kind of speech, and that it is now only a matter of taking the answering on myself. But in each instance a word demanding an answer has happened to me.

We may term this way of perception *becoming aware*.

It by no means needs to be a man of whom I become aware. It can be an animal, a plant, a stone. No kind of appearance or event is fundamentally excluded from the series of the things through which from time to time something is said to me. Nothing can refuse to be the vessel for the Word. The limits of the possibility of dialogue are the limits of awareness.

The Signs

Each of us is encased in an armour whose task is to ward off signs. Signs happen to us without respite, living means being addressed, we would need only to present ourselves and to perceive. But the risk is too dangerous for us, the soundless thunderings seem to threaten us with annihilation, and from generation to generation we perfect the defence apparatus. All our knowledge assures us, "Be calm, everything happens as it must happen, but nothing is directed at you, you are not meant; it is just 'the world', you can experience it as you like, but whatever you make of it in yourself proceeds from you alone, nothing is required of you, you are not addressed, all is quiet."

Each of us is encased in an armour which we soon, out of familiarity, no longer notice. There are only moments which penetrate it and stir the soul to sensibility. And when such a moment has imposed itself on us and we then take notice and ask ourselves, "Has anything particular taken place? Was it not of the kind I meet every day?" then we may reply to ourselves, "Nothing particular, indeed, it is like this every day, only we are not there every day."

The signs of address are not something extraordinary, something that steps out of the order of things, they are just what goes on time and again, just what goes on in any case, nothing is added by the address. The waves of the æther roar on always, but for most of the time we have turned off our receivers.

What occurs to me addresses me. In what occurs to me the world-happening addresses me. Only by sterilizing it, removing the seed of address from it, can I take what occurs to me as a part of the world-happening which does not refer to me. The interlocking sterilized system into which all this only needs to be dovetailed is man's titanic work. Mankind has pressed speech too into the service of this work.

From out of this tower of the ages the objection will be levelled against me, if some of its doorkeepers should pay any attention to such trains of thought, that it is nothing but a variety of primitive superstition to hold that cosmic and telluric happenings have for the life of the human person a direct meaning that can be grasped. For instead of understanding an event physically, biologically, sociologically (for which I, inclined as I always have been to admire genuine acts of research, think a great deal, when those who carry them out only know what they are doing and do not lose sight of the limits of the realm in which they are moving), these keepers say, an attempt is being made to get behind the event's alleged significance, and for this there is no place in a reasonable world continuum of space and time.

Thus, then, unexpectedly I seem to have fallen into the company of the augurs, of whom, as is well-known, there are remarkable modern varieties.

But whether they haruspicate or cast a horoscope their signs have this peculiarity that they are in a dictionary, even if not necessarily a written one. It does not matter how esoteric the information that is handed down: he who searches out the signs is *well up in* what life's juncture this or that sign means. Nor does it matter that special difficulties of separation and combination are created by the meeting of several signs of different kinds. For you can "look it up in the dictionary". The common signature of all this business is that it is for all time: things remain the same, they are discovered once for all, rules, laws, and analogical conclusions may be employed throughout. What is commonly termed superstition that is, perverse faith, appears to me rather as perverse knowledge (1). From "superstition" about the number 13 an unbroken ladder leads into the dizziest heights of gnosis. This is not even the aping of a real faith.

Real faith—if I may so term presenting ourselves and perceiving—begins when the dictionary is put down, when you are done with it. What occurs to me says something to me, but what it says to me cannot be revealed by any esoteric information; for it has never been said before nor is it composed of sounds that have ever been said. It can neither be interpreted nor translated, I can have it neither explained nor displayed; it is not a *what* at all, it is said into my very life; it is no experience that can be remembered independently of the situation, it remains the address of that moment and cannot be isolated, it remains the question of a questioner and will have its answer.

(It remains the question. For that is the other great contrast between all the business of interpreting signs and the speech of signs which I mean here: this speech never gives information or appeasement.)

Faith stands in the stream of "happening but once" which is spanned by knowledge. All the emergency structures of analogy and typology are indispensable for the work of the human spirit, but to step on them when the question of the questioner steps up to you, to me, would be running away. Lived life is tested and fulfilled in the stream alone.

With all deference to the world continuum of space and time I know as a living truth only concrete world reality which is constantly, in every moment, reached out to me. I can separate it into its component parts, I can compare them and distribute them into groups of similar phenomena, I can derive them from earlier and reduce them to simpler phenomena; and when I have done all this I have not touched my concrete world reality. Inseparable, incomparable, irreducible, now, happening once only, it gazes upon me with a horrifying look. So in Stravinsky's ballet the director of the wandering marionette show wants to point out to the people at the annual fair that a pierrot who terrified them is nothing but a wisp of straw in clothes: he tears it asunder—and collapses, gibbering, for on the roof of the booth the *living* Petrouchka sits and laughs at him.

The true name of concrete reality is the creation which is entrusted to me and to every man. In it the signs of address are given to us.

A Conversion

In my earlier years the "religious" was for me the exception. There were hours that were taken out of the course of things. From somewhere or other the firm crust of everyday was pierced. Then the reliable permanence of appearances broke down; the attack which took place burst its law asunder. "Religious experience" was the experience of an otherness which did not fit into the context of life. It could begin with something customary, with consideration of some familiar object, but which then became unexpectedly mysterious and uncanny, finally lighting a way into the lightning-pierced darkness of the mystery itself. But also, without any intermediate stage, time could be torn apart—first the firm world's structure then the still firmer self-assurance flew apart and you were delivered to fulness. The "religious" lifted you out. Over there now lay the accustomed existence with its affairs, but here illumination and ecstasy and rapture held, without time or sequence. Thus your own being encompassed a life here and a life beyond, and there was no bond but the actual moment of the transition.

The illegitimacy of such a division of the temporal life, which is streaming to death and eternity and which only in fulfilling its temporality can be fulfilled in face of these, was brought home to me by an everyday event, an event of judgment, judging with that sentence from closed lips and an unmoved glance such as the ongoing course of things loves to pronounce.

What happened was no more than that one forenoon, after a morning of "religious" enthusiasm, I had a visit from an unknown young man, without being there in spirit. I certainly did not fail to let the meeting be friendly, I did not treat him any more remissly than all his contemporaries who were in the habit of seeking me out about this time of day as an oracle that is ready to listen to reason. I conversed attentively and openly with him—only I omitted to guess the questions which he did not put. Later, not long after, I learned from one of his friends—he himself was no longer alive—the essential content of these questions; I learned that he had come to me not casually, but borne by destiny, not for a chat but for a decision. He had come to me, he had come in this hour. What do we expect when we are in despair and yet go to a man? Surely a presence by means of which we are told that nevertheless there is meaning.

Since then I have given up the "religious" which is nothing but the exception, extraction, exaltation, ecstasy; or it has given me up. I possess nothing but the everyday out of which I am never taken. The mystery is no longer disclosed, it has escaped or it has made its dwelling here where everything happens as it happens. I know no fulness but each mortal hour's fulness of claim and responsibility. Though far from being equal to it, yet I know that in the claim I am claimed and may respond in responsibility, and know who speaks and demands a response.

I do not know much more. If that is religion then it is just *everything*, simply all that is lived in its possibility of dialogue. Here is space also for religion's highest forms. As when you pray you do not thereby remove yourself from this life of yours but in your praying refer your thought to it, even though it may be in order to yield it; so too in the unprecedented and surprising, when you are called upon from above, required, chosen, empowered, sent, you with this your mortal bit of life are referred to, this moment is not extracted from it, it rests on what has been and beckons to the remainder which has still to be lived, you are not swallowed up in a fulness without obligation, you are willed for the life of communion.

Who Speaks?

In the signs of life which happens to us we are addressed. Who speaks?

It would not avail us to give for reply the word "God", if we do not give it out of that decisive hour of personal existence when we had to forget everything we imagined we knew of

God, when we dared to keep nothing handed down or learned or self-contrived, no shred of knowledge, and were plunged into the night.

When we rise out of it into the new life and there begin to receive the signs, what can we know of that which—of him who gives them to us? Only what we experience from time to time from the signs themselves. If we name the speaker of this speech God, then it is always the God of a moment, a moment God.

I will now use a *gauche* comparison, since I know no right one.

When we really understand a poem, all we know of the poet is what we learn of him in the poem—no biographical wisdom is of value for the pure understanding of what is to be understood: the *I* which approaches us is the subject of this single poem. But when we read other poems by the poet in the same true way their subjects combine in all their multiplicity, completing and confirming one another, to form the one polyphony of the person's existence.

In such a way, out of the givers of the signs, the speakers of the words in lived life, out of the moment Gods there arises for us with a single identity the Lord of the voice, the One.

Above and Below

Above and below are bound to one another. The word of him who wishes to speak with men without speaking with God is not fulfilled; but the word of him who wishes to speak with God without speaking with men goes astray.

There is a tale that a man inspired by God once went out from the creaturely realms into the vast waste. There he wandered till he came to the gates of the mystery. He knocked. From within came the cry: "What do you want here?" He said, "I have proclaimed your praise in the ears of mortals, but they were deaf to me. So I come to you that you yourself may hear me and reply." "Turn back," came the cry from within. "Here is no ear for you. I have sunk my hearing in the deafness of mortals."

True address from God directs man into the place of lived speech, where the voices of the creatures grope past one another, and in their very missing of one another succeed in reaching the eternal partner *ability to respond*

Responsibility

The idea of responsibility is to be brought back from the province of specialized ethics, of an "ought" that swings free in the air, into that of lived life. <u>Genuine responsibility exists only where there is real responding.</u>

Responding to what?

To what happens to one, to what is to be seen and heard and felt. Each concrete hour allotted to the person, with its content drawn from the world and from destiny, is speech for the man who is attentive. Attentive, for no more than that is needed in order to make a beginning with the reading of the signs that are given to you. For that very reason, as I have already indicated, the whole apparatus of our civilization is necessary to preserve men from this attentiveness and its consequences. For the attentive man would no longer, as his custom is, "master" the situation the very moment after it stepped up to him: it would be laid upon him to go up to and into it. Moreover, nothing that he believed he possessed as always available would help him, no knowledge and no technique, no system and no programme; for now he would have to do with what cannot be classified, with concretion itself. This speech has no alphabet, each of its sounds is a new creation and only to be grasped as such.

It will, then, be expected of the attentive man that he faces creation as it happens. It happens as speech, and not as speech rushing out over his head but as speech directed precisely at him. And if one were to ask another if he too heard and he said he did, they would have agreed only about an experiencing and not about something experienced.

But the sounds of which the speech consists—I repeat it in order to remove the misunderstanding, which is perhaps still possible, that I referred to something extraordinary and larger than life—are the events of the personal everyday life. In them, as they now are, "great" or "small", we are addressed, and those which count as great, yield no greater signs than the others.

Our attitude, however, is not yet decided through our becoming aware of the signs. We can still wrap silence about us—a reply characteristic of a significant type of the age—or we can step aside into the accustomed way; although both times we carry away a wound that is not to be forgotten in any productivity or any narcotism. Yet it can happen that we venture to respond, stammering perhaps—the soul is but rarely able to attain to surer articulation—but it is an honest stammering, as when sense and throat are united about what is to be said, but the throat is too horrified at it to utter purely the already composed sense. The words of our response are spoken in the speech, untranslatable like the address, of doing and letting—whereby the doing may behave like a letting and the letting like a doing. What we say in this way with the being is our entering upon the situation, into the situation, which has at this moment stepped up to us, whose appearance we did not and could not know, for its like has not yet been.

Nor are we now finished with it, we have to give up that expectation: a situation of which we have become aware is never finished with, but we subdue it into the substance of lived life. Only then, true to the moment, do we experience a life that is something other than a sum of moments. We respond to the moment, but at the same time we respond on its behalf, we answer for it. A newly-created concrete reality has been laid in our arms; we answer for it. A dog has looked at you, you answer for its glance, a child has clutched your hand, you answer for its touch, a host of men moves about you, you answer for their need (2).

Morality and Religion

Responsibility which does not respond to a word is a metaphor of morality. Factually, responsibility only exists when the court is there to which I am responsible, and "self-responsibility" has reality only when the "self" to which I am responsible becomes transparent into the absolute. But he who practises real responsibility in the life of dialogue does not need to name the speaker of the word to which he is responding— he knows him in the word's substance which presses on and in, assuming the cadence of an inwardness, and stirs him in his heart of hearts. A man can ward off with all his strength the belief that "God" is there, and he tastes him in the strict sacrament of dialogue.

Yet let it not be supposed that I make morality questionable in order to glorify religion. Religion, certainly, has this advantage over morality, that it is a phenomenon and not a postulate, and further that it is able to include composure as well as determination. The reality of morality, the demand of the demander, has a place in religion, but the reality of religion, the unconditioned being of the demander, has no place in morality. Nevertheless, when religion does itself justice and asserts itself, it is much more dubious than morality, just because it is more actual and inclusive. Religion as risk, which is ready to give itself up, is the nourishing stream of the arteries; as system, possessing, assured and assuring, religion which believes in religion is the veins' blood, which ceases to circulate. And if there is nothing that can so hide the face of our fellow-man as morality can, religion can hide from us as nothing else can the face of God. Principle there, dogma here, I appreciate the "objective" compactness of dogma, but behind both there lies in wait the—profane or holy—war against the situation's power of dialogue, there lies in wait the "once-for-all" which resists the unforeseeable moment. Dogma, even when its claim of origin remains uncontested, has become the most exalted form of invulnerability against revelation. Revelation will tolerate no perfect tense, but man with the arts of his craze for security props it up to perfectedness.

Section Two: Limitation

The Realms

THE realms of the life of dialogue and the life of monologue do not coincide with the realms of dialogue and monologue even when forms without sound and even without gesture are included. There are not merely great spheres of the life of dialogue which in appearance are not dialogue, there is also dialogue which is not the dialogue of life, that is, it has the appearance but not the essence of dialogue. At times, indeed, it seems as though there were only this kind of dialogue.

I know three kinds. There is genuine dialogue—no matter whether spoken or silent—where each of the participants really has in mind the other or others in their present and particular being and turns to them with the intention of establishing a living mutual relation between himself and them. There is technical dialogue, which is prompted solely by the need of objective understanding. And there is monologue disguised as dialogue, in which two or more men, meeting in space, speak each with himself in strangely tortuous and circuitous ways and yet imagine they have escaped the torment of being thrown back on their own resources. The first kind, as I have said, has become rare; where it arises, in no matter how "unspiritual" a form, witness is borne on behalf of the continuance of the organic substance of the human spirit. The second belongs to the inalienable sterling quality of "modern existence". But real dialogue is here continually hidden in all kinds of odd corners and, occasionally in an unseemly way, breaks surface surprisingly and inopportunely—certainly still oftener it is arrogantly tolerated than downright scandalizing—as in the tone of a railway guard's voice, in the glance of an old newspaper vendor, in the smile of the chimney-sweeper. And the third. . . .

A *debate* in which the thoughts are not expressed in the way in which they existed in the mind but in the speaking are so pointed that they may strike home in the sharpest way, and moreover without the men that are spoken to being regarded in any way present as persons; a *conversation* characterized by the need neither to communicate something, nor to learn something, nor to influence someone, nor to come into connexion with someone, but solely by the desire to have one's own self-reliance confirmed by marking the impression that is made, or if it has become unsteady to have it strengthened; a *friendly chat* in which each regards himself as absolute and legitimate and the other as relativized and questionable; a *lovers' talk* in which both partners alike enjoy their own glorious soul and their precious experience—what an underworld of faceless spectres of dialogue!

The life of dialogue is not one in which you have much to do with men, but one in which you really have to do with those with whom you have to do. It is not the solitary man who lives the life of monologue, but he who is incapable of making real in the context of being the community in which, in the context of his destiny, he moves. It is, in fact, solitude which is able to show the innermost nature of the contrast. He who is living the life of dialogue receives in the ordinary course of the hours something that is said and feels himself approached for an answer. But also in the vast blankness of, say, a companionless mountain wandering that which confronts him, rich in change, does not leave him. He who is living the life of monologue is never aware of the other as something that is absolutely not himself and at the same time something with which he nevertheless communicates. Solitude for him can mean mounting richness of visions and thoughts but never the deep intercourse, captured in a new depth, with the incomprehensibly real. Nature for him is either an *état d'âme*, hence a "living through" in himself, or it is a passive object of knowledge, either idealistically brought within the soul or realistically alienated. It does not become for him a word apprehended with senses of beholding and feeling.

Being, lived in dialogue, receives even in extreme dereliction a harsh and strengthening sense of reciprocity; being, lived in monologue, will not, even in the tenderest intimacy, grope out over the outlines of the self.

This must not be confused with the contrast between "egoism" and "altruism" conceived by some moralists. I know people who are absorbed in "social activity" and have never spoken from being to being with a fellow-man. I know others who have no personal relation except to their enemies, but stand in such a relation to them that it is the enemies' fault if the relation does not flourish into one of dialogue.

Nor is dialogic to be identified with love. I know no one in any time who has succeeded in loving every man he met. Even Jesus obviously loved of "sinners" only the loose, lovable sinners, sinners against the Law; not those who were settled and loyal to their inheritance and sinned against him and his message. Yet to the latter as to the former he stood in a direct relation. Dialogic is not to be identified with love. But love without dialogic, without real outgoing to the other, reaching to the other, and companying with the other, the love remaining with itself—this is called Lucifer.

Certainly in order to be able to go out to the other you must have the starting place, you must have been, you must be, with yourself. Dialogue between mere individuals is only a sketch, only in dialogue between persons is the sketch filled in. But by what could a man from being an individual so really become a person as by the strict and sweet experiences of dialogue which teach him the boundless contents of the boundary?

What is said here is the real contrary of the cry, heard at times in twilight ages, for universal unreserve. He who can be unreserved with each passer-by has no substance to lose; but he who cannot stand in a direct relation to each one who meets him has a fulness which is futile. Luther is wrong to change the Hebrew "companion" (out of which the Seventy had already made one who is near, a neighbour) into "nearest" (3). If everything concrete is equally near, equally nearest, life with the world ceases to have articulation and structure, it ceases to have human meaning. But nothing needs to mediate between me and one of my companions in the companionship of creation, whenever we come near one another, because we are bound up in relation to the same centre.

The Basic Movements

I term basic movement an essential action of man (it may be understood as an "inner" action, but it is not there unless it is there to the very tension of the eyes' muscles and the very action of the foot as it walks), round which an essential attitude is built up. I do not think of this happening in time, as though the single action preceded the lasting attitude; the latter rather has its truth in the accomplishing, over and over again, of the basic movement, without forethought but also without habit. Otherwise the attitude would have only æsthetic or perhaps also political significance, as a beautiful and as an effective lie. The familiar maxim, "An attitude must first be adopted, the rest follows of itself" ceases to be true in the circle of essential action and essential attitude—that is, where we are concerned with the wholeness of the person.

The basic movement of the life of dialogue is the turning towards the other. That, indeed, seems to happen every hour and quite trivially. If you look at someone and address him you turn to him, of course with the body, but also in the requisite measure with the soul, in that you direct your attention to him. But what of all this is an essential action, done with the essential being? In this way, that out of the incomprehensibility of what lies to hand this one person steps forth and becomes a presence. Now to our perception the world ceases to be an insignificant multiplicity of points to one of which we pay momentary attention. Rather it is a limitless tumult round a narrow breakwater, brightly outlined and able to bear heavy loads—limitless, but limited by the breakwater, so that, though not engirdled, it has become finite in itself, been given form, released from its own indifference. And yet none of the contacts of each hour is unworthy to take up from our essential being as much as it may. For no man is without strength for expression, and our turning towards him brings about a reply, however imperceptible, however quickly smothered, in a looking and sounding forth of the soul that are perhaps dissipating in mere inwardness and yet do exist. The notion of modern man that this turning to the other is sentimental and does not correspond to the compression of life today is a grotesque error, just as his affirmation that turning to the other is impractical in the bustle of this life today is only the masked confession of his weakness of initiative when confronted with the state of the time. He lets it dictate to him what is possible or permissible, instead of stipulating, as an unruffled partner, what is to be stipulated to the state of *every* time, namely, what space and what form it is bound to concede to creaturely existence.

The basic movement of the life of monologue is not turning away as opposed to turning towards; it is "reflexion" (4).

When I was eleven years of age, spending the summer on my grandparents' estate, I used, as often as I could do it unobserved, to steal into the stable and gently stroke the neck of my darling, a broad dapple-grey horse. It was not a casual delight but a great, certainly friendly, but also deeply stirring happening. If I am to explain it now, beginning from the still very fresh memory of my hand, I must say that what I experienced in touch with the animal was the Other, the immense otherness of the Other, which, however, did not remain strange like the otherness of the ox and the ram, but rather let me draw near and touch it. When I stroked the mighty mane, sometimes marvellously smooth-combed, at other times just as astonishingly wild, and felt the life beneath my hand, it was as though the element of vitality itself bordered on my skin, something that was not I, was certainly not akin to me, palpably the other, not just another, really the Other itself; and yet it let me approach, confided itself to me, placed itself elementally in the relation of *Thou* and *Thou* with me. The horse, even when I had not begun by pouring oats for him into the manger, very gently raised his massive head, ears flicking, then snorted quietly, as a conspirator gives a signal meant to be recognizable only by his fellow-conspirator; and I was approved. But once—I do not know what came over the child, at any rate it was childlike enough—it struck me about the stroking, what fun it gave me, and suddenly I became conscious of my hand. The game went on as before, but something had changed, it was no longer the same thing. And the next day, after giving him a rich feed, when I stroked my friend's head he did not raise his head. A few years later, when I thought back to the incident, I no longer supposed that the animal had noticed my defection. But at the time I considered myself judged.

Reflexion is something different from egoism and even from "egotism". It is not that a man is concerned with himself, considers himself, fingers himself, enjoys, idolizes and bemoans himself; all that can be added, but it is not integral to reflexion. (Similarly, to the turning towards the other, completing it, there can be added the realizing of the other in his particular existence, even the encompassing of him, so that the situations common to him and oneself are experienced also from his, the other's, end.) I term it reflexion when a man withdraws from accepting with his essential being another person in his particularity—a particularity which is by no means to be circumscribed by the circle of his own self, and though it substantially touches and moves his soul is in no way immanent in it—and lets the other exist only as his own experience, only as a "part of myself". For then dialogue becomes a fiction, the mysterious intercourse between two human worlds only a game, and in the rejection of the real life confronting him the essence of all reality begins to disintegrate.

The Wordless Depths

Sometimes I hear it said that every *I and Thou* is only superficial, deep down word and response cease to exist, there is only the one primal being unconfronted by another. We should plunge into the silent unity, but for the rest leave its relativity to the life to be lived, instead of imposing on it this absolutized *I* and absolutized *Thou* with their dialogue.

Now from my own unforgettable experience I know well that there is a state in which the bonds of the personal nature of life seem to have fallen away from us and we experience an undivided unity. But I do not know—what the soul willingly imagines and indeed is bound to imagine (mine too once did it)—that in this I had attained to a union with the primal being or the godhead. That is an exaggeration no longer permitted to the responsible understanding. Responsibly— that is, as a man holding his ground before reality—I can elicit from those experiences only that in them I reached an undifferentiable unity of myself without form or content. I may call this an original pre-biographical unity and suppose that it is hidden unchanged beneath all biographical change, all development and complication of the soul. Nevertheless, in the honest and sober account of the responsible understanding this unity is nothing but the unity of this soul of mine, whose "ground" I have reached, so much so, beneath all formations and contents, that my spirit has no choice but to understand it as the groundless (5). But the basic unity of my own soul is certainly beyond the reach of all the multiplicity it has hitherto received from life, though not in the least beyond individuation, or the multiplicity of all the souls in the world of which it is one—existing but once, single, unique, irreducible, this creaturely one: one of the human souls and not the "soul of the All"; a defined and particular being and not "Being"; the creaturely basic unity of a creature, bound to God as in the instant before release the creature is to the *creator spiritus*, not bound to God as the creature to the *creator spiritus* in the moment of release.

The unity of his own self is not distinguishable in the man's feeling from unity in general. For he who in the act or event of absorption is sunk beneath the realm of all multiplicity that holds sway in the soul cannot experience the cessation of multiplicity except as unity itself. That is, he experiences the cessation of his own multiplicity as the cessation of mutuality, as revealed or fulfilled absence of otherness. The being which has become one can no longer understand itself on this side of individuation nor indeed on this side of *I and Thou*. For to the border experience of the soul "one" must apparently mean the same as "the One".

But in the actuality of lived life the man in such a moment is not above but beneath the creaturely situation, which is mightier and truer than all ecstasies. He is not above but beneath dialogue. He is not nearer the God who is hidden above *I and Thou*, and he is farther from the God who is turned to men and who gives himself as the *I* to a *Thou* and the *Thou* to an *I*, than that other who in prayer and service and life does not step out of the position of confrontation and awaits no wordless unity, except that which perhaps bodily death discloses.

Nevertheless, even he who lives the life of dialogue knows a lived unity: the unity of *life*, as that which once truly won is no more torn by any changes, not ripped asunder into the everyday creaturely life and the "deified" exalted hours; the unity of unbroken, raptureless perseverance in concreteness, in which the word is heard and a stammering answer dared.

Of Thinking

To all unprejudiced reflection it is clear that all *art* is from its origin essentially of the nature of dialogue. All music calls to an ear not the musician's own, all sculpture to an eye not the sculptor's, architecture in addition calls to the step as it walks in the building. They all say, to him who receives them, something (not a "feeling" but a perceived mystery) that can be said only in this one language. But there seems to cling to *thought* something of the life of monologue to which com-

c

munication takes a second, secondary place. Thought seems to arise in monologue. Is it so? Is there here—where, as the philosophers say, pure subject separates itself from the concrete person in order to establish and stabilize a world for itself—a citadel which rises towering over the life of dialogue, inaccessible to it, in which man-with-himself, the single one, suffers and triumphs in glorious solitude?

Plato has repeatedly called thinking a voiceless colloquy of the soul with itself. Everyone who has really thought knows that within this remarkable process there is a stage at which an "inner" court is questioned and replies. But that is not the arising of the thought but the first trying and testing of what has arisen. The arising of the thought does not take place in colloquy with oneself. The character of monologue does not belong to the insight into a basic relation with which cognitive thought begins; nor to the grasping, limiting and compressing of the insight; nor to its moulding into the independent conceptual form; nor to the reception of this form, with the bestowal of relations, the dovetailing and soldering, into an order of conceptual forms; nor, finally, to the expression and clarification in language (which till now had only a technical and reserved symbolic function). Rather are elements of dialogue to be discovered here. It is not himself that the thinker addresses in the stages of the thought's growth, in their answerings, but as it were the basic relation in face of which he has to answer for his insight, or the order in face of which he has to answer for the newly arrived conceptual form. And it is a misunderstanding of the dynamic of the event of thought to suppose that these apostrophizings of a being existing in nature or in ideas are "really" colloquies with the self.

But also the first trying and testing of the thought, when it is provisionally completed, before the "inner" court, in the platonic sense the stage of monologue, has besides the familiar form of its appearance another form in which dialogue plays a great part, well-known to Plato if to anyone. There he who is approached for judgment is not the empirical self but the *genius*, the spirit I am intended to become, the image-self, before which the new thought is borne for approval, that is, for taking up into its own consummating thinking.

And now from another dimension which even this lease of power does not satisfy there appears the longing for a trying and testing in the sphere of pure dialogue. Here the function of receiving is no longer given over to the *Thou-I* but to a genuine *Thou* which either remains one that is thought and yet is felt as supremely living and "other", or else is embodied in an intimate person. "Man", says Wilhelm von Humboldt in his significant treatise on *The Dual Number* (1827), "longs even for the sake of his mere thinking for a *Thou* corresponding to the *I*. The conception appears to him to reach its definiteness and certainty only when it reflects from another power of thought. It is produced by being torn away from the moving mass of representation and shaped in face of the subject into the object. But the objectivity appears in a still more complete form if this separation does not go on in the subject alone, if he really sees the thought outside himself; and this is possible only in another being, representing and thinking like himself. And between one power of thought and another there is no other mediator but speech." This reference, simplified to an aphorism, recurs with Ludwig Feuerbach in 1843: "True dialectic is not a monologue of the solitary thinker with himself, it is a dialogue between *I* and *Thou*."

But this saying points beyond that "reflecting" to the fact that even in the original stage of the proper act of thought the inner action might take place in relation to a genuine and not merely an "inward" (Novalis) *Thou*. And where modern philosophy is most earnest in the desire to ask its questions on the basis of human existence, situation and present, in some modifications an important further step is taken. Here it is certainly no longer just that the *Thou* is ready to receive and disposed to philosophize along with the *I*. Rather, and pre-eminently, we have the *Thou* in opposition because we truly have the other who thinks other things in another way. So, too, it is not a matter of a game of draughts in the tower of a castle in the air, but of the binding business of life on the hard earth, in which one is inexorably aware of the otherness of the other but does not at all contest it without realizing it; one takes up its nature into one's own thinking, thinks in relation to it, addresses it in thought.

This man of modern philosophy, however, who in this way no longer thinks in the untouchable province of pure ideation, but thinks in reality—does he think in reality? Not solely in a reality framed by thought? Is the other, whom he accepts and receives in this way, not solely the other framed by thought, and therefore unreal? Does the thinker of whom we are speaking hold his own with the bodily fact of otherness?

If we are serious about thinking between *I* and *Thou* then it is not enough to cast our thoughts towards the other subject of thought framed by thought. We should also, with the thinking, precisely with the thinking, live towards the other man, who is not framed by thought but bodily present before us; we should live towards his concrete life. We should live not towards another thinker of whom we wish to know nothing beyond his thinking but, even if the other is a thinker, towards his bodily life over and above his thinking—rather, towards his person, to which, to be sure, the activity of thinking also belongs.

When will the action of thinking endure, include, and refer to the presence of the living man facing us? When will the dialectic of thought become dialogic, an unsentimental, un-relaxed dialogue in the strict terms of thought with the man present at the moment?

Eros

The Greeks distinguished between a powerful, world-begetting Eros and one which was light and whose sphere was the soul; and also between a heavenly and a profane Eros. Neither seems to me to indicate an absolute distinction. For the primal god Desire from whom the world is derived, is the very one who in the form of a "tender elfin spirit" (Jacob Grimm) enters into the sphere of souls and in an arbitrary daimonic way carries out here, as mediator of the pollination of being, his cosmogonic work: he is the great pollen-bearing butterfly of psychogenesis. And the Pandemos (assuming it is a genuine Eros and not a Priapos impudently pretending to be the higher one) needs only to stir his wings to let the primal fire be revealed in the body's games.

Of course, the matter in question is whether Eros has not forfeited the power of flight and is now condemned to live among tough mortals and govern their mortality's paltry gestures of love. For the souls of lovers do to one another what they do; but lame-winged beneath the rule of the lame-winged one (for his power and powerlessness are always shown in theirs) they cower where they are, each in his den, instead of

soaring out each to the beloved partner and there, in the
beyond which has come near, "knowing" (6).

Those who are loyal to the strong-winged Eros of dialogue
know the beloved being. They experience his particular life
in simple presence—not as a thing seen and touched, but from
the innervations to his movements, from the "inner" to his
"outer". But by this I mean nothing but the bipolar experience, and—more than a swinging over and away in the
instant—a contemporaneity at rest. That inclination of the
head over there—you feel how the soul enjoins it on the neck,
you feel it not on your neck but on that one over there, on the
beloved one, and yet you yourself are not as it were snatched
away, you are here, in the feeling self-being, and you receive
the inclination of the head, its injunction, as the answer to the
word of your own silence. In contemporaneity at rest you
make and you experience dialogue. The two who are loyal
to the Eros of dialogue, who love one another, receive the
common event from the other's side as well, that is, they
receive it from the two sides, and thus for the first time understand in a bodily way what an event is.

The kingdom of the lame-winged Eros is a world of mirrors
and mirrorings. But where the winged one holds sway there
is no mirroring. For there I, the lover, turn to this other
human being, the beloved, in his otherness, his independence,
his self-reality, and turn to him with all the power of intention
of my own heart. I certainly turn to him as to one who is
there turning to me, but in that very reality, not comprehensible by me but rather comprehending me, in which I am there
turning to him. I do not assimilate into my own soul that
which lives and faces me, I vow it faithfully to myself and
myself to it, I vow, I have faith (7).

The Eros of dialogue has the simplicity of fulness; the Eros
of monologue is manifold. Many years I have wandered
through the land of men, and have not yet reached an end of
studying the varieties of the "erotic man" (as the vassal of the
broken-winged one at times describes himself). There a lover
stamps around and is in love only with his passion. There one
is wearing his differentiated feelings like medal-ribbons. There
one is enjoying the adventures of his own fascinating effect.
There one is gazing enraptured at the spectacle of his own
supposed surrender. There one is collecting excitement. There
one is displaying his "power". There one is preening himself

with borrowed vitality. There one is delighting to exist simultaneously as himself and as an idol very unlike himself. There one is warming himself at the blaze of what has fallen to his lot. There one is experimenting. And so on and on— all the manifold monologists with their mirrors, in the apartment of the most intimate dialogue!

I have spoken of the small fry, but I have had more in mind the leviathans. There are some who stipulate to the object they propose to devour that both the doing as a holy right and the suffering as a sacred duty are what is to be called heroic love. I know of "leaders" who with their grip not only cast into confusion the plasma of the growing human being but also disintegrate it radically, so that it can no longer be moulded. They relish this power of their influence, and at the same time deceive themselves and their herd into imagining they are moulders of youthful souls, and call on *Eros*, who is inaccessible to the *profanum vulgus*, as the tutelary god of this work.

They are all beating the air. Only he who himself turns to the other human being and opens himself to him receives the world in him. Only the being whose otherness, accepted by my being, lives and faces me in the whole compression of existence, brings the radiance of eternity to me. Only when two say to one another with all that they are, "It is *Thou*", is the indwelling of the Present Being between them (8).

Community

In the view customary to-day, which is defined by politics, the only important thing in groups, in the present as in history, is what they aim at and what they accomplish. Significance is ascribed to what goes on within them only in so far as it influences the group's action with regard to its aim. Thus it is conceded to a band conspiring to conquer the state power that the comradeship which fills it is of value, just because it strengthens the band's reliable assault power. Precise obedience will do as well, if enthusiastic drill makes up for the associates remaining strangers to one another; there are indeed good grounds for preferring the rigid system. If the group is striving even to reach a higher form of society then it can seem dangerous if in the life of the group itself something of this higher form begins to be realized in embryo. For from such a premature seriousness a suppression of the "effective" impetus is feared. The opinion apparently is that the man who whiles away his time as a guest on an oasis may be accounted lost for the project of irrigating the Sahara.

By this simplified mode of valuation the real and individual worth of a group remains as uncomprehended as when we judge a person by his effect alone and not by his qualities. The perversion of thought grows when chatter is added about sacrifice of being, about renunciation of self-realization, where possible with a reference to the favourite metaphor of the dung. Happiness, possession, power, authority, life can be renounced, but sacrifice of being is a sublime absurdity. And no moment, if it has to vouch for its relation to reality, can call upon any kind of later, future moments for whose sake, in order to make them fat, it has remained so lean.

The feeling of community does not reign where the desired change of institutions is wrested in common, but without community, from a resisting world. It reigns where the fight that is fought takes place from the position of a community struggling for its own reality as a community. But the future too is decided here at the same time; all political "achievements" are at best auxiliary troops to the effect which changes the very core, and which is wrought on the unsurveyable ways of secret history by the moment of realization. No way leads to any other goal but to that which is like it.

But who in all these massed, mingled, marching collectivities still perceives what that is for which he supposes he is striving—what community is? They have all surrendered to its counterpart. Collectivity is not a binding but a bundling together: individuals packed together, armed and equipped in common, with only as much life from man to man as will inflame the marching step. But community, growing community (which is all we have known so far) is the being no longer side by side but *with* one another of a multitude of persons. And this multitude, though it also moves towards one goal, yet experiences everywhere a turning to, a dynamic facing of, the other, a flowing from *I* to *Thou*. Community is where community happens. Collectivity is based on an organized atrophy of personal existence, community on its increase and confirmation in life lived towards one other. The modern zeal for collectivity is a flight from community's testing and consecration of the person, a flight from the vital dialogic, demanding the staking of the self, which is in the heart of the world.

The men of the "collective" look down superciliously on the "sentimentality" of the generation before them, of the age of the "youth movement". Then the concern, wide-ranging and deeply-pondered, was with the problem of all life's relations, "community" was aimed at and made a problem at the same time. They went round in circles and never left the mark. But now there is commanding and marching, for now there is the "cause". The false paths of subjectivity have been left behind and the road of objectivism, going straight for its goal, has been reached. But as there existed a pseudo-subjectivity with the former, since the elementary force of being a subject was lacking, so with the latter there exists a pseudo-objectivism, since one is here fitted not into a world but into a worldless faction. As in the former all songs in praise of freedom were sung into the void, because only freeing from bonds was known, but not freeing to responsibility, so in the latter even the noblest hymns on authority are a misunderstanding. For in fact they strengthen only the semblance of authority which has been won by speeches and cries; behind this authority is hidden an absence of consistency draped in the mighty folds of the attitude. But genuine authority, celebrated in those hymns, the authority of the genuine charismatic in his steady response to the lord of Charis, has remained unknown to the political sphere of the present. Superficially the two generations are different in kind to the extent of contradiction, in truth they are stuck in the same chaotic condition. The man of the youth movement, pondering his problems, was concerned (whatever the particular matter at different times) with his very own share in it, he "experienced" his *I* without pledging a self—in order not to have to pledge a self in response and responsibility. The man of the collective undertaking, striding to action, succeeded beforehand in getting rid of himself and thus radically escaping the question of pledging a self. Progress is nevertheless to be recorded. With the former monologue presented itself as dialogue. With the latter it is considerably simpler, for the life of monologue is by their desire driven out from most men, or they are broken of the habit; and the others, who give the orders, have at least no need to feign any dialogic.

Dialogue and monologue are silenced. Bundled together,

men march without *Thou* and without *I*, those of the left who
want to abolish memory, and those of the right who want to
regulate it: hostile and separated hosts, they march into the
common abyss.

Section Three: Confirmation

Conversation with the Opponent

I HOPE for two kinds of readers for these thoughts: for the *amicus* who knows about the reality to which I am pointing with a finger I should like to be able to stretch out like Grünewald's Baptist; and for the *hostis* or *adversarius* who denies this reality and therefore contends with me, because I point to it (in his view misleadingly) as to a reality. Thus he takes what is said here just as seriously as I myself do, after long waiting writing what is to be written—just as seriously, only with the negative sign. The mere *inimicus*, as which I regard everyone who wishes to relegate me to the realm of ideology and there let my thoughts count, I would gladly dispense with.

I need say nothing at this point to the *amicus*. The hour of common mortality and the common way strikes in his and in my ears as though we stood even in the same place with one another and knew one another.

But it is not enough to tell the *adversarius* here what I am pointing at—the hiddenness of his personal life, his secret, and that, stepping over a carefully avoided threshold, he will discover what he denies. It is not enough. I dare not turn aside his gravest objection. I must accept it, as and where it is raised, and must answer.

So now the *adversarius* sits, facing me in his actual form as he appears in accordance with the spirit of the time, and speaks, more above and beyond me than towards and to me, in accents and attitude customary in the universal duel, free of personal relation.

"In all this the actuality of our present life, the conditioned nature of life as a whole, is not taken into account. All that you speak of takes place in the never-never-land, not in the social context of the world in which we spend our days, and by which if by anything our reality is defined. Your 'two men' sit on a solitary seat, obviously during a holiday journey. In a big city office you would not be able to let them sit, they would not reach the 'sacramental' there. Your 'interrupted conversation' takes place between intellectuals who have leisure a couple of months before the huge mass event to spin fantasies of its prevention through a spiritual influence. That

34

may be quite interesting for people who are not taken up with any duty. But is the business employee to 'communicate himself without reserve' to his colleagues? Is the worker at the conveyor belt to 'feel himself addressed in what he experiences'? Is the leader of a gigantic technical undertaking to 'practise the responsibility of dialogue'? You demand that we enter into the situation which approaches us, and you neglect the enduring situation in which everyone of us, so far as we share in the life of community, is elementally placed. In spite of all references to concreteness, all that is pre-war individualism in a revised edition."

And I, out of a deep consciousness of how almost impossible it is to think in common, if only in opposition, where there is no common experience, reply.

Before all, dear opponent, if we are to converse with one another and not at and past one another, I beg you to notice that I do not demand. I have no call to that and no authority for it. I try only to say that there is something, and to indicate how it is made: I simply record. And how could the life of dialogue be demanded? There is no ordering of dialogue. It is not that you *are* to answer but that you *are able*.

You are really able. The life of dialogue is no privilege of intellectual activity like dialectic. It does not begin in the upper story of humanity. It begins no higher than where humanity begins. There are no gifted and ungifted here, only those who give themselves and those who withhold themselves. And he who gives himself to-morrow is not noted to-day, even he himself does not know that he has it in himself, that we have it in ourselves, he will just find it, "and finding be amazed".

You put before me the man taken up with duty and business. Yes, precisely him I mean, him in the factory, in the shop, in the office, in the mine, on the tractor, at the printing-press: man. I do not seek for men. I do not seek men out for myself, I accept those who are there, I have them, I have him, in mind, the yoked, the wheel-treading, the conditioned. Dialogue is not an affair of spiritual luxury and spiritual luxuriousness, it is a matter of creation, of the creature, and he is that, the man of whom I speak, he is a creature, trivial and irreplaceable.

In my thoughts about the life of dialogue I have had to choose the examples as "purely" and as much in the form of paradigm as memory presented them to me in order to make myself intelligible about what has become so unfamiliar, in fact so sunk in oblivion. For this reason I appear to draw my tales from the province which you term the "intellectual", in reality only from the province where things succeed, are rounded off, in fact are exemplary. But I am not concerned with the pure; I am concerned with the turbid, the repressed, the pedestrian, with toil and dull contraryness—and with the break-through. With the break-through and not with a perfection, and moreover with the break-through not out of despair with its murderous and renewing powers; no, not with the great catastrophic break-through which happens once for all (it is fitting to be silent for a while about that, even in one's own heart), but with the breaking through from the status of the dully-tempered disagreeableness, obstinacy, and contraryness in which the man, whom I pluck at random out of the tumult, is living and out of which he can and at times does break through.

Whither? Into nothing exalted, heroic or holy, into no Either and no Or, only into this tiny strictness and grace of every day, where I have to do with just the very same "reality" with whose duty and business I am taken up in such a way, glance to glance, look to look, word to word, that I experience it as reached to me and myself to it, it as spoken to me and myself to it. And now, in all the clanking of routine that I called my reality, there appears to me, homely and glorious, the effective reality, creaturely and given to me in trust and responsibility. We do not find meaning lying in things nor do we put it into things, but between us and things it can happen.

It is not sufficient, dear opponent, first of all to ascribe to me the pathos of "all or nothing" and then to prove the impossibility of my alleged demand. I know neither what all nor what nothing is, the one appears to me to be as inhuman and contrived as the other. What I am meaning is the simple *quantum satis* of that which this man in this hour of his life is able to fulfil and to receive—if he gives himself. That is, if he does not let himself be deceived by the compact plausibility that there are places excluded from creation, that he works in such a place and is able to return to creation when his shift is over; or that creation is outstripped, that it once was but is irrevocably over, now there is business and now it is a case of stripping off all romanticism, gritting the teeth and getting through with what is recognized as necessary. I say—if he does not let himself be deceived.

No factory and no office is so abandoned by creation that a

creative glance could not fly up from one working-place to another, from desk to desk, a sober and brotherly glance which guarantees the reality of creation which is happening—*quantum satis*. And nothing is so valuable a service of dialogue between God and man as such an unsentimental and unreserved exchange of glances between two men in an alien place.

But is it irrevocably an alien place? Must henceforth, through all the world's ages, the life of the being which is yoked to business be divided in two, into alien "work" and home "recovery"? More, since evenings and Sundays cannot be freed of the workday character but are unavoidably stamped with it, must such a life be divided out between the business of work and the business of recovery without a remainder of directness, of unregulated surplus—of freedom? (And the freedom I mean is established by no new order of society.)

Or does there already stir, beneath all dissatisfactions that can be satisfied, an unknown and primal and deep dissatisfaction for which there is as yet no recipe of satisfaction anywhere, but which will grow to such mightiness that it dictates to the technical leaders, the promoters, the inventors, and says, "Go on with your rationalizing, but humanize the rationalizing *ratio* in yourselves. Let it introduce the living man into its purposes and its calculations, him who longs to stand in a mutual relation with the world." Dear opponent, does the longing already stir in the depths—an impulse to great construction or a tiny spark of the last revolution—to fill business with the life of dialogue? That is, in the formulation of the *quantum satis*, the longing for an order of work in which business is so continually soaked in vital dialogic as the tasks to be fulfilled by it allow? And of the extent to which they can allow it there is scarcely an inkling to-day, in an hour when the question which I put is at the mercy of the fanatics, blind to reality, who conform to the time, and of the heralds, blind to possibility, of the impervious tragedy of the world.

Be clear what it means when a worker can experience even his relation to the machine as one of dialogue, when, for instance, a compositor tells that he has understood the machine's humming as "a merry and grateful smile at me for helping it to set aside the difficulties and obstructions which disturbed and bruised and pained it, so that now it could run free". Must even you not think then of the story of Androclus and the Lion?

But when a man draws a lifeless thing into his passionate longing for dialogue, lending it independence and as it were a soul, then there may dawn in him the presentiment of a world-wide dialogue, a dialogue with the world-happening that steps up to him even in his environment, which consists partly of things. Or do you seriously think that the giving and taking of signs halts on the threshold of that business where an honest and open spirit is found?

You ask with a laugh, can the leader of a great technical undertaking practise the responsibility of dialogue? He can. For he practises it when he makes present to himself in its concreteness, so far as he can, *quantum satis*, the business which he leads. He practises it when he experiences it, instead of as a structure of mechanical centres of force and their organic servants (among which latter there is for him no differentiation but the functional one), as an association of persons with faces and names and biographies, bound together by a work that is represented by, but does not consist of, the achievements of a complicated mechanism. He practises it when he is inwardly aware, with a latent and disciplined fantasy, of the multitude of these persons, whom naturally he cannot separately know and remember as such; so that now, when one of them for some reason or other steps really as an individual into the circle of his vision and the realm of his decision, he is aware of him without strain not as a number with a human mask but as a person. He practises it when he comprehends and handles these persons as persons—for the greatest part necessarily indirectly, by means of a system of mediation which varies according to the extent, nature and structure of the undertaking, but also directly, in the parts which concern him by way of organization. Naturally at first both camps, that of capital and that of the proletariat, will decry his masterly attitude of fantasy as fantastic nonsense and his practical attitude to persons as dilettantist. But just as naturally only until his increased figures of production accredit him in their eyes. (By this of course is not to be implied that those increases necessarily come to pass: between truth and success there is no pre-stabilized harmony.) Then, to be sure, something worse will follow. He will be pragmatically imitated, that is, people will try to use his "procedure" without his way of thinking and imagining. But this demoniac element inherent in spiritual history (think only of all the magicizing of religion) will, I think, shipwreck here on the power of discrimination in men's souls. And meanwhile it is to be hoped that a new generation will arise, learning from what is alive, and will take all this in real seriousness as he does.

Unmistakably men are more and more determined by "circumstances". Not only the absolute mass but also the relative might of social objectives is growing. As one determined partially by them the individual stands in each moment before concrete reality which wishes to reach out to him and receive an answer from him; laden with the situation he meets new situations. And yet in all the multiplicity and complexity he has remained Adam. Even now a real decision is made in him, whether he faces the speech of God articulated to him in things and events—or escapes. And a creative glance towards his fellow-creature can at times suffice for response.

Man is in a growing measure sociologically determined. But this growing is the maturing of a task not in the "ought" but in the "may" and in "need", in longing and in grace. It is a matter of renouncing the pantechnical mania or habit with its easy "mastery" of every situation; of taking everything up into the might of dialogue of the genuine life, from the trivial mysteries of everyday to the majesty of destructive destiny.

The task becomes more and more difficult, and more and more essential, the fulfilment more and more impeded and more and more rich in decision. All the regulated chaos of the age waits for the break-through, and wherever a man perceives and responds, he is working to that end.

II

THE QUESTION TO THE SINGLE ONE (9)

Responsibility is the navel-string of creation.—P.B.

The Unique One and the Single One

Only by coming up against the category of the "Single One", and by making it a concept of the utmost clarity, did Søren Kierkegaard become the one who presented Christianity as a paradoxical problem for the single "Christian". He was only able to do this owing to the radical nature of his solitariness. His "single one" cannot be understood without his solitariness, which differed in kind from the solitariness of one of the earlier Christian thinkers, such as Augustine or Pascal, whose name one would like to link with his. It is not irrelevant that beside Augustine stood a mother and beside Pascal a sister, who maintained the organic connexion with the world as only a woman as the envoy of elemental life can; whereas the central event of Kierkegaard's life and the core of the crystallization of his thought was the renunciation of Regina Olsen as representing woman and the world. Nor may this solitariness be compared with that of a monk or a hermit: for him the renunciation stands essentially only at the beginning, and even if it must be ever anew achieved and practised, it is not that which is the life theme, the basic problem, and the stuff out of which all teaching is woven. But for Kierkegaard this is just what renunciation is. It is embodied in the category of the single one, "the category through which, from the religious standpoint, time and history and the race must pass" (Kierkegaard, 1847).

By means of an opposition we can first of all be precisely aware what the single one, in a special and specially important sense, is not. A few years before Kierkegaard outlined his *Report to History* under the title *The Point of View for my Work as an Author*, in whose *Two Notes* the category of the Single One found its adequate formulation, Max Stirner published his book about "The Unique One" (10). This too is a border concept like the single one, but one from the other end. Stirner, a pathetic nominalist and unmasker of ideas, wanted to dissolve the alleged remains of German idealism (as which he regarded Ludwig Feuerbach) by raising not the thinking subject nor man but the concrete present individual as "the exclusive I" to be the bearer of the world, that is, of "his" world.

Here this Unique One "consuming himself" in "self-enjoyment" is the only one who has primary existence; only the man who comes to such a possession and consciousness of himself has primary existence—on account of the "unity and omnipotence of our I that is sufficient to itself, for it lets nothing be but itself". Thus the question of an essential relation between him and the other is eliminated as well. He has no essential relation except to himself (Stirner's alleged "living participation" "in the person of the other" is without essence, since the other has in his eyes no primary existence). That is, he has only that remarkable relation with the self which does not lack certain magical possibilities (since all other existence becomes the haunting of ghosts that are half in bonds, half free), but is so empty of any genuine power to enter into relation that it is better to describe as a relation only that in which not only *I* but also *Thou* can be said. This border product of a German Protagoras is usually underrated: the loss of reality which responsibility and truth have suffered in our time has here if not its spiritual origin certainly its exact conceptual prediction. "The man who belongs to himself alone . . . is by origin free, for he acknowledges nothing but himself," and "True is what is Mine" are formulas which forecast a congealing of the soul unsuspected by Stirner in all his rhetorical assurance. But also many a rigid collective *We*, which rejects a superior authority, is easily understood as a translation from the speech of the Unique One into that of the *Group-I* which acknowledges nothing but itself—carried out against Stirner's intention, who hotly opposes any plural version.

Kierkegaard's Single One has this in common with its counterpoint, Stirner's Unique One, that both are border categories; it has no more in common than this, but also it has no less.

The category of the Single One, too, means not the subject or "man", but concrete singularity; yet not the individual who is detecting his existence, but rather the person who is finding himself. But the finding himself, however primally remote from Stirner's "utilize thyself", is not akin either to that "know thyself" which apparently troubled Kierkegaard very much. For it means a becoming, and moreover in a weight of seriousness that only became possible, at least for the West, through Christianity. It is therefore a becoming which (though Kierkegaard says that his category was used by Socrates "for the dissolution of heathendom") is decisively different from that effected by the Socratic "delivery". "No-one is excluded from being a Single One except him who excludes himself by wishing to be 'crowd'." Here not only is "Single One" opposed to "crowd", but also becoming is opposed to a particular mode of being which evades becoming. That may still be in tune with Socratic thought. But what does it mean, to become a Single One? Kierkegaard's account shows clearly that the nature of his category is no longer Socratic. It runs, "to fulfil the first condition of all religiosity" is "to be a single man". It is for this reason that the "Single One" is "the category through which, from the religious standpoint, time and history and the race must pass".

Since the concept of religiosity has since lost its definiteness, what Kierkegaard means must be more precisely defined. He cannot mean that to become a Single One is the presupposition of a condition of the soul, called religiosity. It is not a matter of a condition of the soul but a matter of existence in that strict sense in which—precisely by fulfilling the personal life— it steps in its essence over the boundary of the person. Then being, familiar being, becomes unfamiliar and no longer signifies my being but my participation in the Present Being. That this is what Kierkegaard means is expressed in the fundamental word that the Single One "corresponds" to God. In Kierkegaard's account, then, the concept "of all religiosity" has to be more precisely defined by "of all religious reality". But since this also is all too exposed to the epidemic sickening of the word in our time, by which every word is at once covered with the leprosy of routine and changed into a slogan, we must go further, as far as possible, and, giving up vexatious "religion", take a risk, but a necessary risk, and explain the phrase as meaning "of all real human dealings with God". That Kierkegaard means this is shown by his reference to a "speaking with God". And indeed a man can have dealings with God only as a Single One, as a man who has become a Single One. This is so expressed in the Old Testament, though there a people too meets the Godhead as a people, that it time and again lets only a named person, Enoch, Noah, "have dealings with Elohim". Not before a man can say *I* in perfect reality—that is, finding himself—can he in perfect reality say *Thou*—that is, to God. And even if he does it in a community he can only do it "alone". "As the 'Single One' he [every man] is alone, alone in the whole world, alone before God." That is—what Kierkegaard, strangely, does not think of—thoroughly unsocratic: in the words "the divine gives me a sign" Socrates's "religiosity" is represented, significant for all ages; but the words "I am alone before God" are unthinkable as coming from him. Kierkegaard's "alone" is no longer of Socrates; it is of Abraham—Genesis 12. 1 and 22. 2, alike demand in the same "Go before thee" the power to free oneself of all bonds, the bonds to the world of fathers and to the world of sons; and it is of Christ.

Clarity demands a further twofold distinction. First, with respect to mysticism. It too lets the man be alone before God but not as the Single One. The relation to God which it thinks of is the absorption of the *I*, and the Single One ceases to exist if he cannot—even in devoting himself—say *I*. As mysticism will not permit God to assume the servant's form of the speaking and acting person, of a creator, of a revealer, and to tread the way of the Passion through time as the partner of history, suffering along with it all destiny, so it forbids man, as the Single One persisting as such, from really praying and serving and loving such as is possible only by an *I* to a *Thou*. Mysticism only tolerates the Single One in order that he may radically melt away. But Kierkegaard knows, at any rate in relation to God, what love is, and thus he knows that there is no self-love that is not self-deceit (since he who loves—and it is he who matters—loves only the other and essentially not himself), but that without being and remaining oneself there is no love.

The second necessary distinction is with respect to Stirner's "Unique One". (For the sake of conceptual precision this expression is to be preferred to the more humanistic ones, such as Stendhal's *égotiste*.)

A preliminary distinction must be made with respect to so-called individualism, which has also produced a "religious" variety. The Single One, the person ready and able for the "standing alone before God", is the counterpart of what still, in no distant time, was called—in a term which is treason to the spirit of Goethe—personality, and man's becoming a Single One is the counterpart of "personal development". All individualism, whether it is styled æsthetic or ethical or religious, has a cheap and ready pleasure in man provided he is "developing". In other words, "ethical" and "religious" individualism are only inflexions of the "æsthetic" (which is as little genuine *æsthesis* as those are genuine *ethos* and genuine *religio*).

Morality and piety, where they have in this way become an autonomous aim, must also be reckoned among the show-pieces and shows of a spirit that no longer knows about Being but only about its mirrorings.

Where individualism ceases to be wanton Stirner begins. He is also, it is true, concerned with the "shaping of free personality", but in the sense of a severance of the "self" from the world: he is concerned with the tearing apart of his existential bindings and bonds, with breaking free from all ontic otherness of things and of lives, which now may only serve as "nourishment" of his selfhood. The contrapuntal position of Stirner's Unique One to Kierkegaard's Single One becomes clearest when the questions of responsibility and truth are raised.

For Stirner both are bound to be false questions. But it is important to see that intending to destroy both basic ideas he has destroyed only their routine forms and thus, contrary to his whole intention, has prepared for their purification and renewal. Historically-minded contemporaries have spoken disparagingly of him as a modern sophist; since then the function of the sophists, and consequently of their like, of dissolving and preparing, has been recognized. Stirner may have understood Hegel just as little as Protagoras did Heraclitus; but even as it is meaningless to reproach Protagoras with laying waste the gardens of the great cosmologist, so Stirner is untouched by being ridiculed as the unsuspecting and profane interloper in the fields of post-kantian philosophy. Stirner is not, any more than the sophists are, a curious interlude in the history of human thought. Like them he is an ἐπεισόδιον in the original sense. In his monologue the action secretly changes, what follows is a new thing—as Protagoras leads towards his contemporary Socrates, Stirner leads towards his contemporary Kierkegaard.

Responsibility presupposes one who addresses me primarily, that is, from a realm independent of myself, and to whom I am answerable. He addresses me about something that he has entrusted to me and that I am bound to take care of loyally. He addresses me from his trust and I respond in my loyalty or refuse to respond in my disloyalty, or I had fallen into disloyalty and wrestle free of it by the loyalty of the response. To be so answerable to a trusting person about an entrusted matter that loyalty and disloyalty step into the light of day (but both are not of the same right, for now loyalty, born again, is permitted to conquer disloyalty)—this is the reality of responsibility. Where no primary address and claim can touch me, for everything is "My property", responsibility has become a phantom. At the same time life's character of mutuality is dissipated. He who ceases to make a response ceases to hear the Word.

But this reality of responsibility is not what is questioned by Stirner; it is unknown to him. He simply does not know what of elemental reality happens between life and life, he does not know the mysteries of address and answer, claim and disclaim, word and response. He has not experienced this because it can only be experienced when one is not closed to the otherness, the ontic and primal otherness of the other (to the primal otherness of the other, which of course, even when the other is God, must not be confined to a "wholly otherness"). What Stirner with his destructive power successfully attacks is the substitute for a reality that is no longer believed: the fictitious responsibility in face of reason, of an idea, a nature, an institution, of all manner of illustrious ghosts, all that in its essence is not a person and hence cannot really, like father and mother, prince and master, husband and friend, like God, make you answerable. He wishes to show the nothingness of the word which has decayed into a phrase; he has never known the living word, he unveils what he knows. Ignorant of the reality whose appearance is appearance, he proves its nature to be appearance. Stirner dissolves the dissolution. "What you call responsibility is a lie!" he cries, and he is right: it is a lie. But there is a truth. And the way to it lies freer after the lie has been seen through.

Kierkegaard means true responsibility when, rushing in a parabola past Stirner, he speaks thus of the crowd and the Single One: "Being in a crowd either releases from repentance and responsibility or weakens the responsibility of the Single One, since the crowd leaves only a fragment of responsibility to him." These words, to which I intend to return, no longer have in view any illusion of a responsibility without a receiver, but genuine responsibility, recognized once more, in which the demander demands of me the entrusted good and I must open my hands or they petrify.

Stirner has unmasked as unreal the responsibility which is only ethical by exposing the non-existence of the alleged receivers as such. Kierkegaard has proclaimed anew the responsibility which is in faith.

And as with responsibility so with truth itself: here the parabolic meeting becomes still uncannier.

"Truth . . . exists only—in your head." "The truth is a—creature." "For Me there is no truth, for nothing passes beyond Me." "So long as you believe in the truth you do not believe in yourself. . . . You alone are the truth." What Stirner undertakes here is the dissolution of *possessed* truth, of "truth" as a general good that can be taken into possession and possessed, that is at once independent of and accessible to the person. He does not undertake this like the sophists and other sceptics by means of epistemology. He does not seem to have been acquainted with the epistemological method; he is as audaciously naive in his behaviour as though Hume and Kant had never lived. But neither would the epistemology have achieved for him what he needed; for it, and the solipsist theory as well, leads only to the knowing subject and not to the concrete human person at which Stirner aims with undeviating fanaticism. The means by which he undertakes the dissolution of possessed truth is the demonstration that it is conditioned by the person. "True is what is Mine." There already lies hidden the fundamental principle of our day, "what I take as true is defined by what I am". To this two sentences may be taken as alternatives or as a combination—to Stirner's horror, certainly, but in logical continuation as an inseparable exposition—first the sentence "And what I am is conditioned by my complexes", and second the sentence "And what I am is conditioned by the class I belong to", with all its variants. Stirner is the involuntary father of modern psychological and sociological relativizings which for their part (to anticipate) are at once true and false.

But again Stirner is right, again he dissolves the dissolution. *Possessed* truth is not even a creature, it is a ghost, a succubus with which a man may succeed in effectively imagining he is living, but with which he cannot live. You cannot devour the truth, it is not served up anywhere in the world, you cannot even gape at it, for it is not an object. And yet there does exist a participation in the being of inaccessible truth—for the man who stands its test. There exists a real relation of the whole human person to the unpossessed, unpossessable truth, and it is completed only in standing its test. This real relation, whatever it is called, is the relation to the Present Being.

The re-discovery of truth, which has been disenthroned in the human world by the semblance of truth, but which is in truth eternally irremovable, which cannot be possessed but which can be served, and for which service can be given by perceiving *and* standing test, is accomplished by Kierkegaard in a paradoxical series of sentences. It begins with the words, "He who communicates it [the truth] is only a Single One. And then its communication is again only for the Single One; for this view of life, 'the Single One', is the very truth." You must listen carefully. Not that the Single One exists and not that he should exist is described as the truth, but "this view of life" which consists in the Single One's existing, and which is hence also simply identified with him. To be the Single One is the communication of the truth, that is, the human truth. "The crowd," says Kierkegaard, "produces positions of advantage in human life," which "overlook in time and the world the eternal truth—the Single One." "You alone are the truth" is what Stirner says. "The Single One is the truth," is what is said here. That is the uncanny parabolic phenomenon of words to which I have referred. In "a time of dissolution" (Kierkegaard) there is the blank point at which the No and the Yes move up to and past one another with all their power, but purely objectively and without consciousness. Now Kierkegaard continues: "The truth cannot be communicated and received except as it were before God's eyes, by God's help; so that God is there, is the medium as he is the truth. . . .

For God is the truth and its medium." Thus "'The Single One' is the truth" and "God is the truth". That is true because the Single One "corresponds" to God. Hence Kierkegaard can say that the category of the "Single One" is and remains "the fixed point which can resist pantheist confusion". The Single One corresponds to God. For "man is akin to the Godhead". In Old Testament language, the Single One realizes the "image" of God precisely through having become a Single One. In the language in which alone a generation, wrestling with the problem of truth, succumbing to it, turning from it, but also exploring it ever anew, can understand the conquest, the Single One existentially stands the test of the appearing truth by "the personal existence expressing what is said" [I would say "what is unsaid"]. There is this human side of truth—in human existence. God is the truth because he is, the Single One is the truth because he reaches his existence.

Stirner has dissolved the truth which is only noetic, and against all his knowledge and desire cleared a space into which Kierkegaard's believed and tested truth has stepped, the truth which can no longer be obtained and possessed by the *noesis* alone, but which must be existentially realized in order to be inwardly known and communicated.

But there is still a third and last contact and repulsion. For Stirner every man is the Unique One if only he discards all ideological ballast (to which for him the religious belongs) and settles down as owner of his world-property. For Kierkegaard "every, absolutely every man" "can and ought" to be "the Single One"—only he must . . . what, indeed, must he? He must become a Single One. For "the matter is thus: this category cannot be taught by precept; it is something that you can *do*, it is an *art* . . . and moreover an art whose practice could cost the artist, in time, his life". But when we investigate closely to see if there is a nearer definition anywhere, even if not precisely one that can be taught by precept, one will be found—no more than one, no more than a single word, but it is found: it is "obey". It is at any rate what is under all circumstances prohibited to Stirner's Unique One by his author. It is easy to discover that behind all Stirner's prohibitions to his Unique One this stands as the real, comprehensive and decisive prohibition. With this one verb Kierkegaard finally thrusts off the spirit which, without either of them knowing, had approached so near, too near, in the time of dissolution.

And yet—the illumination of our time makes it visible— the two, primally different, primally strange to one another, concerning one another in nothing but with one another concerning us, work together, not a hundred years ago but to-day, the one announcing decay as decay, the other proving the eternal structure to be inviolable. To renounce obedience to any usurping lord is Stirner's demand; Kierkegaard has none of his own—he repeats the ancient, misused, desecrated, outworn, inviolable "obey the Lord". If a man becomes the Single One "then the obedience is all right" even in the time of dissolution, where otherwise the obedience is not all right.

Stirner leads out of all kinds of alleys into the open country where each is the Unique One and the world is his property. There they bustle in futile and non-committal life, and nothing comes of it but bustle, till one after the other begins to notice what this country is called. Kierkegaard leads to a "narrow pass"; his task is "where possible to induce the many, to invite them, to stir them to press through this narrow pass, 'the Single One', through which, note well, none passes unless he becomes 'the Single One', since in the concept itself the opposite is excluded". I think, however, that in actual history the way to this narrow pass is through that open country that first is called individual egoism and then collective egoism and, finally, by its true name, despair.

But is there really a way through the narrow pass? Can one really become the Single One?

"I myself do not assert of myself," says Kierkegaard, "that I am that one. For I have indeed fought for it, but have not yet grasped it, and am in the continued fight continually reminded that it is beyond human strength to be 'the Single One' in the highest sense."

"In the highest sense"—that is spoken with a Christian and a christological reference, it manifests the paradox of the Christian task. But it is also convincing to the non-christian. It has in it the assertion that no man can say of himself that he has become the Single One, since a higher sense of the category always remains unfulfilled beyond him; but it also has in it the assertion that every man can nevertheless become a Single One. Both are true.

"The eternal, the decisive, can be worked for only where

one man is; and to become this one man, which all men can, means to let oneself be helped by God." This is a way.

And yet it is not the way; for reasons of which I have not spoken in this section and of which I now have to speak.

The Single One and his Thou

Kierkegaard's "to become a Single One" is, as we have seen, not meant Socratically. The goal of this becoming is not the "right" life, but the entry into a relation. "To become" means here to become *for* something, "for" in the strict sense which simply transcends the circle of the person himself. It means to be made ready for the one relation which can be entered into only by the Single One, the one; the relation for whose sake man exists.

This relation is an exclusive one, the exclusive one, and this means, according to Kierkegaard, that it is the excluding relation, excluding all others; more precisely, that it is the relation which in virtue of its unique, essential life expels all other relations into the realm of the unessential.

"Everyone should be chary about having to do with 'the others', and should essentially speak only with God and with himself," he says in the exposition of the category. Everyone, so it is to be understood, because everyone can be the one.

The joining of the "with God" with the "with himself" is a serious incompatibility that nothing can mitigate. All the enthusiasm of the philosophers for monologue, from Plato to Nietzsche, does not touch the simple experience of faith that speaking with God is something *toto genere* different from "speaking with oneself"; whereas, remarkably, it is not something *toto genere* different from speaking with another human being. For in the latter case there is common the fact of being approached, grasped, addressed, which cannot be anticipated in any depth of the soul; but in the former case it is not common in spite of all the soul's adventures in doubling roles—games, intoxications, dreams, visions, surprises, overwhelmings, over-powerings—in spite of all tensions and divisions, and all the noble and strong images for traffic with oneself. "Then one became two"—that can never become *ontically* true, just as the reverse "one and one at one" of mysticism can never be ontically true. Only when I have to do with another essentially,

THE QUESTION TO THE SINGLE ONE

that is, in such a way that he is no longer a phenomenon of my
I, but instead is my *Thou*, do I experience the reality of speech
with another—in the irrefragable genuineness of mutuality.
Abyssus abyssum clamat—what that means the soul first experiences when it reaches its frontier and finds itself faced by
one that is simply not the soul itself and yet is a self.

But on this point Kierkegaard seems to correct himself. In
the passage in his *Journals* where he asks the question, "And
how does one become a Single One?" the answer begins with
the formulation, obviously more valid in the problem under
discussion, that one should be, "regarding the highest concerns,
related solely to God".

If, in this sentence, the word "highest" is understood as
limiting in its content, then the phrase is self-evident: the
highest concerns can be put only to the highest. But it cannot
be meant in this way; this is clear from the other sentence,
"Everyone should. . . ." If both are held together, then
Kierkegaard's meaning is evident that the Single One has to
do *essentially* (is not "chary") only with God.

But thereby the category of the Single One, which has
scarcely been properly discovered, is already fatefully
misunderstood.

Kierkegaard, the Christian concerned with "contemporaneity" with Jesus, here contradicts his master.

To the question—which was not merely aimed at "tempting"
him, but was rather a current and significant controversial
question of the time—which was the all-inclusive and fundamental commandment, the "great" commandment, Jesus
replied by connecting the two Old Testament commandments
between which above all the choice lay: "love God with all your
might" and "love your neighbour as one like yourself" (11).
Both are to be "loved", God and the "neighbour" (i.e. not
man in general, but the man who meets me time and again in
the context of life), but in different ways. The neighbour is to
be loved "as one like myself" (not "as I love myself"; in the
last reality one does not love oneself, but one should rather
learn to love oneself through love of one's neighbour), to whom,
then, I should show love as I wish it may be shown to me. But
God is to be loved with all my soul and all my might. By
connecting the two Jesus brings to light the Old Testament
truth that God and man are not rivals. Exclusive love to God
("with *all* your heart") is, *because he is God*, inclusive love, ready

to accept and include all love. It is not himself that God creates, not himself he redeems, even when he "reveals himself" it is not himself he reveals: his revelation does not have himself as object. He limits himself in all his limitlessness, he makes room for the creatures, and so, in love to him, he makes room for love to the creatures.

"In order to come to love," says Kierkegaard about his renunciation of Regina Olsen, "I had to remove the object". That is sublimely to misunderstand God. Creation is not a hurdle on the road to God, it is the road itself. We are created along with one another and directed to a life with one another. Creatures are placed in my way so that I, their fellow-creature, by means of them and with them find the way to God. A God reached by their exclusion would not be the God of all lives in whom all life is fulfilled. A God in whom only the parallel lines of single approaches intersect is more akin to the "God of the philosophers" than to the "God of Abraham and Isaac and Jacob". God wants us to come to him by means of the Reginas he has created and not by renunciation of them. If we remove the object, then—we have removed the object altogether. Without an object, artificially producing the object from the abundance of the human spirit and calling it God, this love has its being in the void.

"The matter must be brought back to the monastery from which Luther broke out." So Kierkegaard defines the task of the time. "Monastery" can here mean only the institutional safeguarding of man from an essential relation, inclusive of his whole being, to any others but God. And certainly to one so safeguarded the orientation towards the point called God is made possible with a precision not to be attained otherwise. But what "God" in this case means is in fact only the end-point of a human line of orientation. But the real God lets no shorter line reach him than each man's longest, which is the line embracing the world that is accessible to this man. For he, the real God, is the creator, and all beings stand before him in relation to one another in his creation, becoming useful in living with one another for his creative purpose. To teach an acosmic relation to God is not to know the creator. Acosmic worship of a God of whom one knows, along with Kierkegaard, that it is of his grace "that he wills to be a person in relation to you", is Marcionism, and not even consistent Marcionism; for this worship does not separate the creator and the redeemer as it would have to do if it were consistent.

But one must not overlook the fact that Kierkegaard is not at all concerned to put Luther breaking out of the monastery in the wrong. On one occasion he treats Luther's marriage as something removed from all natural personal life, all directness between man and wife, as a symbolic action, a deed representing and expressing the turning-point of the spiritual history of the west. "The most important thing," he makes Luther say, "is that it becomes notorious that I am married." But behind Luther's marrying Katharina there emerges, unnamed but clear, Kierkegaard's not marrying Regina. "Put the other way round, one could say . . . in defiance of the whole nineteenth century I cannot marry." Here there is added as a new perspective the qualitative difference between historical epochs. Certainly, on Kierkegaard's view it is true for both ages that the Single One should not have to do essentially with any others but God, and according to him, then, Luther speaks not essentially but only symbolically with Katharina; though bound to the world he remains essentially worldless and "alone before God". But the symbolic actions are opposed: by the one the word of a new bond with the world—even if perhaps in the end a bond that is not binding—is spoken to the one century; by the other the word of a new and in any event binding renunciation is spoken to the other century. What is the reason? Because the nineteenth century has given itself up to the "crowd", and "the crowd is untruth".

But now two things are possible. Either the bond with the world preached with his life by Luther is in Kierkegaard's view not binding or "essential" or necessary for the leading of Luther's age to God. But that would make Luther one who lets what is not binding be effective as something that is binding, who has a different thing to say for men than he has for God, and who treats the sacrament as though it were fulfilled outside God; it would make Luther one in whose symbolic action no authority could reside. Or else on the other hand the bond with the world preached with his life by Luther is in Kierkegaard's view binding and essential and necessary for leading to God. Then the difference between the two epochs, which is for the rest indubitably a qualitative one, would have a say in what is basically independent of history, more so than birth and death—the relation of the Single One to God. For the essential quality of this relation cannot be of one kind in the former century and of another in the latter; it cannot in the one go right through the world and in the other go over and beyond the world. Human representations of the relation change, the truth of the relation is unchangeable because it stands in eternal mutuality; it is not man who defines his approach to it but the creator who in the unambiguity of man's creation has instituted the approach.

It is certainly not possible to speak of God other than dialectically, for he does not come under the principle of contradiction. Yet there is a limit of dialectic where assertion ceases but where there is knowledge. Who is there who confesses the God whom Kierkegaard and I confess, who could suppose in decisive insight that God wants *Thou* to be truly said only to him, and to all others only an unessential and fundamentally invalid word—that God demands of us to choose between him and his creation? The objection is raised that the world as a fallen world is not to be identified with the creation. But what fall of the world could be so mighty that it could *for him* break it away from being his creation? That would be to make the action of the world into one more powerful than God's action and into one compelling him.

The essential is not that we should see things as standing out from God nor as being absorbed in him, but that we should "see things in God", the things themselves. To apply this to our relations with creatures: only when all relations, uncurtailed, are taken into the one relation, do we set the ring of our life's world round the sun of our being.

Certainly that is the most difficult thing, and man in order to be able to do it must let himself be helped from time to time by an inner-worldly "monastery". Our relations to creatures incessantly threaten to get incapsulated. As the world itself is sustained in its independence as the world through striving to be closed to God, though as creation it is open to him, so every great bond of man—though in it he has perceived his connexion with the infinite—defends itself vigorously against continually debouching into the infinite. Here the monastic forms of life in the world, the loneliness in the midst of life into which we turn as into hostelries, help us to prevent the connexion between the conditioned bonds and the one unconditioned bond from slackening. This too, if we do not wish to see our participation in the Present Being dying off, is an imperative interchange, the systole to the diastole of the soul;

and the loneliness must know the quality of strictness, of a monastery's strictness, in order to do its work. But it must never wish to tear us away from creatures, never refuse to dismiss us to them. By that it would act contrary to its own law and would close us, instead of enabling us, as is its office, to keep open the gates of finitude.

Kierkegaard does not conceal from us for a moment that his resistance to a bond with the world, his religious doctrine of loneliness, is based on personal nature and personal destiny. He confesses that he "ceased to have common speech" with men. He notes that the finest moment in his life is in the bath-house, before he dives into the water: "I have nothing more to do with the world". He exposes before our eyes some of the roots of his "melancholy". He knows precisely what has brought him to the point of being chary about having to do with others and of essentially speaking only with God and with himself. And yet, as soon as he begins with the "direct" language, he expresses it as an imperative: let *everyone* do so. Continually he points to his own shadow—and wants to leap across it. He is a being excepted and exposed, and certainly so are we all, for so is man as man. But Kierkegaard has moved to the fringe of being excepted and exposed, and maintains equilibrium only by means of the unheard-of balance of his "author's" reticently communicative existence with the complicated safeguards of all the "pseudonyms"; whereas we are not on the fringe, and that is no "not yet" nor any sort of compromising, no shirking of melancholy; it is organic continuance and grace of preservation and significant for the future of the spirit. Kierkegaard behaves in our sight like a schizophrenist, who tries to win over the beloved individual into "his" world as if it were the true one. But it is not the true one. We, ourselves wandering on the narrow ridge, must not shrink from the sight of the jutting rock on which he stands over the abyss; nor may we step on it. We have much to learn from him, but not the final lesson.

Our rejection can be supported by Kierkegaard's own teaching. He describes "the ethical" as "the only means by which God communicates with 'man'" (1853). The context of the teaching naturally keeps at a distance the danger of understanding this in the sense of an absolutizing of the ethical. But it must be understood so that not merely an autarkic ethic but also an autarkic religion is inadmissible; so that as the ethical cannot be freed from the religious neither can the religious from the ethical without ceasing to do justice to the present truth. The ethical no longer appears here, as in Kierkegaard's earlier thought, as a "stage" from which a "leap" leads to the religious, a leap by which a level is reached that is quite different and has a different meaning; but it dwells in the religious, in faith and service. This ethical can no longer mean a morality belonging to a realm of relativity and time and again overtaken and invalidated by the religious; but it means an *essential* action and suffering in relation to men, which are co-ordinated with the essential relation to God. But only he who has to do with men essentially can essentially act and suffer in relation to them. If the ethical is the only means by which God communicates with man then I am forbidden to speak essentially only with God and myself. And so indeed it is. I do not say that Kierkegaard on his rock, alone with the mercy of the Merciful, is forbidden. I say only that you and I are forbidden.

Kierkegaard is deeply conscious of the dubiousness which arises from the negativizing extension of the category of the Single One. "The frightful thing", he writes in his Journal, and we read it, as he wrote it, with fear and trembling, "is that precisely the highest form of piety, to let everything earthly go, can be the highest egoism". Here obviously a distinction is made according to motives, and the idea of egoism used here is an idea of motivation. If we put in its place an objective idea, an idea of a state of affairs, the sentence is changed to a still more frightful one: "Precisely what appears to us as the highest form of piety—to let everything earthly go—is the highest egoism."

Is it true that the Single One "corresponds" to God? Does he realize the "image" of God solely by having become a Single One? One thing is lacking for that to be—and it is the decisive thing.

"Certainly," says Kierkegaard, "God is no egoist, but he is the infinite Ego." Yet thereby too little is said of the God whom we confess—if one dares to say anything at all. He hovers over his creation not as over a chaos, he embraces it. He is the infinite *I* that makes every *It* into his *Thou*.

The Single One corresponds to God when he in his human way embraces the bit of the world offered to him as God embraces his creation in his divine way. He realizes the image when, as much he can in a personal way, he says *Thou* with his being to the beings living round about him.

No-one can so refute Kierkegaard as Kierkegaard himself. Reasoning with and judging himself, he corrects his own spirit from its depths, often before it has uttered itself. In 1843 Kierkegaard enters this unforgettable confession in his Journal: "Had I had faith I would have stayed with Regina." By this he means, "If I had really believed that 'with God all things are possible', hence also the resolution of this—my melancholy, my powerlessness, my fear, my alienation, fraught with destiny, from woman and from the world—then I would have stayed with Regina." But while meaning this he says something different, too, namely, that the Single One, if he really believes, and that means if he is really a Single One (which, as we saw, he has become for the one relation of faith), can and may have to do essentially with another. And behind this there lurks the extreme that he who can and may also *ought to* do this. "The only means by which God communicates with man is the ethical." But the ethical in its plain truth means to help God by loving his creation in his creatures, by loving it towards him. For this, to be sure, one must let oneself be helped by him.

"The Single One is the category through which, from the religious standpoint, time and history and the race must pass." What is this "religious standpoint"? One beside others? The standpoint towards God, gained by standing aside from all others? God one object beside other objects, the chosen one beside the rejected ones? God as Regina's successful rival? Is that still God? Is that not merely an object adapted to the religious genius? (Note that I am not speaking of true holiness for which, as it hallows *everything*, there is no "religious stand-point".) Religious genius? Can there be religious geniuses? Is that not a *contradictio in adiecto*? Can the religious be a specification? "Religious geniuses" are theological geniuses. Their God is the God of the theologians. Admittedly, that is not the God of the philosophers, but neither is it the God of Abraham and Isaac and Jacob. The God of the theologians, too, is a logicized God, and so is even the God of a theology which will speak only dialectically and makes light of the principle of contradiction. So long as they practise theology they do not get away from religion as a specification. When Pascal in a volcanic hour made that stammering distinction between God and God he was no genius but a man experiencing the primal glow of faith; but at other times he was a theological genius and dwelt in a specifying religion, out of which the happening of that hour had lifted him.

Religion as a specification misses its mark. God is not an object beside objects and hence cannot be reached by renunciation of objects. God, indeed, is not the cosmos, but far less is he Being *minus* cosmos. He is not to be found by subtraction and not to be loved by reduction.

The Single One and the Body Politic

Kierkegaard's thought circles round the fact that he essentially renounced an essential relation to a definite person. He did not resign this casually, or in the relativity of the many experiences and decisions of life, or with the soul alone, but essentially. The essential nature of his renunciation, its downright positive essentiality, is what he wants to express by saying, "In defiance of the whole nineteenth century I cannot marry." The renunciation becomes essential through its representing in concrete biography the renunciation of an essential relation to the world as that which hinders being alone before God. Moreover, as I have already said, this does not happen just once, as when a man enters a monastery and has thereby cut himself off from the world and lives outside it as one who has done this; but it is peculiarly enduring: the renunciation becomes the zero of a spiritual graph whose every point is determined in relation to this zero. It is in this way that the graph receives its true existential character, by means of which it has provided the impulse to a new philosophy and a new theology. And certainly there goes along with this secularly significant concreteness of biography the curiously manifold motivation—which is undoubtedly legitimate, and is to be found piecemeal in the soundings of inwardness—of the renunciation which Kierkegaard expresses directly and indirectly, by suggestion and concealment. But beyond that, on a closer consideration it is to be noted that there arises, between the renunciation and an increasingly strong point of view and attitude which is finally expressed with penetrating clarity in the *Two Notes* to the *Report to History*, a secret and unexpressed connexion important for Kierkegaard and for us.

"The crowd is untruth." "This consideration of life, the

Single One, is the truth." "No-one is excluded from becoming a Single One except him who excludes himself by wanting to be crowd." And again, " 'The Single One' is the category of the spirit, of spiritual awakening and revival, and is as sharply opposed to politics as possible." The Single One and the crowd, the "spirit" and "politics"—this opposition is not to be separated from that into which Kierkegaard enters with the world, expressing it symbolically by means of his renunciation.

Kierkegaard does not marry "in defiance of the whole nineteenth century". What he describes as the nineteenth century is the "age of dissolution", the age of which he says that a single man "cannot help it or save it", he can "only express that it is going under"—going under, if it cannot reach God through the "narrow pass". And Kierkegaard does not marry, in a symbolic action of negation, in defiance of this age, because it is the age of the "crowd" and the age of "politics". Luther married in symbolic action, because he wanted to lead the believing man of his age out of a rigid religious separation, which finally separated him from grace itself, to a life with God in the world. Kierkegaard does not marry (this of course is not part of the manifold subjective motivation but is the objective meaning of the symbol) because he wants to lead the unbelieving man of his age, who is entangled in the crowd, to becoming single, to the solitary life of faith, to being alone before God. Certainly, "to marry or not to marry" is the representative question when the monastery is in view. If the Single One really must be, as Kierkegaard thinks, a man who does not have to do essentially with others, then marriage hinders him if he takes it seriously—and if he does not take it seriously then, in spite of Kierkegaard's remark about Luther, it cannot be understood how he as an existing person can be "the truth". For man, with whom alone Kierkegaard is fundamentally concerned, there is the additional factor that in his view woman stands "quite differently from man in a dangerous rapport to finitude". But there is still a special additional matter which I shall now make clear.

If one makes a fairly comprehensive survey of the whole labyrinthine structure of Kierkegaard's thought about renunciation it will be recognized that he is speaking not solely of a hard, hard-won renunciation, bought with the heart's blood, of life with a person; but in addition of the downright positively valued renunciation of the life (conditioned by life with a person) with an impersonal being, which in the foreground of the happening is called "people", in its background "the crowd". This being, however, in its essence—of which Kierkegaard knows or wants to know nothing—refutes these descriptions as caricatures and acknowledges as its true name only that of a *res publica*, in English "the body politic". When Kierkegaard says the category of the "Single One" is "as sharply opposed as possible to politics" he obviously means an activity that has essentially lost touch with its origin the *polis*. But this activity, however degenerate, is one of the decisive manifestations of the body politic. Every degeneration indicates its genus, and in such a way that the degeneration is never related to the genus simply as present to past, but as in a distorted face the distortion is related to the form persisting beneath it. The body politic, which is sometimes also called the "world", that is, the human world, seeks, knowingly or unknowingly, to realize in its genuine formations men's turning to one another in the context of creation. The false formations distort but they cannot eliminate the eternal origin. Kierkegaard in his horror of malformation turns away. But the man who has not ceased to love the human world in all its abasement sees even to-day genuine form. Supposing that the crowd is untruth, it is only a state of affairs in the body politic; how truth is here related to untruth must be part and parcel of the true question to the Single One, and that warning against the crowd can be only its preface.

From this point that special matter can be made clear of which I said that it is an additional reason for Kierkegaard's considering marriage to be an impediment. Marriage, essentially understood, brings one into an essential relation to the "world"; more precisely, to the body politic, to its malformation and its genuine form, to its sickness and its health. Marriage, as the decisive union of one with another, confronts one with the body politic and its destiny—man can no longer shirk that confrontation in marriage, he can only prove himself in it or fail. The isolated person, who is unmarried or whose marriage is only a fiction, can maintain himself in isolation; the "community" of marriage is part of the great community, joining with its own problems the general problems, bound up with its hope of salvation to the hope of the great life that in its most miserable state is called the crowd. He who "has entered on marriage", who has entered into marriage, has been in earnest, in the intention of the sacrament, with the fact that the other *is*; with the fact that I cannot legitimately share in the Present Being without sharing in the being of the other; with the fact that I cannot answer the lifelong address of God to me without answering at the same time for the other; with the fact that I cannot be answerable without being at the same time answerable for the other as one who is entrusted to me. But thereby a man has decisively entered into relation with otherness; and the basic structure of otherness, in many ways uncanny but never quite unholy or incapable of being hallowed, in which I and the others who meet me in my life are inwoven, is the body politic. It is to this, into this, that marriage intends to lead us. Kierkegaard himself makes one of his pseudonyms, the "married man" of the *Stages*, express this, though in the style of a lower point of view which is meant to be overcome by a higher. But it is a lower point of view only when trivialized, there is no higher, because to be raised above the situation in which we are set never yields in truth a higher point of view. Marriage is the exemplary bond, it carries us as does none other into the greater bondage, and only as those who are bound can we reach the freedom of the children of God. Expressed with a view to the man, the woman certainly stands "in a dangerous rapport to finitude", and finitude is certainly the danger, for nothing threatens us so sharply as that we remain clinging to it. But our hope of salvation is forged on this very danger, for our human way to the infinite leads only through fulfilled finitude.

This person is other, essentially other than myself, and this otherness of his is what I mean, because I mean him; I confirm it; I wish his otherness to exist, because I wish his particular being to exist. That is the basic principle of marriage and from this basis it leads, if it is real marriage, to insight into the right and the legitimacy of otherness and to that vital acknowledgement of many-faced otherness—even in the contradiction and conflict with it—from which dealings with the body politic receive their religious ethos. That the men with whom I am bound up in the body politic and with whom I have directly or indirectly to do, are essentially other than myself, that this one or that one does not have merely a different mind, or way of thinking or feeling, or a different conviction or attitude, but has also a different perception of the world, a different recognition and order of meaning, a different touch from the regions of existence, a different faith, a different soil: to affirm all this, to affirm it in the way of a creature, in the midst of the hard situations of conflict, without relaxing their real seriousness, is the way by which we may officiate as helpers in this wide realm entrusted to us as well, and from which alone we are from time to time permitted to touch in our doubts, in humility and upright investigation, on the other's "truth" or "untruth", "justice" or "injustice". But to this we are led by marriage, if it is real, with a power for which there is scarcely a substitute, by its steady experiencing of the life-substance of the other as other, and still more by its crises and the over-coming of them which rises out of the organic depths, whenever the monster of otherness, which but now blew on us with its icy demons' breath and now is redeemed by our risen affirma-tion of the other, which knows and destroys all negation, is transformed into the mighty angel of union of which we dreamed in our mother's womb.

Of course, there is a difference between the private sphere of existence, to which marriage belongs, and the public sphere of existence. *Identification* takes place in a qualitatively different way in each. The private sphere is that with which a man, at any rate in the healthy epochs of its existence, can in all con-creteness identify himself without regard to individual differentiation, such as the bodily and spiritual one between members of a family. This identification can take place by his saying in all concreteness *We, I,* of this family or band of his. (A genuine band stands in this respect on the side of the private sphere, in another respect it is on the side of the public sphere.) And when he says this he means not merely the whole, but also the single persons recognized and affirmed by him in their particular being. Identification with the public sphere of existence, on the other hand, is not really able to embrace the concrete persons in a concrete way. Thus I say of my nation "we", and this can be raised to the power of an elementary "That is I". But as soon as concretion, direction to the persons of whom the nation consists, enters in, there is a cleavage, and knowledge of the unbridgable multiple otherness permeates the identification in a broad stream. If the like happened to a province of private existence then it would either itself become of questionable value or it would pass over into public existence. For the relation to public existence every such test can be a proof and strengthening.

There are, however, two basic attitudes in which identification with public existence wards off the concretion, the direction to actual persons, and either transitorily or enduringly asserts itself. Very different from one another though they are, they often exercise almost the same effect. The one derives from the act of enthusiasm of "historic" hours: the crowd is actualized, enters into the action and is transfigured in it, and the person, overpowered by delirious ecstasy, is submerged in the movement of public existence. Here there is no contesting and impeding knowledge about the otherness of other persons: the transfiguration of the crowd eclipses all otherness, and the fiery impulse to identification can beget a real "family" feeling for the unknown man who walks in a demonstration or in the enthusiastic confusion of the streets runs into one's arms.

The other basic attitude is passive and constant. It is the accustomed joining in public opinion and in public "taking of a position". Here the crowd remains latent, it does not appear as a crowd, but only becomes effective. And, as is known, this happens in such a way that I am either completely excused from forming an opinion and a decision, or as it were convicted, in a murky recess of inwardness, of the invalidity of my opinions and decisions, and in their stead fitted out with ones that are approved as valid. By this means I am not in the least made aware of others since the same thing happens to them and their otherness has been varnished over.

Of these two basic attitudes the first is of such a kind that it snatches us out and away from confrontation with the great form of otherness in public existence, from the most difficult of the inner-worldly tasks, and raises us enthusiastically into the historical paradise of crowds. The second undermines the ground on which confrontation is to be carried out; it rubs out the pathetic signs of otherness and then convinces us by the evidence of our own eyes that uniformity is the real thing.

It is from this point that Kierkegaard's confusion of public existence, or the body politic, with the crowd, is to be understood. He knows the body politic, indeed, also in the form of the State, which is for him, however, only a fact in the world of relativity which is foreign to transcendence; it is respectable, but without significance for the individual's religious relation. And then he knows a crowd which is not respectable, but which has the deepest negative significance, indeed concerning transcendence, but as compact devilry.

This confusion which is in increasing measure heavy with consequences for the thought of our time must be opposed with the force of distinction.

A man in the crowd is a stick stuck in a bundle moving through the water, abandoned to the current or being pushed by a pole from the bank in this or that direction. Even if it seems to the stick at times that it is moving by its own motion it has in fact none of its own; and the bundle, too, in which it drifts has only an illusion of self-propulsion. I do not know if Kierkegaard is right when he says that the crowd is untruth—I should rather describe it as non-truth since (in distinction from some of its masters) it is not on the same plane as the truth, it is not in the least opposed to it. But it is certainly "un-freedom". In what un-freedom consists cannot be adequately learned under the pressure of fate, whether it is the compulsion of need or of men; for there still remains the rebellion of the inmost heart, the tacit appeal to the secrecy of eternity. It can be adequately learned only when you are tied up in the bundle of the crowd, sharing its opinions and desires, and only dully perceiving that you are in this condition.

The man who is living with the body politic is quite different. He is not bundled, but bound. He is bound up in relation to it, betrothed to it, married to it, therefore suffering his destiny along with it; rather, simply suffering it, always willing and ready to suffer it, but not abandoning himself blindly to any of its movements, rather confronting each movement watchfully and carefully that it does not miss truth and loyalty. He sees powers press on and sees God's hands in their supreme power held up on high, that the mortal immortals there below may be able to decide for themselves. He knows that in all his weakness he is put into the service of decision. If it is the crowd, remote from, opposed to, decision which swarms round him, he does not put up with it. At the place where he stands, whether lifted up or unnoticed, he does what he can, with the powers he possesses, whether compressed predominance or the word which fades, to make the crowd no longer a crowd. Otherness enshrouds him, the otherness to which he is betrothed. But he takes it up into his life only in the form of *the* other, time and again the other, the other who meets him, who is sought, lifted out of the crowd, the "companion". Even if he has to speak to the crowd he seeks the person, for a people can find and find again its truth only through persons, through persons standing their test. *That* is the Single One who "changes the crowd into Single Ones"—how could it be one who remains far from the crowd? It cannot be one who is reserved, only one who is given; given, not given over. It is a paradoxical work to which he sets his soul, to make the crowd no longer a crowd. It is to bring out from the crowd and set on the way of creation which leads to the Kingdom. And if he does not achieve much he has time, he has God's own time. For the man who loves God and his companion in one— though he remains in all the frailty of humanity—receives God for his companion.

"The Single One" is not the man who has to do with God essentially, and only unessentially with others, who is unconditionally concerned with God and conditionally with the body politic. The Single One is the man for whom the reality of relation with God as an exclusive relation includes and encompasses the possibility of relation with all otherness, and for whom the whole body politic, the reservoir of otherness, offers just enough otherness for him to pass his life with it.

The Single One in Responsibility

The category of the Single One has changed. It cannot be that the relation of the human person to God is established by the subtraction of the world. The Single One must therefore take his world, what of the world is extended and entrusted to him in his life, without any reduction into his life's devotion; he must let his world partake unabated of its essentiality. It cannot be that the Single One finds God's hands when he stretches his hands out and away beyond creation. He must put his arms round the vexatious world, whose true name is creation; only then do his fingers reach the realm of lightning and of grace. It cannot be that the spirit of reduction reigns in the relation of faith as well. The Single One who lives in his relation of faith must wish to have it fulfilled in the uncurtailed measure of the life he lives. He must face the hour which approaches him, the biographical and historical hour, just as it is, in its whole world content and apparently senseless contradiction, without weakening the impact of otherness in it. He must hear the message, stark and untransfigured, which is delivered to him out of this hour, presented by this situation

as it arrives. Nor must he translate for himself its wild and
crude profaneness into the chastely religious: he must recognize
that the question put to him, with which the speech of the
situation is fraught—whether it sounds with angels' or with
devils' tongues—remains God's question to him, of course
without the devils thereby being turned into angels. It is a
question wondrously tuned in the wild crude sound. And he,
the Single One, must answer, by what he does and does not
do, he must accept and answer for the hour, the hour of the
world, of all the world, as that which is given to him, entrusted
to him. Reduction is forbidden; you are not at liberty to select
what suits you, the whole cruel hour is at stake, the whole
claims you, and you must answer—Him.

You must hear the claim, however unharmoniously it strikes
your ear—and let no-one interfere; give the answer from the
depths, where a breath of what has been breathed in still
hovers—and let no-one prompt you.

This arch-command, for whose sake the Bible makes its God
speak from the very time of creation, defines anew, when it is
heard, the relation of the Single One to his community.

The human person belongs, whether he wants to acknowledge it and take it seriously or not, to the community in
which he is born or which he has happened to get into. But
he who has realized what destiny means, even if it looks like
doom, and what being placed there means, even if it looks like
being misplaced, knows too that he must acknowledge it and
take it seriously. But then, precisely then, he notes that true
membership of a community includes the experience, which
changes in many ways, and which can never be definitively
formulated, of the *boundary* of this membership. If the Single
One, true to the historico-biographical hour, perceives the
word, if he grasps the situation of his people, his own situation,
as a sign and demand upon him, if he does not spare himself
and his community before God, then he experiences the
boundary. He experiences it in such agony as if the boundary-
post had pierced his soul. The Single One, the man living in
responsibility, can carry out his political actions as well—and
of course omissions are also actions—only from that ground of
his being to which the claim of the fearful and kind God, the
Lord of history and our Lord, wishes to penetrate.

It is obvious that for the man living in community the ground
of personal and essential decision is continually threatened by

the fact of so-called collective decisions. I remind you of Kierkegaard's warning: "That men are in a crowd either excuses a man of repentance and responsibility or at all events weakens the Single One's responsibility, because the crowd lets the man have only a fragment of responsibility." But I must put it differently. In practice, in the moment of action, it is only the semblance of a fragment, but afterwards, when in your waking dream after midnight you are dragged before the throne and attacked by the spurned calling to be a Single One, it is complete responsibility.

It must, of course, be added that the community to which a man belongs does not usually express in a unified and unambiguous way what it considers to be right and what not right in a given situation. It consists of more or less visible groups, which yield to a man interpretations of destiny and of his task which are utterly different yet all alike claim absolute authenticity. Each knows what benefits the community, each claims your unreserved complicity for the good of the community.

Political decision is generally understood to-day to mean joining such a group. If this is done then everything is finally in order, the time of deciding is over. From then on one has only to share in the group's movements. One no longer stands at the cross-roads, one no longer has to choose the right action out of the possible ones; everything is decided. What you once thought—that you had to answer ever anew, situation by situation, for the choice you made—is now got rid of. The group has relieved you of your political responsibility. You feel yourself answered for in the group; you are permitted to feel it.

The attitude which has just been described means for the man of faith (I wish to speak only of him here), when he encounters it, his fall from faith—without his being inclined to confess it to himself or to admit it. It means his fall in very fact from faith, however loudly and emphatically he continues to confess it not merely with his lips but even with his very soul as it shouts down inmost reality. The relation of faith to the one Present Being is perverted into semblance and self-deceit if it is not an all-embracing relation. "Religion" may agree to be one department of life beside others which like it are independent and autonomous—it has thereby already perverted the relation of faith. To remove any realm basically from this relation, from its defining power, is to try to remove it from God's defining power which rules over the relation of faith. To prescribe to the relation of faith that "so far and no further you may define what I have to do; here your power ends and that of the group to which I belong begins" is to address God in precisely the same way. He who does not let his relation of faith be fulfilled in the uncurtailed measure of the life he lives, however much he is capable of at different times, is trying to curtail the fulfilment of God's rule of the world.

Certainly the relation of faith is no book of rules which can be looked up to discover what is to be done now, in this very hour. I experience what God desires of me for this hour—so far as I do experience it—not earlier than *in* the hour. But even then it is not given me to experience it except by answering before God for this hour as *my* hour, by carrying out the responsibility for it towards him as much as I can. What has now approached me, the unforeseen, the unforeseeable, is word from him, a word found in no dictionary, a word that has now become word—and it demands my answer to him. I give the word of my answer by accomplishing among the actions possible that which seems to my devoted insight to be the right one. With my choice and decision and action—committing or omitting, acting or persevering—I answer the word, however inadequately, yet properly; I answer for my hour. My group cannot relieve me of this responsibility, I must not let it relieve me of it; if I do I pervert my relation of faith, I cut out of God's realm of power the sphere of my group. But it is not as though the latter did not concern me in my decision—it concerns me tremendously. In my decision I do not look away from the world, I look at it and into it, and before all I may see in the world, to which I have to do justice with my decision, my group to whose welfare I cling; I may before all have to do justice to it, yet not as a thing in itself, but before the Face of God; and no programme, no tactical resolution, no command can tell me how I, as I decide, have to do justice to my group before the Face of God. It may be that I may serve it as the programme and resolution and command have laid down. It may be that I have to serve it otherwise. It could even be—if such an unheard-of thing were to rise within me in my act of decision—that I might be set in cruel opposition to its success, because I became aware that God's love ordains otherwise. Only one thing matters, that as the situation is presented to me I expose myself to it as to the word's manifestation to me, to the very ground where hearing passes into being, and that I perceive what is to be perceived and answer it. He who prompts me with an answer in such a way as to hinder my perceiving is the hinderer, let him be for the rest who he will (12).

I do not in the least mean that a man must fetch the answer alone and unadvised out of his breast. Nothing of the sort is meant; how should the direction of those at the head of my group not enter essentially into the substance out of which the decision is smelted? But the direction must not be substituted for the decision; no substitute is accepted. He who has a master may yield "himself", his bodily person, to him, but not his responsibility. He must find his way to that responsibility armed with all the "ought" that has been forged in the group, but exposed to destiny so that in the demanding moment all armour falls away from him. He may even hold firm with all his force to the "interest" of the group—till in the last confrontation with reality a finger, hardly to be perceived, yet never to be neglected, touches it. It is not the "finger of God", to be sure; we are not permitted to expect that, and therefore there is not the slightest assurance that our decision is right in any but a personal way. God tenders me the situation to which I have to answer; but I have not to expect that he should tender me anything of my answer. Certainly in my answering I am given into the power of his grace, but I cannot measure heaven's share in it, and even the most blissful sense of grace can deceive. The finger I speak of is just that of the "conscience", but not of the routine conscience, which is to be used, is being used and worn out, the play-on-the-surface conscience, with whose discrediting they thought to have abolished the actuality of man's positive answer. I point to the unknown conscience in the ground of being, which needs to be discovered ever anew, the conscience of the "spark" (13), for the genuine spark is effective also in the single composure of each genuine decision. The certainty produced by this conscience is of course only a personal certainty; it is uncertain certainty; but what is here called person is the very person who is addressed and who answers.

I say, therefore, that the Single One, that is, the man living in responsibility, can make even his political decisions properly only from that ground of his being at which he is aware of the event as divine speech to him; and if he lets the awareness of this ground be strangled by his group he is refusing to give God an actual reply.

What I am speaking of has nothing to do with "individualism". I do not consider the individual to be either the starting-point or the goal of the human world. But I consider the human person to be the irremovable central place of the struggle between the world's movement away from God and its movement towards God. This struggle takes place to-day to an uncannily large extent in the realm of public life, of course not between group and group but within each group. Yet the decisive battles of this realm as well are fought in the depth, in the ground or the groundlessness, of the person.

Our age is intent on escaping from the demanding "ever anew" of such an obligation of responsibility by a flight into a protective "once-for-all". The last generation's intoxication with freedom has been followed by the present generation's craze for bondage; the untruth of intoxication has been followed by the untruth of hysteria. He alone is true to the one Present Being who knows he is bound to his place—and just there free for his proper responsibility. Only those who are bound and free in this way can still produce what can truly be called community. Yet even today the believing man, if he clings to a thing that is presented in a group, can do right to join it. But belonging to it, he must remain submissive with his whole life, therefore with his group life as well, to the One who is his Lord. His responsible decision will thus at times be opposed to, say, a tactical decision of his group. At times he will be moved to carry the fight for the truth, the human, uncertain and certain truth which is brought forward by his deep conscience, into the group itself, and thereby establish or strengthen an inner front in it. This can be more important for the future of our world than all fronts that are drawn today between groups and between associations of groups; for this front, if it is everywhere upright and strong, may run as a secret unity across all groups.

What the right is can be experienced by none of the groups of today except through men who belong to them staking their own souls to experience it and then revealing it, however bitter it may be, to their companions—charitably if it may be, cruelly if it must be. Into this fiery furnace the group plunges time and again, or it dies an inward death.

And if one still asks if one may be certain of finding what is right on this steep path, once again the answer is *No*; there is no certainty. There is only a chance; but there is no other. The risk does not ensure the truth for us; but it, and it alone, leads us to where the breath of truth is to be felt.

Attempts at Severance

Against the position outlined here of the Single One in responsibility there is bound to rise up that powerful modern point of view, according to which in the last resort only so-called objectives, more precisely collectives, are real, while significance is attached to persons only as the workers or the tools of the collectives. Kierkegaard's merely religious category, to be sure, may be indifferent to this point of view: according to his category only the person is essential and the objective either has only a secondary existence or, as crowd, is the negative which is to be avoided. If, however, the Single One as such has essentially to do with the world, and even with the world in particular, with the body politic, but not in order, consciously and with the emphasis of faith, henceforth to let himself be used, but in responsibility for that in which before God he participates, then he is bound to be opposed and if possible refuted once for all by that point of view. It can set about this by means of arguments taken from a certain contemporary trend of thought which conforms to the time and is apparently its expedient. It is a trend of which the representatives, first of all, with all their various differences, have in common one object of attack—it may be described as liberalism or individualism or by any other slogan you please. (In this they usually neglect—as, understandably, often happens in cases of this kind—to analyze the attacked "ism" conceptually, nor do they make a distinction between what they mean and what they do not mean, that is, between what is worth contesting and what should be spared. If such an analysis should be applied to, say, "liberalism", individual concepts of varying tendency would arise, towards which it would be possible to adopt a standpoint in quite different clarity and unambiguousness. Thus, for example, there would be libertinism, the poor mode of thought of the released slave who only knows what is or what ought to be permitted to him, to "man"; on the other hand there would be liberism, the mode of thought of the free-born man for whom freedom is the presupposition of binding, of the true personal entry into a binding relation, no more and no less—a mode of thought worthy of being preserved in the treasure-house of the spirit and defended along with it by everyone who knows about the spirit.) But it is more significant that the representatives of this trend have also a common purpose or at least a common effect: they give the political province an exaggerated autonomy, they contrast public life with the rest of life, they remove it from the responsibility of the Single One who takes part in it.

In order to indicate what might be replied to such arguments from the standpoint of the transformed category of the Single One, two examples of the trend of thought under consideration may be discussed, one concerning the philosophy of the State and the other the theology of the State.

But first I precede these with a third example, less important but also rich in teaching, a historiosophical one.

Oswald Spengler wishes to establish the special sphere of the political, as having a value independent of our therefore inaccessible ethics, by classifying man with beasts of prey. If no longer between tamed individuals yet certainly between the groups, conditions (he says) are always, necessarily and normally, like those between packs of beasts. Here, in his existence within the group, man has remained an unweakened beast of prey, and the Single One has to guard against applying standards which are foreign to the particular sphere.

This is a trivialization of a Nietzschian thesis. Nietzsche believed that the important thing is that the power in history should keep faith with its own nature; if that is repressed then degeneration follows. Nietzsche does not move away from a *presupposition*. The important thing is that the power in history keeps faith with itself as with one of the partners in a dialogical event in which even the most forceful activity can signify a shirking of the answer, a refusal to give an answer.

Nietzsche's thesis speaks the language of history, Spengler's the language of biology. Every attempt to interpret human action in biological terms (however much one must remember biological existence when explaining man) is a trivialization; it is a poor simplification because it means the abandoning of the proper anthropological content, of that which constitutes the category of *man*.

Beasts of prey have no history. A panther can indeed have a biography and a colony of termites perhaps even State annals, but they do not have history in the great distinguishing sense which permits us to speak of human history as "world-history". A life of prey yields no history. Man has acquired history by entering fundamentally on something that would be bound to appear to the beast of prey as senseless and grotesque—namely, on responsibility, and thus on becoming a person with a relation to the truth. Hence it has become impossible to comprehend man from the standpoint of biology alone.

"History" is not the sequence of conquests of power and actions of power but the context of the responsibilities of power in time.

Thus the beast of prey thesis means a denial of human essence and a falsification of human history. It is true, as Spengler says in defence of his thesis, that "the great beasts of prey are *noble* creations of the most perfect kind", but this has no power to prove anything. It is a matter of man's becoming in *his* kind, which is conditioned by *his* evolution *and* his history, just as "noble a creation" as they in theirs: that means that he helps to realize that "freedom of the children of God" towards which, as Paul says, all creatures "crane their necks".

More serious consideration must be given to the conceptual definition of the political offered by a well-known Roman Catholic exponent of Constitutional Law, Carl Schmitt. In his view the political has its own criterion, which cannot be derived from the criterion of another realm. It is the distinction between friend and foe which in his view corresponds to "the relatively autonomous criteria of other oppositions, good and evil in the moral sphere, beautiful and ugly in the æsthetic, and so on". The eventuality of a real struggle, which includes the "possibility of physical killing", belongs to the concept of the foe, and from this possibility the life of man acquires "its specifically *political* tension".

The "possibility of physical killing"—really it should be "the intention of physical killing". For Schmitt's thesis carries a situation of private life, the classic duel situation, over into public life.

This duel situation arises when two men experience a conflict existing between them as absolute, and therefore as capable of resolution only in the destruction of the one by the other. There is no reconciliation, no mediation, no adequate expiation, the hand that deals the blow must not be any but the opponent's; but this *is* the resolution. Every classic duel is a masked "judgment of God". In each there is an aftermath of the belief that men can bring about a judgment of God. That is what Schmitt, carrying it over to the relation of peoples to one another, calls the specifically political.

But the thesis rests on an error of method. The essential principle of a realm, the principle that constitutes it as such, cannot be taken from the *labile* state of the formations in this realm, but only from their lasting character. The friend-foe formula derives from the sphere of exposedness of political formations, not from the sphere of their coherence. The radical distinction which Schmitt supposes appears in times in which the common life is threatened, not in times in which it experiences its stability as self-evident and assured. The distinction, therefore, is not adequate to yield the principle of "the political".

But the formula does not even include the whole lability of a political formation. This lability is always twofold—an outer, which is exposed by the neighbour (or attacker become neighbour) pressing on the frontier, and an inner, which is indicated by the rebel. Schmitt calls him the "inner foe", but in this he confuses two fundamentally different kinds of lability. The foe has no interest in the preservation of the formation, but the rebel has—he wants to "change" it: it is precisely *it* he wants to change. Only the former is radical enough to establish the import of the formula. The friend-foe formula comprehends, therefore, only one side of lability and cannot be stretched to include the other.

The oppositions "good and evil in the moral sphere, beautiful and ugly in the æsthetic", which Schmitt sets together with this one, are in distinction from it intended *normatively*, that is, only when the good, the beautiful, are understood in a content of essential significance is there any sense in defining the evil, the ugly. "Friend and foe," however, describes not a normative concept of being but only a concept of an attitude within a situation.

Moreover, it seems to me that behind the common pairs of opposed concepts, good and evil, beautiful and ugly, there stand others in which the negative concept is intimately bound to the positive, being the emptiness to its fulness, the chaos to its cosmos. Behind good and evil as the criteria of the ethical stand direction and absence of direction, behind beautiful and ugly as the criteria of the æsthetic stand form and formlessness. For the realm of the political there is no pair of concepts in the foreground, obviously because it is more difficult, or impossible, to give autonomy to the negative pole in it. I should call the pair in the background order and absence of order, but the concept of order must be freed of the depreciation which sometimes clings to it. Right order is direction and form in the political realm. But these two concepts must not be allowed to petrify. They have their truth only from the conception of a homogeneous *dynamic of order* which is the real principle of the political. The true history of a commonwealth must be understood as its striving to reach the order suited to it. This striving, this wrestling for the realization of true order— wrestling between ideas, plans, outlines of true order that are so different, but also a wrestling that is simultaneously common to them all, not known, not to be expressed—constitutes the political structure's dynamic of order. An order is gained and established again and again as a result. It becomes firm and inclusive, it consolidates itself as well against the resistance of whatever dynamic may be left. It stiffens and dies off, completely renouncing the dynamic which set it going; and yet it keeps its power for the struggle for true order flaring up again. The foe threatens the whole dynamic of order in the commonwealth, the rebel threatens only the order as it is at the time. Every order considered from the standpoint of the whole dynamic is called in doubt. That is the double life of the State: again and again realization of the political structure, again and again its being called in doubt. The "high points of concrete politics" are not, as Schmitt thinks, "at the same time the moments in which the foe is visualized in concrete clarity as the foe"; they are the moments in which an order, in face of the gravest responsibility of the individual confronting himself with it, demonstrates the legitimacy of its static character, its character (however necessarily relative) of fulfilment.

In Schmitt's view all "genuine" political theories presuppose that man is "evil". (Incidentally, why do the theories that do this do it? Since from Schmitt's point of view political theory is only a department of practical politics, the answer along his line would have to be "because it seems to their authors to be politically expedient".) This "evil", indeed, Schmitt ex-

plains as being "in no way unproblematic" and "dangerous"—
and I too take man to be both—but he finds support for the
correctness of his presupposition in the theological doctrine of
the *absolute* sinfulness of man. He has found a weighty
theological associate in Friedrich Gogarten.

Gogarten explains in his *Political Ethics* that all ethical problems receive their ethical relevance only from the political
problem. That is, the ethical is valid as the ethical only by
its connexion with man's political being. In saying this he
abandons Kierkegaard's category of the Single One. Gogarten
believes that he is only fighting against individualism but at
the same time he is fighting against the position of personal life
in the rigour of its total responsibility. If ethical problems
receive their relevance from the political realm, they cannot
also receive them from the religious, not even if the political
has a religious basis. But if they do not receive them from the
religious realm, then we have reached again, within the life of
the "religious" man—even if in a politicized form—the disconnected ethic which Kierkegaard helped us to overcome.
Gogarten may speak in theological terms as emphatically as he
pleases, he narrows down the Single One's fundamental relation
with God when he lets his action receive its validity from some
other source, even if it is from the destiny, considered in itself,
of the community to which the Single One belongs. (And
what else are "ethical problems" but man's questions about
his actions and their meaning?) True as it is that he, the Single
One, cannot win to a legitimate relation with God without a
legitimate relation to the body politic, it is nevertheless also
true that the defining force has to be ascribed not to the latter
but to the former alone. That is, I must always let the boundary
between co-operation and non-co-operation within my relation
to my community be drawn by God. You say that often you
hear nothing? Well, we have to be attentive with the unreserved effort of our being. If even then we hear nothing,
then, but only then, may we turn in the direction Gogarten
indicates. But if we are not attentive or if we hear but do not
obey, then our omission, and not our invoking of some kind of
relation of ethical problems to the political, will persist in
eternity.

In Gogarten's view man is "radically and therefore irrevocably evil, that is, in the grip of evil". The relevance of the
political arises from the fact that "only in the political" does

man have, "in face of this recognition, the possibility of existence". The ethical quality of the State consists "in its warding off the evil to which men have fallen prey by its sovereign power and by its right over the life and property of its subjects". (Incidentally, this is a theological version of the old police-state idea.) For "whence shall the State derive sovereign power if not from the recognition of man's fallen state"?

The concept to which Gogarten refers, of the radical evil of man, his absolute sinfulness, is taken from the realm where man confronts God and is significant there alone. What to my knowledge and understanding is taught by Christian theology, in whose name Gogarten speaks, is that man, more precisely, fallen man, considered as being unredeemed, is "before God" (*coram Deo*) sinful and depraved. I do not see how his being unredeemed can be broken off from its dialectic connexion with redemption (*ab his malis liberemur et servemur*) and used separately. Nor do I see how the concept of being evil can be translated from the realm of being "before God" into that of being before earthly authorities, and yet retain its radical nature. In the sight of God a state of radical evil can be ascribed to man because God is God and man is man, and the distance between them is absolute, and because precisely in this distance and in virtue of it God's redeeming deed is done. In the sight of his fellow-men, of human groups and orders, man, it seems to me, cannot be properly described as simply sinful, because the distance is lacking which alone is able to establish the unconditional. Nothing is changed if a human order is considered as established or empowered by God. For that absolute distance to man, which establishes the unconditional (but at the same time discloses the place of redemption)—the distance from which alone man's radical evil could appear also in face of the body politic—can by no means be bestowed in this way upon the human order. Hence no legitimate use can be made in politics or political theory of the concept of human sinfulness.

In my view, however, man generally is not "radically" this or that.

It is not radicality that characterizes man as separated by a primal abyss from all that is merely animal, but it is his potentiality. If we put him alone before the whole of nature then there appears embodied in him the character of possibility inherent in natural existence and which everywhere else hovers round dense reality only like a haze. Man is the crystallized potentiality of existence. But he is this potentiality in its factual limitation. The wealth of possibility in existence from which the animals are kept away by their exiguous reality is exhibited in man in a sign that is incomprehensible from the standpoint of nature. Yet this wealth of possibility does not hold free sway, so that life might be able time and again to follow on wings the anticipation of spirit, but it is confined within narrow limits. This limitation is not essential, but only factual. That means that man's action is unforeseeable in its nature and extent, and that even if he were peripheral to the cosmos in everything else, he remains the centre of all surprise in the world. But he is fettered surprise, only inwardly is it without bonds; and his fetters are strong.

Man is not good, man is not evil; he is, in a pre-eminent sense, good and evil together. He who eats of him, as he who ate of that fruit, has the knowledge of good and evil together. That is his limitation, that is the cunning of the serpent: he was to become as God, knowing good and evil; but what he "recognizes", what in being mixed up with it he has recognized as something mixed up, is good and evil together: he has become good and evil together; that is the nakedness in which he recognizes himself. The limitation is only factual, it does not transform his essence or destroy God's work. To ascribe to the serpent the power of destruction is to elevate it to rivalry with God and make it for the time superior to him (as Ahriman was for a time to Ormuzd), since it perverts God's creation. But the serpent in the Bible is not that. It is not an opposing god, it is only the creature which desires to undo man by man's own doing. It is the "cunning" creature, the cunning of the secretly poisonous creature which foments disorder; and out of the disorder comes history which, groping and striving and failing, is concerned with God's order. The primal event pointed out by the images of the Bible does not lie under the principle of contradiction: *A* and *not-A* are here strangely concerned with one another.

Good and evil, then, cannot be a pair of opposites like right and left or above and beneath. "Good" is the movement in the direction of home, "evil" is the aimless whirl of human potentialities without which nothing can be achieved and by which, if they take no direction but remain trapped in themselves, everything goes awry. If the two were indeed poles the man who did not see them as such would be blind; but the man would be blinder who did not perceive the lightning flash from pole to pole, the "and".

As a condition of the individual soul evil is the convulsive shirking of direction, of the total orientation of the soul by which it stands up to personal responsibility before God. The shirking can take place from passion or from indolence. The passionate man refuses by his passion, the indolent man by his indolence. In both cases the man goes astray within himself. The real historical dæmonias are the exploiting by historical powers of this shirking.

But the State *as such* cannot indicate the one direction of the hour towards God, which changes time and again by concretion. Only the Single One, who stands in the depth of responsibility, can do that. And indeed a statesman can also be this Single One.

Gogarten puts *the* State in place of the historical State, that is, of the government of the particular time (ἄρχοντες). This government cannot ward off the "evil" as an impersonal State but can do it only on the basis of its own personal responsibility, and is for the rest itself exposed to the dynamic between good and evil. The State is the visible form of authority, and for Gogarten authority is simply what is established, the diaconal; power is full power. But if the establishment of power is taken seriously, theologically and biblically seriously, the establishing turns out to be a precise commission and the power a great duty of responsibility. The Old Testament records, in the history of the kings of Israel and the history of foreign rulers, the degeneration of legitimacy into illegitimacy and of full power into antagonistic power. As no philosophical concept of the State, so likewise no theological concept of the State leads beyond the reality of the human person in the situation of faith. None leads beyond his responsibility—be he servant or emperor—for the body politic as man in the sight of God.

The Question

In the human crisis which we are experiencing to-day these two have become questionable—the person and the truth. We know from the act of responsibility how they are linked together. For the responsible response to exist the reality of the person is necessary, whom the word meets in the happening claiming him; and the reality of the truth is necessary to which the person goes out with united being and which he is therefore able to receive only in the word, as the truth which concerns himself, in his particular situation, and not in any general way.

The question by which the person and the truth have become questionable to-day is the question to the Single One.

The person has become questionable through being collectivized.

This collectivizing of the person is joined in history to a basically different undertaking in which I too participated and to which I must therefore confess now. It is that struggle of recent decades against the idealistic concepts of the sovereign, world-embracing, world-sustaining, world-creating *I*. The struggle was conducted (among other ways) by reference to the neglected creaturely bonds of the concrete human person. It was shown how fundamentally important it is to know in every moment of thought this as well—that the one who thinks is bound, in different degrees of substantiality but never purely functionally, to a spatial realm, to a historical hour, to the genus man, to a people, to a family, to a society, to a vocational group, to a companionship in convictions. This entanglement in a manifold *We*, when known in an actual way, wards off the temptation of the thought of sovereignty: man is placed in a narrow creaturely position. But he is enabled to recognize that this is his genuine width; for being bound means being bound up in relation.

But it came about that a tendency of a quite different origin and nature assumed power over the new insights, which exaggerated and perverted the perception of bonds into a doctrine of serfdom. Primacy is ascribed here to a collectivity. The collectivity receives the right to hold the person who is bound to it bound in such a way that he ceases to have complete responsibility. The collectivity becomes what really exists, the person becomes derivatory. In every realm which joins him to the whole he is to be excused a personal response.

Thereby the immeasurable value which constitutes man is imperilled. The collectivity cannot enter instead of the person into the dialogue of the ages which the Godhead conducts with mankind. Human perception ceases, the human response is dumb, if the person is no longer there to hear and to speak. It is not possible to reduce the matter to private life; only in the uncurtailed measure of lived life, that is, only with the inclusion of participation in the body politic, can the claim be heard and the reply spoken.

The truth, on the other hand, has become questionable through being politicized.

The sociological doctrine of the age has exercised a relativizing effect, heavy with consequences, on the concept of truth, in that it has, in the dependence of the thought processes on social processes, proved the connexion of thought with existence. This relativization was justified in that it bound the "truth" of a man to his conditioning reality. But its justification was perverted into the opposite when its authors omitted to draw the basic boundary line between what can and what cannot be understood as conditioned in this way. That is, they did not comprehend the person in his *total* reality, wooing the truth and wrestling for it. If we begin with the Single One as a whole being, who wishes to recognize with his total being, we find that the force of his desire for the truth can at decisive points burst the "ideological" bonds of his social being. The man who thinks "existentially", that is, who stakes his life in his thinking, brings into his real relation to the truth not merely his conditioned qualities but also the unconditioned nature, transcending them, of his quest, of his grasp, of his indomitable will for the truth, which also carries along with it the whole personal power of standing his test. We shall certainly be able to make no distinction, in what he has, time and again, discovered as the truth, between what can and what cannot be derived from the social factor. But it is an ineluctable duty to accept what cannot be so derived as a border concept and thus to point out, as the unattainable horizon of the distinction made by the sociology of knowledge, what takes place between the underivable in the recognizing person and the underivable in the object of his recognition. This duty has been neglected. Consequently, the political theory of modern collectivisms was easily able to assume power over the principle which lay ready, and to proclaim what corresponded to the (real or supposed) life interests of a group as its legitimate and unappealable truth. Over against this the Single One could no longer appeal to a truth which could be recognized and tested by him.

This marks the beginning of a disintegration of human faith

in the truth, which can never be possessed and yet may be comprehended in an existentially real relation; it marks the beginning of the paralysis of the human search for the truth.

"What I speak of," says Kierkegaard, "is something simple and straightforward—that the truth for the Single One only exists in his producing it himself in action." More precisely, man finds the truth to be true only when he stands its test. Human truth is here bound up with the responsibility of the person.

"True is what is Mine," says Stirner. Human truth is here bound up with the human person's lack of responsibility. Collectivisms translate this into the language of the group: "True is what is Ours."

But in order that man may not be lost there is need of persons who are not collectivized, and of truth which is not politicized.

There is need of persons, not merely "representatives" in some sense or other, chosen or appointed, who exonerate the represented of responsibility, but also "represented" who on no account let themselves be represented with regard to responsibility. There is need of the person as the ground which cannot be relinquished, from which alone the entry of the finite into conversation with the infinite became possible and is possible.

There is need of man's faith in the truth as that which is independent of him, which he cannot acquire for himself, but with which he can enter into a real relation of his very life; the faith of human persons in the truth as that which sustains them all together, in itself inaccessible but disclosing itself, in the fact of responsibility which awaits test, to him who really woos the truth.

That man may not be lost there is need of the person's responsibility to truth in his historical situation. There is need of the Single One who stands over against all being which is present to him—and thus also over against the body politic— and guarantees all being which is present to him—and thus also the body politic.

True community and true commonwealth will be realized only to the extent to which the Single Ones become real out of whose responsible life the body politic is renewed.

III

EDUCATION

"THE development of the creative powers in the child" is the subject of this conference. As I come before you to introduce it I must not conceal from you for a single moment the fact that of the nine words in which it is expressed only the last three raise no question for me.

The child, not just the individual child, individual children, but the child, is certainly a reality. That in this hour, while we make a beginning with the "development of creative powers", across the whole extent of this planet new human beings are born who are characterized already and yet have still to be characterized—this is a myriad realities, but also one reality. In every hour the human race begins. We forget this too easily in face of the massive fact of past life, of so-called world-history, of the fact that each child is born with a given disposition of "world-historical" origin, that is, inherited from the riches of the whole human race, and that he is born into a given situation of "world-historical" origin, that is, produced from the riches of the world's events. This fact must not obscure the other no less important fact that in spite of everything, in this as in every hour, what has not been invades the structure of what is, with ten thousand countenances, of which not one has been seen before, with ten thousand souls still undeveloped but ready to develop—a creative event if ever there was one, newness rising up, primal potential might. This potentiality, streaming unconquered, however much of it is squandered, is the reality *child*: this phenomenon of uniqueness, which is more than just begetting and birth, this grace of beginning again and ever again.

What greater care could we cherish or discuss than that this grace may not henceforth be squandered as before, that the might of newness may be preserved for renewal? Future history is not inscribed already by the pen of a causal law on a roll which merely awaits unrolling; its characters are stamped by the unforeseeable decisions of future generations. The part to be played in this by everyone alive to-day, by every adolescent and child, is immeasurable, and immeasurable is our part if we are educators. The deeds of the generations now approaching can illumine the grey face of the human world or plunge it in darkness. So, then, with education: if it at last rises up and exists indeed, it will be able to strengthen the light-spreading force in the hearts of the doers—how much it can do this cannot be guessed, but only learned in action.

The child is a reality; education must become a reality. But what does the "development of the creative powers" mean? Is *that* the reality of education? Must education become that in order to become a reality? Obviously those who arranged this session and gave it its theme think this is so. They obviously think that education has failed in its task till now because it has aimed at something different from this development of what is in the child, or has considered and promoted other powers in the child than the creative. And probably they are amazed that I question this objective, since I myself talk of the treasure of eternal possibility and of the task of unearthing it. So I must make clear that this treasure cannot be properly designated by the notion of "creative powers", nor its unearthing by the notion of "development".

Creation originally means only the divine summons to the life hidden in non-being. When Johann Georg Hamann and his contemporaries carried over this term metaphorically to the human capacity to give form, they marked a supreme peak of mankind, the genius for forming, as that in which man's imaging of God is authenticated in action. The metaphor has since been broadened; there was a time (not long ago) when "creative" meant almost the same as "of literary ability"; in face of this lowest condition of the word it is a real promotion for it to be understood, as it is here, quite generally as something dwelling to some extent in all men, in all children of men, and needing only the right cultivation. Art is then only the province in which a faculty of production, which is common to all, reaches completion. Everyone is elementally endowed with the basic powers of the arts, with that of drawing, for instance, or of music; these powers have to be developed, and the education of the whole person is to be built up on them as on the natural activity of the self.

We must not miss the importance of the reference which is the starting-point of this conception. It concerns a significant but hitherto not properly heeded phenomenon, which is certainly not given its right name here. I mean the existence of an autonomous instinct, which cannot be derived from others, whose appropriate name seems to me to be the "originator instinct". Man, the child of man, wants to make things. He does not merely find pleasure in seeing a form arise from material that presented itself as formless. What the child desires is its own share in this becoming of things: it wants to be the subject of this event of production. Nor is the instinct I am speaking of to be confused with the so-called instinct to busyness or activity which for that matter does not seem to me to exist at all (the child wants to set up or destroy, handle or hit, and so on, but never "busy himself"). What is important is that by one's own intensively experienced action something arises that was not there before. A good expression of this instinct is the way children of intellectual passion produce speech, in reality not as something they have taken over but with the headlong powers of utter newness: sound after sound tumbles out of them, rushing from the vibrating throat past the trembling lips into the world's air, and the whole of the little vital body vibrates and trembles, too, shaken by a bursting shower of selfhood. Or watch a boy fashioning some crude unrecognizable instrument for himself. Is he not astonished, terrified, at his own movement like the mighty inventors of prehistoric times? But it is also to be observed how even in the child's apparently "blind" lust for destruction his instinct of origination enters in and becomes dominant. Sometimes he begins to tear something up, for example, a sheet of paper, but soon he takes an interest in the form of the pieces, and it is not long before he tries—still by tearing—to produce definite forms.

It is important to recognize that the instinct of origination is autonomous and not derivatory. Modern psychologists are inclined to derive the multiform human soul from a single primal element—the "libido", the "will to power", and the like. But this is really only the generalization of certain degenerate states in which a single instinct not merely dominates but also spreads parasitically through the others. They begin with the cases (in our time of inner loss of community and oppression the innumerable cases) where such a hypertrophy breeds the appearance of exclusiveness, they abstract rules from them, and apply them with the whole theoretical and practical questionableness of such applications. In opposition to these doctrines and methods, which impoverish the soul, we must continually point out that human inwardness is in origin a polyphony in which no voice can be "reduced" to another, and in which the unity cannot be grasped analytically, but only heard in the present harmony. One of the leading voices is the instinct of origination.

This instinct is therefore bound to be significant for the work of education as well. Here is an instinct which, no matter to what power it is raised, never becomes greed, because it is not directed to "having" but only to doing; which alone among the instincts can grow only to passion, not to lust; which alone among the instincts cannot lead its subject away to invade the realm of other lives. Here is pure gesture which does not snatch the world to itself, but expresses itself to the world. Should not the person's growth into form, so often dreamed of and lost, at last succeed from this starting-point? For here this precious quality may be unfolded and worked out unimpeded. Nor does the new experiment lack demonstration. The finest demonstration I know, that I have just got to know, is this Children's Choir led by the marvellous Bakule of Prague, with which our Conference opened. How under his leadership crippled creatures, seemingly condemned to lifelong idleness, have been released to a life of freely moving persons, rejoicing in their achievement, formable and forming, who know how to shape sights and sounds in multiform patterns and also how to sing out their risen souls wildly and gloriously; more, how a community of achievement, proclaimed in glance and response, has been welded together out of dull immured solitary creatures: all this seems to prove irrefutably not merely what fruitfulness but also what power, streaming through the whole constitution of man, the life of origination has.

But this very example, seen more deeply, shows us that the decisive influence is to be ascribed not to the release of an instinct but to the forces which meet the released instinct, namely, the educative forces. It depends on them, on their purity and fervour, their power of love and their discretion, into what connexions the freed element enters and what becomes of it.

There are two forms, indispensable for the building of true human life, to which the originative instinct, left to itself, does not lead and cannot lead: to sharing in an undertaking and to entering into mutuality.

An individual achievement and an undertaking are two very different matters. To make a thing is mortal man's pride; but to be conditioned in a common job, with the unconscious humility of being a part, of participation and partaking, is the true food of earthly immortality. As soon as a man enters effectively into an undertaking, where he discovers and practises a community of work with other men, he ceases to follow the originative instinct alone.

Action leading to an individual achievement is a "one-sided" event. There is a force within the person, which goes out, impresses itself on the material, and the achievement arises objectively: the movement is over, it has run in one direction from the heart's dream into the world, and its course is finished. No matter how directly, as being approached and claimed, as perceiving and receiving, the artist experiences his dealings with the idea which he faces and which awaits embodiment, so long as he is engaged in his work spirit goes out from him and does not enter him, he replies to the world but he does not meet it any more. Nor can he foster mutuality with his work: even in the legend Pygmalion is an ironical figure.

Yes; as an originator man is solitary. He stands wholly without bonds in the echoing hall of his deeds. Nor can it help him to leave his solitariness that his achievement is received enthusiastically by the many. He does not know if it is accepted, if his sacrifice is accepted by the anonymous receiver. Only if someone grasps his hand not as a "creator" but as a fellow-creature lost in the world, to be his comrade or friend or lover beyond the arts, does he have an awareness and a share of mutuality. An education based only on the training of the instinct of origination would prepare a new human solitariness which would be the most painful of all.

The child, in putting things together, learns much that he can learn in no other way. In making some thing he gets to know its possibility, its origin and structure and connexions, in a way he cannot learn by observation. But there is something else that is not learned in this way, and that is the viaticum of life. The being of the world as an object is learned from within, but not its being as a subject, its saying of *I* and *Thou*. What teaches us the saying of *Thou* is not the originative instinct but the instinct for communion.

This instinct is something greater than the believers in the "libido" realize: it is the longing for the world to become present to us as a person, which goes out to us as we to it, which chooses and recognizes us as we do it, which is confirmed in us as we in it. The child lying with half-closed eyes, waiting with tense soul for its mother to speak to it—the mystery of its will is not directed towards enjoying (or dominating) a person, or towards doing something of its own accord; but towards experiencing communion in face of the lonely night, which spreads beyond the window and threatens to invade.

But the release of powers should not be any more than a *presupposition* of education. In the end it is not the originative instinct alone which is meant by the "creative powers" that are to be "developed". These powers stand for human spontaneity. Real education is made possible—but is it also established?—by the realization that youthful spontaneity must not be suppressed but must be allowed to give what it can.

Let us take an example from the narrower sphere of the originative instinct—from the drawing-class. The teacher of the "compulsory" school of thought began with rules and current patterns. Now you knew what beauty was, and you had to copy it; and it was copied either in apathy or in despair. The teacher of the "free" school places on the table a twig of broom, say, in an earthenware jug, and makes the pupils draw it. Or he places it on the table, tells the pupils to look at it, removes it, and then makes them draw it. If the pupils are quite unsophisticated soon not a single drawing will look like another. Now the delicate, almost imperceptible and yet important influence begins—that of criticism and instruction. The children encounter a scale of values that, however unacademic it may be, is quite constant, a knowledge of good and evil that, however individualistic it may be, is quite unambiguous. The more unacademic this scale of values, and the more individualistic this knowledge, the more deeply do the children experience the encounter. In the former instance the preliminary declaration of what alone was right made for resignation or rebellion; but in the latter, where the pupil gains the realization only after he has ventured far out on the way to his achievement, his heart is drawn to reverence for the form, and educated.

This almost imperceptible, most delicate approach, the raising of a finger, perhaps, or a questioning glance, is the other half of what happens in education.

Modern educational theory, which is characterized by tendencies to freedom, misunderstands the meaning of this other half, just as the old theory, which was characterized by the habit of authority, misunderstood the meaning of the first half. The symbol of the funnel is in course of being exchanged for that of the pump. I am reminded of the two camps in the doctrine of evolution, current in the seventeenth and eighteenth centuries, the animalculists, who believed that the whole germ was present in the spermatozoon, and the ovists who believed it was wholly present in the ovum. The theory of the development of powers in the child recalls, in its most extreme expressions, Swammerdam's "unfolding" of the "preformed" organism. But the growth of the spirit is no more an unfolding than that of the body. The dispositions which would be discovered in the soul of a new-born child—if the soul could in fact be analysed—are nothing but capacities to receive and imagine the world. The world engenders the person in the individual. The world, that is the whole environment, nature and society, "educates" the human being: it draws out his powers, and makes him grasp and penetrate its objections. What we term education, conscious and willed, means *a selection by man of the effective world:* it means to give decisive effective power to a selection of the world which is concentrated and manifested in the educator. The relation in education is lifted out of the purposelessly streaming education by all things, and is marked off as purpose. In this way, through the educator, the world for the first time becomes the true subject of its effect.

There was a time, there were times, where there neither was nor needed to be any specific calling of educator or teacher. There was a master, a philosopher or a coppersmith, whose journeymen and apprentices lived with him and learned, by being allowed to share in it, what he had to teach them of his handwork or brainwork. But they also learned, without either their or his being concerned with it, they learned, without noticing that they did, the mystery of personal life: they received the spirit. Such a thing must still happen to some extent, where spirit and person exist, but it is expelled to the sphere of spirituality, of personality, and has become exceptional, it happens only "on the heights". Education as a purpose is bound to be summoned. We can as little return to the state of affairs that existed before there were schools as to that which existed before, say, technical science. But we can and must enter into the completeness of its growth to reality, into the perfect humanization of its reality. Our way is composed of losses that secretly become gains. Education has lost the paradise of pure instinctiveness and now consciously serves at the plough for the bread of life. It has been transformed; only in this transformation has it become visible.

Yet the master remains the model for the teacher. For if the educator of our day has to act consciously he must nevertheless do it "as though he did not". That raising of the finger, that questioning glance, are his genuine doing. Through him the selection of the effective world reaches the pupil. He fails the recipient when he presents this selection to him with a gesture of interference. It must be concentrated in him; and doing out of concentration has the appearance of rest. Interference divides the soul in his care into an obedient part and a rebellious part. But a hidden influence proceeding from his integrity has an integrating force.

The world, I said, has its influence as nature and as society on the child. He is educated by the elements, by air and light and the life of plants and animals, and he is educated by relationships. The true educator represents both; but he must be to the child as one of the elements.

The release of powers can be only a presupposition of education, nothing more. Put more generally, it is the nature of freedom to provide the place, but not the foundation as well, on which true life is raised. That is true both of inner, "moral" freedom and of outer freedom (which consists in not being hindered or limited). As the higher freedom, the soul's freedom of decision, signifies perhaps our highest moments but not a fraction of our substance, so the lower freedom, the freedom of development, signifies our capacity for growth but by no means our growth itself. This latter freedom is charged with importance as the actuality from which the work of education begins, but as its fundamental task it becomes absurd.

There is a tendency to understand this freedom, which may be termed evolutionary freedom, as at the opposite pole from compulsion, from being under a compulsion. But at the opposite pole from compulsion there stands not freedom but communion. Compulsion is a negative reality; communion is the positive reality; freedom is a possibility, possibility regained. At the opposite pole of being compelled by destiny or nature or men there does not stand being free of destiny or nature or men but to commune and to covenant with them. To do this, it is true that one must first have become independent; but this independence is a foot-bridge, not a dwelling-place. Freedom is the vibrating needle, the fruitful zero. Compulsion in education means disunion, it means humiliation and rebelliousness. Communion in education is just communion, it means being opened up and drawn in. Freedom in education is the possibility of communion; it cannot be dispensed with and it cannot be made use of in itself; without it nothing succeeds, but neither does anything succeed by means of it: it is the run before the jump, the tuning of the violin, the confirmation of that primal and mighty potentiality which it cannot even begin to actualize.

Freedom—I love its flashing face: it flashes forth from the darkness and dies away, but it has made the heart invulnerable. I am devoted to it, I am always ready to join in the fight for it, for the appearance of the flash, which lasts no longer than the eye is able to endure it, for the vibrating of the needle that was held down too long and was stiff. I give my left hand to the rebel and my right to the heretic: forward! But I do not trust them. They know how to die, but that is not enough. I love freedom, but I do not believe in it. How could one believe in it after looking in its face? It is the flash of a significance comprising all meanings, of a possibility comprising all potentiality. For it we fight, again and again, from of old, victorious and in vain.

It is easy to understand that in a time when the deterioration of all traditional bonds has made their legitimacy questionable, the tendency to freedom is exalted, the springboard is treated as the goal and a functional good as substantial good. More-over, it is idle sentimentality to lament at great length that freedom is made the subject of experiments. Perhaps it is fitting for this time which has no compass that people should throw out their lives like a plummet to discover our bearings and the course we should set. But truly *their* lives! Such an experiment, when it is carried out, is a neck-breaking venture which cannot be disputed. But when it is talked about and talked around, in intellectual discussions and confessions and in the mutual pros and cons of their life's "problems", it is an abomination of disintegration. Those who stake themselves, as individuals or as a community, may leap and crash out into the swaying void where senses and sense fail, or through it and beyond into some kind of existence. But they must not make freedom into a theorem or a programme. To become free of a bond is destiny; one carries that like a cross, not like a cockade. Let us realize the true meaning of being free of a bond: it means that a quite personal responsibility takes the place of one shared with many generations. Life lived in free-dom is personal responsibility or it is a pathetic farce.

I have pointed out the power which alone can give a content to empty freedom and a direction to swaying and spinning freedom. I believe in it, I trust those devoted to it .

This fragile life between birth and death can nevertheless be a fulfilment—if it is a dialogue. In our life and experience we are addressed; by thought and speech and action, by producing and by influencing we are able to answer. For the most part we do not listen to the address, or we break into it with chatter. But if the word comes to us and the answer proceeds from us then human life exists, though brokenly, in the world. The kindling of the response in that "spark" of the soul, the blazing up of the response, which occurs time and again, to the unex-pectedly approaching speech, we term responsibility. We practise responsibility for that realm of life allotted and en-trusted to us for which we are able to respond, that is, for which we have a relation of deeds which may count—in all our inadequacy—as a proper response. The extent to which a man, in the strength of the reality of the spark, can keep a traditional bond, a law, a direction, is the extent to which he is permitted to lean his responsibility on something (more than this is not vouchsafed to us, responsibility is not taken off our shoulders). As we "become free" this leaning on something is more and more denied to us, and our responsibility must become personal and solitary.

From this point of view education and its transformation in the hour of the crumbling of bonds are to be understood.

It is usual to contrast the principle of the "new" education as "Eros" with that of the "old" education as the "will to power".

In fact the one is as little a principle of education as the other. A principle of education, in a sense still to be clarified, can only be a basic relation which is fulfilled in education. But Eros and the will to power are alike passions of the soul for whose real elaboration a place is prepared elsewhere. Education can supply for them only an incidental realm and moreover one which sets a limit to their elaboration; nor can this limit be infringed without the realm itself being destroyed. The one can as little as the other constitute the educational attitude.

The "old" educator, in so far as he was an educator, was not "the man with a will to power", but he was the bearer of assured values which were strong in tradition. If the educator represents the world to the pupil, the "old" educator represented particularly the historical world, the past. He was the ambassador of history to this intruder, the "child"; he carried to him, as the Pope in the legend did to the prince of the Huns, the magic of the spiritual forces of history; he instilled values into the child or he drew the child into the values. The man who reduces this encounter between the cosmos of history and its eternally new chaos, between Zeus and Dionysos, to the formula of the "antagonism between fathers and sons", has never beheld it in his spirit. Zeus the Father does not stand for a generation but for a world, for the olympic, the formed world; the world of history faces a particular generation, which is the world of nature renewed again and again, always without history.

This situation of the old type of education is, however, easily used, or misused, by the individual's will to power, for this will is inflated by the authority of history. The will to power becomes convulsive and passes into fury, when the authority begins to decay, that is, when the magical validity of tradition

disappears. Then the moment comes near when the teacher
no longer faces the pupil as an ambassador but only as an
individual, as a static atom to the whirling atom. Then no
matter how much he imagines he is acting from the fulness of
the objective spirit, in the reality of his life he is thrown back
on himself, cast on his own resources, and hence filled with
longing. Eros appears. And Eros finds employment in the new
situation of education as the will to power did in the old
situation. But Eros is not a bearer or the ground or the
principle any more than the will to power was. He only
claims to be that, in order not to be recognized as longing, as
the stranger given refuge. And many believe it.

Nietzsche did not succeed in glorifying the will to power as
much as Plato glorified Eros. But in our concern for the
creature in this great time of concern, for both alike we have
not to consider the myths of the philosophers but the actuality of
present life. In entire opposition to any glorification we have to
see that Eros—that is, not "love", but Eros the male and mag-
nificent—whatever else may belong to him, necessarily includes
this one thing, that he desires to enjoy men; and education,
the peculiar essence bearing this name which is composed of
no others, excludes precisely this desire. However mightily an
educator is possessed and inspired by Eros, if he obeys him in
the course of his educating then he stifles the growth of his
blessings. It must be one or the other: either he takes on
himself the tragedy of the person, and offers an unblemished
daily sacrifice, or the fire enters his work and consumes it.

Eros is choice, choice made from an inclination. This is
precisely what education is not. The man who is loving in
Eros chooses the beloved, the modern educator finds his pupil
there before him. From this unerotic situation the *greatness*
of the modern educator is to be seen—and most clearly when
he is a teacher. He enters the school-room for the first time,
he sees them crouching at the desks, indiscriminately flung
together, the misshapen and the well-proportioned, animal
faces, empty faces, and noble faces in indiscriminate confusion,
like the presence of the created universe; the glance of the
educator accepts and receives them all. He is assuredly no
descendant of the Greek gods, who kidnapped those they loved.
But he seems to me to be a representative of the true God. For
if God "forms the light and creates darkness", man is able to
love both—to love light in itself, and darkness towards the light.

If this educator should ever believe that for the sake of education he has to practise selection and arrangement, then he will be guided by another criterion than that of inclination, however legitimate this may be in its own sphere; he will be guided by the recognition of values which is in his glance as an educator. But even then his selection remains suspended, under constant correction by the special humility of the educator for whom the life and particular being of all his pupils is the decisive factor to which his "hierarchic" recognition is subordinated. For in the manifold variety of the children the variety of creation is placed before him.

In education, then, there is a lofty asceticism: an asceticism which rejoices in the world, for the sake of the responsibility for a realm of life which is entrusted to us for our influence but not our interference—either by the will to power or by Eros. The spirit's service of life can be truly carried out only in the system of a reliable counterpoint—regulated by the laws of the different forms of relation—of giving and withholding oneself, intimacy and distance, which of course must not be controlled by reflection but must arise from the living tact of the natural and spiritual man. Every form of relation in which the spirit's service of life is realized has its special objectivity, its structure of proportions and limits which in no way resists the fervour of personal comprehension and penetration, though it does resist any confusion with the person's own spheres. If this structure and its resistance are not respected then a dilettantism will prevail which claims to be aristocratic, though in reality it is unsteady and feverish: to provide it with the most sacred names and attitudes will not help it past its inevitable consequence of disintegration. Consider, for example, the relation of doctor and patient. It is essential that this should be a real human relation experienced with the spirit by the one who is addressed; but as soon as the helper is touched by the desire—in however subtle a form—to dominate or to enjoy his patient, or to treat the latter's wish to be dominated or enjoyed by him other than as a wrong condition needing to be cured, the danger of a falsification arises, beside which all quackery appears peripheral.

The objectively ascetic character of the sphere of education must not, however, be misunderstood as being so separated from the instinct to power and from Eros that no bridge can be flung from them to it. I have already pointed out how very significant Eros can be to the educator without corroding his work. What matters here is the threshold and the transformation which takes place on it. It is not the church alone which has a testing threshold on which a man is transformed or becomes a lie. But in order to be able to carry out this ever renewed transition from sphere to sphere he must have carried it out once in a decisive fashion and taken up in himself the essence of education. How does this happen? There is an elemental experience which shatters at least the assurance of the erotic as well as the cratetic man, but sometimes does more, forcing its way at white-heat into the heart of the instinct and remoulding it. A reversal of the single instinct takes place, which does not eliminate it but reverses its system of direction. Such a reversal can be effected by the elemental experience with which the real process of education begins and on which it is based. I call it experiencing the other side.

A man belabours another, who remains quite still. Then let us assume that the striker suddenly receives in his soul the blow which he strikes: the same blow; that he receives it as the other who remains still. For the space of a moment he experiences the situation from the other side. Reality imposes itself on him. What will he do? Either he will overwhelm the voice of the soul, or his impulse will be reversed.

A man caresses a woman, who lets herself be caressed. Then let us assume that he feels the contact from two sides—with the palm of his hand still, and also with the woman's skin. The twofold nature of the gesture, as one that takes place between two persons, thrills through the depth of enjoyment in his heart and stirs it. If he does not deafen his heart he will have—not to renounce the enjoyment but—to love.

I do not in the least mean that the man who has had such an experience would from then on have this two-sided sensation in every such meeting—that would perhaps destroy his instinct. But the one extreme experience makes the other person present to him for all time. A transfusion has taken place after which a mere elaboration of subjectivity is never again possible or tolerable to him.

Only an inclusive power is able to take the lead; only an inclusive Eros is love. Inclusiveness is the complete realization of the submissive person, the desired person, the "partner", not by the fancy but by the actuality of the being.

It would be wrong to identify what is meant here with the familiar but not very significant term "empathy". Empathy means, if anything, to glide with one's own feeling into the dynamic structure of an object, a pillar or a crystal or the branch of a tree, or even of an animal or a man, and as it were to trace it from within, understanding the formation and motoriality of the object with the perceptions of one's own muscles; it means to "transpose" oneself over there and in there. Thus it means the exclusion of one's own concreteness, the extinguishing of the actual situation of life, the absorption in pure æstheticism of the reality in which one participates. Inclusion is the opposite of this. It is the extension of one's own concreteness, the fulfilment of the actual situation of life, the complete presence of the reality in which one participates. Its elements are, first, a relation, of no matter what kind, between two persons, second, an event experienced by them in common, in which at least one of them actively participates, and, third, the fact that this one person, without forfeiting anything of the felt reality of his activity, at the same time lives through the common event from the standpoint of the other.

A relation between persons that is characterized in more or less degree by the element of inclusion may be termed a dialogical relation.

A dialogical relation will show itself also in genuine conversation, but it is not composed of this. Not only is the shared silence of two such persons a dialogue, but also their dialogical life continues, even when they are separated in space, as the continual potential presence of the one to the other, as an unexpressed intercourse. On the other hand, all conversation derives its genuineness only from the consciousness of the element of inclusion.—even if this appears only abstractly as an "acknowledgement" of the actual being of the partner in the conversation; but this acknowledgement can be real and effective only when it springs from an experience of inclusion, of the other side.

The reversal of the will to power and of Eros means that relations characterized by these are made dialogical. For that very reason it means that the instinct enters into communion with the fellow-man and into responsibility for him as an allotted and entrusted realm of life.

The element of inclusion, with whose recognition this clarification begins, is the same as that which constitutes the relation in education.

The relation in education is one of pure dialogue.

I have referred to the child, lying with half-closed eyes waiting for his mother to speak to him. But many children do not need to wait, for they know that they are unceasingly addressed in a dialogue which never breaks off. In face of the lonely night which threatens to invade, they lie preserved and guarded, invulnerable, clad in the silver mail of trust. Trust, trust in the world, because this human being exists— that is the most inward achievement of the relation in education. Because this human being exists, meaninglessness, however hard pressed you are by it, cannot be the real truth. Because this human being exists, in the darkness the light lies hidden, in fear salvation, and in the callousness of one's fellow-men the great Love.

Because this human being exists: therefore he must be really there, really facing the child, not merely there in spirit. He may not let himself be represented by a phantom: the death of the phantom would be a catastrophe for the child's pristine soul. He need possess none of the perfections which the child may dream he possesses; but he must be really there. In order to be and to remain truly present to the child he must have gathered the child's presence into his own store as one of the bearers of his communion with the world, one of the focuses of his responsibilities for the world. Of course he cannot be continually concerned with the child, either in thought or in deed, nor ought he to be. But if he has really gathered the child into his life then that subterranean dialogic, that steady potential presence of the one to the other is established and endures. Then there is reality *between* them, there is mutuality.

But this mutuality—that is what constitutes the peculiar

nature of the relation in education—cannot be one of inclusion, although the true relation of the educator to the pupil is based on inclusion. No other relation draws its inner life like this one from the element of inclusion, but no other is in that regard like this, completely directed to one-sidedness, so that if it loses one-sidedness it loses essence.

We may distinguish three chief forms of the dialogical relation.

The first rests on an abstract but mutual experience of inclusion.

The clearest example of this is a disputation between two men, thoroughly different in nature and outlook and calling, where in an instant—as by the action of a messenger as anonymous as he is invisible—it happens that each is aware of the other's full legitimacy, wearing the insignia of necessity and of meaning. What an illumination! The truth, the strength of conviction, the "standpoint", or rather the circle of movement, of each of them, is in no way reduced by this. There is no "relativizing", but we may say that, in the sign of the limit, the essence of mortal recognition, fraught with primal destiny, is manifested to us. To recognize means for us creatures the fulfilment by each of us, in truth and responsibility, of his own relation to the Present Being, through our receiving all that is manifested of it and incorporating it into our own being, with all our force, faithfully, and open to the world and the spirit. In this way living truth arises and endures. We have become aware that it is with the other as with ourselves, and that what rules over us both is not a truth of recognition but the truth-of-existence and the existence-of-truth of the Present Being. In this way we have become able *to acknowledge*.

I have called this form abstract, not as though its basic experience lacked immediacy, but because it is related to man only as a spiritual person and is bound to leave out the full reality of his being and life. The other two forms proceed from the inclusion of this full reality.

Of these the first, the relation of education, is based on a concrete but one-sided experience of inclusion.

If education means to let a selection of the world affect a person through the medium of another person, then the one through whom this takes place, rather, who makes it take place through himself, is caught in a strange paradox. What is otherwise found only as grace, inlaid in the folds of life—

the influencing of the lives of others with one's own life—
becomes here a function and a law. But since the educator
has to such an extent replaced the master, the danger has
arisen that the new phenomenon, the will to educate, may
degenerate into arbitrariness, and that the educator may carry
out his selection and his influence from himself and his idea
of the pupil, not from the pupil's own reality. One only needs
to read, say, the accounts of Pestalozzi's teaching method to
see how easily, even with the noblest teachers, arbitrary self-
will is mixed up with will. This is almost always due to an
interruption or a temporary flagging of the act of inclusion,
which is not merely regulative for the realm of education, as
for other realms, but is actually constitutive; so that the realm
of education acquires its true and proper force from the constant
return of this act and the constantly renewed connexion with it.
The man whose calling it is to influence the being of persons
that can be determined, must experience this action of his
(however much it may have assumed the form of non-action)
ever anew from the other side. Without the action of his spirit
being in any way weakened he must at the same time be over
there, on the surface of that other spirit which is being acted
upon—and not of some conceptual, contrived spirit, but all the
time the wholly concrete spirit of this individual and unique
being who is living and confronting him, and who stands with
him in the common situation of "educating" and "being
educated" (which is indeed one situation, only the other is at
the other end of it). It is not enough for him to imagine the
child's individuality, nor to experience him directly as a
spiritual person and then to acknowledge him. Only when he
catches himself "from over there", and feels how it affects one,
how it affects this other human being, does he recognize the
real limit, baptize his self-will in Reality and make it true will,
and renew his paradoxical legitimacy. He is of all men the
one for whom inclusion may and should change from an
alarming and edifying event into an atmosphere.

But however intense the mutuality of giving and taking with
which he is bound to his pupil, inclusion cannot be mutual in
this case. He experiences the pupil's being educated, but the
pupil cannot experience the educating of the educator. The
educator stands at both ends of the common situation, the
pupil only at one end. (In the moment when the pupil is able
to throw himself across and experience from over there, the

educative relation would be burst asunder, or change into friendship.

We call friendship the third form of the dialogical relation, which is based on a concrete and mutual experience of inclusion. It is the true inclusion of one another by human souls.

The educator who practises the experience of the other side and stands firm in it, experiences two things together, first that he is limited by otherness, and second that he receives grace by being bound to the other. He feels from "over there" the acceptance and the rejection of what is approaching (that is, approaching from himself, the educator)—of course often only in a fugitive mood or an uncertain feeling; but this discloses the real need and absence of need in the soul. In the same way the foods a child likes and dislikes is a fact which does not, indeed, procure for the experienced person but certainly helps him to gain an insight into what substances the child's body needs. In learning from time to time what this human being needs and does not need at the moment, the educator is led to an ever deeper recognition of what the human being needs in order to grow. But he is also led to the recognition of what he, the "educator", is able and what he is unable to give of what is needed—and what he can give now, and what not yet. So the responsibility for this realm of life allotted and entrusted to him, the constant responsibility for this living soul, points him to that which seems impossible and yet is somehow granted to us—to self-education. But self-education, here as everywhere, cannot take place through one's being concerned with oneself but only through one's being concerned, knowing what it means, with the world. The forces of the world which the child needs for the building up of his substance must be chosen by the educator from the world and drawn into himself.

The education of men by men means the selection of the effective world by a person and in him. The educator gathers in the constructive forces of the world. He distinguishes, rejects, and confirms in himself, in his self which is filled with the world. The constructive forces are eternally the same: they are the world bound up in community, turned to God. The educator educates himself to be their vehicle.

Then is this the "principle" of education, its normal and fixed maxim?

No; it is only the *principium* of its reality, the beginning of its reality—wherever it begins.

There is not and never has been a norm and fixed maxim of education. What is called so was always only the norm of a culture, of a society, a church, an epoch, to which education too, like all stirring and action of the spirit, was submissive, and which education translated into its language. In a formed age there is in truth no autonomy of education, but only in an age which is losing form. Only in it, in the disintegration of traditional bonds, in the spinning whirl of freedom, does personal responsibility arise which in the end can no longer lean with its burden of decision on any church or society or culture, but is lonely in face of Present Being.

In an age which is losing form the highly-praised "personalities", who know how to serve its fictitious forms and in their name to dominate the age, count in the truth of what is happening no more than those who lament the genuine forms of the past and are diligent to restore them. The ones who count are those persons who—though they may be of little renown—respond to and are responsible for the continuation of the living spirit, each in the active stillness of his sphere of work.

The question which is always being brought forward—"To where, to what, must we educate?"—misunderstands the situation. Only times which know a figure of general validity—the Christian, the gentleman, the citizen—know an answer to that question, not necessarily in words, but by pointing with the finger to the figure which rises clear in the air, out-topping all. The forming of this figure in all individuals, out of all materials, is the formation of a "culture". But when all figures are shattered, when no figure is able any more to dominate and shape the present human material, what is there left to form?

Nothing but the image of God.

That is the indefinable, only factual, direction of the responsible modern educator. This cannot be a theoretical answer to the question "To what?", but only, if at all, an answer carried out in deeds; an answer carried out by non-doing.

The educator is set now in the midst of the need which he experiences in inclusion, but only a bit deeper in it. He is set in the midst of the service, only a bit higher up, which he invokes without words; he is set in the *imitatio Dei absconditi sed non ignoti.*

When all "directions" fail there arises in the darkness over the abyss the one true direction of man, towards the creative Spirit, towards the Spirit of God brooding on the face of the waters, towards Him of whom we know not whence He comes and whither He goes.

That is man's true autonomy which no longer betrays, but responds.

Man, the creature, who forms and transforms the creation, cannot create. But he, each man, can expose himself and others to the creative Spirit. And he can call upon the Creator to save and perfect His image.

IV

THE EDUCATION OF CHARACTER

I

EDUCATION worthy of the name is essentially education of character. For the genuine educator does not merely consider individual functions of his pupil, as one intending to teach him only to know or be capable of certain definite things; but his concern is always the person as a whole, both in the actuality in which he lives before you now and in his possibilities, what he can become. But in this way, as a whole in reality and potentiality, a man can be conceived either as personality, that is, as a unique spiritual-physical form with all the forces dormant in it, or as character, that is, as the link between what this individual is and the sequence of his actions and attitudes. Between these two modes of conceiving the pupil in his wholeness there is a fundamental difference. Personality is something which in its growth remains essentially outside the influence of the educator; but to assist in the moulding of character is his greatest task. Personality is a completion, only character is a task. One may cultivate and enhance personality, but in education one can and one must aim at character.

However—as I would like to point out straightaway—it is advisable not to over-estimate what the educator can even at best do to develop character. In this more than in any other branch of the science of teaching it is important to realize, at the very beginning of the discussion, the fundamental limits to conscious influence, even before asking what character is and how it is to be brought about.

If I have to teach algebra I can expect to succeed in giving my pupils an idea of quadratic equations with two unknown quantities. Even the slowest-witted child will understand it so well that he will amuse himself by solving equations at night when he cannot fall asleep. And even one with the most sluggish memory will not forget, in his old age, how to play with *x* and *y*. But if I am concerned with the education of character, everything becomes problematic. I try to explain to my pupils that envy is despicable, and at once I feel the secret resistance of those who are poorer than their comrades. I try to explain that it is wicked to bully the weak, and at once I see a suppressed smile on the lips of the strong. I try to explain that lying destroys life, and something frightful happens: the worst habitual liar of the class produces a brilliant essay on the destructive power of lying. I have made the fatal mistake of *giving instruction* in ethics, and what I said is accepted as current coin of knowledge; nothing of it is transformed into character-building substance.

But the difficulty lies still deeper. In all teaching of a subject I can announce my intention of teaching as openly as I please, and this does not interfere with the results. After all, pupils do want, for the most part, to learn something, even if not overmuch, so that a tacit agreement becomes possible. But as soon as my pupils notice that I want to educate their characters I am resisted precisely by those who show most signs of genuine independent character: they will not let themselves be educated, or rather, they do not like the idea that somebody wants to educate them. And those, too, who are seriously labouring over the question of good and evil, rebel when one dictates to them, as though it were some long established truth, what is good and what is bad; and they rebel just because they have experienced over and over again how hard it is to find the right way. Does it follow that one should keep silent about one's intention of educating character, and act by ruse and subterfuge? No; I have just said that the difficulty lies deeper. It is not enough to see that education of character is not introduced into a lesson in class; neither may one conceal it in cleverly arranged intervals. Education cannot tolerate such politic action. Even if the pupil does not notice the hidden motive it will have its negative effect on the actions of the teacher himself by depriving him of the directness which is his strength. Only in his whole being, in all his spontaneity can the educator truly affect the whole being of his pupil. For educating characters you do not need a moral genius, but you do need a man who is wholly alive and able to communicate himself directly to his fellow beings. His aliveness streams out to them and affects them most strongly and purely when he has no thought of affecting them.

The Greek word character means *impression.* The special
link between man's being and his appearance, the special connexion between the unity of what he is and the sequence of his
actions and attitudes is impressed on his still plastic substance.
Who does the impressing? Everything does: nature and the
social context, the house and the street, language and custom,
the world of history and the world of daily news in the form of
rumour, of broadcast and newspaper, music and technical
science, play and dream—everything together. Many of these
factors exert their influence by stimulating agreement, imitation, desire, effort; others by arousing questions, doubts,
dislike, resistance. Character is formed by the interpenetration
of all those multifarious, opposing influences. And yet, among
this infinity of form-giving forces the educator is only one
element among innumerable others, but distinct from them all
by his *will* to take part in the stamping of character and by his
consciousness that he represents in the eyes of the growing person
a certain *selection* of what is, the selection of what is "right", of
what *should* be. It is in this will and this consciousness that his
vocation as an educator finds its fundamental expression.
From this the genuine educator gains two things: first, humility,
the feeling of being only one element amidst the fullness of
life, only one single existence in the midst of all the tremendous
inrush of reality on the pupil; but secondly, self-awareness,
the feeling of being therein the only existence that *wants* to
affect the whole person, and thus the feeling of responsibility
for the selection of reality which he represents to the pupil.
And a third thing emerges from all this, the recognition that
in this realm of the education of character, of wholeness, there
is only *one* access to the pupil: his *confidence.* For the adolescent
who is frightened and disappointed by an unreliable world,
confidence means the liberating insight that there is human
truth, the truth of human existence. When the pupil's confidence has been won, his resistance against being educated
gives way to a singular happening: he accepts the educator as
a person. He feels he may trust this man, that this man is not
making a business out of him, but is taking part in his life,
accepting him before desiring to influence him. And so he
learns to *ask.*

The teacher who is for the first time approached by a boy
with somewhat defiant bearing, but with trembling hands,
visibly opened-up and fired by a daring hope, who asks him

what is the right thing in a certain situation—for instance, whether in learning that a friend has betrayed a secret entrusted to him one should call him to account or be content with entrusting no more secrets to him—the teacher to whom this happens realizes that this is the moment to make the first conscious step towards education of character; he has to answer, to answer under a responsibility, to give an answer which will probably lead beyond the alternatives of the question by showing a third possibility which is the right one. To dictate what is good and evil in general is not his business. His business is to answer a concrete question, to answer what is right and wrong in a given situation. This, as I have said, can only happen in an atmosphere of confidence. Confidence, of course, is not won by the strenuous endeavour to win it, but by direct and ingenuous participation in the life of the people one is dealing with—in this case in the life of one's pupils— and by assuming the responsibility which arises from such participation. It is not the educational intention but it is the meeting which is educationally fruitful. A soul suffering from the contradictions of the world of human society, and of its own physical existence, approaches me with a question. By trying to answer it to the best of my knowledge and conscience I help it to become a character that actively overcomes the contradictions.

If this is the teacher's standpoint towards his pupil, taking part in his life and conscious of responsibility, then everything that passes between them can, without any deliberate or politic intention, open a way to the education of character: lessons and games, a conversation about quarrels in the class, or about the problems of a world-war. Only, the teacher must not forget the limits of education; even when he enjoys confidence he cannot always expect agreement. Confidence implies a break-through from reserve, the bursting of the bonds which imprison an unquiet heart. But it does not imply unconditional agreement. The teacher must never forget that conflicts too, if only they are decided in a healthy atmosphere, have an educational value. A conflict with a pupil is the supreme test for the educator. He must use his own insight wholeheartedly; he must not blunt the piercing impact of his knowledge, but he must at the same time have in readiness the healing ointment for the heart pierced by it. Not for a moment may he conduct a dialectical manœuvre instead of the real battle for truth.

But if he is the victor he has to help the vanquished to endure defeat; and if he cannot conquer the self-willed soul that faces him (for victories over souls are not so easily won), then he has to find the word of love which alone can help to overcome so difficult a situation.

2

So far I have referred to those personal difficulties in the education of character which arise from the relation between educator and pupil, while for the moment treating character itself, the object of education, as a simple concept of fixed content. But it is by no means that. In order to penetrate to the real difficulties in the education of character we have to examine critically the concept of character itself.

Kerschensteiner in his well-known essay on *The Concept and Education of Character* distinguished between "character in the most general sense", by which he means "a man's attitude to his human surroundings, which is constant and is expressed in his actions", and real "ethical character", which he defines as "a special attitude, and one which in action gives the preference before all others to absolute values". If we begin by accepting this distinction unreservedly—and undeniably there is some truth in it—we are faced with such heavy odds in all education of character in our time that the very possibility of it seems doubtful.

The "absolute values" which Kerschensteiner refers to cannot, of course, be meant to have only subjective validity for the person concerned. Don Juan finds absolute and subjective value in seducing the greatest possible number of women, and the dictator sees it in the greatest possible accumulation of power. "Absolute validity" can only relate to universal values and norms, the existence of which the person concerned recognizes and acknowledges. But to deny the presence of universal values and norms of absolute validity—that is the conspicuous tendency of our age. This tendency is not, as is sometimes supposed, directed merely against the sanctioning of the norms by religion, but against their universal character and absolute validity, against their claim to be of a higher order than man and to govern the whole of mankind. In our age values and norms are not permitted to be anything but expressions of the life of a group which translates its own needs into the language of objective claims, until at last the group itself, for example a nation, is raised to an absolute value—and moreover to the only value. Then this splitting up into groups so pervades the whole of life that it is no longer possible to re-establish a sphere of values common to mankind, and a commandment to mankind is no longer observed. As this tendency grows the basis for the development of what Kerschensteiner means by moral character steadily diminishes. How, under these circumstances, can the task of educating character be completed?

At the time of the Arab terror in Palestine, when there were single Jewish acts of reprisal, there must have been many discussions between teacher and pupils on the question: Can there be any suspension of the Ten Commandments, i.e. can murder become a good deed if committed in the interest of one's own group? One such discussion was once repeated to me. The teacher asked: "When the commandment tells you 'Thou shalt not bear false witness against thy neighbour', are we to interpret it with the condition, 'provided that it does not profit you'?" Thereupon one of the pupils said, "But it is not a question of my profit, but of the profit of my people." The teacher: "And how would you like it, then, if we put our condition this way: 'Provided that it does not profit your family'?" The pupil: "But family—that is still something more or less like myself; but the people—that is something quite different; there all question of *I* disappears." The teacher: "Then if you are thinking, 'we want victory', don't you feel at the same time, 'I want victory'?" The pupil: "But the people, that is something infinitely more than just the people of to-day. It includes all past and future generations." At this point the teacher felt the moment had come to leave the narrow compass of the present and to invoke historical destiny. He said: "Yes; all past generations. But what was it that made those past generations of the Exile live? What made them outlive and overcome all their trials? Wasn't it that the cry 'Thou shalt not' never faded from their hearts and ears?" The pupil grew very pale. He was silent for a while, but it was the silence of one whose words threatened to stifle him. Then he burst out: "And what have we achieved that way? This!" And he banged his fist on the newspaper before him, which contained the report on the British White Paper. And again he burst out with "Live? Outlive? Do you call that life? We want to live!"

I have already said that the test of the educator lies in conflict with his pupil. He has to face this conflict and, whatever turn it may take, he has to find the way through it into life, into a life, I must add, where confidence continues unshaken—more, is even mysteriously strengthened. But the example I have just given shows the extreme difficulty of this task, which seems at times to have reached an impassable frontier. This is no longer merely a conflict between two generations, but between a world which for several millennia has believed in a truth superior to man, and an age which does not believe in it any longer—will not or cannot believe in it any longer.

But if we now ask, "How in this situation can there be any education of character?", something negative is immediately obvious: it is senseless to want to prove by any kind of argument that nevertheless the denied absoluteness of norms exists. That would be to assume that the denial is the result of reflection, and is open to argument, that is, to material for renewed reflection. But the denial is due to the disposition of a dominant human type of our age. We are justified in regarding this disposition as a sickness of the human race. But we must not deceive ourselves by believing that the disease can be cured by formulæ which assert that nothing is really as the sick person imagines. It is an idle undertaking to call out, to a mankind that has grown blind to eternity: "Look! the eternal values!" To-day host upon host of men have everywhere sunk into the slavery of collectives, and each collective is the supreme authority for its own slaves; there is no longer, superior to the collectives, any universal sovereignty in idea, faith, or spirit. Against the values, decrees and decisions of the collective no appeal is possible. This is true, not only for the totalitarian countries, but also for the parties and party-like groups in the so-called democracies. Men who have so lost themselves to the collective Moloch cannot be rescued from it by any reference, however eloquent, to the absolute whose kingdom the Moloch has usurped. One has to begin by pointing to that sphere where man himself, in the hours of utter solitude, occasionally becomes aware of the disease through sudden pain: by pointing to the relation of the individual to his own self. In order to enter into a personal relation with the absolute, it is first necessary to be a person again, to rescue one's real personal self from the fiery jaws of collectivism which devours all self-hood. The desire to do this is latent in the pain the individual suffers through his distorted relation to his own self. Again and again he dulls the pain with a subtle poison and thus suppresses the desire as well. To keep the pain awake, to waken the desire—that is the first task of everyone who regrets the obscuring of eternity. It is also the first task of the genuine educator in our time.

The man for whom absolute values in a universal sense do not exist cannot be made to adopt "an attitude which in action gives the preference over all others to absolute values". But what one can inculcate in him is the desire to attain once more to a real attitude, and that is, the desire to become a person following the only way that leads to this goal to-day.

But with this the concept of character formulated by Kerschensteiner and deriving, as we know, from Kant is recognized to be useless for the specifically modern task of the education of character. Another concept has to be found if this task is to be more precisely defined.

We cannot conceal from ourselves that we stand to-day on the ruins of the edifice whose towers were raised by Kant. It is not given to us living to-day to sketch the plan for a new building. But we can perhaps begin by laying the first foundations without a plan, with only a dawning image before our mind's eye.

3

According to Kerschensteiner's final definition character is "fundamentally nothing but voluntary obedience to the maxims which have been moulded in the individual by experience, teaching, and self-reflection, whether they have been adopted and then completely assimilated or have originated in the consciousness through self-legislation". This voluntary obedience "is, however, only a form of self-control". At first, love or fear of other people must have produced in man "the *habit* of self-conquest". Then, gradually, "this outer obedience must be transformed into inner obedience".

The concept of habit was then enlarged, especially by John Dewey in his book, *Human Nature and Conduct*. According to

him character is "the interpenetration of habits". Without
"the continued operation of all habits in every act" there
would be no unified character, but only "a juxtaposition of
disconnected reactions to separated situations".

With this concept of character as an organization of self-
control by means of the accumulation of maxims, or as a system
of interpenetrating habits, it is very easy to understand how
powerless modern educational science is when faced by the
sickness of man. But even apart from the special problems of
the age, this concept can be no adequate basis for the construction of a genuine education of character. Not that the educator
could dispense with employing useful maxims or furthering
good habits. But in moments that come perhaps only seldom,
a feeling of blessed achievement links him to the explorer, the
inventor, the artist, a feeling of sharing in the revelation of
what is hidden. In such moments he finds himself in a sphere
very different from that of maxims and habits. Only on this,
the highest plane of his activity, can he fix his real goal, the
real concept of character which is his concern, even though he
might not often reach it.

For the first time a young teacher enters a class independently, no longer sent by the training college to prove his efficiency.
The class before him is like a mirror of mankind, so multiform,
so full of contradictions, so inaccessible. He feels "These
boys—I have not sought them out; I have been put here and
have to accept them as they are—but not as they now are in
this moment, no, as they *really* are, as they can become. But
how can I find out what is in them and what can I do to make
it take shape?" And the boys do not make things easy for him.
They are noisy, they cause trouble, they stare at him with
impudent curiosity. He is at once tempted to check this or
that trouble-maker, to issue orders, to make compulsory the
rules of decent behaviour, to say No, to say No to everything
rising against him from beneath: he is at once tempted to start
from beneath. And if one starts from beneath one perhaps
never arrives above, but everything comes down. But then
his eyes meet a face which strikes him. It is not a beautiful
face nor particularly intelligent; but it is a real face, or rather,
the chaos preceding the cosmos of a real face. On it he reads
a question which is something different from the general
curiosity: "Who are you? Do you know something that concerns me? Do you bring me something? What do you bring?"

In some such way he reads the question. And he, the young teacher, addresses this face. He says nothing very ponderous or important, he puts an ordinary introductory question: "What did you talk about last in geography? The Dead Sea? Well, what about the Dead Sea?" But there was obviously something not quite usual in the question, for the answer he gets is not the ordinary schoolboy answer; the boy begins to *tell a story.* Some months earlier he had stayed for a few hours on the shores of the Dead Sea and it is of this he tells. He adds: "And everything looked to me as if it had been created a day before the rest of creation." Quite unmistakably he had only in this moment made up his mind to talk about it. In the meantime his face has changed. It is no longer quite as chaotic as before. And the class has fallen silent. They all listen. The class, too, is no longer a chaos. Something has happened. The young teacher has started from above.

The educator's task can certainly not consist in educating great characters. He cannot select his pupils, but year by year the world, such as it is, is sent in the form of a school class to meet him on his life's way as his destiny; and in this destiny lies the very meaning of his life's work. He has to introduce discipline and order, he has to establish a law, and he can only strive and hope for the result that discipline and order will become more and more inward and autonomous, and that at last the law will be written in the heart of his pupils. But his real goal which, once he has well recognized it and well remembers it, will influence all his work, is the great character.

The great character can be conceived neither as a system of maxims nor as a system of habits. It is peculiar to him to act from the whole of his substance. That is, it is peculiar to him to react in accordance with the uniqueness of every situation which challenges him as an active person. Of course there are all sorts of similarities in different situations; one can construct types of situations, one can always find to what section the particular situation belongs, and draw what is appropriate from the hoard of established maxims and habits, apply the appropriate maxim, bring into operation the appropriate habit. But what is untypical in the particular situation remains un-noticed and unanswered. To me that seems the same as if, having ascertained the sex of a new-born child, one were immediately to establish its type as well, and put all the children of one type into a common cradle on which not the individual name but the name of the type was inscribed. In spite of all similarities every living situation has, like a new-born child, a new face, that has never been before and will never come again. It demands of you a reaction which cannot be prepared beforehand. It demands nothing of what is past. It demands presence, responsibility; it demands you. I call a great character one who by his actions and attitudes satisfies the claim of situations out of deep readiness to respond with his whole life, and in such a way that the sum of his actions and attitudes expresses at the same time the unity of his being in its willingness to accept responsibility. As his being is unity, the unity of accepted responsibility, his active life, too, coheres into unity. And one might perhaps say that for him there rises a unity out of the situations he has responded to in responsibility, the indefinable unity of a moral destiny.

All this does not mean that the great character is beyond the acceptance of norms. No responsible person remains a stranger to norms. But the command inherent in a genuine norm never becomes a maxim and the fulfilment of it never a habit. Any command that a great character takes to himself in the course of his development does not act in him as part of his conscious-ness or as material for building up his exercises, but remains latent in a basic layer of his substance until it reveals itself to him in a concrete way. What it has to tell him is revealed whenever a situation arises which demands of him a solution of which till then he had perhaps no idea. Even the most universal norm will at times be recognized only in a very special situation. I know of a man whose heart was struck by the lightning flash of "Thou shalt not steal" in the very moment when he was moved by a very different desire from that of stealing, and whose heart was so struck by it that he not only abandoned doing what he wanted to do, but with the whole force of his passion did the very opposite. Good and evil are not each other's opposites like right and left. The evil approaches us as a whirlwind, the good as a direction. There is a direction, a "yes", a command, hidden even in a prohibi-tion, which is revealed to us in moments like these. In moments like these the command addresses us really in the second person, and the Thou in it is no one else but one's own self. Maxims command only the third person, the each and the none.

One can say that it is the unconditioned nature of the address which distinguishes the command from the maxim. In an age which has become deaf to unconditioned address we cannot overcome the dilemma of the education of character from that angle. But insight into the structure of great character can help us to overcome it.

Of course, it may be asked whether the educator should really start "from above", whether, in fixing his goal, the hope of finding a great character, who is bound to be the exception, should be his starting-point; for in his methods of educating character he will always have to take into consideration the others, the many. To this I reply that the educator would not have the right to do so if a method inapplicable to these others were to result. In fact, however, his very insight into the structure of a great character helps him to find the way by which alone (as I have indicated) he can begin to influence also the victims of the collective Moloch, pointing out to them the sphere in which they themselves suffer—namely, their relation to their own selves. From this sphere he must elicit the values which he can make credible and desirable to his pupils. That is what insight into the structure of a great character helps him to do.

A section of the young is beginning to feel today that, because of their absorption by the collective, something important and irreplaceable is lost to them—personal responsibility for life and the world. These young people, it is true, do not yet realize that their blind devotion to the collective, e.g. to a party, was not a genuine act of their personal life; they do not realize that it sprang, rather, from the fear of being left, in this age of confusion, to rely on themselves, on a self which no longer receives its direction from eternal values. Thus they do not yet realize that their devotion was fed on the unconscious desire to have responsibility removed from them by an authority in which they believe or want to believe. They do not yet realize that this devotion was an escape. I repeat, the young people I am speaking of do not yet realize this. But they are beginning to notice that he who no longer, with his whole being, decides what he does or does not, and assumes responsibility for it, becomes sterile in soul. And a sterile soul soon ceases to be a soul.

This is where the educator can begin and should begin. He can help the feeling that something is lacking to grow into the clarity of consciousness and into the force of desire. He can awaken in young people the courage to shoulder life again.

He can bring before his pupils the image of a great character who denies no answer to life and the world, but accepts responsibility for everything essential that he meets. He can show his pupils this image without the fear that those among them who most of all need discipline and order will drift into a craving for aimless freedom: on the contrary, he can teach them in this way to recognize that discipline and order too are starting-points on the way towards self-responsibility. He can show that even the great character is not born perfect, that the unity of his being has first to mature before expressing itself in the sequence of his actions and attitudes. But unity itself, unity of the person, unity of the lived life, has to be emphasized again and again. The confusing contradictions cannot be remedied by the collectives, not one of which knows the taste of genuine unity and which if left to themselves would end up, like the scorpions imprisoned in a box, in the witty fable, by devouring one another. This mass of contradictions can be met and conquered only by the rebirth of personal unity, unity of being, unity of life, unity of action—unity of being, life and action together. This does not mean a static unity of the uniform, but the great dynamic unity of the multiform in which multiformity is formed into unity of character. Today the great characters are still "enemies of the people", they who love their society, yet wish not only to preserve it but to raise it to a higher level. To-morrow they will be the architects of a new unity of mankind. It is the longing for personal unity, from which must be born a unity of mankind, which the educator should lay hold of and strengthen in his pupils. Faith in this unity and the will to achieve it is not a "return" to individualism, but a step beyond all the dividedness of individualism and collectivism. A great and full relation between man and man can only exist between unified and responsible persons. That is why it is much more rarely found in the totalitarian collective than in any historically earlier form of society; much more rarely also in the authoritarian party than in any earlier form of free association. Genuine education of character is genuine education for community.

In a generation which has had this kind of upbringing the desire will also be kindled to behold again the eternal values, to hear again the language of the eternal norm. He who knows inner unity, the innermost life of which is mystery, learns to honour the mystery in all its forms. In an understandable reaction against the former domination of a false, fictitious mystery, the present generations are obsessed with the desire to rob life of all its mystery. The fictitious mystery will disappear, the genuine one will rise again. A generation which honours the mystery in all its forms will no longer be deserted by eternity. Its light seems darkened only because the eye suffers from a cataract; the receiver has been turned off, but the resounding ether has not ceased to vibrate. To-day, indeed, in the hour of upheaval, the eternal is sifted from the pseudo-eternal. That which flashed into the primal radiance and blurred the primal sound will be extinguished and silenced, for it has failed before the horror of the new confusion and the questioning soul has unmasked its futility. Nothing remains but what rises above the abyss of to-day's monstrous problems, as above every abyss of every time: the wing-beat of the spirit and the creative word. But he who can see and hear out of unity will also behold and discern again what can be beheld and discerned eternally. The educator who helps to bring man back to his own unity will help to put him again face to face with God.

V

WHAT IS MAN?

Ne connaîtrons-nous jamais l'homme?—Rousseau

Section One: The Progress of the Question

I: KANT'S QUESTIONS

I

RABBI BUNAM VON PRZYSUCHA, one of the last great teachers of Hasidism, is said to have once addressed his pupils thus: "I wanted to write a book called *Adam*, which would be about the whole man. But then I decided not to write it."

In these naive-sounding words of a genuine sage the whole story of human thought about man is expressed. From time immemorial man has known that he is the subject most deserving of his own study, but he has also fought shy of treating this subject as a whole, that is, in accordance with its total character. Sometimes he takes a run at it, but the difficulty of this concern with his own being soon overpowers and exhausts him, and in silent resignation he withdraws—either to consider all things in heaven and earth save man, or to divide man into departments which can be treated singly, in a less problematic, less powerful and less binding way.

The philosopher Malebranche, the most significant of the French philosophers who continued the Cartesian investigations, writes in the foreword to his chief work *De la recherche de la vérité* (1674): "Of all human knowledge the knowledge of man is the most deserving of his study. Yet this knowledge is not the most cultivated or the most developed which we possess. The generality of men neglect it completely. And even among those who busy themselves with this knowledge there are very few who dedicate themselves to it—and still fewer who successfully dedicate themselves to it." He himself certainly raises in his book such genuinely anthropological questions as how far the life of the nerves which lead to the lungs, the stomach, and the liver, influences the origin of errors; but he too established no doctrine of the being of man.

2

The most forcible statement of the task set to philosophical anthropology was made by Kant. In the *Handbook* to his lectures on logic, which he expressly acknowledged—though he himself did not publish it and though it does not reproduce his underlying notes authentically—he distinguishes between a philosophy in the scholastic sense and a philosophy in the universal sense (*in sensu cosmico*). He describes the latter as "the knowledge of the ultimate aims of human reason" or as the "knowledge of the highest maxim of the use of our reason". The field of philosophy in this cosmopolitan significance may, according to Kant, be marked off into the following questions. "1. What can I know? 2. What ought I to do? 3. What may I hope? 4. What is man? Metaphysics answers the first question, ethics the second, religion the third and anthropology the fourth." And Kant adds: "Fundamentally all this could be reckoned as anthropology, since the first three questions are related to the last." This formulation repeats the three questions of which Kant says, in the section of his *Critique of Pure Reason* entitled *Of the ideal of the supreme good*, that every interest of the reason, the speculative as well as the practical, is united in them. In distinction from the *Critique of Pure Reason* he here traces these questions back to a fourth question, that about the being of man, and assigns it to a discipline called anthropology, by which—since he is discussing the fundamental questions of human philosophizing—only philosophical anthropology can be understood. This, then, would be the fundamental philosophical science.

But it is remarkable that Kant's own anthropology, both what he himself published and his copious lectures on man, which only appeared long after his death, absolutely fails to achieve what he demands of a philosophical anthropology. In its express purpose as well as in its entire content it offers something different—an abundance of valuable observations for the knowledge of man, for example, on egoism, on honesty and lies, on fancy, on fortune-telling, on dreams, on mental diseases, on wit, and so on. But the question, what man is, is simply not raised, and not one of the problems which are implicitly set us at the same time by this question—such as man's special place in the cosmos, his connexion with destiny, his relation to the world of things, his understanding of his fellowmen, his existence as a being that knows it must die, his attitude in all the ordinary and extraordinary encounters with the mystery with which his life is shot through, and so on— not one of these problems is seriously touched upon. The *wholeness* of man does not enter into this anthropology. It is as if Kant in his actual philosophizing had had qualms about setting the question which he formulated as the fundamental one.

A modern philosopher, Martin Heidegger, who has dealt (in his *Kant and the Problem of Metaphysics*, 1929) with this strange contradiction, explains it by the *indefiniteness* of the question, what man is. The way of asking the question about man, he says, has itself become questionable. In Kant's first three questions it is man's *finitude* which is under discussion: "What *can* I know?" involves an inability, and thus a limitation; "What *ought* I to do?" includes the realization that something has not yet been accomplished, and thus a limitation; and "What *may* I hope?" means that the questioner is given one expectation and denied another, and thus it means a limitation. The fourth question is the question about "finitude in man", and is no longer an anthropological question at all, for it is the question about the essence of existence itself. As the basis of metaphysics anthropology is replaced by "fundamental ontology".

Whatever this finding represents, it is no longer Kant. Heidegger has shifted the emphasis of Kant's three questions. Kant does not ask: "What *can* I know?" but "What *can* I *know*?" The essential point here is not that there is something I can do and thus something else that I cannot do; nor is it that there is something I know and thus something else that I do not know; but it is that I *can know* something, and that I can then ask what that is that I can know. It is not my finitude that is under discussion here, but my real participation in knowing what there is to know. And in the same way "What ought I to do?" means that there *is* something I ought to do, and thus that I am not separated from "right" doing, but precisely by being able to *come to know* my "ought" may find the way to the doing. Finally, "What may I hope?" does not assert, as Heidegger thinks, that a "may" is made questionable here, and that in the expectation a want of what may not be expected is revealed; but it asserts, first, that there is something for me to hope (for obviously Kant does not mean that the answer to the third question is "Nothing"), secondly, that I am permitted to hope it, and thirdly, that precisely because I am permitted I can learn what it is that I may hope. That is what *Kant* says. And thus in Kant the meaning of the fourth question, to which the first three can be reduced is, what sort of a being is it which is able to know, and ought to do, and may hope? And the fact that the first three questions can be reduced to this question means that the knowledge of the essence of this being will make plain to me *what*, as such a being, it can know, *what*, as such a being, it ought to do, and *what*, as such a being, it may hope. This also means that indissolubly connected with the finitude which is given by the ability to know *only* this, there is a participation in infinity, which is given by the ability to know at all. The meaning is therefore that when we recognize man's finitude we must *at the same time* recognize his participation in infinity, not as two juxtaposed qualities but as the twofold nature of the processes in which alone man's existence becomes recognizable. The finite has its effect on him and the infinite has its effect on him; he shares in finitude and he shares in infinity.

Certainly Kant in his anthropology has neither answered nor undertaken to answer the question which he put to anthropology—What is man? He lectured on another anthropology than the one he asked for—I should say, in terms of the history of philosophy, an earlier anthropology, one that was still bound up with the uncritical "science of man" of the 17th and 18th centuries. But in formulating the task which he set to the philosophical anthropology he asked for, he has left a legacy.

3

It is certainly doubtful to me as well whether such a discipline will suffice to provide a foundation for philosophy, or, as Heidegger formulates it, a foundation for metaphysics. For it is true, indeed, that I continually learn what I can know, what I ought to do, and what I may hope. It is further true that philosophy contributes to this learning of mine: to the first question by telling me, in logic and epistemology, what being able to know means, and in cosmology and the philosophy of history and so on, what there is to know; to the second question by telling me, in psychology, how the "ought to do" is carried out psychically, and in ethics, the doctrine of the State, æsthetics and so on, what there is to do; and to the third question by telling me, at least in the philosophy of religion, how the "may hope" is displayed in actual faith and the history of faith—whereas it can certainly not tell me what there is to hope, since religion itself and its conceptual elaboration in theology, whose task this is, do not belong to philosophy. All this is agreed. But philosophy succeeds in rendering me such help in its individual disciplines precisely through each of these disciplines *not* reflecting, and not being able to reflect, on the wholeness of man. Either a philosophical discipline shuts out man in his complex wholeness and considers him only as a bit of nature, as cosmology does; or (as all the other disciplines do) it tears off its own special sphere from the wholeness of man, delimits it from the other spheres, establishes its own basic principles and develops its own methods. In addition it has to remain open and accessible, first to the ideas of metaphysics itself as the doctrine of being, of what is and of existence, secondly to the findings of the philosophical branch disciplines, and thirdly to the discoveries of philosophical anthropology. But least of all may it make itself dependent on the latter; for in every one of those disciplines the possibility of its achieving anything in thought rests precisely on its objectification, on what may be termed its "de-humanization", and even a discipline like the philosophy of history, which is so concerned with the actual man, must, in order to be able to comprehend man *as a historical being*, renounce consideration of the whole man—of which the kind of man who is living outside history in the unchanging rhythm of nature is an essential part. What the philosophical disciplines are able to contribute to answering Kant's first three questions, even if it is only by clarifying them, or teaching me to recognize the problems they contain, they are able to do only by *not* waiting for the answer to the fourth question.

Nor can philosophical anthropology itself set itself the task of establishing a foundation either for metaphysics or for the individual philosophical sciences. If it attempted to answer the question *What is man?* in such a general way that answers to the other questions could be derived from it, it would miss the very reality of its own subject. For it would reach, instead of the subject's genuine wholeness, which can become visible only by the contemplation of all its manifold nature, a false unity which has no reality. A legitimate philosophical anthropology must know that there is not merely a human species but also peoples, not merely a human soul but also types and characters, not merely a human life but also stages in life; only from the systematic comprehension of these and of all other differences, from the recognition of the dynamic that exerts power within every particular reality and between them, and from the constantly new proof of the one in the many, can it come to see the wholeness of man. For that very reason it cannot grasp man in that absoluteness which, though it does not speak out from Kant's fourth question, yet very easily presents itself when an answer is attempted—the answer which Kant, as I have said, avoided giving. Even as it must again and again distinguish within the human race in order to arrive at a solid comprehension, so it must put man in all seriousness into nature, it must compare him with other things, other living creatures, other bearers of consciousness, in order to define his special place reliably for him. Only by this double way of distinction and comparison does it reach the whole, real man who, whatever his people or type or age, knows, what no being on earth but he can know, that he goes the narrow way from birth towards death, tests out what none but he can, a wrestling with destiny, rebellion and reconciliation, and at times even experiences in his own blood, when he is joined by choice to another human being, what goes on secretly in others.

Philosophical anthropology is not intent on reducing philosophical problems to human existence and establishing the philosophical disciplines so to speak from below instead of from above. It is solely intent on knowing man himself. This sets it a task that is absolutely different from all other tasks of thought. For in philosophical anthropology man himself is given to man in the most precise sense as a subject. Here, where the subject is man in his wholeness, the investigator cannot content himself, as in anthropology as an individual science, with considering man as another part of nature and with ignoring the fact that he, the investigator, is himself a man and experiences his humanity in his inner experience in a way that he simply cannot experience any part of nature—

not only in a quite different perspective but also in a quite different dimension of being, in a dimension in which he experiences only this one part of all the parts of nature. Philosophical knowledge of man is essentially man's self-reflection (*Selbstbesinnung*), and man can reflect about himself only when the cognizing person, that is, the philosopher pursuing anthropology, first of all reflects about himself as a person. The principle of individuation, the fundamental fact of the infinite variety of human persons, of whom this one is only one person, of this constitution and no other, does not relativize anthropological knowledge; on the contrary, it gives it its kernel and its skeleton. In order to become genuine philosophical anthropology, everything that is discovered about historical and modern man, about men and women, Indians and Chinese, tramps and emperors, the weak-minded and the genius, must be built up and crystallized round what the philosopher discovers by reflecting about himself. That is a quite different matter from what, say, the psychologist undertakes when he completes and clarifies by reference to his own self in self-observation, self-analysis and experiment, what he knows from literature and observation. For with him it is a matter of individual, objectivized processes and phenomena, of something that is separated from connexion with the whole real person. But the philosophical anthropologist must stake nothing less than his real wholeness, his concrete self. And more; it is not enough for him to stake his self as an *object* of knowledge. He can know the *wholeness* of the person and through it the wholeness of *man* only when he does not leave his *subjectivity* out and does not remain an untouched observer. He must enter, completely and in realit into the act of self-reflection, in order to become aware of h man wholeness. In other words, he must carry out this act of entry into that unique dimension as an act of his *life*, without any prepared philosophical security; that is, he must expose himself to all that can meet you when you are really living. Here you do not attain to knowledge by remaining on the shore and watching the foaming waves, you must make the venture and cast yourself in, you must swim, alert and with all your force, even if a moment comes when you think you are losing consciousness: in this way, and in no other, do you reach anthropological insight. So long as you "have" yourself, have yourself as an object, your experience of man is only as of a thing among things, the wholeness which is to be grasped is not yet "there"; only when you *are*, and nothing else but that, is the wholeness there, and able to be grasped. You perceive only as much as the reality of the "being there" incidentally yields to you; but you do perceive that, and the nucleus of the crystallization develops itself.

An example may clarify more precisely the relation between the psychologist and the anthropologist. If both of them investigate, say, the phenomenon of anger, the psychologist will try to grasp what the angry man feels, what his motives and the impulses of his will are, but the anthropologist will also try to grasp what he is doing. In respect of this phenomenon self-observation, being by nature disposed to weaken the spontaneity and unruliness of anger, will be especially difficult for both of them. The psychologist will try to meet this difficulty by a specific division of consciousness, which enables him to remain outside with the observing part of his being and yet let his passion run its course as undisturbed as possible. Of course this passion can then not avoid becoming similar to that of the actor, that is, though it can still be heightened in comparison with an unobserved passion, its course will be different: there will be a release which is willed and which takes the place of the elemental outbreak, there will be a vehemence which will be more emphasized, more deliberate, more dramatic. The anthropologist can have nothing to do with a division of consciousness, since he has to do with the unbroken wholeness of events, and especially with the unbroken natural connexion between feelings and actions; and this connexion is most powerfully influenced in self-observation, since the pure spontaneity of the action is bound to suffer essentially. It remains for the anthropologist only to resign any attempt to stay outside his observing self, and thus when he is overcome by anger not to disturb it in its course by becoming a spectator of it, but to let it rage to its conclusion without trying to gain a perspective. He will be able to register in the act of recollection what he felt and did then; for him memory takes the place of psychological self-experience. But as great writers in their dealings with other men do not deliberately register their peculiarities and, so to speak, make invisible notes, but deal with them in a natural and uninhibited way, and leave the harvest to the hour of harvest, so it is the memory of the competent anthropologist which has, with reference to himself as to others, the concentrating power which preserves what is essential. In the moment of life he has nothing else in his mind but just to live what is to be lived, he is there with his whole being, undivided, and for that very reason there grows in his thought and recollection the knowledge of human wholeness.

II: FROM ARISTOTLE TO KANT

i

THE man who feels himself solitary is the most readily disposed and most readily fitted for the self-reflection of which I am speaking; that is, the man who by nature or destiny or both is alone with himself and his problematic, and who succeeds, in this blank solitude, in meeting himself, in discovering man in his own self, and the human problematic in his own. The times of spiritual history in which anthropological thought has so far found its depth of experience have been those very times in which a feeling of strict and inescapable solitude took possession of man; and it was the most solitary men in whom the thought became fruitful. In the ice of solitude man becomes most inexorably a question to himself, and just because the question pitilessly summons and draws into play his most secret life he becomes an experience to himself.

In the history of the human spirit I distinguish between epochs of habitation and epochs of homelessness. In the former, man lives in the world as in a house, as in a home. In the latter, man lives in the world as in an open field and at times does not even have four pegs with which to set up a tent. In the former epochs anthropological thought exists only as a part of cosmological thought. In the latter, anthropological thought gains depth and, with it, independence. I will give a few examples of both, which offer a glance at a few chapters of the *pre-history* of philosophical anthropology.

Bernhard Grœthuysen (a pupil of my teacher Wilhelm Dilthey, the founder of the history of philosophical anthropology) rightly said of Aristotle, in a work called *Philosophical Anthropology* (1931), that with him man ceases to be problematic, with him man speaks of himself always as it were in the third person, is only a "case" for himself, he attains to consciousness

of self only as "he", not as "I". The special dimension, in
which man knows himself as he can know himself alone, remains unentered, and for that reason man's special place in
the cosmos remains undiscovered. Man is comprehended only
in the world, the world is not comprehended in him. The
tendency of the Greeks to understand the world as a self-
contained space, in which man too has his fixed place, was
perfected in Aristotle's geocentric spherical system. The
hegemony of the visual sense over the other senses, which
appears among the Greeks for the first time, as a tremendous
new factor in the history of the human spirit, the very hegemony
which enabled them to live a life derived from *images* and to
base a culture on the forming of images, holds good in their
philosophy as well. A visual image of the universe (*Weltbild*)
arises which is formed from visual sense-impressions and
objectified as only the visual sense is able to objectify, and the
experiences of the other senses are as it were retrospectively
recorded in this picture. Even Plato's world of ideas is a visual
world, a world of forms that are seen. But it is not before
Aristotle that the visual image of the universe is realized in
unsurpassable clarity as a universe of *things*, and now man is a
thing among these things of the universe, an objectively comprehensible species beside other species—no longer a sojourner
in a foreign land like the Platonic man, but given his own
dwelling-place in the house of the world, not, indeed, in one
of the highest storeys, but not in one of the lower, either, rather
in the respectable middle. The presupposition for a philosophical anthropology in the sense of Kant's fourth question
is lacking here.

2

The first to pose the genuine anthropological question anew,
and in the first person—more than seven centuries after
Aristotle—was Augustine. The solitude out of which he asked
the question can only be understood when one realizes that
that round and unified world of Aristotle had long since
collapsed. It collapsed because the soul of man, divided against
itself, could no longer grasp as truth anything but a world
which was divided against itself. In place of the sphere which
had collapsed there now arose two autonomous and mutually
hostile kingdoms, the kingdom of light and the kingdom of

darkness. We meet them again in almost every system of that widespread and manifold spiritual movement of gnosis, which at that time seized the embarrassed heirs of the great oriental and antique cultures, split the godhead and emptied value from creation; and in the most consistent of these systems, in Manichæism, there is even, consistently, a double earth. Here man can no longer be a thing among things, and he can have no fixed place in the world. Since he consists of soul and body he is divided between the two kingdoms, he is simultaneously the scene and the prize of the struggle. In each man the original man who fell is manifested; in each man the problematic of being is stated in terms of life. Augustine emerged from the school of Manichæism. Homeless in the world, solitary between the higher and the lower powers, he remains homeless and solitary even after he found salvation in Christianity as a redemption that had *already taken place*. So he asks Kant's question in the first person, and not, indeed, as with Kant, as an objectivized problem, which the hearers of his logic lectures could certainly not understand as a question directed to themselves; but he takes up the question of the psalmist again in real address, with another sense and in another tone: *What is man that thou art mindful of him?* He asks for information from one who can give it: *quid ergo sum, Deus meus? quæ natura mea?* He does not mean only himself; the word *natura* says clearly that in his person he means man, that man whom he calls the *grande profundum*, the great mystery. And he even draws that same anthropological conclusion which we have heard in Malebranche; he does it in his famous accusation of men, that they marvel at mountains, at the waves of the sea and the course of the stars, but "relinquish" themselves without being astonished at themselves. This wonder of man at himself, which Augustine demands as a result of his own self-experience, is something quite different from the wonder with which Aristotle in his metaphysic makes all philosophizing begin. The Aristotelian man wonders at man among the rest, but only as a part of a quite astonishing world. The Augustinian man wonders at that in man which cannot be understood as a part of the world, as a thing among things; and where that former wondering has already passed into methodical philosophizing, the Augustinian wondering manifests itself in its true depth and uncanniness. It is not philosophy, but it affects all future philosophy.

In the post-augustinian west it is not the contemplation of nature, as with the Greeks, but faith which builds a new house in the cosmos for the solitary soul. The Christian cosmos arises; and this was so real for every mediæval Christian that all who read the *Divina Commedia* made in spirit the journey to the nethermost spiral of hell and stepped up over Lucifer's back, through purgatory, to the heaven of the Trinity, not as an expedition into lands as yet unknown, but as a crossing of regions already fully mapped. Once again there is a self-enclosed universe, once again a house in which man is allowed to dwell. This universe is still more finite than that of Aristotle, for here finite time too is taken into the image in all seriousness—the finite time of the Bible, which here appears, however, transformed into a Christian form. The pattern of this image of the universe is a cross, whose vertical beam is finite space from heaven to hell, leading right across the heart of the human being, and whose cross-beam is finite time from the creation of the world to the end of days; which makes time's centre, the death of Christ, fall coveringly and redemptively on the centre of space, the heart of the poor sinner. The mediæval image of the universe is built round this pattern. In it Dante painted life, the life of men and spirits, but the conceptual framework was set up for him by Thomas Aquinas. As of Aristotle, so too it is true of Aquinas, though he was a theologian, and therefore in duty bound to know about the real man who says "I" and is addressed as "Thou", that man speaks here "as it were always in the third person". In Aquinas's world-system man is indeed a separate species of a quite special kind, because in him the human soul, the lowest of the spirits, is substantially united with the human body, the highest of physical things, so that man appears as it were as "the horizon and the dividing line of spiritual and physical nature". But Aquinas knows no special problem and no special problematic of human life, such as Augustine experienced and expressed with trembling heart. The anthropological question has here come to rest again; in man, housed and unproblematic, no impulse stirs to questioning self-confrontation, or it is soon appeased.

3

In the late middle ages there already emerged a new earnestness about man as man. The finite world still hedged man safely in; *hunc mundum haud aliud esse, quam amplissimam quandam hominis domum*, says Carolus Bovillus as late as the sixteenth century. But the same Bovillus cries to man: *homo es, sistere in homine*, and thus takes up the motif that had been expressed by the great Cusa before him: *homo non vult esse nisi homo*. This by itself certainly does not imply that man by his nature steps out of and forth from the world. For Cusa there is not a thing which would not prefer its own being to all being and its own way of being to all other ways of being; all that is wishes in eternity to be nothing but itself, but to be this one thing always more perfectly in the way proper to its nature; it is precisely from this that the harmony of the universe grows, for every being contains everything in a special "contraction".

But with man there is also thought, the reason which measures and values. He has in himself all created things, like God; but God has them in himself as the archetypes, man has them in himself as relations and values. Cusa compares God to the coining master of the mint, and man to the money-changer with his scale of values. God can create all, we can know all; we can know all because we too carry all in ourselves potentially. And soon after Cusa, Pico della Mirandola draws from this proud self-assurance the anthropological conclusion, which again reminds us of the words of Malebranche: *nos autem peculiare aliquid in homine quaerimus, unde et dignitas ei propria et imago divinae substantiae cum nulla sibi creatura communis comperiatur*. Here the theme of anthropology already clearly appears. But it appears without that setting of the problematic which is indispensable for the genuine establishment of anthropology—the deadly earnestness of the question about man. Man steps forth here in such autonomy and such consciousness of power that the real question does not step up to him. These thinkers of the Renaissance affirm that man can know, but the Kantian question, *what* he can know, is still quite foreign to them: he can know all. It is true that the last in the series of these thinkers, Bovillus, excepts God: the human spirit cannot reach God, but Bovillus lets the whole universe be known by man, who has been created outside it as its spectator, in fact, as its eye. So securely are these pioneers of a new era still housed in a secure universe. Cusa, it is true, speaks of the spatial and temporal infinity of the universe, and thus deprives the earth of its central position, and destroys in thought the mediæval pattern. But this infinity is only one that is thought, it is not yet beheld and lived. Man is not yet solitary again, he has still to learn again to ask the solitary man's question.

But at the same time as Bovillus was extolling the universe as man's *amplissima domus*, all the walls of the house were in fact already crumbling beneath the blows of Copernicus, the unlimited was pressing in from every side, and man was standing in a universe which in actual fact could no longer be experienced as a house. Man was no longer secure, but though at first he had a heroic enthusiasm for the grandeur of this universe, as with Bruno, then a mathematical enthusiasm for its harmony, as with Kepler, yet finally, more than a century after the death of Copernicus and the publication of his work, the new reality of man proved itself to be more powerful than the new reality of the universe. Pascal, a great scientist, a mathematician and a physicist, young and destined to die early, experienced beneath the starry heavens not merely, as Kant did, their majesty, but still more powerfully their uncanniness: *le silence éternel de ces espaces infinis m'effraie*. With a clarity that has not since then been surpassed he discerns the twin infinities, that of the infinitely great and that of the infinitely small, and so comes to know man's limitation, his inadequacy, the casualness of his existence: *combien de royaumes nous ignorent!* The enthusiasm of Bruno and Kepler which as it were skipped man is here replaced by a terribly clear, melancholy yet believing sobriety. It is the sobriety of the man who has become more deeply solitary than ever before, and with a sober pathos he frames the anthropological question afresh: *qu'est ce qu'un homme dans l'infini?* Cusa's sovereignty, in which man boasted that he carried all things in himself and thus that he could know all things, is opposed here by the insight of the solitary man, who endures being exposed as a human being to infinity: *Connaissons donc notre portée: nous sommes quelque chose, et ne sommes pas tout; ce que nous avons d'être nous dérobe la connaissance des premiers principes, qui naissent du néant; et le peu que nous avons d'être nous cache la vue de l'infini.* But, in this renewal of anthropological thought, from the very fact that self-reflection is carried out with such clarity, there is yielded man's special place in the cosmos. *L'homme n'est qu'un roseau, le plus faible de la nature: mais c'est un roseau pensant. Il ne faut pas que l'univers entier s'arme pour l'écraser: une vapeur, une goutte d'eau, suffit pour le tuer. Mais, quand l'univers l'écraserait, l'homme serait encore plus noble que ce qui le tue, parce qu'il sait qu'il meurt et l'avantage que l'univers a sur lui. L'univers n'en sait rien.* This is not the stoic attitude over again; it is the new attitude of the person who has become homeless in infinity, for here everything depends on the knowledge that man's grandeur is born of his misery, that he is different from all things just because even as he passes away he can be a child of the spirit. Man is the being who knows his situation in the universe and is able, so long as he is in his senses, to continue this knowledge. What is decisive is not that this creature of all dares to step up to the universe and know it—however amazing this is in itself; what is decisive is that he knows the relation between the universe and himself. Thereby from out of the midst of the universe something that faces the universe has arisen. And that means that this "from out of the midst" has its own special problematic.

4

We have seen that the strict anthropological question, which refers to man's specific problematic, becomes insistent in times when as it were the original contract between the universe and man is dissolved and man finds himself a stranger and solitary in the world. The end of an image of the universe, that is, the end of a *security* in the universe, is soon followed by a fresh questioning from man who has become insecure, and homeless, and hence problematic to himself. But it can be shown that a *way* leads from one such crisis to the next, and on to the one after that. The crises have something essential in common, but they are not similar. Aristotle's cosmological image of the universe breaks up from within, through the soul's experience of the problem of evil in its depth, and through its feeling of being surrounded by a divided universe; Aquinas's theological image of the universe breaks up from without, through the universe manifesting itself as unlimited. What causes the crisis is on the one occasion a myth, the dualistic myth of gnosis, on the other occasion it is the cosmos of science itself, no longer clothed with any myth. Pascal's solitude is truly historically *later* than Augustine's; it is more complete and harder to overcome. And in fact something new arises that has not existed before; work is carried out on a new *image* of the universe, but a new *house* in the universe is no longer built. Once the concept of infinity has been taken seriously a human dwelling can no longer be made of the universe. And infinity itself must be included in the image of the universe—which is a paradox, for an image, if it is really an image, is limited, yet now the unlimited itself must enter the image. In other words, when the point is reached where the image ends, the point, say—to use the language of modern astronomy—of the nebulæ, which are a hundred million light-years distant from us, then it must be felt with the utmost urgency that the image does not and cannot end. Incidentally it may be noticed, though it is self-evident, that Einstein's concept of finite space would be by no means fit for rebuilding the universe as a house for man, since this "finitude" is essentially different from that which produced the feeling of the universe as a house. And more, it is certainly possible that this concept of the universe, which has been disclosed by the mathematician's genius, freed from sensuality, can one day become accessible to natural human understanding; but it will no longer be in a position to produce a new *image* of the universe, not even a paradoxical image as the Copernican concept could. For the Copernican concept only fulfilled what the human soul had vaguely felt in the hours when the house of universal space, the Aristotelian or the Thomist, seemed too cramped, and it dared to beat on its walls to see if a window could not be thrown out into a world beyond—it fulfilled it, it is true, in a way which deeply perturbed this same human soul, which cannot help being as it is, once and for all. But Einstein's concept of the universe signifies no fulfilment of the spirit's inkling, but the contradiction of all its inklings and imaginings: this universe can still be thought, but it can no longer be imaged, the man who thinks it no longer really lives in it. The generation which works modern cosmology into its natural thought will be the first, after several millennia of changing images of the universe, which will have to forego the possession of an image of its universe; this very fact, that it lives in a universe which cannot be imaged, will probably be its feeling of the universe, so to speak its image of the universe: *imago mundi nova—imago nulla.*

5

I have far anticipated the course of our investigation.
Let us return to our second example and ask how from
there we reach our age in its special human homelessness
and solitude, and its new setting of the anthropological
question.

The greatest attempt to master the situation of post-
copernican man, as mediated to us by Pascal, was undertaken
shortly after Pascal's death by a man who was destined to die
almost as young. Spinoza's attempt, from the point of view
of our problem, means that astronomical infinity is both unconditionally accepted and stripped of its uncanniness: extension,
of which this infinity is stated and demonstrated, is only one
of the infinitely many attributes of infinite substance, and it is
one of the two which alone we know—the other is thought.
Infinite substance, also called God by Spinoza, in relation to
which this infinity of space can be only one of infinitely many
attributes, *loves*, it loves itself, and it loves itself also, and
especially, in man, for the love of the human spirit for God is
only *pars infiniti amoris, quo Deus se ipsum amat*. Here one may
say that Pascal's question, what is a man in the infinite, is
answered: he is a being in whom God loves himself. Cosmology
and anthropology appear here imposingly reconciled, but the
cosmos has not again become what it was with Aristotle and
Aquinas—a manifold universe, ordered as an image, in which
every thing and every being has its place and the being "man"
feels himself at home in union with them all. A new security
of being in the world is not given; yet for Spinoza this is not
necessary: his devotion to the infinite *natura naturans* lifts him
above the mere outline character of his *natura naturata*, which
is drawn into the system only conceptually, as the aggregate
of the divine modes, and in which the kinds and orders of
being are not really grasped and united. There is no new
house of the universe, no ground-plan of a house and no
material for it: a man accepts his homelessness, his lack of a
universe, because it enables him to have *adæquata cognitio
æternæ et infinitæ essentiæ Dei*, that is, enables him to know how
God loves himself in *him*. A man, however, who knows this
can no longer be problematic to himself.

In Spinoza's intellectual separatedness reconciliation was
effected. But in actual man's concrete life with the actual

world, in the unseparated and inseparable life out of which Pascal spoke and expressed at once man's frailty and the world's terror, it became increasingly difficult to effect it. The age of rationalism, which weakened and adapted Spinoza's objectification of being in which world and man are united, breaks off the point of the anthropological question; but it remains embedded in the flesh and secretly festers.

Certainly, one can point to a man who was a true heir of Spinoza in the post-rationalist age and was made happy by Spinoza's "atmosphere of peace", who was "a child of peace" and minded to keep peace "for ever and ever with the whole world", who grasped and penetrated this world in its living fulness, as a whole which gives us in its synthesis with spirit "the most blissful assurance of the harmony of existence". Gœthe, who in his place in history appears to us in many respects like a glorious lethal euphoria before the end of an age, was undoubtedly still able to live really in the cosmos; but he, who had plumbed the depths of solitude ("I can speak only with God about many things"), was exposed in his inmost being to the anthropological question. Certainly, man to him was "the first conversation which nature holds with God", yet, like Werther, he heard "the voice of the creature completely driven into itself, lacking itself, and falling irresistibly downwards".

6

Kant was the first to understand the anthropological question critically, in such a way that an answer was given to Pascal's real concern. This answer—though it was not directed metaphysically to the being of man but epistemologically to his attitude to the world—grasped the fundamental problems. What sort of a world is it, which man knows? How can man, as he is, in his altered reality, know at all? How does man stand in the world he knows in this way—what is it to him and what is he to it?

In order to understand the extent to which the *Critique of Pure Reason* may be taken as an answer to Pascal's question we must consider the question once more. To Pascal infinite space is an uncanny thing which makes him conscious of the questionable nature of man, exposed as he is to this world. But what stirs and terrifies him is not the newly discovered infinity of space in contrast to the finitude previously believed of it. Rather it is the fact that, by the impression of infinity, any concept of space, a finite no less than an infinite, becomes uncanny to him, for really to try and imagine finite space is as hazardous a venture as really to try and imagine infinite space, and makes man just as emphatically conscious that he is not a match for the world. When I was about fourteen years of age I myself experienced this in a way which has deeply influenced my whole life. A necessity I could not understand swept over me: I had to try again and again to imagine the edge of space, or its edgelessness, time with a beginning and an end or a time without beginning or end, and both were equally impossible, equally hopeless—yet there seemed to be only the choice between the one or the other absurdity. Under an irresistible compulsion I reeled from one to the other, at times so closely threatened with the danger of madness that I seriously thought of avoiding it by suicide. Salvation came to the fifteen year old boy in a book, Kant's *Prolegomena to all Future Metaphysics*, which I dared to read although its first sentence told me that it was not intended for the use of pupils but for future teachers. This book showed me that space and time are only the forms in which my human view of what is, necessarily works itself out; that is, they were not attached to the inner nature of the world, but to the nature of my senses. It further taught that it is just as impossible to all my concepts to say that the world is infinite in space and time as to say that it is finite. "For neither can be inherent in experience", and neither can be situated in the world itself, since the world is given to us only as an appearance "whose existence and connexions take place only in experience". Both can be asserted and both can be proved; between the thesis and the antithesis there exists an irresoluble contradiction, an antinomy of cosmological ideas; being itself is not touched by either. Now I was no longer compelled to torture myself by trying to imagine first the one unimaginable and then the opposite equally unimaginable thing: I could gain an inkling that being itself was beyond the reach alike of the finitude and the infinity of space and time, since it only appeared in space and time but did not itself enter into this appearance. At that time I began to gain an inkling of the existence of eternity as something quite different from the infinite, just as it is something quite different from the finite, and of the possibility of a connexion between me, a man, and the eternal.

Kant's answer to Pascal may be formulated after this fashion: what approaches you out of the world, hostile and terrifying, the mystery of its space and time, is the mystery of your own comprehension of the world and the mystery of your own being. Your question *What is man?* is thus a genuine question to which you must seek the answer.

Here Kant's anthropological question is shown in all clarity as a legacy to our age. No new house in the universe is being planned for man, but he, as the builder of houses, is being required to know himself. Kant sees the age after him in all its uncertainty as an age of self-restraint and self-reflection, as the anthropological age. First—as is clear from that well-known letter of 1793—he saw in the treatment of the fourth question a task which he set himself, and whose resolution was to follow that of the first three questions; he did not really set about it, but he set it in such clarity and urgency that it remained a task set to following generations, till at last our own generation is preparing to place itself in its service.

III: HEGEL AND MARX

I

FIRST, however, there follows such a radical alienation from the anthropological setting of the question as has probably never happened before in the history of human thought. I mean the system of Hegel, that is, the system which has exercised a decisive influence not merely on an age's way of thought but also on its social and political action—an influence which can be characterized as the dispossessing of the concrete human person and the concrete human community in favour of universal reason, its dialectical processes and its objective structures. This influence, as is well-known, has also operated on thinkers who, though deriving from Hegel, have travelled far from him, such as Kierkegaard on the one hand, the critic of modern Christianity, who certainly grasped like no other thinker of our time the significance of the person, but still saw the life of the person entirely in the forms of the Hegelian dialectic as a movement from the æsthetic to the ethical and from there to the religious, and Marx on the other hand, who entered with an unexampled earnestness on the actuality of human society, but considered its development in forms of Hegelian dialectic as a movement from primitive communal economy to private property and from there to socialism.

In his youth Hegel accepted Kant's anthropological setting of the question, which was at that time not published in its final form but whose sense was certainly known to the young man so deeply engaged with Kant. From this point his thought proceeded in a genuinely anthropological fashion, in that he sought to reach, by understanding the organic connexion of the spirit's capacities, what Kant himself knew only as a regulative idea, not as living being, namely, what the young Hegel himself called (about 1798) the "unity of the whole man". What he strove after then has been rightly called an anthropological metaphysic. He took the concrete human person so seriously that it was by him that he demonstrated his conception of man's special position. To illustrate this I quote a beautiful sentence from the notes *The Spirit of Christianity and its Destiny*, which clearly shows the way in which Hegel, going beyond Kant, seeks to penetrate the anthropological problem: "In every man himself there is light and life, he is the property of light; and he is not illumined by a light like a dark body which has only a reflected brilliance, but his own fuel is being kindled and there is a flame of its own." It is worth noticing that Hegel does not speak of a general concept of man here, but of "every man", that is, of the real person from whom genuine philosophical anthropology must seriously begin.

But this setting of the problem will be sought in vain in the later Hegel, in the one, that is, who has influenced a century's thought. I should go so far as to say that the real man will be sought in vain in the later Hegel. If one, for instance, looks through the section in the *Encyclopædia of the Philosophical Sciences* which is entitled "Anthropology", one sees that it begins with statements about what spirit is and signifies, then passes to statements about the soul as substance. There follow valuable references to distinctions within mankind and human life, especially to distinctions of age, of sex, between sleeping and waking, and so on—but without our being able to relate all this to a question about the reality and significance of this human life. Also the chapters about feeling, self-feeling, and habit, give no help, and even in the chapter entitled "The real soul" we learn only that the soul is real as the "identity of the inner with the outer". The systematic philosopher Hegel no longer begins, like the young Hegel, with man, but with universal reason; man is now only the principle in which the universal reason reaches perfect self-consciousness and thus completion. All the contradiction in human life and history does not lead to the anthropological questionableness and question, but presents itself as a "ruse" which the idea makes use of in order to reach its own perfection through the very fact that it overcomes contradiction. The claim is made that Kant's fundamental question *What is man?* is finally answered here; in reality it is obscured, even eliminated. Even the first of Kant's three philosophical questions which precede the anthropological question, the question *What can I know?* is silenced. If man is the place and medium in which the universal reason knows itself, then there is simply no limitation to what man can know. In terms of the idea man knows all things, just as in terms of the idea he realizes all things, that is, all that is in the reason. Both the knowing and the realizing take place in history, in which the perfect State appears as the completion of being and the perfect metaphysic appears as the completion of knowledge. By experiencing both we experience simultaneously and adequately the meaning of history and the meaning of man.

Hegel undertakes to give man a new security, to build a new house of the universe for him. No further house can be built in Copernican space; Hegel builds it in *time* alone, which is "the supreme power of all that is" (1805).

Man's new house is to be time in the form of history whose meaning can be perfectly learned and understood. Hegel's system is the third great attempt at security within western thought; following Aristotle's cosmological attempt and Aquinas's theological attempt it is the logological attempt. All insecurity, all unrest about meaning, all terror at decision, all abysmal problematic is eliminated. The universal reason goes its undeflectable way through history, and knowing man knows this way, rather, his knowledge is the real goal and end of the way in which truth as it realizes itself knows itself in its realization. The stages of the way follow one another in an absolute order: the law of dialectic, in which the thesis is relieved by the antithesis and the antithesis by the synthesis, is sovereign over them. As one goes with sure step from storey to storey and from room to room of a well-built house with its solid foundations and walls and roof, so Hegel's all-knowing man goes through the new world-house, history, whose whole meaning he knows. If only he shares thoroughly in the thought of the new metaphysic his glance is saved from dizziness, for he can survey everything. The young man over whom the dread of the infinite swept since the Copernican revolution, when he opened the window of his room at night and stood solitary in the darkness, is to know peace now; if the cosmos, in its infinite greatness and infinite smallness, denies itself to his heart, the reliable order of history, which "is nothing but the realization of the spirit", takes him and makes him at home. Solitude is overcome, and the question about man is obliterated.

But now there appears a remarkable historical phenomenon. In earlier times it took some centuries for criticism to destroy a cosmic security and to reinvigorate the anthropological question. Now the Hegelian image of the universe had, indeed, tremendous effect for a century, penetrating every realm of the spirit; but the rebellion against it was raised immediately, and with it the demand for an anthropological perspective was renewed. The Hegelian house of the universe is admired, explained, and imitated; but it proves uninhabitable. Thought confirms it and the word glorifies it; but the real man does not set foot in it. In the universe of Aristotle real ancient man felt himself at home; similarly with the real Christian in the universe of Aquinas; the universe of Hegel has never become the real universe for real modern man. In the thought of mankind Hegel succeeded in repressing Kant's anthropological question only for a moment; in the life of man he did not overcome even for a moment the great anthropological unrest which in modern times is first expressed in Pascal's question.

I wish to indicate here only one of the reasons for this phenomenon. An intellectual image of the universe which builds on *time* can never give the same feeling of security as one which builds on space. To grasp this fact we must distinguish sharply between cosmological and anthropological time. We can as it were comprehend cosmological time, that is, make use of the concept of it, as if all time were present in a relative way, even though the future is not given to us at all. Anthropological time, on the other hand, that is, time in respect of actual, consciously willing man, cannot be comprehended, because the future cannot be present, since it depends to a certain extent, in my consciousness and will, on my decision. Anthropological time is real only in the part which has become cosmological time, that is, in the part called the past. This distinction is not identical with Bergson's well-known one, whose *durée* means a flowing present, whereas the anthropological time which I mean functions essentially through the memory—of course, in respect of the present, this is always "open" memory: as soon as we experience something *as time*, as soon as we become conscious of the dimension of time as such, the memory is already in play; in other words, the pure present knows no specific consciousness of time. It is true that we do not know cosmological time as a whole either, in spite of our knowledge of the regular movements of the stars, and so on; but our thoughts may be engaged with it as with something real, even in what we do not know of this, and naturally even in what we do not know of future human actions, since in the moment of thought all their causes are present. With the anthropological future, on the other hand, our thoughts cannot be engaged as with something real, since my decision, which will take place in the next moment, has not yet taken place. The same is true of the decisions of other men, since I know, on the basis of the anthropological concept of man as a consciously willing being, that he cannot be understood simply as a part of the world. Within the boundaries of the human world which is given in the problem of human being there is no certainty of the future. The time which Hegel introduced into the groundwork of his image of the universe, cosmological time, is not actual human time but a time in terms of thought. It lies in the power of human thought but not of living human imagination to incorporate perfection in the reality of what is; it is something which can be thought, but not lived. An intellectual image of the universe, which incorporates "the goal of universal history", has no power in this part of it to give assurance, the unbroken line changes as it were into a dotted line, which even the mightiest philosopher cannot transform for us into a continuous line. The only exception is an image of the universe which is grounded on faith: the power of faith alone can experience perfection as something assured, because it is something guaranteed to us by someone we trust—whom we trust as the guarantor also for what has not yet come to be in our world. In the history of religion we know above all two such great images of the

universe, that of Persian Messianism, in which the future final
and complete victory of light over darkness is guaranteed to
the precise hour, and that of Israelite Messianism, which
rejects such precision because it understands man himself, frail,
contradictory, questionable man himself as an element that
can both contribute to salvation and hinder it; but final and
complete salvation is guaranteed to this form of Messianism as
well, in faith in the saving power of God which carries out in
the midst of history its work on resisting man. In the Christian
picture of the universe, as we saw it in its finished form in
Aquinas, the effect of Messianism persists, though weakened.
In Hegel's system Messianism is secularized, that is, it is
transferred from the sphere of faith, in which man feels himself
to be bound up with the object of his faith, to the sphere of
evident conviction, in which man contemplates and considers
the object of his conviction. This has been repeatedly remarked.
But it has not been sufficiently observed that in such a trans-
ference the element of *trust* cannot be taken over at the same
time. Faith in creation may be replaced by a conviction
about evolution, faith in revelation by a conviction about increasing knowledge, but faith in salvation will not really be
replaced by a conviction about the perfecting of the world by
the idea, since only trust in the trustworthy is able to establish
a relation of unconditional certainty towards the *future*. I say,
not *really* replaced, that is, not in and for real life. For in
mere thought a conviction about the self-realization of an
absolute reason in history does not achieve less, even for man's
relation to the future, than a messianic faith in God; in fact,
it achieves even more, since it is, so to speak, chemically pure
and undisturbed by any kind of adulteration by actuality.
But thought does not have the power to build up man's real
life, and the strictest philosophical certainty cannot endow the
soul with that intimate certitude that the world which is so
imperfect will be brought to its perfection. In the last resort
the problem of the future does not exist for Hegel, since he
saw, in fact, in his own age and in his own philosophy the
beginning of fulfilment, so that the dialectical movement of
the idea through time has really reached its end already. But
what devoted admirer of the philosopher has ever truly shared
in this worldly auto-messianism, that is, not merely with
thought, but—as has continually happened in the history of
religion—with the whole real life?

It is true that there is a significant phenomenon within the sphere of Hegel's influence which seems to contradict what I said about the attitude to the future. I mean Marx's doctrine of history, which is based on the Hegelian dialectic. Here too a certainty with regard to perfection is proclaimed, here too Messianism is secularized; yet real man, in the shape of the modern proletarian masses, has entered into this certainty and made this secularized Messianism his faith. How is this to be understood? What Marx has carried out with Hegel's method can be called a sociological reduction. That is, he does not wish to present any image of the universe; none is necessary any more. (The representation of an image of the universe which Engels later—in 1880—attempted, under the title *Dialectic of Nature*, a quite derivatory rendering of the teaching of Hæckel and other evolutionists, completely contradicts the fundamental restriction made by Marx.) What Marx wants to give the men of his age is not an image of the universe but only an image of society, more precisely, the image of the way by which human society is to reach its perfection. The Hegelian idea or universal reason is replaced by human conditions of production, from whose transformation proceeds the transformation of society. Conditions of production are what are essential and basic for Marx; they are the point from which he starts and to which he retraces everything; there is no other origin and no other principle for him. Certainly, they cannot be considered, like Hegel's universal reason, as the first and the last; sociological reduction means an absolute renunciation of a perspective of being in which there exists a first and a last. In Marx the home in which man can dwell—that is, will be able to dwell when it is ready—is built up on conditions of production alone. Man's world is society. In actual fact a security is established by this reduction which the proletarian masses really did accept and take up into their lives, at least for the duration of an age. When the attempt has been made within Marxism, as by Engels, to eliminate this reduction and to present the proletariat with an image of the universe, the proved vital security has been confused with a completely baseless intellectual security and thus robbed of its genuine force.

Certainly, something else, which is particularly important, is added to the reduction. Hegel perceives the beginning of fulfilment in his own age, in which the absolute spirit reaches its goal. Marx simply cannot see the fulfilment beginning in the heyday of capitalism, which has to be relieved by socialism which brings about the fulfilment. He sees, however, in his age something existing in which fulfilment is manifested and guaranteed—namely, the proletariat. In the existence of the proletariat the elimination of capitalism, the "negation of the negation", is bodily declared. "When the proletariat," says Marx, "proclaims the dissolution of the hitherto existing world-order, then it is only expressing the mystery of its own existence, for it is the actual dissolution of this world-order." By this fundamental thesis Marx is able to provide the proletariat with a security. Nothing else needs to be believed in but its own continuation, till the hour in which its existence becomes its action. The future appears here as bound to the directly experienced present and assured by it. Thought consequently does not have the power to construct man's real life; but life itself has this power, and the spirit has it, if it acknowledges the power of life and joins to it its own power, which is different in nature and effect.

Marx is both right and wrong in this view of the power of social life proper. He is right, since in fact social life, like all life, itself produces the forces which can renew it. But he is wrong, since human life, to which social life belongs, is distinct from all other kinds of life by the power of decision which is distinct from all other kinds of power: this power is different from them all in that it does not appear as quantity, but reveals the measure of its strength only in action itself. It depends on the direction and force of this power how far the renewing powers of life as such are able to take effect, and even whether they are not transformed into powers of destruction. The development depends essentially on something which cannot be explained in terms of the development. In other words, neither in man's personal nor in his social life must anthropological time be confused with cosmological time, not even when the latter is endowed with the form of the dialectical process, as, for example, in Marx's famous statement that capitalist production breeds its negation "with the necessity of a natural process". With all his sociological reduction he does no more than follow in Hegel's tracks and introduce cosmological time—that is, a time which is alien to man's reality—into his consideration of the future. The problem of human decision, as the origin of events and of destiny, including social events and destiny, does not exist here at all. Such a doctrine can persist in power only so long as it does not clash with a moment in history in which the problematic of human decision makes itself felt to a terrifying degree, I mean a moment in which catastrophic events exercise a frightening and paralysing influence over the power of decision, and repeatedly move it to renunciation in favour of a negative élite of men—men who, knowing no inner restraint, do not act as they do from real decision, but only stick to their power. In such situations the man who is striving for the renewal of social life, socialist man, can only share in the decision of his society's destiny if he believes in his own power of decision and knows that it matters, for only then does he actualize, in the effect which his decision has, the highest strength of his power of decision. In such a moment he can only share in the decision of his society's destiny if the view of life which he holds does not contradict his *experience*.

Hegel as it were compulsorily combined the course of the stars and of history into a speculative security. Marx, who confined himself to the human world, ascribed to it alone a security in regard to the future, which is likewise dialectic, but has the effect of an actual security. To-day this security has perished in the ordered chaos of a terrible historical revulsion. Gone is the calm, a new anthropological dread has arisen, the question about man's being faces us as never before in all its grandeur and terror—no longer in philosophical attire, but in the nakedness of existence. No dialectical guarantee keeps man from falling; it lies with himself to lift his foot and take the step which leads him away from the abyss. The strength to take this step cannot come from any security in regard to the future, but only from those depths of insecurity in which man, overshadowed by despair, answers with his decision the question about man's being.

IV: FEUERBACH AND NIETZSCHE

I

WITH Marx we are already in the midst of the anthropological rebellion against Hegel. At the same time we can see in perfect clarity in Marx the peculiar character of this rebellion. There is a return to the anthropological limitation of the picture of the universe without a return to the anthropological *problematic* and setting of the question. The philosopher who so rebelled against Hegel, and as whose pupil in this respect Marx has to be regarded, in spite of all differences and even oppositions between them, is Feuerbach. Feuerbach's anthropological reduction precedes Marx's sociological reduction.

In order to understand aright Feuerbach's struggle against Hegel and its significance for anthropology, it is best to begin with the fundamental question, What is the *beginning* of philosophy? Kant, in opposition to rationalism, and based on Hume, had established cognition as the very first thing for philosophizing men, and thus made the decisive philosophical problem what knowing is and how it is possible. This problem then led him, as we saw, to the anthropological question— what kind of a being is man, who knows in this way? Hegel, perfectly conscious of what he was doing, passed over this first thing. In his view, as he expressed it with complete clarity in the first edition of his *Encyclopædia of the Philosophical Sciences* (1817), there must not be *any* immediate object at the beginning of philosophy, since immediacy is by nature opposed to philosophical thought; in other words, philosophy is not permitted, as with Kant and Descartes before him, to start from the situation of the philosophizing man, but it must "anticipate". He carries out this anticipating in the sentence: "Pure being is the beginning," which is straightway explained as follows: "Now, pure being is pure abstraction." On this basis Hegel is able to make the development of the universal reason, instead of that of human cognition, into the object of philosophy. This is the point where Feuerbach puts in his attack. The universal reason is only a new concept for God; and as theology, when it said "God", only transferred the human essence itself from earth to heaven, so metaphysics, when it says "universal reason", only transfers the human essence from concrete existence to abstract existence. The new philosophy— so Feuerbach formulates it in his manifesto, *Principles of the Philosophy of the Future* (1843)—has as its principle "not the absolute, that is, the abstract, spirit—in short, not reason *in abstracto*, but man's real, whole being". Unlike Kant, Feuerbach wishes to make the whole being, not human cognition, the beginning of philosophizing. In his view nature too is to be understood only as the "basis of man". "The new philosophy", he says, "makes man . . . the exclusive, universal . . . object of philosophy, and thus makes anthropology . . . the universal science." Thus the anthropological reduction, the reduction of being to human existence, is carried out.   One could say that Hegel, in the position he assigns to man, follows the first creation story, that of the first chapter of *Genesis*, of the creation of *nature*, where man is created last and given his place in the cosmos, yet in such a way that creation is not only ended but also completed in its significance now that the "image of God" has appeared; while Feuerbach follows the second creation story, that of the second chapter of *Genesis*, of the creation of *history*, where there is no world but that of man, man in its centre, giving all living things their true name. Never before has a philosophical anthropology been so emphatically demanded. But Feuerbach's postulate does not lead beyond the threshold to which Kant's fourth question led us. More, in one decisive respect we feel that we are not merely no further advanced than with Kant, but actually less advanced. For in Feuerbach's demand the question *What is man?* is not included at all. Indeed, his demand means a renunciation of this question. His anthropological reduction of being is a reduction to *unproblematic* man. But the real man, man who faces a being that is not human, and is time and again over-powered by it as by an inhuman fate, yet dares to know this being and this fate, is not unproblematic; rather, he is the beginning of all problematic. A philosophical anthropology is not possible unless it begins from the anthropological *question*. It can be attained only by a formulation and expression of this question which is more profound, sharp, strict, and cruel than it has ever been before. Nietzsche's real significance lies, as we shall see, in his undertaking of such a deepening and sharpening of the question.

But we must first continue to deal with Feuerbach, for the sake of a matter which is extraordinarily important for the thought of our age about man. By man, whom he considers as the highest subject of philosophy, Feuerbach does not mean man as an individual, but man with man—the connexion of *I* and *Thou*. "The individual man for himself," runs his manifesto, "does not have man's being in himself, either as a moral being or a thinking being. Man's being is contained only in community, in the unity of man with man—a unity which rests, however, only on the reality of the difference between I and Thou." Feuerbach did not elaborate these words in his later writings. Marx did not take up into his concept of society the element of the real relation between the really different *I* and *Thou*, and for that very reason opposed an unreal individualism with a collectivism which was just as unreal. But in those words Feuerbach, passing beyond Marx, introduced that discovery of the *Thou*, which has been called "the Copernican revolution" of modern thought, and "an elemental happening which is just as rich in consequences as the idealist discovery of the I" and "is bound to lead to a new beginning of European thought, pointing beyond the Cartesian contribution to modern philosophy".[1] I myself in my youth was given a decisive impetus by Feuerbach.

2

Nietzsche depends much more solidly on Feuerbach's anthropological reduction than is usually admitted. He falls short of Feuerbach in that he loses sight of the autonomous sphere of the relation between *I* and *Thou* and is content, in respect of inter-human relations, to continue on the line of the French moral philosophers of the seventeenth and eighteenth centuries and complete it by depicting the origin and development of morality. But he far surpasses Feuerbach in that, like no other previous thinker, he brings man into the centre of his thought about the universe, and not, as with Feuerbach, man as a clear and unambiguous being, but rather man as a problematic being; and thereby he endows the anthropological question with an unprecedented force and passion.

The questionableness of man is Nietzsche's real great theme, which engages him from his first philosophical efforts till the end. As early as 1874, in his study of Schopenhauer as an educator, he puts a question which is like a marginal note to Kant's fourth question, and in which our age is mirrored as Kant's age is mirrored in his question: "How can man know himself?" And he adds by way of explanation: "He is something dark and veiled." Ten years later comes an explanation

[1] Karl Heim, *Ontologie und Theologie*, Zeitschrift für Theologie und Kirche, neue Folge XI (1930), 333; Karl Heim, *Glaube und Denken* l.Auflage (1931), 405 ff (in the revised edition of 1934 Heim excised this passage). The English translation, *God Transcendent*, has been made from this third, revised and shortened, and altogether more orthodox edition. For a smiliar point of view see especially Emil Brunner.

of this explanation: man is "the animal that is not yet established". That is, he is not a determined, unambiguous, final species like the others, he is not a finished form, but something that is only becoming. If we regard him as a finished form then he must appear "as the supreme aberration of nature and a self-contradiction", for he is the being which, "in consequence of a violent separation from the animal past", suffers from himself and from the problem of what his life means. But that is only a transition. In truth, man—as Nietzsche finally expresses it in the notes which were brought together posthumously under the title *The Will to Power*—is "as it were an embryo of the man of the future", of the real man, of the real species man. The paradox of the situation consists in the fact that the coming of this real future man is not at all assured; present man, the man of the transition, must first create him out of the material which he himself is. "Man is something fleeting and plastic—one can make of him what one will." Man, *animal* man, "has hitherto had no meaning. His existence on earth has had no goal. 'To what end man?' was a question without an answer". He suffered, "but it was not the suffering itself which was his problem, but that there was no answer to the cry 'To what end this suffering?'" The ascetic ideal of Christianity wishes to free man from the meaninglessness of suffering; it does this by separating him from the foundations of life and leading him towards nothing. It is from life that man must take the meaning which he has to give to himself. But life is "the will to power"; all great humanity and great culture has developed from the will to power and from a good conscience to it. The ascetic ideals, which gave man a "bad conscience", have suppressed this will. The real man will be he who has a good conscience towards his will to power. That is the man we should "create" and "breed", for whose sake we should "overcome" what is called man. Present man is "no goal, but only a way, an episode, a bridge, a great promise". That is what, in Nietzsche's view, distinguished man from all animals: he is "an animal that may promise"; that is, he treats a bit of the future as something dependent on him for which he answers. No animal can do that. This human quality has arisen out of the contractual relation between creditor and debtor, out of the debtor's obligation. The "leading ethical concept of 'guilt' (*Schuld*) took its origin from the very material concept of 'debts'

(*Schulden*)". And human society has elevated by every possible means the quality which has arisen in this way, in order to keep the individual fulfilling his ethical and social duties. As the supreme means it made use of the ascetic ideals. Man must be free of it all, of his bad conscience and of the bad salvation from this conscience, in order to become in truth the way. Now he no longer promises others the fulfilment of his duties, but he promises himself the fulfilment of man.

Whatever of these ideas is meant as an *answer* is wrong. First, the sociological and ethnological presupposition about the history of man's origins is wrong. The concept of guilt is found most powerfully developed even in the most primitive communal forms which we know, where the relation between creditor and debtor is almost non-existent: the man is guilty who violates one of the original laws which dominate the society and which are mostly derived from a divine founder; the boy who is accepted into the tribal community and learns its laws, which bind him thenceforth, learns to promise; this promise is often given under the sign of death, which is symbolically carried out on the boy, with a symbolical re-birth. Just because the man has learned to promise in this way it is possible for the contract-relation in private economy to develop between the debtor who promises and the creditor who is promised.

Secondly, the psychological and historical view of the will to power is wrong. Nietzsche's concept of a will to power is not so unambiguous as Schopenhauer's concept of the will to life, on which it was modelled. Sometimes he understands by it the will to acquire ever more and more power; "all purposive happenings", he says, "can be reduced to the purpose of increasing power"; all that lives strives, in his view, "for power, for increase in power", "for a maximal feeling of power". But another time he defines the will to power as the "insatiable desire to display power, or to employ, to practise power". These are two different things. We may, nevertheless, look on them as the two sides, or the two moments, of the same event. At any rate we know that real greatness in history, in the history of the spirit and of culture, as well as in the history of peoples and of states, cannot be characterized by either of these. Greatness by nature includes a power, but not a will to power. Greatness has an inner powerfulness, which sometimes grows suddenly and irresistibly to power over men, sometimes exerts its effect quietly and slowly on a company that is quietly and slowly increasing, sometimes, too, seems to have no effect at all, but rests in itself, and sends out beams which will perhaps catch the glance only of some far time. But greatness strives neither to "increase" nor to "display" power. The great man, whether we comprehend him in the most intense activity of his work or in the restful equipoise of his forces, is powerful, involuntarily and composedly powerful, but he is not avid for power. What he is avid for is the realization of what he has in mind, the incarnation of the spirit. Of course he needs power for this realization; for power—when we strip the concept of the dithyrambic splendour with which Nietzsche equipped it—means simply the capacity to realize what one wants to realize; but the great man is not avid for this capacity—which is, after all, only a self-evident and indispensable means—but for *what* he wishes to be capable of. This is the point from where we can understand the *responsibility* in which the powerful man is placed, namely whether, and how far, he is really serving his goal; and also the point from where we can understand the seduction by power, leading him to be unfaithful to the goal and yield to power alone. When we see a great man desiring power instead of his real goal we soon recognize that he is sick, or more precisely that his attitude to his work is sick. He overreaches himself, the work denies itself to him, the incarnation of the spirit no longer takes place, and to avoid the threat of senselessness he snatches after empty power. This sickness casts the genius on to the same level as those hysterical figures who, being by nature without power, slave for power, for an ever fresh display of power and an ever fresh increase of power, in order that they may enjoy the illusion that they are inwardly powerful, and who in this striving for power cannot let a pause intervene, since a pause would bring with it the possibility of self-reflection and self-reflection would bring collapse. From this point, too, the connexion between power and culture is to be judged. It is an essential element of the history of almost all peoples that the political leadership which is historically important strives to win and to increase the power of the nation; that is, precisely what, as we saw, has a pathological character in personal life is normal in the relation between the historical representatives of the nation and the nation itself. Now again the characters separate in decisive fashion. It is decisively important whether the man who leads longs in his inmost heart, in his deepest desire and dream, to acquire power for his nation for power's sake, or in order that the nation may attain the capacity to realize what in his view appears as their nature and destiny—what he has discovered in his own soul as the sign of a future which is waiting for this nation, to be realized by it. If a man longs in *this* way for power for his nation then what he does in the service of his will or his vocation furthers, enrichs and renews the national culture; if he longs for national power in itself then he may achieve the greatest successes—what he does will only weaken and paralyse the national culture he wishes to glorify. The heyday of a community's culture is only rarely identical with the heyday of its power: great, genuine, spontaneous cultural productivity mostly precedes the time of intense striving and struggling for power, and the cultural activity which follows that time is mostly only a gathering and completing and imitating—unless a conquered people brings a new elemental cultural force to the powerful conqueror and enters into an association with it in which the people which has becoming politically powerless represents culturally the powerful, male, generative principle. No-one knew more clearly than the historian Jakob Burckhardt that political predominance and the capacity to realize the hidden form, the "idea", thus producing culture, are only seldom compatible. Burckhardt was the man whom Nietzsche admired as he did scarcely any other of his contemporaries, though Burckhardt more and more set him quietly aside. It is noteworthy that the spark which kindled Nietzsche's enthusiasm for the will to power probably came from a lecture by Burckhardt which he heard in 1870. We possess these lectures now in Burckhardt's posthumous book, published with the title *Reflections on World History*, one of the few important books about the powers which determine what we call history. We read there that the real inner incentive for the great historical individual is not love of glory, not ambition, but "the sense of power, which as an irresistible impulse drives the great individual into the light of day". But Burckhardt understands by that something quite different from the will to power in itself. He sees "the characteristic of greatness" in "its carrying out a will which goes beyond the individual". It is possible that the community and the age are unconscious of this will; "the individual knows what the nation's will should really be, and carries it out", because "the force and capacity of infinitely many are concentrated" in him. There appears here, as Burckhardt says, "a secret coincidence of the egoism of the individual" with the greatness of the whole. But the coincidence can be broken up if the means of power which are adopted "react on the individual and in the long run deprive him of the taste for great aims". On the basis of this insight Burckhardt uttered, in another lecture at that time—taking up the words of an earlier historian, Schlosser—the memorable, much-repeated and much-misunderstood words: "Now power in itself is evil, no matter who exercises it. It has no persistence, but is greed and *eo ipso* cannot be fulfilled, hence it is unhappy in itself and is bound to be the cause of unhappiness in others." These words can only be understood in the context of Burckhardt's thoughts, when one notes that he is speaking here of power *in itself*. So long as a man's power, that is, his capacity to realize what he has in mind, is bound to the goal, to the work, to the calling, it is, considered in itself, neither good nor evil, it is only a suitable or an unsuitable instrument. But as soon as this bond with the goal is broken off or loosened, and the man ceases to think of power as the capacity to do something, but thinks of it as a possession, that is, thinks of power in itself, then his power, being cut off and self-satisfied, is evil; it is power withdrawn from responsibility, power which betrays the spirit, power in itself. It corrupts the history of the world. Genuine knowledge of historical reality must rectify in this way Nietzsche's wrong answer to the anthropological question, when he says that man is to be understood, and released from his problematic nature, from the standpoint of the will to power.

As we see, Nietzsche did not give a positive foundation for a philosophical anthropology. But in elevating, as no previous thinker has done, the questionableness of human life to be the real subject of philosophizing he gave the anthropological question a new and unheard-of impulse. Yet it is specially noteworthy that from beginning to end of his thought he endeavoured to overcome the special problem of man in its strict sense. With Augustine, with Pascal, and even with Kant, the pathos of the anthropological question lies in our perceiving something in ourselves that we cannot explain to ourselves from nature and its development alone. For philosophy till Nietzsche, so far as it has an anthropological concern, "man" is not merely a species, but a category. But Nietzsche, who is very strongly determined by the eighteenth century, and whom one would sometimes like to call a mystic of the Enlightenment, does not acknowledge such a category or basic problem. He attempts to follow out a thought indicated by Empedocles, but since then never discussed in a genuinely philosophical fashion: he wants to understand man purely *genetically*, as an animal that has grown out and stepped forth from the animal world. He writes: "We no longer derive man from the 'spirit', we have put him back among the animals." These could be the words of one of the French encyclopædists. But all the same Nietzsche remains deeply conscious of the specifically human questionableness. It is this very questionableness which he wants to explain by the fact of man's breakaway from the animal world and his aberration from his instincts; man is problematic because he is an "overwrought kind of animal" and thus a "sickness" of the earth. For Kant the problem of man is a *frontier* problem, that is, the problem of a being which belongs, certainly, to nature, but not to nature alone, of a being that is established on the frontier between nature and another realm. For Nietzsche the problem of man is a problem of the *edge*, the problem of a being that has moved from within nature to its utmost edge, to the perilous end of natural being, where there begins, not as for Kant the ether of the spirit but the dizzying abyss of nothing. Nietzsche no longer sees in man a being in himself, a "new thing", which has come out of nature but in such a way that the fact and the way of this coming cannot be grasped by concepts of nature; he sees only a *becoming*, "an attempt, a groping, a missing the mark", not precisely a being but at best the pre-form of a being, "the animal that is not yet established", thus an extreme piece of nature, where something new has only begun to grow, which till now has certainly seemed very interesting but, considered in respect of its totality, not really a success. Yet two definite things, he thinks, can arise from this indefinite thing. Either man, in virtue of his "growing morality", which suppresses his instincts, will develop in himself "merely the herd animal" and thus "establish" the animal Man as the species in which the animal world goes into decline, as the decadent animal. Or man will overcome what is "fundamentally amiss" with him, give new life to his instincts, bring to light his unexhausted possibilities, build up his life on the affirmation of the will to power, and breed the superman who will be the real man, the successful new being. For this goal Nietzsche apparently does not think how it could come to pass that such an "ill-bred" animal could pull itself out of the bog of its own ambiguity. He demands conscious breeding on a widespread scale, and does not think of what he himself wrote: "We deny that anything that is being consciously made can be made perfect." We are, however, not concerned here with these inner contradictions in Nietzsche's thought, but with something else. Nietzsche, as we have seen, undertook with passionate earnestness to explain man in terms of the animal world; the specific problem of man does not thereby fade out, but has become more visible than ever. Only, from this point of view, the question ceases to be, *How is it to be understood that there is such a being as man?* but is *How is it to be understood that such a being as man has emerged and stepped forth from the animal world?* But in spite of all the arguments he brought to bear throughout his thought Nietzsche has not made this clear. He has scarcely troubled about what is for us the fundamental anthropological fact and the most amazing of all earthly facts—that there is in the world a being who knows the universe as a universe, its space as space, its time as time, and knows himself in it as knowing it. But that does not mean, as has been asserted, that the world exists "over again" in man's consciousness, but that a *world* in our sense, a unified, spatio-temporal world of the senses, only exists in virtue of man, because only the human person is able to combine into a cosmic unity the data of his own senses and the traditional data of the whole race. Certainly, if Nietzsche had troubled about this fundamental fact it would have led him to the sociology he despised, namely, to the sociology of knowledge and the sociology of tradition, to that of language, and that of the generations—in brief, to the sociology of human thinking together, which Feuerbach had in principle already pointed out. The man who knows a world is man *with* man. The problem which Nietzsche neglected, that such a being exists, is only shifted in his view from the realm of the being of a species to the realm of its becoming. If a being has emerged from the animal world who knows about life and about his own life, then the fact and the manner of this emergence cannot be explained by his place in the animal world or comprehended by concepts of nature. For post-nietzschian philosophy man is more than ever not merely a species, but a category. Kant's question *What is man?* is put to us with new urgency by Nietzsche's passionate anthropological concern. We know that to answer it we must invoke not merely the spirit but also nature to tell us what it has to tell; but we know that we have also to approach another power for information, namely, community.

I say "we know". But it is true that modern philosophical anthropology, even in its most significant representatives, has not yet realized this knowledge. Whether it has turned more to the spirit or more to nature, the power of community has not been invoked. If this power is not invoked the others lead not only to fragmentary knowledge but of necessity also to knowledge which is inadequate in itself.

Section Two: Modern Attempts

I: THE CRISIS AND ITS EXPRESSION

ONLY in our time has the anthropological problem reached maturity, that is, come to be recognized and treated as an independent philosophical problem. Besides philosophical development itself, which led to an increasing insight into the problematic nature of human existence, and whose most important points I have presented, two factors which are connected in many ways with this development have contributed to bringing the anthropological problem to maturity. Before discussing the present situation I must indicate the character and significance of these factors.

The first is predominantly sociological in nature. It is the increasing decay of the old organic forms of the direct life of man with man. By this I mean communities which quantitatively must not be too big to allow the men who are connected by them to be brought together ever anew and set in a direct relation with one another, and which qualitatively are of such a nature that men are ever anew born into them or grow into them, who thus understand their membership not as the result of a free agreement with others but as their destiny and as a vital tradition. Such forms are the family, union in work, the community in village and in town. Their increasing decay is the price that had to be paid for man's political liberation in the French Revolution and for the subsequent establishment of bourgeois society. But at the same time human solitude is intensified anew. The organic forms of community offered to modern man—who, as we saw, has lost the feeling of being at home in the world, has lost cosmological security—a life which had the quality of home, a resting in direct connexion with those like him, a sociological security which preserved him from the feeling of being completely exposed. Now this too slipped away from him more and more. In their outer structure many of the old organic forms remained as before, but they decayed inwardly, they steadily lost meaning and spiritual power. The new community forms which undertook to bring the individual anew into connexion with others, such as the club, the trade union, the party, have, it is true, succeeded in kindling collective passions, which, as is said, "fill out" men's lives, but they have not been able to re-establish the security which has been destroyed. All that happens is that the increased sense of solitude is dulled and suppressed by bustling activities; but wherever a man enters the stillness, the actual reality of his life, he experiences the depth of solitude, and confronted with the ground of his existence experiences the depth of the human problematic.

The second factor can be described as one of the history of the spirit, or better, of the soul. For a century man has moved ever deeper into a crisis which has much in common with others that we know from earlier history, but has one essential peculiarity. This concerns man's relation to the new things and connexions which have arisen by his action or with his co-operation. I should like to call this peculiarity of the modern crisis man's lagging behind his works. Man is no longer able to master the world which he himself brought about: it is becoming stronger than he is, it is winning free of him, it confronts him in an almost elemental independence, and he no longer knows the word which could subdue and render harmless the golem (14) he has created. Our age has experienced this paralysis and failure of the human soul successively in three realms. The first was the realm of technique. Machines, which were invented in order to serve men in their work, impressed him into their service. They were no longer, like tools, an extension of man's arm, but man became their extension, an adjunct on their periphery, doing their bidding. The second realm was the economic. Production, immensely increased in order to supply the growing number of men with what they needed, did not reach a reasonable co-ordination; it is as though the business of the production and utilization of goods spread out beyond man's reach and withdrew itself from his command. The third realm was the political. In the first world war, and on both sides, man learned with ever greater horror how he was in the grip of incomprehensible powers, which seemed, indeed, to be connected with man's will but which threw off their bonds and again and again trampled on all human purposes, till finally they brought all, both on this side and on the other, to destruction. Man faced the terrible fact that he was the father of demons whose master he could not become. And the question about the meaning of this simultaneous power and powerlessness flowed into the question about man's being, which now received a new and tremendously practical significance.

It is no chance, but significant necessity, that the most important works in the sphere of philosophical anthropology appeared in the decade after the first world war; nor does it seem to me to be chance that Edmund Husserl, the man in whose school and methods the most powerful attempts of our time to construct an independent philosophical anthropology made their appearance, was a German Jew, that is, the son of a people which experienced more grievously and fatefully than any other the first of those two factors, the increasing decay of the old organic forms of man's common life, and the pupil and adopted son, as he thought, of a people which experienced more grievously and fatefully than any other the second of the two factors, man's lagging behind his works.

Husserl himself, the creator of the phenomenological method in which the two attempts at a philosophical anthropology of which I shall have to speak, those of Martin Heidegger and Max Scheler, were undertaken, never treated the anthropological problem as such. But in his last, unfinished work, a treatise on the crisis of the European sciences, he made, in three separate sentences, a contribution to this problem which seems to me, in view of the man who uttered them and the time when they were uttered, to be important enough to be adduced and have their truth scrutinized at this point, before we pass to the discussion and criticism of phenomenological anthropology.

The first of the three sentences asserts that the greatest historical phenomenon is mankind wrestling for self-understanding. That is, Husserl says that all the effective events which have again and again, as it is usually put, changed the face of the earth, and which fill the books of the historians, are less important than that ever new effort, which is carried out in stillness and is scarcely noted by the historians, to understand the mystery of man's being. Husserl describes this effort as a wrestling. He means that the human spirit encounters great difficulties, great opposition from the problematic material it is striving to understand—that is, from its own being—and that from the beginning of history it has had to fight them. The history of this struggle is the history of the greatest of all history's phenomena.

Thus Husserl confirms the significance for the growth of

man of the historical course of philosophical anthropology—
the course from question to question, some of whose stages I
have indicated.

The second sentence runs: "If man becomes a 'metaphysical',
a specifically philosophical problem, then he is called in
question as a reasoning thing". These words, whose significance
was particularly stressed by Husserl, are only true, or only
become true, if they mean that the relation of "reason" to non-
reason in man must be called in question. In other words, it
is not a case of considering reason as the specifically human
and considering what is not reason in man as the non-specific,
as what man has in common with non-human beings, as what
is "natural" in man—as has been done again and again,
especially since Descartes. Rather, the depth of the anthropological question is first touched when we also recognize as specifically human that which is not reason. Man is not a centaur,
he is man through and through. He can be understood only
when one knows, on the one hand, that there is something
in all that is human, including thought, which belongs to the
general nature of living creatures, and is to be grasped from
this nature, while knowing, on the other hand, that there is
no human quality which belongs fully to the general nature of
living creatures and is to be grasped exclusively from it. Even
man's hunger is not an animal's hunger. Human reason is to
be understood only in connexion with human non-reason.
The problem of philosophical anthropology is the problem of
a specific totality and of its specific structure. So it has been
seen by Husserl's school, whom Husserl himself, however, was
unwilling to acknowledge as his school at the decisive points.

The third sentence runs: "Humanity in general is essentially
the existence of man in entities of mankind which are bound
together in generations and in society". These words fundamentally contradict the whole anthropological work of the
phenomenological school, both that of Scheler who, though
a sociologist, scarcely noticed man's social connexions in his
anthropological thought, and that of Heidegger, who certainly
recognized that these connexions were primary but treated
them essentially as the great obstacle to man's attainment of
himself. In these words Husserl says that man's essence is
not to be found in isolated individuals, for a human being's
bonds with his generation and his society are of his essence;
we must therefore know what these bonds really mean if

we want to know the essence of man. That is to say that an individualistic anthropology either has as its subject man in a condition of isolation, that is, in a condition not adequate to his essence, or in fact does consider man in his bonds of community, but regards their effects as impairing his real essence, and thus is not thinking of that fundamental communion of which Husserl speaks.

2

Before I pass to the discussion of phenomenological anthropology I must refer to the man to whose influence its individualistic character is largely traceable, namely, Kierkegaard. This influence is admittedly of a special nature. The phenomenological thinkers of whom I have to speak, and pre-eminently Heidegger, have certainly taken over Kierkegaard's mode of thinking, but they have broken off its decisive presupposition, without which Kierkegaard's thoughts, especially those on the connexion between truth and existence, change their colour and their meaning. Moreover, as we shall see, they have broken off not merely the theological aspect of this presupposition but the whole presupposition, including the anthropological aspect, so that the character and thus also the effect of "existential" thought represented by Kierkegaard have been almost converted into their opposite.

In the first half of the nineteenth century Kierkegaard, as a single and solitary man, confronted the life of Christendom with its faith. He was no reformer, again and again he emphasized that he had no "authority" from above; he was only a Christian thinker, but he was of all thinkers the one who most forcibly indicated that thought cannot authorize itself but is authorized only out of the existence of the thinking man. Yet thought in this latter sense was not the important thing for him, he really saw in it only a conceptual translation of faith—either a good or a bad translation. As for faith, he was intensely convinced that it is genuine only when it is grounded in and proved by the existence of the believer. Kierkegaard's criticism of actual Christianity is an inner one; he does not confront Christianity, as, for example, Nietzsche does, with an alleged higher value, and test it by that and reject it. There is for him no higher, and really no other, value. He measures the so-called Christianity lived by Christians against the real

Christianity which they profess and proclaim, and rejects this whole so-called Christian life together with its false faith (false because it is not realized), and its proclamation which has turned into a lie (because it is self-satisfied). Kierkegaard does not acknowledge any faith which is not binding.   The so-called religious man, no matter how great the enthusiasm with which he thinks and speaks of the object of his faith and gives expression to what he considers to be his faith by taking part in religious services and ceremonies, is only imagining that he believes unless the heart of his life is transformed by it, unless the presence of what he believes in determines his essential attitude from the most secret solitude to public action. Belief is a relation of life to what is believed, a relation of life which includes all life, or it is unreal. Obviously that cannot mean that a man's relation to the object of his faith is established, or can be established, by man. To Kierkegaard's insight as to that of all religious thought this connexion is by nature, first, ontic, that is, concerning not merely a man's subjectivity and life but his objective being, and second, like every objective connexion, two-sided, of which, however, we are able to know only one, the human side. But it can be influenced by man— at least in respect of this human side. That is, it depends on the man to a certain extent, which we cannot measure, if or how far his subjectivity enters his life, in other words, if or how far his faith becomes the substance and form of the life he lives. This question is fraught with destiny, because it does not concern a connexion established by man but one by which man is established, and which, constituting human life and giving it its meaning, should not merely be mirrored in the subjectivity of a religious view and a religious feeling, but bodily fulfilled in the wholeness of human life and "become flesh". Kierkegaard calls the striving for this realization and incarnation of faith an existential striving, for existence is the transition from a possibility in the spirit to a reality in the wholeness of the person. For the sake of this question, fraught with destiny, Kierkegaard makes the stages and conditions of life itself, guilt, fear, despair, decision, the prospect of one's own death and the prospect of salvation, into objects of metaphysical thought. He lifts them beyond the sphere of purely psychological consideration, for which they are in-different events within the course of the soul's life, and looks on them as links in an existential process, in an ontic connexion with the absolute, as elements of an existence "before God". Metaphysics here takes possession of the actuality of the living man with a strength and consistency hitherto unknown in the history of thought. Its ability to do this springs from the fact that man is considered not as an isolated being but in the problematic nature of his bond with the absolute. It is not the I, absolute in itself, of German idealism that is the object of this philosophical thought, the I which makes a world for itself by thinking it, it is the real human person, but considered in the ontic connexion which binds it to the absolute. This connexion is for Kierkegaard a real mutual connexion of person with person, that is, the absolute also enters it as a person. Kierkegaard's anthropology is therefore a theological anthropology. But modern philosophical anthropology has been made possible by it. This philosophical anthropology had to renounce the theological presupposition in order to acquire its philosophical basis. The problem was whether it would succeed in doing that without losing at the same time the metaphysical presupposition of the concrete man's bond with the absolute. As we shall see, it did not succeed.

II: THE DOCTRINE OF HEIDEGGER

I

WE have seen, in the discussion of Heidegger's interpretation of Kant's four questions, that he wants to establish as the principle of metaphysics not philosophical anthropology but "fundamental ontology", that is, the doctrine of existence as such. By existence he understands a present being which has a relation to its own being and an understanding of it. Man is the only one whom we know as such a present being. But fundamental ontology does not have to do with man in his actual manifold complexity but solely with existence in itself, which manifests itself through man. All concrete human life which is drawn upon by Heidegger concerns him only because (and in so far as) the modes of relation (*Verhalten*) of existence itself are shown in it, both the relation in which it comes to itself and becomes a self and the relation in and through which it fails to do so.

Even though Heidegger himself does not regard his philosophy or wish it to be regarded as philosophical anthropology, we must nevertheless test the genuineness and correctness of its anthropological content, since in philosophical fashion it draws upon concrete human life, which is the subject of philosophical anthropology; that is, against its intention we must subject it to criticism as a contribution to answering the anthropological question.

At the very beginning we must question Heidegger's starting-point. Is the extraction of "existence" from real human life anthropologically justified? Are statements which are made about this separated existence to be regarded in any way as philosophical statements about actual man? Or does the "chemical purity" of this concept of existence not rather make it impossible for the doctrine to stand up to the real facts of its subject—a test which all philosophy and all metaphysics must be able to pass?

Real existence, that is, real man in his relation to his being, is comprehensible only in connexion with the nature of the being to which he stands in relation. To exemplify what I mean I choose one of the most audacious and profound chapters of Heidegger's book, which treats of man's relation to his death. Here everything is perspective, what matters is how man looks to his end, whether he has the courage to anticipate the *whole* of his existence, which is made fully revealed only in death. But only when the subject of discussion is man's relation to his being is death to be limited to the end-point; if one is thinking of objective being itself, then death is also there in the present second as a force which wrestles with the force of life. The state of this struggle at a given time helps to determine man's whole nature at that moment, his existence at that moment, his attitude towards being at that moment; and if man looks now to his end, the manner of this looking cannot be separated from the reality of death's power in this very moment. In other words, man as existence, as comprehension of being that looks towards death, cannot be separated from man as a creature that begins to die when it begins to live, and that cannot possess life without death, or preserving power without destructive and disintegrative power.

Heidegger abstracts from the reality of human life the categories which originate and are valid in the relation of the individual to what is not himself, and applies them to "exist-

ence" in the narrower sense, that is, to the relation of the
individual to his own being. Moreover he does not do this
merely to enlarge the sphere of their validity; in Heidegger's
view the true significance and depth and import of these
categories is disclosed only in the realm of the individual's
relation to himself. But what we find here is that on the one
hand they are refined, differentiated, and subtilized, and that
on the other hand they are weakened and devitalized.
Heidegger's modified categories disclose a curious partial
sphere of life, not a piece of the whole real life as it is actually
lived, but a partial sphere which receives its independence, its
independent character and laws as it were through having the
circulation of the blood in the organism arrested at some point
and the isolated part examined. We enter a strange room of
the spirit, but we feel as if the ground we tread is the board on
which a game is being played whose rules we learn as we
advance, deep rules which we ponder, and must ponder, but
which arose and which persist only through a decision having
once been reached to play this intellectual game, and to play
it in this very way. And at the same time, it is true, we feel
that this game is not arbitrarily chosen by the player, but he
is under necessity, it is his fate.

2

I take as an example the concept of guilt (*Schuld*). Heidegger,
who always begins from the "everyday" (of which we shall
have to say more later), begins here from the situation presented by the German language, which says that someone
"owes" something to another (*schuldig ist*), and then from the
situation that someone "is answerable" for something (*an
etwas Schuld ist*), from where he advances to the situation that
someone becomes guilty in respect of another (*schuldig wird*),
that is, that he causes a lack in the existence of another, that
he becomes the reason for a lack in the existence of another.
But this too is only indebtedness (*eine Verschuldung*) and not the
original and real guilt (*Schuldigsein*) out of which the indebtedness proceeds and by which it is made possible. Real guilt,
according to Heidegger, consists in the fact that the existence
itself is guilty. The existence is "guilty in the ground of its
being". And the existence is guilty through not fulfilling

itself, through remaining in the so-called "generally human", in "one" (*das Man*), and not bringing its own self, the man's self, into being. The call of conscience sounds into this situation. Who calls? Existence itself. "In conscience the existence calls itself." The existence, which by its guilt has not reached self-being, summons itself to remember the self, to free itself to a self, to come from the "unreality" to the "reality" of existence.

Heidegger is right to say that all understanding of indebtedness must go back to a primal guilt. He is right to say that we are able to discover a primal guilt. But we are not able to do this by isolating a part of life, the part where the existence is related to itself and to its own being, but by becoming aware of the whole life without reduction, the life in which the individual, in fact, is essentially related to something other than himself. Life is not lived by my playing the enigmatic game on a board by myself, but by my being placed in the presence of a being with whom I have agreed on no rules for the game and with whom no rules can be agreed on. This presence before which I am placed changes its form, its appearance, its revelation, they are different from myself, often terrifyingly different, and different from what I expected, often terrifyingly different. If I stand up to them, concern myself with them, meet them in a real way, that is, with the truth of my whole life, then and only then am I "really" there: I am there if I am *there*, and where this "there" is, is always determined less by myself than by the presence of this being which changes its form and its appearance. If I am not really there I am guilty. When I answer the call of present being—"Where art thou?"—with "Here am I," but am not really there, that is, not with the truth of my whole life, then I am guilty. Original guilt consists in remaining with oneself. If a form and appearance of present being move past me, and I was not really there, then out of the distance, out of its disappearance, comes a second cry, as soft and secret as though it came from myself: "Where were you?" *That* is the cry of conscience. It is not my existence which calls to me, but the being which is not I. Now I can answer only the *next* form; the one which spoke can no longer be reached. (This next form can of course sometimes be the same man, but it will be a different, later, changed appearance of him.)

3

We have seen how in the history of the human spirit man again and again becomes solitary, that is, he finds himself alone with a universe which has become alien and uncanny, he can no longer stand up to the universal forms of present being; he can no longer truly meet them. This man, as we recognized him in Augustine, in Pascal, in Kierkegaard, seeks a form of being which is not included in the world, that is, he seeks a divine form of being with which, solitary as he is, he can communicate; he stretches his hands out beyond the world to meet this form. But we have also seen that there is a *way* leading from one age of solitude to the next, that is, that each solitude is colder and stricter than the preceding, and salvation from it more difficult. But finally man reaches a condition when he can no longer stretch his hands out from his solitude to meet a divine form. That is at the basis of Nietzsche's saying, "God is dead". Apparently nothing more remains now to the solitary man but to seek an intimate communication with himself. This is the basic situation from which Heidegger's philosophy arises. And thereby the anthropological question, which the man who has become solitary discovers ever afresh, the question about the essence of man and about his relation to the being of what is, has been replaced by another question, the one which Heidegger calls the fundamental-ontological question, about human existence in its relation to its *own* being.

There remains, however, one irrefragable fact, that one can stretch out one's hands to one's image or reflection in a mirror, but not to one's real self. Heidegger's doctrine is significant as the presentation of the relations to one another of various "beings" abstracted from human life, but it is not valid for human life itself and its anthropological understanding, however valuable its suggestions for this subject.

4

Human life possesses absolute meaning through transcending in practice its own conditioned nature, that is, through man's seeing that which he confronts, and with which he can enter into a real relation of being to being, as not less real than himself, and through taking it not less seriously than himself. Human life touches on absoluteness in virtue of its dialogical character, for in spite of his uniqueness man can never find, when he plunges to the depth of his life, a being that is whole in itself and as such touches on the absolute. Man can become whole not in virtue of a relation to himself but only in virtue of a relation to another self. This other self may be just as limited and conditioned as he is; in being together the unlimited and the unconditioned is experienced. Heidegger turns away not merely from a relation to a divine unconditioned being, but also from a relation in which man experiences another than himself in the unconditioned, and so experiences the unconditioned. Heidegger's "existence" is monological. And monologue may certainly disguise itself ingeniously for a while as dialogue, one unknown layer after the other of the human self may certainly answer the inner address, so that man makes ever fresh discoveries and can suppose that he is really experiencing a "calling" and a "hearing"; but the hour of stark, final solitude comes when the dumbness of being becomes insuperable and the ontological categories no longer want to be applied to reality. When the man who has become solitary can no longer say "Thou" to the "dead" known God, everything depends on whether he can still say it to the living unknown God by saying "thou" with all his being to another living and known man. If he can no longer do this either, then there certainly remains for him the sublime illusion of detached thought that he is a self-contained self; as man he is lost. The man of "real" existence in Heidegger's sense, the man of "self-being", who in Heidegger's view is the goal of life, is not the man who really lives with man, but the man who can no longer really live with man, the man who now knows a real life only in communication with himself. But that is only a semblance of real life, an exalted and unblessed game of the spirit. This modern man and this modern game have found their expression in Heidegger's philosophy. Heidegger isolates from the wholeness of life the realm in which man is related to himself, since he absolutizes the temporally conditioned situation of the radically solitary man, and wants to derive the essence of human existence from the experience of a nightmare.

5

This seems to be contradicted by Heidegger's statement that man's being is by nature *in the world*, in a world in which man is not merely surrounded by things which are his "gear", that is, which he uses and applies, in order to "take care of" what has to be taken care of, but also by men *together with* whom he is in the world. These men are not, like things, mere being, but, like himself, existence, that is, a being that stands in relation to itself and knows itself. They are for him an object not of "care" but of "carefulness", solicitude; moreover they are this by nature, existentially, even when he passes them by and does not trouble about them, when they "do not concern" him, and even when he treats them with complete inconsiderateness. Further, they are by nature the object of his understanding, for only by the understanding of others do cognition and knowledge become possible at all. This is how it is in the everyday, which is Heidegger's point of departure in a way specially important for him. But of the highest level, which he calls real self-being or resolution, more precisely resolution to be a self, he emphasizes that it does not separate existence from its world or isolate it into a freely moving I. "Resolution," he says, "in fact makes the self into a being with what is to hand, taking care each time, and urges it into a life of solicitude with others." Further, "Real life together is the first thing to arise out of the real self-being of resolution." Thus it looks as though Heidegger fully knew and acknowledged that a relation to others is essential. But this is not actually the case. For the relation of solicitude which is all he considers cannot *as such* be an essential relation, since it does not set a man's life in direct relation with the life of another, but only one man's solicitous help in relation with another man's lack and need of it. Such a relation can share in essential life only when it derives its significance from being the effect of a relation which is essential in itself—such as that between mother and child; of course it can lead to such a relation, as when genuine friendship or love arises between the solicitous person and the object of his solicitude. In its essence solicitude does not come from mere co-existence with others, as Heidegger thinks, but from essential, direct, whole relations between man and man, whether those which are objectively based on ties of blood, or those which arise by choice and can either assume

M

objective, institutional forms or, like friendship, shrink from all institutional forming and yet touch the depth of existence. It is from these direct relations, I say, which have an essential part in building up the substance of life, that the element of solicitude incidentally arises, extending after that, beyond the essential relations, into the merely social and institutional. In man's existence with man it is not solicitude, but the essential relation, which is primal. Nor is it any different if we set aside the problem of origin, and undertake the pure analysis of existence. In *mere* solicitude man remains essentially with himself, even if he is moved with extreme pity; in action and help he inclines towards the other, but the barriers of his own being are not thereby breached; he makes his assistance, not his self, accessible to the other; nor does he expect any real mutuality, in fact he probably shuns it; he "is concerned with the other", but he is not anxious for the other to be concerned with him. In an essential relation, on the other hand, the barriers of individual being are in fact breached and a new phenomenon appears which can appear only in this way: one life open to another—not steadily, but so to speak attaining its extreme reality only from point to point, yet also able to acquire a form in the continuity of life; the other becomes present not merely in the imagination or feeling, but in the depths of one's substance, so that one experiences the mystery of the other being in the mystery of one's own. The two participate in one another's lives in very fact, not psychically, but ontically. This is certainly something which comes to a man in the course of his life only by a kind of grace, and many will say that they do not know it; but even he to whom it has not come has it in his existence as a constitutive principle, because the conscious or unconscious *lack* of it plays an essential part in determining the nature and character of his existence. And certainly, in the course of their life many will be given the opportunity of it which they do not fulfil in their existence; they acquire relations which they do not make real, that is, which they do not use to open themselves to another; they squander the most precious, irreplacable and irrecoverable material; they pass their life by. But then this very void penetrates the existence and permeates its deepest layer. The "everyday", in its inconspicuous, scarcely perceptible part, which is nevertheless accessible to an analysis of existence, is interwoven with what is "not the everyday".

But we have seen that, according to Heidegger, even on the highest level of self-being man does not pass beyond "a life of solicitude with others". The level which Heidegger's man can reach is that of the free self which, as Heidegger emphasizes, is not separated from the world, but is only now mature and resolute for right existence with the world. But this mature resolute existence with the world knows nothing of an *essential* relation. Heidegger would perhaps reply that it is only the self which has become free that is really capable of love and friendship. But since self-being is here an ultimate, *the* ultimate, which the existence is able to reach, there is absolutely no starting-point for understanding love and friendship still as essential relations. The self which has become free certainly does not turn its back on the world, its resolution includes the resolve really to be with the world, to act in it and on it, but it does not include the belief that in this life with the world the barriers of the self can be breached, nor even the desire that it should happen. Existence is completed in self-being; there is no ontic way beyond this for Heidegger. What Feuerbach pointed out, that the individual does not have the essence of man in himself, that man's essence is contained in the unity of man with man, has entirely failed to enter Heidegger's philosophy. For him the individual has the essence of man in himself and brings it to existence by becoming a "resolved" self. Heidegger's self is *a closed system*.

6

"Everyone," said Kierkegaard, "should be chary about having dealings with 'others' and should essentially speak only with God and with himself." And he uttered this "should" as he looked to the goal and the task which he set to man, namely, to become a Single One. Heidegger seems to set man the same goal. But with Kierkegaard "to become a Single One" means only the presupposition to entry into a relation with God: only by having become a Single One can man enter into this relation. Kierkegaard's Single One is an open system, even if open solely to God. Heidegger knows no such relation; and since he does not know any other essential relation his "to become a self" means something quite different from Kierkegaard's "to become a Single One". Kierkegaard's man becomes a Single One *for* something, namely for the entry into a relation with the absolute; Heidegger's man does not become a self for something, since he cannot breach his barriers, and his participation in the absolute—so far as there is such a thing for him—consists in his barriers and nothing else.   Heidegger speaks of man becoming "opened" to his self; but this self itself to which he becomes opened is by nature closedness and reserve.   What Kierkegaard says appears here in a modified form: "Everyone should essentially speak only with himself".   But in fact Heidegger leaves out the "should" as well.   What he means is that everyone can essentially speak only with himself; what he speaks with others cannot be essential—that is, the word cannot transcend the individual's essence and transfer him into another essential life, which does not arise but is between the beings and grows by their essential relation with one another.   Heidegger's man is certainly pointed towards being with the world and towards an understanding and solicitous life with others; but in the essentiality of his existence, wherever his existence is essential, he is alone. With Kierkegaard's man anxiety and dread become essential as anxiety about the relation with God and dread lest he miss it.   With Heidegger they become essential as anxiety about the growth of self-being and dread lest it be missed.   In his anxiety and dread Kierkegaard's man stands "alone before God", Heidegger's man stands before himself and nothing else, and— since in the last resort one cannot stand before oneself—he stands in his anxiety and dread before nothing.   In order to become a Single One and to enter into the Single One's relation with the absolute, Kierkegaard's man has to renounce the essential relation to another, as Kierkegaard himself renounced the essential relation to another, to his fiancée—a renunciation which shapes the great theme of his works and journals. Heidegger's man has no essential relation to renounce. In Kierkegaard's world there is a *Thou* spoken with the very being to the other person, even if only to tell this person direct (as in a letter from Kierkegaard to his fiancée long after the engagement was broken off) or indirectly (as often in his books) why the essential relation had to be renounced.   In Heidegger's world there is no such *Thou*, no true *Thou* spoken from being to being, spoken with one's own being.   One does not say this *Thou* to the man for whom one is merely solicitous.

Heidegger's "openness" of the existence to itself thus in truth involves its being finally closed—even though it appears in humane forms—to all genuine bonds with the other and with otherness. This becomes still clearer if we pass from the person's relation to individuals to his relation to anonymous generality, to what Heidegger calls "one" (*das Man*). Here, too, Kierkegaard, with his concept of the "crowd", has anticipated him. The crowd, in which a man finds himself when he tries to advance to self-reflection, that is, the general, the impersonal, the faceless and formless, the average and the levelled down, this "crowd" is "untruth" for Kierkegaard. On the other hand the man who breaks out of it, escapes from its influence and becomes a Single One, is as a Single One the truth. For to Kierkegaard there is no other possibility of man's becoming truth, human (that is, conditioned) truth except by confronting unconditioned or divine truth and entering into the decisive relation with it. One can do this only as a Single One, through having become a person with the complete and independent responsibility of singleness. But one may only become a Single One through disengaging oneself from the crowd, which deprives one of, or at least weakens, personal responsibility. Heidegger takes over Kierkegaard's concept and develops it in the subtlest fashion. But the growth of the Single One—or, as he says, of self-being—has with him lost its goal of entering into relation with divine truth and thereby becoming human truth. The action which engages man's life—freeing himself from the crowd—retains its central place in Heidegger, but it loses its meaning, which is to lead man out beyond himself.

Heidegger's "one" is not something definite, but is the general condition into which we are born. All are this "one", not as an aggregate of individuals but as the faceless and nameless mass in which nothing individual can be recognized. Its real character is to be the "average", and it is with this that the "one" in its being is essentially concerned. "Every title of precedence", says Heidegger, "is noiselessly suppressed. Everything original is smoothed out in a trice as common knowledge. All that was once fought for is now plausible. Every mystery loses its power." The "one" has the tendency to "level" every possibility of being and to reduce human existence to a uniform flatness. Every interpretation of the world and of existence is arranged in advance by the "public". Almost in the same words as Kierkegaard uses Heidegger says that the "one" deprives the actual human life of its responsibility. If it is asked who then is this "one", the answer can only be that it is "no-one". Actual human life is handed over to this mighty no-one, and thus deprived of independence and reality. Instead of being concentrated in the self, it is dispersed in the "one", and has first to find itself. The power of the "one" causes existence to be fully absorbed by it. The life to which this happens flees from itself, from its power to be a self, it misses its own existence. Only the life which "fetches itself back" from this dispersal (which is, incidentally, a gnostic concept by which the gnostics meant the concentration and salvation of the soul which is lost in the world) attains to self-being.

We have seen that Heidegger does not look on the highest level as an isolation, but as resolution to co-existence with others. We have also seen, however, that this resolution only confirms the relation of solicitude on a higher plain, but knows nothing of any essential relation with others or any real *I-Thou* with them which could breach the barriers of the self. Whereas in the relation between persons, a relation is affirmed even for the self which has become free—namely, the relation of solicitude—in Heidegger there is lacking any corresponding reference for the relation to the impersonal "multitude" of men. The "one", and all that belongs to it, the "idle talk", "curiosity" and "ambiguity" which are dominant there and which are shared in by the man who has fallen a prey to the "one"—all this is purely negative, and destructive of the self: nothing positive takes its place; anonymous generality as such is repudiated, but there is nothing to replace it.

What Heidegger says about the "one" and a man's relation to it is right in essential traits. It is also right that a man has to disengage himself from it in order to reach self-being. But something is lacking here, without which what is right in itself becomes wrong.

As we have seen, Heidegger secularizes the Single One of Kierkegaard, that is, he severs the relation to the absolute for which Kierkegaard's man becomes a Single One. And as we have seen, he does not replace this "for" with any other worldly and human "for". He ignores the decisive fact that only the man who has become a Single One, a self, a real person, is able to have a complete relation of his life to the other self, a relation which is not beneath but above the problematic of the relations between man and man, and which comprises, withstands and overcomes all this problematic situation. A *great* relation exists only between real persons. It can be strong as death, because it is stronger than solitude, because it breaches the barriers of a lofty solitude, subdues its strict law, and throws a bridge from self-being to self-being across the abyss of dread of the universe. It is true that the child says *Thou* before it learns to say *I*; but on the height of personal existence one must be truly able to say *I* in order to know the mystery of the *Thou* in its whole truth. The man who has become a Single One—even if we limit ourselves to immanence—is there *for* something: he has become "this Single One" for something, for the perfect realization of the *Thou*.

8

But is there on this level something corresponding to the essential *Thou* in the relation to the multitude of men, or is Heidegger here finally right?

What corresponds to the essential *Thou* on the level of self-being, in relation to a host of men, I call the essential *We*.[1]

The person who is the object of my mere solicitude is not a *Thou* but a *He* or a *She*. The nameless, faceless crowd in which I am entangled is not a *We* but the "one". But as there is a *Thou* so there is a *We*.

Here we have to do with a category essential for our consideration, which it is important to clarify. It cannot be straightway grasped from out of current sociological categories. It is true that a *We* can arise in every kind of group, but it cannot be understood from the life of any single one of the groups. By *We* I mean a community of several independent persons, who have reached a self and self-responsibility, the community resting on the basis of this self and self-responsibility, and being made possible by them. The special character of the *We* is shown in the essential relation existing, or arising temporarily, between its members; that is, in the holding sway

[1] I shall not discuss in this connexion the *primitive We*, to which the essential *We* is related in the same way as the essential *Thou* to the primitive *Thou*.

within the *We* of an ontic directness which is the decisive presupposition of the *I-Thou* relation. The *We* includes the *Thou* potentially. Only men who are capable of truly saying *Thou* to one another can truly say *We* with one another.

As we have said, no particular kind of group-formation *as such* can be adduced as an example of the essential *We*, but in many of them the variety which is favourable to the arising of the *We* can be seen clearly enough. For example, in revolutionary groups we find a *We* most readily among those whose members make it their labour among the people to waken and teach quietly and slowly; in religious groups we find it among those who strive for an unemphatic and sacrificial realization of faith in life. In both cases it is enough to prevent the *We* arising, or being preserved, if a single man is accepted, who is greedy of power and uses others as means to his own end, or who craves for importance and makes a show of himself.

The essential *We* has hitherto been all too little recognized, both in history and in the present, because it is rare, and because group-formations have hitherto been considered mostly in respect of their energies and effects and not their inner structure—though the direction of the energy and the nature of the effects (even if not often their visible and measurable compass) depend most closely on the inner structure.

For more precise understanding I must point out that beside the constant forms of the essential *We* there are also transient forms, which nevertheless merit attention. Among these is to be reckoned, for example, the closer union which is formed for a few days among the genuine disciples and fellow-workers of a movement when an important leader dies. All impediments and difficulties between them are set aside, and a strange fruitfulness, or at all events incandescence, of their life with one another is established. Another transient form is seen when in face of a catastrophe which appears inevitable the really heroic element of a community gathers together within itself, withdraws from all idle talk and fuss, but in it each is open to the others and they anticipate, in a brief common life, the binding power of a common death.

But there are still other, remarkable structures which include men hitherto unknown to one another, and which are at least very close to the essential *We*. Such a structure can arise in, say, a terrorist régime, when adherents of an opinion which is opposed by the régime, hitherto strangers to one another, perceive that they are brothers and meet not as members of a party but in genuine community.

We can see that even in the sphere of the relation to a host of men there is an essential relation which takes up the man who has reached self-being—in fact, can truly take up no-one but him. Here only is the realm where a man is truly saved from the "one". A man is truly saved from the "one" not by separation but only by being bound up in genuine communion.

9

Let us now summarize our comparison of Kierkegaard's man and Heidegger's man.

In virtue of his nature and his situation man has a threefold living relation. He can bring his nature and situation to full reality in his life if all his living relations become essential. And he can let elements of his nature and situation remain in unreality by letting only single living relations become essential, while considering and treating the others as unessential.

Man's threefold living relation is, first, his relation to the world and to things, second, his relation to men—both to individuals and to the many—third, his relation to the mystery of being—which is dimly apparent through all this but infinitely transcends it—which the philosopher calls the Absolute and the believer calls God, and which cannot in fact be eliminated from the situation even by a man who rejects both designations.

The relation to things is lacking in Kierkegaard, he knows things only as similes. In Heidegger it can be found only as a technical, purposive relation. But a purely technical relation cannot be an essential one, since it is not the whole being and whole reality of the thing one is related to which enter into the relation, but just its applicability to a definite aim, its technical suitability. An essential relation to things can only be a relation which regards them in their essential life and is turned towards them. The fact of art can only be understood in the connexion of an essential with a technical relation. Nor is it to the purpose even in an analysis of everyday existence that things should be present only as "gear". The technical is only what can be easily surveyed, easily explained, it is the

co-ordinated. But besides, and in the midst of this, there is a
manifold relation to things in their wholeness, their independence, and their purposelessness. The man who gazes without
purpose on a tree is no less "everyday" than the one who
looks at a tree to learn which branch would make the best
stick. The first way of looking belongs to the constitution of
the "everyday" no less than the second. (Besides, it can be
shown that even genetically, in human development, the
technical does not come first in time, and that what in its late
form is called the æsthetic does not come second.)

The relation to individual men is a doubtful thing to
Kierkegaard, because in his view an essential relation to God
is obstructed by an essential relation to human companions.
In Heidegger the relation to individual men appears only as a
relation of solicitude. A relation of mere solicitude cannot be
essential; in an essential relation which includes solicitude the
essentiality is derived from another realm which is lacking in
Heidegger. An essential relation to individual men can only
be a direct relation from life to life in which a man's reserve is
resolved and the barriers of his self-being are breached.

The connexion with the faceless, formless, nameless many,
with the "crowd", with the "one", appears in Kierkegaard,
and following him in Heidegger, as the preliminary situation
which must be overcome for self-being to be attained. In itself
this is true; that nameless human all and nothing in which we
are immersed is in fact like a negative womb from which we
have to emerge in order to come into the world as a self. But
it is only one side of the truth, and without the other side it
becomes untrue. The genuineness and adequacy of the self
cannot stand the test in self-commerce, but only in communication with the whole of otherness, with the medley of the
nameless crowd. A genuine and adequate self also draws out
the spark of self-being wherever it touches the crowd, it makes
self be bound to self, it founds the opposition to the "one", it
founds the communion of individuals, it shapes the form of
community in the stuff of social life.

Man's third living relation is that which is called respectively
the relation to God or to the Absolute or to the mystery. We
have seen that this is the sole essential relation for Kierkegaard,
while it is completely lacking in Heidegger.

The essential relation to God, which Kierkegaard means,
presupposes, as we saw, a renunciation of every essential

relation to anything else, to the world, to community, to the individual man. It can be understood as a subtraction which, reduced to a crude formula, appears thus: Being—(World + Man)=Object (the object or partner of the essential relation); it comes into existence by leaving out everything except God and myself. But a God reached only by renunciation of the relation to the whole being cannot be the God of the whole being whom Kierkegaard means, cannot be the God who has made and preserves and holds together all that is. Though the history of creation which is left to its own resources may be called separation, the goal of the way can only be communion, and no essential relation to this God can stand outside this goal. The God of Kierkegaard can only be either a demiurge outgrown by and suffering from his creation, or a saviour who is a stranger to creation, approaching it from without and taking pity on it. Both are gnostic figures. Of the three great Christian philosophers of solitude, Augustine, Pascal and Kierkegaard, the first is thoroughly conditioned by gnosticism, the presuppositions of the last touch on it—obviously without his knowing it—and only Pascal has nothing to do with it, perhaps because he comes by way of science and never abandons it, and because science can come to terms with faith but not with gnosis, which itself claims to be the true science.

Heidegger's philosophical secularization of Kierkegaard had to abandon the religious conception of a bond of the self with the Absolute, a bond in real mutual relation of person with person. But neither does it know any other form of a bond between the self and the Absolute or between the self and the dimly apparent mystery of being. The Absolute has its place in Heidegger's philosophy only in the sphere to which the self penetrates in its relation to itself, that is, where the question about the entry into a *connexion* with it ceases to be asked. Heidegger, influenced by Hölderlin, the great poet of this mystery, has undoubtedly had a profound experience of the mystery of being which is dimly apparent through all that is; but he has not experienced it as one which steps before us and challenges us to yield the last thing, so hard fought for, the being at rest in one's own self, to breach the barriers of the self and to come out from ourselves to meet with essential otherness.

Besides man's threefold living relation there is one other, that to one's own self. This relation, however, unlike the others, cannot be regarded as one that is real as such, since the necessary presupposition of a real duality is lacking. Hence it cannot in reality be raised to the level of an essential living relation. This is expressed in the fact that every essential living relation has reached its completion and transfiguration, that to things in art, that to men in love, that to the mystery in religious manifestation, while man's relation to his own life and his own self has not reached, and obviously cannot reach, such a completion and transfiguration. (It could perhaps be maintained that lyric poetry is such a completion and transfiguration of men's relation to his own self. But it is rather the tremendous refusal of the soul to be satisfied with self-commerce. Poetry is the soul's announcement that even when it is alone with itself on the narrowest ridge it is thinking not of itself but of the Being which is not itself, and that this Being which is not itself is visiting it there, perplexing and blessing it.)

For Kierkegaard this relation is given meaning and is consecrated by the relation to God. For Heidegger it is essential in itself and it is the only essential relation. That means, that man can attain to his real life only as a system which in respect of his essential relation is a closed system. In contrast to this, the anthropological view which considers man in his connexion with being must regard this connexion as supremely realizable only in an open system. Connexion can mean only connexion with the integrality of his human situation. Neither the world of things, nor his fellow-man and community, nor the mystery which points beyond these, and also beyond himself, can be dismissed from a man's situation. Man can attain to existence only if his whole relation to his situation becomes existence, that is, if every kind of living relation becomes essential.

The question what man is cannot be answered by a consideration of existence or of self-being as such, but only by a consideration of the essential connexion of the human person and his relations with all being. Consideration of existence or self-being as such yields only the concept and outline of an almost ghostly spiritual being, that possesses, indeed, bodily contents of its basic sensations, its dread of the universe, its anxiety about existence, its feeling of primal guilt, yet possesses even these in a way that has nothing to do with the body. This spiritual being lurks in man, lives its life and settles the accounts of this life with itself; but it is not man, and our question is about man. If we try to grasp man on the far side of his essential connexion with the rest of being then we understand him, as Nietzsche does, to be a degenerate animal, or, as Heidegger does, to be a separated spiritual being. Only when we try to understand the human person in his whole situation, in the possibilities of his relation to all that is not himself, do we understand man. Man is to be understood as the being who is capable of the threefold living relation and can raise every form of it to essentiality.

10

"No age", writes Heidegger in his *Kant and the Problem of Metaphysics*, "has known so much, and so many different things, about man as ours. . . . And no age has known less than ours of what man is." In his book *Being and Time* he has tried to give us a knowledge of man by the analysis of his relation to his own being. This analysis he did in fact give, on the basis of a separation of this relation from all other essential human relations. But in this way one does not learn what man is, but only what the edge of man is. One can also say, one learns what man is on the edge—the man who has reached the edge of being. When I read Kierkegaard in my youth, I regarded Kierkegaard's man as the man on the edge. But Heidegger's man is a great and decisive step out from Kierkegaard in the direction of the edge where *nothing* begins.

III: THE DOCTRINE OF SCHELER

I

THE second significant attempt of our time to treat the problem of man as an independent philosophical problem has likewise come from the school of Husserl: it is the "anthropology" of Scheler.

Scheler, indeed, did not complete his work on this subject, but what has been published of articles and addresses on anthropology, by himself and posthumously, is sufficient to show us his point of view and to make it possible for us to form a judgment.

Scheler expresses clearly the situation in our time from which anthropology starts. "We are the first epoch in which man has become fully and thoroughly 'problematic' to himself; in which he no longer knows what he essentially is, but at the same time also *knows* that he does not know." It is now a case of beginning, in this situation of his extreme problematic condition, with the systematic comprehension of what he is (*Wesen*). Scheler, unlike Heidegger, refuses to abstract from the concreteness of the whole man present to him and to consider his "existence" (*Dasein*), namely his relation to his being (*Sein*), as what is metaphysically the only essential. He has to do with the sheer concreteness of man, i.e. he wants to treat what on his understanding divides man from other living creatures only in connexion with what he has in common with them; and he wants to treat it in such a way that it may be recognizable precisely in relation to what is common, by its standing out in its specific character from what is common.

For such a treatment, as Scheler rightly recognizes, the history of anthropological thought in the widest sense, both the philosophical and the pre-philosophical and extra-philosophical, that is, the "history of man's consciousness of himself", can have only an introductory significance. By means of discussion of all "mystical, religious, theological and philosophical theories of man" freedom·must be won from all theories. "Only," says Scheler, "by being willing to make a complete *tabula rasa* of all traditions about this question, and by learning to look in extreme methodical aloofness and astonishment on the being called man, can we reach tenable insights again."

That is indeed the real, genuine philosophical method, and is especially to be recommended in face of a subject that has become so problematic as this. All philosophical discovery is the uncovering of what is covered by the veil woven from the threads of a thousand theories. Without such an uncovering we shall not be able to master the problem of man at this late hour. But we have to investigate whether Scheler employs with all strictness in his anthropological thought the method which he sets forth. We shall see that he does not. If Heidegger considers instead of the real man only a metaphysical essence and composition, a metaphysical homunculus, Scheler lets his consideration of the real man be permeated by a metaphysic, and moreover one which, though independently achieved and of independent value, is deeply influenced by Hegel and Nietzsche, however much it seeks to rid itself of these influences. But a metaphysic which permeates the consideration in this way can no less than all anthropological theories prevent the glance being directed "in extreme aloofness and astonishment on the being called man".

Of the two named influences it must be said that Scheler's earlier anthropological writings are more determined by Nietzsche, the later more by Hegel. Scheler has followed both, as we shall see, in his over-estimation of the significance of time for the absolute. Nietzsche admittedly wishes to know nothing of the absolute itself, all idea of absoluteness is for him—not essentially different than for Feuerbach—merely a game and a projection of man. But in wanting to find the *meaning* of human life in its transition to a "superman" he establishes so to speak a relative absolute, and this no longer has its content in a supra-temporal being but only in becoming, in time. But for Hegel, at whom Scheler arrives by way of Nietzsche, the absolute itself attains complete and final realization of its own being and consciousness only in man and his perfection. Hegel sees the substance of the universal spirit in its "producing itself", in its "knowing and realizing itself and its truth" in an "absolute process", "step by step", culminating in history. Scheler's metaphysic—which has essentially determined his anthropology in its later form—is to be understood from this starting-point, in the doctrine, namely, of the "ground of things", which "is realized in the temporal course of the world-process", and about the human self as "the only place of the becoming of God which is accessible to us and at the same time a true part of the process of this becoming of God"; so that the becoming is dependent on it and it on the becoming. The absolute, or God, is thereby far more radically than with Hegel introduced into time and made dependent on it. God is not, but he is becoming; thus he is inserted into time, in fact he is its product. And even if there is, in passing, talk about a supra-temporal being which only manifests itself in time, for such a being there is no genuine place in a doctrine of a God who is becoming. There is in truth no other being but that of time, in which the becoming takes place.

This basic assumption of Scheler's metaphysic must, however, by no means be confused with Heidegger's teaching about time as the essence of human existence and thereby of existence in general. Heidegger relates only existence to time and does not overstep the boundary of existence. But Scheler lets being itself be resolved in time. Heidegger is silent about eternity, in which perfection *is*; Scheler denies this eternity.

2

Scheler reached this later metaphysic of his after a Catholic period in which he confessed a theism. All theism is a variety of that conception of eternity for which time can signify only the manifestation and effect but not the origin and development of a perfect being. Heidegger comes from the neighbouring Protestant realm of the same Christian theism. But he only draws a line between himself and theism, Scheler breaks with it.

I wish to insert a personal recollection here, for it seems to me to have a significance that goes beyond the personal. Since my own thoughts over the last things reached, in the first world war, a decisive turning-point, I have occasionally described my standpoint to my friends as the "narrow ridge". I wanted by this to express that I did not rest on the broad upland of a system that includes a series of sure statements about the absolute, but on a narrow rocky ridge between the gulfs where there is no sureness of expressible knowledge but the certainty of meeting what remains, undisclosed. When I met Scheler a few years after the war, after we had not seen one another for some time—he had at that time completed that break with the church's thought, without my knowing— he surprised me by saying, "I have come very near your narrow ridge." In the first moment I was nonplussed, for if there was anything I did not expect from Scheler it was the giving up of the supposed knowledge about the ground of being. But in the next moment I answered, "But it is not where you think it is." For in the meantime I had understood that Scheler did not really mean that standpoint which I had then, and have had since then; he confused it with a point of view which I had cherished and upheld for a long time, and which indeed was not far from his new philosophy of the becoming God. Since 1900 I had first been under the influence of German mysticism from Meister Eckhart to Angelus Silesius, according to which the primal ground (*Urgrund*) of being, the nameless, impersonal godhead, comes to "birth" in the human soul; then I had been under the influence of the later Kabbala and of Hasidism, according to which man has the power to unite the God who is over the world with his *shekinah* dwelling in the world. In this way there arose in me the thought of a realization of God through man; man appeared to me as the being through whose existence the Absolute, resting in its truth, can gain the character of reality. It was this point of view of mine which Scheler meant in his remark; he saw me as still holding it; but it had long since been destroyed in me. He on the other hand surpassed it by his idea of a "becoming of God". But he too had had a decisive experience during the war, which for him was translated into a conviction of the original and essential powerlessness of the spirit.

3

Primal and present being, the world's ground, has according to Scheler two attributes, spirit and impulse. In this connexion one thinks of Spinoza; but with him the two attributes are two of infinitely many, the two which we know. For Scheler the life of absolute being consists in this duality. Further, with Spinoza the two attributes of thought and extension stand to one another in a relation of perfect unity; they correspond to and complete one another. With Scheler the attributes of spirit and impulse stand in a primal tension with one another which is fought out and resolved in the world process. In other words, Spinoza grounds his attributes in an eternal unity which infinitely transcends the world and time; Scheler—in fact though not explicitly—limits being to time and the world process which takes place in time. With Spinoza, when we turn from the world to what is not the world, we have the feeling of an incomprehensible and over-mastering fulness; with Scheler, when we do this, we have the feeling of a meagre abstraction, even a feeling of emptiness. Scheler, who speaks in his lecture on Spinoza of the "air of eternity of the very godhead", which the reader of Spinoza breathes in "in deepest draughts", no longer gives his own reader this air to breathe. In truth the man of our time scarcely knows with living knowledge anything of an eternity which bears and swallows all time as the sea a fleeting wave; though even to him a way to eternal being still stands open, in the content of eternity of each moment into which the whole existence is put and lived.

But in still another important point Scheler differs from Spinoza. He does not, like Spinoza, give the second of his attributes a static denomination, like extension, corporeal or material nature, but the dynamic denomination *impulse*. That is, he substitutes for Spinoza's attributes Schopenhauer's two fundamental principles, the will, which he terms impulse, and the idea, which he terms spirit.

4

With regard to the attribute of spirit in the ground of being, Scheler asserts, in an incidental remark which acquires essential significance for the understanding of his thought, that it is also possible to term this attribute the godhead, *deitas*, in the ground of being. The godhead is thus for him not the world's ground itself, but only one of two opposed principles within it. Moreover it is that of the two which possesses "as spiritual being no kind of original power or force" and hence is not able to exert any kind of positive creative effect. Over against it stands the "almighty" impulse, the world fantasy which is charged with infinitely many images and lets them grow to reality, but in its origin is blind to spiritual ideas and values. In order to realize the godhead with the wealth of ideas and values that are latent in it the world's ground must "lift the brakes" of the impulse, must release it and set the world-process on its course. But since the spirit has no energy of its own it can influence the world-process only by holding ideas and meaning before the primal powers, the life-impulses, and guiding and sublimating them till in ever higher ascent spirit and impulse penetrate one another, impulse being given spirit and spirit being given life. The decisive place of this event is the living being "in which the primal being begins to know and comprehend itself, to understand and to redeem itself", and in which "the relative becoming of God"—namely, man—begins. "Being in itself becomes a being worthy to be called divine existence only to the extent that it realizes, in and through man, the eternal *deitas* in the impulse of world-history."

This dualism, fed on Schopenhauer's philosophy, goes back

to the gnostic idea of two primal gods, a lower, related to matter, who creates the world, and a higher, purely spiritual god who redeems the world. Only, in Scheler's thought the two have become attributes of the one world's ground. This cannot be termed a god, since it contains a godhead only alongside a non-divine principle and is only destined to become a god. But it appears to us as much like a man as any kind of divine image, as the transfigured likeness of a modern man. In this man the sphere of the spirit and the sphere of impulse have fallen apart more markedly than ever before. He perceives with apprehension that an unfruitful and powerless remoteness from life is threatening the separated spirit, and he perceives with horror that the repressed and banished impulses are threatening to destroy his soul. His great anxiety is to reach unity, a feeling of unity and an expression of unity, and in deep self-concern he ponders on the way. He believes he finds it by giving his impulses their head, and he expects his spirit to guide their working. It is a misleading way, for the spirit as it is here can indeed hold ideas and values before, but can no longer make them credible to, the impulses. Nevertheless, this man and his way have found their transfiguration in Scheler's "world's ground".

5

Scheler's idea of the world's ground shows, behind the philosophical influences it has received, an origin in the constitution of the modern soul. This origin has introduced into it a deep and insoluble contradiction. Scheler's basic thesis, which is very understandable from the spirit's experiences in our time, affirms that the spirit in its pure form is simply without any power at all. He comes across this powerless spirit present in primal being itself as its attribute. Thereby he makes an empirically *developed* powerlessness which he comes across into one primally existing. But it is an inner contradiction of his conception of the world's ground that in this the spirit is in origin powerless. The world's ground "releases" the impulse in order that it may produce the world, in order, that is, that the spirit may be realized in the history of this world. But by what force did the world's ground bind its impulse and by what force does it now release it? By what other

than that of the one of its two attributes which seeks for realization, that of the *deitas*, of the spirit? The impulse cannot itself
yield the power to keep itself bound, and if it is to be released
this can only happen by the same power which is so superior to
its power that it could keep it bound. Scheler's conception of
the world's ground demands in fact an original preponderant
power of the spirit—a power so great that it is able to bind
and to release all the motive-force from which the world
proceeds.

It may be objected that this is not a positive creative power
of its own. But this objection rests on a confusion of power and
force—a confusion which, indeed, Scheler himself makes many
times. Concepts are formed from our highest experiences of a
certain kind, which we recognize as being repeated. But our
highest experiences of power are not those of a force which
produces a direct change, but those of a capacity to set these
forces directly or indirectly in motion. Whether we use the
positive expression "to set in motion" or the negative expression
"to release" is irrelevant. Scheler's choice of words veils the
fact that even in his world's ground the spirit has the power
to set the forces in motion.

6

Scheler asserts that in face of his thesis of an original
powerlessness of the spirit the thought of a "creation of the
world from nothing" falls to the ground. He means, of course,
the biblical story of the creation, for which a later theology
has coined the misleading description of a creation from
nothing. The biblical story does not know the idea of "nothing", an idea which would harm the mystery of the "beginning".
The Babylonian epic of the creation of the world makes the
god Marduk strike amazement into the assembly of the gods
by causing a garment to rise up out of nothing; such magic
tricks are alien to the biblical story of the creation. What it
at the very beginning calls "to create" heaven and earth—in
a word that originally means "to hew out"—is left wholly in
mystery, in a process taking place within the godhead. This
process is described falsely by later theology in the language
of bad philosophy, but gnosis draws it out of mystery into the
world and thereby subdues the alogical to the logic which

reigns in the world as such. After this beginning there is a "spirit"—which is, indeed, something quite different from a "spiritual being", namely, the source of all motion, of all spiritual and natural motion—upon the face of the "waters" which are obviously charged with germinal forces, since they can make living beings "swarm forth" from them. The creation by the Word which is reported is not to be separated from the effect of the spirit which sets the forces in motion. Forces are set going, and the spirit has the power over them.

Scheler's "world's ground", too, is only one of the countless gnostic attempts to strip the mystery from the biblical God.

7

But let us turn from the world's origin to its existence, from the divine spirit to our own which is known to us in our experience. What about this?

In man, says Scheler, the spiritual attribute of present being itself is becoming manifest "in the unity of concentration of the person gathering himself to himself". On the ladder of becoming, primal present being, in the building-up of the world, is always more and more bent back on itself, "in order to become aware of itself on ever higher levels and in ever new dimensions, in order finally to possess and to comprehend itself wholly in man". But the human spirit, in which this Hegelian ladder culminates, is, precisely as spirit, in its origin without any power. It acquires power only by letting itself "be supplied with energy" by the life-instincts, i.e. by man's sublimating his instinctive energy to spiritual capacity. Scheler depicts this process in this way: first the spirit guides the will by instilling into it the ideas and values which are to be realized; then the will as it were starves out the impulses of the instinctive life by mediating to them the conceptions they would use in order to attain to an instinctive *action*; finally the will places "the conceptions, appropriate to the ideas and values", "before the waiting instincts" "like bait before their eyes", until they execute the project of will set by the spirit.

Is the man of whose inner life this presentation—based on the concept of modern psycho-analysis—is given, really *man*?

Or is it not rather a certain kind of man, namely that in which the sphere of the spirit and the sphere of the instincts have been made so separate and independent from one another that the spirit from its height can bring before the instincts the fascinating magnificence of ideas, as in gnostic lore the daughters of light appear to the mighty princes of the planets in order to make them burn in love and lose the force of their light?

8

Scheler's description may fit many who are ascetics by a decision of the will and who have reached contemplation by way of asceticism. But the existential asceticism of so many great philosophers is not to be understood as the spirit in them depriving the instincts of life-energy, or having it conveyed into itself. This asceticism is rather to be understood in terms of a high measure of concentrated power having been allotted, and an unqualified mastery lent, to thought in the primal constitution of their life. What happens in them between the spirit and the instincts is not, as with Scheler's man, a struggle conducted from the side of the spirit by great strategical and pedagogic means, against which the instincts offer a resistance which is first violent and is then gradually overcome. But what happens is, as it were, the two-sided carrying-out of an original contract which assures to the spirit unassailable mastery and which the instincts now fulfil—in individual instances grudgingly but in most actually with pleasure.

But the ascetic type of man is not, as seems to Scheler, *the* basic type of spiritual man. This is shown most clearly of all in the realm of art. If you try to understand a man like Rembrandt or Shakespere or Mozart with this type as your starting-point, you will notice that it is precisely the mark of artistic genius that it does not need to be ascetic in its being. It too will have constantly to carry out ascetic acts of denial, of renunciation, of inner transformation; but the real conduct of its spiritual life is not based on asceticism. There is here no endless negotiation between spirit and instincts; the instincts listen to the spirit, so as not to lose connexion with the ideas, and the spirit listens to the instincts so as not to lose connexion with the primal powers. Certainly the inner life of these men does not run in a smooth harmony; in fact it is precisely they who know, as scarcely any other, the dæmonic realm of conflict. But it is a mistaken and misleading implication to identify the dæmons with the instincts; they often have a purely spiritual face. The true negotiations and decisions take place, in the life of these and in general of great men, not between spirit and instincts but between spirit and spirit, between instincts and instincts, between one product of spirit and instinct and another product of spirit and instinct. The drama of a great life cannot be reduced to the duality of spirit and instinct.

It is altogether precarious to want to show, as Scheler does, the being of man and of his spirit on the basis of the philosopher-type, his qualities and experiences. The philosopher is an immensely important human type, but he represents a remarkable exceptional case of the spiritual life rather than its basic form. But even he is not to be understood on the basis of that duality.

9

Scheler wishes to represent to us, in the act of forming ideas, the particular nature of the spirit as a specific good of man, in distinction from technical intelligence which he shares with the animals. He gives this example.

A man has a pain in his arm. The intelligence asks how it has arisen and how it can be removed, and answers the question with the help of science. But the spirit takes the same pain as an example of that character of existence, namely, that the world is shot through with pain, it asks about the nature of pain itself and from there it goes on to ask what the ground of things must be like, that something like pain should be possible at all. That is, man's spirit abolishes the character of reality of the empirical pain which the man has felt. Moreover, the spirit does not merely exclude, as Husserl supposed, the judgment about the actuality of the pain and treat it according to its nature, but it removes "experimentally" the whole impression of reality, it carries out the "basically ascetic act by which reality is stripped off" and thus rises above the pain-tormented impulse of life.

I contest, even in respect of the philosopher, so far as he takes the discovery of a mode of being as the starting-point of his thought, whether the decisive act of forming ideas is of this character. The nature of pain is not recognized by the spirit as it were standing at a distance from it, sitting in a box and watching the drama of pain as an unreal example. The man whose spirit does this may have all sorts of brilliant thoughts about pain, but he will not recognize the nature of pain. This is recognized by pain being discovered in very fact. That is, the spirit does not remain outside and strip off reality, it casts itself into the depth of this real pain, takes up its abode in the pain, gives itself over to the pain, permeates it with spirit, and the pain itself in such nearness as it were discloses itself to him. The recognition does not happen by the stripping off of reality but by the penetration into this definite reality, a penetration of such a kind that the nature of pain is exposed in the heart of this reality. Such a penetration we call spiritual.

The first question is therefore not, as Scheler supposes, "What then really is *pain itself* apart from the fact that *I* feel it *here now*?" There is no "apart from" this fact. The nature of pain is disclosed to me by this very pain that I have here now, its being mine, its being now, its being here, its defined and particular being, the perfected presence of this pain. Under the penetrating touch of the spirit the pain itself as it were communicates with the spirit in dæmonic speech. Pain— and every real happening of the soul—is to be compared not with a drama but with those early mysteries whose meaning no-one learns who does not himself join in the dance. The spirit translates out of the dæmonic speech, which it learned in intimate touch with the pain, into the speech of ideas. It is this translation which takes place in a differentiation and removal from the object. "Contemplating" thought is with the philosopher too, so far as he is really empowered by the being of the world to proclaim it, not first but second.

·The first thing is the discovery of a mode of being in communion with it, and this discovery is pre-eminently a spiritual act. Every philosophical idea springs from such a discovery. Only a man who has communicated in his spirit with the pain of the world in the ultimate depth of his own pain, without any kind of "apart from", is able to recognize the nature of pain. But for him to be able to do this there is a presupposition, that he has already really learned the depth of the pain of other lives—and that means, not with "sympathy", which does not press forward to being, but with great love. Only then does his own pain in its ultimate depth light a way into the suffering of the world. Only participation in the existence of living beings discloses the meaning in the ground of one's own being.

10

But to learn more precisely what spirit is we must not be content with investigating it where it has reached expression in achievement and a calling. It must also be sought out where it is still a *happening*. For the spirit in its original reality is not something that is but something that happens; more precisely, it is something that is not expected but suddenly happens.

Consider a child, especially at the age when it has absorbed speech but not yet the accumulated wealth of tradition in the language. It lives with things in the world of things, with what we adults also know and also with what we no longer know, what has been scared away from us by the wealth of tradition, by concepts, by all that is sure and stable. And suddenly the child begins to speak, it tells its story, falls silent, again something bursts out. How does the child tell what it tells? The only correct designation is *mythically*. It tells precisely as early man tells his myths which have become an inseparable unity composed from dream and waking sight, from experience and "fantasy" (but is fantasy not originally also a kind of experience?). Then suddenly the spirit is there. But without any preceding "asceticism" and "sublimation". Of course the spirit was in the child before it tells its story; but not as such, not for itself, but bound up with "instinct"—and with things. Now the spirit steps forth itself, independently—in the *word*. The child "has spirit" for the first time when it speaks; it has spirit because it wants to speak. Before it now speaks the mythical images were not there separately but inserted and mingled into the substance of life. But now they are there— in the word. Only because the child has the *spiritual instinct* to the word do these images come forward now, and at the same time become independent: they exist and can be spoken. The spirit begins here as an instinct, as an instinct to the word, that is, as the impulse to be present with others in a world of streaming communication, of an image given and received.

Or consider a typical peasant, as he still exists, although the social and cultural conditions for his existence seem to have disappeared. I mean a peasant who all his life seemed able to think only purposively and technically, who bore in mind only what he needed for his work and the immediate condition of his life. But now he begins to age, to have to make an effort to carry out his job. And then it happens that on his day off he can be seen standing there staring into the clouds, and if he is asked he replies, after a while, that he has been studying the weather and you see that it is not true. At the same time he can occasionally be seen with his mouth quite unexpectedly opening—to utter a saying. Before this he had of course uttered sayings, but traditional and known ones, which were mostly humorously pessimistic utterances about "the way of things". He still utters the same kind now, and preferably if something has gone amiss, if he has experienced the "contrary-ness" of things (which Scheler takes as the fundamental nature of all experience of the world), that is, if he has once more experienced the contradiction which reigns in the world. But now he makes, time and again, remarks of a quite different kind, such as were not heard from him earlier, and unknown to tradition. And he utters them staring ahead, often only whispering as though to himself, they can barely be caught: he is uttering his own insights. He does not do this when he has experienced the contrariness of things, but for example when the ploughshare has sunk softly and deeply into the soil as though the furrow were deliberately opening to receive it, or when the cow has been quickly and easily delivered of her calf as though an invisible power were helping. That is, he utters his own insights if he has experienced the *grace* of things, if he has once again experienced despite all contrariness that man participates in the being of the world. Certainly the experience of grace is only made possible by the experience of contrariness and in contrast to it. But here too it holds true that the spirit arises from concord with things and in concord with instincts.

II

In his first anthropological treatise, written during his theistic period, Scheler makes true man begin with the "God-seeker". Between the beast and *homo faber*, the maker of tools and machines, there exists only a difference of degree. But between *homo faber* and the man who begins to go out beyond himself and to seek God there exists a difference of kind. In his last anthropological works, whose underlying position is no longer theism but that idea of a becoming God, the philosopher takes the place of the religious man. Between *homo faber* and the beast, so Scheler expounds here, there exists no difference of kind, for intelligence and the power of choice belong also to the beast. Man's special position is established by means of the principle of spirit as absolutely superior to all intelligence and standing altogether outside all that we call life. Man as a being in the order of living things is "without any doubt a cul-de-sac of nature", while "as a potential spiritual being" he is "the bright and glorious way *out* of this cul-de-sac". Man is therefore "not a static being, not a fact, but only a potential direction of a process".

That is almost exactly the same as Nietzsche says about man, except that here the "spirit" takes the place of Nietzsche's "will to power" which makes man into real man. But the basic definition of a "spiritual" being is for Scheler his existential separability from the organic, from "life" and all that belongs to life. To a certain extent—with the essential limitations I have formulated above—this is true of the philosopher; it is not true of the spiritual existence of man in general, and especially it is not true of spirit as a happening. In his early and in his later works Scheler draws two different lines of division through mankind, but both are inadmissible and full of self-contradiction. If the religious man is something different from the existential actuation of all that lives in the "non-religious" man as dumb need, as stammering dereliction, as despair crying out, then he is a monster. Man does not begin where God is sought, but where God's farness means suffering without the knowledge of what is causing it. And a "spiritual" man, in whom a spirit dwells which is not found anywhere else, and which understands the art of cutting itself free from all life, is only a curiosity. If the spirit as a calling wants to be in its essence something different from the spirit as a happening then it is no longer the true spirit but an artificial product usurping the spirit's place. The spirit is inserted in sparks into the life of all, it bursts out in flames from the life of the most living man, and from time to time there burns somewhere a great fire of the spirit. All this is of *one* being and *one* substance. There is no other spirit but that which is nourished by the unity of life and by unity with the world. Certainly it experiences being separated from the unity of life and being thrown into abysmal contradiction to the world. But even in the martyrdom of spiritual existence true spirit does not deny its primal community with the whole of being; rather it asserts it against the false representatives of being who deny it.

12

The spirit *as a happening*, the spirit I have indicated in the child and the peasant, proves to us that it is not inherent in spirit, as Scheler contends, to arise by repression and sublimation of the instincts. Scheler, as is well-known, takes these psychological categories from Sigmund Freud's ideas, among whose greatest services is that he has formed them. But though these categories have general validity, the central position which Freud gives them, their dominating significance for the whole structure of personal and communal life, and especially for the origin and development of the spirit, is not based on the general life of man but only on the situation and qualities of the typical man of to-day. But this man is sick, both in his relation to others and in his very soul. The central significance of repression and sublimation in Freud's system derives from analysis of a pathological condition and is valid for this condition. The categories are psychological, their dominating power is pathopsychological. It can, indeed, be shown that nevertheless their significance is valid not only for our time but also for others akin to it, that is, for times of a pathological condition similar to our own, times like our own when a crisis is arising. But I know no such deep-reaching and comprehensive crisis in history as ours, and that indicates the extent of the significance of those categories. If I were to express our crisis in a formula I should like to call it the crisis of confidence. We have seen how epochs of security of human existence in the cosmos alternate with epochs of insecurity; but in the latter there still reigns for the most part a *social* certainty, one is borne along by a small organic community living in real togetherness. Being able to have confidence within this community compensates for cosmic insecurity; there is connexion and certainty. Where confidence reigns man must often, indeed, adapt his wishes to the commands of his community; but he must not repress them to such an extent that the repression acquires a dominating significance for his life. They often coalesce with the needs of the community, which are expressed by its commands. This coalescence, indeed, can really take place only where everything really lives with everything within the community, where, that is to say, there reigns not an enjoined and imagined but a genuine and elementary confidence. Only if the organic community disintegrates from within and mistrust becomes life's basic note does the repression acquire its dominating importance. The unaffectedness of wishing is stifled by mistrust, everything around is hostile or can become hostile, agreement between one's own and the other's desire ceases, for there is no true coalescence or reconciliation with what is necessary to a sustaining community, and the dulled wishes creep hopelessly into the recesses of the soul. But now the ways of the spirit are also changed. Hitherto it was the characteristic of its origin to flash forth from the clouds as the concentrated manifestation of the wholeness of man. Now there is no longer a human wholeness with the force and the courage to manifest itself. For spirit to arise the energy of the repressed instincts must mostly first be "sublimated", the traces of its origin cling to the spirit and it can mostly assert itself against the instincts only by convulsive alienation. The divorce between spirit and instincts is here, as often, the consequence of the divorce between man and man.

13

In opposition to Scheler's conception it must be said of the spirit that in its beginning it is pure power, namely man's power to grasp the world, from inner participation in it and from strict and close struggle with it, in picture and sound and idea. First comes man's intimate participation in the world, intimate with it in strife as in peace. Here the spirit as a separate being is not yet present, but it is contained in the force of the primitively concentrated participation. Only with the tremendous impulse not merely to perceive the world in wrestling or in playing with it, but also to grasp it; only with the passion to bind the experienced chaos to the cosmos, does the spirit arise as a separate being. The picture emerges distinctly from the wild flickering light, the sound from the wild tumult of the earth, the idea from the wild confusion of all things: in this way the spirit arises as spirit. But there cannot be imagined any primal stage of the spirit in which it does not wish to express itself: the picture itself strives to be painted on the roof of a cave, and the reddle is at hand, the sound strives to be sung, and the lips are opening in a magic song. Chaos is subdued by form. But form wishes to be perceived by others besides him who produced it: the picture is shown with passion, the singer sings to the listeners with passion. The impulse to form is not to be divorced from the impulse to the word. From participation in the world man reaches participation in souls. The world is bound up, and given order; it can be spoken between man and man, now for the first time it becomes a world between man and man. And again the spirit is pure power; with gesture and words the man of the spirit subdues the resistance of the friends of chaos and gives order to community. The powerlessness of the spirit which Scheler considers to be original is always an accompanying circumstance of the disintegration of community. The word is no longer received, it no longer binds and orders what is human, participation in souls is forbidden to the spirit and it turns aside and cuts free from the unity of life, it flees to its citadel, the citadel of the brain. Hitherto man thought with his whole body to the very finger-tips; from now on he thinks only with his brain. Only now does Freud receive the object of his psychology and Scheler the object of his anthropology— the sick man, cut off from the world and divided into spirit and instincts. So long as we suppose that this sick man is *man*, the normal man, man in general, we shall not heal him.

Here I must break off the presentation and criticism of Scheler's anthropology. In a genetic study it would remain to be shown that the essential difference between man and beast, the difference which establishes the essential life of man, is not his separation from instinctive connexion with things and living beings but on the contrary his different and new way of turning to things and living beings. It would remain to be shown that the primary relation is not the technical relation common to man and beast, above which man then rises, but that man's specific primitive technique, the invention of independent tools suited to their purpose and able to be used again and again, has become possible only through man's new relation to things as to something that is inspected, is independent, and lasting. It would further remain to be shown that in the same way in relation with other men the original and defining characteristic is not the instinctive in general, above which man only later rises in the struggle of the spirit with a turning to men as persons who are there, apart from my need, independent and lasting, and that the origin of speech is to be understood only on the basis of such a turning to others. Here as there a unity of spirit and instinct and a formation of new spiritual instincts obviously stand at the beginning. And here as there man's essential life is not to be grasped from what unrolls in the individual's inner life nor from the consciousness of one's own self, which Scheler takes to be the decisive difference between man and beast, but from the distinctiveness of his relations to things and to living beings.

IV: PROSPECT

IN two significant modern attempts we have seen that an individualistic anthropology, an anthropology which is substantially concerned only with the relation of the human person to himself, with the relation within this person between the spirit and its instincts, and so on, cannot lead to a knowledge of man's being. Kant's question *What is man?* whose history and effects I have discussed in the first part of this work, can never be answered on the basis of a consideration of the human person as such, but (so far as an answer is possible at all) only on the basis of a consideration of it in the wholeness of its essential relations to what is. Only the man who realizes in his whole life with his whole being the relations possible to him helps us to know man truly. And since, as we have seen, the depths of the question about man's being are revealed only to the man who has become solitary, the way to the answer lies through the man who overcomes his solitude without forfeiting its questioning power. This means that a *new* task in life is set to human thought here, a task that is new in its context of *life*. For it means that the man who wants to grasp what he himself is, salvages the tension of solitude and its burning problematic for a life with his world, a life that is renewed in spite of all, and out of this new situation proceeds with his thinking. Of course this presupposes the beginning of a new process of overcoming the solitude—despite all the vast difficulties—by reference to which that special task of thought can be perceived and expressed. It is obvious that at the present stage reached by mankind such a process cannot be effected by the spirit alone; but to a certain extent knowledge will also be able to further it. It is incumbent on us to clarify this in outline.

Criticism of the individualistic method starts usually from the standpoint of the collectivist tendency. But if individualism understands only a part of man, collectivism understands man only as a part: neither advances to the wholeness of man, to man as a whole. Individualism sees man only in relation to himself, but collectivism does not see *man* at all, it sees only "society". With the former man's face is distorted, with the latter it is masked.

Both views of life—modern individualism and modern collectivism—however different their causes may be, are essentially the conclusion or expression of the same human condition, only at different stages. This condition is characterized by the union of cosmic and social homelessness, dread of the universe and dread of life, resulting in an existential constitution of solitude such as has probably never existed before to the same extent. The human person feels himself to be a man exposed by nature—as an unwanted child is exposed—and at the same time a person isolated in the midst of the tumultuous human world. The first reaction of the spirit to the awareness of this new and uncanny position is modern individualism, the second is modern collectivism.

In individualism the human being ventures to affirm this position, to plunge it into an affirmative reflexion, a universal *amor fati*; he wants to build the citadel of a life-system in which the idea asserts that it wills reality as it is. Just because man is exposed by nature, he is an individual in this specially radical way in which no other being in the world is an individual; and he accepts his exposure because it means that he is an individual. In the same way he accepts his isolation as a person, for only a monad which is not bound to others can know and glorify itself as an individual to the utmost. To save himself from the despair with which his solitary state threatens him, man resorts to the expedient of glorifying it. Modern individualism has essentially an imaginary basis. It founders on this character, for imagination is not capable of actually conquering the given situation.

The second reaction, collectivism, essentially follows upon the foundering of the first. Here the human being tries to escape his destiny of solitude by becoming completely embedded in one of the massive modern group formations. The more massive, unbroken and powerful in its achievements this is, the more the man is able to feel that he is saved from both forms of homelessness, the social and the cosmic. There is obviously no further reason for dread of life, since one needs only to fit oneself into the "general will" and let one's own responsibility for an existence which has become all too complicated be absorbed in collective responsibility, which proves itself able to meet all complications. Likewise, there is obviously no further reason for dread of the universe, since technicized nature—with which society as such manages well, or seems to— takes the place of the universe which has become uncanny and with which, so to speak, no further agreement can be reached. The collective pledges itself to provide total security. There is nothing imaginary here, a dense reality rules, and the "general" itself appears to have become real; but modern collectivism is essentially illusory. The person is joined to the reliably functioning "whole", which embraces the masses of men; but it is not a joining of man to man. Man in a collective is not man with man. Here the person is not freed from his isolation, by communing with living beings, which thenceforth lives with him; the "whole", with its claim on the wholeness of every man, aims logically and successfully at reducing, neutralizing, devaluating, and desecrating every bond with living beings. That tender surface of personal life which longs for contact with other life is progressively deadened or desensitized. Man's isolation is not overcome here, but overpowered and numbed. Knowledge of it is suppressed, but the actual condition of solitude has its insuperable effect in the depths, and rises secretly to a cruelty which will become manifest with the scattering of the illusion. Modern collectivism is the last barrier raised by man against a meeting with himself.

When imaginings and illusions are over, the possible and inevitable meeting of man with himself is able to take place only as the meeting of the individual with his fellow-man— and this is how it must take place. Only when the individual knows the other in all his otherness as himself, as man, and from there breaks through to the other, has he broken through his solitude in a strict and transforming meeting.

It is obvious that such an event can only take place if the person is stirred up as a person. In individualism the person, in consequence of his merely imaginary mastery of his basic situation, is attacked by the ravages of the fictitious, however much he thinks, or strives to think, that he is asserting himself as a person in being. In collectivism the person surrenders himself when he renounces the directness of personal decision and responsibility. In both cases the person is incapable of breaking through to the other: there is genuine relation only between genuine persons.

In spite of all attempts at revival the time of individualism is over. Collectivism, on the other hand, is at the height of its development, although here and there appear single signs of slackening. Here the only way that is left is the rebellion of the person for the sake of setting free the relations with others. On the horizon I see moving up, with the slowness of all events of true human history, a great dissatisfaction which is unlike all previous dissatisfactions. Men will no longer rise in re-bellion—as they have done till now—merely against some dominating tendency in the name of other tendencies, but against the false realization of a great effort, the effort towards community, in the name of the genuine realization. Men will fight against the distortion for the pure form, the vision of the believing and hoping generations of mankind.

I am speaking of living actions; but it is vital knowledge alone which incites them. Its first step must be to smash the false alternative with which the thought of our epoch is shot through—that of "individualism or collectivism". Its first question must be about a genuine third alternative—by "genuine" being understood a point of view which cannot be reduced to one of the first two, and does not represent a mere compromise between them.

Life and thought are here placed in the same problematic situation. As life erroneously supposes that it has to choose between individualism and collectivism, so thought erroneously supposes that it has to choose between an individualistic anthropology and a collectivist sociology. The genuine third alternative, when it is found, will point the way here too.

The fundamental fact of human existence is neither the

individual as such nor the aggregate as such. Each, considered by itself, is a mighty abstraction. The individual is a fact of existence in so far as he steps into a living relation with other individuals. The aggregate is a fact of existence in so far as it is built up of living units of relation. The fundamental fact of human existence is man with man. What is peculiarly characteristic of the human world is above all that something takes place between one being and another the like of which can be found nowhere in nature. Language is only a sign and a means for it, all achievement of the spirit has been incited by it. Man is made man by it; but on its way it does not merely unfold, it also decays and withers away. It is rooted in one being turning to another as another, as this particular other being, in order to communicate with it in a sphere which is common to them but which reaches out beyond the special sphere of each. I call this sphere, which is established with the existence of man as man but which is conceptually still uncomprehended, the sphere of "between". Though being realized in very different degrees, it is a primal category of human reality. This is where the genuine third alternative must begin.

The view which establishes the concept of "between" is to be acquired by no longer localizing the relation between human beings, as is customary, either within individual souls or in a general world which embraces and determines them, but in actual fact *between* them.

"Between" is not an auxiliary construction, but the real place and bearer of what happens between men; it has received no specific attention because, in distinction from the individual soul and its context, it does not exhibit a smooth continuity, but is ever and again re-constituted in accordance with men's meetings with one another; hence what is experience has been annexed naturally to the continuous elements, the soul and its world.

In a real conversation (that is, not one whose individual parts have been preconcerted, but one which is completely spontaneous, in which each speaks directly to his partner and calls forth his unpredictable reply), a real lesson (that is, neither a routine repetition nor a lesson whose findings the teacher knows before he starts, but one which develops in mutual surprises), a real embrace and not one of mere habit, a real duel and not a mere game—in all these what is essential does not take place in each of the participants or in a neutral world which includes the two and all other things; but it takes place between them in the most precise sense, as it were in a dimension which is accessible only to them both. Something happens to me—that is a fact which can be exactly distributed between the world and the soul, between an "outer" event and an "inner" impression. But if I and another come up against one another, "happen" to one another (to use a forcible expression which can, however, scarcely be paraphrased), the sum does not exactly divide, there is a remainder, somewhere, where the souls end and the world has not yet begun, and this remainder is what is essential. This fact can be found even in the tiniest and most transient events which scarcely enter the consciousness. In the deadly crush of an air-raid shelter the glances of two strangers suddenly meet for a second in astonishing and unrelated mutuality; when the All Clear sounds it is forgotten; and yet it did happen, in a realm which existed only for that moment. In the darkened opera-house there can be established between two of the audience, who do not know one another, and who are listening in the same purity and with the same intensity to the music of Mozart, a relation which is scarcely perceptible and yet is one of elemental dialogue, and which has long vanished when the lights blaze up again. In the understanding of such fleeting and yet consistent happenings one must guard against introducing motives of feeling: what happens here cannot be reached by psychological concepts, it is something ontic. From the least of events, such as these, which disappear in the moment of their appearance, to the pathos of pure indissoluble tragedy, where two men, opposed to one another in their very nature, entangled in the same living situation, reveal to one another in mute clarity an irreconcilable opposition of being, the dialogical situation can be adequately grasped only in an ontological way. But it is not to be grasped on the basis of the ontic of personal existence, or of that of two personal existences, but of that which has its being between them, and transcends both. In the most powerful moments of dialogic, where in truth "deep calls unto deep", it becomes unmistakably clear that it is not the wand of the individual or of the social, but of a third which draws the circle round the happening. On the far side of the subjective, on this side of the objective, on the narrow ridge, where *I* and *Thou* meet, there is the realm of "between".

This reality, whose disclosure has begun in our time, shows

the way, leading beyond individualism and collectivism, for the life decision of future generations. Here the genuine third alternative is indicated, the knowledge of which will help to bring about the genuine person again and to establish genuine community.

This reality provides the starting-point for the philosophical science of man; and from this point an advance may be made on the one hand to a transformed understanding of the person and on the other to a transformed understanding of community. The central subject of this science is neither the individual nor the collective but man with man. That essence of man which is special to him can be directly known only in a living relation. The gorilla, too, is an individual, a termitary, too, is a collective, but *I* and *Thou* exist only in our world, because man exists, and the *I*, moreover, exists only through the relation to the *Thou*. The philosophical science of man, which includes anthropology and sociology, must take as its starting-point the consideration of this subject, "man with man". If you consider the individual by himself, then you see of man just as much as you see of the moon; only man with man provides a full image. If you consider the aggregate by itself, then you see of man just as much as we see of the Milky Way; only man with man is a completely outlined form. Consider man with man, and you see human life, dynamic, twofold, the giver and the receiver, he who does and he who endures, the attacking force and the defending force, the nature which investigates and the nature which supplies information, the request begged and granted—and always both together, completing one another in mutual contribution, together showing forth man. Now you can turn to the individual and you recognize him as man according to the possibility of relation which he shows; you can turn to the aggregate and you recognize it as man according to the fulness of relation which he shows. We may come nearer the answer to the question what man is when we come to see him as the eternal meeting of the One with the Other.

TRANSLATOR'S NOTES

(1) p. 12. There is a typical example here, which could be multiplied many times, of a play of words in the German which cannot be reproduced in the English. "This is not superstition (*Aberglaube*), but perverse knowledge (*Aberwissen*)." And of course this is more than a *play* of words, since this perverse knowledge leads direct to gnosis, which is very different from the theme, faith.

(2) p. 17. The significance of *responsibility* (and the point of the whole section, indeed of the whole of *Dialogue*) is brought out more acutely in the German than in the English. *Wort, Antwort, antworten, verantworten*, etc., are part of a closely inter-related situation in which speech and response, answering for and being responsible for, and so on, are more intimately connected than the English version can hope to show. If the reader will remember that "responsibility" carries in itself the root sense of being "answerable", then the significance of the "word" in actual life will not be lost. Buber's teaching about the "word" always carries a strict reference to "lived life", and is very far from being an abstraction, theological or other.

(3) p. 21. The German *Genosse*, Hebrew רע, English *companion*, is not the same, Buber means, as the "nearest" (*der Næchste*, the usual word for *neighbour*). In the Septuagint the change of sense had already begun, since the word used there, πλήσιος (Lev. xix. 18), means near, near-dweller; Luther completes the change, and in his as in the English vernacular version of the Bible the real sense of the injunction, to meet the other in real objective love, is dissipated in the notion of "universal unreserve".

(4) p. 22. "Reflexion" for *Rückbiegung* is by no means a perfect rendering. Buber, however, makes clear that he is here describing the essence of the "monological" life, in which the other is not really met as the other, but merely as a part of the monological self, in an *Erlebnis* or inner experience which has no objective import: what happens is that the self "curves back on itself" (cf. *I and Thou*, esp. pp. 115-6, where the same attitude is considered in relation to God).

(5) p. 24. *Ungrund*: for this difficult notion cf. Berdyaev, *Spirit and Reality*, pp. 144-5, where Berdyaev, discussing Boehme's conception of *Ungrund* says:

Ungrund is not being, but a more primeval and deeper stratum of being. *Ungrund* is *nothingness* as distinct from *something* in the category of being; it is not εὐχ ὄν but μή ὄν. But it is not μὴ ὄν in the Greek sense. Boehme goes beyond the limits of Greek thought, of Greek intellectualism and ontology. Like *Eckhart's Gottheit* Boehme's *Ungrund* goes deeper than God.

But for Buber *Ungrund* is less vague and more modest than this, being recognized as the undifferentiated basic unity of the life of the soul.

(6) p. 29. "Knowing" ("*erkennen*") is used in the Biblical sense of lovers "knowing" each other—which of course is not limited to the physical, but means a connexion comprehending the whole being of the beloved.

(7) p. 29. "I vow it faithfully to myself and myself to it. I vow, I have faith": here again the German (*ich gelobe es mir an und mich ihm, ich gelobe, ich glaube*) shows in a way the English cannot the intimate connexion between language and thought.

(8) p. 30. "The indwelling of the Present Being between them": *die Einwohnung des Seienden zwischen ihnen*, refers to the Shekinah or Divine Presence. This usage derives from the Old Testament reference to "the place where the Lord God causes his name to dwell" (cf., e.g. Deut. xii. 11). God comes to be described as "the One who causes his name to dwell there" (scil. the Temple), and then simply as "dwelling" (שכינה). For a full discussion of this usage (which recurs in Buber, as of central significance to his teaching), see Strack-Billerbeck, *Kommentar zum Neuen Testament*, II, 314.

(9) p. 40. *The Question to the Single One*. The German which I have rendered by the cumbrous and none too clear phrase "the Single One" is *der Einzelne*, which is a fairly precise rendering of Kierkegaard's *hiin Enkelte*. It is a pity that in the English translations of Kierkegaard no effort seems to have been made by the translators to avoid the use of the word "individual", which is highly misleading. For every man is *individuum*, but not everyone is an *Einzelner* or *Enkelte*. In fact, the whole course of Kierkegaard's life, and the whole force of his teaching, is directed towards "becoming a Single One", and this is not a natural or biological category but, as Kierkegaard reiterates, it is "the spirit's category", and a rare thing. The reader's complaisance is invited, therefore, as it was decided better to make the English a little odd rather than customary and misleading.

(10) p. 41. All Kierkegaard's works, and a selection of the

Journals, are now available in English. An English translation of Stirner's book, by S. C. Byington, was published under the title *The Ego and his Own*, London (A. C. Fifield) and New York (E. C. Walker), 1913.

(11) p. 51. "Love your neighbour as one like yourself": this departure from the customary rendering of the Authorized Version is again an effort to render the original more precisely (in this case the Hebrew of Lev. xix. 18) in order to keep before the reader the stark objectivity of the command—the other whom you are required to "love" being one with a real life of his own, and not one whom you are invited to "acquire".

(12) p. 69. "The Hinderer" (*der Hinderer*): this is the best rendering of the Hebrew שטן ("Satan"). See, for example, the story of Balaam in *Numbers* XXII, where the *Authorized Version* gives (v. 22) "adversary", and paraphrases (v. 32) by "to withstand". But the true meaning is given in the most concrete rendering that English can supply—short of being imprisoned in a proper name.

(13) p. 69. "Spark": the allusion is to the "Fünklein" of Eckhart. Cf., e.g., "the soul has something in it, a spark of speech (*redelicheit*) that never dies", and "the soul's spark, which is untouched by time and space" (*Meister Eckhart*, ed. Pfeiffer, 1857, pp. 39 and 193). There is an English translation by Evans, *Master Eckhart*, 1924. It is to be noted, however, that in Buber *Fünklein* has throughout a more ethical connotation than in Eckhart.

(14) p. 158. *Golem* is originally a Hebrew word. cf. *I and Thou*, p. 44, 1. 17, where I paraphrased it as "animated clod without soul". The allusion is to the clay figure, possessed of no divine soul, made by a Rabbi in order to prevent attacks on Jews. Its end is either its destruction by the Rabbi, or his by it; for it could only destroy or be destroyed. (cf. H. L. Held, *Das Gespenst des Golem* (1927), pp. 85, 94.)

AFTERWORD

The History of the Dialogical Principle*

by Martin Buber

In all ages it has undoubtedly been glimpsed that the reciprocal essential relationship between two beings signifies a primal opportunity of being, and one, in fact, that enters into the phenomenon that man exists. And it has also ever again been glimpsed that just through the fact that he enters into essential reciprocity, man becomes revealed as man; indeed, that only with this and through this does he attain to that valid participation in being that is reserved for him; thus, that the saying of Thou by the I stands in the origin of all individual human becoming.

This glimpse is expressed in the immediacy of its own language in a letter written in 1775 by Friedrich Heinrich Jacobi to an unknown person (quoted in a letter of 1781 from Jacobi to Lavater). There it says: "I open eye or ear, or I stretch forth my hand, and feel in the same moment inseparably: Thou and I, I and Thou." In the transition to speech, the insight that is stated here is expressed in one of Jacobi's "Pamphlets": "The source of all certainty: you are and I am!" And the mature formulation (1785) reads: "The I is impossible without the Thou." **

---

* Translated by Maurice Friedman. Parts of the sections on Ferdinand Ebner and Karl Jaspers are reprinted with the permission of Random House, Inc., from *The Worlds of Existentialism: A Critical Reader,* edited and with Introductions and a Conclusion by Maurice Friedman (New York: Random House, 1964), pp. 317ff., also translated by Maurice Friedman.

** One may compare this formulation with the 1797 statement of Fichte, which is to be understood, to be sure, in a wholly different context of meaning: "The consciousness of the individual is necessarily accompanied by that of another, that of a Thou, and only under this condition possible."

Only a half century afterward, however, did Ludwig Feuerbach—a thinker of a wholly different nature from Jacobi, but one not entirely uninfluenced by him—succeed in incorporating his knowledge of the primal relationship of I and Thou in complementary philosophical theses. He finds himself at first only in the foreroom of the building that has opened itself to him: "The consciousness of the world is mediated for the I through the consciousness of the Thou." To this, one may join a later sentence, though one that does not actually go beyond Jacobi, that the real I is "only the I that stands over against a Thou and that is itself a Thou over against another I." Soon after this utterance, however, clearly inundated by one of the surging and receding waves of an inspiration of genius, Feuerbach writes, concerning the "mystery of the necessity of the Thou for the I," the statement that manifestly has for him the character of final validity, and at this point he remains without even trying to go further: "Man for himself is man (in the usual sense)—man with man—the unity of I and Thou is God." Here the standpoint of the new way of thinking has gained a firm footing, but in the same instant it is already overstepped in the indefiniteness of a bad mysticism where the philosopher can no longer expect a ground capable of sustaining him. The sentence is clearly, consciously or unconsciously, directed against Jacobi's basic view which leads him in that letter, after he has represented the Thou as an earthly one ("the other as the support of one's own existence; a beloved Thou"), to address God by the same Thou. To this coupling of the human and the divine Thou, Feuerbach does not reply with the demand of a radical renunciation of the concept of God but with the substitution of an anthropological ersatz God. Instead of logically concluding, "The unity of I and Thou is man in the true sense," he introduces a pseudomystical construction that neither he himself nor anyone after him could fill with a genuine content.

The eliminating of this construction from general use is facilitated a short time afterward by Søren Kierkegaard, who preserves at the same time Feuerbach's grasp of reality. The category "to be the Single One" that he placed before his epoch is to be understood, in the strict sense, as the decisive presupposition for the highest essential relationship; for God "wants the Single Ones, only with the Single Ones will he have to do, no matter whether the Single One is exalted or insignificant, splendid or pitiful." But there prevails here, if not fundamentally at least factually, a critical limitation. Kierkegaard demands, to be sure, that man also deal as a Single One with his fellowman, but the relation to his fellowman does not become an essential relationship in that exact sense. It cannot become such for Kierkegaard, no matter how splendidly he knows how to preach about the love of one's neighbor. When Jacobi reported in his letter about his immediacy, he broke into an overflow of feeling the expression of which literally ("Heart! Love! God!") reminds one of Faust's answer to Gretchen—the *Urfaust* stems from just that time indeed. Thus the Thou of the "other" and that of God are brought together, although the danger of a vague intermingling was not altogether avoided. In the most extreme contrast to this, the human Thou in Kierkegaard's existential thought is never transparent into the divine, the bounded never into the boundless. From this No a great question has been posed to the succeeding generations that demands a sober and impartial weighing and response. For the breaking out of the cleft between Thou and Thou threatens to pervert the innermost significance of that discovery of I and Thou. The danger that arose earlier from a seemingly mystical atheism now arises from an almost monadically intended theistic piety.

Only sixty years later,* at the time of the First World War, does the movement begin anew. Out of the experience of the Vesuvian hour, a strange longing awakens for thinking to do justice to existence itself. This longing

---

* A notable statement of William James in the interim (*The Will to Believe*, 1897) should not remain unmentioned. It reads: "The universe is no longer a mere *It* to us, but a *Thou*, if we are religious; and any relation that may be possible from person to person might be possible here."

even seizes the systematic thinkers. It is significant that the vision of the Thou is renewed first of all by the neo-Kantian thinker Hermann Cohen, who, near death in the winter of 1917–1918, wrote the book *Religion der Vernunft aus den Quellen des Judentums* (*The Religion of Reason out of the Sources of Judaism*, 1919). It may be regarded as a continuation of the line of Jacobi when it is recognized here that "only the Thou, the discovery of the Thou, brings me to consciousness of my I" and that it is "the personality" that "is raised by the Thou to the light of day." But something formerly unexpressed in philosophy becomes explicit when it says of the reciprocal relationship of man and God, their "correlation," that it could "not enter into completion if it were not preceded by the inclusive correlation of man and man."

Cohen's astonishing disciple Franz Rosenzweig in that winter had become acquainted with the *Religion der Vernunft* in manuscript form and bore it in mind—without, to be sure, being centrally influenced by it. Rosenzweig did not remove himself so far from Kierkegaard as Cohen did when, in the following summer in the Macedonian trenches, he began to build his *Der Stern der Erlösung* (*Star of Redemption*, 1921). But in the understanding of the Thou as a spoken one, fired by the solid concreteness of his philosophy of speech, he goes notably beyond Cohen. The essential spokenness of the Thou is for him contained in the "Where art Thou?" directed by God to Adam. Interpreting this, he asks: "Where is such an independent Thou, freely standing over against the hiding God, a Thou to whom he can reveal himself as I?" From this point an inner biblical way to that "I have called you by name; you are mine" becomes visible by which God shows himself "as the originator and opener of this whole dialogue between him and the soul." This is Rosenzweig's most significant theological contribution to our subject.*

In February, 1919, the *Star* was completed. But in the

* Franz Rosenzweig must also in this regard be seen in connection with a circle from which, in particular, Hans Ehrenberg and Eugen Rosenstock-Huessy are to be singled out here.

same winter and in the spring following, Ferdinand Ebner, a Catholic schoolteacher in the Austrian province, heavily afflicted by sickness and depression, wrote his "pneumatological fragments," which he collected then in the book *Das Wort und die geistigen Realitäten* (*The Word and the Spiritual Realities*, 1921). Ebner proceeds from the experience of the "solitude of the I" (*Icheinsamkeit*) in that existential sense that it has won in our time: it is for him "nothing original" but the result of the "closing off from the Thou." Starting from here, following the trail of Hamann, but binding the insights more strongly to one another, he penetrates more deeply into the mystery of speech as the ever-new establishment of the relation between the I and the Thou. He acknowledges himself, in a more direct fashion than Kierkegaard, as one who is not able to find the Thou in man. Already in 1917 he had indicated the danger of going under spiritually in the consciousness of this "impossibility." He finds salvation in the thought: "There is only one single Thou and that is just God." To be sure, he also postulates, as does Kierkegaard: "Man shall love not only God but also men." But where it is a question of the authenticity of existence, every other Thou disappears for him before that of God. If we ask here, as with Kierkegaard, about what is finally valid, we stand again before the self-relating individuals who look at the world but are in the last instance acosmic, who love men but are in the last instance ananthropic.

At this point I must speak of myself.

The question of the possibility and reality of a dialogical relationship between man and God had already accosted me in my youth. This dialogue implies a free partnership of man in a conversation between heaven and earth whose speech in address and answer is the happening itself, the happening from above and the happening from below. In particular, since the Hasidic tradition had grown for me into the supporting ground of my own thinking, hence since about 1905, that had become an innermost question for me. In the language of the writings on the dialogical principle that arose many years later, it appears emphatically for the first time* in the autumn of 1907 in the introduction to my book *The Legend of the Baal-Shem*. This introduction was concerned with the radical distinction between myth in the narrower sense (the myth of the mythologists) and legend. It said:

> The legend is the myth of the calling. In pure myth there is no difference of being. . . . Even the hero only stands on another rung than the god, not over against him: they are not the I and the Thou. . . . The god of pure myth does not call, he begets; he sends forth the begotten, the hero. The god of the legend calls, he calls the son of man: the prophets, the saints. . . . The legend is the myth of I and Thou, of caller and called, of the finite that enters into the infinite and of the infinite that needs the finite.**

Here the dialogical relationship is thus exemplified in its highest peak: because even on this height the essential difference between the partners persists unweakened, while even in such nearness the independence of man continues to be preserved.

From this event of the exception, of the extraction, however, my thought now led me, ever more earnestly, to the common that can be experienced by all. The clari-

* Translator's Note: Actually, Buber made use of the language of I and Thou even earlier, as pointed out in the following passage from Maurice Friedman, *Martin Buber: The Life of Dialogue* (New York: Harper Torchbooks, 1960), p. 51 n.b.: "In his essay on Boehme in 1901 Buber writes that Boehme's dialectic of the reciprocal condition of things finds its completion in Ludwig Feuerbach's sentence: 'Man with man—the unity of I and Thou—is God.' ('Ueber Jacob Böhme,' p. 252f.) In 1905 Buber uses the term 'I and Thou' in a discussion of the drama and of the tension of the isolated individual [Buber, 'Die Duse in Florenz,' *Die Schaubühne*, Vol. I, No. 15 (December 14, 1905)]. . . ."

** Translated by Maurice Friedman (New York: Harper & Bros., 1956), p. xiii.

fication took place first of all * here too in connection
with my interpretation of Hasidism: in the Preface written in September, 1919, to my book *Der Grosse Maggid
und seine Nachfolge* (1921), the Jewish teaching was described as "wholly based on the two-directional relation
of human I and divine Thou, on reciprocity, on the
meeting." Soon after, in the autumn of 1919, followed
the first, still unwieldly, draft of *I and Thou.*

There now followed two years in which I could do
almost no work except on Hasidic material, but also—
with the exception of Descartes' *Discours de la méthode,*
which I again took up—read no *philosophica* (therefore,
the works connected with the subject of dialogue by
Cohen, Rosenzweig, and Ebner** I read only later, too
late to affect my own thought). This was part of a procedure that I understood at that time as a spiritual ascesis.
Then I was able to begin the final writing of *I and Thou,*
which was completed in the spring of 1922. As I wrote
the third and last part, I broke the reading ascesis and
began with Ebner's fragments.*** His book showed me,
as no other since then, here and there in an almost uncanny nearness, that in this our time men of different
kinds and traditions had devoted themselves to the search

* Translator's Note: This clarification is also manifest in
other of Buber's writings in 1919. Thus in *Cheruth: Ein Rede
über Jugend und Religion,* Buber wrote: "Man experiences
the Absolute as the great presence that is over against him, as
'Thou' in itself." In *Gemeinschaft* he wrote: "The erection of
new institutions can only have a genuinely liberating effect
when it is accompanied by a transformation of the actual life
between man and man." Cf. Maurice Friedman, *Martin Buber:
The Life of Dialogue,* pp. 41, 46.

** Hermann Cohen, *Religion der Vernunft aus den Quellen
des Judentums* (1919); Franz Rosenzweig, *Der Stern der Erlösung* (1921); Ferdinand Ebner, *Das Wort und die geistigen
Realitäten* (1921). Therefore, Rosenzweig states in one of his
letters (*Briefe,* p. 462) that in December, 1921, I did not yet
know his book.

*** First I happened to see some of them that were published in an issue of *Brenner* and then sent for the book.

for the buried treasure. Soon I also had similar experiences from other directions.

Of the initiators, I had already as a student known Feuerbach and Kierkegaard: Yes and No to them had become a part of my existence. Now there surrounded me in spirit a growing circle of men of the present generations who were concerned, even if in unequal measure, about the one thing that had become for me an ever more vital matter. The basic view of the twofold nature of the human attitude is expressed in the beginning of *I and Thou*. But I had already prepared the way for this view in the distinction presented in my book *Daniel* (1913) between an "orienting," objectifying basic attitude and a "realizing," making-present one. This is a distinction that coincides in its core with that carried through in *I and Thou* between the I-It relation and the I-Thou relation, except that the latter is no longer grounded in the sphere of subjectivity but in that between the beings. But this is the decisive transformation that took place in a series of spirits in the time of the First World War. It announced itself in very manifold meanings and spheres, but the fundamental connection between them, stemming out of the disclosed transformation of the human situation, is unmistakable.

A number of publications from the decade following the aforementioned works must be brought together under this heading as belonging to that period of time in which the clarification was completed.

Out of the circle of Rosenzweig came books of two Protestant thinkers: Hans Ehrenberg's *Disputation I Fichte* (1923) and Eugen Rosenstock-Heussy's *Angewandte Seelenkunde* (1924), by which Rosenzweig, who knew an earlier version of it, was "decisively" influenced in the writing of his book [cf. also Rosenstock-Huessy's *Der Atem des Geistes* (*The Breath of the Spirit*, 1951)].

Out of Protestant theology, Friedrich Gogarten's *Ich glaube an den dreieinigen Gott* (*I Believe in the Three-in-One God*, 1926) must be named first of all. This book understands *history* as "the meeting of Thou and I," but at the same time it clings to the undialectical thesis that "history is God's work" and thus ultimately fails to grasp the character of history as meeting. In the same author's *Glaube und Wirklichkeit (Faith and Reality,* 1928) the teaching that the meeting of Thou and I is reality is treated as simply a constituent part of Reformation Protestantism. Next we have before us here Karl Heim's comprehensive theological-philosophical systematic attempt *Glaube und Denken* (Faith and Thought, 1931), in which the significance of the new direction of thinking is pointed out in the most emphatic manner ("If at first the I-It relationship was to the fore and now the Thou opens to us . . . a far more radical revolution has taken place than the discovery of a new part of the world or the disclosure of a new system of suns. The whole of the space-time It-world, inclusive of all the constellations and nebulae of the Milky Way has entered a new perspective"). Even in the works of Emil Brunner of this period our problem is already included.

Catholic philosophy produced at that time, before all, Gabriel Marcel's *Journal métaphysique* (1927), in which, apparently independently of that which had been said up till then in the German language, the central insight appears to be noted down in its actual coming to be. It is nowhere comparable to the elemental experiences of the Catholic thinker Ebner, for the depths of the kingdom of speech are not touched on here. Still the fact that there recurs here the fundamental thesis of *I and Thou,* that the eternal Thou by its nature cannot become an It, confirms the universality of the spiritual development with which this postscript is concerned.

This development also occurs within "free" philosophy —by which is meant that which no longer, like that of Descartes or Leibniz, is existentially rooted in a reality of faith and therefore fundamentally excludes the concern about the link between the intercourse with the conditioned Thou and the intercourse with the unconditioned Thou. Four works of that period stand in the foreground: Theodor Litt's *Individuum und Gemeinschaft (Individual and Community,* 1924, 1926), Karl Löwith's *Das Individuum in der Rolle des Mitmenschen*

(*The Individual in the Role of Fellowman,* 1928), Eberhard Grisebach's *Gegenwart* (*The Present,* 1928), and Karl Jaspers' *Philosophie* II and III (1932).

For Litt the concept of the "Thou-experience" is decisive; yet he unmistakably goes beyond the sphere of the psychological when he sees, for example, a changed relationship to the world coming "out of the dialectical relation of a true 'dialogos.' "

Löwith's book is the distinctive contribution of phenomenology,* a competent structural analysis, especially penetrating in its evaluation of Wilhelm von Humboldt's great findings in the philosophy of language. But when a door that has not been anticipated seems about to spring open, Löwith cannot refrain from carefully bolting it.

The strict and overly strict logical consistency of the radical critique of Grisebach sacrifices many concrete contents of the Thou relationship to the postulate of the acknowledgment of the Thou of the fellowman in its existential address and response. It remains unnoticed here that in a real meeting with my neighbor, the sheer practice of the hearing of the otherness of the other that Grisebach demands may miss precisely that help that is in question: the unfolding of something that is to be regarded in common. To allow oneself really to be limited by the Thou is important, but it may be much more important to lay oneself open together with him before the

---

* Max Scheler's *Wesen und Formen der Sympathie* (*The Nature and Forms of Sympathy,* 1923), for all its significance, does not belong here because it does not correspond to the character of being of our subject. Sentences like that which states that the "Thou-world" is "precisely as much an independent sphere of being" as that of the outer world sphere, the inner world sphere, the "sphere of the divine," do not transcend the limitations of perspective. [Still there may be mentioned here, although stemming from a later time, the pertinent sections in Ludwig Landgrebe's *Phänomenologie und Metaphysik* (1948), an interpretation of the thought of Husserl.]

Unlimited that limits us both. "Being addressed by the
Absolute," says Grisebach, "is a dogma of the memory."
But what if one is addressed by it in the presence of the
other and just through it? Grisebach adds: "An individual can, by his nature, certainly claim as his possession an
unconditional but never the Unconditioned." His inex-
orable clearness hinders him from recognizing that it is
precisely the real becoming addressed—not, of course, by
the "Absolute," which does not speak, but by the God
who speaks the world to me—that is what burns away all
claim to the possession of an absolute.

Karl Jaspers eminently belongs here through the section on communication in his *Existenzerhellung* (*Philosophie* II) and that on the teaching of the cipher-script in
his *Metaphysik* (*Philosophie* III). Both together form the
exemplary conclusion of a phase of development in which
the "free" philosophy takes possession of the new discovery by reducing it. I say "reducing" because the connection of transcendence with the concrete is treated by
it as arbitrary; the advance to the boundlessness of the
Thou is, in effect, annulled. No longer clinging to any
ground soil of a reality of faith, this philosophy believes
that if it only preserves the basic situation of an existen-
tiality of the philosophizing person, it will be able to
govern unhindered in the new land, and it succeeds after
its fashion.

We have recognized that just the same Thou that goes
from man to man is the Thou that descends from the
divine to us and ascends from us to the divine. It was
and is a question of this that is common to these two relationships otherwise so utterly uncommon. That biblical
union of the love of God and the love of man in the
double command directs our gaze to the transparence of
the finite Thou, but also to the grace of the infinite Thou,
which appears where and as it will. Now, however, our
saying Thou to the divine is censured as illegitimate. Certainly philosophy is inviolably qualified to explain that
"philosophical existence" does not suffer us "to draw
near to the hidden God." But it is not qualified to desig-

nate as "questionable" the prayer that is thus alien to its experience.*

It is not essentially otherwise with the teaching of the reading of the cipher-script. "Signs," we have remarked, "happen to us incessantly, to live means to be addressed," and "What encounters me is an address to me. As that which encounters me, the world happening is an address to me." Something similar seems to be meant when philosophy points out to us the fact that "the world is no direct revelation, but only a speech which, without becoming generally valid, is at times historically perceivable by existence and even then cannot be deciphered once for all," and when, still more pregnantly, it is said of transcendence: "It comes into this world as an alien power from its distant meaning and speaks to existence: it approaches it without ever showing more than a cipher." Only what is presupposed is that, "mythically speaking, the cipher of the devil is as visible as that of the divine." Thereby it becomes clear how differently what is said here and what we have said is meant. What sort of a wonderful "transcendence" is that in which the cipher-scripts become fatally confused! To hold the devil, mythically speaking, in honor, even though he has so much power that with his code he can not only trouble but upset that of God, Jaspers undoubtedly does not do. If the concept of the cipher-script is to have a clear meaning, then a deciphering court must be presupposed that can correctly decipher the script meant for my life, a court that thus will also make such deciphering possible, even though with difficulty. Certainly Jaspers explains here expressly that "the genuine consciousness of transcendence" guards itself against thinking of God "simply as personality." Many men of faith might well agree with

* In the book *Der philosophische Glaube* of 1948 [translated under the title *The Perennial Scope of Philosophy*—trans.], Jaspers expresses himself, to be sure, in a much more positive fashion about prayer, in order to bring the two spheres closer to each other; but he blurs the vital distinction when he understands "speculative assurance"—"where it becomes genuine contemplation"—as the highest form of prayer.

this statement—if only the word "simply" were sufficiently emphasized. For him, this man of faith, God is not simply a person; he is for him *also* person. Out of the infinity of his attributes this one, being a person, also exists among them, God's turning, his entering into intercourse with him, the man of faith. But thus, despite his "simply," Jaspers in no wise wants to be understood. "I shrink back immediately," he continues, "from the impulse to make the godhead a Thou, because I feel that I am offending Transcendence." Thus God may be everything but just not a person, and for the reason, indeed, that personality, *per definitionem,* is "the mode of being that by its nature cannot be alone." As though such a definition must also hold true in the paradox of the absolute Person, when the Absolute, insofar as it can be thought of at all, can appear to thought only as a *complexio oppositorum!* And if it is even valid to say, as Jaspers does, "The divine needs us, men, for communication," then among the teachings of faith in the transcendence, that one does not appear to me unworthy that sees God as having created man for communication with God. Finally, however, it is maintained that "the communication with the godhead" has "the tendency to hinder communication among men," for "communication from self to self as the truly present reality in which Transcendence may speak is paralyzed if Transcendence is brought too close and is degraded by being directly related to as Thou." * One notes: the praying man who humbly ventures to turn in personal immediacy to the superexistent as present to him just thereby degrades it and just thereby cripples in himself the ability to communicate with his fellowmen. Within the unfolding of what seems to be the same idea, here the opposite pole becomes manifest to our insight.

* Translator's Note: For an English translation of the passages in Jaspers' *Metaphysik (Philosophie* III) from which these sentences are taken, see *The Worlds of Existentialism: A Critical Reader,* edited and with Introductions and a Conclusion by Maurice Friedman (New York: Random House, 1964), pp. 264–69.

This philosophical conclusion, which was no termination, was followed by two decades in which many noteworthy works emerged, which must remain undiscussed here, especially in the evaluation of the new vision for intellectual fields such as those of sociology, pedagogy, psychology, psychotherapy, and theory of art. Only one of these works, an important one, to be sure, I cannot renounce going into, for a passage in it seems to make a personal-factual explanation by me necessary. It is Karl Barth's *Kirchliche Dogmatik,* Part Two, the "Doctrine of the Creation" (1948).

For his presentation of the "basic form of humanity," Barth, in all the fullness and original power of his theological thinking, claims the specific acquisition of a spiritual movement, the path of which was broken in the eighteenth and nineteenth centuries by a nonchurch but believing idealist and an unbelieving materialist. In the twentieth century this movement found, in some measure, an adequate expression through the not unimportant participation of a believing Jew. Not that Barth annexes it for Reformation Protestantism, as Gogarten had once done in an almost naïve gesture. He seeks to do justice to the spirit that blows outside of Christianity, practicing himself, in as difficult a sphere as that of theology, the "freedom of the heart" that he himself teaches. Thus he takes over on the one side, naturally in the manner of genuine independent thinking, our recognition of the fundamental distinction between It and Thou and of the true being of the I in the meeting. But on the other side, he cannot rightly acknowledge that such a concept of humanity could have grown on any other ground than the Christological (Jesus Christ as "the man for his fellowmen and thus the image of God"). He asserts, to be sure, that "the theological anthropology which here in its own way goes to this determined end comes to expression in statements which are quite similar to those in which humanity had already reached from entirely other sides (for example, by the heathen Confucius, by the atheist L. Feuerbach, by the Jew M. Buber)." He asks with complete legitimacy: "Shall we, therefore, allow ourselves to hold

back from these statements?" He wants, indeed, to rejoice
in all tranquillity that "in the general direction of our
investigation and presentation we find ourselves in a
certain agreement with the wiser men among the wise of
this world." But he raises—without, of course, wanting
"to insist"—a strong critical question: "whether and how
far they [these "wiser men"] can on their side follow us
in the final and decisive consequences of this conception. . . ." In opposition to this statement I must, to begin with, raise a small reservation of language: is it not,
then, conceivable that these more or less wise men who
are mentioned do not, indeed, "follow" those theologians
("us"), but only because they themselves have already attained in their own seeking to similar, if not exactly the
same, "consequences"? Barth is concerned in this connection about "that freedom of the heart between man and
man as the root and crown of the concept of humanity"—
he finds it missing, just as such, in the non-Christians
whom he has named. What concerns him, therefore, is
that man is man insofar as he is willingly human. "Willingly" in the sense that "unwillingly" is out of the question? Where is this "willingly" to be found and where
not? "Now it does not appear to us," says Barth, "as
though this were the case with Confucius, with Feuerbach, with Buber."

I cannot engage myself in this connection for the exalted, but to me somewhat alien, Confucian teaching or
for the more anthropologically postulative than originally
humane teaching of Feuerbach. But what touches me myself, I cannot here leave unexplained. It would certainly
be disagreeable to be compelled to counter the doubts
that have been raised with one's own certainties. In fact,
however, there need be here just as little talk of my personal thought world as that of Barth. Rather, the Protestant world of faith in Barth's understanding of it stands
over against the Hasidic in my understanding of it. And
there, among the Hasidim—in a world of faith whose
teaching is ultimately the commentary on a lived life—
the "willingly" of the freedom of the heart is not, indeed,
consequence, but certainly the innermost presupposition,

the ground of grounds. One need only hear how it is spoken: "Cleverness without heart is nothing at all. Piety is false." For "the true love of God begins with the love of man." But I would, I could, show Karl Barth here, in Jerusalem, how the Hasidim dance the freedom of the heart to the fellowman.

INDEX

INDEX OF NAMES

INDEX OF SUBJECTS